INTERPRETING PROCLUS

This is the first book to provide an account of the influence of Proclus, a member of the "Athenian Neoplatonic School," during more than one thousand years of European history (*c.* 500–1600). Proclus was the most important philosopher of late antiquity, a dominant (albeit controversial) voice in Byzantine thought, the second most influential Greek philosopher in the later western Middle Ages (after Aristotle), and a major figure (together with Plotinus) in the revival of Greek philosophy in the Renaissance. Proclus was also intensively studied in the Islamic world of the Middle Ages and was a major influence on the thought of medieval Georgia. The volume begins with a substantial essay by the editor summarizing the entire history of Proclus' reception. This is followed by chapters by more than a dozen of the world's leading authorities in the various specific areas covered.

STEPHEN GERSH is Professor of Medieval Studies and Concurrent Professor of Philosophy at the University of Notre Dame. Specializing in the Platonic tradition, he is the author of numerous monographs on ancient, medieval, and modern philosophy of which the most recent are *Reading Plato Tracing Plato* (2005); *Neoplatonism after Derrida: Parallelograms* (2006); and *Being Different: More Neoplatonism after Derrida* (2014). He has edited, among other books, *Medieval and Renaissance Humanism: Realism, Representation, and Reform* (with Bert Roest, 2003); and *Eriugena, Berkeley, and the Idealist Tradition* (with Dermot Moran, 2006).

INTERPRETING PROCLUS

From Antiquity to the Renaissance

EDITED BY

STEPHEN GERSH

CAMBRIDGE
UNIVERSITY PRESS

CAMBRIDGE
UNIVERSITY PRESS

University Printing House, Cambridge CB2 8BS, United Kingdom

One Liberty Plaza, 20th Floor, New York, NY 10006, USA

477 Williamstown Road, Port Melbourne, VIC 3207, Australia

314-321, 3rd Floor, Plot 3, Splendor Forum, Jasola District Centre, New Delhi - 110025, India

79 Anson Road, #06-04/06, Singapore 079906

Cambridge University Press is part of the University of Cambridge.

It furthers the University's mission by disseminating knowledge in the pursuit of education, learning and research at the highest international levels of excellence.

www.cambridge.org
Information on this title: www.cambridge.org/9781108465359

First published 2014
First paperback edition 2018

A catalogue record for this publication is available from the British Library

Library of Congress Cataloging in Publication data
Interpreting Proclus : from antiquity to the renaissance / edited by Stephen Gersh.
pages cm
Includes bibliographical references and index.
ISBN 978-0-521-19849-3 (hardback)
1. Proclus, approximately 410–485. I. Gersh, Stephen.
B701.Z7158 2014
186′.4 – dc23 2014009559

ISBN 978-0-521-19849-3 Hardback
ISBN 978-1-108-46535-9 Paperback

Contents

Contributors

LELA ALEXIDZE, Ivane Javakhishvili Tbilisi State University, Georgia

MICHAEL J. B. ALLEN, University of California, Los Angeles

CRISTINA D'ANCONA, Università degli Studi di Pisa

JOHN M. DILLON, Trinity College Dublin

MARKUS FÜHRER, Augsburg College

STEPHEN GERSH, University of Notre Dame

THOMAS LEINKAUF, Westfälische Wilhelms-Universität Münster

DOMINIC J. O'MEARA, University of Fribourg

PASQUALE PORRO, Université de Paris-Sorbonne

ANNE SHEPPARD, Royal Holloway, University of London

LUCAS SIORVANES, King's College London

CARLOS STEEL, Katholieke Universiteit Leuven, Belgium

MICHELE TRIZIO, Università degli Studi di Bari

Note on editions and translations of Proclus' works

In this volume, the writings of Proclus are cited according to the editions and using the **abbreviations** noted in the following list. This list also notes the English translations that are currently available. Items marked with an asterisk * include translations into French.

De aeternitate mundi, fragments in Philoponus, *De aeternitate mundi contra Proclum*, edited by H. Rabe, Leipzig 1899.

On the Eternity of the World, introduction, translation, and commentary by H. S. Lang and A. D. Macro, Berkeley and Los Angeles 2001.

De arte sacrificali, in *Catalogue des manuscrits alchimiques grecs*, vol. VI, edited by J. Bidez, Brussels 1928 (= ***De arte sacr.***).

On the Priestly Art according to the Greeks, translated by B. Copenhaver, in I. Merkel and A. G. Debus (eds.), *Hermeticism and the Renaissance, Intellectual History and the Occult in Early Modern Europe*, Washington, DC and London 1988, 103–105.

De philosophia chaldaica (Eclogae) in **Oracles chaldaïques, avec un choix de commentaires anciens*, edited by É. des Places, Paris 1971, 205–212 (= ***De phil. chald.***).

Elementatio theologica, *The Elements of Theology, A Revised Text with Translation, Introduction, and Commentary*, edited by E. R. Dodds, Oxford 1933; second edition, Oxford 1963 (= ***El. theol.***).

Hymni, edited by E. Vogt, Wiesbaden 1957 (= ***Hymn.***).

Translated by R. M. van den Berg, in *Proclus' Hymns, Essays, Translations, Commentary*, Leiden 2001.

In primum Alcibiadem*, edited by A.-Ph. Segonds, 2 vols., Paris 1985–1986 (= ***In Alc.*).

Proclus, Alcibiades I, translation and commentary by W. O'Neill, The Hague 1965.

In Platonis Cratylum commentaria, edited by G. Pasquali, Leipzig 1908 (= ***In Crat.***).

On Plato's Cratylus, translated by B. M. Duvick, Ithaca, NY 2007.

In primum Euclidis Elementorum librum commentarii, edited by G. Friedlein, Leipzig 1873 (= ***In Eucl.***).

A Commentary on the First Book of Euclid's Elements, translation, introduction, and notes by G. R. Morrow, Princeton 1970.

In Platonis Parmenidem commentaria, edited by C. Steel, 3 vols., Oxford 2007–2009 (= ***In Parm.***).

Commentaire sur le Parménide de Platon, edited by C. Luna and A.-Ph. Segonds, Paris 2007–.

Commentaire sur le Parménide de Platon, traduction de Guillaume de Moerbeke, edited by C. Steel, 2 vols., Leuven and Leiden 1982–1985.

Commentary on Plato's Parmenides, translation, introduction, and notes by G. R. Morrow and J. M. Dillon, Princeton 1987.

In Platonis Rem Publicam commentarii, edited by W. Kroll, 2 vols., Leipzig 1899–1901 (= ***In Remp.***).

In Platonis Timaeum commentaria, edited by E. Diehl, 3 vols., Leipzig 1903–1906 (= ***In Tim.***).

Commentary on Plato's Timaeus, translated by D. Baltzly, H. Tarrant, D. T. Runia, and M. Share, Cambridge 2007–

Theologia Platonica, Théologie platonicienne, edited by H.-D. Saffrey and L. G. Westerink, 6 vols., Paris 1968–1997 (= ***Theol. Plat.***).

Translated by T. Taylor, London 1816. Reprinted Kew Gardens, NY 1985.

Tria opuscula:

Decem dubitationes circa providentiam, Dix problèmes concernant la providence, in *Trois Études sur la Providence*, vol. I, edited by D. Isaac, Paris 1977 (= ***De dec. dub.***).

Ten Doubts concerning Providence and a Solution of Those Doubts; and On the Subsistence of Evil, translated by T. Taylor, London 1833. Reprinted Chicago 1980.

De malorum subsistentia, De l'existence du mal, in *Trois Études*, vol. III, edited by D. Isaac, Paris 1982 (= ***De mal. sub.***).

On the Existence of Evils, translated by J. Opsomer and C. Steel, Ithaca, NY 2003.

De providentia et fato, Providence, fatalité, liberté, in *Trois Études*, vol. II, edited by D. Isaac, Paris 1979 (= ***De prov.***).

On Providence, translated by C. Steel, Ithaca, NY 2007.

One thousand years of Proclus

An introduction to his reception

Stephen Gersh

To describe the reception of Proclus in European thought in either a narrative or an analytical form is undoubtedly a complicated task. It is well known that a substantial part of the history of Platonism – and indeed, the entirety of that history down to the seventeenth century – is the history of what we nowadays term "Neoplatonism" (together with that of the closely related phenomenon of "Middle Platonism"). It is less well known, although it is a demonstrable historical fact rather than a historian's subjective view, that the influence of Proclus far outweighs that of any other Neoplatonist. That the name of Proclus' predecessor Plotinus tends to come to mind when people who are not among the ranks of academic specialists think of the term "Neoplatonism" results from certain features of the current "hermeneutical situation." These include the respective chronological positions of Plotinus and Proclus that bring the former into the purview of classicists and leave the latter outside it, the fact that – methodologically speaking – the essentials of Plotinus' philosophical position need to be grasped before proceeding to the explanation of Proclus' doctrine, and the two philosophers' respective degrees of potential consistency with the monotheistic Christian worldview, which is greater in the case of Plotinus than it is in that of Proclus. However, there are also good reasons for re-evaluating or "rehabilitating" Proclus at the present time, not the least of which is the enormous extent of his influence in the medieval Latin and Byzantine worlds and in the Renaissance.[1]

In order to avoid the danger of losing sight of the wood for the trees, I will frame a narrative of Proclus' influence within European thought between approximately 500 and 1600 of the Common Era by working along two trajectories. After making a very brief summary of what might be termed the "Proclean diffusion" in both the Greek-speaking and Latin-speaking

[1] One should also not forget Proclus' influence on the philosophy of the Islamic world. Some aspects of this tradition will be noted below.

worlds, I will follow a first trajectory by considering certain general features of the assimilation of Proclus' philosophy without consideration of which the mechanism of the Proclean diffusion cannot be understood. Among these general features, the following seem to me to be the most important: (a) the reading of Proclus in conjunction with Syrianus and Damascius; (b) the concealment of Proclus' doctrine within the writings of "Dionysius the Areopagite"; (c) the exploitation of Proclus' ideas in the context of Aristotelian commentary; (d) the loss or suppression of Proclus' works; and (e) the paraphrasing of Proclus' text in the *Liber de causis*. Having considered these general features of the assimilation of Proclus' philosophy, I will follow a second trajectory by considering the extent to which the diffusion of these ideas was regulated by the availability of specific texts of Proclus either in Greek or in Latin translation. Arranged roughly in order of historical significance the most important texts are: 1. *Elements of Theology*; 2. *Three Opuscula*; 3. *Commentary on Plato's Parmenides*; 4. *Platonic Theology*; 5. *Commentary on Plato's Timaeus*; and 6. Other works. Since my intention is to demonstrate perhaps for the first time[2] that there is a "grand narrative" of Proclus' influence in European thought rather than to study the many separate elements that make up that narrative in detail, this introductory study will endeavor to avoid the cumbersome documentation that might obscure the general outline by stating the main facts in a quasi-dogmatic manner and simply referring the reader to the various chapters in the present volume for the more nuanced and more fully documented treatment. In fashioning my survey, I have obviously relied on all of these, although I have retained a certain editorial privilege in adding information from time to time in order to complete the picture and occasionally (albeit more rarely) in disagreeing with the findings of my colleagues.[3]

General diffusion of Proclus' writings

Regarding the general diffusion of Proclus, one should observe that in *late antiquity* when there was already a geographic and cultural division into

[2] There appear to be no earlier surveys of this question as a whole. A few publications have taken the first steps in studying specific areas within the more general diffusion of Proclus' ideas. See especially Imbach (1978), Kristeller (1987), and Sturlese (1987). The collective volume of Bos and Meijer (1992), although a laudable contribution in its day, made no attempt to identify central themes or cover the ground systematically.

[3] I beg the indulgence of these colleagues on the rare occasions when I do this, pointing out conversely that they are not responsible for all the opinions expressed by their editor.

Greek-speaking and Latin-speaking worlds, a variety of responses to Proclus' work can be discerned. These responses range between overt critique and silent appropriation. In the East we have John Philoponus' *On the Eternity of the World against Proclus* in which nineteen of Proclus' arguments for this important cosmological doctrine – not preserved as a group in any of his extant texts – are considered and refuted.[4] It is unclear whether this document illustrates a conflict between paganism and Christianity or merely a debate among different factions within the classical Platonic tradition. However, it seems to initiate a tradition of controversy surrounding Proclus that definitely takes on the shape of a conflict between orthodox Christianity and "Hellenism" reaching a climax during the twelfth century in Nicholas of Methone's *Anaptyxis (Explanation) of Proclus' Elements of Theology*. Some scholars have suggested – probably on inadequate grounds – that Nicholas' controversial work is influenced by or plagiarized from a late ancient anti-Proclean treatise by Procopius of Gaza. But if Proclus is being overtly attacked in the East he is being silently appropriated in the West. The most important illustration of this is Boethius' use of Proclus' three *Opuscula* and *Commentary on Plato's Timaeus* (and possibly *Hymns*) in the *Consolation of Philosophy* in working out his doctrine of providence and other details of cosmology. Another illustration – albeit a less certain one – is Martianus Capella's possible use of Proclus' commentary on the *Chaldaean Oracles* in connection with the "twice-beyond" deity and the "flower of the soul."

Turning to the medieval *Byzantine tradition* in particular, we should note that Proclus' writings were continuously available in Greek, apart from certain inevitable losses resulting from the passage of time and occasional wanton destruction by hostile religious authorities, from late antiquity down to the Turkish conquest. L. G. Westerink has discovered much evidence regarding the early manuscript transmission of Neoplatonic works including those of Proclus, others have shown the extent of the knowledge of Proclus on the part of Michael Psellos and of several generations of thinkers influenced by Psellos – whether or not one endorses Podskalsky's notion of an actual *Proklos-Renaissance* in the eleventh and twelfth centuries[5] – and others have drawn attention to the editorial activity of George Pachymeres in the late Byzantine period. From these researches it has become clear that "Proclus" was seen as a kind of *bête-noire* of philosophical secularism by the orthodox religious. Evidence of this attitude can be found in documentation regarding the trials of John Italos and Eustratios of Nicaea, in George

[4] See Lang and Macro (2001). [5] See Podskalsky (1976).

Tornikes' funeral oration for Anna Komnena, and in the literature generated by the controversies surrounding Hesychasm – especially the writings of Gregory Palamas, Barlaam of Calabria, and Nikephoros Gregoras – these controversies being echoed in the dispute between George Scholarios and George Gemistos Plethon.

In the medieval *Latin tradition*, Proclus' writings were more of a rarity because any diffusion of his works depended on translation. However, from the middle of the thirteenth century and in the wake of the Arabic and Greek translation movements of the previous century which had brought Aristotle and his commentators into circulation in the West, translators of Plato and Proclus came forward in the persons of William of Moerbeke, Ambrogio Traversari, Pietro Balbi, and George of Trebizond – the latter two responding to commissions by Nicholas of Cusa – and this tradition continued into the Renaissance with Marsilio Ficino and Francesco Patrizi da Cherso. The landmarks in the diffusion of Proclus' philosophy resulting from their translations are undoubtedly Thomas Aquinas' discovery of the dependence of the pseudo-Aristotelian *Book of Causes* upon Proclus' *Elements of Theology*, the use of Proclus in forging a kind of Platonic-Aristotelian synthesis in the work of Henry Bate of Mechelen (Malines), the work of thinkers in the German Dominican tradition such as Dietrich of Freiberg and Berthold of Moosburg, for whom Platonic thought as epitomized by Proclus begins to be elevated above Aristotle, and finally Nicholas of Cusa's *marginalia* on Proclus' texts and original works influenced by Proclus from *On Conjectures* onwards.

Of course, one has to recall that the medieval Byzantine and Latin worlds were not completely isolated from one another. Nicholas of Cusa reports that he achieved his great insight into the "coincidence of opposites" (*coincidentia oppositorum*) during a sea voyage back from Constantinople, and George Gemistos Plethon's presence in the Byzantine delegation at the Council of Florence-Ferrara was said to have given Cosimo de' Medici the idea of founding a kind of Florentine "Academy." The transmission of Proclus' ideas in particular in Eustratios of Nicaea's *Commentary on the Nicomachean Ethics*, books I and VI, which was translated from its original Greek into Latin, and in Boethius' *Consolation of Philosophy*, which was translated from the original Latin into Greek, may be cited as striking examples of cross-fertilization between the Byzantine and Latin traditions.

In connection with each of the five headings under which I have suggested that the features of the assimilation of Proclus' philosophy may be grouped,[6] something should be said – as applicable – about the late ancient,

[6] See p. 2.

the medieval Greek, the medieval Latin, and the Renaissance versions of "Proclus." In accordance with the current state of scholarship, or at least with the present writer's knowledge, these remarks may be considered as sometimes more and sometimes less definitive.

(a) *The reading of Proclus in conjunction with Syrianus and Damascius*

The intellectual relations of Proclus to Syrianus, who preceded him in the ancient Athenian school of Platonism, and to Damascius, who followed him in that school, are of radically different types. There is broad agreement between the teachings of Syrianus and Proclus, the former being cited reverently as "my teacher" (ὁ ἡμέτερος καθηγεμών) by the latter. Any differences between the two philosophers that are apparent to us stem largely from the fact that Syrianus is represented mainly by his *Commentary on Aristotle's Metaphysics* whereas Proclus is known to us mostly through commentaries on Plato and original treatises.[7] The relations between Damascius and Proclus are, however, extremely complex in ranging between broad agreement and outright critique.[8] In his *On First Principles* and *Commentary on the Parmenides*, Damascius on the one hand follows Syrianus and Proclus in maintaining the doctrine of a hierarchy of hypostases consisting of the One, Intellect, Soul, Body, and Matter held in place by the threefold causality of remaining, procession, and reversion. He also follows his predecessors in preserving the exegetical system based on the harmonization of Plato with the *Chaldaean Oracles* and the Orphic poetry together with a belief in the consummation of philosophy through theurgic ritual. On the other hand, Damascius exploits certain internal tensions within the metaphysical approach of Syrianus and Proclus by using an *aporetic* method in order to introduce surreptitiously doctrines that are novel to the Athenian School. These include a more comprehensive interpretation of the nine hypotheses of Plato's *Parmenides*, the notion of an "Ineffable" prior to the One in connection with which he appeals to the authority of Iamblichus, and the notion of the partial soul as becoming temporal even in substance.

A reading of Proclus together with Damascius is characteristic of the Christian theological writings circulating under the name of Dionysius the Areopagite at the end of antiquity. Although the existence of textual parallels between this *pseudo*-Dionysius' *On Divine Names* and the three *Opuscula* of Proclus became part of the case for the definitive dating of the

[7] The extant fragments of Syrianus' most important commentaries on Plato are now conveniently accessible in Klitenic Wear (2011).

[8] On Damascius see the chapter by S. Gersh in the present volume.

Corpus Dionysianum to the fifth to sixth centuries made by nineteenth-century scholars, and although numerous further "liens objectifs" between the two writers – as H.-D. Saffrey has called them[9] – have been disclosed since then, it remains true that certain doctrines of central importance to the Dionysian theology such as the more extreme variety of apophaticism emerging in the final chapter of *On Mystical Theology*, where the Trinity is elevated negatively above both being and non-being, are closer to Damascius' than to Proclus' mode of thinking. Now, it is true that in the writings of medieval Byzantine intellectuals Proclus tends to reappear either on his own as the author of the *Elements of Theology* or else in mere lists of names that reveal very little in a doctrinal sense. However, a case of Proclus appearing together with Syrianus in which the latter takes on an independent role can be found in Barlaam of Calabria's *Solutiones ad Georgium Lapithen.* Here, the discussion turns to the nature of demonstration and illuminative knowledge, and Syrianus' *Commentary on Aristotle's Metaphysics* is the definite albeit unacknowledged source. A case of Proclus together with Damascius according an independent role to the latter occurs in a letter of Cardinal Bessarion to George Gemistos Plethon which mentions both of the ancient philosophers by name. The issue here is the relation between "self-constituted" (αὐθυπόστατα) principles and the First Cause, and the association of this notion with the highest intelligibles follows Damascius rather than Proclus. In the Renaissance, Proclus and Damascius are equally important sources for Francesco Patrizi, whose *Nova de universis philosophia* envisions a hierarchy of first principles in which Proclus' notion of horizontal and vertical series is combined with Damascius' emphasis on the primary role of the "One-All." It is to be noted that Patrizi, instead of considering the deconstructive elements in Damascius' project, adopts a primarily harmonizing view of the relation between the two ancient thinkers.

(b) The concealment of Proclus' doctrine in the writings of "Dionysius the Areopagite"

It was definitively established during the nineteenth century that the Christian theologian who adopted the name of St. Paul's first Athenian convert "Dionysius the Areopagite" as his pseudonym was actually a writer of the fifth to sixth centuries whose doctrine has affinities with those of Proclus and Damascius. It is also well known that the writings of pseudo-Dionysius

9 See Saffrey (1966) and Saffrey (1979).

were suspect in the minds of Christian authorities from the earliest days of their circulation, although they had come to be generally accepted thanks to the efforts of such figures as John of Scythopolis and Maximus the Confessor. Subsequently, this perceived apostolic status gave the *Corpus Dionysianum* the highest theological authority in the Christian churches of both East and West, this authority not being shaken until Valla and Erasmus showed that the style of theological language and the liturgical practices described were quite inconsistent with the early Church.[10]

Given that the author of the *Corpus Dionysianum* for obvious reasons concealed his debt to Proclus by not mentioning the latter's name – although there are some veiled allusions to a teacher called "Hierotheos" who bears a certain resemblance to the Proclus whom we know – medieval Byzantine or Latin readers were placed in a peculiar position regarding the question of how to interpret these texts. The answer to this question depended on whether they also knew Proclus or did not also know Proclus. Medieval Latin writers before the late thirteenth century, when writings of Proclus first became available in Latin translation, simply read Dionysius without having to consider any relation to Proclus. On the other hand, medieval Byzantine writers or medieval Latin writers from the late thirteenth century onwards with some access to Proclus' works had to adopt specific hermeneutical strategies. These involved placing Proclus chronologically after Dionysius and accusing him of plagiarizing and distorting the latter and sometimes also explaining the non-appearance of Dionysius' writings before the late fifth century by saying that the pagan Platonists concealed these works after copying them. This explanation appears first at the end of antiquity in the prologue to the *Corpus Dionysianum* by John of Scythopolis, although the most relevant passage is possibly an interpolation by Philoponus. Subsequent Byzantine writings either treat Dionysius as expounding a spiritually superior version of doctrines that were later stated in a more dialectical form by Proclus – for example, Michael Psellos' *About Theology and the Distinction among the Greeks' Doctrines*, the Aristotelian commentaries of Eustratios of Nicaea, and George Pachymeres' preface to the works of Dionysius – or else establish a radical opposition between the Christian truth of Dionysius and the pagan distortion by Proclus – for example, Nicholas of Methone's *Explanation of Proclus' Elements of Theology* and Gregory Palamas' *150 Chapters*. Latin writings of the later Middle Ages and Renaissance also exemplify these contrasting strategies for dealing with the relation between Dionysius and Proclus, Nicholas of

[10] On pseudo-Dionysius see the chapter by J. M. Dillon in the present volume.

Cusa and Marsilio Ficino stressing the agreement and Thomas Aquinas the disagreements between the two authors.

In actual fact, Dionysius' appropriation of Proclus' teachings is combined with significant transformations of the latter in accordance with the requirements of a Christian theology that also owes a debt to the Cappadocian Fathers. Among these doctrinal modifications are the transformation of Proclus' multiplicity of self-sufficient henads into a multiplicity of divine names, the heightened apophaticism of *On Mystical Theology*, and the substitution of Christian sacraments for the natural symbols of Proclus' theurgy. However, despite these clear distinctions between the two thinkers, Byzantine scholars were always operating at a disadvantage because of their faulty understanding of Dionysius' historical position. For example, much confusion regarding the question of precisely which doctrines belong to Proclus and which to Dionysius is characteristic of the later Hesychast controversy and especially of the exchanges between Nikephoros Gregoras and Gregory Palamas, given that the distinction between the uncreated and unknowable essence of God and the divine energies that can be known or participated, which was so important for the orthodox theology of the day, actually has no real basis in either Dionysius or Proclus.

(c) The exploitation of Proclus' ideas in the context of Aristotelian commentary

Among the major questions that arise in ancient Aristotelian commentaries and continue in their medieval Greek and Latin counterparts, of particular importance are those of establishing the right relation between Aristotle's and Plato's doctrines concerning Forms and universals and of properly understanding the nature of causality in Aristotelianism and Platonism. Proclus is often brought into these discussions as a kind of paradigm of Platonic thinking, recourse to his doctrine being either acknowledged by the mention of his name or indicated by the adoption of technical terminology peculiar to his work. This process of assimilation begins in late antiquity with such works as Ammonius' commentaries on Aristotle's *Categories* and *On Interpretation.*

In the medieval Byzantine world, the *Commentaries on the Nicomachean Ethics, Books I and VI* and the *Commentary on the Posterior Analytics* by Eustratios of Nicaea provide some of the most important examples.[11] In

[11] Among Byzantine Aristotelian commentators, Michael of Ephesus also derives material from Proclus albeit with less further philosophical elaboration than in the case of Eustratios.

quoting or utilizing Proclus in his commentary on *Ethics I*, Eustratios mounts an important defense of Plato's ideal world in the face of Aristotle's critique in which he argues that if all things desire the Good, the Good itself must be above Being. Similarly in commenting on *Ethics VI*, he establishes a clear distinction between Aristotle's abstracted ideas and Platonic transcendent Ideas and endorses the latter understood as the contents of Intellect in the manner of Proclus.[12] In quoting or utilizing Proclus in commenting on both books of the *Ethics*, Eustratios goes to great lengths in maintaining the obviously un-Aristotelian distinction between the discursive thinking of Soul and the non-discursive activity of Intellect in which the discursive thinking engages in a kind of circular dance around a center represented by non-discursive thinking. In connection with the discussions of the theory of Forms, Eustratios is dependent on Proclus' *Elements of Theology*, whereas in connection with that of non-discursive and discursive reason he relies on both the *Elements of Theology* and the *Commentary on Plato's Parmenides*. Of course, Eustratios retains the standpoint of a Christian commentator, sometimes quoting Proclus without issuing a value judgment, sometimes contrasting his view with the Christian one, and sometimes silently assimilating Proclus to his own position. When bringing Proclus into a comparative relation with Christian authorities, Gregory Nazianzen is undoubtedly his favorite point of reference, although in one passage the doctrine of the "flower of the intellect" (νοῦ ἄνθος) is transferred directly from Proclus to Dionysius. Eustratios' *Commentaries on the Nicomachean Ethics* together with their tapestry of Proclean borrowings represent some of the most philosophically sophisticated writing ever to emerge from Byzantium, their importance for the future history of philosophy being increased by their translation into Latin by Robert Grosseteste in the early thirteenth century and their subsequent use as a counterweight to Aristotelianism especially by members of the German Albertist school.

In the Renaissance we can find another striking example of Proclus' doctrines being transmitted by way of Aristotelian commentary in Francesco Patrizi's notion that space is equivalent to light and that both are bodies.[13] Space is equivalent to light because the former and the latter share the three properties of being impassive, extended in interval, and penetrable. This space/light is a body which is, on the one hand, immaterial – because it has the least on a scale of degrees of bulk – and, on the other hand, universal – because it contains the whole cosmos. The argument here is based on a

[12] On Eustratios see the chapter by M. Trizio in the present volume.
[13] For a good discussion of this question see Deitz (1999).

doctrine that is seemingly peculiar to Proclus, being reported in one of Patrizi's favorite texts: the *Corollarium de loco* of Simplicius' *Commentary on Aristotle's Physics.*

(d) *The loss or suppression of Proclus' works*

Among the writings of Proclus, the *Commentary on the Chaldaean Oracles* and the *Commentary on Plotinus' Enneads* are two works whose loss is particularly to be regretted. The importance for Proclus of the *Commentary on the Chaldaean Oracles* is underlined by the report of Proclus' successor and biographer Marinus that his master wanted to leave only the *Timaeus* and the *Chaldaean Oracles* in circulation among ancient books and that he had composed his own commentary on the oracles in the wake of Syrianus' writings on the same topic. Circumstantial evidence suggests that Proclus' commentary in a complete or abridged form was still available in the time of Michael Psellos, who used it in connection with his own project of reconciling the oracles with Christian dogma,[14] and that, although numerous oracles continue to be cited by later Byzantine authors such as Nikephoros Gregoras in his commentary on Synesius, whatever remained of the work was probably incinerated by the religious authorities at the time of John Italos' condemnation. Eventually, a completely new commentary was put together by George Gemistos Plethon – which was in its turn the source of the oracular texts inserted by Marsilio Ficino into his own *Platonic Theology* – although there is evidence of material from Proclus making its way into the Plethonian commentary via Psellos' notes. The differences between Plethon's and the earlier treatment are that Plethon attributes the *Oracles* to "*magi* in the tradition of Zoroaster" rather than to the two Julians mentioned in the *Souda*, removes the Christianizing tendencies of Psellos' version, and maintains the relative simplicity of the original *Oracles*' hypostatic structure in contrast to the increasing ramifications of the Proclus–Psellos version. In addition to the *Chaldaean Oracles*, Proclus also held Plotinus in the highest esteem, quoting him frequently and applying to him the epithets of "the divine" (ὁ θεῖος) or "the most divine" (ὁ θειότατος). It was shown convincingly by L. G. Westerink that Psellos incorporated phrases taken from *Enneads* I together with short glosses couched in Proclean terminology into his theological treatise *De omnifaria doctrina* and that a commentary by Proclus on all or part of the *Enneads* must therefore have been still extant in his day. There is also some evidence

[14] On this point see the chapter by D. O'Meara in the present volume.

that the work continued to be available to the first and second generations of Psellos' followers, since a similar passage has been found in an *Oration* of Eustratios of Nicaea, although it seems to vanish from the historical record after that. The project of interpreting Proclus' philosophy in connection with the Plotinian writings reappears in the Renaissance, albeit without any recovery of the Proclean commentary itself, when Marsilio Ficino produces the first new commentary on the *Enneads* since antiquity. Of particular significance in this connection is the extensive use of Proclus' notion of theurgic "series" (σειραί) in the third book of Ficino's *De vita*, since this book is described by its author as essentially a commentary on Plotinus' *Ennead* IV. 3. 11.

At this point, a peculiar set of historical circumstances that may represent the suppression if not the loss of Proclus' work needs to be considered.[15] According to the *Letter to Joseph the Exarch* by George Scholarios, who was the ideological opponent of George Gemistos Plethon and who later as Patriarch of Constantinople was responsible for destroying most of the latter's *chef d'oeuvre*, Plethon claimed to be following Plutarch, Plotinus, Porphyry, and Iamblichus in his *Laws* while actually concealing his debt to Proclus in order to bolster his own claim to originality. This question of influence raised by Scholarios is a tricky one since Plethon avoids the scissors-and-paste method of citation characteristic of less creative authors. Nevertheless, a close inspection of the theological system of the *Laws* indicates that, despite the general similarity between this work and Proclus' *Platonic Theology* in presenting a systematic philosophical account of polytheism, the differences between Plethon and Proclus are at least as great as the similarities. For instance, the Plethonian theological doctrine avoids the triadic structuring of the divine ranks, depends more heavily on Plato's *Sophist* than on his *Parmenides*, and reduces the tendency towards apophaticism or "negative" theology. Therefore, Plethon was perhaps not concealing his debt to Proclus or suppressing the latter but rather avoiding reference to him on perfectly valid intellectual grounds.

(e) The paraphrasing of Proclus' text in the Liber de causis

The work known as the "Book of Causes" is a translation of an Arabic work entitled "The Discourse on the Pure Good" that was usually attributed by the late medieval Schoolmen either to Aristotle, or to al-Fārābī, or to a combination of the two, although modern scholarship has been able to trace

[15] On Plethon see the chapter by S. Gersh in the present volume.

it back more convincingly to the circle of al-Kindī in the tenth century and perhaps even to al-Kindī himself.[16] Its importance for the western Middle Ages was assured when it was translated into Latin by Gerard of Cremona at Toledo around the third quarter of the twelfth century. Moreover, the combination of the axiomatic form in which the work was written and the obscurity surrounding its literary origins made it possible for the *Book of Causes* to be understood subsequently as the culmination of Aristotle's own theological project and to become a prescribed textbook in the thirteenth-century University of Paris. Finally, thanks to the translation of the *Elements of Theology* into Latin by William of Moerbeke in 1268, Thomas Aquinas was able to discern quite rightly that the Arabic–Latin treatise is heavily dependent on Proclus' work with respect to both form and content.[17]

Given that the *Book of Causes* seems to have originated in a philosophically sophisticated milieu in the Islamic world, it is not surprising to find its author not content to repeat Proclean doctrines in a slavish manner but endeavoring to transform them in accordance with more overtly monotheistic assumptions. Among the most important doctrinal transformations are the replacement of Proclus' One by pure Being as the first principle, the reduction of the *Elements of Theology*'s extensive list of metaphysical principles to a simpler hierarchy consisting of Being, Intellect, and Soul, and the supplementation of Proclus' notion of emanative causality with a theistic notion of creation. For Aquinas, the possibility of comparing the *Book of Causes* with the *Elements of Theology* provided a clearer historical understanding not only of what Aristotle himself may have understood by theology but also of what the Platonists took this discipline to mean. Evidence of Aquinas' heightened historical awareness is provided by his treatise *On Separate Substances* written shortly after the discovery of the literary dependence. In chapters 1 and 2 of this treatise, Aquinas exploits the *Elements of Theology*, albeit without mentioning the name of the treatise or its author, in order to explain the doctrine of "the Platonists" (*Platonici*) according to which there is a hierarchy of separate substances comprising in descending order the unparticipated One or Good, secondary gods equivalent to unities and to Forms, separate intellects, souls of the heavenly bodies, souls of daemons, and human souls. Aquinas himself prefers the more modest Aristotelian repertory of separate substances. However, he is somewhat more sympathetic to the Platonist – the Proclean – doctrines that intellects can understand lower things by participating in

[16] On the *Book of Causes* see the chapter by C. D'Ancona in the present volume.

[17] On Moerbeke see the chapter by C. Steel in the present volume.

the intelligible Forms or gods and also provide a theoretical basis for the observable phenomenon of daemonic possession. The final section of *On Separate Substances* takes on an unintentionally ironic character when Aquinas summarizes the Dionysian doctrine of angelology and states that it is consistent with the Faith, without being in the least conscious that it too is derived from the *Elements of Theology.*

Moerbeke's translation of the *Elements of Theology* and Aquinas' *Commentary on the Book of Causes* together bring Proclus to the attention of many other scholars in the University of Paris and beyond, including Matthew of Acquasparta, Henry of Ghent, Thomas of Sutton, Radulphus Brito, John Duns Scotus, and Thomas Bradwardine. It has been suggested that the practice of quoting propositions of Proclus in commenting on the *Book of Causes* became so widespread in the late thirteenth-century University of Paris *milieu* that the reading of "Proclus" degenerated to the level of collecting clichés.[18] However, this view certainly seems questionable if one takes account of philosophical developments such as James of Viterbo's sophisticated use of the *Elements of Theology* in the context of his treatment of human volition.[19]

The "styles" of Proclus

This brief survey of the general features of the assimilation of Proclus' work in late antiquity, in the medieval Byzantine and Latin worlds, and in the Renaissance should be completed by drawing attention to two overarching assumptions about Proclus' thought on the part of his ever-expanding readership during these periods of history. These assumptions are, first, that Proclus is a representative of extreme rationalism and, second, that he is a representative of extreme paganism.

The first assumption about Proclus' thought – that it represents extreme rationalism – is most apparent among medieval Latin writers. During the period in which the *Elements of Theology* was the only text generally known, Proclus was considered as representing the very epitome of rationalist discourse, although the overtly logical ordering of Proclus' treatise was not considered a sign of weakness in the thirteenth century after Aristotle's logical writings had been adopted as the foundation of the university curriculum. An extreme example of this approach is Berthold of Moosburg's *Exposition of Proclus' Elements of Theology.* The preface to this massive Latin commentary states that Proclus' principal achievements were the reduction

[18] See Sturlese (1987), 270–271. [19] See the chapter by P. Porro in the present volume.

of Platonic philosophy to an axiomatic form in the face of its earlier more rhetorical presentation, and the removal of the metaphorical coverings in which that philosophy had been presented before the time of Plotinus. The axiomatic method of Proclus representing a kind of transposition into the metaphysical sphere of the geometrical method of Euclid had been influential in late antiquity in the case of Boethius' theological treatise *Quomodo substantiae*, and in the later Middle Ages gives rise to such works as Meister Eckhart's *Work of Propositions* and Heimeric de Campo's *Theoremata totius universi.* A less rationalistic and more "mystical" reading of Proclus begins to emerge with the diffusion in translation of his *Three Opuscula* and *Commentary on Plato's Parmenides* somewhat later than that of the *Elements of Theology*, the first real signs of this newer tendency in the interpretation of Proclus appearing as an important secondary motif in Berthold's commentary.

The second assumption about Proclus' thought – that it represents extreme paganism – is most apparent among medieval Byzantine writers. From the time of the earliest references to Proclus on the part of Byzantine intellectuals, throughout the period of the Hesychast controversy, and down to the final years before the Turkish conquest, Proclus was considered as representing the "Hellenic" or pagan religious doctrines in their most undiluted form. Nicholas of Methone's *Explanation of Proclus' Elements of Theology* is the archetypal instance of this approach. In its preface the author establishes an analogy between Proclus' textual construction of 211 propositions and the biblical Tower of Babel, comparing the treatise's "reasonings" (λογισμοί) to the bricks of the tower and the "interconnection" (ἀλληλουχία) of the demonstrations to the tower's cement.[20] Nicholas' conviction that Proclus' doctrine contains parallels to most of the heresies that have beset the Christian Church reflects the mentality that had earlier condemned the teaching of John Italos and would eventually consign Plethon's *Laws* to the flames. There was nothing precisely comparable to this on the medieval Latin side, probably because Proclus' texts were never as widely available in the West as in the East, and also because they came into circulation a little too late to figure among bishop Étienne Tempier's list of condemned propositions at the University of Paris in 1277.

A combination of the assumptions that Proclus is a representative of extreme rationalism and that he is a representative of extreme paganism resurfaces, albeit in a more intellectually generous form, in the Renaissance. At that time Marsilio Ficino, who was definitely familiar with Nicholas of

[20] On Nicholas of Methone see the chapter by M. Trizio in the present volume.

Methone's treatise and possibly also with that of Berthold of Moosburg, came to write his own *Commentary on the Parmenides.*[21] Despite his respect for Proclus' earlier essay in the same genre, Ficino makes a point of distancing himself. In Proclus' reading of the *Parmenides* there is, according to Ficino, on the one hand an excessively mechanical and on the other an excessively realist interpretation of the sequence of logical categories in applying them to orders of gods. The Florentine commentator prefers to interpret the *Parmenides* in line with the other dialogues of Plato as a mixture of play and seriousness. In this manner it seems easier for him avoid the twin pitfalls of extreme rationalism and extreme paganism characteristic of Proclus' approach and also to remain true to the Plotinian-Augustinian outlook that is more compatible with Christian piety.

At this point, our account of Proclus' influence must be brought into greater focus by turning to the *fortuna* of his individual works during the period 500–1600.

1. The *Elements of Theology*

In the Byzantine world, since he explicitly treats Proclus as the pinnacle of Greek philosophy, Michael Psellos provides a good starting-point for considering the influence of the *Elements of Theology.* In the essay *About Intellect*, where Psellos provides a handy summary of the later Neoplatonic doctrine in which he distinguishes the unparticipated from the participating intellects and discusses the relation between intellect and the intelligibles, he concludes by noting that "these are the philosophical doctrines of Proclus concerning intellect in his *Elements of Theology.*" This short essay illustrates one of Psellos' methods of dealing with Proclus' texts, namely by straightforward citation in the manner of a textbook. Elsewhere he either contrasts Proclus' doctrine with Christianity – obviously favoring the latter – or silently assimilates it to Christian doctrine. Both methods can be illustrated with Psellos' theological compendium *De omnifaria doctrina*, which is peppered with citations from the *Elements of Theology* that are here identified as "the chapters" (τὰ κεφαλαῖα).[22] These citations are connected with such doctrines as the three kinds of reversion (making comparison with Dionysius), the eternal nature of intellect in both substance and activity, the infinity of powers (making comparison with Gregory Nazianzen),

[21] On Ficino see the chapter by M. J. B. Allen in the present volume.

[22] On Psellos see the chapter by D. O'Meara in the present volume.

the divine knowledge of divisible things in an indivisible manner, and so forth.

In the next generation John Italos approaches the reading of the *Elements of Theology* in a broadly similar way in his *Questions and Solutions* although he introduces comparisons with Christianity less often and rarely ventures towards outright assimilation.[23] As examples of his use of the "Elements" (Στοιχείωσις) with considerable detachment might be mentioned the references to the triad "according to cause," "according to substance," and "according to participation" (prop. 103), to the irradiations of intellect within soul (prop. 57, corr.), and to the superiority of the cause to the effect (prop. 7), all within the space of the first question. Italos' sixty-eighth question likewise presents an extremely careful summary of the doctrine of the primal hypostases according to "the most theological of the Greeks" (οἱ τῶν Ἑλλήνων θεολογικώτατοι) which interweaves allusions to the *Elements of Theology* with those to other Proclean works and to other late ancient Platonists. John Italos often compares Proclus' doctrines with that of Aristotle: a strategy taken up formally in the next generation by Eustratios in his commentaries on the *Nicomachean Ethics.*

Historians have generally seen Nicholas of Methone's *Explanation of Proclus' Elements of Theology* as a reaction, in the wake of several official condemnations, to the kind of preoccupation with pagan philosophical texts typical of Psellos, Italos, and Eustratios. Since Proclus was seen as the archetypal pagan thinker and the author of the most widely circulated pagan treatise, Nicholas embarks on the major task of refuting Proclus' treatise proposition by proposition. He employs two principal strategies. The first strategy is to show the incompatibility of Proclus' teachings with Christian dogma. Sometimes Nicholas corrects Proclus with scripture, as when the pagan thinker's confusion of "causality" (παραγωγή) and "generation" (γονιμότης) is contrasted with the Christian distinction between God's demiurgic production of other beings and the intra-Trinitarian generation. Elsewhere, he underlines the distinction between Proclus' attribution of self-sufficient status to principles inferior to the Good and Gregory Nazianzen's restriction of this attribute to God, or again emphasizes the difference between Proclus' treatment of intellect, life, and power as things generated by the First Principle and Dionysius' understanding of the latter as attributes of God. Nicholas' second strategy is to show the inconsistency of Proclus' own arguments with one another. For example, he argues that

[23] On John Italos see the chapter by M. Trizio in the present volume.

the placing of a multiplicity of henads before the unity of Being or the positing of a participation in something that is described as unparticipated makes no sense within the context of Proclus' own thinking. In these cases Nicholas often displays a good knowledge of the Aristotelian logical reasoning that was taught in the Byzantine schools.

Before turning to the Latin tradition of the *Elements of Theology*, something should be said about two other streams within this diffusion. The first additional stream of diffusion is represented by Ioane Petritsi's Georgian translation and commentary produced sometime in the twelfth century.[24] Petritsi, who emerged from the tradition of Michael Psellos and John Italos and may even have been a student of the latter in Constantinople, was also the author of a translation of Nemesius and of a commented translation of the Psalms. The importance of his version of the *Elements of Theology* has been generally known for some time since the literalness of the translation enables us to reconstruct a very early stage in the transmission of the Greek text and in one case even to insert an additional proposition (prop. 129).[25] However, in recent years, thanks to the German translation and commentary of L. Alexidze, it has become clear that Petritsi's commentary includes an independent philosophical analysis of considerable merit. The second additional stream of diffusion is a collection of Arabic extracts nowadays thought to have been produced during the tenth century in the circle of al-Kindī. In the wake of an earlier discovery of a few extracts in manuscripts of Cairo and Damascus by A. Badawī, a total of more than twenty propositions of the *Elements of Theology* in Arabic translation falsely attributed to Alexander of Aphrodisias has now been retrieved from *Istanbul, Süleymaniye Kütüphanesi, Carullah 1279* and provided with a modern edition and commentary by G. Endress.[26] This *Proclus Arabus* is connected conceptually and lexically with the Arabic version of Plotinus known for a long time as the *Theology of Aristotle* and, like the latter work, significantly modifies the tone of the original Greek material in the direction of a more insistent monism and creationism congenial to the medieval Muslim readership.[27]

Turning now to the Latin tradition of the late Middle Ages, mention has already been made of the impact of Moerbeke's translation of the *Elements of Theology* in the arts school of the University of Paris during the thirteenth

[24] On Petritsi see the chapter by L. Alexidze in the present volume.

[25] See Alexidze and Bergemann (2009), 20–24, 291, 307. The Greek version conversely has a proposition missing in the Georgian (prop. 149 Dodds).

[26] On the *Proclus Arabus* see the essay by C. D'Ancona in the present volume.

[27] See also most recently Wakelnig (2006).

century and of Thomas Aquinas' and James of Viterbo's exploitation of the relation between the *Book of Causes* and the Greek work from which it derives. However, the most significant influence of Proclus' treatise in the Latin-speaking world was outside both France and the universities.

In the Low Countries, Henry Bate of Mechelen (Malines) inserts numerous citations of the *Elements of Theology* into his encyclopedic work entitled *Speculum divinorum et quorundam naturalium*, employing this material in a manner that is both sympathetic and persuasive.[28] Part VII of the *Speculum* is a defense of Plato's doctrine of Forms against the Aristotelian critique and is in practice a reply to Thomas Aquinas' interpretations. For Bate, as for many of his contemporaries, Proclus is the paradigmatic Platonist, and among the doctrines of the *Elements of Theology* that are exploited here are the explanation of participation in terms of the distinction between unparticipated and participated terms, and the threefold structure of "according to cause," "according to substance," and "according to participation." The strategy of Bate is the opposite of Aquinas' in that he elaborates on the agreement between Proclus and Dionysius. Parts XI–XII of the *Speculum* further Bate's thoroughly non-Thomistic project of reducing the conflict between Plato's and Aristotle's positions to a difference of viewpoint. This section of the encyclopedia also includes an abundance of citations from the *Elements of Theology* in which interpretation of the notion of self-subsistence and the identification of the henads with Ideas are especially prominent themes. But elaborate use of the *Elements of Theology* is not the only notable feature of Henry Bate's *Speculum*, for this encyclopedia is also the only medieval work known to have utilized the three extracts from Proclus' *Commentary on Plato's Timaeus* translated into Latin by William Moerbeke.

Whereas Bate was perhaps an isolated figure in the Low Countries with his devotion to Proclus, in Germany we see the development of an entire tradition in which Platonism gradually increases in importance relative to Aristotelianism, and philosophy gains strength as an independent rational discipline, with Proclus being the primary catalyst in this process. Taking its starting-point from the first tentative but sympathetic approaches to Proclus in the writings of Albert the Great, the latter having cited the first set of propositions in the *Elements of Theology* with respect to the identification of the One and the Good, this radically new development of Platonic philosophy is documented in the writings of Dietrich of Freiberg,

[28] See Steel and van de Vyver (1994), xxxii–lii; and Boese (1990), xvi–xx and xxiv.

Berthold of Moosburg,[29] and – albeit less obviously – in those of Meister Eckhart.

Dietrich of Freiberg includes a total of around fifty citations of the *Elements of Theology* in five works: *On the Blessed Vision*, *On the Knowledge of the Separate Beings*, *On Spiritual Substances*, *On the Animation of the Heaven*, and perhaps most strikingly *On Intellect and the Intelligible.* In a manner typical of this period, Dietrich reads the *Elements of Theology* in very close association with the *Book of Causes.* However, Dietrich is a first-rate philosopher who transforms what he reads into something that is powerfully original albeit with identifiable roots in the work of the Athenian Platonist. For example, he adopts the structure of the four levels of reality in prop. 20 of the *Elements of Theology* – the One (= Dietrich's God), Intellect, Soul, and Body – but combines it with features derived from the *Book of Causes* in order to delineate a procession whereby the first intellect (= Proclus' One) produces the second intellect (= Proclus' Intellect), the second intellect produces the soul of the first celestial sphere and the body of that sphere, the third intellect produces the soul of the second celestial sphere and the body of that sphere, the process continuing down to our agent intellect. Dietrich especially develops the notion of intellection in striking new ways; for example, he introduces the medieval Aristotelian doctrine of the "transcendentals" (*transcendentalia*) at this point by arguing that each created intellect is characterized by being as reversion to self, by truth as reversion to the first intellect, and by goodness as production of the lower. With a radical extension of Proclus' statement that intellect produces by its activity of understanding into a fully developed idealism, Dietrich also formulates a distinction between "conceptional being" (*ens conceptionale*) and "real being" (*ens reale*) that encompasses the entire universe.

Although Meister Eckhart appears to show some knowledge of Dietrich's presentation of Proclus in exploiting the thesis regarding the four levels of reality and in attributing the distinction between *ens conceptionale* and *ens reale* actually to *Proclus*, and although he owes an obvious debt to the Proclus' axiomatic methodology in conceiving his vast and unfinished project of a *Work of Propositions*,[30] major aspects of his thought cannot be shown to depend primarily on Proclus. Nevertheless, the difference between the levels of overt Proclean citation in Dietrich and Eckhart respectively may simply result from the fact that the former has left us distinctively philosophical works in which citation of the *Elements of Theology* would be

[29] On Dietrich of Freiburg and Berthold of Moosburg see the chapter by M. Führer and S. Gersh in the present volume.

[30] For a list of passages in which Eckhart cites or uses Proclus see Sturlese (1987), 280, n. 71.

quite reasonable whereas the latter's extant writings are mostly scriptural commentaries and sermons in which it would be less appropriate to name a pagan master explicitly.

We do not know the precise circumstances that drove Berthold of Moosburg to produce a huge commentary on the *Elements of Theology* in Moerbeke's Latin translation between 1327 and 1361. What is at least clear is that Berthold intends to defend Proclus and therefore move in a direction opposite to that of Nicholas of Methone, who wrote his commentary in order to refute Proclus. As Berthold explains in its *prologus* and *praeambulum*, this work of commentary proceeds on the assumptions that Platonism, which posits the One above Intellect and supra-intellectual cognition, is superior to Aristotelianism, which is preoccupied with being *qua* being and intellectual activity, that Proclus is superior to all other Platonists in reducing a doctrine previously expressed in figurative language to a rigorously dialectical form, and that Proclus' philosophy is in agreement with and represents a more dialectical version of the teaching of Dionysius the Areopagite. The *Expositio super Elementationem theologicam Procli* begins its detailed analysis by noting that the sequence of propositions is unfolded on the basis of two *supposita* that are not stated as such but function by analogy with articles of faith in Christian theology. These are, first, that multiplicity exists and, second, that productivity exists. The analysis then continues by using the sequence of propositions as a kind of massive conceptual grid into which *sententiae* drawn from a wide range of Greek, Latin, and Arabic sources are inserted. These are listed on the first page of the text – having been moved there from the end of the text by the modern editors in line with Berthold's instructions – and include Plato, Aristotle, Hermes Trismegistus, Proclus, Avicenna, Algazel, Alfarabius, the *De causis*, Averroes, Seneca, Cicero, Apuleius, Macrobius, and Maimonides. Since Proclus is explicitly cited within this list for his three *Opuscula* as well as for his *Elements of Physics*, we here find the first documented use of these specific works in a medieval philosophical treatise.

The link between the medieval reading of Proclus and its Renaissance counterpart is most clearly provided on the Latin side by Nicholas of Cusa,[31] just as it is provided most clearly on the Greek side by George Gemistos Plethon. Although Plethon was lauded by Marsilio Ficino as the thinker who inspired Cosimo de' Medici to patronize a Platonic revival in Florence, the extent of his literary relation to Proclus – as noted earlier – is

[31] On Nicholas of Cusa see the chapter by S. Gersh in the present volume.

somewhat unclear. In the case of Nicholas of Cusa there is no such ambiguity. During his early years the future cardinal had studied in the Albertist circle of Cologne with Heimeric de Campo, the author of works such as the *Compendium divinum* and the *Theoremata totius universi*, in which the *Elements of Theology* had been extensively used. Fortunately, we still possess the MS *Bernkastel-Kues, Cusanus 195* containing Moerbeke's translation of the *Elements of Theology* together with Nicholas' own marginal notes. These glosses draw attention particularly to the doctrine of the four levels of reality and to discussions of participation. It is noteworthy that Nicholas makes annotations only as far as proposition 139 and that the glosses are of modest scope in comparison with his massive annotations in the Latin translations of Proclus' *Commentary on Plato's Parmenides* and *Platonic Theology*, which he also owned in manuscript. This should not be taken as evidence that Nicholas thought the *Elements of Theology* to be relatively unimportant. It probably just reflects the fact that this work had been available and commented upon for two hundred years up to and including the work of Berthold of Moosburg, which Nicholas definitely knew, whereas the *Commentary on Plato's Parmenides* had been available but little studied and the *Platonic Theology* was a complete novelty in the Latin-speaking world of the fifteenth century.

There is evidence that the *Elements of Theology* was studied by thinkers of a Platonist inclination during the Renaissance, although perhaps with less intensity than had been the case during the later Middle Ages. Marsilio Ficino made extracts from the Greek text in the MS *Milano, Ambrosianus 329* and also annotations on Nicholas of Methone's *Explanation* in the MS *Paris B. N. gr. 1256*. It is known that Ficino himself made a new Latin translation which has not been found, although extracts from it appear in the glosses in his manuscript of Plotinus' *Enneads*, these extracts showing that he was working quite independently of Moerbeke.[32] Cardinal Bessarion owned manuscripts that represent the two main families into which the textual history of the work has been organized: *Venezia, Marcianus gr. 63* and *Marcianus gr. 403*. Giovanni Pico della Mirandola's manuscript of the *Elements of Theology* is now in the Bodleian Library as MS *Oxford, Laud. graec. 18*. With Francesco Patrizi, the history of the work's reception takes a more dramatic turn. Patrizi not only owned one manuscript – *Milano, Ambrosianus 38* – and copied another – the *Ambrosianus 12* – but also produced a new translation published in Ferrara in 1583. Moreover, in

[32] The point has been proven in a recent study of these glosses by D. Robichaud (communicated privately to the editor). For a different view see the chapter by C. Steel in the present volume.

his principal philosophical work the *Nova de universis philosophia* he makes extensive use of the *Elements of Theology* and other writings of Proclus.[33] A striking feature of Patrizi's approach is the formal application of theorems such as "that unity precedes multiplicity" and "that the cause is superior to the effect," having an obvious derivation metaphysically and methodologically from Proclus' treatise. Moreover, the structure of Patrizi's universe, which consists of the *un'omnia (pater)* followed by – in a kind of horizontal series – the *unitas primaria* (= the Idea of the Good), the *unitas essentiarum*, the *unitas vitarum*, and so on, and also followed by – in a kind of vertical series – the *unitas primaria* again, the *essentia primaria*, the *vita primaria*, and so on, obviously follows Proclus' notions of *seira* and *taxis*.[34] A final noteworthy feature of Patrizi's approach is the verbatim translation into Latin of much of Proclus' technical terminology, ἑνιαίως becoming *uniter*, and ἀπειροδύναμος becoming *infinitipotens*, to name two instances.

2. *Three Opuscula*

The evidence of their diffusion in both the Greek-speaking and Latin-speaking worlds indicates that the treatises *On Providence and Fate*, *Ten Doubts concerning Providence*, and *On the Subsistence of Evils* were Proclus' most widely read works after the *Elements of Theology*. This is undoubtedly because the texts were relatively modest in compass, were produced in a format less academic than that employed in the commentaries, and dealt with matters of common philosophical interest. The popularity of these works was enough to ensure that they were paraphrased or plagiarized by other writers beginning with pseudo-Dionysius in the fifth to sixth centuries and continuing with Isaac Sebastokrator (a relative of Emperor Alexios II Komnenos) in the eleventh century. These two cases of verbatim borrowing have turned out to be especially providential from the viewpoint of modern scholarship, since that of Dionysius has provided the clearest evidence of the perpetrator's non-apostolic status while that of Isaac Sebastokrator has left us the only portions of these texts now extant in the Greek. Also in the Byzantine world, Psellos' *De omnifaria doctrina* draws upon the *Ten Doubts concerning Providence* in order to explain the manner of God's foreknowledge of future contingents and from *On the Subsistence of Evils* for the doctrine of the non-substantiality of evil. In the Latin world there are several striking examples of the exploitation of these *Opuscula*. Ideas

[33] On Patrizi see the chapter by T. Leinkauf in the present volume.
[34] For further details see Deitz (1999).

derived from *Ten Doubts concerning Providence* and *On Providence and Fate* form the nucleus of the extensive arguments near the end of Boethius' *On the Consolation of Philosophy* dealing with the unfolding of the power pre-existing in Providence by things subject to Fate and with the determination of the nature of objects primarily by the nature of the subject that knows them. The fact that in the thirteenth century William of Moerbeke was able to translate the three *Opuscula* into Latin shows that they were at that date still extant in the Greek. Having first left some evidence of their presence in Paris through several passages in James of Viterbo's works,[35] the same *Opuscula* contribute important material to Berthold of Moosburg's commentary on the *Elements of Theology* including certain notions that are typical of Proclus but less prominent in this specific Proclean work: for example, the notion of the *unum in nobis* that was to become the hallmark of the later German mystical tradition. Finally, ideas drawn from *On the Subsistence of Evils* are combined with those notions in pseudo-Dionysius and Boethius that parallel them most closely in order to develop parts of Marsilio Ficino's commentary on Plotinus' *Ennead III. 2: On Providence: First Treatise.*

3. *Commentary on Plato's Parmenides*

There is evidence that some Byzantine intellectuals were familiar with Proclus' *Commentary on Plato's Parmenides.* Given Proclus' intention of defending the Platonic theory of Forms against the Aristotelian critique and the consequently elaborate discussion of those Forms in the first part of his text, it is perhaps not surprising to find Eustratios of Nicaea exploiting the distinction between the discursive thinking of Soul and the non-discursive thinking of Intellect that is associated by Proclus with different levels of Forms. It is interesting to contrast Eustratios' thoroughly Platonic approach to the *Commentary on Plato's Parmenides* with George Pachymeres' Aristotelian appropriation. Apparently, the Greek text was already by the twelfth century preserved in the incomplete form ending within the first hypothesis that we know today, and Pachymeres therefore decided to complete the missing portion in a strictly logical style by ignoring Proclus' own well-documented plan for the interpretation of the first five hypotheses in a theological manner. In fact, when William Moerbeke translated Proclus' commentary into Latin in the 1260s he was able to preserve part of the text in his Latin version that is no longer extant in the

[35] On this point see the chapter by P. Porro in the present volume.

Greek, and it is in the form given to the text by Moerbeke's translation that the *Commentary on Plato's Parmenides* came to exercise its greatest influence on later western thinkers such as Nicholas of Cusa and Marsilio Ficino. Nicholas of Cusa makes explicit citations of Proclus' text concerning the hierarchy of the three principles in his dialogue *On the beryl* and concerning the self-subsistent principles in his sermon-treatise *Tu quis es? (De principio)*, and it is likely that his general treatments of the distinction between non-discursive and discursive thinking, the application of negative language to God, the nature of the relation between opposites, and the disproportion between God and created things reflect the same source at least in part. In Nicholas' case there is also manuscript evidence of his engagement with the *Commentary on Plato's Parmenides*, since a codex of Strasbourg preserves an extract from Moerbeke's translation apparently copied by him in his youth and the MS *Bernkastel-Kues, Cusanus 186* is a complete copy of the same translation containing around 620 marginal annotations made on at least three different occasions. Marsilio Ficino combines the use of Moerbeke's translation with a close study in the original Greek of Plato's own text and abundant use of Proclus' commentary. The influence of this combined study shows itself already in the 1460s when Ficino noted in the *argumentum* attached to his own translation of Plato's *Parmenides* that the work itself is primarily theological in character and has as its principal topic not so much the Ideas discussed in the first part as the One discussed in the second.[36] Some years later Ficino wrote his own extended commentary on the *Parmenides* in which he follows Proclus in his general approach to the negative and affirmative meanings of the various hypotheses but departs from his predecessor in mitigating the polytheistic tendency of the text by insisting that not every conceptual distinction corresponds to a distinction between orders of gods. With Ficino, the character of the *Parmenides* dialogue is seen more to reflect the character of Parmenides' original poem and to represent a mixture of philosophy and poetry, seriousness and playfulness.

4. *Platonic Theology*

Although the *Platonic Theology* was obviously understood by Proclus to be one of the definitive statements of his philosophy, the work's uncompromising polytheism must have limited its readership within the Christian

[36] On this point see the chapter by M. J. B. Allen in the present volume.

intellectual community of the Middle Ages. There are perhaps only one or two verbal echoes to be found in the writings of Byzantine thinkers. Attention has recently been drawn to Eustratios of Nicaea's use of the notion of the "proximity" (γειτνίασις) of Soul to Intellect: an idea seemingly derived from the first book of the *Platonic Theology*.[37] H.-D. Saffrey has examined a passage in Pachymeres' commentary on Dionysius' *On the Celestial Hierarchy* revealing the commentator's familiarity with Proclus' doctrine of the "implacable" (ἀμείλικτοι) gods in *Platonic Theology* V.[38] It is certainly striking that among Byzantine writers neither Nicholas of Methone, whose primary polemical target was the polytheism of Proclus, nor George Gemistos Plethon, who revived the pro-polytheist agenda in the fifteenth century, made any obvious use of this text. Nevertheless, the *Platonic Theology* undergoes a significant revival in the Latin-speaking world of the late Middle Ages and Renaissance. Nicholas of Cusa commissioned Pietro Balbi of Pisa to make a translation of the work into Latin in the late 1450s – the process of translating and commenting on it being reported in dramatic form in Nicholas' dialogue *Concerning the "Non-Other"* of 1461, where Balbi appears as one of the characters – and it is possible that the future cardinal was also the motivating force behind a translation that had been begun but not completed by Ambrogio Traversari before 1439. Evidence of Nicholas' study of the *Platonic Theology* can also be found in the abundant *marginalia* in his personal copy of Balbi's translation which is now the MS *Bernkastel-Kues, Cusanus 185*. He draws attention here to such topics as the ancient tradition of theology in book I, the use of the phrase *non aliud* in book II, the ubiquity of triadic structures in book III, the references to the coincidence of opposites in book IV, and the nature of intellect in book V. There is also a further citation of the work in Nicholas' *De venatione sapientiae* of 1462, where the correspondence of the hierarchy of gods in Proclus with the hierarchy of divine names in Dionysius is noted. In the next generation there is evidence of the study of Proclus' *magnum opus* on the part of Marsilio Ficino, whose mention of Balbi's translation in his letter of 1489 to Martin Prenninger suggests that he may have consulted it and whose lexical notes and detailed summary of the Greek text in the MS *Firenze, Riccardianus 70* show a profound understanding of the latter's contents. The suggestion frequently made that the title if not the doctrine of Ficino's own *Theologia Platonica* was inspired by Proclus is probably

[37] On this point see the chapter by M. Trizio in the present volume.
[38] See Saffrey and Westerink (2003), lxiv–lxvii.

correct. Moreover, in the independent philosophical writings of Ficino, much information of a doxographical kind – for example, concerning the origins of the so-called "ancient theology," the different schools of later Platonists, and their various approaches to the *Parmenides* – seems to have been derived primarily from this text. If Ficino was somewhat wary of the polytheistic tone of Proclus' treatise, his younger contemporary Giovanni Pico della Mirandola was less circumspect, deriving most of the arguments attributed to Proclus in his *900 Conclusions* from book V of the *Platonic Theology*. Finally, evidence of reading this work can be found in the writings of numerous Italian thinkers of the same or immediately subsequent generations, including Agostino Steucho, Giles of Viterbo, and Francesco Patrizi.

5. *Commentary on Plato's Timaeus*

The most unambiguous evidence regarding the study of Proclus' *Commentary on Plato's Timaeus* in the medieval Byzantine world is provided by Michael Psellos, who refers to the discussion of the eternity of the world found in that work in his *De omnifaria doctrina*, and at greater length to the discussion of the mathematical structure of soul in one of his shorter philosophical essays. In the medieval West between the time of Boethius' *On the Consolation of Philosophy*, which seems to depend on this work for the summary of Platonic cosmology in book III, poem 9, and the late thirteenth century, when William of Moerbeke translated three extracts into Latin, Proclus' commentary was completely unknown, the *Timaeus* itself being studied with great zeal by William of Conches, Thierry of Chartres, and others but exclusively in the Latin translation with accompanying commentary by Calcidius. Moerbeke's three extracts come from Proclus' discussion of prayer at the beginning of his second book and were put to good use by Henry Bate of Mechelen (Malines) in parts XI and XXIII of his *Speculum divinorum et quorundam naturalium*, the emphatically Platonic philosophical compendium mentioned earlier.[39] When the entire text of Proclus' *Commentary on Plato's Timaeus* became available in the original Greek to western scholars in the Renaissance, there was naturally an upsurge of interest. Thus, Marsilio Ficino – who had access to two manuscripts of the work: *Firenze, Riccardianus 24* and *Città del Vaticano, Chigianus R VIII 58* – exploits various aspects of its mathematical psychology

[39] For collection and discussion of these fragments see Steel (1985), 559–587.

in his *Commentary on the Nuptial Number in Plato's Republic*, its interpretation of the myth of Atlantis in his *Compendium on the Timaeus*, and its teachings concerning the indissoluble vehicle of the soul, the status of eternity and time, and the daemonic nature of *Fortuna* in his *Commentary on Plotinus' Ennead III*. His younger contemporary Giovanni Pico della Mirandola's *900 Conclusions*, in addition to depending on other works of Proclus for his propositions *secundum Proclum*, uses the *Commentary on Plato's Timaeus* as the primary doxographical source for the propositions *secundum Porphyrium* and *secundum Iamblichum*.

6. Other works

Studies in the history of reception of other works of Proclus in the Byzantine milieu have not progressed very far. Among the meager results to date, one should at least mention A.-Ph. Segonds' discovery of a probable citation of the *Commentary on the First Alcibiades*[40] in George Pachymeres' commentary on Dionysius, and D. O'Meara's of a possible one from the *Commentary on Euclid's Elements* in Psellos' *Chronographia*.[41] During the Renaissance, Marsilio Ficino's reading of the Greek texts of some of Proclus' other writings can be documented. The *Commentary on Plato's Republic* represents an interesting case since the manuscript on which the tradition depends was separated into two parts. Ficino obtained the first part covering dissertations I–XII in 1492 (now *Firenze, Laurentianus 80.9*), and he refers to his translation of extracts from it that are now lost in a letter. However, the second part of the manuscript, which W. Kroll was able to use for his Teubner edition, did not come to light until late in the sixteenth century. Ficino obtained a copy of the *Commentary on the First Alcibiades*, publishing some extracts from it in his own Latin translation in a collection of minor texts by ancient Platonists that he published in 1497. The work had already been quoted in Ficino's *Commentary on Plotinus' Ennead III. 5: On Love* in connection with the notion of self-knowledge. Proclus' *Commentary on Plato's Cratylus* is probably the source of Ficino's own notion of a sublunary Demiurge that he elaborated in conjunction with his reading of a scholion on the *Sophist* that he attributed to Proclus. Ficino also obtained a copy of the essay *On the Hieratic Art*, publishing this in his own Latin translation – under the title of *De sacrificio et magia* – in the same collection of minor Platonic texts published in 1497. This work

[40] See Segonds (1985), cxvii–cxviii. [41] See the chapter by D. O'Meara in the present volume.

had already been utilized quite extensively in Ficino's *De vita*, book III in connection with the notion of theurgic *seirai.* Significant doubt remains whether Ficino knew the *Hymns* or the *Commentary on Euclid's Elements*, the balance of probability being affirmative in the former and negative in the latter case.

Bibliography

Alexidze, L. and Bergemann, L. (eds. and trans.) (2009) *Ioane Petrizi, Kommentar zur Elementatio theologica des Proklos*, Amsterdam and Philadelphia.

Boese, H. (ed.) (1990) Henricus Bate, *Speculum divinorum et quorundam naturalium, XI–XII: On Platonic Philosophy*, introduction and analysis by C. Steel, Leuven.

Bos, E. P. and Meijer, P. A. (eds.) (1992) *On Proclus and His Influence in Medieval Philosophy*, Leiden, New York, and Cologne.

Deitz, L. (1999) "Space, Light and Soul in Francesco Patrizi's *Nova de universis philosophia* (1591)," in A. Grafton and N. Siraisi (eds.), *Natural Particulars, Nature and the Disciplines in Renaissance Europe*, Cambridge, MA, 139–169.

Imbach, R. (1978) "Le (néo-) platonisme médiéval: Proclus latin et l'école dominicaine allemande," *Revue de théologie et de philosophie* 110: 427–448.

Klitenic Wear, S. (2011) *The Teachings of Syrianus on Plato's Timaeus and Parmenides*, Leiden and Boston.

Kristeller, P. O. (1987) "Proclus as a Reader of Plato and Plotinus, and His Influence in the Middle Ages and in the Renaissance," in J. Pépin and H.-D. Saffrey (eds.), *Proclus lecteur et interprète des anciens, Actes du colloque international du Centre National de la Recherche Scientifique, 2–4 octobre 1985*, Paris, 191–211.

Lang, H. S. and Macro, A. D. (2001) *Proclus: On the Eternity of the World*, introduction, translation, and commentary, Berkeley and Los Angeles.

Podskalsky, G. (1976) "Nikolaos von Methone und die Proklosrenaissance in Byzanz (11./12. Jh.)," *Orientalia Christiana Periodica* 42, 509–523.

Saffrey, H.-D. (1966) "Un lien objectif entre le pseudo-Denys et Proclus," *Studia Patristica* 9, Berlin, 98–105. Reprinted in Saffrey (1990), 227–234.

(1979) "Nouveaux liens objectifs entre le pseudo-Denys et Proclus," *Revue des sciences philosophiques et théologiques* 63: 3–16. Reprinted in Saffrey (1990), 235–248.

(1990) *Recherches sur le Néoplatonisme après Plotin*, Paris 1990.

Saffrey, H.-D. and Westerink, L. G. (eds.) (2003) *Proclus: Théologie platonicienne*, vol. v, Paris.

Segonds, A.-Ph. (ed.) (1985) *Proclus: Sur le Premier Alcibiade de Platon*, vol. i, Paris.

Steel, C. (ed.) (1985) *Proclus: Commentaire sur le Parménide de Platon, traduction de Guillaume de Moerbeke*, vol. ii, Leuven.

Steel, C. and van de Vyver, E. (eds.) (1994) Henricus Bate, *Speculum divinorum et quorundam naturalium, VI–VII: On the Unity of Intellect; On the Platonic Doctrine of the Ideas*, Leuven.

Sturlese, L. (1987) "Il dibattito sul Proclo Latino nel medioevo fra Università di Parigi e lo studium di Colonia," in G. Boss and C. Seel (eds.), *Proclus et son influence, Actes du colloque de Neuchâtel, juin 1985*, Zurich, 261–285.

Wakelnig, E. (2006) *Feder, Tafel, Mensch: Al-'Āmirī's Kitāb al-Fuṣūl fī l-Ma'ālim al-ilāhīya und die arabische Proklos-Rezeption im 10. Jh., Texte, Übersetzung und Kommentar*, Leiden and Boston.

PART I

Proclus

CHAPTER I

Proclus' life, works, and education of the soul

Lucas Siorvanes

Biographical sources

Proclus' biography was drafted less than a year after his death by his student and immediate successor, Marinus. It is not just a story of his life, but an account of the Neoplatonic family of meanings "concerning well-being" (περὶ εὐδαιμονίας) also translated "concerning true happiness." Marinus paints a portrait of a philosopher-saint, who fulfilled all the virtues possible for a mortal. His exposition makes liberal use of rhetorical forms and material,[1] while he treats rhetoricians as if he were in Socrates' time. He adopts silence on the violent events of the fifth century AD; except for a handful of dark hints, one could think that Proclus lived in some period of classical antiquity.

The other main source for Proclus' life and character is a collection of fragments from Damascius, who was head of the philosophy School from AD 515 until its forced closure in 529/31 in the reign of Emperor Justinian. He wrote a *Life* of his teacher Isidorus, himself a student of Proclus. It amounts to a *Philosophical History*.[2] Damascius' account is also based on the Neoplatonic theory of virtue but is sensitive to the degree that thinkers fell short of his version of the philosophical ideal. It is full of biting anecdotes about the fifth-century professors. He admires Proclus but receives him more critically. Damascius does mention the personalities and events that punctuated the fifth century's historic changes, from the murdered philosopher Hypatia (AD 415) to Attila the Hun, to Anthemius, the last noteworthy emperor in Rome (467–72), who had attended Proclus' classes, and to the rule of Italy by the Goths (493).

[1] For allusion and rhetoric in Marinus, see Edwards (2000), Saffrey and Segonds (2001).

[2] References to Athanassiadi (1999).

Proclus' life in facts and figures

Proclus (Πρόκλος) was "the head of the philosophy School in Athens"[3] from about the age of twenty-five until his death on April 17, 485. We do not know for sure when he was born: according to the reported lifespan, in 410/11; or, according to a horoscope, on February 7 or 8, 412.

The first biographical fact we have about Proclus is that he lived "a long life of five and seventy years in all (ὅλοις)" (Marinus, *Vita Procli* 3.55–56). The age of seventy-five is repeated in a later chapter (*VP* 26.27–36). But these references to Proclus' lifespan disagree with the date calculated from a horoscope (more on this later).

His parents possessed "significant wealth" (*VP* 4.29), probably inherited,[4] certainly earned by his father, who was "greatly famous in the royal city in the exercise of litigation (δικανική)" (*VP* 8.23–24). M. Edwards suggested that Proclus' father, Patricius, was a Roman aristocrat appointed as a procurator or fiscal magistrate in the imperial capital.[5] His mother was "Marcella, the legitimate wife of Patricius" (*VP* 6.2–4). Siblings are not mentioned. His birth date/year is not given.

Proclus was born in "Byzantium" (*VP* 6.6): the classical Greek name of "Constantinople." At the time of Proclus' birth it was the capital of the Eastern Roman Empire; in his lifetime it became the sole capital of the Roman world, following the end of the empire in Rome in AD 476, during the reign of Emperor Zeno in Constantinople. His parents, however, came from Lycia (southwest Asia Minor). "Soon after he was born," they returned to the city of Xanthus, Lycia, which "became his own homeland" (πατρίδα αὐτοῦ γενομένην) (*VP* 6.15–18). Later records refer to him as Proclus "from Lycia" (Simplicius, *In Physica* 601.15, etc.), or "Lycian" (Proclus' own *Epitaph*; *Suda* P2473).

He was taught by a grammarian in Lycia, but at an unspecified point during his adolescence he travelled to Alexandria in the province of Egypt, to be "able to choose for himself his teachers" (*VP* 8.4–5). One such teacher was a sophist called Leonas, who invited him to live with his family and introduced him to "those who held the reins of Egypt." A grammarian, Orion, of a priestly cast, instructed Proclus in religious practice. Proclus also attended classes in rhetoric and Latin; he was being prepared to follow in his father's profession (*VP* 8.22–23). Leonas was asked by the "governor

[3] *Suda* P2473: οὗτος προέστη τῆς ἐν Ἀθήναις φιλοσόφου σχολῆς.

[4] It depends on the reading of the phrase: "his ancestors (τῶν πατέρων)" (*VP* 4.29).

[5] Edwards (2000), 68, n. 79.

of Alexandria," Theodorus, to visit the capital, and Leonas invited the "eager" Proclus to accompany him (*VP* 9.1–7).

On this visit to his birthplace, Byzantium, something dramatic happened that prompted Proclus to break with his life so far. We are given no human reason, Marinus briefly saying that "the goddess" exhorted him to turn to philosophy and attend the schools in Athens (τὰς Ἀθήνησι διατριβάς) (*VP* 9.11). Probably, he was inspired by the imperial establishment of a Byzantine higher School in 425, which included a chair in philosophy.[6] It was a period fraught with Athenian "Hellenic" aspirations.[7]

When Proclus returned to Alexandria, he stopped the rhetoric lessons (*VP* 9.12–15) and studied Aristotle's logical treatises (*VP* 9.33) with a philosopher Olympiodorus. He studied mathematics with a namesake of Heron, who inducted him into "piety" (θεοσέβεια), a coded reference to the late antique pagan "Hellenism." Proclus made this big change to his life while still a "stripling boy," an adolescent (μειράκιον) (*VP* 9.20). We do not know if his parents approved of it, for they have disappeared from the biography.

Proclus next set off for Athens itself (*VP* 10.5–10). In three chapters Marinus tells us how he was adopted by the Athenian philosophers through a series of events steeped in Neoplatonic meaning. Setting this aside, Proclus profited from a well-connected supporter, whom Marinus almost dismisses. Nicolaus was a Lycian "fellow-citizen," who studied rhetoric (like Proclus) and later became a famous career sophist. From other sources we know that he was brother to a patrician grammarian in Byzantium, and that in Athens he was a student both of Lachares, the scholarch of rhetoric, and of Plutarch, the scholarch of the philosophy School.[8] Lachares had philosophical interests and kept company with the philosopher Syrianus (*VP* 11), who seems to have been deputy leader of the School.[9] Although Proclus was still an adolescent (μειράκιον), after attending a philosophical seminar he impressed both Lachares and Syrianus (*VP* 11.15–23) by his manner of "free expression" (παρρησία), a term indicative of a philosopher, but originally of Athenian free speech.

At this juncture Marinus gives us an age: he was "a youth (νέος) not yet in his twentieth year" (*VP* 12.2) when Syrianus introduced Proclus to the head

[6] Saffrey and Westerink (1968), xi–xii. [7] Siorvanes (1996), 2–4.

[8] Nicolaus from Myra, Lycia, sophist in Byzantium, brother of Dioscorides, grammarian, proconsul, consul and patrician in Byzantium, *Suda* N395, "known to" (i.e. student of) Plutarch of Nestorius, and Proclus, *Suda* N394. Lachares, "worthy of being called a philosopher" (Damascius, *Hist. phil.* 62A), *Suda* L165. See Kennedy (1983), 66–69.

[9] There is insufficient evidence about the School's precise leadership arrangements. Athanassiadi (1999), 231, n. 247, suggested that "successor" was a title of achievement, without necessarily being the School's leader.

of the philosophy School, Plutarch (Nestorius' descendant biologically or as a student). The latter had been responsible for introducing Iamblichean Neoplatonism in Athens. Although Plutarch was "extremely old," he took Proclus in to study Aristotle's *De anima*, and Plato's *Phaedo*, both of these works dealing with the soul. Plutarch's daughter Asclepigeneia (the older) initiated him into the theurgical way (ἀγωγή), "handed down to her by her father from the great Nestorius" (*VP* 28.12–15). Proclus lodged with Plutarch, who "called him frequently his child" (τέκνον) (*VP* 12.17), while Proclus called Plutarch his "forefather/grandfather" (προπάτωρ).[10]

After approximately two years (*VP* 12.28) Plutarch died and "entrusted this youth" and his grandson Archiadas to his successor Syrianus, who invited Proclus "into his house and his philosophic life." Although Proclus later retained his parental property in Xanthus (*VP* 14.18–20), this became his new family: Syrianus his "father" (πατήρ) and the Platonic "succession" (διαδοχή) his life (*VP* 10.15–16; 12.31–36; 29.31–35).

"In less than two full (ὅλοις) years" (*VP* 13.1) Proclus studied with Syrianus "all the treatises of Aristotle, logical, ethical, political, physical, and the theological knowledge that transcends these (i.e. the *Metaphysics*)" (*VP* 13.2–4). When these "lesser mysteries" were sufficiently learned, Syrianus instructed him in the "mystagogy of Plato," so that his education might proceed in "orderly sequence" (see later, on the Neoplatonic system of education). The textbooks on politics had been Aristotle's political treatises, Plato's *Laws* and the *Republic* (*VP* 14.1–3). He worked "night and day," so that he "delivered so much in a short time that when he was still in his twenty-eighth year he wrote many and various commentaries . . . filled with knowledge, especially the one on the *Timaeus*" (*VP* 13.10–17). He reached the "contemplative" grade.

By then Proclus had succeeded Syrianus as head of School, but we are left to infer the circumstances. According to Damascius and Marinus (*VP* 26), after Syrianus had completed the studies on Plato, he asked Proclus and a "colleague,"[11] "Domninus, a Syrian philosopher who was also a successor" (*VP* 26.8), to choose between lectures on the Orphic or the Chaldaean theology. The two disagreed, while Syrianus "did not live very long." At some stage Proclus wrote a "cathartic treatise" against Domninus' "superficial understanding of philosophy" that "distorted" Plato (Damascius, *Historia philosophica* 89).[12]

[10] Marinus, *VP* 29.31–35; Proclus, *In Parm.* 1058.22.

[11] Proclus, *In Tim.* 1.109.31–110.1: " ὁ ἑταῖρος ἡμῶν Δομνῖνος."

[12] In *Suda* D1355.

Marinus does not tell us when Proclus became head of School. It is estimated that he spent six years under philosophical instruction: about three years on Aristotle and three years on Plato.[13] So, he became the leading "Platonic Successor" around the age of twenty-five or twenty-six.

Marinus does offer fascinating glimpses into Proclus' political influence in Athens and cities abroad (*VP* chs. 14–16), his cosmopolitan practices (*VP* 19), his intrepid worship of polytheistic deities under a Christianized regime (*VP* chs. 29–33), his daily schedule (*VP* chs. 22 and 24), and the running and location of the School (*VP* chs. 22–23, 29). The Neoplatonic School flourished at the foot of the Acropolis. Plato's Academy had been located outside the ancient city walls, which Proclus visited to honor the memory of the ancestors' souls (*VP* 36.16–17).

Damascius draws attention to an unexpected fact: Proclus' School was truly wealthy. By contrast, the Alexandrian philosophy School relied on student fees and city grants, and its leader was preoccupied with finances. In Damascius' eyes (*Hist. phil.* 118), Ammonius (former student of Proclus', and son of Proclus' colleague Hermeias) was "a man of sordid greed for gain, who saw everything in money-making terms." Still, the Alexandrian School continued well into the sixth century, after the closure of the Athenian.

> Plato was poor (πένης): he had owned only the garden of the Academy, which was only a tiny portion of the Successors' property. It produced a revenue of just three gold coins, whereas by the time of Proclus the income from the whole property had increased to the amount of 1,000 coins or more . . . as holy lovers of learning at various times bequeathed in their wills property to the School . . . for the leisure (the original meaning of "school" [σχολή]) and tranquillity of the philosophical life. (Damascius, *Hist. phil.* 102)

Assuming it is not a rhetorical device, 1,000 Roman "solidi" of gold annually had the following purchasing power:[14] 1–2 solidi for a year's food subsistence; 4–5 solidi for annual rations for a soldier (the word derived from "solidus") or 30 for full provision; 35-solidi salary for a grammarian or rhetorician, around 100 solidi combining public and private income; 50–90-solidi salary for a doctor-in-chief, or a judge; 188 solidi (1,500 in eight years), exceptionally lucrative teaching funded from public and private sources (Libanius, *Orat.* 1.61); 600-solidi salary for a crown-counsel, fiscal

[13] Saffrey and Westerink (1968), xv–xix; Lloyd (1990), 4–6.

[14] Teachers' salaries from Kaster (1988), 117–118, 122, and n. 120 (quoting Libanius, *Orat.* 1.61); imperial officials' salaries from A. H. M. Jones (1964), vol. 1, 397–398, 447–449, and 509. In addition to these salaries, an imperial official collected all sorts of charges.

advocate (like Proclus' father?); 700–800 solidi for a province governor; 1,000-solidi pension to chief palace minister.

Proclus exercised pastoral care to those under his charge, and to the city, according to the traditional and Neoplatonic views of involvement with the world. In his fortieth year, it is said, he stopped a drought and an earthquake, and he spoke inspired utterances again in his forty-second year, when he attained the virtue of "theurgy" (θεουργία) (*VP* 28).

He led an ascetic life, refrained from eating meat except token meat for religious purposes, and abstained from carnal sex. Damascius records that Proclus was one of four Neoplatonist virgins in a century: Hypatia (*Hist. phil.* 43A), Proclus (56), Marinus (97B), Sarapion (111). Only "some divinity prevented Proclus" from marrying "the most beautiful and noble woman of Alexandria," Aedesia, a philosopher relation of Syrianus (*Hist. phil.* 56). Above all, Proclus stayed active, avoiding "sloth." His daily routine was:

> "He held five, sometimes even more classes of interpretation in a day and generally wrote about seven hundred lines. He held formal conversations (συγγίγνομαι) with the other philosophers, taking the lead, and further, he held evening seminars that were not written up. And he did all these things after a night of his sleepless worship (θρησκεία), and after his venerations (προσκυνῆσαι) to the rising, midday, and setting sun. (*VP* 22.30–37)

During his tenure he tried to lead the philosophical "undisturbed" life (ἀταραξία) (*VP* 20.10–11). But his hot temper was a fact that even Marinus "could not deny" (*VP* 16.10–20). Moreover, Marinus admits that "external events fell on him unexpectedly and those that seemed to be contrary to reason" (*VP* 20.18–20; *VP* 15.15–17), while Proclus speaks of "the many unending troubles" (*Hypotyposis astronomicarum positionum* 1.17–18).

Proclus left Athens for a year and went to Lydia, north of Lycia (*VP* 15.33–35). His return may be dated after Emperor Theodosius' death in 450, or earlier in the 440s.[15] There he made a philosopher friend, to whom, after his return, he addressed the book *Outline of Astronomical Hypotheses*,[16] and who could be the Pericles of Lydia (*VP* 29.17) cited in the *Commentary on Plato's Parmenides* and the *Platonic Theology*. Later Proclus witnessed the removal of Athena's statue from the Parthenon (*VP* 30.5–11) by the Christians, the event perhaps being dated to AD 465.[17]

[15] For AD 450 and later, H.-D. Saffrey, "Allusions anti-chrétiennes chez Proclus, le diadoque platonicien," reprinted in Saffrey (1990), 553–563. For the 440s, Watts (2006), 105.

[16] "Last year when I was with you in middle Lydia": Proclus, *Hyp. Astr.* 1.14.

[17] Frantz (1988), 77. See Lane Fox (2005), 19–50 on the Parthenon's conversion into a church dedicated to the Virgin Mary before AD 490.

Damascius, on the other hand, gives a wealth of worldly reports about the fifth-century AD events, with references to Attila, the emperors Valentinian (Rome) and Theodosius II (Constantinople) (Damascius, *Hist. phil.* 50–51, 115); to Proclus' statesmen students, such as the "Hellenic-minded" Byzantine patrician Anthemius (*Hist. phil.* 51, 77A), who became emperor of the West (but was killed by his Germanic general); to his fellow-student, the philosopher Severus, who was visited in Alexandria by Indian Brahmans and became Anthemius' chief minister in Rome (*Hist. phil.* 51C–D); to the rise of the Ostrogoth leader Theodoric, "who now has supreme rule over the whole of Italy" (*Hist. phil.* 51). In Byzantium Plutarch's student Hierocles (420s/30) had been beaten until he was bathed in blood (*Hist. phil.* 45B). During a rebellion (484–488/9) in the reign of Emperor Zeno, "Hellenic" associates were persecuted. In Alexandria philosophers suffered (*Hist. phil.* 119), and two prominent theurgists Horapollo and Heraiscus were tortured (*Hist. phil.* 117A–C), while Damascius and his teacher Isidorus escaped to join Asclepiodotus of Alexandria, a dear student of Proclus', who flourished in the city of Aphrodisias, in Caria near Lycia.

In his last five years Proclus' health deteriorated, his exceptional adherence to "his harsh and insupportable diet . . . and other acts of endurance (διακαρτερήσεις) having exhausted the natural well-being of his body" (Marinus, *VP* 26.37–41). He thought back to his student days, when the dead Plutarch had appeared to him in a dream and prophesied that the number of Proclus' note-pages on the *Oracles* would count his years: seventy. Later, his reliable powers of recollection were failing him selectively (*VP* 20.11–15).

The philosophy School seems to have been a challenging place (ἀνταγωνίζομαι: Damascius, *Hist. phil.* 54), where Proclus channelled his hot-tempered, competitive ambition for honor (φιλοτιμία) into the pursuit of excellence.[18] Although Marinus was taking on the responsibilities of successor, he was infirm, and Proclus "feared that the true golden chain of Plato might abandon our city of Athena" (Damascius, *Hist. phil.* 98E–F, 97, 151–152). The School's future leadership was being contested by Asclepiodotus, but especially by Hegias and his father, Theagenes, who had compelling connections (Damascius, *Hist. phil.* 99A, 100A, 101, 145A–B). Theagenes was a wealthy archon (chief magistrate) of Athens, "our benefactor," and married to Asclepigeneia (the younger), daughter of Archiadas the grandson of the scholarch Plutarch. The philosophy succession went for a while to Isidorus, who was present as a pallbearer at Proclus' funeral.

[18] Other hot temperaments: Isidorus (Damascius, *Hist. phil.* 15A), Theagenes (*Hist. phil.* 100).

Proclus was buried in a joint grave with Syrianus on the Athenian hill Lycabettus (*VP* 36.24–30). Marinus does inform us of when Proclus died (*VP* 36.1–4, 37.1–12). He triangulates the date from different sources: by reckoning the number of years (124) since the accession of the Hellenists' hero, Emperor Julian (around AD 361); by naming the contemporary Athenian archons; by citing the date and month in Athenian and Latin calendars: April 17. Best of all, Marinus locates the year of Proclus' death between two objective celestial phenomena: eclipses of the sun, one already witnessed (January 14, 484, shortly after sunrise), and one predicted to be observed in Athens. If the latter corresponded to the annular solar eclipse of November 1, 487, Proclus may have died in 486. Although this option would help to resolve the problem of his year of birth, its possibility has been ranked as minor. The most likely candidate is the partial eclipse of May 19, 486.[19] So, we arrive at the date of Proclus' death: April 17, 485.

Symbolism of Proclus' life and ages

Marinus highlights the biographical data for what mattered to the Neoplatonist circle of philosophers. They are presented not simply as literal facts to be verified by exact science, but as meaningful stages in the "procession" of an inspired philosophical soul.

Proclus' birth marked the "descent" of his soul into the mortal "shell." Porphyry estimated Plotinus' time of birth by "reckoning backwards" his lifespan from his time of death, for Plotinus "never told anyone the month in which he was born nor the day of his birth" (Porphyry, *Vita Plotini* 2.35–44). Marinus does not seem to have known Proclus' birthday either, but he similarly furnishes us with the lifespan and time of death. The birthdays they celebrated were the traditional ones of Plato and Socrates as representatives of divine life (Marinus, *VP* 23.15–17, and Porphyry, *VPlot.* 2.40–44).

Before Proclus joined the Athenian School around his twentieth year, he was a "stripling boy" (μειράκιον). In Greek pedagogy and in Plato's *Republic* the term "μειράκιον" signified the age range in which one was fit to sustain rigorous training at preparative stage. The twentieth year corresponded to the age grade of a senior trainee, who can learn comprehensively.[20]

[19] For solar eclipses and possible year of Proclus' death, see Schove (1984), 83, including references to earlier survey works.

[20] On training (ἀγωγή), "adolescent" (μειράκιον) and "youth" (νέος) in philosophical training, e.g. Proclus, *In Parm.* 676.2–39; on μειράκιον Alcibiades as the preparative stage in philosophical training, Olympiodorus, *In Alc.* 180.15–181.7; on child–adolescent–man, twenty years, in Plato,

The subsequent ages of (twenty-one implied), twenty-eight, forty-two, seventy, fall into a pattern of seven: a highly meaningful number in the (Neo)Pythagoreanism known to Proclus and applied to a scheme of the significant ages of man. Moreover, by meaningful coincidence, the twenty-eighth and fortieth years match ages of important events in Plotinus' life.[21] On Proclus' own evidence (*In Parm.* 683.18–27), the Greeks traditionally considered a man older than seventy no longer an elder (πρεσβύτερος) but a geriatric case.[22] The seventieth year seems to have marked the symbolic end of one's intellectual life.

Death signified the release of one's soul from the body, and "return" towards true reality. Marinus celebrates Proclus' death soberly, by recording the eclipses that marked "the departure of the light in philosophy" (*VP* 37.11–12). The reported age when he died, seventy-five, corresponded to the age limit for holding the top office of Examiner in Plato's *Laws* (946c). Seventy-five was also the "icon" of the non-rational psyche living in the realm of generation, as discussed at length in Proclus' *Commentary on Plato's Republic* 2.19–70 (cf. Plato, *Timaeus* 35b–36e). Reaching seventy-five may have symbolized the limit of one's physical capabilities.

The matter of Proclus' horoscope

Towards the end of the biography Marinus concludes the case for Proclus' life by bringing retrospective proof from the "disposition of the stars under which he was born" (*VP* 35); the text contains a set of astronomical data for astrology, of unknown provenance. Marinus had a special interest in mathematics (e.g. Damascius, *Hist. phil.* 97G, Test. III 81; Photius 181), and his surviving works include astronomy and methods of calculation.[23] The

Republic 498a–c, 537a–d, to 539d. On training-ἀγωγή and age-grades, Kennell (1995), 32–39. On number seven and age-grades, Iamblichus, *Theologumena arithmeticae* 55.11–56.7; Philo, *De opificio mundi* 102–106.

21 Proclus completed many commentaries and reached the philosopher's contemplative virtue by the age of twenty-eight (*VP* 13). By fascinating coincidence, this is the very age when Plotinus first felt the impulse to study philosophy at Alexandria (Porphyry, *VPlot.* 3.7–8). Proclus started to reach the highest possible human virtue, the theurgic, in his fortieth year (*VP* 28). By another coincidence, it was the age when Plotinus arrived in Rome (*VPlot.* 3.23–24), where he would establish his philosophy circle. Is Marinus suggesting to his audience that the precocious Proclus surpassed Plotinus?

22 From Hippocrates(?), *Hebdomads* 5–6. According to Aristotle, *History of Animals* 545b25, human males can be fertile until the age of seventy. The symbolism of Proclus' ages was discussed earlier in Siorvanes (1996), 25–26.

23 Marinus' astronomical works, Tihon (1976), 167–184. This, the interpretive and practical astronomical interests of the fifth–sixth-century philosophy schools (the observations conducted in Athens and Alexandria have been well recorded by Neugebauer [1975], 1031–1050), are omitted from A. Jones (1999).

Athenian School's activities in philosophy, astronomy, and its "interpretive" arm, astrology, were the specific targets for the ban as enforced locally on Emperor Justinian's authority (Watts [2006], 128–142).

The horoscope's data have been amended and recalculated with greater precision in relation to the date for which it was cast,[24] but questions remain. Regarding the birth year, are Proclus' lifespan and horoscope two irreducibly different pieces of information?[25] Can they be made to fit by shortening the seventy-five years, so that 485–412 = 73 years? For example, by counting the seventy-five as lunar years, equivalent to seventy-three solar ones (Boissonade citing Fabricius)?[26] Or by making it an aggregate of Proclus' being in his seventieth year (sixty-nine years) plus in the fifth year (four years) thus 69 + 4 = 73 years?[27]

Why was the horoscope cast not for the latitude zone of Byzantium, Proclus' actual birthplace, but for the latitude zone of Rhodes?[28] Rhodes is located close to Xanthus (Lycia), Proclus' parental place, which "became his own native land," "soon after" his birth. Was it procured in Proclus' youth (A. Jones [1999])?

Horoscopes were calculated from astronomical tables spanning long periods of time, and they were often produced many years after the person's birth.[29] Horoscopes of dead natives offered a comparison of the chart's predictions with the person's actual life, but with a hindsight that benefited from over-abundant possible explanations.[30] Was the horoscope "set out" (ἐξεθέμην; *VP* 35.1–5) after Proclus' death to corroborate the fulfillment of his destiny as presented in his biography or to complete the hagiography (Siorvanes [1996])? Interpretation is a horoscope's *raison d'être*. There were artificial and fictional horoscopes, whose astronomical positions were made up to be astrologically consistent.[31]

Since Galileo's time, the Proclus horoscope studies have concentrated on the astronomical data but have not researched what mattered more: the meaning. Relevant sources that can be consulted include: Firmicus

24 A. Jones (1999), 81–88.
25 Évrard (1960), 137–141, contains a useful survey of the problem's suggested solutions.
26 In the Prolegomena (xxiv) of Boissonade's edition (1814) of Proclus' biography. Mentioned in Évrard (1960).
27 Saffrey and Segonds (2001), 73, n. 4, 173, n. 5, and on the background of the horoscope studies see their appendix, 185–201.
28 Neugebauer (1975), 1031–1050. Neugebauer and Van Hoesen (1959), 135–136, horoscope L412.
29 I thank Mossman Roueché for the discussions on the contexts of late ancient philosophical accounts. See Roueché (2011), 1–30, on the *Handy Tables*, and retrospective horoscope casting.
30 Beck (2007), 93–100, on post-mortem astrology.
31 Examples in the fifth century: of artificial horoscope: Neugebauer and Van Hoesen (1959), 134, horoscope L401; of purely fictitious horoscope in Nonnus' *Dionysiaka*, see their p. vii.

Maternus, who knew of Plotinus; Porphyry's astrological work; Paulus of Alexandria (fourth century), and the commentary on Paulus probably derived from lecture notes of the sixth-century Alexandrian Neoplatonist, Olympiodorus. Proclean material can be sought in his major commentaries *On Plato's Republic* and *On Plato's Timaeus*.

Here are some questions to investigate. Does the horoscope correlate with what we know about Proclus from biographies (e.g. his temper, love of work)? What life changes, character profile, profession, and suchlike, emerge from the horoscope's amended data compared with the raw data? What are the meanings for Proclus' "lot" (κλῆρος; *VP* 35.3) of Fortune, and "lot" of Daimon? What would be the readings for Proclus' length of life, according to his "lot," "ascendant," "starter of life," and "destroyer" signifiers? The "length-of-life" astrological calculation was most complex and dangerous: it was punished as high treason if attempted on emperors.

Neoplatonic education and Proclus' biography

For Proclus, philosophical education was a form of induction of the soul by degrees (e.g. *VP* 22.1–15), based on Plato's scheme of graded knowledge (*Republic* books 6–7). It was intended to stimulate the soul to think of her innate truths, to learn in the manner proposed by the Platonic theory of recollection. Doing philosophy was not just a cerebral affair. Since Plato, it was "the gymnastics of the soul" (*Rep.* 498b). Since the Hellenistic schools it was an ἀγωγή (see on Proclus' work: περὶ ἀγωγῆς), a training-up in virtue, a course of living.

The training required natural ability, experience in abstract thinking, and desire for learning.[32] In the stage of "the lesser mysteries" the students were taught Aristotle on logic and language, developed their ethical and political grounding, and were exposed to Aristotle's physical topics. With the mathematics of arithmetic, geometry, music (harmonics), and astronomy they crossed the "bridge" from the sense-perceived to the intelligible domain, indicated by Aristotle's "theology," the *Metaphysics*. On the Plato course, the students read a carefully chosen selection of the Platonic dialogues (typically twelve) entering "the greater mysteries" or "mystagogy." They studied both the logical anatomy and theological significance of the principles of being. Reading Homer was an allegorical way of

[32] Proclus, *In Parm.* 927.20–36.

understanding the soul's journey in the material world (e.g. the *Odyssey*), and of encountering revealed knowledge of the gods.[33]

Marinus wrote Proclus' *Life*, not as a biographical history (*VP* ch. 2), but as an exemplar of the Neoplatonic conception of the soul's journey, through training in ascending degrees of virtue, to true happiness (εὐδαιμονία). One starts with (*VP* 3.1–7) the basic qualities that nature (φύσις) and one's parents endow, that early training inculcates, and that the soul possesses (*VP* ch. 3, chs. 4–5). Then, one cultivates ethics (*VP* chs. 7–13) as exemplified by the political, social virtues (*VP* chs. 14–17). Next comes the "cathartic" virtue, which cleanses the soul from bodily considerations and restores it (*VP* chs. 18–21), ready for the rigors of intellectual contemplation: the "theoretical" virtue (*VP* chs. 22–25). This culminates in the contemplation of unity, which substantiates intelligible being but transcends it. "Beholding" (θεωρία) leads to revealed knowledge. Orphic and "Chaldaean" literature aid the soul towards theurgy (*VP* chs. 26–33).[34]

Proclus' works and the curriculum

As his biography tells us, Proclus could write 700 lines a day. About a third of his writings survive (roughly eighteen of fifty-four titles), numbering at least 1,093,884 words[35] (without counting the fragments surviving elsewhere and pieces in non-Greek). In volume it surpasses the Aristotle corpus (1,015,272 words), and in total Proclus would have competed with the superlative Galen corpus of 2,608,974 words. The works' word-counts are owed to the database of the Thesaurus Linguae Graecae, University of California at Irvine.

Our sources consist of manuscripts that survive in Greek, in Arabic, and in Latin. Our knowledge of Proclus' works has benefited enormously from the devotion of Professors L. G. Westerink, H.-D. Saffrey, A. Segonds, and C. Steel. For the works that have not survived, references can be found in Proclus, in Marinus, in treatises of his colleagues (e.g. Hermeias), his students (e.g. Ammonius), their students (e.g. Asclepius, Damascius, John Philoponus, Olympiodorus, Simplicius), and others. Byzantine collections such as Photius' *Library* (ninth century), the encyclopedic *Suda* lexicon (tenth century), and Arabic sourcebooks such as Ibn al-Nadim's *Kitab*

[33] Sheppard (1980); Lamberton (1986).

[34] Read further: Edwards (2000), O'Meara (2003), O'Meara (1989), Saffrey and Segonds (2001), Westerink, Trouillard, and Segonds (1990).

[35] Goulet (2007), 29–61.

al-Fihrist (tenth century) offer intriguing references to the reception of Proclus and to otherwise unknown pieces of his work.

We can divide his works according to form, audience, or subject, or according to date of composition (up to Proclus' early thirties [*Commentary on Plato's Timaeus* and "much else"], middle [*on Fate, Existence of Evils*], and late in his life [*Commentary on Plato's Parmenides*, the *Platonic Theology*]). Although he did distinguish different types of interpretation, such as ethical, physical, logical, and theological, his monographs, essays, and commentaries address much the same areas of study. To him, even the hymns are philosophical, addressing the principle(s) whither one's soul aims to "return."[36]

Here, his works are listed by their connection to topics of Proclus' curriculum (his polemic against Domninus has not survived: "πραγματεία καθαρτικὴ ἢ ἐπιγραφὴ τῶν δογμάτων τοῦ Πλάτωνος"; ref. *Suda* D1355). In this way I can present in context Proclus' missing works and offer relevant alternatives and/or further references. Their provenance has been verified afresh with the primary sources.

Proclus taught and wrote on Aristotle, Plato, Euclid, Ptolemy, Homer, and others. The curriculum started with a general but very methodical introduction to the aims, definitions, and sources of philosophy. This course covered the different schools of Greek philosophy (including Hedonism), and the different ways by which philosophical material can be examined. In the Aristotle-dominated syllabus, "five are the degrees of philosophy: logic, ethics, physics, mathematics, theology" (Elias, *In Categorias Aristotelis* 121.5–8, and Olympiodorus, *Prolegomena* 9.31–10.25). For the Plato syllabus, the academic Neoplatonists were well aware that Plato's dialogues could be arranged chronologically. However, as philosophers, they selected those whose central theme fitted their "scope" of study (Anonymous, *Prolegomena in Platonis philosophiam* 24–26, 21–23).

Note on marginal symbols used: bullet point indicates an extant or reported Proclus work; "-" no known work by Proclus; ">" see (also) under another curricular topic; "?" unresolved or other attribution.

Introductory level

- Proclus, *Joint and Comparative Reading* (συνανάγνωσις) of philosophy, including *Introduction to Aristotle in Ten Chapters* (ref. Elias, *In Cat.*

[36] Proclus considered Plato's *Timaeus* to be a hymn to the Demiurge of the world (Proclus, *Theol. Plat.* 5.20.75.10–16). Proclus' *Commentary on Plato's Parmenides* starts with a hymn in prose to the gods. On Proclus' hymns, see Van den Berg (2001).

107.3–26 and ff.). This "Proclean treatise" (σύνταγμα Πρόκλειον) is not extant. Can be reconstructed from Ammonius, Olympiodorus, John Philoponus, Simplicius, "David and Elias" on *Prolegomena* and on the *Categories*.[37]

- Porphyry, *Introduction* (*Isagoge*) (Εἰσαγωγή) to Aristotelian logic. Proclus, *Commentary* (ref. Asclepius, *In Metaph.* 142.36–37): not extant. Compare commentary by "Ammonius."
- Proclus, *Outline (ὑποτύπωσις) of the Platonic Philosophy* (ref. John Lydus, *De Mensibus*, 2.8.59, 4.7.25–26. Cf. Proclus, *In Alc.* 10.3–11.17): elements extant in lecture notes produced in sixth-century Alexandria, the *Prolegomena to Platonic Philosophy*.[38]

The "lesser mysteries"

Logic, inclusive of language[39]

> Aristotle, *Categories*. See under Introductory level: Proclus, *Introduction to Aristotle* (ref. Elias, *In Cat.* 107.24–26), and Proclus, *Commentary on Porphyry's Isagoge.*
Compare commentaries by "Ammonius," Olympiodorus, John Philoponus, Simplicius, David/Elias.

- Aristotle, *On Interpretation*. Proclus, *Commentary* (ref. Ammonius, *In De interpr.* 1.6–11; 181.30–32; Stephanus, *In De interpr.* 46.25–47.12): not extant.
  Compare commentary by Ammonius, and Proclus, *Commentary on Plato's Cratylus*.[40]
- Aristotle, *Prior Analytics*. Proclus, *Commentary* (ref. *Commentaria in Aristotelem Graeca* [*CAG*] 4.6 "Ammonius," *In Anal. pr.* 43.30–31; 31.24; 39.2):[41] not extant.
  Compare commentaries by "Ammonius," John Philoponus.
- Aristotle, *Posterior Analytics*. Proclus, *Commentary* (ref. Philoponus, *In Anal. post.* 111.31–112.36):[42] not extant.
  Compare commentary by John Philoponus (and pseudo-Philoponus).

37 In Westerink (1962), see especially xxvi–xxxii, and on the profound direction of Proclus, xxxii–xli. Cf. Lloyd (1990), 4–11; Wildberg (1990), 33–51.

38 Westerink (1962); and Westerink, Trouillard, and Segonds (1990).

39 On Proclus cited by Alexandrians as the primary authority on Aristotelian language theory, see Duvick (2007), Introduction, 2.

40 On similarities between Ammonius, *In De interpr.* and Proclus, *In Crat.*, see Sheppard (1987), 137–152.

41 Correcting reference to "Philoponus *Anal. pr.* 40,30–31" etc., in Westerink (1962), xii, which has been repeated in Westerink, Trouillard, and Segonds (1990), and in other publications.

42 Further reading, Haas, Leunissen, and Martijn (2010), includes a paper on Proclus.

Ethics: general (including Aristotle, Stoics, Pythagorean Exhortations)

- Studied. No commentary by Proclus on Aristotelian or Stoic ethics. Compare Simplicius, *Commentary on Epictetus' Handbook.*

• Proclus, *Commentary on the Pythagorean Golden Verses* (in Latin, *Carmina aurea*) (ref. Arabic *Fihrist*, of Syriac translation); perhaps from an earlier source: partly extant in Arabic translation.

> Proclus, *Commentary on Hesiod's "Works and Days."* The work's "scope" suggests it aimed to educate and calm the passions.[43] See also below under Revealed religion and literature.

• Proclus, *Commentary on Plotinus' Enneads* (ref. Damascius, *In Parm.* 4.14.5–8 (Combès); "David/Elias," *In Isagoge, CAG* 18.2, xxi; preamble attached to Iamblichus, *Myst.* 1.1–10; scholion at Proclus, *In Remp.* 2.371.18; *Catalogus Astrologorum Graecorum*, vol. v.1, 189.28–190.5): short fragments extant, mostly on *Ennead* 1, incl. 1.8 on the origin of evils.[44]

On matters affecting ethical choice:[45]

• Proclus, *Ten Doubts concerning Providence* (13,405 words), Latin translation, a Greek version by the Byzantine Isaac Komnenos.

• Proclus, *On Providence, Fate and What Depends on Us, A Reply to Theodorus, the Mechanist* (5,479 words),[46] Latin translation, also Greek version.

• Proclus, *On the Existence of Evils* (9,437 words), Latin translation, also Greek version.

Ethics: Politics

- Studied Aristotle's political treatises, Plato's *Republic* and *Laws* (ref. Marinus, *VP* chs. 13–14). No commentary on Aristotle's *Politics* or *Nicomachean Ethics* (called "political science," *Eth. Nic.* 1.2).

43 I thank Robbert van den Berg for the comment.

44 See also notes 45 and 46 on Proclus, *On Providence*. According to Porphyry's thematic arrangement of Plotinus, the first *Ennead* concerns the "less weighty problems," "ethical." Topics on providence impacted on ethical choice: "what depends on us," and topics regarding the union of soul with body (cf. Proclus, *Elements of Theology*, props. 184–211) have a strong ethical dimension. The fragment in David, *Prolegomena and Commentary on Porphyry's Isagoge* (1904) *CAG* 18.2, xxi, refers to *eudaimonia* and cites Proclus as commenting that well-being does not avoid the terrible things but perseveres (ἐγκαρτερεῖ) through them. This was an old moral saying from Lucian on *Anacharsis* (38.18) or on training.

45 These three monographs are speculatively placed here, since they were intended for a wider philosophical audience than the few advanced students: see Opsomer and Steel (2003), Introduction, 1. The treatise on the problem of evil gives some idea of what Proclus may have written in his *Commentary on Plotinus' Ennead* 1.8: see Opsomer and Steel (2003), Introduction, 4.

46 See Steel (2007), Introduction, 1–2. For the connection with topics discussed in Proclus' *Commentary on Plato's Republic*, the problem of human responsibility in a deterministic universe, the Stoic discussion of "what depends on us" = responsibility and free choice, see Steel (2007), Introduction, 5–7.

Compare Proclus, *Investigation of the Objections of Aristotle, in the Second Book of the Politics, to Plato's Republic*, essay in Proclus, *Commentary on Plato's Republic* (2.360ff.) under Plato Dialogues, Ethical: Political.

- Proclus, *On the Way of Life* (περὶ ἀγωγῆς) (ref. *Suda* P2473); possibly on political ἀγωγή to mystical union (cf. Proclus, *In Remp.* 1.81.3ff.; 1.84.25–26; 2.66.11–19; *In Tim.* 3.351.19–29). Two books: not extant.[47]

Aristotelian physical topics (including *On the Soul*)

- Proclus, *Elements of Physics* (7,688 words). With a set of initial terms and fifty-two propositions, it presents a demonstrative account, drawing on Aristotle's *Physics* and *On the Heavens*, with a Neoplatonic aim. Some topics appear in the Arabic *Fihrist* as separate titles, *On the Indivisible*, *Definition of the Origins of Natural Phenomena*.
- Aristotle, *Physics*, *On the Heavens*, etc.: studied. Relevant Proclus fragments, including from *Investigation of the Objections of Aristotle to Plato's Timaeus* (see below) and *On the Nature of Place* (περὶ τῆς τοῦ τόπου φύσεως) (ref. Proclus, *In Remp.* 2.199.22, and scholion at 2.380.30), appear in commentaries on Aristotle by Simplicius, John Philoponus, Olympiodorus.
- Proclus, *Letter to Aristocles*. Fragment of a discussion on place and on materiality of the heavens (ref. Simplicius, *In Phys.* 9.615.15): not extant. On Proclus' physics, see also under Plato: Second Cycle, Physics: *Timaeus*.
- Aristotle, *On the Soul* (*De anima*): studied, no known commentary by Proclus.
  Compare commentaries by John Philoponus and pseudo-Simplicius.
  For references to *De anima*, see also in commentaries on Plato's *Phaedo*.

Mathematics, inclusive of astronomy

- *Introduction to the Arithmetic of Nicomachus*. Proclus "believed he had the soul of Nicomachus" (ref. Marinus, *VP* 28.34–36). Perhaps lectures passed on to Ammonius.

[47] The term "ἀγωγή" took the meanings of education, conduct, method, etc. See the Hellenistic schools' concern with "how to live"; Pyrrho and Sextus Empiricus on skepticism as "ἀγωγή" = way of life; and Stoic work "περὶ ἀγωγῆς" by Cleanthes. On Stoic interpretation of ἀγωγή, see Kennell (1995), e.g. p. 100 on philosophical training in virtue (ἀρετή) for the purpose of attaining true happiness (εὐδαιμονία). Without all this precedent, Dodds (1963), xiv, identified "περὶ ἀγωγῆς" solely with theurgical elevation. But Proclus in most of his writings uses "ἀγωγή" to mean training, discipline, method, or way: e.g. political ἀγωγή, dialectical, mathematical, etc.; the mystical "leading-up" sense is accentuated at the initiatory level/mode (cf. ἱερατικὸς τρόπος τῆς ἀγωγῆς . . . μὴ μόνον αὐτὸ μαθηματικῶς θεωρῆσαι καὶ διαλεκτικῶς, ἀλλὰ καὶ ἱερατικῶς, *In Remp.* 2.66.11–19).

Compare commentaries by Asclepius of Tralles, John Philoponus.

- Proclus, *Commentary on Euclid's Elements*, book I (84,453 words). Influential treatise on the status of mathematics, read by Copernicus and in Galileo's circle, quoted by Kepler. Treatise includes many important theorems, e.g. on Parallel Lines, which may be listed indiscriminately as separate titles.

\- Aristoxenus, *Harmonic Elements*, book I (see Proclus, *In Tim.* 2.169.17–26, 2.183.13–22): no commentary by Proclus.
Compare Porphyry, *Commentary on Ptolemy's Harmonics.*

- Proclus, *Outline (ὑποτύπωσις) of the Astronomical Hypotheses* (24,977 words). Critical assessment of the authoritative astronomer Ptolemy.

> See Proclus, *Compilation (συναγωγή) of the Mathematical Concepts of the Timaeus*, under Plato: Second Cycle: *Timaeus.*
Attributed to Proclus:

> "Proclus Ouranodromos" (ref. *Catalogus Astrologorum Graecorum* vol. VI, p. 82, ed. Kroll, 1903): two fragments of this claimed work. Not a treatise title: derived from the epithet "οὐρανοδρόμε Πρόκλε," which occurs in Byzantine scholia on *Hesiod's Works and Days* (one fragment is extracted from a scholion) accompanying the introduction of Proclus, *Commentary on Hesiod* (see under Literary works).[48]

? *Paraphrase of Ptolemy's Tetrabiblos*, *Anonymous Commentary on Ptolemy's Tetrabiblos*; *Sphaera* (text from first-century BC astronomer Geminus).

? *On Eclipses*: sixteenth-century Latin translations "ex Proclo." Perhaps sourced from chapters on Eclipses from the *Tetrabiblos* and/or *Astrologia Dialogus*, e.g. chs. 10–12.

Aristotle's *Metaphysics*

\- Studied. No work by Proclus. Compare commentary by Syrianus.[49]

The "greater mysteries" in two cycles

First cycle of Plato's Dialogues: from knowledge of self to that of the Good
Preparatory

- *Alcibiades* I. Proclus, *Commentary* (68,762 words): survived to *Alc.* page 116b, source for the rest in commentary by Olympiodorus.

[48] A prolegomenon on Hesiod's *Works and Days* ascribed to Proclus, followed by Byzantine scholia (*Poetae minores Graeci*, vol. II, Gaisford): "οὐρανοδρόμε Πρόκλε" in scholion 1.218 (p. 34.3).

[49] See Helmig (2008), 31–52, esp. 40 on shared argumentation between Proclus, *Commentary on Plato's Parmenides* 980.29–981.31, and Syrianus, *Commentary on Aristotle's Metaphysics* 161.14–20, etc.

Ethical: Political

- *Gorgias*. Proclus, *Commentary* (ref. Proclus, *In Remp.* 2.139.18–20, obliquely *In Remp.* 2.140.23–25 and 2.178.3–6), Syriac translation (ref. Arabic *Fihrist*): none extant.
  Compare commentary by Olympiodorus.
- *Republic*. Proclus, *Commentary on Plato's Republic* (167,711 words).[50] A joint and comparative reading (συνανάγνωσις) of diverse essays, including on definition of justice, value of Homeric myths in philosophy, Aristotle's objections.

Purificatory (cathartic)

- *Phaedo*. Proclus, *Commentary* (ref. Marinus, *VP* 12; Proclus, *In Remp.* 2.179.12–15, 2.183.23–25, obliquely, *In Remp.* 2.178.3–6; affirmatively, Elias, *In Isag.* 2.10–11); Arabic translation by Ibn Zur'a (ref. Arabic *Fihrist*): none extant.
  Compare commentaries by Damascius, Olympiodorus.
  On cleansing and restoring the soul from bodily considerations, see:
- Proclus, *On Plato's Three Proofs of Immortality* (ref. Priscianus, *Solutionum ad Chosroem* ch. 1, pp. 47–49; Arabic *Fihrist*): arguments preserved in Arabic and Latin.

Theoretical: Logical

- *Cratylus*. Proclus, *Commentary* (28,788 words): survived (to 407cd) in notes from a student.[51]
- *Theaetetus*. Proclus, *Commentary* (ref. Marinus, *VP* 38.14–15, "he liked it greatly"; Proclus, *In Tim.* 1.255.25–26): not extant.[52]

Theoretical: Physical

- *Sophist*. Proclus, *Commentary* (ref. Proclus, *In Parm.* 774.26): not extant, but elements of it in Proclus, *Commentary on Plato's Parmenides*.[53]
  Compare commentary by the chief Renaissance Neoplatonist, Ficino.[54]

[50] A reading of Plato's *Republic* is speculatively placed here, although it would disturb the Neoplatonic teaching order *Alcibiades–Gorgias–Phaedo*: see Jackson and Tarrant (1998), 4–5. Plato's *Republic* did not have a fixed position in the Neoplatonic curriculum. According to the *Prolegomena to Platonic Philosophy*, ch. 26, "the divine Proclus excluded . . . the *Republic* because it consists of many discourses and is not written in dialogic manner." Proclus had studied it together with Plato's *Laws* and Aristotle's "political" treatises. However, in a flexible curriculum, topics from the *Republic* could be read in addition to *Gorgias*. On the whole subject, read O'Meara (2003). I thank Dominic O'Meara for his comment regarding the placing of the *Republic*.

[51] For its many links, see Van den Berg (2008).

[52] Sedley (1996), 79–103.

[53] Steel (1992), 51–64; Marback (1994), 30–49.

[54] Allen (1989).

- *Statesman* (*Politicus*). No separate commentary, but see Proclus' interpretation in the *Platonic Theology*, book 5, chs. 6–8.[55]
  Compare the Renaissance Ficino, who continued the Neoplatonic linking of the *Sophist* with the *Statesman.*

Theoretical: Theological

- *Phaedrus.* Proclus, *Commentary* (ref. "On the Palinode," Proclus, *In Parm.* 949.39, 1088.27; *In Remp.* 2.282.12–17, 2.312.3, 2.339.15–16; "On the Palinode of *Phaedrus*," Proclus, *In Remp.* 2.309.20–23), cf. *Theol. Plat.* book 4:[56] not extant.
  Compare commentary by Proclus' colleague, Hermeias.
- *Symposium.* Proclus, *Discourse of Diotima* (ref. scholion at Proclus, *In Remp.* 2.371.14): not extant.
  Compare commentary by the Renaissance Neoplatonist, Ficino.

Completion of first cycle

- *Philebus.* Proclus, *Commentary* (ref. Damascius, *Hist. Phil.* 38A): not extant. Read Proclus, *Platonic Theology*, book 3, chs. 8–14. Compare commentary by Damascius.
  On the Good, see also:
- Proclus, *On the Three Monads.* "As we said in the book (βιβλίον) on these three monads" (ref. Proclus, *In Remp.* 1.295.24–25); the three monads of the Good are beauty, truth, symmetry (Proclus, *In Remp.* 1.295.18–28; cf. Proclus, *In Tim.* 2.267.20, *Plat. Theol.* 3, ch. 18; Damascius, *In Phileb.* 2.3–4, 237.1–244.6ff.): not extant.
- Proclus, *The First Good* (ref. Arabic *Fihrist).* If it is not an Arabic version of the *Elements of Theology* (see under Neoplatonic "theology"), it may be Proclus' untitled "*monobiblon*" (ref. Damascius, *De principiis* 1.86.16–17): none extant.[57]

Second cycle of Plato's Dialogues: knowledge of the cosmos and the divine

[55] Dillon (1995), 364–374.

[56] On Proclus' *Platonic Theology* and Plato's *Phaedrus*, Sheppard (2000), 415–423.

[57] In the *Fihrist*, Proclus' *The First Good* is differentiated from Proclus' *Elements (of Theology)*, but the latter was also known in the Arabic world as Aristotle's book on *The Pure Good.* For Proclus, the Good is the Neoplatonic first principle, identical with the One: see Neoplatonic "theology" in Proclus, *El. theol.*, props. 12–13, 119; *Theol. Plat.* book 2, chs. 7–8. Damascius, *De principiis* 1.86.16–17 (Westerink and Combès) mentions a monograph by Proclus, "ὁ φιλόσοφος Πρόκλος ἐν τῷ μονοβίβλῳ," in a discussion about knowledge of the One.

"Summit" of Physics

- *Timaeus*. Proclus, *Commentary* : extant in Greek (325,501 words) to *Tim.* page 44cd (total pages 92c); extant Arabic translation of Proclus, *Commentary* on *Tim.* 89e–90c.
- Proclus, *Investigation of the Objections (ἀντιρρήσεις, ἀντειρημένα) of Aristotle to Plato's Timaeus* (ref. Proclus, *In Tim.* 2.278.27–29, 279.2; John Philoponus, *De aet. mundi* 31.11, 82.14, 138.21, 167.4, etc. to 626.3; Simplicius, *In Cael.* 7.38.4); possibly a preliminary to the *Commentary*: not extant.
- Proclus, *Compilation (συναγωγή) of the Mathematical Concepts of the Timaeus* (ref. Proclus, *In Tim.* 2.76.24); possibly an appendix to the *Commentary*: not extant.

  On Proclus' views of the cosmos, see also:
- Proclus, *On the Eternity of the World.* On Plato's *Timaeus*, arguing that the cosmos must be eternal like its creator, not finite in time (interpretation of certain first- to second-century AD Platonists). Known as "Eighteen Arguments against the Christians" . . . "Proclus is the second after Porphyry to move his defiling and insulting tongue against the Christians" (ref. Byzantine *Suda* P2473) (text also translated in Arabic): extant as part of John Philoponus, *On the Eternity of the World against Proclus*.
- Proclus, *On Light* (περὶ φωτὸς) (ref. John Philoponus, *De aet. mundi* 18.19–19.16, noted by Saffrey and Westerink [1968], lviii): not extant.

"Summit" of Theology

- *Parmenides*. Proclus, *Commentary* (177,636 words) and conclusion of the "first hypothesis" extant in Latin.

  On Neoplatonic "theology" as "first philosophy":
- Proclus, *Elements of Theology* (28,278 words): Proclus' most read book, demonstrating the Neoplatonic metaphysics in 211 propositions.[58]
- Proclus, *Platonic Theology* (149,543 words): the fruit of the *Parmenides* interpretation.[59] *Platonic Theology* is Proclus' crowning opus.

Revealed religion and literature

- Proclus, *Commentary on Chaldaean Philosophy* (1502 words): a sample is extant.

[58] Placed by thematic association. Being a systematic guide to the main levels of being and the soul's relation to body, Proclus' *Elements of Theology* could have been discussed at an earlier stage, or as a preparation to the study of Plato's "theology."

[59] I thank Fr. Saffrey for Saffrey (1984), 1–12. See Steel (2000), 373–398.

- Proclus, *On the Hieratic Art* (1048 words), on theurgy: a small part extant, and perhaps from:
- A larger work on *Mythical Symbols*[60] (ref. Proclus, *In Remp.* 2.109.1–2; cf. *In Remp.* 2.65.3 "in the hieratic art"): not extant.
- Proclus, *On the Mother of the Gods* (ref. Marinus, *VP* 33):[61] not extant.
- Notes on Syrianus, *Theology of Orpheus* (ref. Marinus, *VP* 27), and a work labeled *Agreement of Orpheus, Pythagoras, Plato* (ref. Byzantine *Suda*, ascribed both to Proclus and Syrianus): not extant.
- Proclus, *On the Gods in Homer* (ref. Byzantine *Suda*, ascribed both to Proclus and Syrianus): not extant.
- Proclus, *Commentary on the Whole of Homer* (ref. Byzantine *Suda* P2473): not extant.
  Compare essays on Homer in Proclus, *Commentary on Plato's Republic.* For specimen Neoplatonic allegorical reading, Porphyry, *The Cave of the Nymphs in the Odyssey.*
- Proclus, *Commentary on Hesiod's "Works and Days"* (ref. Byzantine *Suda* P2473): an introduction and assorted scholia extant.

? Scholarship assigns these works to a namesake "Proclus" (ref. Byzantine source Photius' *Library* 239.318–322): *Chrestomathy Grammatica*, an outline on reading Homer (also ref. in *Suda*, under Proclus); *On the Epistolary Style*, on letter writing.

- Proclus, *Hymns* 1–7 (to Athena, Aphrodite, *et al.*) (1151 words).
- Proclus, *Epigrams* (three, of which two are theurgical verses, *VP* 28) and his own *Epitaph* (*VP* 36).

Bibliography

Allen, M. J. (1989) *Icastes, Marsilio Ficino's Interpretation of Plato's "Sophist,"* Berkeley and Los Angeles.

Athanassiadi, P. (1999) *Damascius: The Philosophical History*, Athens.

Baltzly, D. (2006) "Pathways to Purification: The Cathartic Virtues in the Neoplatonic Commentary Tradition," in H. Tarrant and D. Baltzly (eds.), *Reading Plato in Antiquity*, London, 169–184.

Beck, R. (2007) *A Brief History of Ancient Astrology*, Oxford.

Berg, van den, R. (2001) *Proclus' Hymns, Essays, Translations, Commentary*, Leiden.

(2008) *Proclus' Commentary on the Cratylus in Context: Ancient Theories of Language and Naming*, Leiden.

60 Suggested by Dodds (1963), xiv.

61 Beutler (1957) added a lost work (#43) on Hekate, whose reference is found in Marinus, *VP* 28.16–18. On Hekate's place in Proclus' system see Proclus, *Theol. Plat.* 6.11.51.20–27.

Beutler, R. (1957) "Proklos," in Pauly-Wissowa (ed.), *Realenkyklopaedie der klassischen Altertumswissenschaft* 32/1, cols. 186–247.
Blumenthal, H. J. (1984) "Marinus' *Life of Proclus*: Neoplatonist Biography," *Byzantion* 54: 469–494.
Boissonade, J. F. (ed.) (1814) *Marini Vita Procli*, Leipzig.
Dillon, J. (1993) *Alcinous: The Handbook of Platonism*, Oxford.
(1995) "The Neoplatonic Exegesis of the Statesman Myth," in C. J. Rowe (ed.), *Reading the Statesman*, Sankt Augustin, 364–374.
Dodds, E. R. (ed. and trans.) (1963) *Proclus: The Elements of Theology*, 2nd edn., Oxford.
Duvick, B. (trans.) (2007) *Proclus: On Plato's Cratylus*, Ithaca, NY.
Edwards, M. (2000) *Neoplatonic Saints: The Lives of Plotinus and Proclus by Their Students*, Liverpool.
Évrard, É. (1960)"La date de la naissance de Proclus le néoplatonicien," *Antiquité Classique* 29: 137–141.
Fowden, G. (1982) "The Pagan Holy Man in Late Antique Society," *Journal of Hellenic Studies* 102: 33–59.
Frantz, A. (1988) *The Athenian Agora, Late Antiquity: AD 267–700*, Princeton.
Gerson, L. P. (2005) *Aristotle and Other Platonists*, Ithaca, NY.
Goulet, R. (2007) "La conservation et la transmission des textes philosophiques grecs," in C. D'Ancona (ed.), *The Libraries of the Neoplatonists*, Leiden, 29–61.
Haas, F. A., Leunissen, M., and Martijn, M. (eds.) (2010) *Interpreting Aristotle's Posterior Analytics in Late Antiquity and Beyond*, Leiden.
Helmig, C. (2008) "Proclus and Other Neoplatonists on Universals and Predication," *Documenti e studi sulla tradizione filosofica medievale* 19: 31–52.
Jackson, R. and Tarrant, H. (trans.) (1998) *Olympiodorus the Younger of Alexandria 6th cent: Commentary on Plato's Gorgias*, Leiden.
Jones, A. (1999) "The Horoscope of Proclus," *Classical Philology* 94/1: 81–88.
Jones, A. H. M. (1964) *The Later Roman Empire, 284–602*, Oxford.
Kaster, R. A. (1988) *Guardians of Language: The Grammarian and Society in Late Antiquity*, Berkeley.
Kennedy, G. A. (1983) *Greek Rhetoric under Christian Emperors*, Princeton.
Kennell, N. (1995) *The Gymnasium of Virtue*, Chapel Hill, NC.
Lamberton, R. (1986) *Homer the Theologian, Neoplatonist Allegorical Reading and the Growth of the Epic Tradition*, Berkeley, Los Angeles, and London.
Lane Fox, R. (2005) "Movers and Shakers," in A. Smith (ed.), *The Philosopher and Society in Late Antiquity*, Swansea, 19–50.
Lloyd, A. C. (1990) *The Anatomy of Neoplatonism*, Oxford.
Marback, C. (1994) "Rethinking Plato's Legacy, Neoplatonic Readings of Plato's *Sophist*," *Rhetoric Review* 13/1: 30–49.
Masullo, R. (1985) *Marino di Neapoli: Vita di Proclo*, Naples.
Neugebauer, O. (1975) *A History of Ancient Mathematical Astronomy*, part 2, Berlin.
Neugebauer, O. and Van Hoesen, H. B. (1959) *Greek Horoscopes*, Philadelphia.
O'Meara, D. J. (1989) *Pythagoras Revived. Mathematics and Philosophy in Late Antiquity*, Oxford.

(2003) *Platonopolis, Platonic Political Philosophy in Late Antiquity*, Oxford.
Opsomer, J. and Steel, C. (trans.) (2003) *Proclus on the Existence of Evils*, Ithaca, NY.
Roueché, M. (1990) "The Definitions of Philosophy and a New Fragment of Stephanus the Philosopher," *Jahrbuch der Österreichischen Byzantinistik* 40: 107–128.
(2011) "Stephanus the Alexandrian Philosopher, the *Kanon* and a Seventh-Century Millennium," *Journal of the Warburg and Courtauld Institutes* 74: 1–30.
Saffrey, H.-D. (1984) "La Théologie platonicienne de Proclus, fruit de l'exégèse du Parménide," *Revue de théologie et de philosophie* 116: 1–12.
(1990) *Recherches sur le Néoplatonisme après Plotin*, Paris.
Saffrey, H.-D. and Segonds, A.-Ph. (eds.) (2001) *Marinus: Proclus ou sur le Bonheur*, Paris.
Saffrey, H.-D. and Westerink, L. G. (eds.) (1968) *Proclus: Théologie platonicienne*, vol. 1, Paris.
Schove, D. J. (1984) *Chronology of Eclipses and Comets, AD 1–1000*, Woodbridge, Suffolk.
Sedley, D. N. (1996) "Three Platonist Interpretations of the 'Theaetetus'," in C. Gill and M. M. McCabe (eds.), *Form and Argument in Later Plato*, Oxford, 79–103.
Sheppard, A. D. R. (1980) *Studies on the 5th and 6th Essays of Proclus' Commentary on the Republic*, Göttingen.
(1987) "Proclus' Philosophical Method of Exegesis: The Use of Aristotle and the Stoics in the Commentary on the Cratylus," in J. Pépin and H.-D. Saffrey (eds.), *Proclus: lecteur et interprète des anciens, Actes du colloque international du CNRS, Paris 2–4 octobre 1985*, Paris, 137–152.
(2000) "Plato's *Phaedrus* in the *Theologia Platonica*," in A.-Ph. Segonds and C. Steel (eds.), *Proclus et la Théologie platonicienne*, Leuven and Paris, 415–423.
Siorvanes, L. (1996) *Proclus. Neo-Platonic Philosophy and Science*, New Haven, CT.
Sorabji, R. (2006) "The Transformation of Plato and Aristotle," in H. Tarrant and D. Baltzly (eds.), *Reading Plato in Antiquity*, London, 185–193.
Steel, C. (1992) "Le *Sophiste* comme texte théologique dans l'interprétation de Proclus," in E. P. Bos and P. A. Meijer (eds.), *Proclus and His Influence in Medieval Philosophy*, Leiden, 51–64.
(2000) "Le *Parménide* est-il le fondement de la *Théologie platonicienne?*," in A.-Ph. Segonds and C. Steel (eds.), *Proclus et la Théologie platonicienne*, Leuven and Paris, 373–398.
(trans.) (2007) *Proclus: On Providence*, Ithaca, NY.
Tihon, A. (1976) "Notes sur l'astronomie grecque au Vie siecle: Marinus de Naplouse. Un commentaire au Petit commentaire de Theon," *Janus* 63: 167–184.
Watts, E. (2006) *City and School in Late Antique Athens and Alexandria*, Berkeley, and Los Angeles.

Westerink, L. G. (1962) *Anonymous Prolegomena to Platonic Philosophy*, Amsterdam.
Westerink, L. G., Trouillard, J., and Segonds, A.-Ph. (eds.) (1990) *Prolégomènes à la philosophie de Platon*, Paris.
Wildberg, C. (1990) "Three Neoplatonic Introductions to Philosophy: Ammonius, David, Elias," *Hermathena* 149: 33–51.

CHAPTER 2

Proclus as exegete

Anne Sheppard

The work of Proclus, like that of many other philosophers of late antiquity, is presented primarily in the form of exegesis. This chapter will survey not only Proclus' philosophical exegesis but also his exegesis of Euclid and Ptolemy, of Homer and Hesiod, of the *Chaldaean Oracles* and the Orphic poems. We might think of exegesis as primarily an activity concerned with texts but for Proclus the whole world and the activity of human beings within it can be read, "like a book," as we might say. At the end of the chapter I shall consider Proclus' exegesis of divine names and theurgic rites and the way in which exegesis is fundamental to his view of the world overall.

I begin by considering the principles which underlie Proclus' exegesis of texts of all kinds. At the beginning of the *Platonic Theology*, in I.2.10.1–4 Saffrey–Westerink, Proclus declares his intention to "discover the clear meaning of what has been expressed in a riddling way by appealing to other evidence drawn not from assumptions foreign to Plato's thought but from the writings which are most certainly Plato's own." In doing so, he appeals to a principle often associated with the interpretation of Homer – "clarifying Homer from Homer" (Ὅμηρον ἐξ Ὁμήρου σαφήνιζειν) – which is first attested by an earlier Neoplatonist with a strong interest in exegesis, namely Porphyry in his *Quaestiones Homericae* (297.16 Schrader), although it may go back to the Hellenistic scholar Aristarchus. Similar principles can be found in Cicero and in Galen and are applied to Biblical exegesis by both Clement of Alexandria and Origen.[1] Two things are worth noting about this principle of explaining difficult passages in an author's work by appeal to parallels drawn from that same author: first, such a principle implies that the body of work by a given author is treated as a consistent unity. Proclus, like other Neoplatonists, assumed that Plato's work formed such a unity and was not troubled by concerns about matters such as

[1] See Mansfeld (1994), 148–149, 178–179, 204–205.

chronological development. At the same time, he did apparently accept that some of the works ascribed to Plato are not by him.[2] Second, Proclus, like others, aims at clarification of "what has been proposed in a riddling way." The mention of "riddles" (αἰνίγματα) indicates that what Proclus has in mind is exposition of passages that require allegorical interpretation.[3]

The concern for unity and the interest in allegorical interpretation may also be seen in another fundamental principle which Proclus applies to the interpretation of Plato in particular. Proclus follows Iamblichus in holding that every Platonic dialogue has one overall aim or theme (σκοπός). So, for example, he believes that the *Timaeus* is concerned with the physical world and that passages such as the Atlantis story must therefore be understood as allegories relating to that world.[4] Proclus and his contemporaries justified this principle by appealing to Plato's own remarks at *Phaedrus* 264c, where Socrates says that "every speech should hold together as a self-contained body, like a living creature."[5] While it may be attractive to modern readers to see this principle primarily as a concern for literary unity,[6] Proclus is not primarily a literary critic and for him the principle has deeper implications. Ultimately, for Proclus, the point is not just that the Atlantis story reflects the concerns of the *Timaeus* as a whole or that the *Timaeus* in turn reflects other works of Plato. In Proclus' eyes, Plato's entire corpus presents and reflects the underlying unity of the whole world as it was understood by the Neoplatonists. For Proclus the texts of Plato, Euclid, Homer, Hesiod, the *Chaldaean Oracles*, and the Orphic poems all reveal underlying philosophical truths. I shall return to the significance of this at the end of the chapter, after detailed discussion of Proclus' exegesis of all these different kinds of text.

Philosophical exegesis

Much of Proclus' surviving work consists of commentaries on Plato. We have partial commentaries on the *First Alcibiades*, the *Timaeus* and the *Parmenides*, as well as a summary of some of his commentary on the *Cratylus* and a collection of essays on the *Republic*. The lengthy commentary on the *Timaeus* deals with less than half of the dialogue, down to 44d, while the

[2] See Anon. *Proleg. Plat. phil.* 26.1–6 (Westerink 1962).
[3] For the connection of αἴνιγμα and the verb αἰνίττομαι with allegorical interpretation in both classical and Patristic authors, see Buffière (1956), 45–59; Sheppard (1980), 145; Struck (2004), 39–50, 170–177.
[4] *In Tim.* I.4.6–26, 78.12–19, 205.4–16 (Diehl 1903–1906). See also Cleary (2006), 135–150.
[5] Cf. Hermias, *In Phaedrum* 9.6–10 (Couvreur 1901) and the comments in Bielmeier (1930), 23.
[6] See Coulter (1976), 73–94.

commentary on the *Parmenides* deals with the text only down to 142a, again less than halfway through the dialogue. Likewise the material we have from the commentary on the *Cratylus* goes only to 407c, covering twenty-four out of the fifty-seven Stephanus pages of Plato's text, and the commentary on the *First Alcibiades* breaks off in the middle of a discussion of 116a–b, having commented on thirteen out of thirty-two Stephanus pages. It seems reasonable to assume that in all these cases Proclus did in fact discuss the whole dialogue, but that his commentaries have not survived in full.[7] The *First Alcibiades*, often treated as spurious in modern times,[8] was accepted as genuine by the Neoplatonists and was the first dialogue read in the standard curriculum of the pagan Neoplatonic schools.[9] The *Timaeus* and the *Parmenides* formed the culmination of that curriculum and according to Proclus' biographer, Marinus, the *Timaeus* was the dialogue which Proclus regarded as the most important.[10] These three commentaries are clearly related to Proclus' teaching activity in the Platonic school at Athens. The *Cratylus* too was one of the dialogues read in the standard Neoplatonic curriculum. The commentary we have consists of excerpts, made by a later author from a full commentary.[11] We are thus somewhat further removed from Proclus' lecture room when we read this text than when we read the commentaries on the *First Alcibiades*, the *Parmenides*, or the *Timaeus* but, like them, this commentary too reflects the activity described by Marinus in the following passage:

> In his seminars he explained everything in detail ably and clearly and set it all down in writing. He had an immense love of hard work: he used to give five classes of exegesis on the same day – sometimes even more – and generally wrote around 700 lines. He then went straight into discussions with the other philosophers and in the evening gave additional seminars that were not recorded in writing. (*Life of Proclus*, ch. 22)

It is worth noting here that Marinus specifically describes Proclus' main teaching activity as exegesis, using the Greek verb ἐξηγεῖτο. The commentaries of the sixth-century Alexandrian Neoplatonist Olympiodorus, which, like those of Proclus, derive from teaching, are divided into individual lectures, each of which is further subdivided into general interpretation

7 Two fragments of later parts of the *Timaeus* commentary survive in Greek as well as a substantial fragment in Arabic commenting on *Tim.* 89c3–90c7. See Luna and Segonds (2012), 1576 and Arnzen (2013).

8 But see Denyer (2001), 14–26.

9 See Anon. *Proleg. Plat. phil.* 26 (Westerink 1962), especially lines 23–26 and Proclus, *In Alc.* 11 (Segonds 1985–1986).

10 Marinus, *Life of Proclus*, ch. 38 (Saffrey, Segonds, and Luna 2001).

11 See Pasquali (1908), v–vii and Van den Berg (2008), 94.

(θεωρία) and study of individual words or phrases (λέξις). Proclus' commentaries similarly distinguish between general discussion (τὰ πράγματα) and study of particular details (ῥήματα / καθ' ἕκαστα) but the division is less mechanical and the text is not divided into lectures. It has been suggested that this difference between Proclus and Olympiodorus reflects the difference between the two thinkers, or the different nature of their audiences.[12] It might also indicate that Proclus' commentaries, while originating in the classroom, were worked over and revised before the written version was finalized in a way that those of Olympiodorus were not.

The work known as Proclus' commentary on the *Republic* is in fact a collection of sixteen essays plus an additional discussion of Aristotle's objections to Plato in *Politics* 2. Strangely, the *Republic* did not form part of the standard curriculum in the Neoplatonic schools of late antiquity[13] but the essays we have may still be related to Proclus' activity as a teacher. Essays 1–5, 7, 8, 10–12, 14, and 15 all belong together. Some have suggested they formed a course of introductory lectures on the *Republic*, perhaps for a general audience of "serious amateurs."[14] Yet it has also been argued that essays 1, 3, 4, and 5 presuppose philosophical knowledge and expertise and that essay 1 in particular is addressed to an audience of exegetes, or future exegetes.[15] Whatever the intended audience for these essays, it is worth noting that the heading for the first essay uses the term συνανάγνωσις, "reading in class," and that in the opening lines of the essay Proclus addresses his audience as "you."[16] Essay 6 derives from a special lecture given at the annual celebration of Plato's birthday.[17] Essay 16 is a commentary on the Myth of Er in *Republic* 10.[18]

Proclus also wrote commentaries on other Platonic dialogues which have not survived. He himself refers to commentaries on the *Theaetetus*, on the myths in the *Gorgias* and the *Phaedo*, and on Socrates' "palinode" in the *Phaedrus*.[19] Later authors mention commentaries on the *Phaedo*, on

[12] See Festugière (1971), 551–574.

[13] This seems to be the correct interpretation of the statement in Anon. *Proleg. Plat. phil.* 26.6 (Westerink 1962) that Proclus "excluded" (ἐκβάλλει) the *Republic*. See Westerink, Trouillard, and Segonds (1990), lxvii–lxviii.

[14] See Gallavotti (1929), 208–219 and Gallavotti (1971), 41–54; Sheppard (1980), ch. 1; Mansfeld (1994), 36 and 88 (where the phrase "serious amateurs" is used).

[15] See Abbate (1995), 17.

[16] See Mansfeld (1994), 22–23 and Proclus, *In Remp.* I.1.5–7 and I.5.3–9 (Kroll 1899–1901). Mansfeld believes there is no reason not to ascribe the heading for the essay to Proclus himself.

[17] See Proclus, *In Remp.* I.69.23–4 (Kroll 1899–1901) and Sheppard (1980), 29–34.

[18] For a fuller account of the Commentary on the *Republic* see Sheppard (2013).

[19] See Proclus, *In Tim.* I.255.25–26 (Diehl 1903–1906), *In Remp.* II.139.19–20, 179.13, 183.24 (Kroll 1899–1901), *In Parm.* 949.31–32, 1088.21–23 (Steel 2007–2009). Two passages in the *Parmenides*

the whole of the *Phaedrus*, on the *Philebus*, and on Diotima's speech in the *Symposium*.[20] These were all dialogues read as part of the Neoplatonic curriculum mentioned above. Interestingly, some of Proclus' own references to exegesis of these dialogues are more easily interpreted as references to oral teaching than to published commentaries. The phrase at *In Parm.* 1128.29 "as we showed in expounding the *Phaedrus*" (ὡς ἐδείκνυμεν ἐξηγούμενοι τὸν Φαῖδρον) could well be an allusion to oral teaching while the words at *In Tim.* III.295.3–4 "we have also shown this in our discussions about the *Phaedrus*" (καὶ τοῦτο δέδεικται μὲν ἡμῖν ἐν ταῖς εἰς Φαῖδρον συνουσίαις) must be an allusion to a lecture or a seminar rather than to a written commentary.[21] Similarly the commentary on the *Phaedrus* written by Proclus' fellow-student Hermias appears to be based on the lectures by Syrianus which Hermias and Proclus both attended and includes some comments and questions posed by Proclus.[22]

The systematic *Platonic Theology* offers exegesis of Plato of a rather different kind. In this work, in six books, Proclus offers a discursive account of his metaphysical system and attempts to show that all aspects of it can be found in the works of Plato. He sets out the plan for the work in *Theol. Plat.* I.2.9.8–19: first the general notions about the gods, "as transmitted by Plato"; next the ranks, characteristics, and procession of the gods "defining them in Plato's manner and referring everything to the assumptions of the *theologoi*,"[23] and finally the hypercosmic and encosmic gods "celebrated here and there in Plato's works." This is indeed the plan which he follows although the text we have comes to an end with the account of the hypercosmic gods in book VI. The account of the general notions about the gods in book I classifies the attributes of the gods in groups of three according to the Platonic dialogue which, according to Proclus, deals with each group, referring back to the *Laws* in chapters 14–16, the *Republic* in chapters 18–21, the *Phaedrus* in chapters 22–24, and the

commentary which allude to exegesis of the *Sophist* have been taken as referring to a commentary by Proclus on that dialogue but in my view neither passage offers firm evidence; see *In Parm.* 774.17–20 and 1174.18–25 (Steel 2007–2009), with the discussion in Luna and Segonds (2007), xxvi–xxx.

20 Olympiodorus, *In Phd.* 9 §2, 8–9 (Westerink 1976); Elias, *In Isagogen Porphyrii* 2.10–11 (Busse 1900); Philoponus, *De aet. mundi* 248.23–24, 251.8–10, 253.16 (Rabe 1899); Damascius, *Vita Isid.* 42 (Zintzen 1967); schol. in Remp. II.371.14.

21 See Lamberz (1987), 4–5.

22 Hermias records Proclus' interventions in the discussion at *In Phdr.* 92.6–7 and 154.28–30 (Couvreur 1901). See Bielmeier (1930), 30–33 and Bernard (1997), 4–19. Bernard argues that Hermias is more independent of Syrianus than has usually been thought.

23 For Proclus the *theologoi* are the other sources of divine wisdom, primarily Homer, Hesiod, Orpheus, and the *Chaldaean Oracles*.

Phaedo in chapters 26 and 27. In the same way the lengthy account of the gods as they appear at the different levels of Proclus' system, starting with the One in book II and working down the system to the hypercosmic gods in book VI, constantly relates these gods, who are also metaphysical entities, to specific passages of Plato. Exegesis of the hypotheses of the *Parmenides* plays a crucial role in structuring Proclus' theological and metaphysical system but other Platonic texts such as the myth in the *Phaedrus* are also important sources for his exposition.[24]

In *Theol. Plat.* I.4 Proclus distinguishes between four modes of theological exposition practiced by Plato, inspired, dialectical, symbolic, and iconic (i.e. using images, εἰκόνες). He links the inspired mode of exposition with the *Phaedrus*, the dialectical with the *Sophist* and the *Parmenides*, the symbolic with the mythical parts of the *Gorgias*, *Symposium*, and *Protagoras*, and the iconic with the *Timaeus* and the *Statesman.* He goes on to describe the symbolic mode as Orphic, the iconic as Pythagorean, the inspired as appropriate to theurgy, and the dialectical as peculiar to the work of Plato. In its context this passage offers both a programmatic statement about how Proclus will interpret particular dialogues within the *Platonic Theology* and a way of harmonizing differences between dialogues by appealing to the different modes of exposition. At the same time this theory of modes of exposition offers a way of harmonizing Plato with other texts and with the rites of theurgy. The theory also appears in the commentary on the *Parmenides,* at 645.7–647.18, in a preliminary discussion of the literary style (χαρακτήρ) of that dialogue. Elsewhere Proclus does not consistently distinguish between symbolic, iconic, and inspired modes of discourse but he is consistent in taking the approach to Plato which lies behind that distinction, seeking to smooth over difficulties within the text, rather like a modern interpreter appealing to the principle of charity, and seeking also to demonstrate agreement between Plato and what he regards as the other sources of truth.[25]

In commenting on Plato, Proclus draws extensively on earlier exegesis by a wide range of authors. For example, in the commentary on the *Timaeus* he reports the views of the second-century Platonists Atticus and Numenius and the third-century literary critic Cassius Longinus as well as

24 For a summary of the contents, plan, and method of the *Platonic Theology* as well as a full account of its relationship to exegesis of the *Parmenides*, see Saffrey and Westerink (1968–1997), vol. I, lx–lxxxix. On the question whether the *Theol. Plat.* as we have it is complete, see their vol. VI, xxxv–xliv. Cf. Steel (2000), 373–397.

25 See Pépin (2000), 1–14; Gersh (2000), 15–27; and Sheppard (2000), 415–423. Cf. also Steel (2005), 209–225, especially 220–225.

those of Plotinus, Porphyry, Iamblichus, Theodorus of Asine, and others. Pride of place is always given to the views of Syrianus, with whom Proclus rarely disagrees. This feature of Proclus' commentaries has meant that, like the Alexandrian Neoplatonist commentaries on Aristotle, they have often been treated primarily as a source for the views of earlier philosophers. However, again like the Aristotelian commentators, Proclus is not simply recording earlier views. He engages actively with the tradition of commentary on the texts under discussion, adjudicating between rival interpretations and drawing on a very wide range of material from the Greek cultural tradition. He not only considers large issues of philosophical interpretation but also addresses detailed points concerning particular words. Sometimes he comments on matters such as Plato's style or his skill in characterization, using the vocabulary and approach of the literary critical tradition.[26] He interprets both the Atlantis story at the beginning of the *Timaeus* and the myth of Er at the end of the *Republic* as allegories, treating them in the same way as he treats Homer or the Orphic poems.[27]

Many of these features of Proclus' exegesis of Plato can be seen in the discussion of the spherical shape of the universe, at *In Tim.* II.68.6–79.14. He starts by quoting the relevant lemma from the *Timaeus*, 33b1–8, and then proceeds to offer three Platonic "proofs" of the spherical shape of the cosmos. The first proof develops the point made by Plato at *Timaeus* 33b2–4, that the appropriate shape for the living cosmos which includes all living things within itself is the spherical one which includes all other shapes. The second proof expands on the idea that the spherical shape is particularly appropriate or fitting (πρέπον), appealing not only to a passage in Plato's *Laws* (898a–b) but also to Parmenides' comparison of reality to a sphere in fr. 8.43–44 and to Empedocles, interpreting the latter along Neoplatonic lines.[28] The third proof picks up Plato's use of the word συγγενής, "akin," in *Timaeus* 33b2 and argues that spherical shape is akin to the cosmos, to the demiurge, and to the paradigm which provides the demiurge with the model for the physical world. Proclus supports his argument by referring to two lines from Orphic poetry, to the remarks about shape in *Parmenides* 137d–e, and to *Iliad* 18.401, a line which describes the jewelry made by Hephaestus, understood by both Proclus and Syrianus as referring allegorically to enmattered forms, fashioned by Hephaestus as

[26] See Walsdorff (1927), ch. IV, 9, especially 91–108; Sheppard (1980), 117–119 and 124–129; Steel (2005); Sheppard (forthcoming).

[27] Cf. n. 4 above. On Proclus' interpretation of the myth of Er, see Cürsgen (2002), 169–364.

[28] On Proclus' interpretation of the Presocratics see Westerink (1987), 105–112.

demiurge of the sensible world.[29] He uses an allusion to the *Chaldaean Oracles* to contrast the activity of Hephaestus with that of the demiurge in the *Timaeus*.

Having expounded his three proofs, Proclus turns to discuss a problem raised by the text: why did Plato say it is necessary that the cosmos should have a spherical shape? His answer leads him initially into discussion of issues about the relationship between the sphere and other shapes, with reference to what follows in the *Timaeus* about the formation of bodies from the five regular solids. The problem under discussion was evidently traditional and Proclus goes on to spend a couple of pages reporting Iamblichus' arguments on the matter (72.6–73.26) before turning to a summary of material found in Aristotle, *De caelo* 2.4 in the course of which he makes fleeting reference to Plato's *Statesman* 270a (73.26–75.18). He then turns to mathematical arguments for the spherical shape of the cosmos, referring to "the views of experts in this field" (75.18–76.29). The material here finds parallels in the work of the mathematical writers Geminus, Cleomedes, and Theon of Smyrna as well as in Ptolemy. Towards the end of this section of his commentary Proclus refers to Plato's own discussion of polyhedra in *Timaeus* 53c–56b and to mathematicians who use the demonstrations of Euclid and Archimedes respectively.

Up to this point Proclus has been concentrating on the first part of the lemma, 33b1–4. The last part of his commentary on it, 76.29–79.14, picks up some particular details from 33b5–8, with another reference to *Laws* 898b, quotation of a line of Pindar which Plato himself quotes at *Theaetetus* 173e6, reference back to an earlier passage of the *Timaeus* (30b1–3), quotation of a phrase from *Laws* 757b, quotation of a sentence from the work attributed to Timaeus of Locri which Proclus took to be a genuine source independent of Plato's *Timaeus*, and reference back to his own account of the arguments in Aristotle's *De caelo*.[30]

Both in his commentaries on Plato and in the *Platonic Theology* Proclus treats Plato's work as a unified corpus. He regularly addresses the difficulties which arise in reconciling apparently conflicting passages either within or between dialogues. So, for example, *In Parm.* 648.1–658.22 deals in part with a problem which is familiar to modern interpreters of Plato, namely the differences between the views of dialectic in *Republic* 7, the

[29] Cf. Sheppard (1980), 68.

[30] Baltzly (2007), 124–138 provides an English translation of this passage and helpful notes, although I think he is mistaken in not marking 79.15 as moving to discussion of a fresh lemma. See also Festugière (1967), 101–114.

Phaedrus, and the *Sophist*. Proclus is concerned not only to argue that Plato's conception of dialectic is the same in all three dialogues but also to reconcile an apparent contradiction between *Republic* 7.534e, 537e–539d and *Sophist* 253e on the one hand and *Parmenides* 135e on the other. Because he is commenting on the *Parmenides* he starts not with the question of how to reconcile the method of collection and division which appears in the *Sophist* and the *Phaedrus* with the remarks about dialectic in *Republic* 7 but with the conflict between Parmenides' encouragement of the young Socrates to engage in dialectical exercises like those of Zeno and the view expressed by Socrates in *Republic* 7 that dialectic is not a suitable activity for those who are young and lacking in experience.

Characteristically, Proclus argues that there are three different kinds of dialectical activity suitable for different interlocutors. One kind is an exercise for training the young, used by Socrates in the *Theaetetus* and the *Lysis*; another is the contemplation of the intelligible world and the Platonic Forms – according to Proclus here this second kind of dialectical activity is what Plato has in mind not only in *Republic* 7 but also in the *Phaedrus* and the *Sophist* – while the third kind is what Socrates uses to expose the pretensions of the sophists in dialogues such as the *Gorgias* and the *Protagoras* and in arguing with Thrasymachus in *Republic* 1. We might suppose that Parmenides' remarks to the young Socrates at the beginning of the *Parmenides* would imply that any dialectic in that dialogue is an activity of the first kind, but that would conflict with Proclus' view of the dialogue's overall theme and significance.[31] He therefore claims that the Socrates of the *Parmenides* is a special case, capable of the second kind of dialectical activity despite his youth. He pulls in the account of hypothetical method in the *Phaedo* and argues that this too belongs under the second kind. Because Proclus pays close attention to the wording of Plato's text, the use of the word ἀδολεσχία ("babbling") at *Parmenides* 135d5 gives him particular problems. His method of dealing with it is again characteristic: he points out, quite correctly, that Parmenides says this term is used by "the many" and also considers other passages in Plato where the word is used.

In this example Proclus interprets the views of dialectic found in different Platonic dialogues in such a way as to present Plato's views as a unified body of doctrine, allowing for differing dialectical practices by

[31] At *In Parm.* 630.26–643.4 (Steel 2007–2009) Proclus argues firmly against interpreters who regard the *Parmenides* as an exercise in logical method and in favor of a metaphysical interpretation, particularly that put forward by Syrianus.

claiming (not unreasonably) that Plato recognizes more than one kind of dialectical activity while insisting that the different uses of dialectic can be fitted into an interpretive framework of just three specific kinds. He moves easily from one dialogue to another, showing a close knowledge of a wide range of Platonic texts. It was that command of Platonic texts, both on the large scale and in detail, which made it possible for Proclus to compose the *Platonic Theology* in addition to commenting on particular dialogues.[32]

Students in the Neoplatonic schools of late antiquity began by studying Aristotle, before going on to Plato. Marinus reports that Proclus himself followed such a course of study[33] and we do have some evidence for Proclus' exegesis of Aristotle. The commentary on Aristotle's *De interpretatione* by Proclus' pupil Ammonius has connections with Proclus' own commentary on Plato's *Cratylus* and may reflect Proclus' teaching of the *De interpretatione.*[34] A scatter of references in the Alexandrian Neoplatonist commentaries on Aristotle provides evidence for Proclus' views on some of the issues which arise in expounding the *Organon.* Mention is also made of a work of Proclus which was a general introduction to the study of Aristotle, probably covering a standard set of preliminary general points.[35] Proclus' only surviving work on Aristotle is the *Elements of Physics*, a selective summary of books VI and VIII of Aristotle's *Physics* and book I of the *De caelo.* The occasion and purpose of this work are unclear; Proclus might have composed it for his students, to assist them in grasping Aristotle's ideas about the physical world before they moved on to Plato.[36] There is also some rather sparse evidence for Proclus commenting on Plotinus, insufficient for us to determine the context and nature of his exegesis of the *Enneads.*[37]

32 Strictly speaking, *In Parm.* 648.1–658.22 (Steel 2007–2009) is part of Proclus' introduction to the commentary. He repeats the views expressed here when he comes to comment on 135d, at *In Parm.* 989.1–992.22 (Steel 2007–2009), and again at *Theol. Plat.* I.9.39.7–40.18 (Saffrey and Westerink 1968–1997).

33 Marinus, *Life of Proclus*, ch. 13 (Saffrey, Segonds, and Luna 2001).

34 See Sheppard (1987), 137–151.

35 Of the references listed in Westerink (1962), xii, n. 22 = Westerink, Trouillard, and Segonds (1990), xiii, n. 18, Asclepius 142.36–37 (Hayduck 1888), Ammonius, *In De int.* 1.6–11 (Busse 1897), Stephanus, *In De int.* 46.25–47.12 (Hayduck 1885), and Philoponus, *In Anal. post.* 111.31–112.36 (Wallies 1909) can all be understood as references to oral teaching while Philoponus, *In Anal. pr.* 40.30–31 (Wallies 1905) seems to be a mistake as Proclus is not mentioned there. On the passage which refers to Proclus' introduction to the study of Aristotle, Elias (or David) *In Cat.* 107.24–26, see Mansfeld (1994), 22–23.

36 See Ritzenfeld (1912) vi–viii; O'Meara (1989), 177–179; Nikulin and Kutash (2003), 183–221; Opsomer (2009), 193–203.

37 See Westerink (1959), 1–10, reprinted in Westerink (1980), 21–30.

Exegesis of Euclid and Ptolemy

Proclus' surviving works include a commentary on the first book of Euclid's *Elements* and a short work on astronomy, the *Hypotyposis*, much of which presents the hypotheses of Ptolemy's *Almagest*.[38] The commentary on Euclid, like Proclus' commentaries on Plato, derives from teaching. *In Eucl.* 200.11–18, 210.17–28, 272.12–14, and 375.9 all allude to an audience of beginning students although much of the material in the commentary seems suitable for a more advanced audience. Perhaps the more advanced material was introduced when Proclus wrote up his lectures on Euclid to produce a full commentary.[39] His interest in Euclid is primarily philosophical and the prologues to the commentary include some important discussions of the nature of mathematical objects and of the role of imagination (φαντασία) in enabling us to visualize such objects.[40] He draws extensively but critically on earlier commentaries, referring both to mathematicians such as Hero and Pappus and to a wide range of philosophers including Aristotle, Speusippus, Eudemus, Porphyry, Theodorus of Asine, Plutarch of Athens, and, of course, Syrianus.[41] Proclus comments in detail on the definitions, postulates, axioms, and propositions set out in the first book of the *Elements*, applying similar methods of exegesis to those he uses in expounding Plato. So, for example, in commenting on definition I,1 and definition I,3 he deals with conflicting interpretations of the order of generation and priority of the mathematical concepts of point, line, surface, and solid by arguing that the "arithmetical" or Pythagorean interpretation applies in the immaterial world while the "geometrical" or Platonic one applies in the world of material things. At the same time his commentary on definition I,1 also mentions a different solution to the problem of these conflicting interpretations which is developed further in commenting on definition I,6. He now suggests that Euclid's definitions are "images" (εἰκόνες) which should be understood allegorically. This approach makes it possible to apply the "geometrical," Platonic approach to both the material and the immaterial, understanding the former as an image of the latter.[42]

Proclus' attitude to Ptolemy is rather different from his view of Plato, Aristotle, or Euclid. He seeks to maintain the view of astronomy presented

[38] It has also been suggested that some of the scholia on Euclid derive from Proclus: see Mansfeld (1998), 26–28.

[39] See Morrow (1970), xxiv–xxvi and xxxi–xxxii, where Morrow suggests that Proclus did lecture on the other books of Euclid but "lacked the time to put his comments into a form suitable for a larger circle of philosophical readers."

[40] See esp. *In Eucl.* 3.1–18.4 and 49.4–56.22 (Friedlein 1873).

[41] Cf. Morrow (1970), xxvii–xxviii.

[42] See Glasner (1992), 320–333.

by Plato in *Republic* 7.530 and is thus committed both to saying that true astronomy is concerned with the divine and to denying astronomical phenomena such as the precession of the equinoxes, which had been discovered between Plato's time and his own. The main purpose of the *Hypotyposis* is therefore to argue against Ptolemy but in order to do so Proclus has to provide a summary of Ptolemy's views.[43]

Exegesis of Homer

Proclus' exegesis of Homer can be found primarily in the sixth essay of his commentary on the *Republic.* Here he responds to Plato's criticisms of Homer in *Republic* 2, 3, and 10 in a number of different ways, including offering detailed exegesis of the passages of Homer which Plato singles out for criticism in *Republic* 2 and 3.[44] There was a long tradition of defending many of these passages, which Proclus picks up and develops. So, for example, at *In Remp.* I.115.1–117.21 Proclus discusses the deceitful dream sent by Zeus to Agamemnon at the beginning of *Iliad* 2. Plato in *Republic* 2.383a7–8 regards this passage as problematic since it contradicts the principle he has just laid down, that the gods are without falsehood and do not deceive human beings. Proclus starts his discussion of the deceitful dream with the traditional response, found in the Homeric scholia attributed to Porphyry, that the fault lay not in Zeus but in Agamemnon, who misunderstood the word πασσυδίῃ ("with all the army") used by the dream and attacked the Trojans without Achilles.[45] He then reports the view of Syrianus, that this response fails to take account of Zeus's providence and his desire to punish the Greeks for their behavior to Achilles. Syrianus was apparently prepared to admit that Zeus does deceive Agamemnon, for his eventual good. Finally Proclus offers a further solution to the problem, putting together the traditional response and the rather different view of Syrianus. He argues that the falsehood arises in Agamemnon because of his nature, in accordance with divine will and for Agamemnon's own good; the falsehood does not actually come from the gods.[46]

Proclus' main way of defending Homer against Plato is through allegorical interpretation. For example, in *In Remp.* I.87–95 he argues that the Theomachy described in *Iliad* 20, like other mythical theomachies, should

[43] See Segonds (1987), 319–334 and Siorvanes (1996), 279–293.

[44] See Sheppard (1980); Lamberton (1986), 180–232; Kuisma (1996); Struck (2004), 238–253.

[45] πασσυδίῃ in Homer in fact means "with all speed" but Proclus understands it in the sense of "with all the army" found in some prose writers from Xenophon onwards.

[46] Cf. the way in which Origen wrestles with the problem of the hardening of Pharaoh's heart in *De principiis* III.1.8–14 and elsewhere, discussed as a problem of exegesis by Harl (1967), 260–268.

be understood in terms of Neoplatonic metaphysics as representing the contrasting forces that bring about procession and reversion, division and reunification. He reconciles the account of the gods fighting one another in *Iliad* 20 with passages such as *Odyssey* 6.41–46 describing the peace and calm of the gods' dwelling on Olympus by pointing out that at the highest level of metaphysics the divisions which appear at lower levels no longer exist. Here he is not only claiming that, rightly understood, Homeric poetry and Platonic philosophy are not in conflict but is also treating the Homeric poems in the same way as he treats the Platonic corpus, as a consistent body of material in which contradictions can be reconciled by appealing to different levels within his system. It is also worth noting that Proclus does not consider the Theomachy of *Iliad* 20 in isolation. He discusses it alongside the battle between Zeus and the Giants popular in Greek literature and art and the less well-known Orphic myth of the fight between the Titans and Dionysus.

Like the Theomachy, Hera's deception of Zeus and their union on Mount Ida, vividly recounted in *Iliad* 14.153–351 and censured by Plato in *Republic* 3.390b–c, was much discussed by defenders of Homer before Proclus. In *In Remp.* I.132–140 Proclus draws on Syrianus to offer a detailed allegory of the episode in terms of Neoplatonic metaphysics. He deals with another scandalous Homeric union, the story of Ares and Aphrodite told in *Odyssey* 8.266–369, in the same way at *In Remp.* I.141–143. All these allegories are based on Proclus' assumption that Homeric poetry is capable of revealing fundamental truths, the same truths which can be found in the philosophy of Plato. In order to grasp these truths we need to read both Homer and Plato in the right way. The aim of Proclus' exegesis of Homer is to show us how to engage in such reading.

Just as Proclus resolves apparent contradictions in both Homer and Plato by claiming that different passages apply to different levels within his system, so he argues that the inconsistency between Plato's severe criticisms of Homer as dangerously mimetic in *Republic* 10, the respect with which Theognis is cited at *Laws* 1.630a, and the apparent praise of inspired poetry in both *Phaedrus* 245a and the *Ion* is to be explained by postulating a hierarchy of three types of poetry: much of Homer is inspired poetry of the kind praised by Plato in the *Phaedrus* and, according to Proclus, in the *Ion*, while *Laws* 1.630a refers to a second kind of poetry, concerned with giving moral advice, and the criticisms of *Republic* 10 apply only to mimetic or imitative poetry, the third and lowest kind.[47]

[47] *In Remp.* I.177.7–199.28 (Kroll 1899–1901). Proclus never considers that the praise of poetic inspiration in the *Ion* might be ironical.

In accordance with this belief that much of Homer is inspired and should be interpreted allegorically, Proclus throughout his works cites lines and passages of Homer as revealing fundamental truths. We have already seen that the description of the jewellery made by Hephaestus, in *Iliad* 18.401, appears in the discussion of the spherical shape of the cosmos at *In Tim.* II.70.21–26.[48] Elsewhere, at *In Tim.* II.27.16–28.7, Proclus alludes to Hephaestus' role in the story of Ares and Aphrodite in *Odyssey* 8 in a context where he is expounding what he takes to be the god's role in binding together opposites in the physical world. In *In Tim.* I.142.14–144.18 Plato's mention of Hephaestus at *Timaeus* 23e1 leads Proclus to give a lengthy account of the god's place in his metaphysical and theological scheme. This account refers not only to Homer but also to the Orphic myth of the mirror of Dionysus, as well as using a term borrowed from the *Chaldaean Oracles* (ἐργοτεχνίτης – "craft-worker").[49] Proclus is reading the *Iliad* and the *Odyssey* in the light of his version of Neoplatonism while at the same time treating Homeric lines and episodes as confirmation of the truth of his philosophy.

We can see Proclus combining allegorical interpretation of Homer and allegorical interpretation of Plato in a passage from the *Parmenides* commentary, *In Parm.* 1036.24–1038.30, discussing 137b–c, where Parmenides suggests that the youngest of his interlocutors should be the one to answer his questions. Proclus interprets Parmenides' four interlocutors, Zeno, Socrates, Pythodorus, and Aristoteles, as beings at different levels in the metaphysical hierarchy; Aristoteles, the youngest, is at the lowest level, that of a soul which can be led up to higher levels and then carried down again into the material world. Proclus first draws a parallel with the different levels of initiation in mystic rites and then compares Parmenides' desire for a brief rest while his questions are being answered with the unwearied and providential nature of the gods. He illustrates that unwearied and providential nature by referring to the beginning of *Iliad* 4 where the gods are served nectar by Hebe. He goes on to interpret Aristoteles' readiness to identify himself as the youngest interlocutor as an instance of the way in which souls and lower-level gods particularize the generic intellection of higher divine beings and backs up this allegorical treatment of the character in Plato with an allegory of *Iliad* 24.74–77. There Hera asks for "one of the gods" to call Thetis to her, and the call is answered by Iris. Proclus sees

[48] Cf. above pp. 63–64 and n. 27.

[49] Cf. also *Theol. Plat.* VI.22.97.15–17 (Saffrey and Westerink 1968–1997) and the further references given in Saffrey–Westerink's note on that passage in their vol. VI, 177.

this as parallel to Aristoteles' responding to Parmenides and interprets both passages as allegories of relationships between entities at different levels.

Exegesis of Hesiod, the *Chaldaean Oracles*, and the Orphic poems

When Plato criticizes the poets in *Republic* 2, he starts, at 377d–378a, by objecting to the stories of Kronos' castration of Ouranos and Zeus's deposition of Kronos as told in Hesiod's *Theogony.* Proclus does mention Hesiod as well as Homer at *In Remp.* I.72.2–3, at the beginning of the sixth essay. That essay goes on to concentrate on the defense of Homer, but there is every reason to think that Proclus would interpret the account of the gods and their activities given in Hesiod's *Theogony* in the same allegorical way as he interprets the treatment of the gods in Homer. The *Theogony* receives little detailed exegesis by Proclus, perhaps because he was more interested in the Orphic account of theogony. However, he did devote time to commenting on the *Works and Days*, reworking the scholia of Plutarch of Chaeronea and adding material of his own. In part we may see Proclus' concern with the *Works and Days* as reflecting his broad interest in all aspects of Greek culture, not just in philosophy. In his first scholion (1.1–18) he contrasts the *Theogony*, concerned, according to Proclus, with the principles of divine providence, with the *Works and Days*, which aims at the moral benefit of its readers and has an educational aim (σκοπός). The statement that readers "should begin with this work" (ἀπὸ τούτου προσήκει τοῦ συγγράμματος ἄρχεσθαι) suggests that Proclus' exegesis of Hesiod too belongs to some kind of teaching context. The actual scholia tend to emphasize the moral meaning of the text, and also show some interest in arithmology. Scholia LXVIII–XCIII offer an interpretation of the myth of the five ages which differs from those found elsewhere in Proclus, in *In Remp.* II.75.12–78.11 and *In Crat.* CXXIX.[50] It looks as though Proclus regarded the *Works and Days* not as inspired poetry but as belonging to the second of the three kinds of poetry described at *In Remp.* I.177.7–199.28.[51]

[50] All three interpretations regard Hesiod's "golden race" as symbolic of the intellectual life (νοερὰ ζωή) but diverge from each other in their interpretations of the rest of the myth. The relationship of the three interpretations to each other has not been adequately studied.

[51] In taking this view I follow R. M. van den Berg and C. Faraggiana di Sarzana, rather than P. Marzillo. See Van den Berg, "Proclus on Hesiod's *Works and Days* and "didactic" poetry" (2014); the review by Van den Berg and Koning (2011) of Marzillo (2010); Faraggiana di Sarzana (1987), 21–32. Faraggiana di Sarzana 31 argues that study of Plutarch's commentary on the *Works and Days* formed part of Proclus' "programme culturel pour les débutants," alongside Euclid's *Elements.*

The *Suda* attributes works on *Orphic Theology* and on the *Agreement of Orpheus, Pythagoras, and Plato with the Chaldaean Oracles* to both Syrianus and Proclus while Marinus reports that Proclus composed a commentary on the *Chaldaean Oracles* but left only notes on the Orphic poems (chs. 26–27). Whatever the relationship of Proclus' writings on the *Chaldaean Oracles* and the Orphic poems to those of Syrianus, it is clear that Proclus both studied and taught all this material.[52] He himself refers to his commentary on the *Chaldaean Oracles* at *In Remp.* I.40.21–22. The few surviving fragments confirm, unsurprisingly, that Proclus interpreted the *Oracles* in terms of his own psychology and metaphysics.[53] In his other exegetical works he alludes frequently to both the *Chaldaean Oracles* and the Orphic poems, interpreting them allegorically in such a way as to harmonize them with both Plato and Homer. We have already seen how Proclus uses two lines from Orphic poetry in his discussion of the spherical shape of the universe, at *In Tim.* II.68.6–79.14, considers the Orphic myth of the fight between the Titans and Dionysus alongside the theomachy of *Iliad* 20 in *In Remp.* I.87–95, and combines allusions to Homer, Orphic poetry, and the *Chaldaean Oracles* in his account of Hephaestus at *In Tim.* I.142.14–144.18.

In the *Platonic Theology* the *Chaldaean Oracles* play a particularly important role in book IV. Here Proclus gives an account of the intelligible and intellectual gods, presented primarily through exegesis of the myth in the *Phaedrus* and the second hypothesis of the *Parmenides*. A phrase from the *Chaldaean Oracles*, "they both think and are objects of thought" (νοοῦντα νοεῖται), is used in the very first paragraph of IV.1, at 6.11, as evidence of the existence of these gods while at the end of the chapter, at 10.17–18, Proclus is keen to point out that he is not reading them into Plato from elsewhere (οὐχ ἡμεῖς ταῦτα φέροντες ἀλλαχόθεν τῷ Πλάτωνι προσάγομεν). He devotes IV.9 to arguing that the *Chaldaean Oracles* accord with the *Phaedrus* myth and IV.39 to reconciling particular triads of gods mentioned in the *Chaldaean Oracles* with the *Parmenides*. In IV.10 Proclus argues that the "region above the heavens" (ὑπερουράνιος τόπος) of *Phaedrus* 247c corresponds to the three Nights in Orphic theology.

Theol. Plat. V deals with the intellectual gods and is structured around the Orphic version of the myth of Kronos. Although Proclus' main concern is to find the intellectual gods in a range of Platonic texts, particularly the *Timaeus* and the *Parmenides*, he explicitly argues in V.10 that Plato's references to Kronos agree with Orphic doctrine and in both V.3.16.24–17.7 and V.35 he fits the Couretes into his system by combining the way

52 Cf. Praechter (1926), 253–264, reprinted in Praechter (1973), 222–233.

53 See des Places (1971), 202–212 and 225–226.

they are depicted in Orphic poetry with references in both Plato and the *Chaldaean Oracles*.[54]

Exegesis of divine names and theurgic rites

Proclus applies his methods of exegesis not only to texts but also to the names of the gods and the rites of theurgy. *In Crat.* LXXI takes Plato's own use of Homer in *Cra.* 391–392 as the starting-point for an extended discussion of the names of the gods. Proclus there distinguishes between divine names, used by the gods themselves, and man-made names. Of the latter, some are the products of divine inspiration while others are the product of human knowledge (ἐπιστήμη) or of sense perception and opinion. This distinction allows Proclus to interpret the different names of the gods in Homer, Orphic poetry, and the *Chaldaean Oracles* as applying at different levels. He takes the etymologies of Plato's *Cratylus* completely seriously and discusses them at length, treating the dialogue as a source of wisdom about the gods.[55] A similar distinction between divine and man-made names can be found in *In Remp.* I.169.25–170.26[56] and in the discussion of the names of the cosmos in *In Tim.* I.272.7–274.32.

The *Chaldaean Oracles* provided Proclus and other post-Iamblichean Neoplatonists with a theoretical basis for the rites of theurgy. These rites themselves were understood by Proclus as having symbolic significance, as we can see from two passages in which he offers an interpretation of a theurgic rite, *In Remp.* I.152.7–153.3 and *Theol. Plat.* IV.9.30.17–31.5. In the first passage Proclus, following Syrianus, interprets the funeral rites performed by Achilles for Patroclus in *Iliad* 23 as representing the theurgic rite of "immortalization" (ἀπαθανατισμός) and at the same time expounds the symbolic significance of the theurgic rite, for example treating the cup from which Achilles pours his libation as the cup used by the theurgist which symbolizes the "source of souls," that is, the mixing bowl of *Timaeus* 41d.[57] In the second passage another theurgic rite, the simulated burial of an initiate leaving only the head exposed, is interpreted in terms of the *Phaedrus* myth.[58]

Several times in the *Cratylus* commentary Proclus compares divine names to statues of the gods (ἀγάλματα). At *In Crat.* LI.19.12–24, it becomes clear

54 For detailed accounts of Proclus' treatment of the Orphic theogony and of his use of the *Chaldaean Oracles* in the *Platonic Theology*, see Brisson (1987), 43–104 and Brisson (2000), 109–162.

55 See Van den Berg (2008), 161–197.

56 On this passage see Sheppard (1980), 138–139.

57 See Sheppard (1980), 76–77 and Lewy (2011), 184–185 and 207. Proclus discusses the interpretation of the mixing bowl at length in *In Tim.* III.246.29–250.28 (Diehl 1903–1906).

58 See Lewy (2011), 204–207 and Dodds (1965), 43, n. 1.

that what Proclus has in mind are the statues used for theurgic animation. When Proclus deals with the names of the gods he always has in mind the names used in particular texts. His approach to the rituals of theurgy is also that of an exegete, seeking connections between these rituals and his authoritative texts.[59]

The comparison of divine names to statues of the gods reappears in the *Platonic Theology*, at I.29.124.12–125.2. Here Proclus draws an analogy between the activity of the demiurge in producing copies of the primary forms in matter and the activity of the human intellect in fashioning likenesses of all things, especially of the gods, representing the uncompounded by things in combination, the simple by the variegated and the unified through multiplicity. This way of talking recalls the terms in which Proclus, like Plotinus and others before him, describes how myths offer symbolic presentations of higher, divine truths, setting out what in reality is eternally unified as a narrative account following a temporal sequence.[60] In this particular passage Proclus goes on to say that this is the way in which human intellect forms names for divine beings and to compare that with the way in which theurgists summon the gods by means of the tokens or "symbols" (σύμβολα) placed in the statues they are animating. For Proclus the whole world is like a vast theurgic statue. If we follow the analogy through, philosophy itself becomes a form of exegesis: when a Neoplatonic philosopher expounds the structure of reality he is engaged in the same kind of activity as when he explains the meaning of divine names, theurgic rites, or authoritative texts.[61]

Conclusion

We can see from the surviving fragment of Proclus' work *On the Hieratic Art* that theurgy was based on the traditional idea of cosmic sympathy. Proclus there explains how particular stones, plants, and animals have an inherent connection to the sun, for instance, and others to the moon. The

[59] Cf. *In Crat.* XXX.11.1–6, XCVI.47.12–16 (Pasquali 1908) and Van den Berg (2008), 110–111, 140–142, 175.

[60] See Plotinus, *Enn.* III.5.9.24–26 and IV.3.9.14–20 (Henry and Schwyzer 1964–1982); Sallustius, *Concerning the Gods and the Universe* 8.14–16 (Nock 1926); Proclus *In Remp.* I.77.13–27 and 139.30–140.6 (Kroll 1899–1901).

[61] For the world as a theurgic statue, cf. *Theol. Plat.* I.5.23.22–24.11 (Saffrey and Westerink 1968–1997), *In Tim.* 273.10–18 (Diehl 1903–1906), *In Parm.* 847.19–23 (Steel 2007–2009) and *In Remp.* II.212.20–213.12 (Kroll 1899–1901) with the comments of Gersh (2000), 26–27 and Van den Berg (forthcoming). For further discussion of the analogy between the world and a text, and additional references, see Sheppard (forthcoming).

heliotrope, the plant which naturally turns towards the sun, is a particularly clear example.[62] If we took this text on its own as a full account of the theory underlying theurgy we might suppose that such a theory depended on the likeness of the (theurgic) symbol to that which it symbolizes and was therefore quite limited in its application. However, in many other passages, including the one from *Theol. Plat.* I.29 mentioned above, Proclus extends his theory of symbols much more widely and allows for the possibility that opposites can represent by opposites.[63] This extension of the theory of symbolism could also be justified by the Neoplatonic principle that "Everything is in everything, but in each according to its nature" (πάντα ἐν πᾶσιν, οἰκείως δὲ ἐν ἑκάστῳ).[64] It opens the way for flexible, multi-layered exegesis of the kind described in this chapter.

When he comments on the texts which he regarded as fundamentally in accord with one another – the dialogues of Plato, the *Elements* of Euclid, the poetry of Homer and Hesiod, the *Chaldaean Oracles*, and the Orphic poems – Proclus treats them all as expressions of the same philosophical truths, referring readily from one to another, sometimes presupposing the Neoplatonic interpretation of a passage, sometimes explaining that interpretation more fully, depending on the context. Exegesis is fundamental to his way of doing philosophy, not only because so much of his time was spent on teaching through expounding texts but also because he saw the whole world as a system of symbols; for him the philosophy he found in Plato was the key to understanding that system.

Bibliography

Abbate, M. (1995) *Proclo: Commento alla Repubblica, Dissertazione I, III, IV, V*, Pavia.

Arnzen, R. (2013) "Proclus on Plato's *Timaeus* 89c3–90c7," *Arabic Sciences and Philosophy* 23: 1–45.

Baltzly, D. (2007) *Proclus: Commentary on Plato's Timaeus*, vol. III, Cambridge.

Berg, R. M. van den (2008) *Proclus' Commentary on the Cratylus in Context*, Leiden and Boston.

(2014) "Proclus on Hesiod's *Works and Days* and "Didactic" Poetry," *Classical Quarterly* N.S. 64: 383–397.

(forthcoming) "Theurgy in the Context of Proclus' Philosophy," in d'Hoine and Martijn (forthcoming).

[62] See Bidez (1928), I.148.10–18. [63] See especially *In Remp.* I.198.15–19 (Kroll 1899–1901).

[64] See *Elements of Theology* prop. 103 (Dodds 1963), with Dodds' commentary and cf. *On the Hieratic Art* 148. 6 (Bidez 1928).

Berg, R. M. van den and Koning, H. H. (2011) Review of Marzillo (2010), *Bryn Mawr Classical Review* 2011.08.54.

Bernard, H. (1997) *Hermeias von Alexandrien: Kommentar zu Platons "Phaidros,"* Tübingen.

Bidez, J. (ed.) (1928) "Proclus, *De arte sacrificiali,*" in *Catalogue des manuscrits alchimiques grecs*, vol. VI, Brussels.

Bielmeier, A. (1930) *Die neuplatonische Phaidrosinterpretation*, Paderborn.

Brisson, L. (1987) "Proclus et l'Orphisme," in Pépin and Saffrey (1987), 43–104.

(2000) "La place des *Oracles chaldaïques* dans la *Théologie platonicienne*," in Segonds and Steel (2000), 109–162.

Buffière, F. (1956) *Les mythes d'Homère et la pensée grecque*, Paris.

Busse, A. (ed.) (1897) Ammonius, *In Aristotelis De interpretatione commentarius (Commentaria in Aristotelem Graeca* 4.5), Berlin.

(ed.) (1900) Elias, *In Porphyrii Isagogen et Aristotelis Categorias commentaria (Commentaria in Aristotelem Graeca* 18.1), Berlin.

Cleary, J. J. (2006) "Proclus as a Reader of Plato's *Timaeus*," in H. Tarrant and D. Baltzly (eds.), *Reading Plato in Antiquity*, London, 135–150.

Coulter, J. A. (1976) *The Literary Microcosm, Theories of Interpretation of the Later Neoplatonists*, Leiden.

Couvreur, P. (ed.) (1901) Hermias, *In Platonis Phaedrum scholia*, Paris.

Crouzel, H. and Simonetti, M. (eds.) (1978–1984) Origen, *Traité des principes*, 5 vols., Paris.

Cürsgen, D. (2002) *Die Rationalität des Mythischen*, Berlin and New York.

Denyer, N. (ed.) (2001) *Plato: Alcibiades*, Cambridge.

Des Places, E. (ed.) (1971) *Oracles chaldaïques*, Paris.

d'Hoine, P. and Martijn, M. (eds.) (forthcoming) *All from One. A Guide to Proclus*, Oxford.

Diehl, E. (ed.) (1903–1906) Proclus, *In Platonis Timaeum commentaria*, 3 vols., Leipzig.

Dodds, E. R. (ed. and trans.) (1963) *Proclus: The Elements of Theology*, 2nd edn., Oxford.

(1965) *Pagan and Christian in an Age of Anxiety*, Cambridge.

Faraggiana di Sarzana, C. (1987) "Le commentaire à Hésiode et la paideia encyclopédique de Proclus," in Pépin and Saffrey (1987), 21–32.

Festugière, A. J. (1963) "Modes de composition des commentaires de Proclus" *Museum Helveticum* 20: 77–100. Reprinted in Festugière (1971), 551–74.

(1967) *Proclus: Commentaire sur le Timée*, vol. III, Paris.

(1971) *Études de philosophie grecque*, Paris.

Friedlein, G. (ed.) (1873) Proclus, *In primum Euclidis elementorum librum commentarii*, Leipzig.

Gallavotti, C. (1929) "Eterogeneità e cronologia dei commenti di Proclo alla Repubblica," *Rivista di filologia e d'istruzione classica* 57: 208–219.

(1971) "Intorno ai commenti di Proclo alla Repubblica," *Bollettino del Comitato per la Preparazione dell'Edizione Nazionale dei Classici Greci e Latini*, N.S. 19: 41–54.

Gersh, S. (2000) "Proclus' Theological Methods. The Programme of *Theol. Plat.* I.4," in Segonds and Steel (2000), 15–27.

Glasner, R. (1992) "Proclus' Commentary on Euclid's Definitions I,3 and I,6," *Hermes* 120: 320–333.

Harl, M. (1967) "La mort salutaire du Pharaon selon Origène," in *Studi in onore di Alberto Pincherle*, Rome.

Hayduck, M. (ed.) (1885) Stephanus, *In Aristotelis De interpretatione commentarius (Commentaria in Aristotelem Graeca 15)*, Berlin.

(ed.) (1888) Asclepius, *In Aristotelis Metaphysicorum libros A–Z commentaria (Commentaria in Aristotelem Graeca 6.2)*, Berlin.

Henry, P. and Schwyzer, H. R. (eds.) (1964–1982) Plotinus, *Opera*, 3 vols., Oxford.

Kroll, W. (ed.) (1899–1901) Proclus, *In Platonis Rem Publicam commentarii*, 2 vols., Leipzig.

Kuisma, O. (1996) *Proclus' Defence of Homer*, Helsinki.

Lamberton, R. (1986) *Homer the Theologian, Neoplatonist Allegorical Reading and the Growth of the Epic Tradition*, Berkeley, Los Angeles, and London.

Lamberz, E. (1987) "Proklos und die Form des philosophischen Kommentars," in Pépin and Saffrey (1987), 1–20.

Lewy, H. (2011) *Chaldaean Oracles and Theurgy*, 3rd edn., Paris.

Luna, C. and Segonds, A.-Ph. (eds.) (2007) *Proclus: Commentaire sur le Parménide de Platon*, vol. 1.i, Paris.

(2012) "Proclus de Lycie," in R. Goulet (ed.), *Dictionnaire des philosophes antiques*, vol. vb, Paris, 1546–1657.

Manitius, C. (ed.) (1974) Proclus, *Hypotyposis astronomicarum positionum*, Stuttgart.

Mansfeld, J. (1994) *Prolegomena*, Leiden, New York, and Cologne.

(1998) *Prolegomena mathematica*, Leiden, Boston, and Cologne.

Marzillo, P. (2010) *Der Kommentar des Proklos zu Hesiods "Werken und Tagen,"* Tübingen.

Morrow, G. R. (1970) *Proclus: A Commentary on the First Book of Euclid's Elements*, Princeton.

Nikulin, D. and Kutash, E. (2003) "*Physica more geometrico demonstrata:* Natural Philosophy in Proclus and Aristotle," *Proceedings of the Boston Area Colloquium in Ancient Philosophy* 18: 183–221.

Nock, A. D. (ed.) (1926) *Sallustius: Concerning the Gods and the Universe*, Cambridge.

O'Meara, D. J. (1989) *Pythagoras Revived. Mathematics and Philosophy in Late Antiquity*, Oxford.

Opsomer, J. (2009) "The Integration of Aristotelian Physics in a Neoplatonic Context: Proclus on Movers and Divisibility," in R. Chiaradonna and F. Trabattoni (eds.), *Physics and Philosophy of Nature in Greek Neoplatonism*, Leiden and Boston, 193–203.

Pasquali, G. (ed.) (1908) Proclus, *In Platonis Cratylum commentaria*, Leipzig.

Pépin, J. (2000) "Les modes de l'enseignement théologique dans la *Théologie platonicienne*," in Segonds and Steel (2000), 1–14.

Pépin, J. and Saffrey, H.-D. (eds.) (1987) *Proclus: lecteur et interprète des anciens, Actes du colloque international du CNRS, Paris 2–4 octobre 1985*, Paris.

Praechter, K. (1926) "Das Schriftenverzeichnis des Neuplatonikers Syrianos bei Suidas," *Byzantinische Zeitschrift* 26: 253–264. Reprinted in Praechter (1973), 222–233.

(1973) *Kleine Schriften*, Hildesheim and New York.

Rabe, H. (ed.) (1899) Philoponus, *De aeternitate mundi contra Proclum*, Leipzig.

Ritzenfeld, A. (ed.) (1912) Proclus, *Institutio physica*, Leipzig.

Saffrey, H.-D. and Westerink, L. G. (eds.) (1968–1997) *Proclus: Théologie platonicienne*, 6 vols., Paris.

Saffrey, H.-D., Segonds, A.-Ph., and Luna, C. (eds.) (2001) *Marinus: Proclus ou sur le bonheur*, Paris.

Segonds, A.-Ph. (ed.) (1985–1986) *Proclus: Sur le Premier Alcibiade de Platon*, 2 vols., Paris.

(1987) "Proclus et l'astronomie," in Pépin and Saffrey (1987), 319–334.

Segonds, A.-Ph. and Steel, C. (eds.) (2000) *Proclus et la Théologie platonicienne, Actes du colloque international de Louvain, 13–16 mai 1998, en l'honneur de H.-D. Saffrey et L. G. Westerink*, Leuven and Paris.

Sheppard, A. D. R. (1980) *Studies on the 5th and 6th Essays of Proclus' Commentary on the Republic*, Göttingen.

(1987) "Proclus' Philosophical Method of Exegesis: The Use of Aristotle and the Stoics in the Commentary on the *Cratylus*," in Pépin and Saffrey (1987), 137–151.

(2000) "Plato's *Phaedrus* in the *Theologia Platonica*," in Segonds and Steel (2000), 415–423.

(2013) "Proclus' Place in the Reception of Plato's *Republic*," in A. D. R. Sheppard (ed.), *Ancient Approaches to Plato's Republic*, London, 107–115.

(forthcoming) "Literary Theory and Aesthetics" in d'Hoine and Martijn (forthcoming).

Siorvanes, L. (1996) *Proclus. Neo-Platonic Philosophy and Science*, New Haven, CT.

Steel, C. (2000) "Le *Parménide* est-il le fondement de la *Théologie platonicienne*?," in Segonds and Steel (2000), 373–398.

(2005) "Le jugement de Proclus sur le style du Parménide," in J. Dillon and M. Dixsaut (eds.), *Agonistes. Essays in Honour of Denis O'Brien*, Aldershot, 209–225.

(ed.) (2007–2009) Proclus, *In Platonis Parmenidem commentaria*, 3 vols., Oxford.

Struck, P. T. (2004) *Birth of the Symbol. Ancient Readers at the Limits of Their Texts*, Princeton and Oxford.

Wallies, M. (ed.) (1905) Philoponus, *In Aristotelis Analytica priora commentaria* (*Commentaria in Aristotelem Graeca* 13.2), Berlin.

(ed.) (1909) Philoponus, *In Aristotelis Analytica posteriora commentaria* (*Commentaria in Aristotelem Graeca* 13.3), Berlin.

Walsdorff, F. (1927) *Die antiken Urteile über Platons Stil*, Bonn and Leipzig.

Westerink, L. G. (1959) "Exzerpte aus Proklos' Enneaden-Kommentar bei Psellos," *Byzantinische Zeitschrift* 52: 1–10. Reprinted in Westerink (1980), 21–30.

(ed.) (1962) *Anonymous: Prolegomena to Platonic Philosophy*, Amsterdam.

(ed.) (1976) Olympiodorus, in *The Greek Commentaries on Plato's Phaedo*, vol. 1, Amsterdam and New York.

(1980) *Texts and Studies in Neoplatonism and Byzantine Literature*, Amsterdam.

(1987) "Proclus et les Présocratiques," in Pépin and Saffrey (1987), 105–112.

Westerink, L. G., Trouillard, J., and Segonds, A.-Ph. (eds.) (1990) *Prolégomènes à la philosophie de Platon*, Paris.

Zintzen, C. (ed.) (1967) Damascius, *Vitae Isidori reliquiae*, Hildesheim.

CHAPTER 3

Proclus as theologian

Stephen Gersh

Proclus' "Platonic" theology

In a manner comparable with that of the Christian doctrine already evolved by his own time, Proclus' theology is based on the twin sources of revelation and reason.[1] For Proclus, the philosophical appropriation of revelation takes place in the first instance through the formal exegesis of Plato's dialogues, among which the *Parmenides* and the *Timaeus* are considered to have almost universal importance, the *Philebus* and the *Phaedrus* also becoming crucial documents in certain contexts.[2] The philosophical appropriation of revelation also depends on the formal exegesis of certain writers on whom Plato himself is thought to have relied. Sometimes Proclus cites philosophers such as "Timaeus of Locri," who is presumed to have specifically inspired Plato's own dialogue *Timaeus*, as did earlier sources.[3] However, he more often refers generically to "the theologians" (θεόλογοι), who can be identified by the content of their citations as the authors of the "Orphic"[4] or the Homeric poetry.[5] Given that the most profound insights can only be achieved by a philosopher who also practices theurgic ritual, the studies of Plato and these earlier philosophers and theologians must be supplemented and indeed guided by a careful study of the revelation

[1] The term "theology" is used throughout this chapter in what I take to be the Proclean sense of the term: a study whose object is the gods and whose method depends on revelation. "Philosophy" is a term for a more generic practice that includes the study of the gods and things other than the gods and that depends less heavily on revelation. However, it is important to bear in mind (and indeed the meaning of a work such as Proclus' *Elements of Theology* cannot be grasped without doing so): (1) that theology can be extended to study things that are not themselves gods but depend on gods through participation; (2) that philosophy remains dependent on theology because of the metaphysical relation between its own and theology's objects and because of the inescapably non-demonstrable character of many of its premises.

[2] On Proclus' formal organization of methods of theological exegesis see Gersh (2000).

[3] See Proclus, *In Tim.* I. 1, 8–16 and I. 8, 21–27 (Diehl 1903–1906).

[4] See Proclus, *Theol. Plat.* V. 3, 16. 24–28 and V. 35, 127. 8–15 (Saffrey and Westerink 1968–1997). On Proclus' interpretation of Orphic poetry see Brisson (1987).

[5] See *Theol. Plat.* V. 24, 91.4–6 (via Plato).

that is the most important of all because it comes from the gods themselves: the *Chaldaean Oracles*.[6] Finally, the synthesis of all these revelations is most often not claimed for himself but attributed by Proclus in a self-effacing manner to "my teacher" (ὁ ἡμέτερος καθηγεμών) Syrianus, the greatest of the earlier commentators on Plato, the oracles, and many other texts.[7]

Given the methodological dichotomy of revelation and reason, it is important to understand that even Plato's writings fall primarily into the first category rather than the second in Proclus' eyes.[8] It is true that writings of Plato such as the *Parmenides* provide us with models of rational procedure that are worthy of imitation. In the extant portion of his commentary on that dialogue Proclus explains in some detail that the method of dialectic illustrated there is superior to the Aristotelian syllogistic and why it is so superior. However, the abundant testimonies regarding the no longer extant but more important section of the commentary make clear where the real importance of the *Parmenides* lies. It is most valuable because of the "intellectual intuitions" (νοεραὶ ἐπιβολαί)[9] in which the various deductions regarding the One yield not just properties of real things but "symbols" (συνθήματα) of different orders of gods.[10] Careful study of the wording of Proclus' text shows us what is at issue here. *Epibolai* are the points at which the normally discursive reasoning of our partial soul transcends itself with momentary incursions into the non-discursive realm of intellect, while *sunthēmata* are the verbal or visual symbols which are employed in theurgic ritual and whose enigmatic meanings can be explored by meditative reflection. Thus, the inner meaning of the *Parmenides* is both non-discursive and theurgic. According to Proclus, when Plato is thinking most profoundly he is invariably in agreement with the *Chaldaean Oracles*,[11] the obvious inconsistencies between these two doctrines being resolved on the assumption that Plato is actually *concealing* his true teaching.[12]

6 See *Theol. Plat.* V. 13, 43. 26–44. 2; V. 22, 82. 15–17; V. 32, 117. 23–118. 3; V. 35, 130. 2–11. That the revelation here comes directly from the gods is stated at *Theol. Plat.* V. 35, 130. 2–4. The primacy of this direct revelation is compatible with its later date relative to Plato. See *Theol. Plat.* V. 35, 130. 3. On the *Chaldaean Oracles* and Proclus see Saffrey (1981), Brisson (2000), and Van Liefferinge (1999).

7 See *Theol. Plat.* I. 1, 7. 3–4; I. 8, 33. 20–25; III. 15, 52. 18–22; etc.

8 The opposite is assumed by the medieval readers of Proclus, and indeed also by many unwary modern interpreters.

9 *Theol. Plat.* III. 4, 16. 15–16.

10 See *Theol. Plat.* V. 37, 135. 14–18; V. 37, 137. 24–25. Cf. V. 37, 137. 1–5 (σύμβολον).

11 See, for example, *Theol. Plat.* V. 35, 130. 2–11. Cf. *Theol. Plat.* III. 21, 73. 21–74. 22. When Plato agrees with the oracles, he has not just an intellectual grasp but a "divine intellect" (ἔνθεος νοῦς). See *Theol. Plat.* V. 36, 132. 4–5.

12 See *Theol. Plat.* V. 3, 17. 22–18. 28.

The rational element of philosophical thinking operates by arguing syllogistically on the basis of axioms drawn from the common store of Platonic and Aristotelian notions and then applying the results of these deductive procedures to the doctrines stated in the revealed texts. Moreover, the relation between Proclus' two main theological texts: the *Elements of Theology* and the *Platonic Theology* to a considerable extent reflects this relation between deductive procedure and revealed doctrine. It must be admitted that the parallelism is not complete since, although the *Elements of Theology* applies deductive method to axioms and practices no formal exegesis of texts, the *Platonic Theology* practices formal exegesis throughout[13] but also applies deductive method in various contexts.[14] Nevertheless, treating the *Elements of Theology* as a model of deductive method and the *Platonic Theology* as a model of formal exegesis and examining the manner in which the dialectical conclusions of the former work are used to organize the theological systematization of the latter will perhaps provide the illuminating insights into the fundamental structure of Proclus' theology sought by the present study. It is perhaps of some historical interest to note that in extracting axiomatic material from the *Elements of Theology* and then using this as a formal template for understanding the exegetical content of the *Platonic Theology*, we will be following in the footsteps of Proclus himself but running counter to Giovanni Pico della Mirandola. A thousand years after the ancient Greek writer, the "Conclusions according to Proclus" (*conclusiones secundum Proclum*) section of Pico's *Nine-Hundred Conclusions* provides one of the most interesting later readings of the *Platonic Theology* by using the latter itself as a source of *axiomatic* material to be applied in the service of a new philosophy.[15]

However, the project of extracting axiomatic material from the *Elements of Theology* and then using this as a formal template for understanding the exegetical content of the *Platonic Theology* has to begin by making certain strategic decisions. In particular, one must decide what the most important philosophical ideas in the *Elements of Theology* are and which order for presenting them to the reader is the best. The answers to these two questions

[13] At the risk of some simplification, we can say that in the *Platonic Theology* – which is of course emphatically a study of *Plato's* (rather than anybody else's) theology, book I makes a comprehensive survey of Plato's dialogues, book II concentrates heavily on the *Parmenides*, book III on the *Philebus* and *Timaeus*, book IV on the *Phaedrus*, book V on the *Timaeus*, and book VI on the *Phaedrus* and *Timaeus*.

[14] For a good example of deductive procedure in the *Platonic Theology* see *Theol. Plat.* III. 2, 6. 14–11. 15, where axioms concerning similarity, multiplicity, overlapping extension, and participation are used in order to prove certain facts about the gods or henads.

[15] See Farmer (1998), 315–333.

are by no means self-evident, since the *Elements of Theology* consists of a sequence of 211 propositions together with their proofs in which neither are the main axioms distinguished from the other propositions nor are the logical deductions unfolded in a unidirectional sequence.[16] Moreover, the discussion begins by studying the levels of reality in a hierarchy descending from the One, shifts to examining the general principles of causality from different angles and in an order that seems somewhat arbitrary, and then returns to studying the levels of reality from the henads, down through intellects, to souls. The approach of the present chapter will be to use the descending hierarchical structure of the *Platonic Theology* as an initial guide for organizing the propositions of the *Elements of Theology* into groups dealing with that hierarchy, and then to introduce the propositions dealing with those general principles of causality stated in the *Elements of Theology* that seem most relevant to the understanding of each level of reality as one descends.[17] It is important to bear in mind in the course of this reading of the *Elements of Theology* that Proclus is throughout his treatise pursuing a fundamentally *affirmative* theology articulated with a *discursive* method.[18] Therefore, his formulation of propositions about the One or gods simultaneously assumes that these principles transcend the property of unity and the possibility or necessity of demonstration.[19]

The discussion of Proclus' theology through a juxtaposition of his two most relevant texts in the present chapter will be divided into five segments dealing with: the basic module of Proclus' system (limit, infinity, the mixed); the One (or the monad of the unity series); the henads (or the unity series); Intellect (or the monad of the intellect series); and the intellects (or the intellect series), in each case first considering the axiomatic material in

[16] Berthold of Moosburg suggests that the entire argument of the *Elements of Theology* depends on two unstated axioms (or *supposita*): "that multiplicity exists," and "that productivity exists." These are indemonstrable and correspond to the *articuli fidei* in Christian doctrine. Assuming them leads to the conclusions that "the One exists" (props. 1–6) and that "the Good exists" (prop. 7) respectively. See Berthold, *Expos. in El. theol.* 1 (71. 3–7) (Pagnoni-Sturlese and Sturlese 1984) together with the discussion in Gersh (2001), 500.

[17] There is some circularity in this process of reading as there must be in all authentic hermeneutic exercises. However, closer reflection will show that the circularity is actually only a minor element in this particular case.

[18] There are only occasional allusions to the ineffability of the One: for example, at *El. theol.*, prop. 162, pr., 140. 33–142. 1. In fact, the references to ineffability are almost exclusively in the part of the text dealing with the *henads*.

[19] The *Platonic Theology* can be said to "correct" the *Elements of Theology* from both of these viewpoints. For example, see *Theol. Plat.* III. 8, 31. 11–13 for denial of the attribute "one" to the first principle; see *Theol. Plat.* V. 17, 62. 4–63. 19 for evidence that discursive thinking arises below the level of the intellectual gods.

the *Elements of Theology* and secondly applying this to the exegetical content of the *Platonic Theology*.[20] The structural relation between the order of discussion here proposed for the *Elements of Theology* and the book division of the *Platonic Theology* might be tabulated as follows:[21]

	Theol. Plat.	*El. theol.*
II	One (negative)	–
III	Being / beings	One / henads = One (affirmative)
IV	Life / lives	–
V	Intellect / intellects	Intellect / intellects
VI	–	Soul

Although the nature of Proclus' theology does lend itself to a systematic exposition of this kind, the reader needs to be alerted to certain complications below the surface of the narrative. In particular, one must realize that the attributes of the different levels of reality from the One downwards in the *Platonic Theology* are determined according to the narrative sequence of Plato's *Parmenides*,[22] and that tensions frequently arise between the internal metaphysical "logic" of Proclus' theological system and the requirement of compliance with the "letter" of this authoritative Platonic text.[23] To mention just one example here, the notions of continuity and similarity that underlie the system from the start (prop. 103) emerge only in one of the subsequent lemmas of the dialogue (147c–d).

Limit, unlimited, and the mixed

A set of propositions dealing with the relations between being, limit, infinity, and power seems to play a particularly important role in the attempt by the *Elements of Theology* to delineate the whole of reality as a hierarchy of causes and effects. Here Proclus argues that all beings are composed of "limit" (πέρας) and "unlimited" (ἀπειρία) (prop. 89),[24] that a First Limit and a First Unlimited subsist in themselves prior to those beings

[20] Owing to the spatial constraints of the present chapter, the second text will be subjected to sampling rather than exhaustive analysis.

[21] Book I of the *Platonic Theology* is excluded from the tabulation since it does not, as do the later books, concentrate on discussing the gods assigned to one specific level of reality.

[22] The definitive analysis of this question can be found in Saffrey and Westerink (1968–1997), vol. 1, lxxv–lxxxix. See also Saffrey (1984), Dillon (1987), and Steel (2002).

[23] Problems of this kind probably explain George Gemistos Plethon's decision, in formulating his own version of "Platonic" theology in the *Laws* almost a thousand years later, to avoid using the *Parmenides* as his exegetical basis. See Alexandre (1858), lviii–lxiv.

[24] The text actually has the Greek ἄπειρον in prop. 89 and ἀπειρία in props. 90ff. But no conceptual distinction seems to be intended by this change of term.

(prop. 90), that the First Unlimited is equivalent to "unlimited power" (ἄπειρος δύναμις) (prop. 91), that the multitude of powers is derived from the First Unlimited (prop. 92), and that the First Unlimited is equivalent to "power-in-itself" (αὐτοδύναμις) (prop. 92, proof). A further proposition – together with its proof – states that primal Being communicates limit and lack of limit to other beings because it is itself the primal "mixed" (μικτόν) of limit and unlimited (prop. 102).

These propositions are themselves framed by two further groups of propositions dealing with notions of participation and of order. In the first group, Proclus argues that there are "unparticipated terms" (ἀμέθεκτα) that produce from themselves "participated terms" (μετεχόμενα) (prop. 23), and that there is a descending order of superiority between unparticipated terms, participated terms, and "participating terms" (μετέχοντα) (prop. 24), these points being illuminated by a previous proposition stating that there will always be an "order" (τάξις) of terms dependent on a "monad" (μονάς) in the cases described (prop. 21). In the second group, Proclus argues that every unparticipated term "*qua* unparticipated" (ᾗ ἀμέθεκτόν ἐστι) is self-caused (prop. 99), and that every unparticipated term is dependent on the "First Principle of everything" (ἡ μία τῶν πάντων ἀρχή) (prop. 100), these points being clarified by a previous proposition stating that the cause of each order communicates its "distinctive property" (ἰδιότης) to the entire order (prop. 97). A final proposition stating that the first members of any order "have the form of the terms preceding them" (μορφὴν ἔχει τῶν πρὸ αὐτῶν) (prop. 112) completes the picture.

By summarizing the content of the propositions mentioned above, we can arrive at something like a "basic module" of the architectural construct that represents Proclus' theology. Having assumed that a well-known discussion in Plato's *Philebus* applies to the theory of Forms and the principles underlying that theory, Proclus finds a triadic structure which represents at the same time the diffusion of power[25] and the formation of being[26] to be the ultimate basis of reality. Here, the members of the triad themselves are sometimes called limit, unlimited, and mixed[27] and sometimes the unparticipated, [initial] participated, and [further] participated term,[28] while the first member of this triad has the ambivalent status[29] of being both separate from[30] and conjoined with the other terms.[31] Moreover, this triadic structure corresponds to an unspecified number of terms forming a

[25] Proclus, *El. theol.*, props. 91–92 (Dodds 1933). [26] *El. theol.*, props. 89–90 and 102.
[27] *El. theol.*, props. 89–92 and 102. [28] *El. theol.*, props. 23–24 and 99–100.
[29] *El. theol.*, prop. 112. [30] *El. theol.*, props. 23–24 and 99–100.
[31] *El. theol.*, prop. 97.

series derived from a monad.[32] The vast complexity of Proclus' system can, by understanding it as a sequence of rhythmic derivations from the basic module, be reduced to this relatively simple form.

Some preliminary remarks are necessary concerning the "power" (δύναμις) that has already been mentioned and the "activity" (ἐνέργεια) that is closely connected with it.[33] In general, Proclus understands the causal process as involving – from the viewpoint of the cause – a "surplus" (περιουσία) of power in the cause[34] from which it "gives something" (δίδωσί τι)[35] while "remaining in itself" (μένον ἐφ᾽ἑαυτοῦ)[36] and – from the viewpoint of the effect – the "reception" (ὑποδέχεσθαι) of a power[37] which has "become less powerful" (ἐλάττω δύνασθαι)[38] according to the "suitability" (ἐπιτηδειότης) of the effect.[39] According to Proclus' theory of causation, the power at the point of emission from the cause is "complete" (τελεία)[40] and is associated with the cause's actuality,[41] whereas the power at the point of reception is "incomplete" (ἀτελής)[42] and associated with the effect's potentiality.[43] However, the Aristotelian principle that the cause "is actually what the effect is potentially" (κατ᾽ἐνέργειαν ὂν ὃ τοῦτο δυνάμει ἐστίν)[44] is combined here with the Platonic assumption that the cause, in the proper sense of that term, "is transcendent" (ἐξῄρηται) with respect to the effect.[45]

Power and activity generally occur together in Proclus' unfolding of the structure of reality.[46] However, the fact that power tends to be associated more closely with the First Unlimited and activity more closely with the First Mixed included within the fundamental module[47] leads to important consequences. Having stated in the *Elements of Theology* that every cause "has activity" (ἐνεργεῖ) that is both prior to and subsequent to its effect,[48] Proclus explains this proposition in the accompanying proof and corollary by arguing that, given a descending order in which each term is effect of the previous and cause of the subsequent, there is a *continuous* diminution of power but *overlapping* extensions of activities.[49] This situation presumably

32 *El. theol.*, props. 21, 97, and 112.

33 On power and activity in Proclus' metaphysical system see Gersh (1973), 27–48 and 81–102; Gersh (1978), 27–45. See also Steel (1996).

34 *El. theol.*, prop. 27, 30. 25–26.

35 *El. theol.*, prop. 58, pr., 56. 19–20.

36 *El. theol.*, prop. 26, 30. 10–11.

37 *El. theol.*, prop. 150, 132. 1–2.

38 *El. theol.*, prop. 61, pr., 58. 19.

39 *El. theol.*, prop. 71, pr., 68. 9–11.

40 *El. theol.*, prop. 78 + pr., 74. 8–17.

41 *El. theol.*, prop. 77, 72. 20–23.

42 *El. theol.*, prop. 78 + pr., 74. 8–17.

43 *El. theol.*, prop. 77, 72. 20–23.

44 *El. theol.*, prop. 77, 72. 20–21.

45 *El. theol.*, prop. 75, 70. 28–29.

46 For example, see *El. theol.* 78, 74. pr., 9–10.

47 For examples of this notion, see below.

48 *El. theol.*, prop. 57, 54. 23–24.

49 For instance, the One's power is before Intellect's power, Intellect's power is before Soul's power, and Soul's power is before Nature's power, whereas Intellect is active both before and after Soul (in

arises from the disparity between the indeterminacy and the determinacy that power and activity respectively derive from their structural function within the basic module.[50]

The basic module appears as a whole or in part on almost every page of Proclus' *Platonic Theology*. It is most explicit in the early chapters of book III, where in the descending hierarchical order of divinity the first group of the so-called intelligible gods is described in detail and a reading of the *Philebus* obscures the author's more usual dependence on the *Parmenides*.[51] The first three principles mentioned here are limit, infinity, and mixed, and Proclus emphasizes that limit and infinity have the ambivalent status of being both transcendent of and coordinate with the mixed,[52] the point being important because the architectonics of his system depends on a combination of sequencing and subdivision of terms. Although in these early chapters of book III, limit, infinity, and mixed are all described as "henads,"[53] the situation becomes more complicated as we read on in Proclus' treatise. Here, we discover that an analogous triad divides the entire pantheon,[54] subdivides its three terms into three further terms, and then subdivides these further terms in a similar manner, yielding a basic structure of twenty-seven terms.[55] The terminology of "intelligible," "intelligible-and-intellectual," and "intellectual" most often applied to this primary division is relatively stable.[56] However, the larger or smaller subdivisions can be characterized as monad, dyad, and triad,[57] as father, power, and intellect,[58] as remaining, procession, and

intellectual and inanimate things respectively), and the One active both before and after Intellect and Soul (in unity and privation respectively). Although "before" clearly indicates magnitude in the case of power and extension in the case of activity, Proclus maintains that magnitude and extension coincide.

50 And presumably also from the continuity and discreteness that they similarly derive.

51 Damascius bases one of his criticisms of Proclus on the misuse of the *Philebus* in this context. He prefers to speak of the "One-All" (ἓν πάντα), the "All-One" (πάντα ἕν) and the "Unified" (ἡνωμένον). See *De princ.* II. 39. 7–25.

52 *Theol. Plat.* III.10, 41. 16–42. 12.

53 See *Theol. Plat.* III. 9, 36. 13–15 for limit and unlimited. Cf. III. 12, 45. 23–25 and III. 14, 49. 5–6. Proclus' text is more ambiguous with respect to the henadic status of the mixed because at *Theol. Plat.* III. 14, 51. 11–15 and elsewhere he treats both the first terms of triads and also complete triads as gods. *Theol. Plat.* III. 14, 49. 12–18 suggests the possibility of the mixed as a henad. On the three primal henads in Proclus see Van Riel (2001).

54 Pico della Mirandola sees this triadicity as one of the most important features of the *Platonic Theology*. See *Conclusiones* "secundum Proclum" 9, 11, 13–14, 24, 27–30, 32–33, 35, 48–49, and 52. On participation between triadic terms see *Concl.* 45.

55 Not exactly twenty-seven (3 x 3 x 3) because the third group of nine terms is actually seven.

56 For example, see *Theol. Plat.* III. 28, 100. 1–102. 6; V. 1, 6. 1–9. 8.

57 *Theol. Plat.* III. 9, 37. 21–38. 7.

58 *Theol. Plat.* III. 21, 73. 19–21. Cf. *Theol. Plat.* V. 13, 42. 22–44. 17; V. 16, 52. 9–25. "Father" is sometimes replaced by *huparxis*. See *Theol. Plat.* III. 9, 39. 15–18, etc.

reversion,[59] and as being, life, and intellect.[60] The choice seems to depend on whether the structure is viewed as dynamic or stable and as a larger or smaller subdivision,[61] although purely exegetical criteria sometimes play a role.[62]

The relations suggested by the *Elements of Theology* between the notions of limit, unlimited, and mixed on the one hand and those of participation and order on the other also underlie much of the structuration in the *Platonic Theology.* However, the precise location of the *amethekta* ("unparticipated") terms has been puzzling commentators from at least the time of Nicholas of Methone.[63] The problem is basically as follows: If one is confronted with a triad of (e.g.) intelligible, life, and intellect where each term is subdivided into a further triad of intelligible, life, and intellect, is (e.g.) the "unparticipated" intellect the third term of the main division or the third term of the first subdivision? The former option would logically give the unparticipated intellect the most prominent position in the intellectual hierarchy whereas the latter option would with equal logic give it the highest position in that scheme. Proclus' response to this difficulty is ambivalent. In most cases Proclus refers to the first, second, and third terms of the main division as unparticipated intelligible, unparticipated life, and unparticipated intellect respectively.[64] However, in certain contexts he is prepared to describe the third term of the first subdivision as the unparticipated intellect.[65] It is the disparity between these two usages that forces him to countenance the possibilities of speaking of the same term as both unparticipated and participated[66] and also of a plurality of unparticipated intellects.[67] Finally, Proclus refers in a more generic way to the entire structure divided into intelligible, life, and intellect as an "unparticipated apportionment" (ἀμέθεκτος μοῖρα).[68]

59 *Theol. Plat.* III. 9, 35. 19–24. Cf. *Theol. Plat.* III. 8, 32. 13–33. 2; III. 12, 45. 13–16; III. 12, 46. 13–15; III. 13, 48. 5–6; and III. 14, 49. 14–18 for various applications of this triad.

60 *Theol. Plat.* III. 9, 35. 19–24.

61 The triad of remaining, procession, and reversion is preferred in more dynamic contexts, the other triads in more static ones. The triad of father, power, and intellect is applied primarily but not exclusively to the smallest subdivision. Contrast *Theol. Plat.* III. 21, 73. 19–21 and V. 17, 60. 19–22 with *Theol. Plat.* V. 13, 42. 22–44. 17 and V 16, 52. 9–25.

62 The triad of father, power, and intellect comes from the *Chaldaean Oracles.*

63 See Nicholas of Methone, *Anaptyxis* 70. 8–19 (Angelou 1984).

64 For unparticipated intelligible (i.e. being) see *Theol. Plat.* III. 28, 100. 11; V. 1, 8. 13; for unparticipated life see *Theol. Plat.* V.1, 8. 4–5; for unparticipated intellect see *Theol. Plat.* V. 13, 44. 4–5; V. 23, 84. 19–20; V. 25, 93. 17–19. It is this sense of unparticipated that is implied in passages such as *Theol. Plat.* III. 6, 28. 3–21, where Proclus speaks of the presence of a multiplicity of henads in a single unparticipated term.

65 See *Theol. Plat.* V. 25, 93. 17–19.

66 See *Theol. Plat.* III. 6, 28. 3–21.

67 See *Theol. Plat.* V. 37, 134. 15–18.

68 See *Theol. Plat.* III. 6, 28. 9–10. The same approach underlies the notion of unparticipated causality appearing at *Theol. Plat.* III. 8, 31. 14–32. 5. Ficino in his intelligent summary of the text in

The unfolding of the structure of reality in terms of the interrelation of power and activity that was so central to the *Elements of Theology* is also a feature of the *Platonic Theology* although power and activity tend to be understood more statically as the second and third terms of a triadic structure in the longer work.[69] The relation between limit and infinity on the one hand and form and matter on the other is the particular topic of chapter 10 of *Platonic Theology* III. Here, it emerges that both sets of terms represent an opposition of complete power (= activity) and incomplete power (= potentiality), but that the opposition in the case of limit and unlimited covers the entire emanative continuum between complete and incomplete power whereas that in the case of form and matter occurs within that continuum and at a lower level.[70] The doctrine of the *Elements of Theology* that, given a descending order in which each term is effect of the previous and cause of the subsequent, there is a *continuous* diminution of power but *overlapping* extensions of activities reappears in the *Platonic Theology*. The axiom itself is restated in chapter 2 of book III[71] and is later applied to the relation between the activities of Zeus-Demiurge in himself and through the lower gods.[72]

The One or Good

The *Elements of Theology* begins with a sequence of thirteen propositions that deal explicitly with the first hypostasis of Plotinus' system, although frequent references to participation show the applicability of the concepts elaborated also to the Platonic Forms and particulars. Within this group, propositions 1–6 relate more closely to the "One" of Plato's *Parmenides*[73] and propositions 7–12 more closely to the "Good" of Plato's *Republic*,[74] proposition 13 establishing the identity of the One and the Good that is assumed by Plotinus in accordance with Plato's oral teaching.[75] There is a danger of misunderstanding the function of this group of propositions. As Proclus explains elsewhere, the terms "One" and "Good" do not denote what is really first or ultimate, since the latter is beyond denotation as

the MS *Firenze, Riccardianus 70* entitled *ordo divinorum apud Platonem secundum Proclum*, gets around the problem by speaking of all nine subdivisions of Being as "unparticipated beings," all nine subdivisions of Life as "unparticipated lives," and so forth. The text is printed in Saffrey (1959), 171.

69 See Romano (2000).

70 *Theol. Plat.* III. 10, 40. 10–41.15.

71 *Theol. Plat.* III. 2, 9. 12–10. 14.

72 *Theol Plat.* V. 18, 69. 17–21. Cf. *Theol. Plat.* V. 18, 64. 3–14 and V. 18, 66. 26–67. 13.

73 See especially Plato, *Parm.* 157b ff. where the relation between the multitude and unity is discussed.

74 See Plato: *Rep.* VI. 509bc. Proclus describes the Good, recalling Plato's terminology, as "beyond beings" (ἐπέκεινα τῶν ὄντων) at *El. theol.*, prop. 8, pr., 8. 32.

75 See Aristotle, *Metaph. N.* 4, 1091b.

such.[76] Therefore, the sequence of thirteen propositions beginning the *Elements of Theology* really concerns *either* the First Limit included in the basic module *or* – more precisely – the incipient relation between the First Limit, the First Infinity, and the First Mixed.[77]

Propositions 1–6 attempt to demonstrate that the multitude of subsistent things "participates in some manner" (μετέχει πῃ) in unity (prop. 1), that this multitude is both a unity and not a unity (prop. 2), that the multitude "becomes" (γίνεσθαι) a unity by participation (prop. 3), that this multitude – now called "the unified" (τὸ ἡνωμένον) – is other than "the One itself" (τὸ αὐτοέν) (prop. 4), that this multitude is "posterior to" (δεύτερον) the One (prop. 5), and that this multitude consists partly of "unified things" (ἡνωμένα) and partly of "henads" (ἑνάδες) (prop. 6).[78] With respect to propositions 1–6 the following points are perhaps worth noting. First, terminological distinctions are maintained between unity and the One itself when referring to the One, and between unity of the multitude, the unified, and the henads when referring to things subsequent to the One. Second, the immanent relation between the One and subsequent things in props. 1–4 is complemented by a transcendent relation in prop. 5. Third, the relation between the multitude and unity expressed by the negation "not" is a relation of otherness. Fourth, the static contrast between the non-unity and unity of the multitude in prop. 2 is complemented by a dynamic contrast in prop. 3. Finally, the qualified reference (πῃ) to participation in prop. 1 probably results from the ambivalent status of the first term in the basic module which is *un*participated strictly speaking. Several of the proofs also contain noteworthy points. The proof of prop. 1 is based on the rejection of an infinite regress of terms and therefore distinguishes the One clearly from the infinity of the second term in the basic module. The comment within the proof of prop. 6 that the unifieds participate in the One itself whereas the henads do not so participate again alludes to the ambivalent status of the first term in the basic module.

The next group of propositions begins with a statement of the fundamental assumption underlying Neoplatonic thought: namely, that every

[76] See *Theol. Plat.* III. 8, 32. 11–13, etc.

[77] See *Theol. Plat.* III. 8, 31. 13–20. Cf. *Theol. Plat.* III. 17, 57. 6–58. 11 on the relation between eternity and the "one" and III. 24, 83. 20–84. 23 on the "one-being."

[78] The importance of the relation between props. 1–6 (relating to the first principle as "One") on the one hand, and prop. 7 (relating to the first principle as "Good") on the other plays an important role in Berthold of Moosburg's reading of the treatise. See n. 16 above.

cause[79] is "superior" (κρεῖττον) to its effect (prop. 7).[80] Further propositions attempt to prove that the Good itself[81] is superior to a multitude of subsistent things that "somehow participate in" (ὁπωσοῦν μετέχει) goodness (prop. 8), and that the Good itself[82] is superior to that multitude of subsistent things that are specifically "self-sufficient" (αὐτάρκης) (prop. 10).[83] This group of propositions continues with a statement of another fundamental assumption underlying Neoplatonic thought: namely that all "existent things" (ὄντα) derive from a single "first cause" (αἰτία πρώτη) (prop. 11). This in its turn leads to the further conclusion that all existent things derive from a first "principle and cause" (ἀρχὴ καὶ αἰτία) that is "the Good" (τὸ ἀγαθόν) (prop. 12). The following points should be noted with respect to propositions 7–12. First, terminological distinctions are maintained between the primal good and the simply good when referring to the Good, and between the self-sufficient and the not self-sufficient when referring to things subsequent to the Good. Second, the arguments about participation and superiority applied to the Good in props. 8 and 10 respectively parallel the similar arguments applied to the One in props. 1 and 5 respectively. Third, the qualified reference (ὁπωσοῦν) to participation in prop. 8 results from the ambivalent status of the first term in the basic module which is strictly speaking *un*participated. Several of the proofs also contain noteworthy points. The proofs of props. 7 and 11 are based on the rejection of an infinite regress of terms and therefore distinguish the Good clearly from the infinity of the second term in the basic module. Comments within the proofs of props. 8 and 9 introduce the notion of the Good's final causality by referring to the "striving" (ἐφίεσθαι) towards it of subsequent things.

Almost all of these notions are applied at some point in elaborating the complex system of the *Platonic Theology*, beginning of course with the idea running through the entire text that the gods (as the supreme principles) are equivalent to henads (as the most unitary principles). Here, I simply draw attention to the explicit assumption of the inverse

79 Strictly speaking every "productive cause" (παρακτικόν) is superior to its effect. Proclus works with a dichotomy of "producer" (παράγον) and "produced" (παραγόμενον), the verb *paragein* – seemingly first employed by Plotinus – denoting precisely the relation between the (superior) cause and the (inferior) effect which is the fundamental structural component of the Neoplatonic system.

80 See p. 86 above.

81 This abbreviates Proclus' "the primal good that is nothing else than good" (τὸ πρώτως ἀγαθὸν καὶ ὃ μηδέν ἐστιν ἄλλο ἢ ἀγαθόν).

82 This paraphrases Proclus, "the simply good" (τὸ ἁπλῶς ἀγαθόν).

83 An intermediate proposition has established the distinction between self-sufficient and not self-sufficient things together with the superiority of the former over the latter (prop. 9).

relation between multiplicity and superiority underlying Proclus' argument from analogy that just as the highest within the orders of souls govern the most simple bodies, and the highest within the intellectual orders govern the most universal souls, so do the highest within the orders of the gods govern the most simple beings.[84] It is also worth noting that in order to follow the distribution of the properties of unity and goodness through the various divine orders, Proclus is forced to make some complicated maneuvers in his use of concepts and terminologies. With respect to unity, he notes that "infinite multiplicity" (ἄπειρον πλῆθος) occurs in the third triad of the intelligible gods whereas "number" (ἀριθμός) appears in the first triad of the intelligible-and-intellectual divinities, the latter having the additional feature of being "distinct" (διακεκριμένον).[85] With respect to goodness, Proclus notes that "intelligible goodness" (ἀγαθότης νοητή) occurring in the first triad of the intelligible gods represents a "fullness of divine self-sufficiency and power" (πλήρωμα τῆς θείας αὐταρκείας καὶ τῆς θείας δυνάμεως) which is superior to any "idea" (ἰδέα).[86] The position with regard to unity results from the dependence of Proclus' theology on exegesis of the *Parmenides*, the position with regard to goodness from the same theology's lack of dependence on exegesis of the *Republic*.

The henads

In accordance with the system of structural analogies that dominates Proclus' theology, just as the primal Intellect is followed by secondary intellects, and just as the primal Soul is followed by secondary souls, so is the primal One followed by secondary ones.[87] The doctrine regarding these secondary ones – usually called "henads" (ἑνάδες) or "gods" (θεοί) – is set out in propositions 113–165 of the *Elements of Theology*. Its most important features can

84 See *Theol. Plat.* III. 5, 19. 25–30.

85 *Theol. Plat.* IV. 28, 81. 3–9. Cf. *Theol. Plat.* IV. 27, 79. 16–80. 6. The distinctness resides in the fact that the multiplicity may be specified: for example, in terms of the triad or the hebdomad that are the prevailing numerical aspects of Proclus' theological system. For a good summary of triadic structure see *Theol. Plat.* V. 2, 9. 16–10. 18; for hebdomads see especially *Theol. Plat.* V. 2, 10. 19 – V. 4, 20. 21 and V. 36, 131. 12–133. 28. Fourfold structure is less important but occurs in connection with the Forms. See *Theol. Plat.* III. 27, 98. 10–99. 9.

86 *Theol. Plat.* III. 28, 101. 5–15. The "idea" would presumably not occur until the third triad of the intelligible gods.

87 The doctrine of a series of ones coordinated with *the* One was an innovation introduced by Syrianus (although there had already been a slightly different attempt to grapple with the implications of polytheism on the part of Iamblichus). Clearly the innovation of Syrianus demonstrates the extent to which the notion of continuity was dominating metaphysical thinking. See p. 85.

perhaps be summarized by considering what Proclus has to say first about the status and second about the function of these principles.[88]

The status attributed by the *Elements of Theology* to the henads is ambivalent in that they are sometimes more closely associated with the One but sometimes more closely associated with beings. The assimilation of the henads to the One is suggested in a few passages where Proclus argues that the entire divine order is "unitary" (ἑνιαῖος),[89] and that everything divine is "primarily and maximally simple" (ἁπλοῦν πρώτως καὶ μάλιστα),[90] the clear assumption being that the henads are collectively as well as individually unitary. The assimilation of the henads to beings occurs more frequently although there seems to be a further complication. On the one hand, Proclus argues that, since every plurality nearer to the One is lesser in quantity but greater in power, henads are less numerous than beings;[91] on the other hand, he maintains that, since one henad is participated immediately by one being, the number of participated henads is identical with the number of participating beings.[92] The explanation of the disparity between these two statements seems to be that the henads are being associated in the former case with phases of the sequential cycle of intellect's remaining, procession, and reversion – that is, the monadic intellect and the series of intellects – but in the latter case with the subdividing cycle of intellect's remaining, procession, and reversion – that is, the intellect completing the triad of being, life, intellect.[93] I will mark the ambivalent status of the henads by using the graphic form *henad(s)* to express their closer association with the One and the expression *henads-beings* to express their closer association with beings.

The function assigned by the *Elements of Theology* to the henads is to initiate the causality of the universe by conferring on existent things distinctive properties and the interrelation between properties.[94] The basis of this functionality is the "distinctive property" (ἰδιότης) possessed by each henad, this distinctive property being (a) what defines it *as a henad*,[95]

88 The doctrine of henads has attracted the attention of scholars in recent years, although the various attempts to map the entire structure of henadic participation are mostly unconvincing. See especially Butler (2005), Butler (2008a), Butler (2008b), Chlup (2012), 112–136. A more modest and realistic attempt to understand the religious role of the henads is Guérard 1982.

89 *El. theol.*, prop. 113, 100. 5.

90 *El. theol.*, prop. 127, 112. 25–26.

91 *El. theol.*, prop. 62, 58. 22–23 + corr., 58. 30–32.

92 *El. theol.*, prop. 135, 120. 1–4.

93 For more detail on this point see pp. 99–101 below. The first approach predominates in the *Elements of Theology*; and the second, in the *Platonic Theology*.

94 For a good analysis of this aspect of the henads see Butler (2005).

95 See *El. theol.*, props. 114, pr., 100. 22–25; 118, 104. 5–7; 129, pr., 114. 20–22; 138, 122. 7–8; and 145, 128. 1–2.

(b) what defines it as a henad *of a certain type*,[96] and (c) what defines it as *this henad*.[97] In accordance with this functionality, the henads confer on beings not only their distinctive properties – since the highest members of each type of being "are referred to the gods so that in every order there are terms analogous with the gods that maintain and preserve the secondary terms"[98] – but also the interrelation between those properties – since it is through the gods' agency that "everything is in sympathy with everything else, the secondary things pre-existing in the primary and primary things manifested in the secondary,"[99] these two functions representing opposing aspects of the henads' unifying power.[100] Three further aspects of the henads' function are of particular importance. First, the henads exercise causality while entering into no "relation" (σχέσις) with the beings that they cause.[101] However, here one must take account of a distinction between the causal activity of the *henad(s)* which is transcendent with respect to subsequent beings and the causal activity of the *henads-beings* which is coordinate with respect to subsequent beings.[102] Second, given that the One and henads subsist prior to Intellect and intellects, the causal activity of the henads can be called "providence" (πρόνοια).[103] Third, the henads exercise causality through the production of beings that are "*self-* (αὐτο-) determining principles," their self-determination implying the threefold cycle of remaining, procession, and reversion in both its subdividing and its sequential forms.[104] It is precisely because of their *self-hood* that these

[96] See *El. theol.*, prop. 150 + pr., 132. 1 – prop. 159 + pr., 140. 4. The types are "paternal" (πατρικός), "maternal" (μητρικός), and so forth, depending on their relations to the primal limit and unlimited.

[97] See *El. theol.*, props. 125, 110. 29–32; 145, pr., 128. 5–16. These types of distinctive property will ultimately not be distinct from one another because of the inherent unity of the henadic order.

[98] *El. theol.*, prop. 139 + pr., 122. 25–27 τοῖς θεοῖς ἀνεῖται . . . ἵνα ἐν πάσῃ τάξει τὰ τοῖς θεοῖς ἀναλογοῦντα συνεκτικὰ καὶ σωστικὰ τῶν δευτέρων ὑπάρχῃ.

[99] *El. theol.*, prop. 140, pr., 124. 14–18 συμπαθῆ πάντα πᾶσιν, ἐν μὲν τοῖς πρώτοις τῶν δευτέρων προϋπαρχόντων, ἐν δὲ τοῖς δευτέροις τῶν πρώτων ἐμφαινομένων.

[100] I.e. the uniqueness of each secondary being and the unification among secondary beings.

[101] *El. theol.*, prop., 122 + pr., 108. 1–24. The henads are here said to cause "through their essence" (τῷ εἶναι). For a similar description of causality on the part of intellect see above.

[102] See *El. theol.*, prop. 141+ pr., 124. 19–26.

[103] See *El. theol.*, prop. 120, pr. 106, 5–7, where providence is defined as "the activity prior to Intellect" (ἡ πρὸ νοῦ ἐνέργεια).

[104] See n. 93. The type of self-determining principle most frequently discussed by Proclus is the "self-constituted" (αὐθυπόστατος) principle. For the theory of such principles see *El. theol.*, prop. 40 + pr., 42. 8 – prop. 55 + pr., 55. 3. However, Proclus can also speak of a "self-sufficient" (αὐτάρκης), "self-perfect" (αὐτοτελής), or "self-living" (αὐτόζως) principle. The important points are that all these principles involve the notion of selfhood, are interconnected in sense, and imply the cycle of remaining, procession, and reversion. The subdividing cycle is implied at *El. theol.*, props. 190 + pr., 166. 1–25 (discussing self-constitution, self-life, and self-knowledge). The sequential cycle is suggested at *El. theol.*, prop. 64 + pr., 60. 20–62. 12 (discussing self-perfection). For further consideration of this question see Gersh (1978), 125–137 and below.

principles exhibit the greatest affinity to the Good[105] and by implication with the henads also.

Awareness of the henads' ambivalent status in being associated sometimes more closely with the One and sometimes more closely with beings is crucial to the understanding of the *Platonic Theology* as a whole.[106] Although a close association of the henads with the One is probably to be assumed throughout book II and occasionally elsewhere,[107] the treatise as a whole implies the complementary association of the henads with beings. This is because the work unfolds predominantly as an exercise in affirmative theology and as an exegesis of the *second* hypothesis of the *Parmenides* taking its starting-point from the "one-being" (ἓν ὄν).[108] A passage in chapter 21 of book III where the henad corresponding to the first term of the triad of father, power, and intellect is said to be "intelligible" (νοητόν) on the grounds that deity is inherently participable brings this undercurrent of affirmative theology to the fore.[109]

The henads' role in conferring on existent things distinctive properties and the interrelation between properties is clarified particularly by the discussion of the causality exercised by Zeus/the Demiurge (= the third term of the first triad of intellectual gods).[110] Proclus here develops a complicated theory according to which Zeus is said to have a "dyadic character" (τὸ δυοειδές).[111] This character manifests itself in his relations not only with Kronos and Rhea (= the first and second terms of the first triad of intellectual gods) – as reflected in the accusative cases of his two cultic names: Δία and Ζῆνα[112] – but also with a mysterious seventh divinity (= unique term

105 See *El. theol.*, prop. 40, pr., 42. 16–17 and 42. 27–29 (on self-sufficiency).

106 On the problems associated with this aspect of Proclus' theory see Butler (2008a).

107 At *Theol. Plat.* I. 3, 15. 5–6 the One is described as "the secret unification of all the divine henads" (ἡ πασῶν τῶν θείων ἑνάδων ἀπόκρυφος ἕνωσις). Another index of the close association of the henads with the One is Proclus' tendency to describe the One itself as a henad. For example, see *Theol. Plat.* I. 3, 14. 14–15; I. 4, 18. 18; I. 25, 110. 4. At *Theol. Plat.* II. 11, 65. 12 the One is called simply "the henad of henads" (ἑνὰς ἑνάδων).

108 On the "one-being" see *Theol. Plat.* III. 4, 15. 9–15. Negative theology plays a significant role only in book II (although there are traces of it in isolated passages elsewhere: for example, *Theol. Plat.* IV. 11, 35. 11–38. 27 (concerning the supercelestial place of the *Phaedrus*) and V. 28, 102. 12–105. 14 (concerning the Demiurge of the *Timaeus*).

109 *Theol. Plat.* III. 21, 74. 23–75. 3. Proclus is here applying a principle stated in *El. theol.*, prop. 112, 98. 33–34.

110 For the identification of Zeus and the Demiurge see *Theol. Plat.* V. 25, 96. 18–24 (where the *Politicus* is the main source).

111 *Theol. Plat.* V. 22, 82. 8–10.

112 On the two names see *Theol. Plat.* V. 22, 78. 26–79. 17 and V. 22, 83. 11–26, where Zeus is said to obtain limit and final causality (δι' ὅ) from Kronos, infinity and vitality (ζωή) from Rhea.

replacing the third triad of intellectual gods).[113] Zeus and/or the seventh divinity is said to be responsible for distinguishing the intellectual order of gods from the preceding and subsequent orders, the terms within the intellectual order from one another, and indeed the status of the discriminatory god himself.[114] The process described here is understood to be the meaning of the *Chaldaean Oracle* that refers to a "flashing with intellectual cuts" (νοεραῖς ἀστράπτουσα τομαῖς),[115] although Proclus attempts to confirm this direct revelation by the gods with the passage in the *Timaeus* referring to the Demiurge's cutting of the psychic substance into seven portions.[116]

The various additional aspects of the henads' function described in the *Elements of Theology* can also be exemplified in Proclus' treatment of the intellectual gods in his larger treatise. Thus, exercise of causality while entering into no "relation" (σχέσις) with the beings that they cause is exemplified particularly in the case of the Couretes (= second triad of intellectual gods). These gods[117] – who are also called the "immaculate" (ἄχραντοι) gods[118] – are said to preserve the status of the divine substance as "unmixed with respect to secondary things" (ἄμικτον . . . πρὸς τὰ δεύτερα) and also the inflexibility of the divine powers and activities.[119] The providence of the henads is illustrated by Proclus' interpretation of the myth of the *Politicus*, where the two revolutions of the world are said to represent two activities of Zeus/the Demiurge, namely, the elevation of souls towards intellect, which is under the rule of providence, and their inclination towards nature, which is according to the order of fate.[120] Exercise of causality through the production of beings that are self-determining principles is exemplified particularly in the cases of Kronos and Zeus (= first and third terms of the first triad of intellectual gods).[121] The god Kronos[122] is said, by being both

[113] This is called the "separating divinity" (διακριτικὴ θεότης) at *Theol. Plat.* V. 3, 17. 15–16 and the "seventh monad" (ἑβδόμη μονάς) at *Theol. Plat.* V. 36, 131. 19–20.

[114] *Theol. Plat.* V. 3, 17. 15–21 and V. 36, 131. 17–24. At V. 36, 133. 16–22 the distinguishing activity also involves the assignation of being, life, and intellect to lower realities.

[115] *Oracula Chaldaica*, fr. 1. 4 (des Places 1971) quoted at *Theol. Plat.* V. 13, 43. 27; V. 36, 132. 13; and V. 36, 133. 15–16.

[116] See *Theol. Plat.* V. 36, 133. 3–28.

[117] Proclus here interprets the *Parmenides*, where it says that this order of gods has the attributes of being "in motion and at rest" (κινεῖσθαι καὶ ἑστάναι). See *Theol. Plat.* V. 38, 142. 1.

[118] See *Theol. Plat.* V. 33, 121. 20; V. 33, 122. 20–21, etc.

[119] *Theol. Plat.* V. 33, 122. 2–6 and V. 33, 122. 11–13. These gods also have the more specific function of protecting the transcendence of the Demiurge and the Forms. See *Theol. Plat.* V. 34, 123. 24–124. 14.

[120] See *Theol. Plat.* V. 25, 92. 1–13.

[121] For the following details as applied to Zeus see *Theol. Plat.* V. 37, 134. 18–21.

[122] Proclus here interprets the *Parmenides*, where it says that this order of gods has the attributes of being "in itself and in another" (ἐν αὑτῷ καὶ ἐν ἄλλῳ). See *Theol. Plat.* V. 37, 134. 11.

dependent on the causality of a prior principle – as its "paternal intellect" (πατρικὸς νοῦς) – and the initiator of causality for subsequent terms – as their "intellectual father" (πατὴρ νοερός)[123] – to combine subdividing and sequential activity.[124]

Intellect

In Plotinus' system, the second hypostasis is "Intellect" (νοῦς). An alteration of the doctrine of first principles by the introduction of "Being" (ὄν) and "Life" (ζωή) as intermediate hypostases between the One and Intellect was sometimes suggested by the late ancient Platonists themselves and has been the subject of much debate among modern scholars.[125] However, the Plotinian view regarding the "intellective" character of the second hypostasis was essentially maintained by later thinkers. In the *Elements of Theology* the order of the One and henads is immediately followed by that of Intellect and intellects. Moreover, the fundamental doctrine of causality elaborated there – the next topic to consider in any account of Proclus' theology – makes little sense outside an *intellective* context. In fact, this doctrine represents probably the most complete expression of the basic module.

Several propositions in the *Elements of Theology* deal with the role of "similarity" (ὁμοιότης). Thus, "Every procession is accomplished through the similarity of secondary to primary terms,"[126] and "Every reversion is accomplished through the similarity of the reverting terms to that to which they revert."[127] Another proposition in the same treatise emphasizes the notion of "wholeness" (ὁλότης). Thus, "Every series of wholes is referable to an unparticipated principle and cause."[128] A connection between the notions of similarity and wholeness is established by a proposition and proof explaining the similarity between the higher principles as a combination of sameness and otherness,[129] and by a further proposition explaining the relation between all existents as a combination of either (a) sameness and

[123] *Theol. Plat.* V. 37, 134. 21–135. 13. Cf. *Theol. Plat.* 136. 20–137. 18.

[124] *Theol. Plat.* V. 37, 138. 12–139. 4. Proclus notes that these activities correspond to the gods' "swallowing" (καταπίνειν) as described in the myths. See nn. 93 and 104.

[125] The ancient Platonists themselves seem to have discussed this question most often in the context of controversies between various members of the "school."

[126] *El. theol.*, prop. 29, 34. 3–4 πᾶσα πρόοδος δι' ὁμοιότητος ἀποτελεῖται τῶν δευτέρων πρὸς τὰ πρῶτα.

[127] *El. theol.*, prop. 32, 36. 3–4 πᾶσα ἐπιστροφὴ δι'ὁμοιότητος ἀποτελεῖται τῶν ἐπιστρεφομένων πρὸς ὃ ἐπιστρέφεται.

[128] *El. theol.*, prop. 100, 90. 1–2 πᾶσα μὲν σειρὰ τῶν ὅλων εἰς ἀμέθεκτον ἀρχὴν καὶ αἰτίαν ἀνατείνεται.

[129] *El. theol.*, prop. 30, pr. 34. 23–27.

difference or (b) whole and part.[130] Underlying all these statements is an implicit assumption of the connection between mind and hermeneutics. As a general rule, similarity is not a logical category but a hermeneutic category. Moreover, the *Elements of Theology* makes extensive use of a threefold distinction between wholes "before the parts" (πρὸ τῶν μερῶν), "of the parts" (ἐκ τῶν μερῶν), and "in the part" (ἐν τῷ μέρει)[131] depending on a process of "designation by a mark" (χαρακτηρίζεσθαι) and the isolation of "the predominant feature" (τὸ ἐπικρατοῦν),[132] both of which require an interpretive act. Therefore, wholeness is also a hermeneutic rather than a logical category in this context. But, if Proclus posits such an essential connection between the causal and hermeneutic processes, we should not be surprised to find that his notion of causality implies a degree of mind-dependence.

The clearest synthesis of Proclus' ideas concerning similarity and wholeness is perhaps to be found in his proposition – one of the most important in the *Elements of Theology* – that "all things are in all things, but in each according to its proper nature" (πάντα ἐν πᾶσιν, οἰκείως δὲ ἐν ἑκάστῳ).[133] This synthesis is fully elaborated in the propositions dealing with the order of Intellect and intellects.[134] However, it also underlies the various propositions concerning the "intellective Forms" (νοερὰ εἴδη).[135] For Proclus, every intellect is a plenitude of Forms,[136] although – since the continuum between unity and multitude is also that between complete and incomplete power – the highest Intellect is at least in theory equivalent to a single Form.[137]

130 *El. theol.*, prop. 66, 62. 24–25. On these alternatives see below.

131 See *El. theol.*, prop. 67, 64. 1–2. This proposition is one stage in an important series (props. 66–74) studying the relation between wholeness and Form. For reasons that will be examined below, the conclusion that wholeness mediates between "Being" (τὸ ὄν) and "the Forms" (τὰ εἴδη) (*El. theol.*, prop. 74, corr., 70. 22–27) does not reduce the mind-dependency of wholeness.

132 See *El. theol.*, prop. 170, pr., 148. 23–27 and prop. 180 + pr., 158. 11–18.

133 *El. theol.*, prop. 103, 92. 13. Judging from the number of axioms drawn from the *Platonic Theology* and dealing with this question in his *Nine-Hundred Conclusions*, Pico sees this principle as the most important in Proclus' philosophy. See Pico, *Concl. sec. Procl.* 1, 3, 16, 18, 21, and 48.

134 *El. theol.*, props. 166–183. It is worth noting that the association of the dichotomy of whole and part with intellect brings into focus the latter's non-discursive aspect. This is because the notions of "whole before the parts" and "whole in the part" are articulated in defiance of the law of contradiction. The association of the dichotomy of sameness and otherness with intellect does not in itself emphasize the non-discursiveness of the latter. However, the implicit identification of these two dichotomies in most contexts renders the whole process a non-discursive activity of thought. On intellect's non-discursiveness see especially *El. theol.*, prop. 170 + pr., 148. 4–27 and prop. 176 + pr., 154. 3–34.

135 Proclus also envisions certain "intelligible Forms" (νοητὰ εἴδη). On these see below.

136 *El. theol.*, prop. 177, 156. 1. In practice, the simplification process stops at the number 4.

137 *El. theol.*, prop. 177, pr., 156. 5–15.

The points that we have been considering are important underlying assumptions of Proclus' doctrine of causality. However, the most visible feature of that doctrine is the triad of "remaining" (μονή), "procession" (πρόοδος), and "reversion" (ἐπιστροφή) that this later Platonist uses in order to replace the two-directional motion by which Intellect is produced from the One in Plotinus' system, this triad being the most common expression of the basic module in the *Elements of Theology*.[138] That a kind of cycle is involved emerges from the proposition: "Everything that proceeds from any principle and reverts has a cyclic activity,"[139] the cycle resulting from the fact that whatever proceeds does so from a principle to which it also reverts[140] and whatever reverts does so to a principle from which it also proceeds.[141] That the cycle embodies a threefold distinction emerges from the proposition: "Every effect remains in its cause, proceeds from it, and reverts to it."[142] Now, Proclus' explanation of the nature of each of the three moments within the cyclic process presents certain problems.[143] The nature of the relation between remaining and procession is clarified when he comments in one of the proofs that what is produced remains in its producer "to the extent that it has an element of sameness" (ᾗ μὲν ἄρα ταὐτόν τι) with it and proceeds from its producer "to the extent that it has an element of otherness" (ᾗ δὲ ἕτερον).[144] In other words, two opposing logical relations of sameness and otherness ground the first two moments of the causal cycle.[145] However, the nature of the relation between procession and reversion is more obscure, given that both moments are associated with the non-logical relation of similarity.[146] The differences seem to be that (a) reversion alone is associated with "appetite" (ὄρεξις);[147] (b) as relations, procession has a downward direction and reversion an upward direction;[148]

138 On the causal cycle see Gersh (1973), 49–80; Gersh (1978), 45–81.

139 *El. theol.*, prop. 33, 36. 11–12 πᾶν τὸ προϊὸν ἀπό τινος καὶ ἐπιστρέφον κυκλικὴν ἔχει τὴν ἐνέργειαν.

140 *El. theol.*, prop. 31, 34. 28–29.

141 *El. theol.*, prop. 34, 36. 20–22.

142 *El. theol.*, prop. 35, 38. 9–10 πᾶν τὸ αἰτιατὸν καὶ μένει ἐν τῇ αὐτου αἰτίᾳ καὶ πρόεισιν ἀπ' αὐτῆς καὶ ἐπιστρέφει πρὸς αὐτήν.

143 We will adopt the term "moment" provisionally in order to denote something that has not yet been specified quasi-spatially as an "aspect" or quasi-temporally as a "phase."

144 *El. theol.*, prop. 30, pr., 34. 23–25.

145 One says "ground" because other factors – the transformation of power, the implicit identification with whole and parts, etc. – are also involved.

146 See props. 29, 34. 3–4 and 32, 36. 3–4 discussed earlier. The fact that both moments can be associated with similarity is undoubtedly possible precisely because of its non-logical character.

147 See *El. theol.*, props. 31, pr., 34. 30–36. 2; 32, pr., 36. 6; 35, pr., 38. 17, etc. The end of the appetitive process is "conjunction/union" (συναφή). See *El. theol.*, props. 32, pr., 36. 5; 35, pr., 38. 17–21; 36, pr., 40. 1–2, etc.

148 Here, various terms compounded with the prefix *ana-* are employed. See *El. theol.*, prop. 35, 38. 18 "upward tension" (ἀνάτασις) and *El. theol.* 35, 38. 23 "resolution" (ἀναλύειν).

(c) as powers, procession is in transition to incompleteness and reversion in transition to completeness;[149] and (d) reversion alone cannot be expressed in strictly logical terms.

Given that the triad of remaining, procession, and reversion is the most common expression of the basic module, it occurs within Proclus' system not only as a single structure but also as a multiplicity of structures. With respect to the latter, one proposition of the *Elements of Theology* states that "Everything that proceeds from a multitude of causes passes through the same number of terms in reverting as in proceeding,"[150] and the proof of another proposition that "there are greater and lesser cycles, some reversions being to immediately prior terms, and some to the higher, right up to the principle of all things."[151] The multiple structure is normally configured as a monad and a series of terms to which the threefold cycle is applied in either a "subdividing" or a "sequential" form.[152] The subdividing version of the cycle – where the remaining, procession, and reversion within the cycle can each be articulated into a further remaining, procession, and reversion – is indicated in the situation where intellect knows "the prior to itself" (τὰ πρὸ αὑτοῦ) and thereby "itself" (ἑαυτόν).[153] The sequential version of the cycle – where the cycle of remaining, procession, and reversion is followed by a further cycle of remaining, procession, and reversion – is assumed in two cases:[154] namely, where a primary Intellect, primary Soul, and primary Nature are connected as monads of separate series,[155] and where a primary Intellect and secondary intellect(s)[156] are connected as monad and non-monadic term(s) within a single series.[157] With respect to the subdividing and sequential cycles, it should be noted that (a) the progressions of terms in both cases involve a gradual lowering of their status;[158] (b) the primary

[149] See *El. theol.*, props. 36, 38. 30–32 and 37, 40. 7–9.

[150] *El. theol.*, prop. 38, 40. 17–18 πᾶν τὸ προϊὸν ἀπό τινων πλειόνων αἰτίων, δι' ὅσων πρόεισι, διὰ τοσούτων καὶ ἐπιστρέφεται.

[151] *El. theol.*, prop. 33, pr. 36. 16–19 μείζους δὲ κύκλοι καὶ ἐλάττους, τῶν μὲν ἐπιστροφῶν πρὸς τὰ ὑπερκείμενα προσεχῶς γινομένων, τῶν δὲ πρὸς τὰ ἀνωτέρω καὶ μέχρι τῆς πάντων ἀρχῆς.

[152] See nn. 93 and 104.

[153] To be more precise, it has simultaneously "the intelligible from which it comes" (νοητόν . . . ἀφ' οὗ ἐστιν) and "the intelligible that is itself" (νοητόν . . . ὅ ἐστι). See *El. theol.*, prop. 167, 144. 22–25 and pr., 146. 1–15.

[154] These correspond to what modern interpreters (but not Proclus himself) call the "vertical" and "horizontal" series.

[155] See *El. theol.*, prop. 21, corr., 24. 22–33, prop. 22, corr., 26, 16–21.

[156] Or a primary Soul and secondary soul(s), or a primary Nature and secondary nature(s).

[157] This is the structure most frequently described in the *Elements of Theology*. To illustrate this, prop. 179 + pr., 158. 3–10 should be combined with the theory developed through props. 108–111 + pr., 96. 9–98. 32 and props. 162–165 + pr., 140. 28–144. 8. For combination of the two sub-versions of the sequential version see *El. theol.*, props. 181–183 + pr., 158. 19–160. 20.

[158] At *El. theol.*, prop. 97 + pr., 86. 8–19 this is called "remission" (ὕφεσις) or "declension" (ὑπόβασις).

distinction between the two cycles is based on the reversion which has to *precede* any further articulation in the sequential but not in the subdividing version;[159] and (c) the two progressions of terms can be combined or even translated into one another.

Proclus' elaboration of a theory of causality based on certain underlying assumptions regarding similarity and wholeness provides a good illustration of the tension between the internal metaphysical logic of his theological system and the requirement of compliance with the letter of an authoritative Platonic text. Now, it is undeniable that the notions of similarity and wholeness are equally fundamental to Proclus' theory of causation. However, although wholeness is an attribute of one of the highest levels of divinity (the second triad of the intelligible gods), is mentioned in one of the earlier lemmata of the *Parmenides*' second hypothesis (at 142c–d), and is discussed in book III of the *Platonic Theology*,[160] similarity and dissimilarity are attributes of a much lower level of the divine world (the hypercosmic gods), are only mentioned in a later lemma of the second hypothesis (at 147c–d), and are not discussed until *Platonic Theology* VI.[161]

The triad of remaining, procession, and reversion that is the most visible feature of Proclus' theory of causation and is the most common expression of the basic module from which his system is constructed provides an illustration of the ingenuity with which the later Platonist often responds to the kind of tension between metaphysical and exegetical requirements just mentioned. In actual fact, the first two moments of the triad[162] constitute an expression of the "Greatest Kinds" (μέγιστα γένη) that represent the theory of Forms in Plato's *Sophist* and enter into the composition of soul in his *Timaeus*, given that any effect remains in its cause in a moment of "rest" (στάσις) and "sameness" (ταυτότης) and proceeds from its cause in a moment of "motion" (κίνησις) and "otherness" (ἑτερότης). From the *Platonic Theology* we discover that all five *genē*[163] are distributed in different ways throughout the orders of intelligible, intelligible-and-intellectual, and intellectual gods. Thus, (1) in the first triad of intelligible gods there is being; in the middle triad, motion and rest – since the "eternity" (αἰών) that

159 For the latter see *El. theol.*, prop. 37 + pr., 40. 7–16 – where the things "generated by reversion" (κατ' ἐπιστροφὴν ὑφιστάμενα) are in an *ascending* scale of completeness; and for the former combine *El. theol.* 37, pr., 40. 12 – where reversion leads to completeness – and *El. theol.* 25 + pr., 28. 21–30. 4 – where completeness leads to procession.

160 See *Theol. Plat.* III. 25, 86. 16–89. 2.

161 See *Theol. Plat.* VI. 14, 68. 1–72. 9.

162 The third moment is handled in a different way. See above.

163 The presence also of the fifth kind: "being" (ὄν) at all levels of reality subsequent to the One is obviously unproblematic.

"remains" (μένει) in the One[164] is located there; and in the last triad, sameness and difference; (2) in the first triad of the intelligible-and-intellectual gods there is being – colorless, shapeless, and intangible in nature;[165] in the middle triad, motion and rest; and in the last triad, sameness and difference; (3) in the first triad of the intellectual gods there is being; in the middle triad, motion and rest; and in the last monad, sameness and difference – since distinction by means of "intellectual cuts" (νοεραὶ τομαί) occurs there.[166] Proclus explains that the five kinds are present everywhere but not everywhere in the same manner in accordance with the principles of similarity and wholeness. It is not until the third monad of the intellectual sphere that "all the kinds and forms first blaze forth" (πρῶτον μὲν ἐκλάμπει τὰ γένη πάντα καὶ τὰ εἴδη) because this level is "primarily characterized" (μάλιστα χαρακτηρίζεται) by otherness, has allotted to it the lower boundary of the universal hypostases, and is the source from which the "participated intellect" (μετεχόμενος νοῦς) and the multi-formed orders of souls proceed.[167] However, the manner in which Proclus locates the Greatest Kinds within his system broadly parallels that in which he locates the Forms in general. As required by the exegesis of the *Timaeus*, the Forms are manifested in a more unitary way in the Intelligible Living Creature (= the third triad of the intelligible gods)[168] and in a more divided way in the Demiurge (= the third term of the first triad of the intellectual gods).[169]

If the *Elements of Theology* treats the triad of remaining, procession, and reversion either as a single structure or as a multiple structure and, when it is a multiple structure, either in a "subdividing" or a "sequential" form, the *Platonic Theology* – as we have already noted more generally in connection

164 According to *Timaeus* 37d.

165 I.e. the "supercelestial place" (ὑπερουράνιος τόπος) of *Phaedrus* 247c–d.

166 On this notion of intellectual cuts see above. According to the full account of the intellectual domain in *Theol. Plat.* V. 30, 109. 2–113. 12, the first triad (Kronos, Rhea, Zeus) is predominantly characterized by being, the second triad (Couretes) by rest and motion, and the seventh divinity by difference. Within the first triad Kronos is associated predominantly with being, Rhea with rest and motion, and Zeus with sameness and difference. Cf. also *Theol. Plat.* V. 2, 7. 12–17.

167 *Theol. Plat.* V. 30, 111. 18–23. This passage also explains that Zeus as Demiurge in his turn assigns the Greatest Kinds in different ways to subsequent things according to their status.

168 *Theol. Plat.* III. 14, 51. 20–52. 11 and III. 19, 64. 14–67. 19. At the higher level there are only four Forms.

169 See *Theol. Plat.* V. 12, 41. 14–18. At the lower level there is a complete range of Forms. For the relation between the higher and lower sets of Forms see *Theol. Plat.* V. 17, 62. 4–63. 19; V. 27, 99. 15–100. 17; and V. 27, 101. 15–26. Study of these texts is enough to show that the gods or henads in the strict sense are not identifiable with Forms. The gods associated with Forms at *Theol. Plat.* III. 19, 65. 14–67. 2 and III. 27, 96. 24–97. 15 are clearly "gods" in the looser sense of beings participating in divinity.

with the expansion of the basic module, and more specifically in connection with the transcendence and immanence of limit, infinity, and mixture and with the exemplification of self-determination by Kronos and Zeus – tends to present the triad predominantly in its multiple and subdividing form.[170] This is presumably because the multiple and sequential form becomes more significant only after the transition has taken place from the universal and unparticipated to the partial and participated ranks of intellects and souls and this, strictly speaking, falls outside the subject matter of the *Platonic Theology*.

Intellects

Throughout the *Elements of Theology* the level of reality corresponding to Plotinus' second hypostasis is conceived of as a monadic Intellect and a series of intellects dependent upon it, the resulting structure being configured in accordance with the basic module and articulated further through an application of the threefold cycle of remaining, procession, and reversion in its sequential form. A sequence of eighteen propositions is devoted specifically to this topic. Among these, prop. 166 distinguishes the unparticipated Intellect from the participated intellects; props. 167–180 describe the characteristics of intellects in general – props. 176–178 being an insertion dealing with the relation between intellects and Forms; and props. 181–183 classify participated intellects according to the lower principles that participate them. More rarely in the *Elements of Theology* the level of reality corresponding to Plotinus' second hypostasis is conceived of as an evolving triad of being, life, and intellect, the resulting structure again being configured in accordance with the basic module and articulated further through an application of the threefold cycle of remaining, procession, and reversion in its subdividing form.[171]

At first sight, the very positing of a triad of "being" (ὄν), "life" (ζωή), and "intellect" (νοῦς) seems to call into question what we have termed the intellective character of all causality in Proclus. Now, it is true that being seems to be contrasted as a first term with intellect as a third term when the later Platonist argues that "All things participating intellect are dependent

170 See above.

171 The relation between the triad of remaining, procession, and reversion used throughout the *Elements of Theology* and the triad of being, life, and intellect introduced in a few passages should always be borne in mind. Both triads are expressions of the basic module, the former seeming to represent the dynamic relation between successive hypostases and the latter successive hypostases that are themselves dynamically related.

on unparticipated Intellect, those participating life on unparticipated Life, and those participating being on unparticipated Being. Among these terms, Being is prior to Life, and Life to Intellect."[172] The same conclusion can be drawn when he argues that "Unparticipated terms subsist prior to participated terms. So that Being that is in itself and in an unparticipated manner must exist prior to the being that is conjoined with intellect, since the former is intelligible not as coordinated with Intellect but as perfecting it in a transcendent way."[173] However, a number of considerations point to the fact that Being cannot in the last analysis be separated from Intellect in a totally non-intellective sense.[174] First, Proclus argues for the conclusion that every intellect has its substance, power, and activity in eternity from the premise that the intelligible, intellection, and intellect are "identical" (ταὐτόν).[175] Second, he clearly identifies the being of the triad of Being, Life, and Intellect with the "intelligible" (νοητόν) *of* the Intellect. This leads to the further consequences that (a) Intellect and its intelligible are "one in number" (ἓν κατ' ἀριθμόν) or else simply "the same" (ταὐτόν);[176] (b) it is possible to speak of the first in the series as "the intelligible intellect" (νοῦς νοητός);[177] and (c) the intelligible of the Intellect is identified with that "essence" (εἶναι) of Intellect in the context where it produces subsequent things "by being what it is" (κατὰ τὸ εἶναι ὅ ἐστι).[178]

This intellective character of all causality is confirmed on the basis of the *Platonic Theology* not only through the prominence of the main triad of intelligible, intelligible-and-intellectual, and intellectual gods throughout the text but also by Proclus' normal preference for speaking of the triad of "intelligible" (νοητόν), life, and intellect rather than that of "being" (ὄν, οὐσία), life, and intellect.[179] Passages referring to the henads as intelligibles

[172] *El. theol.*, prop. 101, 90. 17–19 πάντων τῶν νοῦ μετεχόντων ἡγεῖται ὁ ἀμέθεκτος νοῦς, καὶ τῶν τῆς ζωῆς ἡ ζωή, καὶ τῶν τοῦ ὄντος τὸ ὄν. αὐτῶν δὲ τούτων τὸ μὲν ὂν πρὸ τῆς ζωῆς, ἡ δὲ ζωὴ πρὸ τοῦ νοῦ. In this passage Proclus only speaks explicitly of unparticipated *Intellect*. For unparticipated Life see *El. theol.*, prop. 188, 164. 15–19. For unparticipated Being and Life see *El. theol.*, prop. 190, 166. 17–18.

[173] *El. theol.*, prop. 161, pr., 140. 23–27 τὰ δὲ ἀμέθεκτα πρὸ τῶν μετεχομένων ὑφέστηκεν. ὥστε καὶ τοῦ συζύγου πρὸς τὸν νοῦν ὄντος προϋπάρχει τὸ καθ' αὑτὸ καὶ ἀμεθέκτως ὄν. νοητὸν γάρ ἐστιν οὐχ ὡς τῷ νῷ συντεταγμένον, ἀλλ' ὡς τελειοῦν ἐξῃρημένως τὸν νοῦν. This point develops an argument running through props. 161–164, 140. 14–142. 25.

[174] Damascius discusses this question at *De principiis* II. 104. 17–106. 15 (Westerink and Combès 1986–1991), revealing the importance of the *Chaldaean Oracles*' authority at this point.

[175] *El. theol.*, prop. 169, 146. 24–148. 3. The two triads are identical with one another and with the triad of being, life, intellect.

[176] See *El. theol.*, props. 167, 144. 22–23; 169, 146. 26; and 174, 152. 10.

[177] See *El. theol.*, prop. 167, pr., 146, 9.

[178] *El. theol.*, prop. 174 + pr., 152. 8–15. Cf. *El. theol.*, prop. 172, pr., 150. 19.

[179] See pp. 87–88 above.

point to the same conclusion.[180] Moreover, certain general metaphysical principles underpinning Proclus' theological system such as the dependence of reversion upon the hermeneutical category of "similarity" (ὁμοιότης) imply that causality is at least partially mind-dependent. That there is an irreducibly idealistic element in Proclus' theology is not surprising when the historical evolution of the latter is considered, since the hierarchy of gods disclosed by the second hypothesis of the *Parmenides* and forming the ground plan of the *Platonic Theology* is clearly a subdivision of rather than an addition to the Plotinian hypostasis of Intellect. Medieval readers of Proclus such as Dietrich of Freiberg, Berthold of Moosburg, and Nicholas of Cusa were therefore correct in understanding their source in this manner, despite the frailty of the textual tradition on which their interpretation had to depend.

Bibliography

Alexandre, C. (ed.) (1858) *Pléthon: Traité des Lois, Ou recueil des fragments, en partie inédits, de cet ouvrage*, trans. A. Pellissier, Paris.

Angelou, A. D. (ed.) (1984) *Nicholas of Methone: Refutation of Proclus' Elements of Theology*, Leiden and Athens.

Barbanti, M. di Pasquale and Romano, F. (eds.) (2002) *Il Parmenide di Platone e la sua tradizione*, Catania.

Brisson, L. (1987) "Proclus et l'Orphisme," in Pépin and Saffrey (1987), 43–104.

(2000) "La place des *Oracles chaldaïques* dans la *Théologie platonicienne*," in Segonds and Steel (2000), 109–162.

Butler, E. (2005) "Polytheism and Individuality in the Henadic Manifold," *Dionysius* 23: 83–104.

(2008a) "The Gods and Being in Proclus," *Dionysius* 26: 93–113.

(2008b) "The Intelligible Gods in the Platonic Theology of Proclus," *Methexis* 21: 131–143.

Chlup, R. (2012) *Proclus, An Introduction*, Cambridge.

Combès, J. (1976) "Négativité et procession des principes chez Damascius," *Revue des études augustiniennes* 22: 114–133. Reprinted in Combès (1989), 101–129.

(1989) *Études néoplatoniciennes*, Grenoble; 2nd edn., Grenoble 1996.

Des Places, É. (ed.) (1971) *Oracles chaldaïques, avec un choix de commentaires anciens*, Paris.

Diehl, E. (ed.) (1903–1906) Proclus, *In Platonis Timaeum commentaria*, 3 vols., Leipzig.

Dillon, J. M. (1987) "Proclus and the Parmenidean Dialectic," in Pépin and Saffrey (1987), 165–175.

[180] See p. 95 above.

Dodds, E. R. (ed. and trans.) (1933) *Proclus: The Elements of Theology*, Oxford; 2nd edn., Oxford 1963.

Farmer, S. A. (1998) *Syncretism in the West, Pico's 900 Theses (1486), The Evolution of Traditional Religious and Philosophical Systems, With Text, Translation and Commentary*, Tempe, AZ.

Gersh, S. (1973) *Kinēsis Akinētos, A Study of Spiritual Motion in the Philosophy of Proclus*, Leiden.

(1978) *From Iamblichus to Eriugena: An Investigation of the Prehistory and Evolution of the Pseudo-Dionysian Tradition*, Leiden.

(2000) "Proclus' Theological Methods. The Programme of *Theol. Plat.* I. 4," in Segonds and Steel (2000), 15–27. Reprinted in Gersh (2005).

(2001) "Berthold von Moosburg on the Content and Method of Platonic Philosophy," in J. A. Aersten, K. Emery, and A. Speer (eds.), *Nach der Verurteilung von 1277, Philosophie und Theologie an der Universität von Paris im letzten Viertel des 13. Jahrhunderts = Miscellanea Mediaevalia* 28, Berlin and New York, 493–503. Reprinted in Gersh (2005).

(2005) *Reading Plato, Tracing Plato: From Ancient Commentary to Medieval Reception*, Aldershot.

(2014) *Being Different, More Neoplatonism after Derrida*, Leiden.

Guérard, C. (1982) "La théorie des hénades et la mystique de Proclus," *Dionysius* 6: 73–82.

Pagnoni-Sturlese, M.-R. and Sturlese, L. (eds.) (1984) Berthold von Moosburg, *Expositio super Elementationem theologicam Procli, prologus, propositiones 1–13*, with Introduction by K. Flasch, Hamburg.

Pépin, J. and Saffrey, H.-D. (eds.) (1987) *Proclus: lecteur et interprète des anciens, Actes du colloque international du CNRS, Paris 2–4 octobre 1985*, Paris.

Romano, F. (2000) "L'ideé de causalité dans la *Théologie platonicienne* de Proclus," in Segonds and Steel (2000), 325–337.

Romano, F. and Cardullo, R. L. (eds.) (1994) *Dunamis nel Neoplatonismo, Atti del I. Colloquio Internazionale del Centro di Ricerca sul Neoplatonismo, Università degli Studi di Catania, 6–8 ottobre 1994*, Florence.

Romano, F. and Taormina, D. P. (eds.) (1994) *Hyparxis e hypostasis nel Neoplatonismo, Atti del II. Colloquio Internazionale del Centre di Ricerca sul Neoplatonismo, Università di Studi di Catania, 1–3 ottobre 1992*, Florence.

Saffrey, H.-D. (1959) "Notes platoniciennes de Marsile Ficin dans un manuscrit de Proclus (Cod. Riccardianus 70)," *Bibliothèque d'Humanisme et de Renaissance* 21: 161–184. Reprinted in Saffrey (1987), 69–94.

(1981) "Les Néoplatoniciens et les Oracles chaldaïques," *Revue des études augustiniennes* 27: 209–225. Reprinted in Saffrey (1990), 63–79.

(1984) "La théologie platonicienne de Proclus, fruit de l'exégèse du Parménide," in *Revue de théologie et de philosophie* 116: 1–12. Reprinted in Saffrey (1990), 173–184.

(1987) *Recherches sur la tradition platonicienne au Moyen Âge et à la Renaissance*, Paris.

(1990) *Recherches sur le néoplatonisme après Plotin*, Paris.

Saffrey, H.-D. and Westerink, L. G. (eds.) (1968–1997) *Proclus: Théologie platonicienne*, 6 vols., Paris.
Segonds, A.-Ph. and Steel, C. (eds.) (2000) *Proclus et la Théologie platonicienne, Actes du colloque international de Louvain, 13–16 mai 1998, en l'honneur de H.-D. Saffrey et L. G. Westerink*, Leuven and Paris.
Steel, C. (1994) "*Hyparxis* chez Proclus," in Romano and Taormina (1994), 79–100.
(1996) "Puissance active et puissance receptive chez Proclus, in Romano and Cardullo (1996), 121–137.
(2002) "Une histoire de l'interprétation du *Parménide* dans l'Antiquité," in Barbanti and Romano (2002), 11–40.
Van Liefferinge, C. (1999) *La Théurgie, Des Oracles chaldaïques à Proclus*, Liége.
Van Riel, G. (2001) "Les hénades de Proclus sont-elles composées de limite et d'infinité?," *Revue des sciences philosophiques et théologiques* 85: 417–432.
Westerink, L. G. and Combès, J. (eds.) (1981–1986) *Damascius: Traité des premiers principes*, 3 vols., Paris.

PART II

The influence of Proclus

II.1 *Late antiquity*

CHAPTER 4

"Dionysius the Areopagite"

John M. Dillon

At some time around the end of the fifth century CE an enterprising Christian controversialist (probably of moderate Monophysite convictions), but highly educated in the intricacies of contemporary Platonism (probably in the school of Ammonius at Alexandria, but possibly also at Athens, with the successors of Proclus), published a series of remarkable works, under the pseudonym of "Dionysius the Areopagite" – thus seeking boldly to upstage the whole late Platonist system by implying that this first-century Athenian convert of St. Paul had anticipated every aspect of it.

In a series of works of great theoretical and linguistic complexity – *The Divine Names* (*DN*), *The Mystical Theology*, *The Celestial Hierarchy* (*CH*), *The Ecclesiastical Hierarchy* (*EH*), along with a collection of nine letters, among which *Letter* 4 is important for an (albeit rather devious) statement of his position on the nature of Christ, and *Letter* 9 as a statement of his theory of the symbolic interpretation of Scripture – "Dionysius" sets before us a conspectus of his (lightly) Christianized version of Procline Neoplatonism. We are also given various intimations of "lost" works, such as *The Symbolic Theology*, *The Theological Representations*, *The Properties and Ranks of Angels*, and a treatise *On the Soul*, as to the existence of any of which we beg leave to doubt. We also hear about a revered mentor, Hierotheus, about whom he speaks in tones interestingly reminiscent of Proclus' references to his master Syrianus (e.g. *CH* 201A; *EH* 376D; 392A; 424C), who is himself the author of a number of works, and a number of disciples and correspondents.

It is probably futile to speculate on the precise identity of this remarkable figure, but he can be situated with great probability, I feel, within the circle of the controversial Monophysite theologian and ecclesiastical statesman, Severus of Antioch. The works of Dionysius first come to notice at a conference held in Constantinople in 532 between a group of Orthodox followers of the Council of Chalcedon, led by Bishop Hypatius of Ephesus, and a group of partisans of Severus, where the Severians adduce

"Dionysius" as an authority, and Hypatius expresses some skepticism as to the provenance of the works cited. However, Dionysius survived this first test, and a commentary composed on the corpus shortly afterwards by John of Scythopolis seems to have confirmed his credentials.

Though there will probably never be agreement on the precise identity of this remarkable figure, it seems pretty safe to say at least that such figures as Severus, and probably also John of Scythopolis, were well acquainted with him, and in sympathy with what he was trying to achieve.

I propose in the present context merely to focus on certain salient features of Dionysius' system, in order to examine how far they may be seen to be dependent on doctrines of Proclus. Dionysius, it must be said, will not necessarily have been exclusively dependent on Proclus for his knowledge of Platonism. He may well have been in a position to have read works of Plotinus, Porphyry, and Iamblichus for himself, and he may also have been acquainted with Damascius, but we are here concerned properly with Proclus (and by implication with his immediate mentor Syrianus), so I will confine myself largely to him. It should also be specified that Dionysius is much more than the slavish plagiarist that he has sometimes been accused of being; he is quite capable of adapting Neoplatonic doctrine to his purposes. We, however, must be primarily concerned with the nature of his borrowings.

Let us start with Dionysius' doctrine of the first principle, which for him is to be coordinated with the God of Jewish and Christian Scripture. This principle, however, retains a good deal of the features of the Neoplatonic One, while also (necessarily, in view of the demands of the Judeo-Christian tradition) extending in some respects into the realm of the second Platonist principle, Intellect. This in turn involves a certain conflation of the subject matters of the first and second hypotheses of Plato's *Parmenides*, as we shall see.[1]

If we consider his main work, *The Divine Names*, we may discern a definite pattern in the sequence of names which affords a clue to Dionysius' conception of the nature and function of God – at once an ineffable and transcendent Unity, about which nothing can properly be said, and an actively providential and creative Trinity, which can be characterized in multiple ways.[2] It has been the insight of a number of scholars, disputing

[1] On this topic, see Corsini (1962).

[2] I am much indebted here to the previous insights of such scholars as H.-U. von Balthasar (Balthasar 1962), E. von Ivanka (Ivanka 1964), and most recently C. Schäfer (Schäfer 2006), while venturing to differ from them on certain details – on a topic on which doubtless no definitive solution can be reached.

the previous consensus that the sequence of names is largely random or even chaotic, that what Dionysius is trying to do in *The Divine Names* is to portray, first the essence, and then the various powers or activities of God, in a definite order, mirroring the (Neoplatonic) system of procession (πρόοδος) and return (ἐπιστροφή), along with, in between these two processes, a moment of "rest" (μονή), portraying God's "remaining" in the midst of his creation.

The Divine Names begins with a series of chapters (1–3) addressing the issue of God's essence, namely that he is One (ch. 1), but also threefold and triune (ch. 2), all the while emphasizing that none of these epithets can be taken as properly describing him, but rather as characterizing our relation to him. There follows then a series of chapters (4–7), presenting, in order, the names Good – with its associated epithets of "Light," "Love" (ἀγάπη), "Beautiful," "Ecstasy" (or at least "stepping forth," ἔκστασις), and "Yearning" (ἔρως) – and then the triad Being, Life, and Wisdom (σοφία, standing in as a scripturally endorsed equivalent for the more properly Platonist "Intellect," νοῦς). These embody the various aspects of God's *proodos*, or providential emanation, to establish the universe, where the latter three are plainly adapted from the Proclean (and previous Neoplatonic) doctrine,[3] with which Dionysius is well acquainted. According to this doctrine these three "moments" of the intelligible world, or alternatively, of God's activity, relate to progressively more restricted and refined levels of entity, to wit, beings in general, living beings, and intelligent beings.

The series of epithets following in chs. 8–11 have occasioned a somewhat greater degree of uncertainty. In ch. 8 we find "Power," "Justice," "Salvation," and "Redemption" (ἀπολύτρωσις, cf. 1 Cor. 1:30), followed in ch. 9 by a series of pairs of epithets, "Greatness/Smallness, Sameness/Difference, Similarity/Dissimilarity, Rest/Motion," picking up a selection of the epithets alternately denied and asserted of the One in the first two hypotheses of the *Parmenides*, but also corresponding largely to the five "greatest genera" of the *Sophist.* There follow in ch. 10 the names "Omnipotent" (παντοκράτωρ), "Ancient of Days" (παλαιὸς ἡμερῶν), but to this latter is conjoined "young" (νέος), introducing the idea, borrowed from *Parm.* 151e ff., that the One, or God, must be both older and younger than itself. Lastly, ch. 11 deals with the epithet "Peace," seen as symbolizing God's unificatory, stabilizing, and harmonizing activity in the world. On the whole, this succession of epithets can reasonably be viewed, I think, as celebrating

[3] Cf. e.g. Procl. *El. theol.*, props. 35 and 57 (Dodds 1963).

aspects of God's salutary presence in the world, his *monē*, emphasizing his creation and ordering of the world, prior (logically) to the movement of *epistrophē*, the "return" of all creation to its first principle.

This, in turn, is the theme of the final two chapters (12–13), covering the epithets "Holy and Holies, King of Kings, Lord of Lords, God of Gods, King forever" (ch. 12) – these double epithets, it seems, emphasizing God's role as a *source* for these qualities, to which they can be related back; followed by "Perfect" and "One" (ch. 13), epithets which bring us back to the opening chapters.

All this, it must be said, is presented less than perspicuously by Dionysius – imitating in this, as acutely suggested by Christian Schäfer,[4] the "associative" style of his putative mentor St. Paul rather than the methodical procedure of Proclus, but the scheme is clear enough nonetheless.

Let us start by looking at his treatment of God "in himself," as set out in the first two chapters. He begins by asserting God's absolute ineffability and transcendence of all epithets, in a manner reminiscent of the end of the first hypothesis of the *Parmenides* (142a), and indeed of Proclus' commentary on that in the *In Parmenidem.* Here is a passage from ch. 1 of *The Divine Names* (588B):

> Just as the senses can neither grasp nor perceive the things of the mind, just as representation and shape cannot take in the simple and the shapeless, just as corporeal form cannot lay hold of the intangible and unstructured[5] formlessness of incorporeals, by the same standard of truth beings are surpassed by the infinity beyond being, intelligences by that oneness which is beyond intelligence. Indeed the inscrutable One is out of the reach of every rational process, nor can any words come up to the inexpressible Good, this Unity (ἑνάς) that is unitive of all unity, this supra-existent Being, mind beyond mind, word beyond speech, it is gathered up by no discourse, by no intuition, by no name, in a way distinct from any other being, cause of existence for all other things, while itself non-existent as transcending existence, it alone could give an authoritative account of what it really is (trans. Lubhéid [1987], emended).

This characteristically Dionysian meditation on the superiority of the One to any naming reflects, though without close verbal parallels, Proclus' treatment of the topic in his commentary on *Parm.* 142a: "Therefore no name or description or knowledge or sensation or opinion applies to it."

[4] Schäfer (2006), 51.

[5] Dionysius here borrows a pair of epithets, ἀναφὴς καὶ ἀσχημάτιστος, employed by Plato at *Phdr.* 247c to describe the supracelestial realm.

"Apparently not." At *In Parm.* VII 48 (Klibansky and Labowsky 1953), Proclus says the following:

> Again, what can be known is the object either of sense-perception or of opinion or of scientific knowledge. For all cognition is either without concepts or with concepts; and, if the latter, it either brings in causes or makes no mention of causes. So we have three kinds of cognition: sense-perception, opinion and scientific knowledge. And so what is completely unapprehended by us is neither scientifically knowable nor judgeable nor perceptible.
>
> Now, starting from the kinds of cognition in ourselves, we must also take their totalities and realise that all being known is denied of the One. For how could what is beyond all that exists be sensibly perceived? And how could it be the object of opinion, when it is not such as in one way to be, and in another way not? And how can what has no cause be an object of science?

On the other hand, however, Dionysius' first principle is not only a transcendent and ineffable henad, it is also a triad, and this is the focus of ch. 2 of *The Divine Names*. This in effect necessitates that Dionysius, in Platonist terms, combine the conclusions of the first two hypotheses of the *Parmenides* as relating to the same entity in different aspects, a development that Proclus would not approve,[6] but which is necessary from Dionysius' point of view as a Christian apologist. A useful passage summarizing his position occurs in the course of ch. 7, 869c–872b, in the course of an exegesis of the divine name "Wisdom" (σοφία):

> Following on this we must enquire as to how, if God cannot be grasped by mind or sense-perception, or indeed is not an existent entity at all, how do we know him?
>
> In response, the truth might be that we cannot know God from his own nature, since this is unknowable and is beyond the reach of mind or of reason, but rather from the structuring (διάταξις) of everything, because everything is, in a sense, projected out from him, and this order possesses certain images and semblances of his divine paradigms, we ascend as far as our capacities allow, in due order, to that which is beyond all things (ἐπέκεινα πάντων), and we pass by way of the removal and the transcending of all things and by way of discerning him as the cause of all things. Hence God is known as inherent in all things and as distinct from all things.
>
> He is known, then, both through knowledge and through unknowing (ἀγνωσία). Of him there is conception, reasoned account (λόγος), understanding, touch, perception, opinion, imagination, name, and many other things; and on the other hand he cannot be conceived of, nor spoken of, nor

[6] Indeed, he explicitly deplores it at *In Parm.* VI 1070, 15ff. (Luna and Segonds 2007–2011), taking aim in particular at Porphyry, the only Platonist known to have advocated this position.

> named. He is not one of the things that are, and he cannot be known in any of them. He is all things in all things, and he is no thing among things. He is known to all from all things, and he is known to no one from anything (trans. Lubhéid, emended).

In this blending of the first and second hypotheses of the *Parmenides* to generate a series of paradoxical characterizations of God, Dionysius cannot be said to be particularly close to Proclus – if anything, he would seem to be indebted to some extent rather to Porphyry – but that is a consequence of the doctrinal position on the nature of the Christian God which he has to maintain. His philosophical affiliations become plainer, however, when one turns to the details of the process of procession (πρόοδος) and return (ἐπιστροφή) that structures God's relation to his creation. Dionysius certainly adopts this concept from Neoplatonism, but, as has been noted,[7] with the interesting variant that he posits the stage of "rest" or "stabilization" (μονή) not as the primal moment, representing the first principle's remaining within itself, but rather as a stage coming between procession and return, representing God's creative and providential "stabilization" of the cosmos. Even this apparent distortion of the model, however, can be seen as having a Platonist ancestry. There is a notable proof-text from Plato's *Laws* (IV 715e), much favoured by Proclus,[8] where the Athenian Stranger quotes an Orphic verse, to the effect that "God holds in his hands the beginning, middle, and end of all things," and this, along with a similar passage in the second hypothesis of the *Parmenides* (145ab), could be taken as equating the "middle" which God holds in his power with a stage of "rest" or stabilization between God's outpouring of his blessings in *proodos* and his recall of all things to himself in *epistrophē*, during which the world is established as a cosmos. The *monē* which is the original state of the first principle "it itself" can be taken for granted, it seems.

There is a nice passage in ch. 4 of *The Divine Names* (700AB), which illustrates Dionysius' "personalizing" of the Neoplatonic doctrine in a Christian direction:

> The Good returns all things to itself and gathers together whatever may be scattered, for it is the divine source and unifier of the sum total of things. Each being looks to it as a source, as the agent of cohesion, and as an objective. The Good, as Scripture testifies, produced everything and it is the ultimately perfect cause. In it "all things hold together"[9] and are maintained

[7] E.g. by Schäfer (2006), 59ff. [8] Cf. e.g. *In Parm.* VI 1113 (Cousin 1864).

[9] Here an artfully introduced quotation from Col. I:17: "He is before all things, and in him all things hold together."

> and preserved as if in some almighty receptacle. All things are returned to it as their own goal. All things desire it: everything with mind and reason seeks to know it, everything sentient yearns to perceive it, everything lacking perception has a living and instinctive longing for it, and everything lifeless and merely existent turns, in its own fashion, for a share of it.[10]

Once that has been recognized, the essentially Neoplatonic nature of Dionysius' portrayal of God's relation to his creation should be clear enough. Clearer still, in its relation to Proclean doctrine, is Dionysius' employment of the triad of Being–Life–Wisdom (this last standing in for Intellect, as being more scripturally respectable), as structuring principles of *proodos*, as set out in chs. 5–7 of *The Divine Names*. Dionysius sets out his position at the beginning of ch. 5 (816B):

> We must go on now to the name of "Being," which is rightly applied by theology to Him who truly is. But I must point out that the purpose of what I have to say is not to reveal that supra-essential (ὑπερούσιος) Being in so far as it is supra-essential, for this is something beyond words, something unknown and wholly unrevealed, something above unity itself. What I wish to do is to sing a hymn of praise for the being-making (οὐσιοποιός) procession of the absolute divine Source of being into the total domain of Being.
>
> The divine name of "Good" tells of all the processions of the universal Cause; it extends to beings and to non-beings, and that Cause is superior to beings and non-beings. The name "Being" extends to all beings which are, and it is beyond them. The name of "Life" extends to all living things, and it is beyond them. The name "Wisdom" reaches out to everything which has to do with understanding, reason, and sense-perception, and it is above all these (trans. Lubhéid, emended).

We discern here a theory of the progressively more specialized spheres of influence of a sequence of causal principles. This is a doctrine that is stated in general terms by Proclus in prop. 57 of the *Elements of Theology* in relation to the One, Intellect, and Soul, but in a more specialized mode in relation to the "moments" of Being, Life, and Intellect proper within the hypostasis of Intellect in prop. 101,[11] and also in his *Alcibiades Commentary* (*In Alc.* 319, 12 – 322, 17, on *Alc.* 115a1–9), backed up by Olympiodorus, reporting on Proclus' doctrine in his commentary (*In Alc.* 109, 15 – 110, 13, Westerink): Being extends its influence to all existents of whatever sort, Life

10 We can discern here an adumbration of the triad Being–Life–Intellect.

11 "All things which participate intelligence are preceded by the unparticipated Intelligence, those which participate life by Life, and those which participate being by Being; and of these three unparticipated principles Being is prior to Life, and Life to Intelligence."

only to living things, and Intellect only to rational beings. Here Dionysius adopts this schema, prefixing to it "Good" in the role of the One in Proclus' more general theory, as relating even to non-being, in the guise of Matter, and according the latter triad their Proclean roles, though without formally admitting them to be a triad.

Another adaptation of a very distinctive Syrianic-Proclean system of triads occurs in Dionysius' account of the structure of the angelic world in the *Celestial Hierarchy.* In that work, from 200D onwards to 261D, Dionysius sets out the succession, or *hierarchia* (a term which he seems to have invented), of the divine orders of beings in a series of triads, interestingly reminiscent of that proposed for the intelligible realm by Syrianus and faithfully adopted by Proclus.[12] For Syrianus and Proclus, we may recall, the intelligible realm comes to be divided into a sequence of three levels: an intelligible triad of entities, an intelligible-intellective triad (each element of these subdivided into further triads), and an intellective hebdomad, consisting of two triads and a seventh entity, the so-called "membrane" (ὑπεζωκώς). However, what we basically have is a sequence of triads. This is reflected in Dionysius, as follows (200D):

> The Word of God (θεολογία) has provided nine explanatory designations for the heavenly beings, and my own divine initiator (ὁ θεῖος ἡμῶν ἱεροτελεστής) has divided these into three triadic groups. According to him, the first group is forever around God and is said to be permanently united with Him ahead of any of the others and with no intermediary (ἀμέσως). Here, then, are the most holy "Thrones," and orders said to be many-eyed and many-winged, called in Hebrew the Cherubim and Seraphim; following the tradition of Scripture, he says that they are found immediately around God and in a proximity enjoyed by no other. This threefold group, says my distinguished teacher (ὁ κλεινὸς ἡμῶν καθηγεμών), forms a single hierarchy which is truly first and whose members are of equal status (ὁμοταγῆ). No other is more like the divine or receives more directly the first enlightenment from the Deity. The second group, he says, is made up of "Authorities," "Dominions," and "Powers"; and the third, at the end of the heavenly hierarchies, is the group of angels, archangels and principalities (trans. Lubhéid, emended).

Such a triadic system as this for the heavenly realm has really no warrant in Scripture, and it is remarkable that Dionysius should have felt moved to propound it. One can only imagine that he was profoundly impressed by the elaborate structuring of the spiritual realm developed by the Athenian

[12] It is notable, indeed, that Dionysius is at pains to attribute this scheme to his revered master Hierotheus, in very much the same terms as Proclus uses to attribute doctrines to Syrianus (cf. in particular ὁ κλεινὸς ἡμῶν καθηγεμών at 201C).

School, and resolved to match it by imposing a triadic order on the rather chaotic assemblage of angelic entities surrounding the God of Christianity.

The highest triad in fact corresponds well to the highest, noetic, level of the Proclean system, since that is presented as being particularly closely connected with the realm of the One, with the multiplicity characteristic of the realm of Intellect still in a "hidden" mode, "because it receives its primary determination from unity proper to the gods (θεῖα ἕνωσις)."[13] This seems to be reflected in Dionysius' presentation of his first triad.

As regards the third and lowest triad, there is no reason for Dionysius to follow the Neoplatonists in making the curious postulation of a hebdomad – which in the Neoplatonic case is probably designed as a sort of spiritual anticipation of the seven planetary gods. What is most interesting, though, is a reference which Dionysius makes to the angels as "henads." At *DN* 588B, first of all, near the beginning of the work, he describes God as "a unity conferring unity on every unity" (ἑνὰς ἑνοποιὸς πάσης ἑνάδος) – a pretty general characterization, admittedly, which need mean nothing more than that God is responsible for the degree of unity which is present in every being, at whatever level of reality; but then, much later, in ch. 8, at 892D, we find him talking of "the immortal lives of the angelic henads (ἀγγελικαὶ ἑνάδες)," which the power of God preserves unharmed. Now, once again, it may be that Dionysius means "unities" here only in a general sense, but it seems to me possible that, having in effect conflated the realms of the One and of Intellect in the Neoplatonic system (which enables him to introduce the Trinity into the realm of the One), he sees fit also to assimilate the various classes of angelic being, which in Neoplatonist terms would be inhabitants of the realm of Intellect, to the divine henads of the Syrianic-Proclean system, which are inhabitants of the realm of the One. This would at any rate be a logical consequence of his position, and it also enables him to, as it were, "streamline" the Neoplatonic universe by subsuming the complex layers of divine reality under the providential activity of God himself, thus producing a more monistic system, suitable to the Christian perspective.[14]

If Dionysius' use of the term *henas* smacks somewhat of creative distortion of Neoplatonic terminology, his usage in another crucial area is much more notable. A salient feature of later Neoplatonism, from Iamblichus onwards, was the elevation of theurgy (θεουργία), the performance of rituals to attract the favor of the gods, to a status matching that of

[13] Cf. Proclus, *Plat. Theol.* III 24 (Saffrey and Westerink 1968–1997).

[14] This tendency is well brought out by Perl (2007).

theologia, or the philosophical analysis of the nature of God and the gods. As Iamblichus propounds it in book I of the *De mysteriis*, in response to the vexatious queries of Porphyry, the theoretical stance behind theurgy is that the efficacy of the rituals is not a consequence of any compulsion exerted on the gods by the theurgist (as would be the assumption underlying vulgar magic), but rather the result of a cooperation between the gods, who are essentially benevolent, and the theurgist, who knows the correct means of drawing down their beneficent powers.[15] This position would be entirely endorsed by Proclus. There are many passages scattered throughout his works testifying both to his practice of theurgy and to his appreciation of the principles underlying it. I select just two, one from the *Timaeus* commentary, and one from that on the *Parmenides:*

> And further, just as the theurgist (*telestēs*), by attaching certain symbols to statues, makes them more receptive (*epitēdeiotera*) to participation in higher powers, even so the Universal Nature, in shaping the bodies as receptacles for souls by means of natural reason-principles (φυσικοὶ λόγοι), sows one or other body with a receptivity for the reception of one kind of soul or another, some souls being better and others worse.[16] (*In Tim.* I 51, 25–30)

> And then they smiled,[17] as if in admiration of Socrates. This action is a symbol of their goodness, for they were not dispirited by Socrates' objections, but rejoiced at finding a worthy recipient of their doctrines. And thus Parmenides is moved to address Socrates "when he had finished." In this phrase also Plato has given us a divine symbol. When a man is anticipating the appearance of the divine, he must exert himself to stir up the divine spark within him in preparation for participating in higher beings; but when the illumination from above is at hand he must be silent, and this is what Socrates does. Having aroused himself for the reception of these men's insight, having by his words unfolded and exhibited his fitness for partaking of it, he stops speaking and begins to receive the midwifely instructions that they give him. (*In Parm.* 781, 3–21)

Here the emphasis is very much on the theurgist's humble preparation of himself to receive the divine inspirations or illuminations, not on any constraining of the higher powers. What we have portrayed here is a perfect cooperation between divine benevolent activity and human expertise in maximizing receptivity.

[15] Cf. the useful discussion of Shaw (1995).

[16] This is part of a comment on *Tim.* 18de (Burnet 1900–1907), where the question of how suitable souls get into suitable bodies is being discussed.

[17] Sc. Parmenides and Zeno. This is part of a comment on *Parm.* 130a.

With this theurgic tradition Dionysius appears to separate off the divine activity from the human, and to denominate the former *theourgia*, thus subtly altering the connotation of the compound "god-work" to cause it to mean "work *of the gods*," rather than "work on the gods," as in the Hellenic tradition.[18] The latter, human component he renames *hierourgia.*

The following passage from the *Ecclesiastical Hierarchy* (429CD) illustrates well the relation between *theourgia* and *hierourgia* for Dionysius:

> The sacred scriptural tablets[19] have a lesson for those capable of being divinized (τοῖς πρὸς θέωσιν ἐπιτηδείοις). They teach that God himself gives substance and arrangement to everything that exists, including the legal hierarchy and society . . . they praise the divine works of the man Jesus (τὰς ἀνδρικὰς Ἰήσους θεουργίας)[20] . . . and the sacred writings about the divine songs, which have as an aim to praise all the divine words (θεολογίαι) and divine works (θεουργίαι) and to celebrate the sacred words (ἱερολογίαι) and operations (ἱερουργίαι) of divine men, form a universal song and exposition of divine things, granting to those chanting the sacred words sacredly the ability to receive and distribute the entire rite of the hierarchy (ἱεραρχικὴ τελετή).

Of course, for Dionysius, the "hierurgic rites" are the sacraments, but these fulfill the same role and possess the same rationale as the rites of the Iamblichean or Procline theurgist. At the beginning of the *Ecclesiastical Hierarchy* (372AB), Jesus is identified as the true source of every theurgic act:

> Indeed the Word of God teaches those of us who are its disciples that in this fashion – though more clearly and more intellectually – Jesus enlightens the blessed entities superior to us,[21] Jesus who is the most divinely transcendent and super-essential mind, the source and essence of the entire hierarchy, all holiness, every theurgic act, who is the ultimate in divine power and makes them as similar as possible to his own light.

The hierarch, then – that is to say, the bishop – derives his power from Jesus himself. The rites (the sacraments) derive from him, even as, in Iamblichean theory, they derive from the gods in general, and when the rites take place in a liturgical setting, the hierarch, like the Iamblichean

[18] Basically, this involves understanding the implied genitive as subjective rather than objective.
[19] One of Dionysius' ways of referring to the books of the Old Testament.
[20] We may discern here, I think, a subtle suggestion of Dionysius' basically monophysite position.
[21] Dionysius uses here an expression, κρείττονες οὐσίαι, to refer to the angelic realm, which seems a variant of the standard Iamblichean/Proclean term, κρείττονα γένη, to refer to the daemonic realm.

theurgist, can tap into the divine power to enact the *theourgia*, as we learn later in the work (*EH* 436c):

> The most sacred performers of the sacred operations (ἱερουργοί) and lovers of visions (φιλοθεάμονες)[22] reverently beholding the most holy of rites (ἁγιωτάτη τελετή), sing with a universal hymn the cause that is the worker of good and bestower of good, by whom the salvific rites are revealed to us, to enact (ἱερουργοῦσαι) the sacred divinization of those being perfected.

Thus, then, are the Platonists "corrected," and their theory made to serve a higher cause.

One final topic may be noted, as it has long[23] constituted the "smoking gun" linking Dionysius to Proclus, and that is his adoption of the distinctive Proclean doctrine on the nature and status of evil in the universe. Even here, though, we must acknowledge[24] Dionysius' originality in his adaptation of his source, which is Proclus' treatise *On the Existence of Evils*. Proclus' position – as distinction from that of Plotinus, whom he criticizes – is that evil can have no place in the universe as an entity in itself, since all things, insofar as they partake in existence, are generated by the Good, and the Good cannot generate evil. Evil can therefore only subsist in an incidental way, as a *parhypostasis*, a parasitical existence. This formulation suits Dionysius very well, as we shall see.

Only occasionally is Dionysius in verbal agreement with Proclus, but his doctrinal position is the same, though he makes his points in a less scholastically exact way. For example, at *De malorum substantia* 2, 23–32, Proclus argues as follows:

> If, then, the Good is, as we say, beyond Being and is the source of beings – since everything, in whatever way it exists and is generated, strives for the Good according to its nature – how then could evil be any one thing among beings, if it is actually excluded from such a desire? Thus it is far from true to say that evil exists because "there must be something that is completely contrary to the Good."[25] For how could that which is completely contrary to something desire the nature that is contrary to it? Now, it is impossible that there is any being which does not strive for the Good, since all beings have been generated and exist because of that desire and are preserved through it.

Dionysius seems to be reflecting this basic tenet of Proclus' theory in the following passage of *The Divine Names* (716cd):

[22] Dionysius here employs a Platonic term, ultimately deriving from *Rep.* V 476ab (Burnet 1900–1907), though in a positive (Neoplatonic) sense.

[23] In fact, since the researches of J. Stiglmayr in 1895. See Stiglmayr (1895), 253–273.

[24] As is justifiably insisted upon by Christian Schäfer in his recent monograph (Schäfer 2006).

[25] A reference to Plato, *Tht.* 176a (Burnet 1900–1907).

> Now, if it is the case that things which have being also have a desire for the Beautiful and the Good, if all their actions are done for what seems to be a good, and if all their intentions have the Good as their source and goal (for nothing does what it does by looking at the nature of evil), what place is left for evil among the things that have being, and how can it exist at all if it is bereft of good purpose? Furthermore, if all the things that have being come from the Good, and if the Good itself transcends Being, then that which is not in Being is also in the Good.
>
> Evil is not a being; for if it were, it would not be totally evil. Nor is it a non-being; for nothing is completely a non-being, unless it is said to be in the Good in the sense of beyond-being. For the Good is established far beyond and above simple being and non-being. Evil, by contrast, is not among the things that have being, nor is it among what is not in being. It is more alien to the Good and more non-existent (ἀνουσιώτερον) even than non-being itself (trans. Lubhéid, emended).

What is most useful to Dionysius, as a radical monist, in Proclus' theory is the idea that, since all that exists, by the very fact of existing, strives for the Good, there is simply no room for evil as an entity in its own right; it can only be parasitical on something essentially positive, an aberration or failure of function.

This has been necessarily a rather partial survey of Dionysius' relation to Neoplatonic philosophy, and in particular to that of Syrianus and Proclus, but it should be sufficient to indicate the remarkable blend of dependence and originality that he employs. His use of language, it must be said in conclusion, mirrors his doctrinal position. While he makes extensive use of standard Neoplatonist technical vocabulary, such as *proodos* and *epistrophē*, *agathotēs*, *diakosmēsis*, *ellampsis*, *henōsis*, *hyperkosmios*, *kryphios*, *noētos/noeros*, *symbolon*, or *teletē*, he also concocts numerous neologisms, many of a thoroughly bizarre nature – compounds with the prefixes *hyper-* or *auto-*, or the suffixes *–arkhia* or *–nymia* – which seem designed to somehow "trump" the Neoplatonists at their own game, and demonstrate the superiority of Christian philosophy in the linguistic area also. It seems all of a piece with the exuberance of his exercise in intellectual "oneupmanship," an exercise which, after a slightly rocky start in the 530s, succeeded in bamboozling both the learned and the pious for over a millennium.

Bibliography

Balthasar, H. Urs von (1962) *Herrlichkeit, Eine theologische Ästhetik*, Einsiedeln.

Burnet, J. (ed.) (1900–1907) *Plato: Timaeus, Parmenides, Theaetetus*. In *Platonis Opera*, Oxford.

Corsini, E. (1962) *Il trattato "De divinis nominibus" dello pseudo-Dionigi e i commenti neoplatonici al Parmenide*, Turin.
Cousin, V. (ed.) (1864) *Procli philosophi Platonici opera inedita*, 2nd edn., Paris.
Dodds, E. R. (ed. and trans.) (1963) *Proclus: The Elements of Theology*, 2nd edn., Oxford.
Heil, G. and Ritter, A. M. (eds.) (1991) Pseudo-Dionysius, *De caelesti hierarchia, De ecclesiastica hierarchia, in Corpus Dionysiacum*, vol. II, Berlin and New York.
Ivanka, E. von (1964) *Plato Christianus, Übernahme und Umgestaltung des Platonismus durch die Väter*, Einsiedeln.
Klibansky, R. and Labowsky, C. (eds.) (1953) *Parmenides usque ad finem primae hypothesis nec non Procli Commentarium in Parmenidem pars ultima adhuc inedita interprete Guillelmo de Moerbeka*, London.
Lubhéid, C. (trans.) (1987) *Pseudo-Dionysius: The Complete Works*, New York and Mahwah.
Luna, C. and Segonds A.-Ph. (eds.) (2007–2011) *Proclus: Commentaire sur le Parménide de Platon*, Paris.
Perl, E. (2007) *Theophany: the Neoplatonic Philosophy of Dionysius the Areopagite*, Albany, NY.
Saffrey, H.-D. and Westerink, L. G. (eds.) (1968–1997) *Proclus: Théologie platonicienne*, 6 vols., Paris.
Schäfer, C. (2006) *Philosophy of Dionysius the Areopagite: An Introduction to the Structure and the Content of the Treatise On the Divine Names*, Leiden and Boston.
Shaw, G. (1995) *Theurgy and the Soul: The Neoplatonism of Iamblichus*, University Park, PA.
Stiglmayr, J. (1895) "Der neuplatoniker Proclus als Vorlage des sogen. Dionysius Areopagita in der Lehre vom Uebel," *Historisches Jahrbuch* 16: 253–273.
Suchla, B. R. (ed.) (1990) Pseudo-Dionysius, *De divinis nominibus*, in *Corpus Dionysiacum*, vol. I, Berlin and New York.
Westerink L. G. (1956) *Olympiodorus: Commentary on the First Alcibiades of Plato*, Amsterdam.
(ed.) (1965) Proclus, *Commentarius in Alcibiadem I*, Amsterdam.

EXCURSUS 4A

Damascius and Boethius

Stephen Gersh

Boethius and Damascius were approximate contemporaries who illustrate the wide diffusion of Proclus' writings and doctrines in the late fifth and early sixth centuries.[1] These two thinkers are particularly interesting because they not only illustrate, in the immediate aftermath of Proclus' own works, different possibilities in the reception of the latter's ideas but also constitute extreme cases within this range of possibilities. Apart from being representatives of the Latin and Greek traditions respectively – a fact that had repercussions with respect to their own later influence – Boethius' connection with the School of Athens was perhaps only literary or stylistic whereas Damascius was physically present there as the last formally appointed head of the School; Boethius was a committed and practicing Christian while Damascius remained resolutely pagan during the period of Christian ascendancy; Boethius adopted Proclus' doctrines in an unmodified form in appropriate contexts whereas Damascius took every opportunity to criticize those doctrines or reduce them to *aporia*; Boethius integrated specific teachings of Proclus into a broader Augustinian framework while Damascius treated Proclus' teachings as the broad framework into which more specific views of Iamblichus and others could be inserted; and last but not least Boethius' teaching and its Proclean components exercised influence throughout the medieval period whereas the contribution to philosophy of Damascius was forgotten until at least the Renaissance.

Although these facts regarding the two thinkers are now generally agreed among scholars, the connection between *Boethius* and Proclus has been less obvious in the past. The most convincing evidence for this relationship is provided by Boethius' discussion of providence and fate in *De consolatione philosophiae* many details of which seem to have been taken directly from Proclus' *Tria opuscula* (and especially *De decem dubitationibus circa*

[1] Boethius was born *c.* 480 and died *c.* 524; Damascius was born *c.* 460 and died after 538. For biographical information about the two thinkers see Gersh (1994) and Hoffmann (1994).

providentiam and *De providentia et fato*), although the possibility that some of Boethius' later Neoplatonic doctrine came to him also by way of an Aristotelian commentary (perhaps by Ammonius) that had already integrated Proclean material cannot be totally excluded. The explanation of the relationship between providence and fate in terms of enfolding and unfolding is one of Boethius' most important ideas in *De consolatione*. The technical basis of this approach is laid down in Proclus' *Tria opuscula*,[2] where there are references to the enfolding of the unembodied and embodied souls in one another that reflects their freedom or lack of freedom,[3] and to the unfolding of the power pre-existing in providence by things subject to providence according to their differing capacities.[4] The explanation of the possibility of foreknowledge of future contingents in terms of grades of perception is another important theme of Boethius' *De consolatione*. The essential components of this solution are also laid out in Proclus' *Tria opuscula*, where we find arguments to the effect that knowledge in the knower is characterized according to the latter's essential nature,[5] that this principle applies to different faculties such as intellect, reason, imagination, and sense,[6] and that the One knows all things according to its own proper nature.[7]

However, of perhaps the greatest historical-philosophical significance are the contrasts that become apparent at least in the extant works of Boethius and Damascius with respect to (1) their choice of philosophical methodologies and (2) their preference for specific texts of Plato, both of which constitute particular orientations towards Proclus.

Philosophical methodologies

Boethius was sufficiently Aristotelian in his outlook to hold that philosophical contradictions can be resolved by further conceptual refinement, and that the power and success of discursive and propositional thinking can be exhibited by such conceptual refinement. This approach seems to be in line with a work such as Proclus' *Elements of Theology*. The Boethian text that most illustrates it is the theological tractate *Quomodo substantiae*, which consists of an introductory section where the author, having first

[2] The most recent edition is Isaac (1977–1982), vol. II.
[3] Proclus, *De prov.* 2. 4, 10–19 (Isaac 1977–1982), vol. II.
[4] Proclus, *De dec. dub.* 3. 10, 30–41 (Isaac 1977–1982), vol. I.
[5] Proclus, *De dec. dub.* 2. 7, 20–23. [6] *De dec. dub.* 1. 3, 1–20. [7] *De dec. dub.* 2. 7, 29–48.

appealed to the model of mathematical discourse, sets out nine axioms.[8] Among these axioms (i) distinguishes two kinds of "common notion of the mind" (*communis animi conceptio*): the kind obvious to all and that obvious to the educated only; (ii) contrasts "existence" (*esse*) and "the existent" (*id quod est*) and notes that existence is "not yet" (*nondum*) whereas the existent is established by receiving "the form of being" (*essendi forma*); (iii) notes that existence cannot participate whereas the existent can participate; (iv) notes that existence contains nothing besides itself whereas the existent contains something besides its existence; (v) contrasts "being something" (*esse aliquid*) and "being something in so far as it exists" (*esse aliquid in eo quod est*) and notes that being something is equivalent to accident whereas being something in so far as it exists is equivalent to substance; (vi) contrasts "the existent" (*id quod est*) and "existence in itself" (*id quod est esse*) and notes that the existent participates in existence in itself; (vii) contrasts "something's existence" (*esse suum*) and "something's existence as that something" (*id quod est suum*) and notes that a simple thing has its existence as identical with its existence as that something; (viii) notes that a composite thing has its existence as distinct from its existence as that something; and (ix) notes that diversity repels whereas similarity attracts. The introductory section stating the nine axioms is followed by a main section in which these axioms are said to be applied to the solution of a specific problem,[9] although the precise manner of doing so is left to the reader to guess. The problem might be summarized as follows: Things which exist are good. But are they good by means of participation or according to their own substance? Either alternative produces difficulties: if by participation, then the connection between existence and goodness is weakened; if according to substance, then the distinction between the supreme Good (or supreme Being) and other things becomes problematic.[10]

[8] Boethius, *Quomodo substantiae* 4–48 (Moreschini 2005). A full commentary on this text is now available in Galonnier (2007). On the axiomatic method in this work see Solère (2003). Schrimpf (1966) has explored its historical influence.

[9] *Quo. subst.* 49ff.

[10] At *In Isagogen Porphyrii, editio secunda* 10, 158. 21–11, 167. 20 (Schepss and Brandt 1906), Boethius provides another fine illustration of how he tackles the broader issue of whether philosophical contradictions can or cannot be resolved. Here, one of the questions about universals that Porphyry had raised but not answered in his *Isagoge* was whether genera and species are real things or reside in the understanding alone, and Boethius announces an attempt "to release and untie a knot of doubt" (*dubitationis nodum absolvere atque explicare*) in this connection. The knot (i.e. the *aporia* or impasse) results from the fact that the following conflicting lines of argument are equally possible. On the one hand, genera and species are not real things. A real thing is either one or many, and genera and species – for various reasons explained – can be neither one nor many. On the other hand, genera and species are not only in the understanding and also true. Understanding of something is

Damascius took a different approach. In *On First Principles* we have abundant illustration of his conviction that philosophical contradictions cannot always be resolved by further conceptual refinement, and that investigation of the highest principles should be conducted in terms of *aporiai* rather than axioms.[11] Laying down an implicit challenge to a program such as that carried out in Proclus' *Elements of Theology*, Damascius begins his treatise by arguing that statements regarding the First Principle or "Ineffable" (τὸ ἀπόρρητον) must not only take a negative form but a double negative form.[12] One can posit that the principle of all things is either beyond all things or else included among them, and that all things are either together with the principle or else subsequent to it. However, in both cases an *impasse* (ἀπορία) results. If one combines the view that the principle of all things is beyond all things with the view that all things are subsequent to it, all things will not really be *all things*. Conversely, if one combines the view that the principle of all things is included among all things with the view that all things are together with the principle, the principle will not really be a *principle*.[13] The result is that the One is *neither* all things *nor* not-all things. This argument is applied to other possible predications that one might venture with respect to the First Principle: for example, one must deny that it is a "first" and then deny the denial of its primacy;[14] deny that it is "beyond" and then deny the denial of its transcendence;[15] deny that it is "one" and then deny the denial of its unity;[16] and deny that it is "true" and then deny the denial of its truth.[17] For Damascius, these applications of double negation are really just the inaugural stage of a total "reversal" (περιτροπή) of all discourse[18] with respect to the Ineffable in which we are really operating with the names

either as the thing is constituted or not as the thing is constituted. If genera and species are as the thing is constituted, then they are real – which was rejected by the earlier argument. If genera and species are not as the thing is constituted, then they are false. After some further discussion Boethius concludes, by resorting to the Aristotelian doctrine as interpreted by Alexander of Aphrodisias whereby genera and species are real but only to the extent that they coincide with the particulars subsumed under them, and also are understood as true only to the extent that they are abstracted from the particulars, that "the entire problem is solved" (*omnis . . . quaestio dissoluta est*) (167. 7–8).

11 On the aporetic method of Damascius see Combès (1981). Interesting but more speculative discussions can be found in Rappe (1998a) and Rappe (1998b).

12 For historical notes on the doctrine of the Ineffable see Linguiti (1990) and Lilla (1991–1992). Quite typically, Damascius here appeals to the authority of Iamblichus rather than that of Syrianus and Proclus.

13 *De principiis* I. 1. 4–2. 20 (Westerink and Combès 1986–1991). For a more detailed analysis of this section see Dillon (1996), 124–126.

14 *De princ.* I. 4, 14–16.

15 *De princ.* I. 4, 14–16.

16 *De princ.* I. 18, 9–13; I. 20, 5.

17 *De princ.* I. 15, 6–12.

18 *De princ.* I. 21, 15–20; *De princ.* I. 22, 11–19. Cf. *De princ.* I. 8, 12–15 and I. 26, 3–5.

and concepts of our own intellectual "travails" (ὠδῖνες) with respect to *It.*[19] Adopting an idea from Proclus' interpretation of the conclusion of the first hypothesis of the *Parmenides*, Damascius sees the reversal of discourse as leading to a "silence" (σιγή). By this he seems to mean not that we should abandon the traditional philosophical approach to the highest principles but that we should henceforth pursue it in a more "sigetic" manner.[20] In other words, all dogmatic assertions regarding first principles must, in a paradoxical manner, be held simultaneously in a state of suspension.

Textual preferences

An important poem towards the end of Boethius' *De consolatione philosophiae* III performs the extraordinary technical feat of compressing the teaching of Plato's *Timaeus* as seen through Proclus' commentary on that dialogue into about fifty hexameter lines.[21] The dynamic-logical causal principles underlying the structure of reality and the structure of reality itself underpinned by those dynamic-logical causal principles are both presented in exactly the manner of the ancient commentator. In connection with the dynamic-logical principles, the doctrine of Proclus is followed very closely. Boethius refers to the initial remaining constituting stability or identity of cause and effect by speaking of the Father of the cosmos as "remaining stable" (*stabilis manens*),[22] to the "procession" or motion of differentiation between cause and effect by describing the Father as "ordering to go" (*ire iubere*), as "conferring motion on all things" (*dare cuncta moveri*), and as "leading all things from a higher paradigm" (*cuncta superno ducere ab exemplo*),[23] and to the "reversion" or motion of assimilation between cause and effect by speaking of the Father as "making

[19] *De princ.* I. 8, 12–15. It is important to note that this does not lead to subjectivism – as has often been suggested in modern scholarly works such as Hoffmann (1997) – but rather to a *performative* ontology surpassing the objective subjective disjunction as such.

[20] This fits in with his interpretation of Plato's *Parmenides*. See below.

[21] It is perhaps only because Boethius' dependence on Proclus has been established beyond reasonable doubt with respect to both the doctrine of Providence and Fate in *De consolatione philosophiae* IV, prose 6 and the teaching regarding Love in *De cons. phil.* IV, verse 6 that we are really justified in treating the cosmology of *De cons. phil.* III, verse 9 as a summary not of Plato's *Timaeus* simply but also of Proclus' commentary on that dialogue. The relationship between the two texts was correctly understood although perhaps not sufficiently demonstrated by Klingner (1921), 38–67. For further elaboration of the theory that Boethius is primarily dependent on Proclus for the Platonism of this hymn see Beierwaltes (1983) and Gersh (2012), 117–120. Solère (2003) has argued in considerable detail that *De consolatione* is influenced throughout by Proclus' *Commentary on Plato's Timaeus*, and that there is continuity of method between Boethius' *De consolatione philosophiae* and *Quomodo substantiae* and between both of these works and Proclus.

[22] *De cons. phil.* III, *metrum* 9, 3 (Moreschini 2005).

[23] *De cons. phil.* III, *m.* 9, 3, 6–7.

things return towards him" (*conversas facere reverti*).[24] In connection with the structure of reality, the doctrine of Proclus is again followed albeit with some simplification in order to facilitate Christianization. Here we find a hierarchical order of terms comprising God (or *a* god), Soul and souls, Body and bodies, and Matter, the first term being the cause of all the subsequent terms.[25] Boethius refers to this god as the "Father" (*pater*) who has a relation to the Good[26] in which he is characterized as "the instantiated Form of the supreme Good" (*insita summi forma boni*) and as himself the "fount of goodness" (*fons boni*),[27] a relation to intellect and reason in which he is characterized as "the deep Mind" (*mens profunda*) and as the one who "governs all things with (his) reason" (*ratione gubernare*) and "sustains things with (his) mind" (*mente gerere*),[28] and a relation to the paradigm in which he is described as "leading things from the exemplar" (*ducere ab exemplo*).[29] The poem also provides some information about Soul, Body, and Matter. Soul is characterized either singly as "the mediate soul of threefold nature" (*triplicis media naturae anima*) or collectively as "souls and lesser lives" (*animae vitaeque minores*),[30] whereas Body and Matter are referred to as "the elements" (*elementa*) and as "flowing matter" (*materia fluitans*) respectively.[31]

If Boethius provides a summary of cosmology according to the *Timaeus* in which the intertext of Proclus is a prominent factor, Damascius performs a similar task with respect to the theological doctrine of the *Parmenides.* We know from the anonymous *Prolegomena to Platonic Philosophy* that the *Timaeus* and *Parmenides* were held to represent the definitive summaries of Platonic doctrine in the domains of physics and theology respectively.[32] Since it was the doctrine regarding the intelligible world of the Platonists rather than that concerning their sensible world that was the more problematic for Christians, we should not be surprised in discovering

[24] *De cons. phil.* III, *m.* 9, 21 – the reference here is specifically to souls. The passage should be compared with two further texts in which the logical aspects of the remaining, procession, and reversion are also apparent: *De cons. phil.* IV, prose 6, 34–42, where the cause is Providence and the effect or product is Fate, and *De cons. phil.* IV, verse 6, 44–48, where the cause is the Creator God (or *a* producing god) and the effects or products are created things in general.

[25] The hypostasis of Intellect that comes between the One and Soul in Proclus is assimilated to God as it is in the thought of Augustine, whom Boethius here and elsewhere treats as the highest authority. See below regarding the "deep Mind."

[26] *De cons. phil.* III, *m.* 9, 22.

[27] *De cons. phil.* III, *m.* 9, 5, 23.

[28] *De cons. phil.* III, *m.* 9, 1, 8, 16.

[29] *De cons. phil.* III, *m.* 9, 7.

[30] *De cons. phil.* III, *m.* 9, 13–14, 18.

[31] *De cons. phil.* III, *m.* 9, 5, 10.

[32] See Anonymous, *Prolegomena to Platonic Philosophy* 10. 26, 39. 18–21 (Westerink, Trouillard, and Segonds 1990).

that Boethius the Christian and Damascius the pagan have diametrically opposed preferences among these texts.

It is in his extensive *Commentary on the Parmenides* that Damascius makes some of his most important philosophical innovations. Here he initiates a break with the entire tradition of ancient metaphysics and approaches the position of a contemporary deconstructionist, on the one hand, by elaborating his thinking within the "margins" of Proclus' writings and, on the other,[33] by introducing an element of "the ineffable" into all discourse and the reality mirrored by discourse.[34] He elaborates his thinking within the margins of Proclus' writings when he develops for the first time within the ancient tradition a convincing metaphysical explanation, not just of the first five hypotheses in the second half of the dialogue but of all nine hypotheses. Earlier thinkers up to and including Proclus had either failed to establish a clear connection between the first group of five hypotheses and the last group of four, or had failed to establish metaphysical correlates for all nine hypotheses.[35] Damascius responds to the challenge by treating the hypothetical structure as a whole as pivoting around hypothesis three (neither all nor nothing and both all and nothing = the human soul) in two groups: first, the group formed by hypothesis one (ineffable Nothing according to excess: the One),[36] hypothesis two (the All of the One-Being), hypothesis four (the All of the materiate forms), and hypothesis five (ineffable Nothing according to defect: Matter);[37] and second, the group formed by hypothesis seven (Nothing of absurdity with respect to the One), hypothesis six (the All of phenomena), hypothesis eight (the All of phantasms), and hypothesis nine (Nothing of absurdity with respect to the Others),[38] the pivoting of the second group also around hypothesis three being the main innovation with respect to Proclus' approach. Damascius introduces an element of the ineffable into all discourse and the reality mirrored by discourse when he argues in *De principiis* that Plato never mentioned the Ineffable as First Principle in his *Parmenides* because he was engaged in a kind of enactment of its ineffability through discourse[39] – a practice which Damascius perhaps imitated in beginning his own commentary on

[33] For a discussion of the relation between Damascius and his predecessor see Combès (1987).

[34] This represents another aspect of the *impasse* mentioned above. On the relationship between Damascius and deconstruction see Gersh (2014).

[35] Proclus narrates the history of this problem at *Commentarius in Parmenidem* 1052. 25–1064. 14 (Steel 2007–2009), vol. III.

[36] Strictly speaking, the Ineffable of the One.

[37] Strictly speaking, the Ineffable of Matter.

[38] For an excellent summary of Damascius' interpretation of the hypotheses see Combès (1975).

[39] *De princ.* I. 9, 10–22. Cf. *De princ.* I. 55, 9–19.

that dialogue with a discussion of the *second* hypothesis.[40] Damascius also introduces this element of the ineffable into discourse and reality when he indicates in passages of *On First Principles* and of the *Commentary on the Parmenides* that the Ineffable is in proximity[41] either to "the One" (τὸ ἕν) treated primarily in hypothesis one[42] or to "the Others" (τὰ ἄλλα) treated primarily in hypothesis five[43] – an approach which treats the First Principle of the Ineffable less as a unity of some kind excluding duality – as in the system of the later Platonists up to and including Proclus – than as a kind of "One-Fold" representing an irreducible unity–duality. The elaboration of his thinking within the margins of Proclus' writing and the introduction of an element of the ineffable into all discourse and the reality mirrored by discourse are two inseparable aspects of a single philosophical strategy that works itself out in Damascius' major philosophical writings. This strategy is seen at its best when he challenges the most fundamental principles of Proclus' metaphysics, arguing, for instance, that any attempt to distinguish the members of the causal triad of remaining, procession, and reversion leads to a division of terms *ad infinitum*,[44] or that the human soul cannot plausibly be distinguished into a substantial part that remains above and an active part that descends into body.[45]

Bibliography

Beierwaltes, W. (1983) "Trost im Begriff, Zu Boethius' Hymnus 'O qui perpetua mundum ratione gubernas,'" in H. Bürkle and G. Becker (eds.), *Communicatio fidei, Festschrift für Eugen Biser zum 65. Geburtstag*, Regensburg, 241–251.

Combès, J. (1975) "Damascius lecteur du Parménide," *Archives de philosophie* 38: 33–60. Reprinted in Combès (1989), 63–99.

(1981) "La théologie aporétique de Damascius," in *Néoplatonisme, Mélanges offerts à Jean Trouillard = Les cahiers de Fontenay 19–22*, 125–139. Reprinted in Combès (1989), 199–221.

40 It was perhaps because of a failure to understand the "silence" with regard to the first hypothesis that begins this text that, for a long time, the *De principiis* itself was seen to be the beginning and the *Commentary on the Parmenides* the continuation of a single work entitled "Problems and Solutions regarding First Principles."

41 For this mode of expression see *De princ.* I. 84, 18–19, where the One is said to be "obscured by the closeness" (τῇ γειτονήσει ἐπιλυγάζεσθαι) of the Ineffable.

42 See *De princ.* I. 85, 1–3; II. 10, 25–26; II. 11, 16–19; II. 22, 11–II. 23, 6; II. 23, 9–12.

43 See *Commentarius in Parmenidem* IV. 68. 15; IV. 71. 3–9; IV. 77. 17–21 (Westerink and Combès 2002–2003).

44 See Gersh (1978), 76–81.

45 See Steel (1978), 79–116 (and especially 98–102). Damascius also developed a highly original theory concerning time. See Sambursky and Pines (1971) and Galperine (1980).

(1987) "Proclus et Damascius," in G. Boss and G. Seel (eds.), *Proclus et son influence, Actes du colloque de Neuchâtel, juin 1985*, Zurich, 221–246. Reprinted in Combès (1989), 245–271.

(1996) *Études néoplatoniciennes*, Grenoble; 2nd edn., Grenoble 1996.

Dillon, J. M. (1996) "Damascius on the Ineffable," *Archiv für die Geschichte der Philosophie* 78: 120–129.

Galonnier, A. (2007) *Boèce: Opuscula sacra, texte latin de l'édition de Claudio Moreschini, introduction, traduction et commentaire*, 2 vols., Louvain-la-Neuve.

Galperine, M.-C. (1980) "Le temps intégral selon Damascius," *Les études philosophiques*: 325–341.

Gersh, S. (1978) *From Iamblichus to Eriugena, An Investigation of the Prehistory and Evolution of the Pseudo-Dionysian Tradition*, Leiden.

(1994) "Boethius," in R. Goulet (ed.), *Dictionnaire des philosophes antiques*, vol. II, Paris, 117–122.

(2012) "The First Principles of Latin Neoplatonism: Augustine, Macrobius, Boethius," *Vivarium* 50: 113–138.

(2014) *Being Different, More Neoplatonism after Derrida*, Leiden.

Hoffmann, P. (1994) "Damascius," in R. Goulet (ed.), *Dictionnaire des philosophes antiques*, vol. II, Paris, 541–593.

(1997) "L'expression de l'indicible dans le néoplatonisme grec de Plotin à Damascius," in C. Lévy and Pernot L. (eds.), *Dire l'évidence, philosophie et rhétorique antiques*, Paris, 335–390.

Isaac, D. (ed. and trans.) (1977–1982) *Proclus: Trois études sur la Providence*, 3 vols., Paris.

Klingner, F. (1921) *De Boethii consolatione philosophiae*, Berlin. Reprinted Hildesheim 2005.

Lilla, S. (1991–1992) "La teologia negativa dal pensiero greco classico a quello patristico e bizantino," *Helikon* 31–32: 3–72.

Linguiti, A. (1990) *L'ultimo platonismo greco, principi e conoscenza*, Florence.

Moreschini, C. (ed.) (2005) Boethius, *De consolatione philosophiae, Opuscula theologica*, Leipzig.

Rappe, S. (1998a) "Damascius' Skeptical Affiliations," *The Ancient World* 29: 111–125.

(1998b) "Scepticism in the Sixth Century? Damascius' Doubts and Solutions Concerning First Principles," *Journal of the History of Philosophy* 36: 337–363.

Sambursky, S. and Pines, S. (1971) *The Concept of Time in Late Neoplatonism, Texts with Translation, Introduction and Notes*, Jerusalem.

Schepss, G. and Brandt, S. (eds.) (1906) Boethius, *In Isagogen Porphyrii commenta*, Vienna and Leipzig.

Schrimpf, G. (1966) *Die Axiomenschrift des Boethius (De hebdomadibus) als philosophisches Lehrbuch des Mittelalters*, Leiden.

Solère, J.-L. (2003) "Bien, cercles et hebdomades: Formes et raisonnement chez Boèce et Proclus," in A. Galonnier (ed.), *Boèce ou la Chaîne des Savoirs, Actes du colloque international de la Fondation Singer-Polignac, Paris 8–12 juin 1999*, Louvain-la-Neuve and Paris, 55–110.

Steel, C. (1978) *The Changing Self: A Study on the Soul in Later Neoplatonism: Iamblichus, Damascius, and Priscianus*, Brussels.

(ed.) (2007–2009) Proclus, *In Platonis Parmenidem commentaria*, 3 vols., Oxford.

Westerink, L. G. and Combès, J. (eds. and trans.) (1986–1991) *Damascius: Traité des premiers principes*, 3 vols., Paris.

(eds. and trans.) (2002–2003) *Damascius: Commentaire du Parménide de Platon*, 4 vols., Paris.

Westerink, L. G., Trouillard, J., and Segonds, A.-Ph. (eds.) (1990) *Prolégomènes à la philosophie de Platon*, Paris.

PART II.2 *Medieval Islamic philosophy*

CHAPTER 5

The Liber de causis

Cristina D'Ancona

Proclus' theology in Arabic

The statutes of the Paris University promulgated on March 19 of the year 1255 list among the works by Aristotle to be studied in the Faculty of Arts a *Liber de causis*.[1] Even more telling is the *Compendium examinatorium parisiense*, a program of the curricular works by an anonymous master of the same faculty dated from the thirties or the forties of the thirteenth century. The *Compendium* states that metaphysics should be studied on three books: the *Metaphysica vetus*, the *Metaphysica nova*, and the *Liber de causis*, where

> agitur de substantiis divinis in quantum sunt principia essendi et influendi unam in alteram, secundum quod ibidem habetur quod omnis substantia superior influit in suum causatum.[2]

As everyone knows from Thomas Aquinas onwards,[3] the *De causis* is by no means an Aristotelian work. Its author, Thomas says, was a Muslim philosopher who elaborated on Proclus' *Elements of Theology*,[4] not without adapting them to his religious creed and metaphysical convictions; he also felt free to shorten, cut, and paste parts of Proclus' work.[5]

[1] Denifle and Chatelain (1889), 278.

[2] This document has been discovered by Grabmann (1928), 30–37 and Grabmann (1934), 211–229. Edition by C. Lafleur (1992), § 10. On the threefold articulation of the metaphysical science (*Metaphysica vetus, nova, De causis*) see de Libera (1997), 61–88.

[3] Saffrey (1954), 3.1–10.

[4] The translation from Greek of the *Elements of Theology* made by the Flemish Dominican William of Moerbeke, the great translator of the second half of the thirteenth century, allowed Thomas to compare in detail the *De causis* and its source. See Boese (1985); Boese (1987); Brams and Vanhamel (1989) with detailed references to previous literature.

[5] At times, Thomas is quite unhappy with the outcome of this abridgment: apropos the axiom *Omnis intelligentia intelligit res sempiternas quae non destruuntur neque cadunt sub tempore* (prop. 11), whose sources are two propositions of the *El. theol.* (172 and 173), he remarks: *ex quibus duabus propositionibus auctor huius libri conflavit unam; et dum brevitati studuit, obscuritatem induxit* (73.21–23 Saffrey).

Even after Thomas' discovery of its spurious nature, the *Liber de causis* did not cease to be commented upon – a fact which suggests that its appeal was, at least to some extent, independent of Aristotle's alleged authorship. Indeed, the influence of some of its tenets extended far and wide:[6] the *De causis* has been labeled as a *source de la métaphysique au Moyen Âge* by no less a scholar than H. D. Saffrey OP.[7] In what follows I will first outline the main data about this work; then I will focus on the philosophical reasons that granted it, at least for a while, the status of the pinnacle of Aristotle's *Metaphysics*.[8]

The Origins of the Liber de causis

The information provided by the Latin sources about the Arabic origins of the *De causis*[9] was confirmed in 1882, when the *editio princeps* of the Arabic text was published, under the title *Book on the Pure Good*, by the German patrologist Otto Bardenhewer[10] on the basis of the sole manuscript housed in a western library and known at that time: Leiden, Bibliotheek der Rijksuniversiteit, *Oriental* 209.[11] Baffled by the fact that the Muslim philosophers of the Middle Ages never refer explicitly to the *De causis*, whereas the Latin authors are familiar with it, scholars in the past advanced the hypothesis that the Arabic original had been composed in Spain.[12] As

6 The *Liber de causis* is known beyond the academic milieu: Dante Alighieri quotes some of its most famous axioms (like *prima rerum creatarum est esse*) in various works: *Convivio*, *De Monarchia*, *Epistle to Cangrande*. See D'Ancona and Taylor (2003), 599–647, in particular 646–647.

7 Saffrey (1963).

8 Both Albert the Great and Giles of Rome label the *De causis* as the pinnacle of the *Metaphysics*, even though both (for different reasons) do not believe it to be Aristotle's; see Fauser (1993), 60.3–5 (*iste liber prime philosophie coniungendus est, ut finalem ex isto recipiat perfectionem*), followed by Aegidius Romanus (1550), Proem., Y–Z.

9 The Latin readers were informed about the origins of the *De causis* by the text itself, which contains two loan words from Arabic (*alachili*, from *al-ʿaql*, "intellect," and *yliathim*, from *ḥilya*, "shape"). The translation from Arabic into Latin was the work of Gerard of Cremona, the famous translator active in Toledo between 1144 and 1187. Immediately after his death, his *socii* compiled a biography and a list of his translations, which included the *De causis*. This list, first edited in 1851, has been repeatedly examined; the most recent study is by Burnett (2001). Gerard's translation is edited: see Pattin (1966). For more details on the Latin translation, see D'Ancona and Taylor (2003), 610–617. In what follows, the propositions of the *Liber de causis* after the fourth will be quoted as 4[5], 5[6], and so on, because most manuscripts of the Latin version split the long proposition 4 into two; since some Latin commentaries follow this order (among them, that of Thomas), it is customary to refer to the double numbering.

10 Bardenhewer (1882). Another edition has been provided by Badawī (1955), 1–33; critical edition by Taylor (1981).

11 This manuscript is dated 593 H/1197 AD; description by Bardenhewer (1882), 4–9. Two further manuscripts of the Arabic *De causis* have been discovered since then: see Rosenthal (1961) and Taylor (1982).

12 Munk (1859), 159.

a matter of fact, the idea of the western origins of the *Liber de causis* was grounded less on this argument *e silentio* than on a detailed account by Albert the Great, who in his own *De causis et processu universitatis a prima causa* credits a certain "David Iudaeus" with the creation of the *De causis* out of a selection of metaphysical aphorisms by Aristotle, al-Fārābī, Avicenna, and al-Ġazālī, to which he added his own commentaries.[13] Albert's account places the origins of the *De causis* against the backdrop of the trilingual Toledo, where a certain "Avendauth israelita philosophus," easily identified with Albert's "David,"[14] acted as the learned collaborator of Dominicus Gundissalinus for the Latin version of Avicenna's *De anima*.[15]

Notwithstanding the oddities implied in it,[16] this reconstruction has been definitively ruled out only when a substantial advancement in the knowledge of the Greco-Arabic translations has been achieved, thus paving the way for the discovery of the true origins of the *Liber de causis*.

In 1947 ʿA. Badawī published, on the basis of a Cairo manuscript and another one housed in Damascus, a series of Arabic versions of Aristotle, Alexander of Aphrodisias, and Themistius, plus some writings by Yaḥyā ibn ʿAdī and Avicenna.[17] Among the works of the Arabic Alexander published by Badawī, three short texts soon appeared to be in reality theorems 15, 16, and 17 of Proclus' *Elements of Theology* in Arabic translation.[18] Almost at the same time G. C. Anawati OP carefully compared the axioms of the *De causis* with the *Elements of Theology* edited by E. R. Dodds in 1933,[19] coming to the conclusion that the dependence of the *De causis* upon it was often literal, although countenancing doctrinal modifications at times

[13] Fauser (1993), 59. 9–15 Fauser: *Accipiemus igitur ab antiquis quaecumque bene dicta sunt ab ipsis, quae ante nos David Iudaeus quidam ex dictis Aristotelis, Avicennae, Algazelis et Alpharabii congregavit, per modum theorematum ordinans ea, quorum commentum ipsemet adhibuit, sicut et Euclides in geometricis fecisse videtur.*

[14] "Avendauth israelita, philosophus" is the name of the translator of Avicenna's *De anima* together with Gundissalinus (see the following note); at one and the same time, some of the manuscripts of the Latin *De causis* mention "Avendauth," "Auever," or "David" as the author. See d'Alverny (1954) (reprinted in d'Alverny 1993).

[15] Van Riet (1972), 4.21–23; see also d'Alverny (1989).

[16] Albert's account implies that a copy of the *Elements of Theology* was present in Muslim Spain, that "David/Avendauth" created out of it the *Arabic* text of the *De causis*, and that immediately after this work was translated from Arabic into Latin, not by "David/Avendauth" himself – a translator! – but by Gerard of Cremona (see above, n. 9), who in addition should have been unaware of the authorship of the text he translated, since in the list of his *socii* the *De causis* features as Aristotle's.

[17] Badawī (1947).

[18] Two scholars, independently of one another, realized that this "Alexander" was in fact Proclus: Lewin (1955); Pines (1955) (reprinted in Pines 1986). It is worth noting that two of these propositions had already been acknowledged by Thomas Aquinas as the sources of prop. 15 of the *De causis*: see Saffrey (1954), 88.7–12.

[19] See below, n. 31.

decisive, as in the case of the idea of creation. To this he added a seminal lexicon, pointing to terminology as the key to understanding the origins and purpose of the *De causis*.[20]

The existence of an Arabic translation of many more propositions of the *Elements of Theology* than the three edited by Badawī came to light little by little. Pines[21] had already called attention to the testimonies of the ancient Arabic bio-bibliographic sources about a "Theology" by Proclus and one by Alexander, allegedly translated by the tenth century physician Abū 'Uṯmān al-Dimašqī.[22] Further manuscripts containing Proclus' propositions in Arabic under Alexander's name were discovered, in addition to that which had served as the basis of Badawī's edition. In particular, a manuscript of the Süleymaniye library in Istanbul came to light[23] that contains more than twenty propositions of the *Elements of Theology*, intermingled with some of Alexander's genuine *Quaestiones*; this compilation bears the title *What Alexander Extracted from Aristotle's Book Called "Theology," i.e. "discourse on Divinity."*[24]

From all this rich but quite unpromising material G. Endress, in his 1973 edition of the *Proclus Arabus*,[25] extracted a picture which, being based on in-depth analysis of the translation technique, terminology, and doctrinal adaptations, shed light at one and the same time on the beginning of Arabic philosophy and on the origins of the *De causis*. Endress came to the conclusion that, although attributed to Abū 'Uṯmān al-Dimašqī, the Arabic version of Proclus' *Elements of Theology* reaches back to an earlier stage of the translations from Greek into Arabic. It was in the "circle of al-Kindī"[26] that Proclus' *Elements of Theology* were translated, and the terminology as well as the doctrinal adaptations show striking parallels with another famous Neoplatonic work widespread in Arabic under Aristotle's name: the pseudo-*Theology*. The comparison between the Arabic rendering of the Greek words and sentences in both works allows the reader of the *Proclus Arabus* to ascertain that, to put it in Endress' words,

> Closely related to the so-called *Theology of Aristotle* and other Arabic excerpts from Plotinus is a translation of selections from the *Elements of Theology* of

[20] Anawati (1956); Anawati (1974b). Both studies have been reprinted in Anawati (1974a). Anawati was the first to state clearly that the Arabic Plotinus, i.e. the *Theology of Aristotle*, is an important source of the *De causis*; on this point, see also Taylor (1986) and D'Ancona (1989).

[21] Pines (1955).

[22] On this translator see the entry by Endress (1995).

[23] *Istanbul, Süleymaniye Kütüphanesi, Carullah 1279*, ff. 60v–66v. This manuscript was discovered by Rosenthal (1955).

[24] Van Ess (1965), especially 344–346; van Ess (1966).

[25] Endress (1973). See also Endress (2012b).

[26] Endress (1997).

> Proclus (Στοιχείωσις θεολογική). In the Arabic manuscript tradition, most of these are being presented as alleged excerpts by Alexander of Aphrodisias from the "Theology" of Aristotle. These convey a monotheistic, creationist interpretation of the Neoplatonic system, which served al-Kindī as a philosophic paradigm of the Muslim *tawḥīd*.[27]

Since Endress' groundbreaking book, further traces of the Arabic version of Proclus' *Elements of Theology* have been discovered.[28] If the fact that the *De causis* depends upon this version is firmly established in scholarship, there is no scholarly consensus about the nature of this relation. One may think that the *De causis*, with its 31 propositions versus the 211 of the *Elements of Theology* and its amateurish propensity for repetitions, is the outcome of an unskilled compilation of scattered parts of the Arabic Proclus.[29] Alternatively, one may think that the procedure of cutting and pasting parts of Proclus' propositions shows by itself that the author of the *De causis* had a plan in his mind.[30] In both cases the question arises what, if any, was the purpose in reworking two Neoplatonic writings about the suprasensible principles – the *Enneads* and the *Elements of Theology* – so that the former became the *Theology of Aristotle*, and the latter the *Book by Aristotle on the Exposition of the Pure Good.*

The *Liber de causis* as "Aristotle's" account of the suprasensible principles

As shown by Dodds, the structure of Proclus' *Elements of Theology* rests on the idea that reality proceeds from unity to multiplicity.[31] From the viewpoint of its layout, this "complete system of 'theology' in the Aristotelian sense of 'first philosophy' or metaphysic"[32] is structured into axioms. From the viewpoint of its contents, it is shaped by the topic of the descent from the pure unity of the first principle to the multiplicity of the intra-mundane souls. Within this framework the *Elements of Theology* fall, according to Dodds, into two main sections: one which "introduces successively the

[27] Endress (1997), 53–54. See also Endress (2007).
[28] Zimmermann and Brown (1973); Pines (1986); Zimmermann (1994). Another version of the *De causis* has been discovered by S. Oudaimah in a manuscript housed in Istanbul: see Thillet and Oudaimah (2001–2002). For the various interpretations of the relation of this text with the *De causis*, see D'Ancona and Taylor (2003), 602–603 and Endress (2012b), 1668.
[29] Zimmermann (1986), especially 130–131; Taylor (1992).
[30] This is the opinion advanced in D'Ancona (1989).
[31] Dodds (1933), 187: "The order of exposition of the *Elements of Theology* is an order of progression from the simpler to the more complex."
[32] Dodds (1933), x.

general metaphysical antitheses with which Neoplatonism operated – unity and plurality, cause and consequent, the unmoved, the self-moved and the passively mobile, transcendence and immanence, declension and continuity, procession and reversion, *causa sui* and *causatum*, eternity and time, substance and reflection, whole and part, active and passive potency, limit and infinitude, being, life and cognition," and the other which "expounds in the light of these antitheses the relations obtaining within each of the three great orders of spiritual substance, gods or henads, intelligences, and souls."[33] If we turn to the *Liber de causis*, we immediately realize that it begins with a synthesis of some propositions located towards the middle of the first section, in the subsets labeled by Dodds as "Grades of Causality" and "Whole and Parts." Proposition 1 of the *Liber de causis* states that

> Every primary cause infuses its effect more powerfully than does a universal second cause. Now, when a universal second cause removes its power from a thing, the universal first cause does not withdraw its power from it. This is because the universal first cause acts on the effect of the second cause before the universal second cause, which follows the effect, acts on it. So when the second cause which follows the effect acts, its act is not independent of the first cause, which is above it. And when the second cause is separated from the effect that follows it, the first cause, which is above it, is not separated from the effect, because it is its cause. We find an example of this in being, living, and man, for it is necessary that something be first of all being, next a living thing, and afterward a man. Therefore, living is man's proximate cause and being is its remote cause. Being then is more powerfully the cause of man than is living, because it is the cause of living, which is the cause of man. Likewise, when you assert rationality to be the cause of man, being is more powerfully the cause of man than is rationality, because it is the cause of his cause. The indication of this is that, when you remove the rational power from a man, a man does not remain, but living, breathing, and sensible remain . . . The first cause aids the second cause in its activity, because the first cause also effects every activity that the second cause effects, although it effects it in another way [which is] higher and more sublime . . . It is, therefore, now clear and plain that the remote cause is more powerfully the cause of a thing than the proximate cause that follows it, and that the remote cause infuses the thing with its power, conserves it, and is not separated from it by the separation of its proximate cause. Rather, it remains in it and adheres to it powerfully, as we have shown and explained (trans. Taylor).[34]

[33] Dodds (1933), x. See Luna and Segonds (2012), especially 1610–1613.

[34] Bardenhewer (1882), 58.3–61.9 = Pattin (1966), 134.1–138.70, English trans. by Taylor in Guagliardo, Hess, and Taylor (1996), 5–7. All translations by Taylor utilized in the present chapter are taken from this volume. See also Taylor (2012).

This proposition has been created by the author of the *De causis* out of Proclus' props. 56[35] and 70.[36] Keeping in mind that only some of the 211 propositions of the *Elements of Theology* have come down to us in Arabic translation, one may well think that if the *De causis* begins with Proclus' prop. 56, it is because its author did not have at his disposal any proposition prior to it. However, on closer inspection he proves to be acquainted with prop. 11 of the *Elements of Theology*,[37] and this elicits the conclusion that he *decided* to begin with the topic of the causal priority of the highest principle. To this effect, he mixed up two propositions of the *Elements of Theology*; more importantly, he took a new start with respect to his Greek source: instead of the opposition one–multiple, it is the primacy of the remote, transcendent First Cause that sets the tone in the *Liber de causis*. As we shall see, this overarching principle will surface once again at the end of the text, when the causality of the One will be described as the power that reaches even the individual beings of the world of coming-to-be and passing away. Here, at the beginning of the "exposition of the Pure Good" by "Aristotle" – so runs the title of the Arabic *De causis*[38] – the author lays emphasis on the unique status of this causal power, that presupposes nothing while everything else presupposes it. As we shall see in a moment, this unique causal power is the power to create.

Proposition 2 of the *De causis* deepens the impression of a purposeful selection of topics from the *Elements of Theology*: it combines Proclus' props. 88 and 87 with one another and makes use also of props. 169 and 191, in order to describe the relation between the suprasensible principles and eternity or time. This selection goes hand in hand with an important modification of Proclus' wording and doctrine. According to the *Elements*

35 *El. theol.* 54.4–6 (Dodds 1933): "All that is produced by secondary beings is in a greater measure produced from those prior and more determinative principles from which the secondary were themselves produced" (trans. Dodds, 55).

36 *El. theol.* 66.14–27 (Dodds 1933): "For the higher cause begins its operation upon secondary beings before its consequent, and is present concomitantly with the presence of the latter, and is still present and operative when the consequent has ceased to operate . . . Thus, for example, a thing must exist before it has life, and have life before it is human. And again, when the logical faculty has failed it is no longer human, but it is still a living thing, since it breathes and feels; and when life in turn has abandoned it existence remains to it, for even when it ceases to live it still has being. So in every case. The reason is that the higher cause, being more efficacious, operates sooner upon the participant . . . and in the activity of the secondary the higher is co-operative, because all the effects of the secondary are concomitantly generated by the more determinative cause; and where the former has withdrawn the latter is still present" (trans. Dodds, 67).

37 *El. theol.*, prop. 11, 12.15–17 (Dodds 1933) is reflected in prop. 5[6] of the *Liber de causis*, 70.2–7 (Bardenhewer 1882) = 147.32–148.40 (Pattin 1966).

38 This is the title in the extant Arabic manuscripts; an ancient Arabic source alludes to our text with the title that appears in most Latin manuscripts, namely, "Book of Causes"; for a discussion of this point, one may see D'Ancona (2011a).

of Theology, true being (i.e. the intelligible reality) can be either above eternity, or on the same level as it, or below it as one of its participants.[39] Instead, the *Liber de causis* applies Proclus' tripartition to the First Cause, Intellect, and Soul. By the same token, the First Cause turns out to be that pure and underived Being which is even above eternity: a move which shows how substantially the author of the *De causis* parts company with Proclus, whose first principle is located not only beyond Being, but also beyond the supra-essential henads.[40]

> Every higher being is higher than eternity and before it or is with eternity or is after eternity and above time. The being that is before eternity is the First Cause, since it is the cause of eternity.[41] The being that is with eternity is Intelligence,[42] since it is second being. Existing in a single state, it neither undergoes change nor is subject to destruction. The being that is after eternity and above time is the soul,[43] since it is lower on the horizon of eternity and above time.[44] The indication that the first cause is before eternity itself is that being in eternity is acquired. And I say that all eternity is being but not all being is eternity. So being is more common than eternity.[45] The First Cause is above eternity because eternity is its effect. The Intelligence is placed at eternity because it is coextensive with eternity and neither changes nor is subject to destruction. The soul is joined to eternity in a lower way,

39 *El. theol.* 80.15 (Dodds 1933): "There is true Being both prior to and in Eternity, and there is also true Being which participates Eternity" (trans. Dodds, 81).

40 The One of the Neoplatonic sources of the *De causis* (Proclus and Plotinus) is said to to be the pure, underived Being also in prop. 4, 65.7–10 (Bardenhewer 1882) = 142.44–49 (Pattin 1966); prop. 8[9], 78.8–79.1 (Bardenhewer 1882) = 157.98–178.2 (Pattin 1966); prop. 15[16], 88.10–89.1 (Bardenhewer 1882) = 169.86–87 (Pattin 1966) and 89.4–10 (Bardenhewer 1882) = 170.93–171.5 (Pattin 1966); prop. 17[18], 94.2–6 (Bardenhewer 1882) = 173.42–44 (Pattin 1966); prop. 19[20], 96.1–3 (Bardenhewer 1882) = 178.16–19 (Pattin 1966); prop. 31[32], 116.4–6 (Bardenhewer 1882) = 200.83–201.88 (Pattin 1966). This is a substantial modification with respect to Neoplatonic metaphysics, whose starting-point is the identity between the "one" of Plato's *Parmenides* and the Good "beyond being" of *Republic* VI; the modification occurs already in the Arabic adaptation of Plotinus, one of the sources of the *De causis* (I have tried to argue this point in D'Ancona [2000b] 51–97).

41 To this sentence, which substantially alters Proclus' doctrine, nothing corresponds in the *Elements of Theology*. It has a striking parallel in pseudo-Dionysius' *Divine Names*; for more details, one may see D'Ancona (1992a) and D'Ancona (1990).

42 Compare *El. theol.* 169, 146.24–25 (Dodds 1933): "Every Intelligence has its existence, its potency and its activity in eternity" (trans. Dodds, 147).

43 Cf. *El. theol.* 191, 166.26–27 (Dodds 1933): "Every participated soul has an eternal existence but a temporal activity" (trans. Dodds, 167).

44 This expression does not come from Proclus, but from the Arabic version of *Enn.* IV 4[28], 2.16–17, where Plotinus' τῆς ψυχῆς ἐν οἷον ἐσχάτοις τοῦ νοητοῦ κειμένης is rendered as "she is placed on the horizon of the intelligible world (*fī ufuqi l-'ālami l-'aqliyyi*)" (Badawī [1966], 33.14, trans. G. Lewis in Henry and Schwyzer [1959], 67).

45 Cf. *El. theol.* 87, 80.22 (Dodds 1933): "Thus Being is participated by a greater number of terms than Eternity" (trans. Dodds, 81).

since it is more susceptible to impression than is Intelligence, and it is above time, since it is the cause of time[46] (trans. Taylor, slightly modified).[47]

Having established the primacy of the First Cause and the hierarchy of the principles that come after it – Intellect, which is true, eternal being, and Soul, which belongs to the intelligible realm but in a lower way, in so far as it is connected to time also – the *De causis* proceeds to state that the transcendent First Cause does not limit itself to being the first item of a causal chain: indeed, it *creates* the derivative levels of reality.[48] The primacy of the remote cause means, as explained in prop. 1, that the highest principle produces what is essential for the effect, while secondary principles do nothing other than add more specific characteristics. In obedience to this rule, prop. 3 of the *De causis* states that the First Cause creates the *esse* of the Soul. It does so through the mediation of Intellect.[49]

Implying, as it does, that the creative power of God has recourse to a mediation, the axiom *Causa prima creavit esse animae mediante intelligentia* is one of the most debated in the process of the Latin reception of the *De causis.* Even more important for present purposes is the fact that the Proclean model is abandoned in favor of the Plotinian one. Instead of having the supra-essential henads and the divine "series" that spring from them[50] as the intermediate principles between the One and the many, the reader is presented with the typically Plotinian idea[51] that the first and

[46] Once again, this sentence does not come from the *Elements of Theology*, but from the Arabic Plotinus: see Badawī (1966), 31.9–10: "and the reason for her knowing the thing without time is that she is above time because she is the cause of time" (trans. Lewis in Henry and Schwyzer [1959], 65; loosely related to IV 4[28], 1.21–25).

[47] *Liber de causis*, prop. 2, 61.11–63.3 (Bardenhewer 1882) = 138.71–139.97 (Pattin 1966), English trans. by R. C. Taylor, 12–13.

[48] Creation features in the *De causis* as the mode of causality peculiar of the First Cause: see, in addition to the passages from props. 3 and 17[18] quoted below in the text, pp. 146–147, the following passages: prop. 4, 65.4–5 (Bardenhewer 1882) = 142.37–38 (Pattin 1966); prop. 8[9], 78.2–5 (Bardenhewer 1882) = 156.85–157.90 (Pattin 1966); prop. 15[16], 88.10–89.1 (Bardenhewer 1882) = 169.86–87 (Pattin 1966), and 89.4–10 (Bardenhewer 1882) = 170.93–171.5 (Pattin 1966); prop. 21[22], 99.6–100.1 (Bardenhewer 1882) = 182.73–82 (Pattin 1966), which is worth quoting in full: "And what is complete among us, although it is self-sufficient, nevertheless cannot create anything else, nor [can it] infuse anything from itself at all. Therefore, if this is so among us, then we say that the First Cause is neither diminished nor merely complete. Rather, it is above the complete because it creates things and infuses them with goodnesses with a complete infusion, because it is goodness without limit or dimensions" (English trans. by R. C. Taylor, 128).

[49] *Liber de causis*, prop. 3, 63.5–65.2 (Bardenhewer 1882) = 139.98–14.36 (Pattin 1966), English trans. by R. C. Taylor, 19–20.

[50] For a concise account of this structure of Proclus' universe, see *El. theol.* 145, 128.1–21 (Dodds 1933).

[51] This topic is especially prominent in *Ennead* V 1[10], which was translated into Arabic and has been one of the most influent among the Plotinian writings in Arabic philosophy; for more details on the Arabic tradition of this treatise, one may see D'Ancona (2012).

immediate offspring of the One is Intellect.[52] According to the *Liber de causis*, there are no more principles than One, Intellect, and Soul in the divine realm.[53] Soul features at the end of prop. 2 as that principle which is below Intellect but above time, namely the world of coming-to-be and passing away; then, in prop. 3, the author of the *De causis* borrows from prop. 201 of the *Elements of Theology* the description of the world-soul of his system:

> Every noble soul has three activities, for its activities consist of animate activity, intellectual activity, and divine activity. The activity is divine because soul provides for nature with the power present in it from the First Cause. Its activity is intellectual because [soul] knows things through the power of the Intelligence present in it. And, the activity is animate because soul moves the first body and all natural bodies, since it is the cause of the motion of bodies and the cause of nature's activity (trans. Taylor).[54]

At this point, the author abandons the *Elements of Theology* for a while and inserts a sentence of his own:

> Soul carries out these activities only because it is an image of a higher power. This is because the First Cause created the being of soul with the mediation of Intelligence. As a result, soul came to carry out a divine activity. Thus, after the First Cause created the being of soul, it placed it as something subject to Intelligence on which it carries out its activities (trans. Taylor, slightly modified).[55]

This sentence parts company with Proclus on two counts: first, the First Cause is said to *create*, thus paving the way to describe the primacy of its causal power as the uniqueness and priority of that action whose effect is the *esse* of the derivative levels of reality, while the secondary principles operate only *per modum formae*, a mode of causality which presupposes the *esse* of the effect. This point, implied in the statement quoted above, is made in prop. 17[18].

[52] See below, p. 148 and D'Ancona (1990).

[53] As we shall see below, this does not prevent the author of the *De causis* from asserting the existence of several separate substances of intellectual nature, as well as of many individual souls; but he shares with Plotinus the absence of any principle between the One and Intellect.

[54] *Liber de causis*, prop. 3, 63.5–9 (Bardenhewer 1882) = 139.98–140.10 (Pattin 1966), English trans. by R. C. Taylor, 19. Cf. *El. theol.* 201, 176.1–5 (Dodds 1933): "All divine souls have a threefold activity, in their threefold capacity as souls, as recipients of a divine intelligence, and as derived from gods: as gods, they exercise providence towards the universe, in virtue of their intellectual life they know all things, and in virtue of the self-movement proper to their being they impart motion to bodies" (trans. Dodds, 177).

[55] *Liber de causis*, prop. 3, 64.2–4 (Bardenhewer 1882) = 140.13–18 (Pattin 1966), English trans. by R. C. Taylor, 19.

> Now let us repeat and say that the First Being is at rest and the cause of causes. If it gives being to all things, then it gives [it] to them by way of creation. And the first life gives life to those which are under it, not by way of creation, but by way of form. Likewise, Intelligence gives knowledge and the remaining things to those which are under it only by way of form, not by way of creation, because this belongs to the First Cause alone (trans. Taylor, slightly modified).[56]

Second, the transmission of God's causal power is entrusted to Intellect alone, rather than to the supplementary levels in the hierarchy of the supra-sensible principles added by post-Plotinian Neoplatonists, especially Proclus. Following Plotinus' lead, the author of the *De causis* sticks to a tripartite hierarchy, as we have seen in prop. 2 (quoted above, pp. 144–145). The First Cause, Intellect, and Soul are the three principles of his universe.[57] Every time he finds in the *Elements of Theology* a feature of Proclus' henads that fits with his ideas about God – such as ineffability, omnipresence, or providence – he refers that feature to the First Cause itself. Although his monotheistic allegiance might count as a strong reason for him to get rid of Proclus' henads, even more important is the influence of Plotinus: as a matter of fact, his sincere faith in God Almighty[58] did not prevent him from glibly defining the Intellect as "divine"[59] or crediting the Soul with a "divine" action, as in the passage quoted above, whilst meticulously eliminating the henads in favor of the direct creation of the Intellect by the One.[60]

However, the *De causis* is first and foremost an adaptation of the *Elements of Theology*, and some philosophical ideas peculiar to Proclus are reflected in it. Among them, the most important is the priority of "being" with respect to every other intelligible reality. The first mix of Limit and Infinite, Being is for Proclus the highest in the triad of the meta-principles of the intelligible realm, which it composes together with Life and Intellect.[61] This topic is reflected in the *Liber de causis*, but the author made an effort

56 *Liber de causis*, prop. 17[18], 92.10–93.4 (Bardenhewer 1882) = 174.54–61 (Pattin 1966), English trans. by R. C. Taylor, 111.

57 On this, one may see D'Ancona (1992b).

58 Formulaic expressions such as "God blessed and sublime" and the like are frequent in the *De causis* as well as in the *Plotiniana arabica*.

59 *Liber de causis*, prop. 18[19], 93.6–8 (Bardenhewer 1882) = 174.63–68 (Pattin 1966); the source is *El. theol.* 111, 98.18–19 (Dodds 1933); prop. 22[23], 100.5–6 (Bardenhewer 1882) = 183.90–92 (Pattin 1966); the source is *El. theol.* 134, 118.20 (Dodds 1933).

60 See, for instance, the clear-cut formula of prop. 22[23], 100.8–9 (Bardenhewer 1882) = 183.97–99 (Pattin 1966): *Et intelligentia est primum creatum est est plus similis Deo sublimi, et propter illud regit res quae sub ea sunt.*

61 *El. theol.*, prop. 138, 122.7–12 (Dodds 1933): "Of all the principles which participate the divine character and are thereby divinized the first and highest is Being. For if, as has been shown, Being

to reshape this doctrine within the framework of his own hierarchy of principles. He agrees with the primacy of Being, ultimately derived from Proclus' prop. 138: for him *prima rerum creatarum est esse et non est ante ipsum creatum aliud.*[62] For him, this primacy fits with the uniqueness of God's causal power, which he understands as the production of the *esse* of the effect: an action that falls exclusively within the province of the First Cause. However, he is not ready to renounce the priority of Intellect among all the creatures: Intellect is for him that *primum creatum* which is *plus similis Deo sublimi,*[63] the unique intermediary cause between the First Principle and the rest of God's creatures. In order to force Proclus' Being to collapse with Intellect, he takes his opportunity with the definition of Being as πλῆθος ἑνιαῖον (prop. 138, p. 122.13 Dodds). If Being is such a "unitary manifold," says Proclus, it is because it is composed of Limit and Infinite (prop. 138, p. 122.14 Dodds), and the *Liber de causis* endorses this idea, with the sole modification of changing Proclus' Being into the *esse creatum.*[64] Immediately after, we read the following sentence, which has no counterpart in Proclus' prop. 138:

> All the part of it that follows the First Cause is *achili*, that is Intelligence, complete and ultimate in power and all the other goodnesses (trans. Taylor, slightly modified).[65]

In this way, the highest level of Being turns out to be the most perfect among the separate substances: that Intellect which is "complete and ultimate in power," the forerunner of Avicenna's First Intellect. After this sentence, clearly reminiscent of the passages of the Arabic Plotinus[66] that assert the immediate derivation of Intellect from the One, the author of the

is beyond both Intelligence and Life, since next to the One it is the most universal cause, it must be the highest participant. It has more of unity than Intelligence or Life, and is therefore necessarily more august. And prior to it there is no further principle save the One" (trans. Dodds, 123).

[62] *Liber de causis*, prop. 4, 65.4–5 (Bardenhewer 1882) = 142.37–38 (Pattin 1966). The source of this proposition is *El. theol.*, prop. 138, quoted in the preceding note.

[63] See above, n. 60.

[64] *Liber de causis*, prop. 4, 65.7–11 (Bardenhewer 1882) = 142.44–53 (Pattin 1966); English trans. by R. C. Taylor, 28: "it came to be so only because its nearness to the pure Being and the true One in which there is no multiplicity of any sort. Although created being is one, nevertheless it comes to be multiple because it receives multiplicity. And it became many only because, although it is simple and there is nothing among created things more simple than it, it is nevertheless composed of the finite and infinite."

[65] *Liber de causis*, prop. 4, 66.1–2 (Bardenhewer 1882) = 143.54–57 (Pattin 1966); English trans. by R. C. Taylor, 28.

[66] See, for instance, ps.-*Theol. Arist.* VII, 85.8–11 (Badawī 1966), loosely related to *Enn.* IV 8[6], 6.1–4: "If the First One is like that, that is, a true cause, then its effect is a true effect, and if it is a true light then the recipient of that light is a true recipient, and if it is a true good and the good emanates, then that on which it emanates is true also. If this is so, then it was necessary that the creator should

De causis has recourse to props. 170, 177, and 180 of the *Elements of Theology* in order to create a hierarchy of intellectual substances according to the degree of universality of the intelligible forms that they contemplate.[67] A similar rule of declension from universality to particularity, from simplicity to multiplicity, allows him to maintain that Soul is followed by individual, lower souls: in this way, a complete cosmic scheme is outlined in prop. 4[5], namely, a hierarchy of levels of being which proceed from one another, starting from the first Intellect immediately next to the One and reaching the sublunar world, where our souls are dwelling.[68] This procession implies the causal influence of each higher degree on the lower one: *et intelligentiae primae influunt super intelligentias secundas bonitates quas recipiunt a causa prima et intendunt bonitates in eis usquequo consequuntur ultimam earum.*[69]

The continuity in the chain of being does not undermine the transcendence of the First Cause.[70] The author is strongly committed to the

not be alone without creating any sublime thing to receive his light, that is, the mind" (English trans. G. Lewis in Henry and Schwyzer (1959), 243).

67 *Liber de causis*, prop. 4, 66.2–5 (Bardenhewer 1882) = 142.44–53 (Pattin 1966); English trans. by R. C. Taylor, 28–29: "And the intelligible forms in it are more extensive and more powerfully universal. The part of it that is lower is also an intelligence, though it is below the former intelligence in completeness, power, and goodnesses. The intelligible forms in it are not as extended in their breadth as they are in the former intelligence. First created being is wholly intelligence, yet intelligence in it is diverse in the way we have said. And because intelligence is diversified, the intelligible form there becomes diverse."

68 *Liber de causis*, prop. 4[5], 67.4–69.3 (Bardenhewer 1882) = 145.86–146.13 (Pattin 1966); English trans. by R. C. Taylor, 37: "The first higher intelligences which follow the first cause impress second, steadfastly abiding forms which are not destroyed, so that they might need to be repeated again. The second intelligences impress declining, separable forms, such as the soul . . . Every soul that receives more power from an intelligence is stronger in its impression. What is impressed by it is fixed, abiding steadfastly, and its motion is regular, continuous motion. But that [soul] in which the power of an intelligence is less is below the first souls in impression, and what is impressed by it is weak, evanescent and destructible. Nevertheless, although it is so, its impression still persists through generation." The topic of the permanence of the lower beings not individually but only as species does not come from Proclus, but directly from the Arabic Plotinus, and indirectly from Alexander of Aphrodisias. For the direct source, compare ps.-*Theol. Arist.* VII, p. 87.10–12 (Badawī 1966) (elaborating on *Enn.* IV 8[6], 6.26–28): "the sensible things are perishable essences, for they are pictures and likenesses of the true essences; their maintenance and their continuation by genesis and procreation is in order that they may abide and continue in imitation of the permanent continuing things of the mind" (English trans. G. Lewis in Henry and Schwyzer [1959], 245); for Alexander of Aphrodisias, see *Quaest.* III 5, p. 89.20–24 Bruns. This doctrine is reflected also in Alexander's treatise *On the Principles of the Universe*, lost in Greek but extant in Arabic, and partly preserved in the Istanbul MS mentioned above (see n. 23), where Proclus' propositions are intermingled with Alexander's *Questions*. For the topic of the permanence through generation, see Genequand (2001) 84, 4–11.

69 *Liber de causis*, prop. 4[5], 67.2–4 (Bardenhewer 1882) = 144.82–85 (Pattin 1966).

70 The *De causis* borrows also from prop. 122 of the *Elements of Theology*, where the divine henads are credited with omnipresence, but without hampering their transcendence: "All that is divine both exercises providence towards secondary existences and transcends the beings for which it provides: its providence involves no remission of its pure and unitary transcendence, neither does its separate

topic of the separatedness of the First Principle: having outlined the cosmic hierarchy, he goes back to the first, transcendent cause and formulates another proposition, where he claims that beyond all the degrees of the *esse superius* – the First Intellect and the intellectual substances, the Soul and the individual souls – a unique principle stands, whose separatedness is so absolute that no description can be made of it.

The well-known axiom *causa prima superior est omni narratione*[71] is grounded in Proclus' prop. 123 and mirrors its claim of the ineffability of the supra-essential henads,[72] but the *De causis* takes a completely new turn with respect to the *Elements of Theology* and their enumeration of the prerogatives of the divine henads. At the end of prop. 5[6], a sentence that – once again – has no counterpart in Proclus affirms that the ineffable First Cause, although exceeding any possibility to be known because of its perfect simplicity, is "signified" through Intellect:

> The First Cause is signified only from the second cause, which is the Intelligence and is referred to by the name of its first effect, but only in a higher and better way because the effect has, further, what belongs to the cause, but in a more sublime, better, and nobler way, as we have shown (trans. Taylor, slightly modified).[73]

The author of the *De causis* proves to be keenly aware of the theological implications of the claim that the First Cause is beyond description. The term for "description" is *ṣifa* (pl. *ṣifāt*), and the denial of the *ṣifāt Allāh* – the "attributes" of God – reveals his willingness to take into account the theological debate of his times.[74] To deny that God can be described by means of the attributes that we commonly use for denotating things serves the purpose of purifying the idea of God from the anthropomorphic features so frequent in the Qur'ān; does this imply that God is not knowing (*'alīm, ḥakīm*),[75] so paving the way to the denial of divine remuneration

unity annul its providence" (108.1–4 Dodds 1933, trans. p. 109), a sentence which runs as follows in the *De causis*, prop. 19[20], 95.2–5 (Bardenhewer 1882) = 177. 97–2 (Pattin 1966): "The First Cause rules all created things without being mixed with them. This is because rule does not weaken its unity, exalted over every thing, and does not destroy it, nor does the essence of its unity, separated from other things, prevent it from ruling things" (English trans. by R. C. Taylor, 120).

71 *Liber de causis*, prop. 5[6], 69.8 (Bardenhewer 1882) = 14.22 (Pattin 1966).

72 *El. theol.*, prop. 123, 108.25–110.9 (Dodds 1933).

73 *Liber de causis*, prop. 5[6], 71.6–9 (Bardenhewer 1882) = 149.59–64 (Pattin 1966); English trans. by R. C. Taylor, 46.

74 On the divine attributes in early Muslim theology see Allard (1965); Frank (1969) (reprinted in Frank [2007]). On the Neoplatonic source of the denial of attributes in God, see Frank (1965) (reprinted in Frank [2005], same pagination). For a comparison with the coeval philosophic literature in Arabic, one may see D'Ancona (2000a).

75 The two terms quoted are the most frequent in the Qur'ān to refer to God's omniscience: see Gimaret (1998), 253–278.

for the human behavior? By no means. Philosophy provides the key to understanding that, although absolutely transcendent with respect to any description, the First Cause can be known, in a sense: if not in itself, at least through Intellect, its first and highest creature. This is why after prop. 5[6] another description of the separate substances follows, and we find in the *De causis* a set of propositions devoted to Intellect and the intellectual separate substances (6[7]–12[13]), and then again two propositions on the soul (13[14]–14[15]).

The endorsement of Plotinus' theory of the direct emanation of Intellect from the One is especially prominent in prop. 8[9]. It states that the First Cause cannot be contained within the limits of any formal determination: the First Cause has no *yliathim*, a loan word for the Arabic *ḥilya* ("shape") which conveys, through the two-step process of translation from Greek into Arabic and from Arabic into Latin, the Greek μορφή.[76] Beyond any form, the First Principle cannot be known. As we have just seen in prop. 5[6], it stands alone, in its transcendence of any kind of knowledge, albeit of intellectual nature: this is the doctrine shared by the Neoplatonic school in its entirety and reflected in prop. 123 of the *Elements of Theology*. What is typically Plotinian, and is reflected in prop. 8[9] of the *De causis*, is the idea that the One, ἄμορφον καὶ ἀνείδεον in itself, has the Intellect as its first and most revealing image, ἄγαλμα τὸ πρῶτον ἐκφανέν: a tenet that Proclus would never have agreed upon, but that features in as many words in the *Liber de causis*.[77] Nevertheless, the author did not refrain from introducing a significant change with respect to Plotinus. The reason why the First Cause is beyond any Form is for him that it is pure Being: *et intelligentia est habens yliathim quoniam est esse et forma et similiter anima est habens yliathim et natura est habens yliathim, et causae quidem primae non est yliathim quoniam ipsa est esse tantum.*[78]

The absolute simplicity of the *esse tantum*, however, does not prevent it from being endowed with science and knowledge, provided that one is

76 This word appeared to the Latin readers to be connected with *hyle*, thus making the *Liber de causis* cite the doctrine of universal hylomorphism. See Taylor (1979).

77 In addition to the passage quoted above, n. 60, see *Liber de causis*, prop. 8[9], 78.2–5 (Bardenhewer 1882) = 156.85–157.90 (Pattin 1966): *Et causa quidem prima non est intelligentia neque anima neque natura, immo est supra intelligentiam et animam et naturam, quoniam est creans omnes res. Verumtamen est creans intelligentiam absque medio et creans animam et naturam et reliquas res mediante intelligentia.*

78 *Liber de causis*, prop. 8[9], 78.8–79.1 (Bardenhewer 1882) = 157.98–158.2 (Pattin 1966). There is no scholarly consensus about the sources of this doctrine, which features also in the Arabic adaptation of Plotinus, but parts company with both Plotinus and Proclus' doctrine of the One beyond being. According to Thillet (1971); Pines (1971); and Taylor (1998), this doctrine can be traced back to Porphyry; according to the present writer, it can be traced back to the pseudo-Dionysian *Divine Names* (D'Ancona [1995c]).

aware that there is no common measure between this "science" and that of creatures, even of the separate intellectual substances among the latter:

> Divine knowledge is not like intellectual knowledge, nor is it like the soul's knowledge. Rather, it is above the intelligence's knowledge and the soul's knowledge because it creates the various kinds of knowledge. The divine power is above all intellectual, animated, and natural power because it is the cause for every power (trans. Taylor, slightly modified).[79]

The cause of every power, God is said to be infinite.[80] Once again, what was for Proclus a principle subordinated to the One but higher than Being – the πρώτη ἀπειρία – becomes in the *Liber de causis* a feature of the One itself. First, the dependence of every power from the First Infinite is stated.[81] Then, this First Infinite is identified as the First Cause itself:

Ens autem primum creans est infinitum primum purum[82]

The modification is substantial: instead of pointing to the omnipresence and priority to Being of the principle ἀπειρία, as Proclus does, the author of the *De causis* maintains here that all the powers that are infinite depend upon a First Cause whose infinite power is the cause of theirs. A convoluted sentence follows, which combines Proclus' tenet that all the ἄπειροι δυνάμεις depend upon the principle of αὐτοαπειρία with the topic of the infinity of the separate intellectual substance, reminiscent of the eternity of the celestial nature stated in Aristotle's *De caelo* – a pivotal text in the circle of al-Kindī, and one which states in as many letters, in its Arabic version, that the "spiritual reality" is "unchanging and unalterable, perfect, complete and perpetual in eternity."[83] In the *Liber de causis* the First Being, that is, the pure One and God Almighty, is above infinity; as for the first created being, that is, the separate intellectual substance, it is endowed with infinity *propter suam acquisitionem ab infinito primo puro*. The author insists that infinity does not prevent it from being created and dependent upon the First Being: *ens primum est quod ponit res quibus non est finis.*

79 *Liber de causis*, prop. 8[9], 78.5–8 (Bardenhewer 1882) = 157.91–97 (Pattin 1966), English trans. by R. C. Taylor, 65.

80 *Liber de causis*, prop. 15[16], 88.2–3 (Bardenhewer 1882) = 168.70–72 (Pattin 1966): "All the unlimited powers are dependent upon the first infinite, which is the power of powers," English trans. by R. C. Taylor, 103.

81 The source of the passage of the *De causis* quoted in the preceding note is *El. theol.* 92, 82.23–24 (Dodds 1933): "The whole multitude of infinite potencies is dependent upon one principle, the First Infinity" (trans. Dodds, 83).

82 *Liber de causis*, prop. 15[16], 88.10–89.1 (Bardenhewer 1882) = 169.86–87 (Pattin 1966).

83 See Endress (2012a): the quotation, p. 280 (from the Arabic version of *De caelo* I 9, 279a30–35).

> This is because, if for powerful beings there is no limit, due to their acquisition [of infinity] from the first pure infinite, due to which they are beings, and if the first being itself is that which determines things for which there is no limit, then without doubt it is above the infinite. But the first created being, namely, Intelligence, is not the infinite, but rather it is called "what is infinite" and is not called "what is itself that which is not finite." Therefore, the First Being is the measure of first intellectual beings and of second sensible beings because it is that which has created beings and measured them with a measure appropriate to every being (trans. Taylor, slightly modified).[84]

The cosmological implications of this move are clear, once it is taken for granted that God's causality expands on all the creatures through the mediation of Intellect: the system of the separate substances whose circular motion has neither beginning nor end depends upon the infinite power of the First Cause itself, and it grants the effusion of the divine power onto the world of coming-to-be and passing away.

> And the remaining simple goodnesses, such as life, light, and their like, are the causes of all things that have goodnesses, because the infinite is from the First Cause. And the first created [being] is the cause of all life, and similarly the remaining goodnesses, which descend from the First Cause upon the first created [being], which is the Intelligence, then descend upon the remaining intelligible and corporeal effects with the mediation of the Intelligence (trans. Taylor, slightly modified).[85]

If the eternity of the celestial substance comes straightforwardly from Aristotle's *De caelo*, the topic of the cosmic "providence" granted through the perfection and regularity of the celestial movements is typical of Alexander of Aphrodisias. This topic is reflected in some of the *Questions* of the Arabic Alexander that are intermingled with the *Proclus Arabus*.[86] In the *Liber de causis* the hierarchy of the degrees of being according to their duration is established on the basis of Proclus' distinction between two kinds of perpetuity: the perpetual steadfastness without time which is typical of the intelligible realm, and the perpetual process with no beginning nor end, which characterizes the celestial substance.[87] This distinction allows

[84] *Liber de causis*, prop. 15[16], 89.1–9 (Bardenhewer 1882) = 169.88–170.00 (Pattin 1966), English trans. by R. C. Taylor, 104.

[85] *Liber de causis*, prop. 15[16], 90.1–6 (Bardenhewer 1882) = 171.6–14 (Pattin 1966), English trans. by R. C. Taylor, 104.

[86] I have tried to argue for the connection between the pseudo-*Theology of Aristotle*, the *Liber de causis*, and Alexander's *Quaest.* II 3 and II 19 in D'Ancona (2011b).

[87] *El. theol.*, prop. 55, 52.30–54.3 (Dodds 1933): "From this is apparent that the perpetuity we spoke of was of two kinds, the one eternal, the other in time; the one a perpetual steadfastness, the other

the *De causis* to set up a tripartite hierarchy below the transcendent First Cause: the intelligible realm which is eternal and immobile, the celestial spheres endowed with sempiternal movement, and the sublunar world ruled by time, where some substances begin and come to an end while time continues to flow.

> Therefore, it is already clear that among substances there are some that are sempiternal above time. And among them there are sempiternal [substances] equal to time and time does not overreach them. And among them there are [some] that are bounded by time, and time overreaches them from the higher of them down to the lower of them, and [these] are substances that fall under generation and corruption (trans. Taylor).[88]

Having descended the chain of being until he has reached the sublunar world, the author of the *Liber de causis* shows a specific concern for soul. We have just seen him adopting the distinction of Proclus' prop. 55 between the two kinds of perpetuity – a proposition located in the first part of the *Elements of Theology*, where the basic rules of Proclus' universe are set. Now, he has recourse to prop. 106, which provides him with the distinction between those beings whose οὐσία and ἐνέργεια are both eternal, and those beings whose οὐσία is eternal, whereas the ἐνέργεια falls under time.[89] Such substances, which steer a middle course between what is eternal and what is generated and corruptible, are the individual souls. Within the sublunar world our souls perform their activities in time; nevertheless, their substance is eternal. The last proposition of the *Liber de causis* borrows from Proclus' prop. 107 the idea that if there is such a thing, namely a thing which is eternal in some of its features and temporal in some others, it is at one and the same time "being" and "becoming."[90] For Proclus, this paves the way for making the world of becoming depend upon Soul, which is both "being" and "becoming"; for making Soul depend upon what is totally eternal, the latter, in turn, depend on the principle Eternity, and Eternity, in turn, depend on Being.[91] This was not the conclusion the author of the

a perpetual process; the one having its existence concentrated in a simultaneous whole, the other diffused and unfolded in temporal extension; the one entire in itself, the other composed of parts each of which exists separately in an order of succession" (trans. Dodds, 53–55).

88 *Liber de causis*, prop. 29[30], 113.5–8 (Bardenhewer 1882) = 198.34–42 (Pattin 1966), English trans. by R. C. Taylor, 154.

89 *El. theol.*, prop. 106, 94.21–31 (Dodds 1933), reflected in *Liber de causis*, prop. 30[31], 113.10–115.6 (Bardenhewer 1882) = 198.43–200.72 (Pattin 1966).

90 *El. theol.*, prop. 107, 94.32–96.3 (Dodds 1933), reflected in *Liber de causis*, prop. 31[32], 115.8–116.6 (Bardenhewer 1882) = 200.73–201.88 (Pattin 1966).

91 *El. theol.*, prop. 107, 96.3–8 (Dodds 1933): "From this it is apparent that coming-to-be, which is temporal even in its existence, is dependent upon that which shares partly in Being, partly in

De causis was looking for. He did not want to conclude his handbook on rational theology without boldly reaffirming that even the lowest among the substances are embraced underneath the power of the unique omnipresent First Cause. To this end, he combines Proclus' prop. 107 with prop. 116, where we are told that every god is participable except the One. The way in which the author of the *De causis* creates his general conclusion out of these two propositions is instructive. The chain of beings of Proclus' prop. 107 turns out to be the assessment of the universal dependence of every being upon the First Being, that is the First Cause:

> Therefore, it is already clear from what we have said that everything that comes to be, falling under time in its substance, has a substance that depends on the pure Being, which is both the cause of durability and the cause of all things, whether sempiternal or destructible (trans. Taylor).[92]

The First Cause is indeed the One, which is the cause of the unity of everything, being itself that unique principle which does not owe its unity to anything else. Proclus' prop. 116 provides the demonstration that there must be an unparticipated principle and that it cannot but be unique;[93] nevertheless, the last sentence of the *De causis* is, once again, independent of Proclus:

> Iam ergo manifestum est et planum quod omnis unitas post unum verum est acquisita creata, verumtamen unum verum purum est creans unitates, faciens acquirere non acquisitum, sicut ostendimus.[94]

By these words "Aristotle" makes his "Exposition of the Pure Good" agree with the Muslim *tawḥīd*, the doctrine of God's unicity, provided that it is interpreted philosophically, as the claim of the divine transcendence and perfect simplicity. The same fictitious "Aristotle" had announced, in the Prologue of his "Theology," that after having written the *Metaphysics* he was going to compose the *Uṯūlūǧiyyā* – a Greek word meaning "discourse on the Divinity."[95]

coming-to-be, participating at once Eternity and Time; and this latter is dependent upon the fully eternal; and the fully eternal upon Eternity; and Eternity upon Being, which is pre-eternal" (trans. Dodds, 97).

92 Guagliardo, Hess, and Taylor (1966), 161.

93 *Liber de causis*, prop. 31[32], 116.7–118.2 (Bardenhewer 1882) = 201.89–202.11 (Pattin 1966); the source is *El. theol.* 116, 102.13–25 (Dodds 1933).

94 *Liber de causis*, prop. 31[32], 118.2–5 (Bardenhewer 1882) = 202.12–203.16 (Pattin 1966).

95 The author of the Prologue of the ps.-*Theology* claims that he had already completed an account of the four causes – matter, form, efficient cause, and perfection – in his "Book on which is after the Physics": ps-*Theol. Arist.*, 5.1–2 Badawī (1966), trans. G. Lewis (quoted 1966), 486. Later on (p. 5.12 Badawī) the author refers again to the *Metaphysics* as to his own work, this time under the title *maṭāṭāfūsīqā*.

> Now our aim in this book is the first discourse on the Divine Sovereignty, and the explanation of it, and how it is the First Cause, eternity and time being beneath it, and that it is the cause and the originator of causes, in a certain way, and how the luminous force steals from it over mind and, through the medium of mind, over the universal celestial soul, and from mind, through the medium of soul, over nature, and from soul, through the medium of nature, over the things that come to be and pass away. This action arises from it without motion; the motion of all things comes from it and is caused by it, and things move towards it by a kind of longing and desire (trans. Lewis, slightly modified).[96]

Anyone who is ready to compare the *Theology* and the *De causis* realizes that the aim that "Aristotle" sets for himself in this passage is better exemplified in the *De causis* than in the reworking of the Plotinian treatises, and this even though what is typical of the *De causis* if compared with the *Elements of Theology* comes, in fact, from the Arabic Plotinus. Elsewhere I have tried to argue that the procedures of reorganization of Plotinus' treatises and of Proclus' propositions are very similar to one another, and that in both cases they bear the hallmarks of an attitude that, amateurish as it might be if compared with the Greek sources used, is nevertheless typical of a philosopher. I also ventured to suggest that the philosopher who authored the reworking of both the Arabic Plotinus and the Arabic Proclus was al-Kindī.[97] One may remark that this flies in the face of the fact that there are topics on which the *De causis* and al-Kindī are at odds: in his personal works, al-Kindī is explicitly committed against the eternity of the celestial sphere, which is on the contrary asserted in the *De causis*. However, the *De causis* is allegedly *Aristotle's* book on rational theology, not *Kindī's*; and the latter frames much of his exposition of metaphysics against the backdrop of the idea that he will endorse Greek philosophy, especially Aristotle's, not without adapting it, if necessary.[98] To discuss this point would go beyond the limits of this chapter; in addition, I am not sure that identifying the author is really an important issue about the *De causis*. What is worth noting, instead, is that the curricular position assigned to the *De causis* in the Latin universities of the Middle Ages reflects, without any acquaintance with the pseudo-*Theology* on the part of the medieval readers,[99] the status

96 Ps.-*Theol. Arist.* 6.7–12 (Badawī 1966), trans. Lewis, 487. The slight modification consists in sticking, in the first sentence, to the reading of some manuscripts of the pseudo-*Theology* (followed by Badawī [1966], 6.7) which read "first discourse" instead of "discourse."

97 D'Ancona (1995b) and D'Ancona (2001b); see also D'Ancona (2011b).

98 Abū Rīda (1950), I, 102.1–4 and 103.10–12; English trans. by Ivry (1974), 57–58.

99 The pseudo-*Theology* was translated into Latin in 1519.

of the pinnacle of the metaphysics that, in the fiction of the Prologue, had been granted to Neoplatonic theology by "Aristotle" himself.

Bibliography

Abū Rīda, M. 'A. (ed.) (1950) *Rasā'il al-Kindī al-falsafiyya*, Cairo.

Aegidius Romanus (1550) *Super Librum de causis*, Venice. Reprinted Frankfurt a. M. 1968.

Allard, M. (1965) *Le problème des attributs divins dans la doctrine d'al-Aš'arī et de ses premiers grands disciples*, Beirut.

Alverny, M.-T. d' (1954) "Avendauth?," in *Homenaje a Millás Vallicrosa*, Barcelona, vol. 1, 19–43. Reprinted in d'Alverny (1993).

(1989) "Les traductions à deux interprètes, d'arabe en langue vernaculaire et de langue vernaculaire en latin," in G. Contamine (ed.), *Traduction et traducteurs au Moyen Âge*, Paris, 193–206.

(1993) *Avicenne en Occident. Recueil d'articles . . . réunis en hommage à l'auteur*, Paris.

Anawati, G. C. (1956) "Prolégomènes à une nouvelle édition du *De causis* arabe (*Kitāb al-ḫayr al-maḥḍ*)," in *Mélanges Louis Massignon*, Damascus, vol. 1, 73–110.

(1974a) *Études de philosophie musulmane*, Paris.

(1974b) "Le néoplatonisme dans la pensée musulmane. État actuel des recherches," in *Plotino e il neoplatonismo in Oriente e in Occidente. Atti del convegno internazionale, Accademia Nazionale dei Lincei, Roma 5–10 ottobre 1970*, Rome, 339–405.

Badawī, 'A. (1947) *'Arisṭū 'inda l-'arab. Dirāsāt wa-nuṣūṣ ġayr manšūra*, Cairo.

(ed.) (1955) *al-Aflāṭūniyya al-muḥdaṯa 'inda l-'Arab*, Cairo.

(ed.) (1966) *Aflūṭīn 'inda l-'arab. Plotinus apud Arabes. Theologia Aristotelis et fragmenta quae supersunt*, Cairo. Translation by G. Lewis in Henry and Schwyzer (1959).

Bardenhewer, O. (ed.) (1882) *Die pseudo-aristotelische Schrift Ueber das reine Gute bekannt unter dem Namen Liber de causis*, Freiburg in Breisgau. Reprinted Freiburg im Breisgau and Frankfurt 1961.

Boese, H. (1985) "Wilhelm von Moerbeke als Übersetzer der *Stoicheiosis theologike* des Proclus," *Abhandlungen der Heidelberger Akademie der Wissenschaften, Philos.-Hist. Klasse* 5, Heidelberg.

(ed.) (1987) Proclus, *Elementatio theologica translata a Guillelmo de Morbecca*, Leuven.

Brams, J. and Vanhamel, W. (eds.) (1989) *Guillaume de Moerbeke. Recueil d'études à l'occasion du 700e anniversaire de sa mort (1286)*, Leuven.

Burnett, C. (2001) "The Coherence of the Arabic–Latin Translation Program in Toledo in the Twelfth Century," *Science in Context* 14: 249–288.

D'Ancona, C. (1989) "Le fonti e la struttura del *Liber de causis*," *Medioevo* 15: 1–38.

(1990) "*Cause prime non est yliathim. Liber de Causis*, prop. 8[9]: le fonti e la dottrina," *Documenti e studi sulla tradizione filosofica medievale* 1: 327–351.

(1992a) "*Esse quod est supra eternitatem.* La Cause première, l'être et l'éternité dans le *Liber de causis* et dans ses sources," *Archives d'histoire doctrinale et littéraire du Moyen Âge* 59: 41–62.

(1992b) "La doctrine de la création *mediante intelligentia* dans le *Liber de causis* et dans ses sources," *Revue des sciences philosophiques et théologiques* 76: 209–233.

(1995a) *Recherches sur le Liber de causis.* Paris.

(1995b) "al-Kindī et l'auteur du *Liber de causis*," in D'Ancona (1995a), 155–193.

(1995c) "La doctrine néoplatonicienne de l'être entre l'Antiquité tardive et le Moyen Âge. Le *Liber de causis* par rapport à ses sources," in D'Ancona (1995a) 121–153.

(2000a) "*Causa prima superior est omni narratione.* Il tema delle *ṣifāt Allāh* nel primo neoplatonismo arabo," *Oriente Moderno* 19/ 80: 519–555.

(2000b) "L'influence du vocabulaire arabe: *Causa prima est esse tantum*," in Hamesse and Steel (1998), 51–97.

(2001) "Pseudo-*Theology of Aristotle*, Chapter I: Structure and Composition," *Oriens* 36: 78–112.

(ed.) (2007) *The Libraries of the Neoplatonists, Proceedings of the Meeting of the European Science Foundation Network, "Late Antiquity and Arabic Thought"*. . . Leiden.

(2011a) "Nota sulla traduzione latina del *Libro di Aristotele sull'esposizione del Bene Puro* e sul titolo *Liber de causis*," in S. Perfetti (ed.), *Scientia, fides, theologia: Studi di filosofia medievale in onore di Gianfranco Fioravanti*, Pisa, 89–101.

(2011b) "La *Teologia* neoplatonica di 'Aristotele' e gli inizi della filosofia arabo-musulmana," in Goulet and Rudolph (2011), 135–190.

(2012) "Le traité de Plotin *Sur les trois substances qui sont des principes* dans le corpus néoplatonicien arabe," *Studia graeco-arabica* 2: 303–324.

D'Ancona, C. and Taylor, R. C. (2003) "Le *Liber de causis*," in R. Goulet (ed.), *Dictionnaire des philosophes antiques*, Supplement to vol. 1, Paris, 599–647.

Denifle, H. and Chatelain, É. (eds.) *Chartularium Universitatis Parisiensis*, vol. 1, Paris and Brussels (repr. 1964).

Dodds, E. R. (ed. and trans.) *Proclus: The Elements of Theology*; 2nd edn., Oxford 1963.

Endress, G. (ed.) (1973) *Proclus Arabus. Zwanzig Abschnitte aus der Institutio Theologica in arabischer Übersetzung*, Wiesbaden and Beirut.

(1995) "Sa'īd b. Ya'kūb al-Dimashkī," in *Encyclopedia of Islam*, 2nd edn., vol. VIII, cols. 858–859.

(1997) "The Circle of al-Kindī. Early Arabic Translations from the Greek and the Rise of Islamic Philosophy," in Endress and Kruk (1997), 43–76.

(2007) "Building the Library of Arabic Philosophy: Platonism and Aristotelianism in the Sources of al-Kindī", in D'Ancona (2007), 319–350.

(2012a) "Platonizing Aristotle. The Concept of 'Spiritual' (*rūḥānī*) as a Keyword of the Neoplatonic Strand in Early Arabic Aristotelianism," *Studia graeco-arabica* 2: 269–283.

(2012b) "Proclus de Lycie. Œuvres transmises par la tradition arabe," in R. Goulet (ed.), *Dictionnaire des philosophes antiques*, vol. vb, Paris, 1657–1674.

Endress, G. and Kruk, R. (eds.) (1997) *The Ancient Tradition in Christian and Islamic Hellenism, Studies on the Transmission of Greek Philosophy and Sciences dedicated to H. J. Drossaart Lulofs on his Ninetieth Birthday*, Leiden.

Fauser, W. (ed.) (1993) *Alberti Magni Opera omnia . . . 17/2: De causis et processu universitatis a prima causa*, Münster.

Frank, R. M. (1965) "The Neoplatonism of Jahm ibn Safwān," *Le Muséon* 78: 395–424. Reprinted in Frank (2005).

(1969) "The Divine Attributes according to the Teaching of Abū 'l-Hudhayl al-'Allāf," *Le Muséon* 82: 451–506. Reprinted in Frank (2007).

(2005) *Philosophy, Theology and Mysticism in Medieval Islam. Texts and Studies on the Development and History of Kalām*, vol. I, ed. D. Gutas, Aldershot.

(2007) *Early Islamic Theology: The Mu'tazilites and al-Ash'arī. Texts and Studies on the Development and History of Kalām*, vol. II, ed. D. Gutas, Aldershot.

Genequand, C. (2001) *Alexander of Aphrodisias on the Cosmos*, Leiden, Boston, and Cologne.

Gimaret, D. (1998) *Les noms divins en Islam. Exégèse lexicographique et théologique*, Paris.

Goulet, R. and Rudolph, U. (eds.) (2011) *Entre Orient et Occident. La philosophie et la science gréco-romaines dans le monde arabe*, Entretiens sur l'Antiquité Classique 57, Fondation Hardt, Vandœuvres and Geneva.

Grabmann, M. (1928) "Mittelalterliche lateinische Aristotelesübersetzungen und Aristoteleskommentaren in Handschriften spanischer Bibliotheken," *Sitzungsberichte der Bayerischen Akademie der Wissenschaften, philos.-philol. und hist. Klasse* 5, Munich. Reprinted in M. Grabmann, *Gesammelte Akademieabhandlungen*, Paderborn, Munich, and Vienna (1979), vol. I, 391–402.

(1934) "Eine für Examinazwecke abgefasste Questionensammlung der Pariser Artistenfakultät aus der ersten Hälfte des XIII. Jahrhunderts," *Revue néoscolastique de philosophie* 36: 211–229.

Guagliardo, V. A., Hess, C. R., and Taylor, R. C. (eds. and trans.) (1996) *St. Thomas Aquinas: Commentary on the Book of Causes*, Washington, DC.

Hamesse, J. and Steel, C. (eds.) (1998) *L'élaboration du vocabulaire philosophique au Moyen Âge. Actes du Colloque International de Louvain-la-Neuve et Leuven, 12–14 septembre 1998 organisé par la S.I.E.P.M.*, Turnhout, 51–97.

Henry, P. and Schwyzer, H.-R. (eds.) (1959) *Plotini Opera*, vol. II, *Enneades IV–V, Plotiniana Arabica*, Paris and Leuven.

Ivry, A. L. (trans.) (1974) *Al-Kindi's Metaphysics, A Translation of Ya'qūb ibn Isḥāq al-Kindī's Treatise "On First Philosophy" (fī al-Falsafah al-Ūlā)*, with introduction and commentary, Albany, NY.

Kraye, J., Ryan, W. F., and Schmitt, C. B. (eds.) (1986) *Pseudo-Aristotle in the Middle Ages, The Theology and Other Texts*, London.
Lafleur, C. (ed.) (1992) *Le guide de l'étudiant d'un maître anonyme de la faculté des arts de Paris au XIIIe siècle: édition critique provisoire du ms. Barcelona, Arxiu de la Corona d'Aragó, Ripoll 109, ff. 143ra–158va*, Laval.
Lewin, B. (1955) "Notes sur un texte de Proclus en traduction arabe," *Orientalia Suecana* 4: 101–108.
Libera, A. de (1997) "Structure du corpus scolaire de la métaphysique dans la première moitié du XIIIe siècle", in C. Lafleur and J. Carrier (eds.), *L'enseignement de la philosophie au XIIIe siècle. Autour du "Guide de l'étudiant" du ms. Ripoll 109. Actes du colloque international*, Turnhout, 61–88.
Luna, C. and Segonds, A.-Ph. (2012) "Proclus de Lycie," in R. Goulet (ed.), *Dictionnaire des philosophes antiques*, vol. vb, Paris, 1546–1657.
Munk, S. (1859) *Mélanges de philosophie juive et arabe*, Paris (repr. 1982).
Pattin, A. (ed.) (1966) "Le *Liber de causis*. Édition établie à l'aide de 90 manuscrits avec introduction et notes," *Tijdschrift voor Filosofie* 28: 90–203.
Pines, S. (1955) "Une version arabe de trois propositions de la *Stoicheiosis theologike* de Proclus," *Oriens* 8: 195–203. Reprinted in *The Collected Works of Shlomo Pines*, vol. II: *Studies in Arabic Versions of Greek Texts and in Mediaeval Science*, Jerusalem and Leiden, 1986, 278–286.
(1971) "Les textes arabes dits plotiniens et le courant 'porphyrien' dans le néoplatonisme grec," in Schuhl and Hadot (1971), 303–317.
(1986) "Hitherto Unknown Arabic Extracts from Proclus' *Stoicheiosis Theologike* and *Stoicheiosis Physike*," in *The Collected Works of Shlomo Pines*, vol. II: *Studies in Arabic Versions of Greek Texts and in Mediaeval Science*, Jerusalem and Leiden, 287–293.
Rosenthal, F. (1955) "From Arabic Books and Manuscripts V: A One-Volume Library of Arabic Philosophical and Scientific texts in Istanbul," *Journal of the American Oriental Society* 75: 14–23.
(1961) "From Arabic Books and Manuscripts VII: Some Graeco-Arabica in Istanbul," *Journal of the American Oriental Society* 81: 7–12.
Saffrey, H.-D. (ed.) (1954) Thomas d'Aquin, *Super Librum de causis expositio*, Fribourg and Leuven (2nd edn. 2002).
(1963) "L'état actuel des recherches sur le *Liber de causis* comme source de la métaphysique au Moyen Âge," in A. Zimmermann (ed.), *Die Metaphysik im Mittelalter = Miscellanea medievalia*, vol. II, Berlin, 267–281.
Schuhl, P. M. and Hadot, P. (eds.) (1971) *Le néoplatonisme. Actes du colloque international du CNRS Royaumont 9–13 juin 1969*, Paris.
Taylor, R. C. (1979) "St. Thomas and the *Liber de causis* on the Hylomorphic Composition of Separate Substances," *Medieval Studies* 41: 506–513.
(1981) "The *Liber de causis (Kalām fī maḥḍ al-khayr)*, A Study of Medieval Neoplatonism," Diss. University of Toronto.
(1982) "Neoplatonic Texts in Turkey: Two Manuscripts Containing Ibn Ṭufayl's *Ḥayy Ibn Yaqẓān*, Ibn al-Sīd's *Kitāb al-Ḥadā'iq*, Ibn Bājja's *Ittiṣāl al-'Aql bi-l-Insān*, the *Liber de causis* and an Anonymous Neoplatonic Treatise on Motion," *Mélanges de l'Institut dominicain d'études orientales* 15: 251–264.

(1986) "The *Kalām fī maḥḍ al-khayr* (*Liber de causis*) in the Islamic Philosophical Milieu," in Kraye, Ryan, and Schmitt (1986), 37–52.

(1992) "A Critical Analysis of the Structure of the Kalām fī maḥḍ al-khair (*Liber de causis*)", in Morewedge, P. (ed.), *Neoplatonism and Islamic Thought*, Albany, NY, 11–40.

(1998) "Aquinas, the *Plotiniana Arabica* and the Metaphysics of Being and Actuality," *Journal of the History of Ideas* 59: 217–239.

(2012) "Primary Causality and ibdāʿ in the *Liber de causis*," in A. Mensching-Estakhr and M. Städtler (eds.), *Wahrheit und Geschichte. Die gebrochene Tradition metaphysischen Denkens. Festschrift zum 70. Geburtstag von Günther Mensching*, Würzburg, 113–136.

Thillet, P. (1971) "Indices porphyriens dans la pseudo-*Théologie d'Aristote*," in Schuhl and Hadot (1971), 293–302.

Thillet, P. and Oudaimah, S. (eds.) (2001–2002) "Proclus arabe. Un nouveau *Liber de causis*? Présenté, édité et traduit par P. T. et S. O.," *Bulletin d'études orientales* 53–54: 293–368.

Van Ess, J. (1965) "Jüngere orientalistische Literatur zur neuplatonischen Überlieferung im Bereich des Islam," in K. Flasch (ed.), *Parusia. Studien zur Philosophie und zur Problemgeschichte des Platonismus, Festgabe für J. Hirschberger*, Frankfurt a. M., 333–350.

(1966) "Über einige neue Fragmente des Alexander von Aphrodisias und des Proklos in arabischer Übersetzung," *Der Islam* 42: 148–168.

Van Riet, S. (ed.) (1972) *Avicenna Latinus. Liber de anima seu sextus de naturalibus, Édition critique de la traduction latine médiévale*, vol. 1, Leuven and Leiden.

Zimmermann, F. W. (1986) "The Origins of the So-Called *Theology of Aristotle*," in Kraye, Ryan, and Schmitt (1986), 110–240.

(1994) "Proclus Arabus Rides Again," *Arabic Sciences and Philosophy* 4: 9–51.

Zimmermann, F. W. and Brown, V. B. (1973) "Neue arabische Übersetzungstexte aus dem Bereich der spätantiken griechischen Philosophie," *Der Islam* 50: 313–324.

PART II.3 *Medieval Byzantine philosophy*

CHAPTER 6

Michael Psellos

Dominic J. O'Meara

Introduction

Proclus, it has been suggested, experienced a veritable "renaissance" in Byzantium in the eleventh and twelfth centuries, a renaissance due in large part to the efforts of Michael Psellos.[1] The extent of this renaissance will be discussed by M. Trizio in the next chapter. In this chapter I will try to describe Psellos' pioneering work in inspiring this renewed interest in Proclus. Psellos (1018 – after 1078) is in many respects perhaps the most remarkable of Byzantine philosophers.[2] Coming from a well-connected background in Constantinople – he provides a fascinating description of his family in his *Epitaphium ad matrem* – he managed, thanks to his literary talents, to secure the patronage of the emperor Constantine IX Monomachos (1042–1055) and was named by the emperor "Head of the Philosophers," a title which seemed to have involved teaching philosophy. Psellos was also interested in many other subjects – rhetoric, law, medicine, music, poetry, Christian theology, among other things – and was also active in promoting and writing in these fields. The stature he created and cultivated for himself as a master of rhetoric, philosophy, and the sciences enabled him to remain close to the life of the Byzantine imperial court in Constantinople in which, in his opinion, he played no insignificant part. His political career had its ups and downs. At one point he had to retire temporarily to the cover of monastic life (1054), where he took the monastic name Michael. He managed to return later to the imperial court and continued to share in imperial politics. We know little about the last part of his life. As well as composing his *Chronographia*, a very interesting account of the imperial history of his time, Psellos produced an immense body of work, of which there is as yet no complete catalogue, which included his correspondence, poems, rhetorical show-pieces, theological

[1] Podskalsky (1976), a fundamental study of the subject.
[2] Duffy (2002). On Psellos' life see Kaldellis (2006), 3–16.

writings, polemical tracts, and many scientific and philosophical treatises and commentaries reflecting in part at least his teaching.[3]

In a well-known passage in the *Chronographia*, Psellos describes his intellectual education and indicates in particular the importance that Proclus had in this education. It will be appropriate then to start with an analysis of the way in which Psellos himself, in this passage, sees his relation to Proclus. An attempt will then be made to identify the particular works of Proclus which Psellos read and used in his own writings. Finally we will consider the various ways in which Psellos used Proclus and the attitudes he expressed in doing this. In what follows, a survey based on presently available information will be offered, a survey which must remain incomplete since, in the case of Proclus, significant works of Proclus known to Psellos are no longer extant (as we will see), and, in the case of Psellos, a number of his writings remain unpublished or have not yet been published in a reliable and usable form.

Proclus the great haven

In describing in the *Chronographia* (VI, 36ff.) how he attracted the patronage of the emperor, Psellos describes in some detail the education which brought him this patronage. This education included studies in rhetoric and in philosophy. As regards philosophy (36), this involved logic, physics, mathematics, and "first philosophy" (metaphysics). At that time, Psellos claims (37), philosophy was dying: he alone, by himself, revived it, not finding worthy teachers for this purpose. Or rather, Psellos mentions, he did have teachers, passing from inferior to better ones and thence passing to their superiors, Aristotle and Plato.

> From there, as if completing a cycle (*periodon*), I came to a Plotinus, a Porphyry and an Iamblichus, after which I progressed to the most admirable Proclus, as if arriving in a great haven, where I sought all science and accuracy of thoughts. After this, intending to ascend to first philosophy and to be initiated to pure science, I took up first the knowledge of incorporeals in what is called mathematics, which have an intermediate rank between the nature that concerns bodies and the thought that is free of relation to bodies.[4]

Psellos then goes on to describe how he passed from his mathematical studies to higher philosophy, to a wisdom transcending demonstration,

[3] For a listing, see Moore (2005).

[4] *Chronographia* (= *Chron.*) VI, 38 (Del Corno, Impellizzeri, Criscuolo, and Ronchey 1984) (Sewter's English translation here is somewhat misleading).

which only an inspired intellect can know, reading "certain ineffable books" (40) which he happened to come across, not, however, claiming to have reached perfect knowledge in such matters. Psellos then goes on to speak of his studies in rhetoric and in another, superior philosophy, namely that of Christian revelation (42).

The passage which I have just summarized and quoted should probably not be taken as a straightforward autobiographical narrative. One element which might meet with some skepticism is Psellos' claim that he "revived" philosophy by himself, that philosophy was reborn through him. The claim seems exaggerated. Yet it cannot be denied that Psellos took an unprecedented interest in the manuscripts of the ancient philosophers, that he exploited these manuscripts extensively in composing his own works, and that, as we will see, he merits a place in the long line of Platonist philosophers who, through some remarkable intellectual sympathy, gave rebirth to Platonism: Numenius, Plotinus, and Eriugena before Psellos; Plethon and Ficino after. Perhaps Psellos' teachers set him on the path of a passion which carried him much further, in a lone search and study of neglected philosophical manuscripts.

Another element of Psellos' narrative which might provoke doubt is the schematic way in which he presents his former teachers, as if they constituted a hierarchy, the inferior teacher being followed by a superior one, an ascending hierarchy going up from persons to books (we presume!), the books of Aristotle, Plato, the Neoplatonists, culminating with Proclus. The fact that Aristotle precedes Plato in Psellos' list of teachers is probably not without significance: in the curriculum of late antique Neoplatonism, a cycle of studies in Aristotle preceded the study of Plato, since Aristotle was considered to be a preparation for (and inferior to) Plato. The Neoplatonic commentators on Plato naturally follow Plato and it is important that Proclus appears as the culmination of the list. This suggests that Proclus corresponds, for Psellos, to the summit of philosophy.

A further element in Psellos' narrative which echoes the curricular practices of the late antique Neoplatonic schools is the fact that he structures his philosophical studies according to the division of philosophy and the pedagogical principles followed by these schools. They divided philosophy into logic (the instrument of philosophy), practical philosophy (ethics, politics), and theoretical philosophy (physics, mathematics, and metaphysics, "first philosophy"), a division which also represented a progression in which mathematics functions as an intermediate between physics and metaphysics, facilitating the transition to the knowledge of transcendent incorporeal reality. It seems somewhat unlikely that Psellos' actual education corresponded to that offered in a late antique Neoplatonic school. But such an education, as he read of it, would have seemed to him an ideal, allowing him to structure and retell the story of his own studies as the story of an ideal education.[5] Here also, it seems, Proclus is a central figure: he provided, as if a "great haven," "all science." The image of a great haven[6] suggests not only the security and calm that Psellos could find in Proclus' works, after the uncertainties and troubles in traversing other books, but also the availability of all necessary provisions: in Proclus Psellos could find knowledge relating to all parts of philosophy.

In view of these somewhat propagandistic and idealizing aspects of Psellos' account of his education we might ask to what extent the realities of Psellos' knowledge and use of Proclus correspond to what he says in the passage of the *Chronographia*. Which works of Proclus did Psellos actually read and how did he use these works?

Proclus' works in Psellos

It is not possible to be completely sure about the list of works of Proclus which Psellos actually read. One reason for this is that sometimes passages in Psellos seem full of Proclean terms and concepts, without corresponding exactly to a specific text in Proclus. It is as if Psellos had assimilated Proclus so thoroughly that he could write without any close dependence on a particular source passage in Proclus. Thus we can sometimes find various parallel texts in Proclus, without being certain about identifying Psellos' precise source. Psellos could also read works by Proclus which have since disappeared, which means that, here again, we are not always in a position to be able to identify his source. However, there are cases where we can be quite sure. The following is a fairly conservative list of these cases.

The *Elements of Theology* is probably Psellos' favourite Proclean text. He names the text by its title a number of times[7] and uses it extensively in his philosophical, theological, and rhetorical works, citing propositions taken from throughout the work.[8] He sometimes uses the same propositions

[5] Podskalsky (1976), 516 describes the account given by Psellos as a "Manifest des wahren Philosophiestudiums." Compare the account Psellos gives of his studies in *Ep. ad matr.* 27–30.

[6] The image is of course a literary commonplace. Its use by Psellos in the *Chronographia* is analyzed by Littlewood (2006), 28–30, and its use by Proclus (who does not, however, use the term *limne*, Psellos' term, but that of *hormos*) in a metaphysical context is discussed by Van den Berg (2000).

[7] *Philosophica minora* (= *PM*) II, 21.31–32 (O'Meara 1989); *Theologica* (= *T*) I, 7.46; 11.22–23 (Gautier 1989).

[8] *T* I, 22.38–39; 54.132–136; 62.27ff.; 105.88–95; *T* II, 18.34; 33.9–17 (Westerink and Duffy 2002); *PM* I, 36.481–506 (Duffy 1992); *PM* II, 21.3–23.15; *Orationes panegyricae* (= *OP*) 2.514 (Dennis 1994b) (this list is not exhaustive).

repeatedly[9] and makes considerable use of the book in composing the little encyclopedia, the *De omnifaria doctrina* (= *OD*), which, in various versions, he dedicated to his imperial patrons.[10] This makes it likely that Proclus' *Elements of Theology* was not just a convenient source of philosophical knowledge for Psellos: he could also use it in his teaching, or at least as providing materials for his teaching.

Another work of Proclus which Psellos names[11] and which he found very useful is the *Commentary on Plato's Timaeus*, from which he compiled extracts explaining the abstruse mathematics of Plato's account in the *Timaeus* of the making of the soul.[12]

With regard to mathematics it seems that Psellos also consulted Proclus' *Commentary on Euclid*. Although, as far as I know, he does not name this work, he does appear to be using it, for example in the passage quoted above from the *Chronographia*, where he also cites, as does Proclus' commentary, a passage of the (pseudo-) Platonic *Epinomis*.[13]

Proclus' three monographs (known as the *Tria opuscula*), the *De decem dubitationibus*, the *De providentia*, and the *De malorum subsistentia*, also provided philosophical materials for Psellos in the *OD* and in other texts.[14] Of these the *De providentia* is named by title.[15]

A lost work of Proclus that Psellos has been shown to be using is the *Commentary on Plotinus*. Psellos make extensive use of Plotinus' *Enneads*. But in some chapters of the *OD* as well as in another philosophical text we read phrases taken from *Ennead* I, 1, followed by commentary which must be that of Proclus.[16] No further parts of this commentary have been found in Psellos and we know nothing about how, and how much, he had access to the commentary.

Another lost work by Proclus which Psellos seems in some way to have been able to use was the *Commentary on the Chaldaean Oracles*. Psellos was fascinated with Chaldaean philosophy as interpreted by Proclus and we can find many references to Proclus in this connection throughout his work. Perhaps the "ineffable books" to which the passage in the *Chronographia*

9 See *T* I, 54.133–134 and 57.95–96.

10 *De omnifaria doctrina* (= *OD*) chs. 16, 21–30, 101 (Westerink 1948).

11 *OD* ch. 157; *T* I, 54.120–123 (Gautier 1989).

12 *OD* chs. 51–54; *PM* II, nos. 4–6. The question of the authorship of the *Commentary on Plato's Psychogony* attributed to Psellos in Migne, *Patrologia graeca* 122, 1077–1101 (it is also attributed to Soterichus in some manuscripts) remains to be examined.

13 See *PM* I, 3.53–60; *Chron.* VI, 38–39 (Del Corno, Impellizzeri, Criscuolo, and Ronchey 1984) (compare Proclus, *In Eucl.* 3.1ff.; Psellos' reference to the *Epinomis* 991e is found in Proclus, *In Eucl.* 42.11–12).

14 *OD* chs. 17, 94–97, 100, 195–197; *PM* II, no. 26.

15 *T* II, 18.35–37.

16 Westerink (1959); *OD* chs. 31–36 and *PM* II, no. 14.

refers included Proclus' commentary. Psellos himself produced a commentary on Chaldaean oracles, which includes explanations of Proclean origin.[17] He also composed various versions of a summary of Chaldaean philosophy.[18] However, the precise relation between all of this material and Proclus' lost *Commentary on the Chaldaean Oracles* is not clear. Did Psellos use Proclus' *Commentary* directly?[19] Proclus' *Commentary* seems to have been a massive affair, over one thousand pages: could Psellos still find it? Did he read it all? Or did he just have access to an abridged version of it[20] or perhaps merely a part of it? Was his knowledge indirect, through some intermediary source, for example Procopius of Gaza's (lost) refutation of Proclus?[21] Since Proclus' work is lost, it is difficult to settle these matters. Extracts from Proclus' *Chaldaean Philosophy* have been found in manuscripts linked to Psellos and his school, and corresponding passages have been found in Psellos' writings.[22] Are these extracts derived from Proclus' *Commentary*? We also have a work by Proclus entitled *On Hieratic Art*, which Psellos uses as a source for Chaldaean doctrine.[23] What is the relation of this work to Proclus' *Commentary*? The situation, it can be seen, is very complex[24] and we probably do not have the information necessary for clarifying it completely. I will return to the subject below, but perhaps we can at least say for the moment that Proclus' *Commentary on the Chaldaean Oracles* was an important source of information for Psellos, whether he had direct or indirect access to it, to a part or to the whole of it, and that he was eager to gather any other texts he could find in Proclus on Chaldaean lore.

It is likely that Psellos had access to and used other lost texts of Proclus, for example in composing his chapters on psychology and on the hierarchy of virtues in the *OD*.[25] But here we can do little more than speculate.

As regards other writings by Proclus which have survived, at least in part, in particular the *Commentaries* on the *Alcibiades*, on the *Cratylus*, on the *Republic*, and on the *Parmenides* and the monumental *Platonic Theology*, even if Psellos does not, as far as I know, name them explicitly or evidently quote from them,[26] it seems quite likely that he consulted them, at least in

[17] *PM* II, no. 38.

[18] *PM* II, nos. 39–41; other summaries of Chaldaean philosophy are found throughout Psellos' work; see the list in Lewy (1978), 473–479.

[19] Lewy (1978), 477. [20] Kroll (1894), 3–5. [21] See Westerink (1942). [22] See next section.

[23] See below, n. 47. [24] I examine the subject in more detail in O'Meara (2011b).

[25] See Westerink (1959), 22 and 29.

[26] See *T* II, 29.9–10, which C. Luna and A. Segonds are confident is a quotation from Proclus, *In Parm* (in their introduction to Proclus, *In Parm.* cdxviii); however, the editors of *T* II are more cautious and merely refer for comparison ("cf.") to Proclus. The use of texts such as the *In Parm.* and *In*

part, such was his curiosity and diligence in making use of the manuscripts of Greek philosophy that he could find.

Psellos' use of Proclus' works

Psellos was an avid reader not only of Proclus, but also of Plotinus, Porphyry, Iamblichus, Syrianus, Philoponus, Simplicius, Olympiodorus, and others. But the survey I have proposed above tends to confirm Psellos' indications in the *Chronographia* that he could find in Proclus "all science": physics, mathematics, metaphysics, "hieratic art," perhaps psychology and ethics. That Proclus was also for him the culmination of philosophy is confirmed in other texts, where Psellos calls Proclus the "most philosophical" (of philosophers) and the most "theological" among them.[27] But why this preference for Proclus as a philosopher? It will be necessary in this regard to deal first with the following questions: In what ways did Psellos make use of Proclus? How did he integrate Proclus in the world of a Byzantine Christian intellectual of the eleventh century?

Before approaching these matters, it will be useful to take note of the way in which Psellos worked in composing his philosophical writings.[28] At a first stage Psellos (and perhaps also some of his pupils) collected excerpts taken from a wide range of philosophical manuscripts. This material, some of which we can still see in an important Oxford manuscript (Barocci 131), provided a sort of database from which Psellos could derive content for producing short didactic pieces on various themes. These didactic pieces, in some cases, could be composed as if they were letters written in response to a query, Psellos merely adding a few introductory lines to the selected extracts (often neither identified as such, nor identified as to their source), together with perhaps a few critical remarks and some concluding words. These materials (or the manuscripts from which they were drawn) could also provide content for some of Psellos' theological pieces or for his more formal philosophical and rhetorical works. Psellos also works in this way with the texts of Proclus, which allows us to see what he selects from Proclus and how he integrates it in his teaching and writing. In the following I will survey the ways in which Psellos uses Proclus' different works, going from

Alc. by Byzantine authors who studied with Proclus or with his successor John Italos, in particular Eustratius of Nicaea, Michael of Ephesos (see next chapter) and Petritsi (see below, Chapter 8) also makes it likely that this use began with Psellos himself. See Steel (2002).

27 *T* I, 105.88; 22.38–39; see *Orationes forenses* (= *OF*) 1.290–292 (Dennis 1994a).

28 I discuss this in more detail in O'Meara (1998).

the collection of excerpts from them to the compilation of didactic texts and the composition of more formal pieces.

The Elements of Theology

We might begin with a more formal piece, Psellos' *OD*. This little encyclopedia covers in short chapters a range of topics going from God, the Trinity, the angels, to intellect, soul, the virtues, nature, the body, matter, meteorological and natural phenomena. Various sources of information are used on these topics, but the more philosophical chapters on the metaphysical order constituted by God, intellect, soul are excerpted from Proclus' *Elements of Theology*: on the infinity of God (*OD* ch. 16, using Proclus' props. 86, 152, 154, 155, 158); on intellect (*OD* chs. 21–28, using Proclus' props. 166–178); on soul (*OD* ch. 30, using Proclus' props. 184–197). Towards the end of the encyclopedia, Psellos returns to Proclus' *Elements of Theology*, excerpting passages for the chapters on the return of all things to the divine (*OD* ch. 101, using Proclus' prop. 39) and on eternity and time (*OD* ch. 107, using Proclus' prop. 104). The general structure of being roughly corresponds to that which Psellos elsewhere[29] derives from the *Elements of Theology* (props. 20–22), without naming his source: God, the henads, Being, intellect, soul, form, and matter. In the *OD*, Proclus' metaphysical doctrines seem to fit seamlessly with Christian teaching: the phrases on divine infinity taken from Proclus (who is not named) in ch. 16 are joined to a passage from Gregory of Nazianzen (who is named). And Proclus' metaphysics of universal return to the divine, in *OD* ch. 101 (where Proclus is named) is presented as having been said before and more accurately by (the pseudo-) Dionysius.

With this we might compare two short didactic pieces, presented as if they are letters, *On Intellect* (*Philosophica minora* II, 10) and *On Soul* (*PM* II, 11), where Psellos uses the same range of propositions from Proclus' *Elements of Theology* as that used in the *OD* on the same subjects. However, the material selected is not always the same: some of the Proclus of the *OD* chapters is not in the two letters, which include, however, some Proclus not in the *OD*. Furthermore, in the letter *On Intellect*, Psellos indicates that he is summarizing the philosophical opinions of "the Greeks" and names his source, Proclus' *Elements of Theology*. In the letter *On Soul*, Psellos adds that some of these Greek doctrines agree with "our oracles" (i.e. Christian

[29] *T* I, 62.27–49.

revelation), but that there is more that is bitter in them than is sweet.[30] The bitter is identified in the second half of the letter (22.22) as the "most ridiculous things" which follow, namely extracts from Proclus' props. 196, 198–211 concerning soul's astral vehicle (*ochēma*), cosmic soul, and the divine souls which accompany the gods. In the corresponding chapter of the *OD* (ch. 30), these "ridiculous things" are not included, the chapter ending with an extract from Proclus which also concludes the first part of the letter *On Soul*.[31] Finally, in comparing the use of the same materials from Proclus' *Elements of Theology* in the two letters and in the *OD*, we can note that Proclus' polytheism remains in the two letters but becomes monotheism in the *OD*.[32]

The comparison of these two letters with the *OD* thus suggests two modalities in the integration of Proclus' text: the compilation of excerpts to produce didactic pieces, in which Psellos presents the philosophical opinions of "the Greeks," with indications of what is unacceptable for a Christian; and the reuse of these excerpts in what is acceptable in them in a metaphysical system which, Psellos claims, harmonizes with Christian theology (Gregory of Nazianzus) or is anticipated by it (pseudo-Dionysius).[33]

Comparable results concerning the use of Proclus' *Elements of Theology* can be reached in examining other works of Psellos. For example, in his treatise *On the Theology and Critique of Greek Doctrines* (*PM* II, 35), Psellos quotes a series of Proclus' propositions (35, 39, 81, 90, 103, 109) and of Porphyry's *Sentences*, Proclus being named and compared with the pseudo-Dionysius, who, Psellos claims, said the same things before Proclus, Proclus giving them a more precise, syllogistic expression (119.1–3). But, here also, not all is good: Psellos rejects some of Proclus' doctrines (e.g. 119.13), finds some useful (118.19) and some indifferent, neither true nor false in relation to Christian revelation (119.24–25). In a more ambitious formal piece *On the Twenty-Four Letters* [of the alphabet] (*PM* I, 36), Psellos uses Proclus' props. 124, 117, 125, 160, and 131, not naming his source but mentioning their demonstrative evidence (485) and naming Dionysius as having philosophized most accurately about these things (507–8).

30 *PM* II, 11, 22.3–4. On the theme in Psellos of the bitter and sweet in the Greek heritage, see Duffy (2001).

31 See also *PM* II, 119.9–12 and 119.25–120.2.

32 Compare *El. theol.* 162, 2–3 with *PM* II, 11, 22.9 and *OD* 30, 4–5.

33 Even then, however, Proclus takes his precautions, warning his imperial patron in the Epilogue of the *OD* that he may not have completely succeeded in purifying the Greek doctrines he has included in the work.

The Commentary on Plato's Timaeus

For the question of the immortality of soul in the *OD* (chs. 51–54), in what sense soul has immortality and in what sense soul is generated, Psellos turns to Proclus' *Commentary on Plato's Timaeus*, which is used to report the opinion of "Plato," finally named in ch. 54 and compared, without criticism, to St. Paul (54.5). The extremely difficult mathematical account of the generation of the soul (*psychogonia*) in Plato's *Timaeus* is not included in the *OD*, perhaps as not suitable to the elementary character of the work. But it is treated elsewhere, in three didactic pieces (*PM* II, 4–6), where Psellos, in providing an exegesis of the passages in Plato, does not mention his source (Proclus' *Commentary*) and shows, it appears, great mathematical virtuosity.

Proclus' *Commentary on Plato's Timaeus* is named in *OD* ch. 157 on the question of the eternity of the world. "Our" (Christian) doctrine that the world is neither ungenerated nor indestructible is first stated and then contrasted with the view, of Aristotle and Plato. The chapter ends with a report of Proclus' view, as argued in the *Commentary*, that the world is both ungenerated and generated.

Finally, Proclus' *Commentary on Plato's Timaeus* appears to be the main source of Psellos' treatise *Greek Dispositions concerning Divine Demiurgy and Differences of the Individual Characteristics of the Superior Genera* (*PM* II, 36). Here, however, in reporting the views of "the Greeks," Psellos uses Proclus (and other Neoplatonic sources) more loosely, more widely, and in a more synthetic way: the excerpts have given way to a more formal and continuous account.

The Tria opuscula

Coming back to the *OD*, when discussing (ch. 19) the question of how God (who is unchanging) knows changing things, Psellos makes use of Proclus' *De decem dubitationibus* (7–8), applying Proclus' solution (Proclus is not named) to the example of God's (fore-) knowledge of Adam's disobedience. The same text of Proclus (3–4) is used again later (ch. 96), on the hierarchy of knowledge going from divine providence down to human sense perception, and (ch. 96), on the necessity of evil according to Plato's *Timaeus* (Proclus, *De dec. dub.* 28). The theme of evil is also dealt with in the next chapters (*OD* 97, 98, 100), where Psellos uses Proclus' treatment of the subject in *De malorum subsistentia* (9–10): there is no absolute evil; matter is not evil; the angels are not evil (on angels Psellos also refers in ch. 98 to

Gregory of Nazianzus). Psellos used the same texts of Proclus elsewhere, in a short didactic piece *On Evil* (*PM* II, 26), where the non-existence of evil and its coming about in the relation between things which are good is explained (using *De dec. dub.* 30). Like the pseudo-Dionysius before him, Psellos found in Proclus a way of explaining evil so as to show its possibility in a reality created by an absolute good, God. Finally, in *OD* chs. 195–197, Psellos makes use of Proclus again, of the *De malorum subsistenta* (23–24) and of the *De providentia* (15–18, 24–29), on the levels of soul and of life and the purification and ascent of the soul to the vision of God. The ascent to this vision is also described in a short piece *On the Soul* (*PM* II, 1), in language that is Proclean.

The Commentary on the Chaldaean Oracles

We know very little about the immense work on the Chaldaean oracles composed by Proclus. It obviously discussed the Chaldaean oracles, but in what sense was it a "commentary" on them? Marinus' description of the work (*Life of Proclus* 26) is somewhat vague: a title is not given for the work, which appears to have been a compilation in which Proclus brought together the exegeses of his predecessors (in particular those of Porphyry and Iamblichus), with appropriate critical appreciation, elaborating other Chaldaean subjects (*hypotheseis*) and most important commentaries (*hypomnēmata*) on the oracles themselves. The work thus appears to have been a vast synthesis of materials, including explanation of the oracles themselves, the exegesis provided by Proclus' predecessors, and other Chaldaean topics. Probably derived in some way from this thousand-page synthesis are the six pages of excerpts, entitled *By Proclus. From the same Chaldaean Philosophy*,[34] which are found in a Vatican manuscript (*Vaticanus graecus 1026*) which also includes, just before, texts of Psellos on the Chaldaean oracles (*PM* II, 38 and 39). It is thus very likely that these excerpts from Proclus (Excerpta Vaticana = *Exc. Vat.*) come from Psellos' school and probable that Psellos himself had made them. We find a good number of these excerpts again in Psellos' compilation *Various Greek Opinions on Soul* (*PM* II, 9), where Proclus is named at the beginning, with no other comment than that "some of the Greeks dare even to discuss clearly our [Christian] mysteries" (17.17–18). The order of the excerpts in this compilation follows that of the *Exc. Vat.* Parts of the *Exc. Vat.* can also be found

[34] Edition and French translation in des Places' edition of the Chaldaean oracles, 206–212. A contemporary of Psellos, Symeon Seth, refers to Proclus' exegesis of "Chaldaean Philosophy" (Faraggiana di Sarzana (1990)).

in Psellos' *Commentary on the Chaldaean Oracles* (*PM* II, 38), but here the order in which the excerpts are used does not exactly follow that of the *Exc. Vat.*, and, in one case, the excerpt is given in a fuller and more accurate version than that found in *PM* II, 9.[35] It thus appears that both works of Psellos make use of the *Exc. Vat.*, probably in an earlier, more extensive version.[36] Could this version have been extensive enough to provide Psellos with the Proclean materials for the composition of his *Commentary on the Chaldaean Oracles* (*PM* II, 38)? Can Psellos' *Commentary* (some twenty pages long) allow us to reconstruct a good deal more of Proclus' lost work than we have in the *Exc. Vat.*?

Psellos' *Commentary* consists of a series of Chaldaean oracles, each oracle being provided with an explanation (*exegesis*). There is no introduction or conclusion and the series of oracles follows no evident order.[37] Sometimes Psellos adds to what must be a Proclean exegesis some comparison with Christian doctrine, showing incompatibility (e.g. 127.19–23) or partial correspondence with Christian theology (e.g. 131.10–14). The *Commentary* is composed then of two parts: (a) the series of oracles, each often followed first by its Proclean exegesis and then, in some cases, (b) by Psellos' comments on the relation of this to Christian theology. Part (a) of the *Commentary*, we might conclude, would be what Psellos excerpted from (a version of) Proclus' lost work.

However, the situation would seem to be more complicated than this. At one point Psellos cites some words of Plotinus as if they were a Chaldaean oracle (128.18) and at another point (132.13) adds a line to a Chaldaean oracle that must have been part of a comment by Proclus, as if it were part of the oracle.[38] Some oracles are quoted in the *Exc. Vat.*, but the excerpts do not have the form of a series of exegeses of particular oracles. One wonders then if Psellos, using as his source a fuller version of the *Exc. Vat.*, might not have intervened more actively, isolating particular oracles (or what he thought were such in Proclus) and then selecting Proclean exegesis for each. In a sense, then, Psellos might actually have *created* a commentary on the Chaldaean oracles, such as no longer existed at his time, on the basis of

35 Compare *Exc. Vat.* 211.21–24 with *PM* II, 9, 20.12–13 and with *PM* II, 38, 144.21–24.

36 Thus a quotation from Proclus in *PM* II 38, 143.14–18 is also found in *PM* II, 9, 19.1–7 but is missing in *Exc. Vat.* Other quotations from Proclus in Psellos which may derive from a more extensive version of the *Exc. Vat.* are: *OF* I. 311–341 (Dennis 1994a); *T* I, 19.74–75; 47.43–46; *Scripta minora* (= *SM*) I, 248.1–249.9 (Kurz and Drexl 1936).

37 Plethon, in his commentary on the Chaldaean oracles, oracles which he took from Psellos, gave them another order, omitted some, and corrected the meter of others; see the edition by Tambrun-Krasker and Tardieu (1995).

38 This fact is eliminated in des Places' edition.

Proclean materials like those preserved in the *Exc. Vat.* Further support for this hypothesis is provided by the observation that Psellos seems to have used other sources of information besides (a more extensive version of) the *Exc. Vat.* The clearest case is the exegesis of Chaldaean oracle 10. Here (142.21) Psellos first says that the doctrine of the oracle is Christian and true. The exegesis that is then given corresponds closely to *OD* ch. 101, where Psellos refers to Proclus' *Elements of Theology* (prop. 39) and says that pseudo-Dionysius said the same things more clearly before.[39] Another case may be the exegesis of Chaldaean oracle 103 (143.20–144.2), where Psellos appears to be using Proclus' *De providentia* (in particular 13).[40]

Psellos also produced a short summary of the Chaldaean system in various versions, as short didactic pieces (*PM* II, 39–41), or as part of more literary works.[41] The ultimate origin of at least some of the information contained in these summaries may be Proclus' lost work, which might easily have included such doctrinal syntheses. However, one of these summaries appears in conjunction with what must be an excerpt from Procopius' (lost) critique of Proclus.[42] Valuable information which Psellos is alone in giving us on the supposed divine inspiration of the Chaldaean oracles[43] must also have come, directly or indirectly, from Proclus.

Proclus' lost work may also be the ultimate source of a text entitled *By Proclus. On the Hieratic Art of the Greeks.*[44] The mention of "the Greeks" in the title suggests that the text is an excerpt made by Psellos[45] or by someone like him. Psellos himself refers in a didactic piece to Proclus' exegesis of the "hieratic art,"[46] and he uses Proclus' text in some of his works.[47] Psellos' short piece *On Sacrificial Art* (*PM* II, no. 42) seems to be related to this Proclean material and to have the same origin.[48] In these texts the Chaldaean sacrificial art is explained in terms of a Proclean conception of the close linking of all levels of reality, including the vegetal and mineral, and the use of this linking in making corresponding and appropriate sacrifices.

39 See also *PM* II, 118.24–119.3.
40 Compare also *OD* ch. 105.
41 See the extracts collected in des Places' edition of the Chaldaean oracles, 218, 221–222 (= *PM* I, 3. 125–134), 223 (= *T* I, 23. 36–55).
42 *T* I, 23.36–55; Westerink (1942); see *OF* 1.294.
43 *PM* I, 46.44–51.
44 Published by Bidez (1928).
45 As suggested by Bidez in his edition.
46 *T* II, 37.32–35; the reference in *PM* I, 36.32–34 to Proclus writings on *mageion* may be to the same work.
47 *PM* I, 16.29–30 and 222–240 ; *PM* II, 38, 125.3–5; *T* I, 11.25–28; 51.38–42; 61.15ff.; see *Orationes hagiographicae* (= *OH*) 4.679–683 (Fisher 1994).
48 Bidez 155.

Conclusion

In the previous section we have explored Psellos' philosophical workshop, so to speak, identifying the specific Proclean materials he collected and selected and the various ways in which he worked up these materials in his writings. Psellos' works give us a rare opportunity to carry out such an exploration, which allows us to draw conclusions, not only as to what Psellos knew of Proclus' work and how he used it, but also as to how he viewed Proclus as a philosopher.

Proclus, it emerges, provided Psellos with an elaborate metaphysical system which could be adapted, with some modifications, to Christian theology. Psellos was aware, of course, of the difference, for example, between the Christian Trinity and the absolute unity of the Neoplatonic first principle.[49] But the general structure of reality, going from the first cause, to intellect, soul, nature, body, matter, could be adopted, even if particular points concerning different parts of this structure might require correction. Psellos could accept Proclus' explanations of God's infinity, God's foreknowledge of contingent things, the return of things and of the soul to God, and evil. The agreement of Proclus on such matters with the pseudo-Dionysius could serve to give Proclus some theological support. In his comments Psellos notes Proclus' clarity, accuracy, and demonstrative explanation. Such qualities apply best to the *Elements of Theology*, where Psellos found an extremely useful metaphysical system. Perhaps Proclus was the "most philosophical" of philosophers on these grounds, as providing a scientific account of the highest part of philosophy, "first" philosophy.

The metaphysical chain of beings of the *Elements of Theology* extends beyond the realm of the divine (the domain covered by Proclus' manual), down to the lowest levels of material reality. Hierarchical continuity is maintained by the use of intermediate levels which link the lower with the upper.[50] Soul is a pivotal intermediary, linking transcendent intelligible reality with the material world. Through Proclus' *Commentary on Plato's Timaeus* and his work on Chaldaean philosophy, Psellos had an extremely detailed view of the lower, material reaches of the hierarchy of being and of the intermediate position of soul. However, this mediation which, in Proclus, establishes the unity and continuity of all things, becomes, in Psellos,

[49] See, for example, *PM* I, 3.212–215; 46.100–110; Gemeinhardt (2001).

[50] For the general principle see Proclus, *El. theol.*, prop. 132. The importance of this principle in Psellos is very well brought out by Jenkins (2006). See also Proclus, *El. theol.*, prop. 190, quoted by Psellos, *OP* 2.513–515.

the locus of tensions which are characteristic of him:[51] tensions between the superior theoretical life, the life of knowledge (soul by itself), and the practical life (soul in body); between the ascetic life (which he admired in his mother and father)[52] and the political life (which he preferred);[53] between pure philosophy and a philosophy joined to rhetoric.

To these tensions in Psellos we should add the one between the philosophy of the "Greeks" and Christian doctrine. Here also Psellos is a mediator torn between conflicting forces.[54] An appearance of resolution is attained by the tactic of separating the acceptable from the ridiculous in pagan philosophy and affirming the absolute authority of Christian doctrine. But Psellos seems to be far too interested in pagan religious practices. Here again, Proclus' importance is clear: in Proclus' work on Chaldaean philosophy Psellos could find a philosophically organized and interpreted mass of information on sacrificial rituals, demonology, and magic. Psellos appears to be fascinated by this material, transmits it to his students, and on occasion makes a show of it in his more formal pieces. His explanation to his students of his interest is that the wise man should not neglect ancient lore (*logoi*).[55] The explanation is somewhat cursory. Psellos was playing with fire (perhaps encouraged by the curiosity and sympathy of some of his entourage), as John Italos, his pupil and successor, condemned and reduced to silence in 1082, would discover.

Bibliography

Barber, C. and Jenkins, D. (eds.) (2006) *Reading Michael Psellos*, Leiden.

Bazán, F. (trans.) (1991) *Oráculos caldeos con una selección de testimonios de Proclo, Pselo y M. Italico*, Madrid.

Berg, R. van den (2000) "Towards the Paternal Harbour, Proclean Theurgy and the Contemplation of the Forms," in A.-Ph. Segonds and C. Steel (eds.), *Proclus et la Théologie platonicienne*, Paris, 425–443.

Bidez, J. (ed.) (1928) "Proclus, *De arte sacrificiali*," in *Catalogue des manuscrits alchimiques grecs*, vol. VI, Brussels, 148–151 (edition with translation and notes [in modern Greek] by P. Kalligas, Athens 2009).

Criscuolo, U. (ed. and trans.) (1989) *Michael Psellos: Epitaphium in matrem. Autobiografia, Encomio per la madre*, Naples (translation in Kaldellis [2006]).

Del Corno, D., Impellizzeri, S., Criscuolo, U., and Ronchey, S. (eds. and trans.) (1984) Michael Psellos, *Chronographia*, Milan.

51 As pointed out by Jenkins (2006), 143–148.
52 See O'Meara (2014). 53 See O'Meara (2011a).
54 The following is discussed at greater length in O'Meara (1998) 438–439, where more references are provided.
55 *PM* II, 42, 153.2–4.

Dennis, G. (ed.) (1994a) Michael Psellos, *Orationes forenses et acta*, Stuttgart.
(ed.) (1994b) Michael Psellos, *Orationes panegyricae*, Stuttgart.
Des Places, E. (ed. and trans.) (1971) *Oracles chaldaïques, avec un choix de commentaires anciens*, Paris.
Duffy, J. (ed.) (1992) Michael Psellos, *Philosophica minora*, vol. I, Leipzig.
(2001) "Bitter Brine and Sweet Fresh Water: The Anatomy of a Metaphor in Psellos," in C. Sode and S. Takács (eds.), *Novum Millennium, Studies in Byzantine History and Culture Dedicated to Paul Speck*, Aldershot, 89–96.
(2002) "Hellenic Philosophy in Byzantium and the Lonely Mission of Michael Psellos," in K. Hierodiakonou (ed.), *Byzantine Philosophy and Its Ancient Sources*, Oxford, 129–156.
Faraggiana di Sarzana, C. (1990) "Una testimonianza bizantina finora ignorata sulla *Filosofia caldaica* di Proclo," *Prometheus* 16: 279–283.
Fisher, E. (ed.) (1994) Michael Psellos, *Orationes hagiographicae*, Stuttgart.
Gautier, P. (ed.) (1989) Michael Psellos, *Theologica*, vol. I, Leipzig.
Gemeinhardt, P. (2001) "Die Trinitätslehre des Michael Psellos," *Theologie und Philosophie* 76: 509–529.
Jenkins, D. (2006) "Psellos' Conceptual Precision," in Barber and Jenkins (2006), 131–151.
Kaldellis, A. (2006) *Mothers and Sons, Fathers and Daughters, The Byzantine Family of Michael Psellos*, Notre Dame.
Kroll, W. (ed.) (1894) *De oraculis chaldaicis*, Breslau. Reprinted Hildesheim 1962.
Kurz, E. and Drexl, F. (eds.) (1936) Michael Psellos, *Scripta minora*, Milan.
Lewy, H. (1978) *Chaldaean Oracles and Theurgy*, new edition by M. Tardieu, Paris.
Littlewood, A. (2006) "Imagery in the *Chronographia* of Michael Psellos," in Barber and Jenkins (2006), 13–56.
Moore, P. (2005) *Iter Psellianum, A Detailed Listing of Manuscript Sources for All Works attributed to Michael Psellos*, Toronto.
O'Meara, D. J. (ed.) (1989) Michael Psellos, *Philosophica minora*, vol. II, Leipzig.
(1998) "Aspects du travail philosophique de Michel Psellus (*Philosophica minora*, vol. II)," in C. Collatz and C. Dummer (eds.), *Dissertatiunculae criticae (Festschrift G. C. Hansen)*, Würzburg, 431–439.
(2011a) "Political Philosophy in Michael Psellos: The Chronographia Read in Relation to His Philosophical Work," in K. Hierodiakonou and B. Byden (eds.), *The Many Faces of Byzantine Philosophy*, Athens.
(2011b) "Psellos' *Commentary on the Chaldaean Oracles* and Proclus' Lost Commentary," in H. Seng (ed.), *Platonismus und Esoterik in byzantinischem Mittelalter und italienischer Renaissance*, Heidelberg.
(2014) "L'ascension mystique néoplatonicienne chez Michel Psellos" (forthcoming).
Parry, K. (2006) "Reading Proclus Diadochus in Byzantium," in H. Tarrant and D. Baltzly (eds.), *Reading Plato in Antiquity*, London, 223–235.
Podskalsky, G. (1976) "Nikolaos von Methone und die *Proklosrenaissance* in Byzanz," *Orientalia Christiana Periodica* 42: 509–523.
(1977) *Theologie und Philosophie in Byzanz*, Munich.

Steel, C. (2002) "Neoplatonic Sources in the Commentaries on the *Nicomachean Ethics* by Eustratius and Michael of Ephesus," *Bulletin de philosophie médiévale* 44: 51–57.
Tambrun-Krasker, B. and Tardieu, M. (eds. and trans.) (1995) *Plethon: Magika logia . . . Oracles chaldaïques*, Athens and Paris.
Westerink, L. G. (1942) "Proclus, Procopius, Psellus," *Mnemosyne* 10: 275–80. Reprinted in Westerink (1980), 1–6.
(ed.) (1948) Michael Psellos, *De omnifaria doctrina*, Nijmegen.
(1959) "Exzerpte aus Proklos' Enneaden-Kommentar bei Psellos," *Byzantinsche Zeitschrift* 52: 1–10. Reprinted in Westerink (1980), 21–30.
(1980) *Texts and Studies in Neoplatonism and Byzantine Literature*, Amsterdam.
Westerink, L. G. and Duffy, J. (eds.) (2002) Michael Psellos, *Theologica*, vol. II, Stuttgart.

CHAPTER 7

Eleventh- to twelfth-century Byzantium

Michele Trizio

Although it is only after the thirteenth and fourteenth centuries that we witness a considerable increase in the number of manuscripts containing Proclus' works, thanks in part to the work of intellectuals such as George Pachymeres (1242–*c.* 1310),[1] Proclus was regularly read and even admired by Byzantine intellectuals of the eleventh to twelfth centuries as one of the most important philosophers of late antiquity. When considering the development of ancient philosophy, Byzantine scholars such as Michael Psellos refer to Proclus' work as the greatest height ever attained by Hellenic wisdom.[2] Psellos' pupil John Italos seems to believe that Proclus not only exemplifies authentic Platonism but also represents the standard view of the "Greek" philosophers on this or that particular issue. Others went even further than this in endorsing Proclus' views with little concern for their incompatibility with Christian dogmata. This provoked a reaction by ecclesiastic authority and more conservative theologians, who saw a threat in Proclus and his Byzantine readers. This array of attitudes is embodied by three of the most relevant Proclus interpreters of the eleventh and twelfth centuries, John Italos, Eustratios of Nicaea, and Nicholas of Methone.

John Italos

It has been stated repeatedly that the condemnation of John Italos (1082),[3] Michael Psellos' pupil and consul of the philosophers after him, was

1 Among the exceptions to this trend is Proclus' commentary on the *Timaeus*, which is preserved in earlier manuscripts. See Westerink and Combès (1986), lxxiv. Pachymeres is known for having copied Proclus' commentaries on the *Parmenides* and the *Alcibiades I*. On the first, preserved in the *Parisinus gr.* 1810, see Westerink (1989), x–xi; Steel (1999), 288–291; Steel and Macé (2006), 77–99. On the latter, preserved in the *Neapolitanus gr.* 339 (III. E. 17), see Segonds (1985b), cxii–cxv. On Pachymeres' Neoplatonic scholarship, see Golitsis (2008), 60.

2 Michael Psellos, *Chronographia* 6, 38, 284,1–4 (Del Corno, Impellizzeri, Criscuolo, and Ronchey 1984).

3 On Italos' biography, see Skoulatos (1980), 150–153, n. 90; Rigo (2001). We have no reason to believe, as do most scholars after Joannou (1956a), 11–13, that Italos was of Norman origin.

intended as a condemnation of the eleventh-century Neoplatonic trend in Byzantium.[4] Certainly the ecclesiastical authorities had regarded Neoplatonism as highly problematic since the time of Psellos.[5] However, the "charges" (*anathēmata*) against Italos contained in the *Synodikon* are directed more towards a set of generic philosophical standpoints contradicting Christian dogmata (including views such as the eternity of matter and the mortality of the soul, which were often associated with Aristotle) than towards undermining one school of ancient philosophy, such as Neoplatonism, in favor of another.[6] Political reasons may also lurk behind Italos' condemnation: Italos' acquaintance with members of the Doukas family and with their anti-Komnenian entourage are likely to have caused a reaction by the new emperor Alexios I Komnenos (1081–1118), who, together with his brother Isaac Sebastokrator, was the driving force behind Italos' final condemnation.[7]

Italos' *damnatio memoriae* is reflected in the poor circulation of his work[8] and the depiction of his character in Anna Komnena's *Alexias*, which portrays him as a deceiving sophist, fond of Aristotle's philosophy as well as Proclus', using a stereotyped vocabulary to discriminate against him for his Italian origins.[9] Even though it is commonly accepted that the *anathēmata* against Italos do not reflect on his thought philologically,[10] modern scholars often tend to reproduce the Byzantine view of Italos as a mediocre scholar whose philosophy was unoriginal and who was unversed in theology; according to this view, Italos nevertheless attempted to reconcile Christianity with ancient philosophy in a new way and rationalized the Christian dogmata in the same way as did thirteenth-century medieval Latin masters.[11] Little work has been done on the institutional context of Italos' activity and on its reflection in Italos' philosophical treatises, which were probably addressed to students and members of the royal family,

4 See e.g. Cacouros (2007), 178–179.
5 See e.g. Gouillard (1976), 315–321.
6 For text of the *Synodikon* concerning Italos, see Gouillard (1967), 56–71, 188–202. On the trial itself, see Clucas (1981), to be updated with Gouillard (1983), (1985), and Darrouzès (1984). See also Browning (1975). 11–15.
7 Anna Komnena, *Alexias* V, 9, 5 (Leib 1943). Cf. Gouillard (1985), 167; Angold (2000), 50–54.
8 See Rigo (2001), 65.
9 See Anna Komnena, *Alexias* V, 8, 1–8 (Leib 1943). On Anna's depiction of Italos, see Arabatzis 2002. On Anna's discriminating vocabulary, see Hunger (1987), 39. The same *topos* concerning Italos' Italian origin is present in the Lucianesque *Timarion*, 44, 1117–1123 (Romano 1974) (twelfth century).
10 See e.g. Stéphanou (1933), 421; Joannou (1956a), 26–29; Gouillard (1976), 310–315; Clucas (1981), 140–162.
11 This view, though to a different extent, does seem to pervade most contributions on Italos, for instance, Uspenskij (1891); Salaville (1930), 141–145; Stéphanou (1933); Stéphanou (1949), 119; Dujčev (1939); Joannou (1956a); Lauritzen (2007).

such as emperor Michael VII Doukas himself.[12] Nor has Italos' conception of himself with respect to the ancient philosophical tradition been sufficiently investigated: whether Italos is merely reporting and discussing ancient philosophical standpoints as a matter of relative interest or is actually endorsing them as a reflection of his own philosophical views.[13]

Given that this issue cannot be fully addressed in the present chapter, I shall simply point out, as an example, that Italos' preference for Greek philosophy is declared accidentally (*Quaestiones quodlibetales* 43, 2–3) in the introduction to a treatise addressed to Michael's brother, Andronikos Doukas, although Greek philosophy is compared with that of Assyria and Egypt here and not with Christianity. Instead, formulations such as "according to the ancient philosophers or as the Greeks say" (κατὰ τοὺς ἔξω σοφούς or ὡς Ἕλληνές φασι) introduce Italos' treatment of a philosophical problem and make it clear that he is reporting antique philosophical standpoints, rather than his own.[14]

Proclus' name appears, along with that of Iamblichus, in the documents of the trial against Italos, as the latter rightly or wrongly used the form ἐπιστρέφειν ("to revert"), with all its Neoplatonic flavor, to describe the Son's conversion to the Father.[15] As a matter of fact, Proclus is frequently quoted by Italos in his philosophical treatises. Just as does his pupil Eustratios, Italos often identifies the position of the "Platonists" (οἱ ἀπὸ πλάτωνος) with that of Proclus, as if the latter exemplified authentic Platonism.[16] The same holds true for Italos' references to the positions of the "Greek wise men," which are always described using Proclus' phrasing,[17] as well as for the expression "the Greek theologians" (οἱ παρ' αὐτοῖς θεολόγοι), which reflects Psellos' description of Proclus as the "chief of the most theological of the Greeks."[18] All of these references introduce Proclus' opinions on various matters and can hardly be regarded as reflecting Italos' own thought. Moreover, his claim that in dealing with issues

[12] Moreover, it is clear that among the philosophical treatises edited by Joannou there is some material, such as *Quaestiones quodlibetales* 44 (Joannou 1956b), that does not belong to Italos himself, but rather to his students.

[13] See e.g. Wolska (1957) and Von Ivánka (1958) on Joannou (1956b). See also the stimulating observations of Giocarinis (1964), 167, n. 24. An attempt at discussing this issue is sketched in Clucas (1981), 162–168. For overview on Italos' thought, see Niarchos (1978) (unavailable to me).

[14] Cf. e.g. John Italos, *Quaest. quod.* 4, 6, 24; 5, 8, 36; 68, 138; 90, 13 (Joannou 1956b).

[15] See Gouillard (1985), 147, 199–203.

[16] John Italos, *Quaest. quod.* 3, 4, 5–6; 42, 52, 29 (Joannou 1956b). Many other occurrences of this kind are not signaled in Joannou's *apparatus fontium*.

[17] E.g. John Italos, *Quaest. quod.* 5, 8, 36; 24, 25, 4; 68, 113, 138; 90, 136, 13 (Joannou 1956b).

[18] E.g. John Italos, *Quaest. quod.* 7, 9, 10; 68, 109, 1 (Joannou 1956b). See Michael Psellos, *Theologica* 22, xxx, 39 (Gautier 1989).

such as the self-subsistence of a substance one should consider what the Greek philosophers said, "for they are the masters of this science . . . even though often their teachings contradict our pious dogmas," demonstrates Italos' aim of discussing philosophical issues through consideration of the opinions of ancient philosophical authorities on the same matters and, concomitantly, his careful professional ethics,[19] reflecting concerns similar to those of Psellos in noting the restrictions a Christian should observe when treating ancient philosophical matters.[20]

Italos explicitly mentions Proclus' *Elements of Theology* (prop. 67) when discussing the whole and parts theory (*Quaest. quod.* 15, 16, 6–13), which he links to Proclus' idea of a thing's threefold modes of existence, κατ' αἰτίαν, καθ' ὕπαρξιν, κατὰ μέθεξιν ("according to cause, according to substance, according to participation), contained in the same work (prop. 65). By the same token, reflecting similar Proclean statements from this work,[21] Italos' reference (*Quaest. quod.* 68, 113, 9–21) to particular souls imitating that which is prior to them – on the grounds that the "World Soul" (ἡ τοῦ παντὸς ψυχή) imitates that which is prior to it, "although it would be impious to state that the world is animated, there being no obstacle to providing an interpretation of this" (*Quaest. quod.* 68, 113, 138–141) – is not presented as Italos' view, but as an opinion "according to the pagan philosophers" (κατὰ τοὺς ἔξω σοφούς), once again a probable reference to Proclus.[22] Furthermore, in mentioning the Neoplatonic distinction between causes and concomitant causes, which should have been corrected by a Christian author through identification of the true causes with God alone,[23] Italos makes it clear that such a distinction stems from Plato, probably on the grounds that such an attribution is supported by the Neoplatonists themselves.[24]

All of these examples suggest that in many respects Italos' attitude had more in common with that of the modern historian of philosophy than with the approach to this that is characteristic of classical and late ancient philosophers. A somewhat more autonomous reference to Proclus is made

19 See John Italos, *Quaest. quod.* 7, 9, 6–9 (Joannou 1956b). On this and other similar passages, see Gouillard (1976), 313–314. Obviously this statement by Italos has nothing to do with the thirteenth-century Averroist double truth theory, as claimed by Podskalsky (1977), 115.

20 E.g. Michael Psellos, *Theologica* 74, 297, 145–149 (Gautier 1989). On this Psellos' concern, see Lemerle (1977), 195–258.

21 Proclus, *El. theol.*, prop. 204, 178, 31–33 (Dodds 1963a). See below.

22 *El. theol.*, 57, 56, 8–11 (Dodds 1963a).

23 See below for Nicholas of Methone's interpretation of this distinction.

24 Italos' account is very close to that of Proclus, *In Tim.* 1, 263, 19–30 (Diehl 1903–1906). See also Simplicius, *In Physica* 3, 16–19 (Diels 1882). The distinction between causes and concomitant causes might be traced back, in its general terms, to Plato, *Phaedo* 99a; *Timaeus* 46d (Burnet 1900–1907).

in Italos' treatment of the aforementioned whole and parts theory and its relation to the notion of wholeness (*Quaest. quod.* 90). Despite a reference (*Quaest. quod.* 90, 136, 10–13) to the "pagan philosophers" and the idea that the cause is superior to that which it causes,[25] Italos seems to elaborate on several hints contained in Proclus' work, identifying the whole-before-parts with the mode of existence κατ' αἰτίαν, the whole-of-parts with the mode καθ' ὕπαρξιν and the whole-in-parts with the mode κατὰ μέθεξιν. In fact, though it is reminiscent of props. 65–67 of the *Elements of Theology*, Italos' argument regards the whole-before-parts as a paradigmatic cause (*Quaest. quod.* 90, 136, 7) rather than as Proclus' form of each thing pre-existing in the cause.[26] What follows, however, reflects Proclus' metaphysics more closely: "every procession," writes Italos (*Quaest. quod.* 90, 136, 19–20), explaining the manner in which that which is caused is found in the cause, "takes place through likeness of the secondary to the primary, and of things after these to the secondary" (Πᾶσα πρόοδος δι' ὁμοιότητα γίνεται τῶν δευτέρων πρὸς τὰ πρότερα καὶ τῶν μετὰ ταῦτα πρὸς τὰ δεύτερα). As a matter of fact, prop. 29 of Proclus' *Elements of Theology* reads as follows: "all procession is accomplished through likeness of the secondary to the primary" (**Πᾶσα πρόοδος δι' ὁμοιότητος** ἀποτελεῖται **τῶν δευτέρων πρὸς τὰ πρῶτα**).

The passage in Italos' writing most relevant to the contemporary accusations made against him is perhaps *Quaest. quod.* 86, which has been connected with the charge of accepting the transmigration of the soul and the denial of the resurrection of the body.[27] However, taking a cue from John Damascene's discussion on resurrection as found in his *De fide orthodoxa*,[28] Italos here merely states in philosophical terms that the form is that which defines the essence of a thing, whereas matter is subject to change and corruption. Thus there is no obstacle, Italos maintains, to admitting the resurrection of bodies, for they are resurrected without their corruptible components, such as nails or hairs, as they are materially present in the living body.[29] Nor does Italos support the Platonic metempsychosis[30] or

[25] See Proclus, *El. theol.*, props. 7; 75 (Dodds 1963a).
[26] Proclus, *El. theol.*, prop. 67, 64, 3–4 (Dodds 1963a).
[27] See Lauritzen (2009), 162, on the basis of *Synodikon orthodoxiae* 57, 193–194 (Gouillard 1967); Anna Komnena, *Alexias* 5, 9, 7, 12 (Leib 1943). Yet, this Italos treatise seems a better fit for the content of *Synodikon orthodoxiae* 59, 225–228 (Gouillard 1967).
[28] John Damascene, *Exposition of the Orthodox Faith* 100, 234,2–239,131.
[29] See John Italos, *Quaest. quod.* 86, 134, 13–15 (Joannou 1956b). Astonishingly, probably through a common but unidentified Greek source, this very same argument is literally present in Augustine, *Enchiridion* XXIII, 89, 97, 58–77 (Evans 1969).
[30] In this regard I agree with Clucas (1981), 157–158. Lauritzen (2009), 162 holds the opposing view.

diverge on this point, namely the resurrection of the body, from his master Michael Psellos, who is the very source of this treatise by Italos.[31]

Another interesting text (*Quaest. quod.* 92, 145, 22–36) discusses causality with respect to matter. Here Italos supports his conclusion, that matter cannot have been caused without intermediaries, with props. 58 and 59 of Proclus' *Elements of Theology*, stating that causation involving a greater number of causes leads to something more composite than that involving fewer causes.[32] On this basis, Italos tackles the idea that the First Principle and matter are equally simple, the First Cause producing matter directly, in a way that is reminiscent of the late ancient debate on matter reported in Proclus' criticism of Plotinus' view on matter-evil.[33] Interestingly, Italos (*Quaest. quod.* 92, 145, 24–29) rejects Proclus' conception of matter as produced by the One directly[34] through Plotinus' view that, since matter is evil, it cannot be good or produced by the Good, for in this manner that which causes matter would itself be evil.[35] But to state that matter is produced through intermediaries would be inappropriate as well, Italos writes (*Quaest. quod.* 92, 145, 29–34): "if so, matter will neither be some last being, nor the worst, as they believe, nor simple. In fact, as has already been said, that which is produced by a greater number of causes is not simple but derives from some other things and is worse than it" (καὶ εἰ τοῦτο, οὐκ ἔσται τι τῶν ὄντων ἔσχατον οὐδὲ χεῖρον, ὡς οἴονται, οὐδὲ ἁπλοῦν· τὸ γὰρ ἐκ πλειόνων αἰτίων ὡς εἴρηται παρηγμένον οὐχ ἁπλοῦν, ἀλλ' ἔκ τινων ἄλλων, καὶ τούτων ἐκείνου χειρόνων). Here, the argument is once again derived from props. 58 and 59 of Proclus' *Elements of Theology*, dealing with the question of how something is simple or composite according to the number of causes producing it. Italos rejects the possibility that matter is composite and also Proclus' idea that "the last being is, like the first, perfectly simple,"[36] on the grounds that according to the same Proclus: "if the extremes of being are produced by fewer and simpler causes, the

[31] See Michael Psellos, *Philosophica minora* II, 28, 103, 16–104, 13 (O'Meara 1989). The editor of this text rightly suggests that Psellos' reference (Michael Psellos, *Phil. min.* II, 28, 104, 1–2 [O'Meara 1989] = John Italos, *Quaest. quod*, 86, 134, 9–10 [Joannou 1956b]) to form as that which characterizes men's essence is found in Plotinus, *Enneads* VI, 3, 9, 32–36 (Henry and Schwyzer 1951–1973).

[32] Compare John Italos, *Quaest. quod.*, 92, 145, 22–24 (Joannou 1956b) (καὶ πᾶν τὸ ἐκ πλειόνων παρηγμένον αἰτίων εἶναι σύνθετον, καὶ ἁπλοῦν τὸ μὴ ἐκ τοιούτων) with Proclus, *El. theol.*, prop. 59, 56, 28–29 (Dodds 1963a) (**Πᾶν τὸ** ὑπὸ **πλειόνων αἰτίων παραγόμενον συνθετώτερόν** ἐστι τοῦ ὑπὸ ἐλαττόνων παραγομένου).

[33] Plotinus, *Enn.* I, 8, 7, 16–23. On Plotinus' view on this subject see O'Meara (1997), (2005). For Proclus' answer see Proclus, *De mal. subs.* 5–6, 179, 35–183, 26 (Boese 1960). On Proclus' criticism of Plotinus' view see Opsomer (2001), (2007).

[34] Proclus, *De mal. subs.* 35, 218, 6–10 (Boese 1960); *In Tim.* 1, 384, 30–385, 17 (Diehl 1903–1906); *El. theol.* 59, 56, 36–37 (Dodds 1963a).

[35] Cf. Opsomer (2007), 174–176.

[36] Proclus, *El. theol.* 58, 56, 36–37 (Dodds 1963a).

intermediate existences by more, the latter will be composite. For the last being is, like the first, perfectly simple, because it proceeds from the first alone; but the one is simple as being above all composition, the other as being beneath it."[37] So, implies Italos, if one admits that matter is created through intermediaries, not only can it not be simple, but it cannot be composite either, for matter as the last term is, likewise according to Proclus, beneath composition itself.[38]

The conclusion of Italos' discussion of matter is somewhat interesting (*Quaest. quod.* 92, 145, 35–36): "therefore, matter, in the way they [*sc.* the pagan philosophers] state its existence, does not exist." This, together with the title of Italos' treatise as transmitted by the manuscript tradition of the text ("Treatise demonstrating that matter does not exist in the way the Greek philosophers say"), demonstrates that Italos is not really denying God's free will by admitting creation through intermediaries.[39] On the contrary, according to the previously mentioned approach – the discussion of ancient philosophical standpoints according to their inner principles and methods – Italos is attempting to demonstrate the internal contradictions of ancient philosophical views of matter: if one starts from the philosophers' assumptions, contends Italos, then one will reach the paradoxical conclusion that matter does not exist, for be it simple or composite, directly or indirectly produced, from all these opinions will follow an inconsistency.[40]

In another text Italos claims (*Quast. quod.* 4, 6, 14–16) that "we have often said and will now repeat that knowledge exists as a mediation between the knower and what is known, and in the knower knowledge coincides with and becomes similar to it" (εἴρηται πολλάκις ἡμῖν καὶ νῦν ῥηθήσεται, ὡς ἡ γνῶσις μεταξὺ γινώσκοντός τε καὶ γινωσκομένου ὑπάρχει καὶ ἐν τῷ γινώσκοντι καὶ σύνδρομος αὐτῷ καὶ αὐτῷ ἐοικυῖα). This statement almost literally echoes Proclus' reference in his commentary on the *Timaeus* to truth as conformity between the knower and the known, where he writes: "that is why truth is the conformity of the knower with that which is known" (καὶ διὰ τοῦτο καὶ ἀλήθεια εἶναι ἡ πρὸς τὸ γινωσκόμενον ἐφαρμογὴ τοῦ γιγνώσκοντος).[41] There is an even greater correspondence with a passage from Proclus' *On Ten Doubts concerning Providence* as reported

[37] Proclus, *El. theol.* 58, 56, 30–32 (Dodds 1963a).
[38] John Italos, *Quaest. quod.* 92, 145, 34–35 (Joannou 1956b).
[39] This view is held by Lauritzen (2009) 163.
[40] This has been ignored by Joannou (1956a), 66–78.
[41] Proclus, *In Tim.* 2, 287, 3–5 (Diehl 1903–1906). This passage will be quoted by Italos' pupil Eustratios and attributed to Aristotle himself, in *In VI Ethica Nicomachea* 268, 19–21 (Heylbut 1892). Italos' passage might also refer to Proclus, *In Parm.* 899, 14–17 (Steel, Mace, and d'Hoine 2008).

by Italos' master, Michael Psellos, in his treatise on the predetermination of death: "for knowledge, which is intermediate between the known and the knower, starts from the knower, is rolled up in the known, and is rendered similar to the known" (ὡς ἡ γνῶσις μέση οὖσα τοῦ γινωσκομένου καὶ τοῦ γινώσκοντος ὥρμηται μὲν ἀπὸ τοῦ γινώσκοντος, εἵλειται δὲ περὶ τὸ γινωσκόμενον καὶ ὡμοίωται τῷ γινώσκοντι).[42] It is striking not only that Italos borrows from Proclus through such an indirect source as Psellos, but that the content of this statement is itself, despite its Proclean derivation, rather harmless from the perspective of Orthodoxy,[43] simply reproducing the standard theory on truth traditionally endorsed by late ancient commentators.[44]

Italos seems to be very careful in dealing with ancient philosophical material. When discussing the aforementioned idea, ascribed to the ancient philosophers, that the soul imitates that which is prior to it in the same way as the World Soul participates in the principle prior to it,[45] Italos tackles (*Quaest. quod.* 68, 113, 145–146) Proclus' view on the manifold of souls as originating from and reverting to the primal Soul[46] and the related metaphysical principle that every manifold must refer to a first term of a series. For, "if something exists in the whole, then the same thing must also be considered to exist in the parts" (*Quaest. quod.* 68, 113, 146–150).[47] Italos' comment that (*Quaest. quod.* 68, 113, 146) "as a matter of fact we do not espouse this" – Proclus' idea that a manifold soul must be traced back to a unique Primal Soul – clearly demonstrates the author's disassociation from the subject under discussion, probably due to Christian concerns.[48]

This last reference may be used to sketch some concluding remarks on Italos' treatment of Neoplatonism and, in particular, Proclus.[49] As I said before, a general study of Italos' methodology is still lacking and the present contribution is in no way intended to produce definitive conclusions on this topic. Having said that, one could argue concerning Italos' interpretation

42 Michael Psellos, *De omnifaria doctrina*, app. 1, 101, 35–37 (Westerink 1949), quoting from Proclus, *De dec. dub.* I, 2, 7, 13, 2–4 (Boese 1960).

43 As a matter of fact precisely this Psellian passage will later be quoted by Nicholas of Methone, author of the twelfth-century *Refutation of Proclus' Elements of Theology*. Cf. Lackner (1985b), lx–lxi.

44 See e.g. David, *Prolegomena philosophiae* 4, 10–13 (Busse 1904); Simplicius, *In Categorias* 12, 32–13, 4 (Kalbfleisch 1907); Philoponus, *In De anima* 73, 6–8 (Hayduck 1897); *In Categorias* 81, 29–31 (Busse 1898). This theory might be traced back to Aristotle's view on truth as the conformity between definition and object. cf. e.g. Aristotle, *Topica* VI, 10, 148b1–3 (Ross 1958).

45 See above. 46 Proclus, *El. theol.*, prop. 21, 24, 25–27 (Dodds 1963a).

47 See e.g. Proclus, *In Parm.* 1112, 20–27 (Steel, Mace, and d'Hoine 2009).

48 On this passage see also Gouillard (1976), 314.

49 For more information on Italos' Neoplatonic sources, particularly regarding his position on universal concepts, see Ierodiakonou (2009).

of Proclus that, like Psellos, Italos regards Proclus as the most authoritative philosopher, best exemplifying ancient philosophical views on certain issues. Yet there is almost no evidence to suggest that Italos went further than this, endorsing Proclus' views as his own. Not only is Italos generally cautious in introducing ancient philosophical views, stressing that these cannot be reconciled with Orthodoxy but, when discussing issues such as matter or the World Soul, he rejects several of Proclus' standpoints. Since most references to Proclus are taken from the *Elements of Theology*, one could argue that Italos' interest in Proclus is a rather scholastic one, in the sense that Proclus is only used in regard to the general principles of his metaphysics, which are stated plainly and clearly in the *Elements of Theology*. On the contrary, Italos' pupil, Eustratios of Nicaea, seems to have considered Proclus in a much more favorable light, expounding this philosopher's views as if they were still valid.

Eustratios of Nicaea (*c.* 1050–*c.* 1120)

We know relatively little of Eustratios of Nicaea's biography. His extant works suggest that he was a court theologian to emperor Alexios I Komnenos (1081–1118) involved in the most relevant theological controversies of his day.[50] More importantly, he commented on book II of Aristotle's *Posterior Analytics* and on books I and VI of the *Nicomachean Ethics*, probably at the request of Alexios' daughter Anna Komnena (1083–1153), who is generally regarded as the patron of a philosophical circle engaged in commenting on Aristotelian works that had not been commented on previously.[51] Yet, since we lack sufficient evidence linking the existence of such a circle or project directly to Anna, it is safer to refer these commentaries to Anna's private interests in ancient literature, as testified by Anna herself in *Alexias* and in the funeral oration written for her by George Tornikes.[52]

Eustratios, whom Anna praises as a brilliant dialectician,[53] is first mentioned in the official documents on John Italos' trial as a pupil of Italos and master in one of Constantinople's schools.[54] Italos' ghost was to haunt Eustratios later, in 1117, when he himself was charged with heresy for his

[50] On Eustratios' biography and bibliography see Skoulatos (1980), 89–91; Cacouros (2000).
[51] See Browning (1962) (reprinted 1977).
[52] See Mullet (1984) 178; Frankopan (2009). Darrouzès (1970), 282, n. 69 raises doubts concerning the connection between Eustratios and Anna.
[53] Anna Comnena, *Alexias* XIV, 8, 9, 10–11 (Leib 1943).
[54] See Gouillard (1985), 159. See also Gouillard (1976), 308.

views on Christology.[55] In fact, Eustratios' main persecutor, Niketas of Heraclea,[56] would recall Eustratios' acquaintance with Italos as a sign of his misconduct and unreliability.[57] More importantly, Niketas of Seida,[58] another of Eustratios' persecutors, in order to achieve greater rhetorical emphasis, would bring up Proclus and Simplicius among other pagan authors as the genesis of Eustratios' alleged theological mistakes.[59]

As a matter of fact, Eustratios' theological writings contain several references to Neoplatonic doctrines. One example is Eustratios' attempt to explain Christ's assumption of human nature by referring to the Plotinian view, as reported in Proclus' lost commentary on the *Enneads*, that the soul remains unaffected by the union with the body and that embodied souls are just an "appearance of the soul" (ἴνδαλμα τῆς ψυχῆς).[60] By means of this example, Eustratios intends to demonstrate that, insofar as it remains self-subsisting and self-perfect, the divinity of the divine *Logos* remains unaffected by its union with the human body in the incarnation. In the same context Eustratios explains Christ's attributes of life and truth and their mode of existence in the *Logos* made flesh by claiming that "that which lives, lives by participating in life; that which is rational is such by having reason and thinking, every term that participates being secondary to the participated" (ζῶον δὲ τὸ ζῶον ὡς μετέχον ζωῆς, καὶ λογικὸν τὸ λογικὸν ὡς λόγον ἔχον καὶ διανοούμενον· ὕστερον δ' ἅπαν τὸ μετέχον ἐστὶ τοῦ μετεχομένου),[61] a statement that resembles prop. 24 of Proclus' *Elements of Theology*: "all that participates is inferior to the participated, and this latter to the unparticipated" (Πᾶν τὸ μετέχον τοῦ μετεχομένου καταδεέστερον, καὶ τὸ μετεχόμενον τοῦ ἀμεθέκτου).

Indeed, one may contend that here Eustratios is merely using Proclus as a tool to support his theological standpoints. Eustratios' strategy may nevertheless have appeared hazardous in the eyes of his contemporaries. This is the impression one gets when reading Eustratios' statement that "the divinity is everywhere, but according to the nature proper to each thing" (Πανταχοῦ μὲν ἡ θεότης, ἀλλ' οἰκείως πρὸς ἕκαστον), which is a Christian

55 On Eustratios' trial see Joannou (1952), (1954), and (1958), to be corrected by Darrouzès (1966); Grumel and Darrouzès (1989), 460–461, n. 1003.

56 On Niketas see Browning (1963), 15–17.

57 Niketas of Heraclea, *Oratio apologetica* 304, 4–15 (Darrouzès 1966); Niketas Choniates, *Thesaurus orthodoxae fidei, Patrologia Graeca* (henceforth *PG*), 140, 135–136.

58 On Niketas of Seida, see Zeses (1976), 7–20.

59 Niketas of Seida, Λόγος κατὰ Εὐστρατίου Νικαίας, 10, 6–12 (Zeses 1976).

60 Eustratios, *Oratio secunda de Spiritu Sancto* 80, 20–27 (Demetracopoulos 1866) (Proclus' commentary on the *Enneads* is witnessed by Michael Psellos, *Phil. min.* II, 14, 74, 10–11 (O'Meara 1989). See Westerink (1942).

61 Eustratios, *Or.* VII, 184, 2–4 (Demetracopoulos 1866).

version of prop. 103 of Proclus' *Elements of Theology*, "All things are in all things, but in each according to its proper nature" (Πάντα ἐν πᾶσιν, **οἰκείως** δὲ ἐν **ἑκάστῳ**).[62] Furthermore, the title of Eustratios' treatise against the Armenians promises to reject monophysitism "by means of logical, physical and theological arguments" (ἐκ λογικῶν καὶ φυσικῶν καὶ θεολογικῶν ἐπιχειρήσεων), that is to say by referring to the three Proclean methods of inquiry[63] which had just been reiterated by scholars such as Michael Psellos and Eustratios' former master John Italos.[64] Unsurprisingly, then, Proclus is the omnipresent shadow behind Eustratios' commentaries on books I and VI of Aristotle's *Nicomachean Ethics* and book II of the *Posterior Analytics*. His preference for this Neoplatonic author is generally apparent in Eustratios' views on such important issues as the nature of causation and intellection.

With respect to causation, Eustratios accepts Proclus' distinction between causes and concomitant causes, relying (276, 21–22) on prop. 75 from Proclus' *Elements of Theology* in defending the view that only the first causes are true causes "for they are the only ones that transcend that which they cause" (ὅτι καὶ μόνα τῶν αἰτιατῶν ἐξῄρηται). However, probably as a result of religious concerns, Eustratios simplifies Proclus' hierarchical structure of reality by eliminating intermediaries such as the henads and the different orders of Gods and souls, but his general attitude towards Proclus' metaphysics remains a positive one; for instance, while describing the souls' noetic reversion to the First Cause, Eustratios (*In VI EN*, 348, 36) maintains that this transpires "through intermediary realms" (διὰ τῶν μέσων διακόσμων), an expression used by Proclus to describe the different realms or planes of being.[65] Discussing the eternal realities (*In VI EN*, 293, 15–19) – those which, according to Eustratios, are described in Plato's *Timaeus* as always self-identical and imperishable[66] – Eustratios writes (294, 14–16): "for through these creation is spread to the earthly realities and providence extends unto the very last beings" (ὡς δι' αὐτῶν μέσων εἰς τὰ τῇδε χωρεῖν τὴν ποίησιν καὶ τὴν πρόνοιαν μέχρι καὶ τῶν

[62] This Proclean standpoint arises in the writings of pseudo-Dionysius several times, but never in a way suggesting Eustratios' direct dependence upon pseudo-Dionysius.

[63] Proclus, *In Tim.* 1, 8, 4–5 (Diehl 1903–1906); *In Parm.* 912, 30–31; 1039, 9–11 (Steel, Mace, and d'Hoine 2008; 2009). See also Ammonius, *In Isagogen* 45, 5–15. On this, see Sheppard (1987); Gersh (2000); and Martijn (2010), 7–10, 67–71.

[64] Michael Psellos, *Theologica* 54, 211, 107–110 (Gautier 1989); John Italos, *Quaest. quod.* 4, 5, 4–6, 5 (Joannou 1956b).

[65] Proclus, *Theol. Plat.* 6, 26, 16–17 (Saffrey and Westerink 1968–1997); *In I Alcibiadem* 112, 92, 2–4 (Segonds 1985a); *In Eucl.* 6, 11–13 (Friedlein 1873).

[66] Plato, *Timaeus* 28a (Burnet 1900–1907). See also *Lexicon Suidae* Π, 1709, 17–28 (Adler 1928–1935).

ἐσχάτων διήκουσαν). Specialists in Neoplatonism will immediately recognize the Proclean vocabulary inherent in this argument on causation and providence. For example, in his *Platonic Theology* Proclus argues that the father and creator of the universe is celebrated throughout the *Timaeus*, as he "illuminates the paternal power and providence which extends from above until the last terms of the Whole" (πατρικὴν ἐμφαίνοντος δύναμιν καὶ **πρόνοιαν**, ἄνωθεν ἄχρι **τῶν ἐσχάτων** τοῦ παντὸς **διήκουσαν**);[67] or, as Proclus states in his commentary on the *Parmenides*, since a property such as greatness is found in the lower realms of being, "therefore this property extends from above unto the very last terms" (ἄνωθεν ἄρα **διήκει καὶ μέχρι τῶν ἐσχάτων**).[68]

Eustratios accepts this Neoplatonic top-down model of causation and its associated vocabulary. While stating that the soul must remain in a close relationship with Intelligence, the commentator adds (*In VI EN*, 317, 30–32): "so that the processions of beings also derive from the First Cause as in a chain, where the lower term is always connected with that superior to it and maintains a certain similarity with it" (ἵνα καὶ τῶν ὄντων αἱ πρόοδοι ἐκ τῆς πρώτης αἰτίας καθ' εἱρμὸν γίνοιντο, ἀεὶ τοῦ ὑφειμένου συναπτομένου τῷ πρὸ αὐτοῦ καί τινα πρὸς ἐκεῖνο κεκτημένου ὁμοίωσιν). This passage summarizes Proclus' theory of causation, as is clear from the notion of "chain" (εἱρμός)[69] and the reference to "similarity" (ὁμοίωσις) as the trait peculiar to the entire process.[70] In another passage (*In VI EN*, 288–18–21) Eustratios states that "the substance of each existing being is considered according to its procession from the productive cause, whereas its perfection is considered from the perspective of its reversion to the productive cause following the desire of striving for it, insofar as each thing zealously attempts to imitate the productive cause according to its measure" (Ἑκάστου τῶν ὄντων ἢ γινομένων ἡ μὲν οὐσία κατὰ τὴν ἐκ τοῦ ποιητικοῦ αἰτίου θεωρεῖται πρόοδον, ἡ δὲ τελειότης κατὰ τὴν πρὸς ἐκεῖνο ἐπιστροφὴν τῆς πρὸς ἐκεῖνο ἀντιποιουμένου ἐφέσεως κἀκεῖνο κατὰ μέτρον μιμεῖσθαι σπουδάζοντος). One would not be wrong to trace this argument back to Proclus' *Platonic Theology*, where it is stated that

67 Proclus, *Theol. Plat.* 5, 102, 5–7 (Saffrey and Westerink 1968–1997).

68 Proclus, *In Parm.* 854, 22–23 (Steel, Mace, and d'Hoine 2008). See also *In Parm.* 996, 1–5 (Steel, Mace, and d'Hoine 2008); *In Tim.* 1, 190, 8–12 (Diehl 1903–1906); *Theol. Plat.* 3, 41, 12–14 (Saffrey and Westerink 1968–1997).

69 See e.g. Proclus, *In Remp.* 2, 240, 25–27 (Kroll 1899–1901); *Theol. Plat.* 6, 14, 5–10 (Saffrey and Westerink 1968–1997).

70 See e.g. Proclus, *Theol. Plat.* 6, 78, 23–29 (Saffrey and Westerink 1968–1997); *El. theol.*, prop. 29; prop. 132, 29–30 (Dodds 1963a). This statement of Eustratios is in general reminiscent of Proclus, *Theol. Plat.* 5, 103, 1–7 (Saffrey and Westerink 1968–1997), where the general rules mentioned by Eustratios are applied to the particular case of the different orders of gods.

"in fact, all things remain, proceed and revert upon the One... Thus, union provides all secondary things with a stable and non-proceeding transcendence of their cause; subordination determines the procession of beings and their separation from the unparticipated and first monad; desire accomplishes the reversion of the existing things and their circular motion towards the ineffable" (Πάντα γὰρ καὶ μένει καὶ πρόεισιν καὶ ἐπιστρέφεται πρὸς τὸ ἕν . . . καὶ ἡ μὲν ἕνωσις μόνιμον ἐνδίδωσι τοῖς δευτέροις ἅπασι καὶ ἀνεκφοίτητον τῆς ἑαυτῶν αἰτίας ὑπεροχήν, ἡ δὲ ὕφεσις τὴν πρόοδον τῶν ὄντων ἀφορίζει καὶ τὴν ἀπὸ τῆς ἀμεθέκτου καὶ πρωτίστης ἑνάδος διάκρισιν, ἡ δὲ ἔφεσις τὴν ἐπιστροφὴν τῶν ὑποστάντων καὶ τὴν εἰς τὸ ἄρρητον ἀνακύκλησιν τελειοῖ).[71]

While comparing Aristotle's standpoints with those of the "followers of Plato," Eustratios avoids the late ancient topos of harmony between Plato and Aristotle.[72] In this the commentator samples Plato in a way that occasionally makes it impossible to distinguish between Eustratios' exposition of Plato's views and the commentator's own views.[73] More importantly, when presenting the Platonists' doctrine, Eustratios identifies it with that of Proclus. For example, in his commentary on book II of the *Posterior Analytics* (*In II An. post.* 195, 28–30), Eustratius writes that "thus, the wholes before parts are, as the Platonists say, monadic principles: from each of them stems the series coordinated to it" (αἱ μὲν οὖν πρὸ τῶν μερῶν ὁλότητες, ὡς οἱ περὶ Πλάτωνα λέγουσιν, αἱ ἀρχικαὶ μονάδες εἰσίν, ἐξ ὧν ἑκάστης ὁ σύστοιχος αὐτῇ ἀριθμὸς ἀπογεννᾶται). This passage introduces a long discussion of the whole and parts theory derived from props. 67, 68, and 69 of Proclus' *Elements of Theology* and, more importantly, is reminiscent of Proclus' statement in the *Platonic Theology* "that it is necessary that each monad causes the series coordinated to it" (ὡς ἀνάγκη πᾶσαν μονάδα παράγειν **ἀριθμὸν αὐτῇ σύστοιχον**).[74]

But Eustratios' most famous Plato-Aristotle doxography, which attracted the attention of thirteenth-century Latin readers of the *Nicomachean Ethics*, introduces Eustratios' passionate defense of the Platonic Ideal Good in opposition to Aristotle's critique of it.[75] Here, Eustratios writes that the

71 Proclus, *Theol. Plat.* 2, 41, 20–28 (Saffrey and Westerink 1968–1997). See also *El. theol.*, prop. 37, 10–16 (Dodds 1963a). By the same token, Eustratios' sentence (*In VI EN*, 288, 20–21) (Heylbut 1892) κἀκεῖνο κατὰ μέτρον μιμεῖσθαι σπουδάζοντος is reminiscent of Proclus' emphasis on participation as taking place according to the different degrees of capacity of each term of the causation process. See e.g. Proclus, *El. theol.*, prop. 142, 3–7 (Dodds 1963a).

72 On this *topos*, see Karamanolis (2006).

73 This has already been recognized by Lloyd (1987), 345.

74 Proclus, *Theol. Plat.* 3, 7, 29–8, 1 (Saffrey and Westerink 1968–1997). On the role of Proclus' whole and parts theory in Eustratios, see Lloyd (1987).

75 On this text and its Latin tradition, see Giocarinis (1964); Mercken (1990), 415–419, 441–444.

existence of the ideas is the major point of disagreement between the Platonists and Aristotle (*In I EN*, 41, 29–30), and contends (40, 22–23) that the Platonists "introduce the ideas as enhypostatic divine thoughts." He goes on supporting this view with Proclus' aforementioned theory of the whole and parts (*In I EN*, 40, 34–35), and assimilates Proclus' whole-before-parts to the Platonic ideas, which Eustratios indifferently calls divine thoughts, forms, and universals that transcend the forms in particulars and later-born concepts, that is, concepts derived by abstraction from the data of sense perception (*In I EN*, 40, 24–27).[76] Unsurprisingly, Proclus is the source of Eustratios' account of the Platonic identification of the First Principle with the First and Highest Good (*In I EN*, 40, 17–18), "insofar as it is the substantial Good that is the object of desire for all things" (ὡς οὐσιῶδες ἀγαθὸν οὗ πάντα ἐφίεται), echoing Proclus' commentary on the *Republic*, where the author comments on Socrates' identification of the supreme object of all sciences with the Good: "for this object is the Good, the object of desire for all things" (ὡς ἄρα τοῦτό ἐστιν **τὸ ἀγαθόν, οὗ πάντα ἐφίεται**).[77]

Eustratios deliberately refers to Proclus' vocabulary, in order to counter Aristotle's definition of the good in book I of the *Nicomachean Ethics* as that which everything desires, on the basis that Proclus himself criticizes this Aristotelian definition by using the same words of the Stagirite.[78] This is confirmed by Eustratios' subsequent claim (*In I EN*, 45, 28–29) that the "word τἀγαθόν," present in the Aristotelian lemma "further, since 'good' is said in as many sense as 'being'" (ἔτι δ' ἐπεὶ τἀγαθὸν ἰσαχῶς λέγεται τῷ ὄντι),[79] is taken by the Platonists "in the sense of the first and universal Good" (ἐπὶ τοῦ πρώτου καὶ καθόλου ἐτίθετο), while the expression "that which all things desire" (οὗ πάντα ἐφίεται), which opens book I of this Aristotelian work, is taken as referring to "the most universal and supreme Good" (τὸ καθολικώτατον δηλοῖ καὶ πρώτιστον), in order to conclude that (45, 30–31) "as a matter of fact, if everything desires it (i.e. the Good), then it is by necessity above all things" (εἰ γὰρ πάντα ἐκείνου ἐφίεται, ὑπὲρ τὰ πάντα ἐξ ἀνάγκης ἐστί). Specialists in Neoplatonism will easily trace this sentence back to Proclus' statement in the *Elements of Theology* that "in fact if all beings desire the Good, it is clear that the First Good is beyond

76 On this passage, see Giocarinis (1964), 172–174.

77 Proclus, *In Remp.* 1, 269, 12 (Kroll 1899–1901). See also Eustratios, *In I EN* 43, 11–14 (Heylbut 1892), where the author ascribes to Plato the identification of the First and Supreme Good with the One. Compare this passage with Michael Psellos, *Theol.* 4, 17, 91–93 (Gautier 1989).

78 Aristotle, *Eth. Nic.* I, 1, 1094a2–3 (Bywater 1962): διὸ καλῶς ἀπεφήναντο **τἀγαθόν, οὗ πάντ' ἐφίεται.**

79 Aristotle, *Eth. Nic.* I, 6, 1096a23–24 (Bywater 1962).

existing things" (**εἰ γὰρ πάντα** τὰ ὄντα τοῦ ἀγαθοῦ **ἐφίεται**, δῆλον ὅτι τὸ πρώτως ἀγαθὸν ἐπέκεινά ἐστι τῶν ὄντων),[80] which demonstrates once again that, when reporting the position of the "Platonists," Eustratios refers to Proclus. Unsurprisingly, then, some lines earlier (*In VI EN*, 45, 15–18), the commentator had borrowed Proclus' distinction between secondary goods, which can be attained by this or that being, and the "common Good," in the sense of the primal and transcendent Good, participated in by secondary goods.[81]

The identification of the standard Platonic standpoints with Proclus remains in Eustratios' theory of intellection and concept-formation and here, too, Eustratios means Proclus when referring to "Platonists." While accounting for the different standpoints, Platonic and Aristotelian, concerning mathematical objects, Eustratios rightly contends (*In VI EN*, 320, 21–24) that according to Aristotle these are known "by abstraction" (ἐξ ἀφαιρέσεως),[82] whereas "this standpoint did not please the Platonists who speculate on this topic, for according to them that which is derived by abstraction is worse than the data of sense perception and physical realities, for they are derived from these and are later-born" (ἀλλὰ τοῦτο οὐκ ἤρεσκε τοῖς Πλατωνικῶς περὶ τοῦτο δοξάζουσι, διότι τὰ ἐξ ἀφαιρέσεως τῶν αἰσθητῶν ἐστι καὶ φυσικῶν χείρονα, ὡς ἐξ αὐτῶν τὴν γένεσιν ἔχοντα καὶ ὑστερογενῶς αὐτῶν ὑφιστάμενα). This paraphrases Proclus' argument against later-born concepts, the Aristotelian concepts derived from sense perception, as being a reliable base for knowledge, as elaborated in his commentary on the *Parmenides*, where Proclus writes: "in fact, we will surely not contemplate later-born concepts. In fact, these are less noble than the data of sense perception and the common elements inherent in them" (οὐ γάρ που περὶ τῶν ὑστερογενῶν ποιησόμεθα τὴν θεωρίαν· ταῦτα γὰρ αὐτὰ τῶν αἰσθητῶν ἐστιν ἀτιμότερα καὶ τῶν ἐν αὐτοῖς κοινῶν).[83]

Apparently, Eustratios' dependence upon Proclus' *Parmenides* commentary is foreshadowed by the author's ascription of the doctrine of ideas to "the followers of Parmenides and Plato," a periphrasis that refers to the same Proclus as commentator of Plato's *Parmenides*.[84] Thus, from this work by Proclus, Eustratios borrows the description (*In I EN*, 47, 4–11) of the

80 Proclus, *El. theol.*, prop. 8, 8, 31–32 (Dodds 1963a).

81 Proclus, *El. theol.*, prop. 8, 8, 32–9, 8 (Dodds 1963a). For further evidence of Eustratios' dependence upon Proclus, see Giocarinis (1964), 183–190.

82 See Aristotle, *Physica* II, 2, 193b36–194a1 (Ross 1959).

83 Proclus, *In Parm.* 980, 10–13; 892, 31–35; 894, 26–895, 1 (Steel, Mace, and d'Hoine 2008). On Eustratios' account of the Platonic and Aristotelian standpoints on mathematical objects, see Trizio (2009a), 72–80.

84 See Steel (2002).

two modes of existence of the forms, in the separate Intelligence and in the particular soul. The latter possesses in a partial manner the forms that are unified within the Intelligence and grasps the forms by dancing around the Intelligence in a circle.[85] This very same argument is put forward by Eustratios in his commentary on book VI of the *Nicomachean Ethics* as his own view. Here the commentator remarks on the transient nature of knowledge proper in the particular soul and contends (*In VI EN*, 317, 26–28) that, while transcending the lower potencies, the soul "can grasp each of the intelligibles in a simple manner, though not simultaneously and eternally as the Intelligence properly so-called grasps them, but one by one, within a temporal dimension and passing from one to the other" (ἑκάστῳ τῶν νοητῶν ἁπλῶς ἐπιβάλλειν δύναται, οὐκ ἀθρόον οὐδ᾿ ἐν αἰῶνι ὡς ὁ κυρίως νοῦς καταλαμβάνων αὐτὰ ἀλλὰ καθ᾿ ἓν καὶ ἐν χρόνῳ καὶ μεταβαίνων ἀφ᾿ ἑτέρου εἰς ἕτερον). Elsewhere (*In VI EN*, 303, 23–25) Eustratios insists that the soul can indeed grasp the intelligibles, "although not all together and all at once like the Intellect which is so in its substance but embraces all things one by one and knows them singularly" (εἰ καὶ μὴ ἀθρόως καὶ ὁμοῦ ὡς ὁ καθ᾿ ὕπαρξιν, ἀλλὰ καθ᾿ ἓν περιεχομένη τὰ πάντα καὶ νοοῦσα καθ᾿ ἕκαστον). Both of these passages derive from Proclus: the former from his commentary on the *Timaeus*, where he writes that reason does not grasp "all things all at once, but passes from one to the other" (οὐ πάντα δὲ ἅμα, ἀλλὰ μεταβαίνων ἀπ᾿ ἄλλων ἐπ᾿ ἄλλα);[86] the latter from his commentary on the *Parmenides*, where he writes that the soul "does not present itself as a whole to the intelligible contents of the intelligence all at once, for by its nature it cannot discern them all together" (**οὔτε** γὰρ ὅλην αὐτὴν **ὁμοῦ** τοῖς τοῦ νοῦ παράγειν νοήμασιν· **οὐ** γὰρ **ἀθρόως** αὐτὰ πέφυκεν ὁρᾷν).[87]

Most Proclean doctrines discussed in Eustratios' commentary on book I of the *Nicomachean Ethics* – and presented by him as Platonic – are reiterated as Eustratios' own views in his commentary on book VI of the same work. More importantly, in the commentary on this later book Proclus' influence is even more distinct. For example, Eustratios maintains that, when free from the passions, the soul is illuminated "by its proximity to the Intelligence" (τῇ πρὸς νοῦν γειτνιάσει), which is a verbatim quotation from Proclus' *Platonic Theology*, where Proclus writes that the soul receives

[85] See Giocarinis (1964) 191; Steel (2002), 52–53. The general principle stated here can be traced back to Proclus, *El. theol.*, prop. 194, 168, 30 (Dodds 1963a).

[86] Proclus, *In Tim.* I, 246, 1–9 (Diehl 1903–1906).

[87] Proclus, *In Parm.* 1165, 24–25 (Steel, Mace, and d'Hoine 2009) (English translation by Morrow and Dillon [1987], 517, slightly modified). On these passages, see Trizio (2009a), 90–99; Trizio (2009b), 86–94.

"a vigilant life from its proximity to the Intelligence" (τὴν ἄγρυπνον ζωὴν ἐκ τῆς **πρὸς** τὸν **νοῦν** ἔχει **γειτνιάσεως**).[88] More importantly, Eustratios defends (*In VI EN*, 303, 19–21) the thesis that the soul "*qua* soul acts by unfolding" (ὡς μὲν ψυχὴ ἀνειλιγμένως ἐνεργεῖ) the intelligible content within discursive reasoning and syllogisms; whereas the soul "as participating in the Intelligence grasps the intelligibles in a simple manner" (ὡς δὲ μετέχουσα νοῦ ἁπλῶς ἐπιβάλλει). Not only is ἀνειλιγμένως the technical Proclean term to describe the soul as containing all forms in an unfolded manner,[89] but the very distinction between the two operations of the soul derives from Proclus' commentary on the *Timaeus*, where reason "*qua* reason acts in a transient manner" (**ὡς μὲν** λόγος **ἐνεργεῖ** μεταβατικῶς), that is to say discursively, whereas reason "as having intellection acts with simplicity" (**ὡς δὲ** νοῶν μετὰ **ἁπλότητος**).[90]

One striking example of Eustratios' identification with Proclus' doctrines is the following: in his commentary on book II of the *Posterior Analytics* Eustratios (*In II An. post.* 257, 24–32) first presents two different concept-formation theories – Aristotle's induction from the particulars and Plato's recollection – and then announces his own solution, which is a jigsaw puzzle of pieces put together from Proclus' works (*In II An. post.* 257, 35–37): "in the hierarchy of forms that which comes directly after a thing participates more clearly in that which comes directly before it. Thus, since the soul comes directly after the Intelligence, it participates in the Intelligence more than that which is further from It" (ἐν τῇ τάξει τῶν εἰδῶν τὰ προσεχῶς μετά τι μετέχει τρανότερον τοῦ προσεχῶς πρὸ αὐτῶν. ἐπεὶ οὖν ἡ ψυχὴ προσεχῶς μετὰ νοῦν, μετέχει τοῦ νοῦ μᾶλλον ἤπερ τὰ πόρρω τοῦ νοῦ). As a matter of fact, in the *Elements of Theology* (prop. 193) one may read that "every soul derives its proximate existence from an Intelligence" (πᾶσα **ψυχὴ προσεχῶς** ἀπὸ **νοῦ** ὑφέστηκεν). Eventually, going against Platonic metempsychosis, Eustratios will defend the Christian view that the soul was created together with the body.[91] At the same time and against Aristotle, in accounting for the origin of the principles of our knowledge, he consistently supports innatism with Proclus' vocabulary, as when he states that (*In II*

[88] Proclus, *Plat. Theol.* 1, 66, 23–24 (Saffrey and Westerink) see also Eustratios, *In VI EN*, 317, 19 (Heylbut 1892). On Eustratios' theory of the intellect and intellection, see also Ierodiakonou (2005) 80–81; Trizio (2009a) 98–99; Jenkins (2009), 120–128.

[89] See e.g. Proclus, *In Parm.* 897, 27–29 (Steel, Mace, and d'Hoine 2008). See also *In Eucl.* 16, 10–16 (Friedlein 1873), where Proclus uses διῃρημένως in a similar context.

[90] Proclus, *In Tim.* 1, 246, 6–7 (Diehl 1903–1906).

[91] On this passage see Ierodiakonou (2005), 80–81.

An. post. 257, 37–38) the self-evident principles of demonstrations that are present in the soul are "echoes" (ἀπηχήματα) of the Intelligence.[92]

Understandably, given the enormous number of Proclus quotations used by Eustratios in expounding his view on concept-formation and on the status of the universals, this view can hardly be considered the token of a nominalistic position, or of a conceptualistic one. These latter interpretations may explain passages where Eustratios applies the traditional threefold distinction between universals – before the many, in the many and after the many – to specific problems such as the presence of two natures (divine and human) in one and the same subject (Christ).[93] However, when discussing the properties that characterize a universal proper, Eustratios appears loyal to his favorite Neoplatonic source in stating that universality does not depend on thought. Moreover, universals in the proper sense and described in Platonic terms as self-identical and self-subsisting beings with a certain causative power are not thought-dependent entities.[94]

Often Eustratios shapes his arguments with quotations from Christian authors, such as Gregory of Nazianzus.[95] However, pseudo-Dionysius the Areopagite is only once mentioned explicitly in Eustratios' commentaries (*In I EN*, 4, 37–38), with regard to the image of the "bloom of the intellect,"[96] which can be traced back to Proclus' reading of the Chaldaean Oracles.[97] In fact, just before referring to the bloom of the intellect, Eustratios had written (*In I EN*, 4, 37) that after becoming intelligent the soul "becomes divine as it is united with God in accordance with the One present in it" (θεοειδὴς ὡς θεῷ ἑνωθεῖσα κατὰ τὸ ἐν αὐτῇ ἐγκείμενον ἕν). Doubtless this passage derives from Proclus' assertion that the soul bears an image of the One which it must awake, "or how could we possibly become closer to the One, if we do not rouse up the One in the soul, which is in us as a kind of image of the One < . . . >? And how are we to make this One and the bloom of the soul shine forth unless we first of all act intellectually?" ("Η πῶς ἐγγυτέρω τοῦ ἑνὸς ἐσόμεθα, μὴ τὸ ἓν τῆς ψυχῆς ἀνεγείραντες, ὅ ἐστιν ἐν ἡμῖν οἷον εἰκὼν τοῦ ἑνὸς < . . . >; Πῶς δ' ἂν τὸ

92 On the Proclean background of this idea, see Ierodiakonou (2005), 81, n. 30; Trizio (2009a), 92.

93 For a summary of the different interpretations of Eustratios' view on universals, see Ierodiakonou (2005), 72.

94 Eustratios, *In VI EN*, 292, 28–293, 19 (Heylbut 1892). See Trizio (2009a), 104–105.

95 See Trizio (2009a), 101.

96 As a matter of fact this image is found only in the scholia to the *Ecclesiastic Hierarchy*. See Rorem and Lamoureux (1998), 118.

97 Proclus, *Eclogae De philosophia chaldaica*, fr. 4, 11 (des Places 1971).

ἓν αὐτὸ τοῦτο καὶ τὸ ἄνθος τῆς ψυχῆς ἀναλάμψαι ποιήσαιμεν, εἰ μὴ κατὰ νοῦν πρότερον ἐνεργήσαιμεν;)[98]

The latter passage presents ideas so close to Eustratios' own that we may ponder whether Eustratios is attempting to dissimulate the Proclean roots of his statement by ascribing it to the authority of the orthodox Dionysius – a question which, I believe, can be answered in the affirmative. Proclus dominates Eustratios' commentaries on Aristotle to such an extent that highly educated readers of the time could hardly have overlooked the strong Neoplatonic flavor of the commentator's arguments. These readers, who may most probably be identified as people closely related to the imperial court, rhetorically called φιλόλογοι by Eustratios,[99] must have shared the same literary tastes as Eustratios, including his fondness for Proclus and Plutarch, the latter's name being mentioned explicitly twice in his commentaries on the *Nicomachean Ethics*.[100]

Eustratios does not merely copy and paste from Proclus, but – and in so doing his usage of this author differs considerably from that of Italos – he re-elaborates Proclus' passages and shapes them to fit the structure of his own arguments.[101] All reference to Proclus' different orders of gods and souls is missing. Yet this attitude, suggestive of the author's religious concern, never becomes a reconciliation of Proclus with Christianity. Quite the contrary, the commentator is deliberately ambiguous on many crucial points: he posits the existence of a separate Intelligence, which he does not clearly identify with the Divine Intellect. Like Proclus, he speaks of the One in the soul, and when talking about Forms, he regards them as both intelligible contents in the separate Intelligence and as self-subsisting entities.[102]

Between Eustratios' death (*c.* 1120) and Nicholas of Methone's *Refutation of Proclus' Elements of Theology* (later 1150s–early 1160s) no Byzantine scholar seems to have endorsed Proclus' standpoints to the extent that Eustratios did. In his commentaries on books V, IX, and X of the *Nicomachean Ethics*, Michael of Ephesos (eleventh to twelfth centuries), whose biography remains mysterious, also refers to the Neoplatonists, though not as extensively as Eustratios.[103] Furthermore, Isaac the Sebastokrator, who may be identified either as Anna Komnena's uncle or as her brother,

[98] Proclus, *In Parm.* 1071, 19–24 (Steel, Mace, and d'Hoine 2009). English translation by Morrow and Dillon (1987), 425–425 (slightly modified).

[99] See Eustratios, *In VI EN*, 294, 28 (Heylbut 1892).

[100] Eustratios *In I EN*, 5, 15; *In VI EN*, 331, 32 (Heylbut 1892). On Plutarch's importance for the Byzantine *cursus studiorum*, see Wilson (1996), 151.

[101] For a case study of this Eustratios attitude, see Trizio (2009a), 92–93.

[102] On this, see Trizio (2009a), 103.

[103] See Luna (2001), 2–32; Steel (2002), 54–57.

adopted a rather different strategy when re-editing Proclus' *Tria opuscula*, christianizing Proclus' treatises on evil and providence in a way that leaves no doubt as to the author's aim of providing a fully Christian explanation of these issues.[104] When compared with these two case studies, Eustratios' assumption of the outlines of Proclus' Neoplatonism appears to be a unique case in twelfth-century Byzantium and is the main reason for his influence in the medieval Latin West. In fact, thirteenth-century scholars such as Albert the Great (†1280) will relate Eustratios' Neoplatonism to that of such Arabic sources available in Latin at the time as the *Liber de causis*. Considering the Proclean background of this latter work and Eustratios' general fondness for Proclus, such a link must have appeared obvious in the eyes of such a medieval master.[105]

Nicholas of Methone

The biography of Nicholas, bishop of Methone († *c.* 1166), is somewhat mysterious. A *Life of Nicholas* that circulated in the nineteenth century accompanied by a fine portrait of Nicholas himself was nothing less than the work of Constantine Simonides, the famous forger.[106] A look at Nicholas' work, which, besides a hagiographical work, includes several anti-Latin treatises and a refutation of the heresy of the Patriarch of Antioch, Sotericos Panteugenos, suggests that he must have been directly involved in the most relevant controversies of his time as a theologian closely related to the emperor Manuel I Komnenos (1143–1180).[107]

Nicholas' main work, the *Refutation of the Elements of Theology by the Platonic Philosopher Proclus the Lycian* (Ἀνάπτυξις τῆς Θεολογικῆς Στοιχειώσεως Πρόκλου τοῦ Λυκίου πλατωνικοῦ φιλοσόφου), is no less controversial than Nicholas' biography. In fact, the refutation of chapter 146 of the *Elements of Theology*, which includes a quotation from Gregory of Nazianzus, as found in the modern edition of Nicholas' work, corresponds to a fragment preserved in the manuscript *Vat. gr.* 1096 (f. 61r) under the name of Procopius of Gaza (*c.* 460/470–*c.* 528).[108] Thus, for a long time it had been thought that Nicholas merely plagiarized an otherwise unknown

104 See Boese (1960), xxii–xxiii.

105 See Trizio (2009b), 95–104.

106 The forgery was discovered by Sp. Lampros and the news was published in Draeseke (1898). On Simonides' skill in portrait see Janko (2009), 407–410. The scarce information concerning Nicholas' life is diligently collected in Angelou (1984b), ix–xxiii.

107 On Nicholas' work see Angelou (1984b), xxv–xliv. On the theological controversies under Manuel I Komnenos, see Magdalino (1993), 279–290, 316–412.

108 The fragment was discovered by Mai (1831), 274–275 (= *PG* 87/2, 2792E–H). The manuscript was later described by Stiglmayr (1899), 296–301 and Mercati (1931), 218–223.

Refutation of Proclus actually written by Procopius,[109] for the latter's pupil Choricius informs us that Procopius committed himself to defending the Christian dogma and rejecting pagan philosophy.[110] However, frequent references to pseudo-Dionysius the Areopagite, the anti-Latin undertones of the Ἀνάπτυξις, and the several cross-references to other works of Nicholas seem to exclude Procopius of Gaza as the veritable author of this work.[111]

It has nevertheless been suggested more recently that the Ἀνάπτυξις is an original work by Nicholas, based upon some earlier lost material by Procopius.[112] In fact – and this is one of the main arguments favoring this view – deliberate plagiarisms of Procopian works by Byzantine scholars were frequent,[113] although there are also cases of Byzantine works accidentally transmitted under the name of Procopius.[114] More importantly, the manuscript *Vat. gr.* 1096 (mostly a fourteenth-century anti-Palamite *catena*) contains two fragments of the Ἀνάπτυξις, ch. 146 ($52r_{12}$–$52v_{18}$; 61r) and ch. 139 ($108r_{15-17}$), the latter of which is in a fragmentary form.[115] The same excerpt from ch. 139 can be found in another manuscript under the name of Procopius, *Vat. gr.* 604 (f. $46r_{36-44}$), copied by the same hand that copied the two previously mentioned chapters of the Ἀνάπτυξις in *Vat. gr.* 1096.[116] Since these excerpts show few variant readings, it has been proposed that the copyist had access to two different manuscripts or versions of a lost Procopian refutation of Proclus' *Elements of Theology*, which Nicholas later incorporated into his Ἀνάπτυξις.[117]

However, this view should be tested against some paleographic evidence. We are in the lucky position of knowing who copied these excerpts in the two Vatican manuscripts, namely, the fourteenth-century anti-Palamite, Isaak Argyros.[118] The hand of an anonymous close collaborator and member of Isaak's circle is also found in the first part of *Vat. gr.* 626, probably

109 See Roussos (1893) 57ff.; Draeseke (1895) and (1897); Krumbacher (1897), 85; Tatakis (1949), 38; Aly (1957); Whittaker (1975), 311; Chauvot (1986), 87–88; Matino (2005) 17, n. 31. Procopius' authorship of the Ἀνάπτυξις is also accepted in Geerard (1979), 7440.

110 Choricius, *Opera* VIII 21, 117, 12–22 (Foerster and Richstieg 1929). See also Michael Psellos, *Orationes forenses* 1, 287–299 (Dennis 1994).

111 Stiglmayr (1899); Bardenhewer (1901), 478; Dodds (1963b), xxxi, n. 1; Beck (1959), 415 and 624; Podskalsky (1976); Angelou (1984b), xliii–xliv; Rorem and Lamoreaux (1998), 10, n. 7.

112 Amato (2010).

113 Amato (2010), 8–10.

114 See the lament for the collapse of Hagia Sophia edited in Michael Psellos, *Oratoria minora* 35 (Littlewood 1985). On this see Wuerthle (1917); Mango (1988), 167–169. According to this latter contribution, this text cannot be ascribed to Psellos either.

115 On the existence of two versions of ch. 146 in the *Vat. gr.* 1096, see Stiglmayr (1899), 299 and Mercati (1931), 265–266.

116 See Bianconi (2008), 354 and Amato (2010), 11.

117 See Amato (2010), 10–12.

118 On Isaak, see Trapp *et al.* (1976–1996), 1285. On Isaak's library see Mercati (1931), 229–242, 264–266.

the earliest manuscript containing the Ἀνάπτυξις.[119] Here, however, the attribution of the Ἀνάπτυξις to Nicholas, found in the upper margin of f. 121r, belongs to a later hand, suggesting that Isaak and his fellows had access to an acephalous version of the Ἀνάπτυξις. Because of this, Isaak himself may have conjectured the Procopian authorship of the fragments which he had copied in the two aforementioned Vaticani.[120]

Although there is still room for further findings,[121] the Ἀνάπτυξις clearly reflects the intellectual climate of Nicholas' time, which is characterized by frequent complaints among twelfth-century Byzantine intellectuals about the spreading of Proclus' work. Around the time of the composition of the Ἀνάπτυξις, George Tornikes' *Funeral Oration on Anna Comnena* cautiously states that the princess admired Proclus and Iamblichus but preferred Dionysius the Areopagite and his alleged master Hierotheus.[122] Byzantine scholars such as Theodore Prodromos were questioned concerning their fondness for pagan philosophy.[123] Moreover, some years after the composition of the Ἀνάπτυξις, the consul of the philosophers Michael of Anchialos openly announced that he would confine his teaching to Aristotle's logical and natural works.[124] Since these accounts are mostly rhetorical, it is difficult to identify "those who regard as worthy of study the chapters of Proclus the Lycian called 'Elements of Theology,'" mentioned by Nicholas (2, 6–7) as the target of the Ἀνάπτυξις. These might have been erudite readers from the intellectual elite of the Komnenian society who concealed their fondness for Proclus by leaving no trace of it in their writings.

Nicholas' Ἀνάπτυξις aims at testing the different propositions of the *Elements of Theology* against Christian dogmata, in order to show their incompatibility with the latter. Thus, he corrects Proclus' statement that "every cause properly so-called transcends its result" (prop. 75), and the related distinction between causes and concomitant causes which Eustratios of Nicaea accepted without reservation,[125] by stating that God is the only true cause transcending creation (77, 21–22). He also argues that this principle does not apply to intra-trinitarian causation, where the Father is the cause of the Son and the Holy Spirit, for this process does not

119 On this manuscript see Devreesse (1950), 33–34; Turyn (1964), 107–108.
120 See Bianconi (2008), 354.
121 See Westerink 1942 on Psellos' quotation from an alleged Procopian refutation of Proclus' commentary on the Chaldean Oracles.
122 George Tornikes, *Oratio* 14, 299, 24–26 (Darrouzès 1970).
123 See Theodore Prodromos, *Poem.* 59 (Hörandner 1974). On this see Magdalino (1993), 390–391.
124 Michael of Anchialos, *Oratio aditialis* 190, 105–108 (Browning 1961). For further documents concerning twelfth-century opposition to Proclus and Hellenic philosophy, see Browning (1975); Angelou (1984b), lvii–lviii; Magdalino (1993), 332–335; Kaldellis (2007), 225–282, (2009), (2012).
125 See above.

involve transcendence of the cause (78, 2–4). Yet, Nicholas agrees with Proclus in admitting that the instrument cannot limit the maker's creation – something that "should also be used against Eunomius, who regards the Son as instrumental cause and the Father as the cause properly so-called and the productive one of the Son Himself" (78, 10–12).

By the same token, probably because he could find the same distinction in pseudo-Dionysius the Areopagite,[126] Nicholas accepts Proclus' three modes of existence as stated in the *Elements of Theology*, κατ' αἰτίαν, καθ' ὕπαρξιν, κατὰ μέθεξιν (prop. 65), but rejects the multiplicity of causes as something that denies God's role as the universe's sole cause (68, 10–12). Furthermore, whilst conceding that "every soul is an incorporeal substance and separable from the body" (prop. 186) Nicholas remarks (163, 19–26) that this only holds true for the rational souls and not for the irrational. Otherwise, suggests Nicholas (163, 26–164, 5), cribbing from Nemesius of Emesa's *De natura hominis*, one should admit the transmigration of souls from men into animals and vice-versa – a view rejected not only by Christians (as witnessed in one of the articles of Italos' condemnation in the *Synodikon*),[127] but also by Hellenic philosophers such as Iamblichus.[128]

Like other Byzantine scholars, such as George Pachymeres,[129] Nicholas explains the similarities between Proclus and pseudo-Dionysius on the grounds that the latter was master to the former, who nevertheless "intermingled the seeds of devotion with grievous devilry" (117, 27–28). Unsurprisingly, Nicholas refers to pseudo-Dionysius as a corrective to Proclus' views. For example, confronting prop. 158 ("all elevative causes among the gods differ both from the purificatory causes and from the conversive kinds"), Nicholas comments that (142, 12–18) these three types of causes are found in the one and only God, and he supports his view that these powers of the intellectual and divine orders come from God Himself by quoting pseudo-Dionysius' *Celestial Hierarchy*.[130]

Only a few passages are quoted from Gregory Nazianzen, one of the authorities most invoked by Nicholas, although these passages are referred to more than once in the Ἀνάπτυξις. Thus, Gregory's statement – originally intended to defend the Christian metaphysical notion of monarchy against the "Greeks" – that "the monad which existed from the beginning and is moved into a dyad, rests as a Triad"[131] is introduced in several

[126] Pseudo-Dionysius, *Epistulae* 9.2, 18–22 (Heil and Ritter 1991).
[127] *Synodikon* 57, 194 (Gouillard 1967).
[128] Nemesius, *De natura hominis* 2, 34, 18–35, 14 (Morani 1987).
[129] George Pachymeres, *Proemium in opera Dionysii*, *PG* 3: 116A.
[130] Pseudo-Dionysius, *De caelesti hierarchia* 106, 22–23 (Heil and Ritter 1991).
[131] Gregory Nazianzen, *Oratio* 29, 2, 130, 11–12 (Barbel 1963).

passages within the Ἀνάπτυξις. This stresses the transcendence of the intra-Trinitarian procession vis-à-vis the other processions of beings from the First Cause or else refers the notion of "unmoved" proper to God alone (5, 10–11; 20, 26–27; 133, 20–22). Furthermore, Nicholas (12, 30–31) refers to Gregory's famous description of God as that which "contains the whole being, holding it in Himself, like an endless and boundless ocean of reality"[132] in order (1) to qualify the notion of primal Good mentioned in Proclus' statement that "All that in any way participates in the Good is subordinate to the primal Good, which is nothing else but good" (prop. 8); and (2) to reject (49, 1–3; 59, 16–18) Proclus' arguments that "All that proceeds from another cause is subordinate to principles which get their substance from themselves and have a self-constituted existence" (prop. 40) and "All that is produced by secondary beings is in a greater measure produced from those prior and more determinate principles from which the secondary were themselves derived" (prop. 56). In fact these Proclean arguments contradict God's role as the only cause of the universe.

Against Proclus' theory that "All that is divine has a substance which is goodness, a potency which has the character of unity, and a mode of knowledge which is secret and incomprehensible to all secondary beings alike" (prop. 121), Nicholas once again maintains that all this applies only to God. He supports this view (117, 11–12) by referring to Gregory Nazianzen's statement that God "is not known in Himself, but from His properties, as sense perception collects them one after the other in order to obtain one single image of the truth."[133] Finally, Proclus' prop. 198 in the *Elements of Theology* which states that "All that participates in time but has perpetuity of movement is measured by periods" is refuted by Nicholas, somewhat naively, on the grounds that there is an inherent contradiction between being in time and perpetuity of movement, as suggested by Gregory's saying that "that which is time according to us is eternity for the eternal realities" (174, 7–8).[134]

It is unfortunate that those who appealed to these quotations from Gregory as evidence favoring the Procopian authorship of the Ἀνάπτυξις[135] did not realize the importance of this author for the Byzantine anti-Latin polemicists like Nicholas. Most quotations from this Church Father present in the Ἀνάπτυξις – for instance, that used for the controversial refutation of prop. 146 of the *Elements of Theology* which resulted in a debate on the authorship of the Ἀνάπτυξις ("the monad which existed since the

[132] Gregory Nazianzen, *Or.* 38, *PG* 36, 317B.
[133] Gregory Nazianzen, *Or.* 38, *PG* 36, 317BC.
[134] Gregory Nazianzen, *Or.* 38, *PG* 36, 320B.
[135] See e.g. Whittaker (1975).

beginning and is moved into a dyad, rests as a Triad")[136] – are present in a vast number of anti-Latin writings by Nicholas and other Byzantine scholars and used as a tool to defend the procession of the Holy Spirit *ex solo patre*.[137] But even before Nicholas the aforementioned quotation from Gregory is diligently mentioned in the *Panoplia dogmatica* by the eleventh- to twelfth-century court theologian Euthymios Zigabenos[138] and also appears in the anti-iconoclastic writings of Euthymios' contemporary Eustratios of Nicaea.[139] Further discussions of this quotation from Gregory can be found in Michael Psellos' theological writings[140] and in John Italos' philosophical treatises.[141]

Often Nicholas ridicules Proclus, introducing a comment of his with the formula "well, well" (116, 12), or addressing him ironically, as in the author's rhetorical comment on prop. 164 ("All those henads are supramundane whereof all the unparticipated souls enjoy participation"). Here, he comments: "if the unparticipated soul is one, oh wisest Proclus, in what sense do you say 'all' as referred to many of them?" (145, 8–9).[142] Nicholas is more interested in rejecting Proclus' view as incompatible with Christian truths than in delving more deeply into Proclus' thought. Had he done so, he would probably have understood how it is possible for Proclus to maintain, for example, that "every soul take its proximate origin from an intelligence" (prop. 193), and at the same time that "every soul is self-animated" (prop. 189) in the sense that it is self-constituted. In fact, eager to refer the notion of self-constitution to God alone, Nicholas does not realize – or is not interested in admitting – that there is no contradiction between deriving from something and being self-constituted in Proclean metaphysics.[143] Yet, Nicholas still concedes that the soul is self-constituted in the same way that Aristotle regards substance as self-subsistent vis-à-vis the accidents (167, 18–21; 24–26).[144] This is the very same argument that he uses (49, 11–13) in relation to Proclus' more general statement that "All that proceeds from another cause is subordinate to principles which get their substance from themselves and have a self-constituted existence" (prop. 40).

[136] See above.

[137] Nicholas of Methone, *Oratio* 7, 317, 17–20 (Demetracopoulos 1866). See also Gregory Palamas, *De processione spiritus sancti orationes duae*, I, 20, 13–16 (Chrestou 1962); Mark Eugenicus, *Testimonia spiritum sanctum ex patre procedere probantia*, n. 54 (Petit 1977).

[138] Euthymios Zigabenos, *Panopolia dogmatica*, *PG* 130, 61D.

[139] Eustratios, *Or.* 6, 152, 31–153, 2 (Demetracopoulos 1866).

[140] Michael Psellos, *Theol.* 20, 76, 2–3 (Gautier 1989).

[141] John Italos, *Quaest. quod.* 69, 115, 36–29 (Joannou 1956b).

[142] On this comment see Dodds (1963a), 284.

[143] See also Dodds (1963a), 299.

[144] Aristotle, *Metaphysica* V, 30, 1025a30–32 (Ross 1924).

Whereas pseudo-Dionysius is used to correcting Proclus' theology, the bishop of Methone uses Aristotle in order to correct him philosophically. Eustratios of Nicaea had charged Aristotle with sophistry for having criticized Plato's Ideal Good, which he himself defended with Proclus' words.[145] Nicholas reverses this, and uses Aristotle to counter Proclus, someone he considers (3, 16–17) to be an "insolent youth." Thus, in rejecting Proclus' belief that "if the potency of any finite body is infinite, it is incorporeal" (prop. 96), Nicholas notes that this contradicts Aristotle's denial of the existence of an infinite body (94, 23–24).[146] Commenting on prop. 14 of the *Elements of Theology* ("All that exists is either moved or unmoved; and if the former, either by itself or by another, that is, intrinsically or extrinsically: so that everything is unmoved, intrinsically moved, or extrinsically moved"), Nicholas claims (19, 23–26) that it contradicts not only Aristotle but the other philosophers as well, for here Proclus – against Aristotle's *De interpretatione*[147] – identifies the notion of "all" with that of "being universal." Finally, both in the Ἀνάπτυξις (160, 18–21) and in his writing against Soterichos Panteugenos, Nicholas refers to Aristotle's definition of the Platonic ideas as "twittering" (τερετίσματα).[148] He thereby makes his contribution to that suppression of Plato and the Platonic tradition in favor of Aristotle being attempted by the intellectual establishment at the time.[149]

Nicholas' strategy in criticizing Proclus consists of denying entities other than God any causative power in order to avoid polytheism. So, under the authority of pseudo-Dionysius, Nicholas (79, 10–12) contends that the ideas of beings are not self-subsistent realities, but God's "divine and good volitions."[150] Interestingly, in his writing against Soterichos Panteugenos, Nicholas endorses the same view by stating that even Plato did not regard the ideas as a self-subsisting hypostasis,[151] a view that is reminiscent of Eustratios of Nicaea's claim that the ideas are "enhypostatic" in the Divine Intellect according to the Platonists.[152]

The link with Eustratios is problematic. Concerning the notion of ἀρχικὰ αἴτια, the Ἀνάπτυξις refers (95, 26) to a ζήτημα ("a treatise")

145 Eustratios, *In I EN*, 45, 32–38; 50, 30–33 (Heylbut 1892).
146 Aristotle, *Physica* 205b35–206a7 (Ross 1959). See Dodds (1963a), 250.
147 Aristotle, *De Interpretatione* 17b12 (Minio-Paluello 1949).
148 Nicholas of Methone, *Or.* 6, 324, 19–23 (Demetracopoulos 1866).
149 See Magdalino (1993), 332.
150 Pseudo-Dionysius, *De divinis nominibus* 188, 6–10 (Suchla 1990).
151 Nicholas of Methone, *Or.* 6, 324, 9–19 (Demetracopoulos 1866).
152 Eustratios, *In I EN*, 40, 22–27 (Heylbut 1892).

on the many gods propounded by "the martyr Eustratios," which investigates the consequences of admitting several principal causes by considering "whether these are all equal in their substance and power and in every way, or whether, among these, some are more important while others are less" (πότερον ἴσα πάντα καὶ κατ' οὐσίαν καὶ κατὰ δύναμιν καὶ πάντῃ αὐτὰ ἢ τὰ μὲν μείζω, τὰ δὲ ἐλάττω). Contrary to the modern editor's opinion, this reference is not to the eleventh–twelfth-century bishop of Nicaea and Aristotle commentator, but rather to the martyr Eustratios and the Passio SS Eustratii et Sociorum, a text dated as early as the ninth century.[153] Nicholas, however, also knew and quoted Eustratios, the bishop of Nicaea. It may not have been so problematic to quote Eustratios at the time of the Ἀνάπτυξις' composition, since by then the former bishop of Nicaea had been rehabilitated and used as a theological authority at the synod of the Blanchernai (1156).[154] In fact, a passage from Eustratios' treatise against iconoclasm is surely the source of Nicholas' statement that God is that which "limits everything, although He is not limited by anything" (143, 2–3).[155]

The Ἀνάπτυξις does not appear to have exercised great influence among the later generations of Byzantine theologians, even though they were just as concerned about the spread of profane learning as Nicholas was.[156] As a matter of fact, Barlaam the Calabrian used Proclus at length in his dispute with Gregory Palamas in the fourteenth century.[157] It may be fruitful to study the refutation of ch. 139 in the *Vat. gr.* 1096 ($108r_{15-27}$), there attributed to Procopius and included within the refutation of the pro-Palamite John VI Kantacouzenos by the anti-Palamite copyist, Isaak Argyros. These fragments of the Ἀνάπτυξις contain some interesting clues concerning the soul's participation and union with the Divine nature, which is said to take place κατὰ χάριν. Since the participants in the fourteenth-century Palamite controversy debated this topic heatedly, the Ἀνάπτυξις may well have been useful source material in some way or other. However, it would seem that this was not enough to confer on the the Ἀνάπτυξις the status of a reference work among the Byzantine scholars of the time.

153 See Lackner (1988).

154 See Magdalino (1993), 279. A series of syllogisms from Eustratios' work are found in Andronikos Kamateros' *Sacred Arsenal* (in Monacensis Graecus 229, ff. 1–309, 82v–84v), written not many years after the Ἀνάπτυξις. I am indebted for this information to the modern editor of Kamateros' work, Alessandra Bucossi.

155 See Eustratios, *Or.* 6, 153, 8–9 (Demetracopoulos 1866).

156 For an overview on Proclus in Byzantium see Benakis (1987).

157 See Sinkewicz (1981), (1982); Trizio (2011).

Bibliography

Adler, A. (ed.) (1928–1935) *Suidae lexicon*, 4 vols., Leipzig.

Aly, W. (1957) "Prokopios von Gaza," in *Paulys Real-Encyklopädie der klassischen Altertumwissenschaft* 23/1, Stuttgart, cols. 259–273.

Amato, E. (2010) "Sul discusso plagio della *Refutatio Procli Institutionis theologicae* di Procopio di Gaza ad opera di Nicola di Metone: nuovi apporti della tradizione manoscritta," *Medioevo Greco* 10: 5–12.

Angelou, A. D. (ed.) (1984a) *Nicholas of Methone: Refutation of Proclus' Elements of Theology*, Leiden and Athens.

(1984b) "Introduction," in Angelou (1984a), ix–lxxx.

Angold, M. (2000) *Church and Society under the Comneni*, Cambridge.

Arabatzis, G. (2002) "Blâme du philosophe, Éloge de la vraie philosophie et figures rhétoriques: le récit d'Anne Comnène sur Jean Italos revisité," *Byzantinische Zeitschrift* 95/2: 403–415.

Barbel, J. (ed.) (1963) *Gregor von Nazianz: Die fünf theologischen Reden*, Düsseldorf, 170–216.

Bardenhewer, O. (1901) *Patrologie*, Freiburg im Breisgau.

Beck, H. G. (1959) *Kirche und theologische Literatur im byzantinischen Reich*, Munich.

Benakis, L. (1987) "Neues zur Proklos-Tradition in Byzanz," in G. Boss and G. Seel (eds.), *Proclus et son influence. Actes du colloque de Neuchâtel, juin 1985*, Neuchâtel, 241–253.

Bianconi, D. (2008) "La controversia palamitica. Figure, libri, testi, mani," *Segno e Testo* 6: 337–376.

Boese, H. (ed.) (1960) *Procli Diadochi: Tria opuscula (De providentia, libertate, malo), latine Guillelmo de Moerbeka vertente et graece ex Isaacii Sebastocratoris aliorumque scriptis collecta*, Berlin.

Browning, R. (1961) "A New Source on Byzantine–Hungarian Relations in the Twelfth Century, The Inaugural Lecture of Michael ὁ τοῦ Ἀγχιάλου as Ὕπατος τῶν φιλοσόφων," *Balkan Studies* 2: 173–214.

(1962) "An Unpublished Funeral Oration on Anna Comnena," *Proceedings of the Cambridge Philological Society* 188: 1–12. Reprinted in Browning (1977).

(1963) "The Patriarchal School at Constantinople in the Twelfth Century," *Byzantion* 33: 11–40.

(1975) "Enlightment and Repression in Byzantium in the Eleventh and Twelfth Centuries," *Past and Present* 69: 3–23. Reprinted in Browning (1977).

(1977) *Studies on Byzantine History, Literature and Education*, London.

Burnet, J. (ed.) (1900–1907) *Platonis Opera*, 5 vols., Oxford.

Busse, A. (ed.) (1891) Ammonius, *In Porphyrii Isagogen sive Quinque voces*, Berlin.

(ed.) (1898) *Philoponi (olim Ammonii) in Aristotelis categorias commentarium*, Berlin.

(ed.) (1904) *Davidis prolegomena et in Porphyrii Isagogen commentarium*, Berlin.

Bywater, I. (ed.) (1962) *Aristotelis Ethica Nicomachea*, 2nd edn., Oxford.

Cacouros, M. (2000) "Eustrate de Nicée," in R. Goulet (ed.), *Dictionnaire de philosophes antiques*, vol. III, Paris, 378–388.

(2007) "Survie culturelle et rémanence textuelle du néoplatonisme à Byzance. Élémente generaux-éléments portant sur la logique," in C. D'Ancona (ed.), *The Libraries of the Neoplatonists*, Leiden, 177–210.

Cereteli, G. (ed.) (1924) *Ioannis Itali opuscula selecta*, vol. I, Tbilisi.

Chauvot, A. (1986) *Procope de Gaza/Priscien de Césarée: Panégyriques pour l'empereur Anastase Ier*, Bonn.

Chrestou, P. K. (1962) *Γρηγορίου τοῦ Παλαμᾶ συγγράμματα*, vol. I, Thessalonica.

Clucas, L. (1981) *The Trial of John Italos and the Crisis of Intellectual Values in Byzantium in the Eleventh Century*, Munich.

Darrouzès, J. (1966) *Documents inédits d'ecclésiologie byzantine*, Paris.

(ed.) (1970) *Georges et Demetrios Tornikes: Lettres et discours*, Paris.

(1984) Review of L. Clucas, *The Trial of John Italos and the Crisis of Intellectual Values in Byzantium in the Eleventh Century, Revue des études byzantines* 42: 317–318.

Del Corno, D., Impellizzeri, S., Criscuolo, U., and Ronchey, S. (eds.) (1984) *Michael Psellos: Imperatori di Bisanzio (Cronografia)*, Milan.

Dennis, G. T. (1994) *Michaelis Pselli orationes forenses et acta*, Stuttgart.

Devreesse, R. (1950) *Codices Vaticani Graeci*, vol. II: *Codices 330–603*, Vatican City.

Demetracopoulos, A. (ed.) (1866) Ἐκκλησιαστικὴ Βιβλιοθήκη, vol. I, Leipzig.

Des Places, É. (ed.) (1971) *Oracles chaldaïques, avec un choix de commentaires anciens*, Paris.

Diehl, E. (ed.) (1903–1906) *Procli Diadochi in Platonis Timaeum commentaria*, 3 vols., Leipzig.

Diels, H. (ed.) (1882) *Simplicii in Aristotelis physicorum libros octo commentaria*, vol. I, Berlin.

Dodds, E. R. (ed. and trans.) (1963a) *Proclus: The Elements of Theology*, 2nd edn., Oxford.

(1963b) "Introduction," in Dodds (1963a), ix–xlvii.

Draeseke, J. (1895) "Nikolaos von Methone als Bestreiter des Proklos," *Theologische Studien und Kritiken* 68: 589–616.

(1897) "Prokopios' von Gaza Widerlegung des Proklos," *Byzantinische Zeitschrift* 6: 55–91.

(1898) "Zu Nikolaos von Methone," *Zeitschrift für Wissenschaftliche Theologie* 41: 402–411.

Dujčev, J. (1939) "L'umanesimo di Giovanni Italo," *Studi bizantini e neoellenici* 5: 432–435.

Evans, E. (ed.) (1969) Aurelius Augustinus, *Enchiridion ad Laurentium de fide et spe et caritate*, Turnhout.

Foerster, R. and Richstieg, E. (eds.) (1929) *Choricii Gazei Opera*, Leipzig.

Frankopan, P. (2009) "The Literary, Cultural and Political Context for the Twelfth-Century Commentary on the *Nicomachean Ethics*," in C. Barber (ed.), *Medieval Greek Commentaries on the Nicomachean Ethics*, Leiden, 45–62.

Friedlein, G. (ed.) (1873) *Procli Diadochi in primum Euclidis elementorum librum commentarii*, Leipzig.

Gauthier, P. (ed.) (1989) *Michaelis Pselli theologica*, vol. I, Leipzig.

Geerard, M. (ed.) (1979) *Clavis Patrum Graecorum*, vol. III, Turnhout.

Gersh, S. (2000) "Proclus' Theological Methods. The Programme of *Theol. Plat.* I 4," in A.-Ph. Segonds and C. Steel (eds.), *Proclus et la Theologie platonicienne. Actes du colloque international de Louvain, 13–16 mai 1998, en l'honneur de H. D. Saffrey et L. G. Westerink*, Leuven and Paris, 15–27.

Giocarinis, K. (1964) "Eustratius of Nicaea's Defense of the Doctrine of Ideas," *Franciscan Studies* 24: 159–204.

Golitsis, P. (2008) "Georges Pachymère comme didascale. Essai pour une reconstitution de sa carrière et de son enseignement philosophique," *Jahrbuch der Österreichischen Byzantinistik* 58: 53–68.

Gouillard, J. (ed.) (1967) "Le *Synodikon de l'Orthodoxie*. Édition et commentaire," *Travaux et mémoires* 2: 1–316.

(1976) "La religion des philosophes," *Travaux et mémoires* 6: 305–324.

(1983) Review of L. Clucas, *The Trial of John Italos and the Crisis of Intellectual Values in Byzantium in the Eleventh Century*, *Byzantinische Zeitschrift* 76: 31–33.

(1985) "Le procès officiel de Jean l'Italien. Les Actes et leurs sous-entendus," *Travaux et memoires* 9: 133–174.

Grumel, V. and Darrouzès, J. (eds.) (1989) *Les regestes des actes du patriarchat de Constantinople*, vol. I: *Les actes des patriarches, fasc. II et III: Les regestes de 715 à 1206*, Paris.

Hayduck, M. (ed.) (1897) *Ioannis Philoponi in Aristotelis de anima libros commentaria*, Berlin.

(ed.) (1907) *In Aristotelis analyticorum posteriorum librum secundum commentarium*, Berlin.

Heil, G. and Ritter, A. M. (eds.) (1991) *Corpus Dionysiacum*, vol. II: *Pseudo-Dionysius Areopagita: De caelesti hierarchia, De ecclesiastica hierarchia, De mystica theologia, Epistulae*, Berlin.

Henry, P. and Schwyzer, H.-R. (1951–1973) *Plotini Opera*, 3 vols., Leiden.

Heylbut, G. (ed.) (1892) *Eustratii et Michaelis et anonyma in ethica Nicomachea commentaria*, Berlin.

Hörandner, W. (ed.) (1974) *Theodoros Prodromos: Historische Gedichte*, Vienna.

Hunger, H. (1987) *Graeculus perfidus – Ἰταλὸς ἰταμός, Il senso dell' alterità nei rapporti greco-romani ed italo-bizantini*, Rome.

Ierodiakonou, K. (2005) "Metaphysics in the Byzantine Tradition: Eustratios of Nicaea on Universals," *Quaestio* 5: 67–82.

(2009) "John Italos on Universals," *Documenti e studi sulla tradizione filosofica medievale* 18: 231–248.

Janko, R. (2009) "The Artemidorus Papyrus," *The Classical Review* 59/2: 403–410.

Jenkins, D. (2009) "Eustratios of Nicaea's 'Definition of Being' Revisited," in C. Barber and D. Jenkins (eds.), *Medieval Greek Commentaries on the Nicomachean Ethics*, Leiden and Boston, 111–130.

Joannou, P. (1952) "Eustrate de Nicée: trois pièces inédites de son proces (1117)," *Revue des études byzantines* 10: 24–34.

(1953) "La doctrine de l'"illumination' dans l'ontologie et l'épistémologie du XIe siècle (Jean Italos)," *Studi bizantini e neoellenici*, 7: 130–131.

(1954) "Der nominalismus und die menschliche psychologie Christi: Das *semeioma* gegen Eustratios von Nikaia," *Byzantinische Zeitschrift* 47: 358–378.

(1956a) *Christliche Metaphysik in Byzanz*, vol. I: *Die Illuminationslehre des Michael Psellos und Joannes Italos*, Ettal.

(ed.) (1956b) Johannes Italos, *Quaestiones quodlibetales (Ἀπορίαι καὶ λύσεις)*, Ettal.

(1958) "Le sort des évêques hérétiques réconciliés: un discours inédit de Nicétas de Serres contre Eustrate de Nicée," *Byzantion* 28: 1–30.

Kalbfleisch, K. (ed.) (1907) *Simplicii in Aristotelis categorias commentarium*, Berlin.

Kaldellis, A. (2007) *Hellenism in Byzantium. The Transformations of Greek Identity and the Reception of the Classical Tradition*, Cambridge.

(2009) "Classical Scholarship in Twelfth-Century Byzantium," in C. Barber and D. Jenkins (eds.), *Medieval Greek Commentaries on the Nicomachean Ethics*, Leiden and Boston, 1–43.

(2012) "Byzantine Philosophy Inside and Out: Orthodoxy and Dissidence in Counterpoint," in K. Ierodiakonou (ed.), *The Many Faces of Byzantine Philosophy*, Athens, 129–151.

Karamanolis, G. E. (2006) *Plato and Aristotle in Agreement? Platonists on Aristotle from Antiochus to Porphyry*, Oxford.

Kotter, P. B. (ed.) (1973) *Die Schriften des Johannes von Damaskos*, vol. II: *Expositio fidei*, Berlin.

Kroll, W. (ed.) (1899–1901) *Procli Diadochi in Platonis rem publicam commentarii*, 2 vols., Leipzig.

Krumbacher, K. (1897) *Geschichte der byzantinischen Literatur von Justinian bis zum Ende des oströmischen Reiches (527–1453)*, 2nd edn., Munich.

Lackner, W. (ed.) (1985a) *Nikephoros Blemmydes: Gegen die Vorherbestimmung der Todesstunde*, Athens and Leiden.

(1985b) "Einleitung," in Lackner (1985a), xv–xciv.

(1988) Review of A. D. Angelou (ed.), *Nicholas of Methone: Refutation of Proclus' Elements of Theology*, Athens 1984, *Jahrbuch der Österreichischen Byzantinistik* 38: 476–478.

Lauritzen, F. (2007) "The Debate on Faith and Reason," *Jahrbuch der Österreichischen Byzantinistik* 57: 75–82.

(2009) "Psello discepolo di Stetato," *Byzantinische Zeitschrift* 101/2: 715–725.

Leib, B. (ed.) (1943) *Anna Comnène: Alexiade*, vol. II, Paris.

Lemerle, P. (1977) "Le gouvernement des philosophes," in *L'enseignement, les écoles, la culture*, in P. Lemerle, *Cinq études sur le XIe siècle byzantin*, Paris, 195–258.

Littlewood, A. R. (ed.) (1985) *Michaelis Pselli oratoria minora*, Leipzig.

Lloyd, A. C. (1987) "The Aristotelianism of Eustratios of Nicaea," in J. Wiesner (ed.), *Aristoteles, Werk und Wirkung*, vol. II, Berlin, 341–351.

Luna, C. (2001) *Trois études sur la tradition des commentaires anciens à la Metaphysique d'Aristote*, Leiden, Boston, and Cologne.
Magdalino, P. (1993) *The Empire of Manuel I Komnenos*, Cambridge.
Mai, A. (1831) *Classicorum auctorum e Vaticanis codicibus editorum tomus IV, complectens scripta aliquot Oribasii, Procopii, Isaei, Themistii, Porphyrii, Philonis, Aristidis, et alia quaedam, curante Angelo Maio*, Rome.
Mango, C. (1988) "The Collapse of St. Sophia, Psellus and the Etymologicum Genuinum," in J. Duffy and J. Peradotto (eds.), *Gonimos, Neoplatonic and Byzantine Studies Presented to Leendert G. Westerink at 75*, New York, 167–174.
Martijn, M. (2010) *Proclus on Nature. Philosophy of Nature and Its Methods in Proclus' Commentary on Plato, Timaeus*, Leiden.
Matino, G. (2005) *Procopio di Gaza: Panegirico per l'imperatore Anastasio*, Naples.
Mercati, G. (1931) *Notizie di Procoro e Demetrio Cidone, Manuele Caleca e Teodoro Meliteniota: ed altri appunti per la storia della teologia e della letteratura bizantina del secolo XIV*, Vatican City.
Mercken, H. P. F. (1990) "The Greek Commentators on Aristotle Ethics," in R. Sorabji (ed.), *Aristotle Transformed. The Ancient Commentators and Their Influence*, London, 407–444.
Minio Paluello, L. (ed.) (1949) *Aristotelis categoriae et liber de interpretatione*, Oxford.
Morani, M. (ed.) (1987) *Nemesii Emeseni de natura hominis*, Leipzig.
Morrow, G. R. and Dillon, J. M. (eds.) (1987) *Proclus' Commentary on Plato's Parmenides*, Princeton.
Mullet, M. (1984) "Aristocracy and Patronage in the Literary Circles of Comnenian Constantinople," in M. Angold, *The Byzantine Aristocracy, IX to XIII Centuries*, Oxford, 173–201.
Niarchos, G. (1978) "God, the Universe and Man in the Philosophy of John Italos," Diss. Oxford.
O'Meara, D. J. (ed.) (1989) *Michaelis Pselli philosophica minora*, vol. II, Leipzig.
(1997) "Das Böse bei Plotin (*Enn.* I, 8)," in T. Kobusch and B. Mojsisch (eds.), *Platon in der abendländischen Geistesgeschichte, Neue Forschungen zum Platonismus*, Darmstadt, 33–47.
(2005) "The Metaphysics of Evil in Plotinus, Problems and Solutions," in J. M. Dillon (ed.), *Agonistes, Essays in Honour of Denis O'Brien*, Aldershot, 179–185.
Opsomer, J. (2001) "Proclus vs Plotinus on Matter (*De mal. subs.* 30–7)," *Phronesis* 46: 154–188.
(2007) "Some Problems with Plotinus' Theory of Matter/Evil. An Ancient Debate Continued," *Quaestio* 7: 165–189.
Petit, L. (ed.) (1977) *Marci Eugenici Metropolitae Ephesi opera anti-unionistica*, vol. X/2, Rome, 34–59.
Podskalsky, G. (1976) "Nikolaos von Methone und die *Proklosrenaissance* in Byzanz (11./12. Jh.)," *Orientalia Christiana Periodica* 42: 509–523.
(1977) *Philosophie und Theologie in Byzanz*, Munich.
Rigo, A. (2001) "Giovanni Italo," in *Dizionario biografico degli italiani*, vol. LVI, Rome, 62–67.

Romano, R. (ed.) (1974) *Pseudo-Luciano: Timarione*, Naples.

Rorem, P. and Lamoreaux, J. C. (1998) *John of Scythopolis and the Dionysian Corpus. Annotating the Areopagite*, Oxford.

Ross, W. D. (ed.) (1924) *Aristotle's Metaphysics*, 2 vols., Oxford.

(ed.) (1958) *Aristotelis Topica et Sophistici Elenchi*, Oxford.

(ed.) (1959) *Aristotelis Physica*, Oxford.

Roussos, D. (1893) *Τρεῖς Γαζαῖοι. Συμβολαὶ εἰς τὴν ἱστορίαν τῆς φιλοσοφίας τῶν γαζαίων*, Constantinople.

Saffrey, H.-D. and Westerink, L.-G. (eds.) (1968–1997) *Proclus: Théologie platonicienne*, 6 vols., Paris.

Salaville, S. (1930) "Philosophie et théologie ou épisodes scholastiques à Byzance de 1059 à 1117," *Échos d'Orient* 29: 132–156.

Segonds, A.-Ph. (ed.) (1985a) *Proclus: Sur le Premier Alcibiade de Platon*, Paris.

(1985b) "Introduction," in Segonds (1985a), vii–cxxxix.

Sheppard, A. (1987) "Proclus' Philosophical Method of Exegesis: The Use of Aristotle and the Stoics in the Commentary on the *Cratylus*," in J. Pépin and H.-D. Saffrey (eds.), *Proclus: lecteur et interprète des anciens*, Paris, 137–151.

Skoulatos, B. (1980) *Les personnages byzantinis de l'Alexiade. Analyse prosopographique et synthèse*, Louvain-la-Neuve and Leuven.

Sinkewicz, R. E. (1981) "The Solutions Addressed by Barlaam the Calabrian to George Lapithes and Their Philosophical Context," *Mediaeval Studies* 43: 151–217.

(1982) "The Doctrine of the Knowledge of God in the Early Writings of Barlaam the Calabrian," *Mediaeval Studies* 44: 181–242.

Steel, C. (1999) "Proclus comme témoin du texte du Parménide," in R. Beyers, J. Brams, D. Sacré, and K. Verrycken (eds.), *Tradition et traduction. Les textes philosophique et scientifiques grecs au Moyen Âge Latin*, Leuven, 281–303.

(2002) "Neoplatonic Sources in the Commentaries on the *Nicomachean Ethics* by Eustratius and Michael of Ephesus," *Bulletin de philosophie médiévale* 44: 51–57.

Steel, C. and Macé, C. (2006) "Georges Pachymère Philologue: le commentaire de Proclus au Parménide dans le manuscrit Parisinus gr. 1810," in M. Cacouros and M.-H. Congordeau (eds.), *Philosophie et science à Byzance de 1204 à 1453. Les textes, les doctrines et leur transmission*, Leuven, 77–100.

Steel, C., Mace, C., and d'Hoine, P. (2008) *Procli in Platonis Parmenidem commentaria*, vol. II, Oxford.

(2009) *Procli in Platonis Parmenidem commentaria*, vol. III, Oxford.

Stéphanou, E. (1933) "Jean Italos. L'immortalité de l'âme et la résurrection," *Échos d'Orient* 32: 413–428.

(1949) *Jean Italos, philosophe et humaniste*, Rome.

Stiglmayr, J. (1899) "Die Streitschrift des Prokopios von Gaza gegen den Neuplatoniker Proklos," *Byzantinische Zeitschrift* 8: 263–301.

Suchla, B. R. (ed.) (1990) *Corpus Dionysiacum*, vol. I: *Pseudo-Dionysius Areopagita, De divinis nominibus*, Berlin and New York.

Tatakis, B. (1949) *La philosophie byzantine*, Paris.

Trapp, E., Walther, R., Beyer, H.-V., and Hunger, H. (1976–1996) *Prosopographisches Lexikon der Palaiologenzeit*, 1.–12. Fasz., Addenda zu Fasz. 1.–8., Addenda zu Fasz. 1.–12., Abkürzungsverzeichnis und Gesamtregister, Vienna.

Trizio, M. (2009a) "Neoplatonic Source-Material in Eustratios of Nicaea's Commentary on Book VI of the *Nicomachean Ethics*," in C. Barber and D. Jenkins (eds.), *Medieval Greek Commentaries on the Nicomachean Ethics*, Leiden and Boston, 71–109.

(2009b) "'Qui fere in hoc sensu exponunt Aristotelem.' Notes on the Byzantine Sources of the Albertinian Notion of 'Intellectus Possessus'," in L. Honnefelder, H. Möhele, and S. Del Barrio (eds.), *Via Alberti. Texte-Quellen-Interpretationen*, Münster, 79–110.

(2011) "'Una è la verità che pervade ogni cosa.' La sapienza profana nelle opere perdute di Barlaam Calabro," in A. Rigo and P. Ermilov (eds.), *The Philosophical Background of Byzantine Theology*, Turnhout.

Turyn, A. (1964) *Codices Graeci Vaticani saeculis XIII et XIV scripti annorumque notis instructi*, in *Civitate Vaticana (Codices e Vaticanis Selecti quam Simillime Expressi* 28), Vatican City.

Uspenskij, T. (1891) "*Filosofičeskoe dviženije v XI i XII v.*," *Žurnal Ministerstva Narodnago Prosveščenija* 277: 102–159, 283–324.

Von Ivánka, E. (1958) Review of P. Joannou, *Christliche Metaphysik in Byzanz, Byzantinische Zeitschrift* 51/2: P–382.

Westerink, L. G. (1942) "Proclus, Procopius, Psellus," *Mnemosyne* 10: 275–280.

(ed.) (1949) Michael Psellos, *De omnifaria doctrina*, Nijmegen.

(1989) "Introduction," in T. A. Gadra, S. M. Honea, P. M. Stinger, G. Umholtz, and L. G. Westerink (eds.), *George Pachymeres: Commentary on Plato's Parmenides (Anonymous Sequel to Proclus' Commentary)*, Athens, ix–xix.

Westerink, L. G. and Combès, J. (1986) "Introduction," in *Damascius. Traité des premiers principes*, vol. 1, Paris, ix–xxvi.

Whittaker, J. (1975) "Proclus, Procopius, Psellus and the Scholia on Gregory of Nazianzus," *Vigiliae Christianae* 29/4: 309–313.

Wilson, N. G. (1996) *Scholars of Byzantium*, 2nd edn., London.

Wolska, W. (1957) Review of P. Joannou, *Christliche Metaphysik in Byzanz, revue des études byzantines* 15: 281–285.

Wuerthle, P. (1917) *Die Monodie des Michael Psellos auf den Einsturz der Hagia Sophia*, Paderborn.

Zeses, T. (1976) Νικήτα Σεΐδου Λόγος κατὰ Εὐστρατίου Νικαίας (= Ἐπιστημονικὴ Ἐπετηρὶς Θεολογικῆς Σχολῆς 19, Supplement), Thessalonica.

EXCURSUS 7A

George Gemistos Plethon

Stephen Gersh

Among historians of ideas, the Byzantine thinker George Gemistos Plethon is most famous for his influence on Italian Renaissance philosophy. The preface to Ficino's *Commentary on Plotinus' Enneads* says that at the time of the Council of Florence, Cosimo de' Medici often listened to the Greek philosopher called Gemistos Plethon – who was "like a second Plato" (*quasi Plato alter*) – and was inspired by him with the idea of founding a kind of Academy.[1] Plethon's activities at the Council of Florence-Ferrara are reported independently of Ficino in the *Memoirs* of Sylvester Syropoulos. Perhaps most importantly, Plethon is known to have composed in Greek his treatise "How Aristotle Differs from Plato" (Περὶ ὧν Ἀριστοτέλης πρὸς Πλάτωνα διαφέρεται [often known by its Latin title *De differentiis*]) at the request of Italian colleagues. Although this work played a major role in bringing Platonism to the top of the philosophical agenda in western Europe, it does not particularly illuminate the question of the relation between Proclus and Plethon, which is our present topic.[2] Much more

[1] Ficino was undoubtedly very familiar with Plethon's thought although he does not mention the Greek writer's name on many occasions. The MS *Firenze, Riccardianus graecus 76* includes the texts of Plethon's *On How Aristotle Disagrees with Plato, Reply to Scholarios, Treatise on Virtues, Treatise on Providence* (i.e. *Laws* II. 6), *Funeral Oration for Helen, Funeral Oration for Cleopa* together with Julian's *Discourse on King Helios* and the Greek text and Ficino's translation of Synesius' *De insomniis*, these items having extensive annotations many of which are clearly by Ficino. That Ficino was familiar with Plethon's Μαγικὰ Λόγια is shown by the Latin translations of oracle texts that he made for insertion in his *Platonic Theology*, and Tambrun (2006), 247–259 has recently made a case for Ficino's use of the Plethonian commentary as well. Her further argument on p. 243 that a passage in Ficino's *Commentary on Dionysius' On Divine Names* (Ficino [1576], 1047) noting Plethon's view that God *is not* beyond Being and contrasting it unfavorably with that of Dionysius proves that Ficino was also familiar with the *Laws* is less compelling, since the relevant Plethonian doctrine also appears in the *Reply to Scholarios*, which Ficino had read and annotated.

[2] Plethon appears in modern works dealing with intellectual history for two main reasons: first, because of his contribution to the rise of the "Plato–Aristotle debate" in the Renaissance; and second, because of the "mystery" surrounding his advocacy of a completely pagan theology in fifteenth-century Byzantium. Since the question of Plethon's intellectual relation to Proclus is no more intimately connected with the second issue than it is with the first, we propose to set it aside here. However, Plethon's cordial relations with many Christian intellectuals and his role in

important for us are Plethon's "Oracles of the *Magi* who follow Zoroaster" (Μαγικὰ λόγια τῶν ἀπὸ Ζωροάστρου μάγων [his commented version of the *Chaldaean Oracles*]) and the surviving fragments of his "On Laws" (Περὶ Νόμων).[3] The first work is a study of moral psychology that embodies a strong tendency towards theurgy, the second a treatise of political philosophy whose surviving fragments explore the religious foundations of an ideal state. Both works expound an overtly pagan theology in metaphysical language and issue prescriptions for the liturgical practices that introduce this theology into the realm of practical affairs.[4]

However, the main evidence of a direct engagement with Proclus on Plethon's part is contained in his correspondence with his disciple Cardinal Bessarion.[5] At one point the Cardinal seeks his former teacher's views

the official Byzantine delegation at the Council of Ferrara-Florence would suggest that, whatever the impact of his doctrine may have been in some quarters of the establishment, he himself saw Christian and pagan theologies at least in the strictly theoretical sense as complementary rather than competing ideologies.

3 For a discussion of the circumstances surrounding the deliberate destruction of the manuscript of the *Laws* by George Scholarios as Patriarch of Constantinople after the Turkish conquest see Alexandre (1858), xliii–lvi. A description of the surviving fragments of Plethon's *chef-d'oeuvre* and of their provenance can be found in Masai (1956), 393–401.

4 The question of the relation between Plethon and Proclus is discussed at least briefly in most if not all the previous scholarly literature concerning the Byzantine thinker – for instance, see Carabă (2010), 62–63 – although items are often simply repeated from earlier secondary sources. Among earlier treatments of a more specialized nature, the essay of Nikolaou (1982) concentrating on the psychology is perhaps the most valuable. More recently there has been an extensive discussion of the question in Tambrun (2006), 153–168. This author first lists the points of agreement between Plethon and Proclus. Although some valuable information is provided, the usefulness of this section is diminished by the fact that many of Tambrun's "points communs" are simply indications of Plethon's agreement with late ancient Platonism in general (e.g. that there is a single first principle, that the sensible world is not produced directly by the first principle but through the intermediary of the intelligible world, that there is a unitary multiplicity of gods); others are expressed in such vague terms that the nature of the agreement (or sometimes, in reality, the disagreement) between the two thinkers is obscured (e.g. that each order of gods is formed by the primordial principles of limit and infinity, that each order of gods is derived from a single principle, and that each god has his own rank); while others are either misleading or inaccurate (e.g. that the Forms are the gods). The handling of the points of disagreement between Plethon and Proclus is more successful. Tambrun here rightly notes that exegesis of Plato's *Parmenides* plays a central role in Proclus' theology but not in that of Plethon, that the hierarchy of gods in Plethon begins at a "lower level" if the Proclean hierarchy is taken as the norm, that there is an intermediate order of henads between the first principle and the intelligible sphere in Proclus only, that the organizing principle of the divine orders is dichotomy in Plethon's theology but not in that of Proclus, and that a higher type of matter is introduced into the intelligible world in Plethon only. These points will be reinforced in the present study, although it will be necessary to take issue with one important point that Tambrun makes (in line with most earlier scholarship), namely that "Pléthon procède exclusivement par voie de théologie affirmative" (p. 156).

5 Another piece of evidence often quoted in this connection is a passage in George Scholarios' *Letter to the Exarch Joseph* (Alexandre [1858], app. 424. 4–13). Here, with respect to a passage in the first book of the *Laws* where its author had listed those whom he deemed to be the most important ancient philosophical authorities, Scholarios comments that Plethon had picked up ideas scattered

regarding four philosophical *quaestiones* of which the first question concerns the Demiurge of the heaven, and the second the nature of unparticipated and participated terms.[6] Plethon's reply to the first question mentions Proclus by name and criticizes him for complicating the intelligible sphere in his placing of the Demiurge in the fourth position after the First Principle – this is said to have resulted from Proclus' attempt to assimilate Plato to the Orphic myths.[7] His reply to the second *quaestio* does not mention an author's name but provides an insightful reading of an unmistakably Proclean doctrine by saying that the same principles can be understood as participated or unparticipated from different viewpoints.[8]

When we turn to Plethon's major writings, we see that the Byzantine thinker's approach varies between the extremes of following Proclus on a precise textual level and of either ignoring his views or contradicting them explicitly. More importantly, we discover the basis of Plethon's strategy with respect to using Proclus: namely, to adopt the Proclean model of metaphysical theology but without the latter's interpretation of the *Parmenides*. In so doing, Plethon almost completely rejects the triadic theological structure which underlies that interpretation, although he does to some extent retain the negative theology. This approach is apparently based on two ideas about the history of philosophy: first, that the "Zoroastrian" oracles contain pre-Platonic doctrine copied by the Platonists;[9] second, that Proclus expounds a Platonism contaminated with Christian features derived from Dionysius the Areopagite. Given that Plethon wishes to excavate a Platonism that is free of later Christian accretions, he will accept the elements of Platonism

in the numerous writings of Proclus but, despite acknowledging his agreement with Plutarch, Plotinus, Iamblichus, and Porphyry, never mentions Proclus' name. This was presumably in order to avoid having to share the credit for inventing his doctrine with somebody else, suggests Scholarios, although other readers who are familiar with Proclus and condemn his teachings will similarly recognize the true source of Plethon's teaching. Given that Scholarios was a lifelong ideological opponent of Plethon, and that the accusation of following "Proclus" had been a kind of cliché in Byzantium for at least four centuries, this passage is not a reliable starting-point for a real discussion of the relation between Plethon and Proclus.

6 Bessarion, *Letter to Plethon* in Mohler (1923), 455. 1ff. There is a slight disparity between Bessarion's first question, which deals with Proclus' doctrine of the self-constituted principles (τὰ αὐθυπόστατα) and mentions the title of the *Elements of Theology* (Στοιχείωσις Θεολογική), and Plethon's reply, which deals rather with the topic of the Demiurge in Plato's *Timaeus*.

7 Plethon, *Letter to Bessarion* in Mohler (1923), 458. 24–459. 12.

8 *Ep. ad Bess.* 460. 7–9. This letter contains some further references to Proclus. Proclus' doctrine denying the convertibility of Being and the One or Good is briefly but explicitly brought into a discussion of synonymy and homonymy in Plethon's reply to Bessarion's third question. See *Ep. ad Bess.* 460. 32–461.1. Proclus' doctrine that that which is self-moved is a mediating term between that which is unmoved and that which is moved by another is mentioned at the end of Plethon's reply to the first question. See *Ep. ad Bess.* 460. 1–5.

9 In parallel fashion, Plethon believes that Timaeus of Locri (whom he uses as source in *On Differences*) is pre-Platonic.

that are seemingly authenticated by the *Oracles* but reject those elements that seem to derive from the Dionysian theology.[10]

For Plethon as for Proclus, causation represents a kind of cyclic process involving on the one hand a relation between the overflowing of active power (δύναμις) on the part of the cause and the conversion of potentiality into actuality (ἐνέργεια) on that of the effect,[11] and on the other hand a relation between the procession (προϊέναι, πρόοδος) and the reversion (ἐπιστρέφειν, ἐπιστροφή) in which the same effects acquire differentiation from and assimilation to their causes respectively. Many examples of the attribution of active power to both Zeus and Hera and of potentiality to Hera can be found in the theological system of the *Laws*, and a clear description of the conversion of potentiality to actuality in the case of images in the human soul occurs in the commentary on the *Oracles*. The gods of three lower ranks are said to proceed from Zeus in several passages in the *Laws* and the second god is said to proceed from the highest god in the commentary on the *Oracles*. At one point Plethon notes that the so-called hypercosmic gods are both differentiated from one another and unified with one another, as befits things that "proceed from a single cause and revert again to the same end" (ἔκ τε μιᾶς προϊόντες ἀρχῆς, καὶ ἐς ταὐτὸν αὖ τέλος . . . ἐπιστρεφόμενοι).[12] In one of the addresses to the gods forming part of the liturgy in the *Laws*, human beings are described as reverting first towards Poseidon and last towards Zeus as they utter prayers to the deities of Olympus.[13] Certain peculiarities of Plethon's treatment of power and activity and of procession and reversion should be noted. In an apparent strategy of avoiding the technical usages of the Greek philosophical schools in the relevant sections of the *Laws*, Plethon usually expresses the notion of being in actuality with ἔργῳ rather than ἐνεργείᾳ.[14] It is a desire to avoid the introduction of triadic configurations that probably

[10] It is worth noting that Plethon treats the *Chaldaean Oracles* as a witness to a doctrine pre-dating Plato, a view in which he probably departed from Psellos but is followed by Ficino and other Renaissance writers. The situation with Proclus is different. Although Proclus treats the Orphic poetry as a witness to an ancient theology of this kind, he knows that the *Chaldaean Oracles* were produced many centuries after Plato, their authority stemming rather from the fact of their direct revelation by the gods to the theurgists. See Proclus, *Theol. Plat.* V. 35, 130. 2–4 (Saffrey and Westerink 1968–1997). Disagreement over the historical position of the *Oracles* is probably another reason why Plethon tries to distance himself from Proclus. On the myths about "ancient theology" see Dannenfeldt (1957), Bertozzi (2003), and Panaino (2003).

[11] Active power here has the characteristic of emanative overflow, although Plethon follows the practice of Proclus in employing not the actual term "emanation" but various periphrases. Thus at *Leges* I. 5, 44. 16–17 (Alexandre 1858) Plethon speaks of the "superabundance" (περιουσία) of the gods' goodness using a standard Proclean term closely associated with the overflowing of the cause.

[12] *Leg.* I. 5, 50. 6–20. [13] *Leg.* III. 34, 160. 25–27 and III. 34, 162. 19–20.

[14] See e.g. *Leg.* III. 15, 104. 28. The same usage occurs in *On Differences* (Lagarde 1973), 337. 10.

leads him to avoid the association of procession and reversion with an initial term: remaining (μένειν, μονή) which is very frequent in Proclus' writings.[15] Finally, Plethon reveals a propensity towards expressing the notion of procession by employing the perfect rather than the present tense of προϊέναι that is perhaps more typical of Damascius than of Proclus.[16]

Plethon's dependence on the *Elements of Theology* for this treatment of causation seems particularly to be revealed by the beginning of the so-called "third afternoon address to the gods" in *Laws*, book III.[17] Here, the address is directed towards Zeus as having no cause other than himself, and Plethon presents the assumption of the priority of unity over multiplicity that underlies his theory of causation in an overtly dialectical manner. There must be a primal unity alone from which other things proceed. There could not be a primal term that was simultaneously unity and multiplicity, because there would have to be a prior principle that brought the unity and multiplicity together. On the other hand, there could not simultaneously be a primal unity and a primal plurality, because there would be no continuity between the unity and the multiplicity. Here, it is relatively easy to discern a general style of argumentation typical of the *Elements of Theology* and a sequence of explicit verbal allusions to the proofs of propositions 1 and 4 of Proclus' treatise.[18]

Plethon proposes several divisions of reality as a whole – conceived of as a divine realm – in his *Laws*.[19] At one point, he divides the gods into four γένη (genera, kinds): two of "hypercosmic" (ὑπερουράνιοι) gods – inhabiting Olympus and inhabiting Tartarus; and two of "encosmic" (ἐντὸς οὐρανοῦ) gods – celestial and terrestrial.[20] Elsewhere, he speaks of the "triple form" (τριττὸν εἶδος) of the entire "generated being" (γενητὴ οὐσία): that of the "eternal" (αἰώνιον), which is "immobile" (ἀκίνητον) and having neither past nor future; that of the "temporal and everlasting" (ἔγχρονον . . . ἀΐδιον), which is mostly "immobile "(ἀκίνητον) but having neither beginning nor end; and that of the "temporal and mortal"

[15] Although Plethon does use μένειν in the usual Proclean sense without associating it with procession and reversion in passages such as *Leg.* I. 5, 48. 17; I. 5, 52. 27; and *Magika logia* 12, 9. 16 (Tambrun-Krasker and Tardieu 1995).

[16] See e.g. *Leg.* III. 34, 150. 11–12 and *Mag. log.* 19, 14. 3 (Tambrun-Krasker and Tardieu 1995).

[17] *Leg.* III. 34, 168. 21ff.

[18] See especially Proclus, *El. theol.*, prop. 4, 4. 12–15 and prop. 1, 2. 1–5 (Dodds 1933).

[19] For general discussion of Plethon's theology and metaphysics see Couloubaritsis (1997) and Blum (2003).

[20] *Leg.* I. 5, 54. 16–56. 25. The gods inhabiting Olympus are called the legitimate offspring and those inhabiting Tartarus the illegitimate offspring of Zeus. See *Leg.* I. 5, 48. 8–16. For a list of Plethon's gods and a discussion of his probable mythological sources see Tambrun (2006), 146–153.

(ἔγχρονον . . . θνητόν), which has beginning and end[21] – these three kinds being explicitly said to correspond to the hypercosmic, to the encosmic and everlasting, and to the encosmic and mortal gods of the previous text.[22] Finally, he refers to the threefold μοῖρα ("apportionment")[23] of divinity: one part being of Zeus, another "projected" (προβεβληκυῖα) immediately from him, and another projected mediately,[24] these apparently corresponding to the Olympian, to the Tartarean, and to the encosmic and everlasting gods of the first text. The details added by Plethon to the enumeration of this division are relatively easy to comprehend: for example, that Zeus is completely outside the division, that he has produced the first subdivision himself and somehow delegated the lower subdivisions to other gods, and that Zeus has bound the divisions to one another. However, three aspects of the division of reality are worthy of special note because of the historical-philosophical issues that they raise. First, it is highly significant that the *mode of classification* is dyadic rather than triadic, given that Proclus' *Platonic Theology* employs a triadic system in a similar context. In Proclus the system starts from a triadic division into intelligible, intelligible-and-intellectual, and intellectual beings, and it proceeds to further subdivisions in order to produce a number of terms sufficient to correspond to notions emerging from the dialectic of Plato's *Parmenides*. Plethon's radically different approach is brought out clearly by a passage in which Zeus is said to make his divisions of terms according to contraries with no μέσον ("mediate term") left between them,[25] this replacement of the triadic with a dyadic approach being perhaps the first indication of his desire to distance himself from the Christian and Dionysian contamination of Platonism that he perceived to underlie Proclus' doctrine. Second, one should draw attention to the *principium divisionis* at work in Plethon's presentation of the levels of reality. Here the beings are subdivided according to modes of temporality: on the one hand according to eternity – transcending temporality itself – and temporality, and on the other hand according to everlastingness – coextensive with temporality itself – and mortality.[26] In contrast to the previous case, Plethon here exploits an analysis which is a commonplace

[21] *Leg.* III. 15, 94. 23–96. 8. Cf. *Leg.* III. 15, 116. 2–14. Similarly, he says that the world made by Zeus is divided into three φύσεων γένη: immobile and eternal; mobile, everlasting, and temporal; and inferior and mortal (*Leg.* III. 34, 180. 10–17).

[22] *Leg.* III. 34, 132. 20–24.

[23] Significantly for Plethon, the word μοῖρα also has the connotation of "fate."

[24] *Leg.* III. 34, 142. 17–21.

[25] *Leg.* III. 15, 94. 18–23.

[26] Other texts introduce a further *principium divisionis* – which is in fact necessary to establish the distinction between the Olympian and Tartarean beings – namely, the type of relation to subsequent beings. Thus, the Olympians govern temporal and everlasting beings, and the Tartareans temporal and mortal beings. See *Leg.* III. 15, 104. 13ff.

in Proclus' writings and in later Neoplatonism generally.[27] Third, it is of great significance that the terms classified are both Forms and gods, since Proclus' *Platonic Theology* deals with gods as distinct from Forms. In Proclus, the system distinguishes between different levels of Forms and situates these exclusively within the third or intellective terms of the various triads of gods in order to integrate the teaching of Plato's *Timaeus* concerning the Paradigm and Demiurge into the metaphysical structure. The radically different approach of Plethon is brought out most clearly by the passage quoted above in which Zeus's division according to contraries is said to be one that applies to εἴδη ("Forms"),[28] the removal of the distinction between gods and Forms being perhaps again motivated by the desire to return from the doctrine of Proclus and its underpinnings of Dionysian Christianity to an earlier type of Platonism.[29]

One thing that is particularly striking about Plethon's theological system is the extent to which his discussion seems to have been elaborated as a kind of affirmative theology, with neither the balancing of affirmative and negative methods nor the prioritization of the negative method typical of the pagan and Christian Neoplatonic traditions. If this is so, perhaps we have a further illustration of Plethon's attempt to distance himself from that part of Proclus' thought that centers on interpretation of the *Parmenides.* However, a wider reading of Plethon's works shows that this is not a completely adequate analysis of the situation.[30] In an interesting text that has apparently been transmitted to us independently of the *Laws* entitled the *Prayer to the One God*, Plethon addresses the first principle – the Zeus of the *Laws* – as that "ocean of goodness that cannot be investigated, cannot be scrutinized, and cannot be expressed" (ἀνεξιχνίαστον . . . ἀνεξερεύνητον

[27] Tambrun (2006), 167 quotes some passages from Proclus in which this teaching is summarized, although such distinctions are widespread in the philosophical literature.

[28] For the identification of gods with Forms see also *Leg.* I. 5, 46. 16–21.

[29] It seems likely that this entire system of divisions is based on Plethon's reading of the *Magika logia.* For the principle of dichotomy see *Mag. log.* 10, 8. 11–18 (Tambrun-Krasker and Tardieu 1995) on the right and left sides of the soul's "bed," which is the underlying χώρα of these διαφοραί. For the identification of the hypercosmic, encosmic, and everlasting, and encosmic and mortal realms with Horomazes, Mithra, and Ahriman in Zoroaster's cosmology as reported by Plutarch see *Mag. log.* 34, 19. 9–22 (Tambrun-Krasker and Tardieu 1995).

[30] In the discussion to follow we must take issue with Tambrun (2006), 173–185, who argues at length – in line with a traditional interpretation – that Plethon has an affirmative theology without its negative counterpart, and that this position marks his departure from both the pagan Neoplatonism of Proclus and the Christian version in Dionysius. However, the facts (i) that Plethon avoids the Proclean-Dionysian *Parmenides* interpretation, and (ii) that the *Laws* take a primarily affirmative approach do not in themselves prove that Plethon was totally averse to negative theology. On the so-called exclusively affirmative theology of Plethon see also Siniossoglou (2011), 43, 223–250, who uses this as part of an implausible broader argument attempting to prove that Plethon actually succeeds in returning to a kind of authentic (i.e. pre-Neoplatonism) Platonism. Cf. (2011), 190–193.

καὶ ἄφατον τῆς ἀγαθότητος πέλαγος).[31] The text is remarkable because it presents a kind of negative-theological counterpart to the numerous affirmative-theological prayers in the *Laws*, although the actual negations are applied to terms that are not common in either Proclus or Dionysius. We do not know the precise context in which this prayer was written, but it is clear that this venture into negativity on Plethon's part is not an isolated one. In the commentary on the *Zoroastrian Oracles* indeed, we find applications of negation to cognition from the viewpoint of both the subject and the object. These applications are broadly in line with the teaching of Proclus whose commentary on the *Chaldaean Oracles* was known to Plethon either directly or through the intermediary of Psellos.

There is perhaps only one point at which Plethon departs significantly from the model of basic causation derived from Proclus, namely in applying that model specifically to the questions of providence and fate.[32] The Byzantine thinker agrees with his predecessor that the gods "foresee" (προνοεῖν) everything and plan everything for "the best" (τὸ βέλτιστον)[33] but disagrees with him in accepting the logical conclusion from the hierarchical structure of the Neoplatonic system that causation is equivalent to determination.[34] In the chapter of the *Laws* dealing with "fate" (εἱμαρμένη), Plethon argues that everything in the world is "determined" (ὥρισται), for if anything arose without being determined, either (a) something would be produced "without a cause" (ἄνευ αἰτίου), or (b) the cause would act "without necessity and without determination" (οὐκ ἀνάγκῃ, οὐδ' ὡρισμένως).[35] In response to various objections to such a theory of which its incompatibility with human freedom seems to be the most troublesome,[36] Plethon develops in the same chapter, elsewhere in the *Laws*, and in the commentary on the *Oracles* an extremely subtle approach to the relation between freedom and necessity in the human context. This seems to be based first on the assumption that in the chain of causes and effects, the human soul is free in

31 Alexandre (1858), app. 1, 273. 5–7.

32 In this paragraph we will argue that the traditional view of Plethon as advocating a total determinism is too extreme and that his position with respect to the relation between determination and freedom is actually more nuanced. The traditional view of Plethon's aims makes nonsense of the role of prayer, which is very extensive within the liturgy of the *Laws*. It also relies exclusively on the chapter on Fate (*Leg.* II. 6) without taking account of statements of a different tone elsewhere.

33 See *Leg.* I. 5, 44. 16–18, where πρόνοια is explicitly identified with εἱμαρμένη.

34 See *Leg.* II. 6, 66. 15–16, where Zeus as first principle is identified with ἀνάγκη. However, since necessity is said to be equivalent to determination and Zeus is said to be alone without determination (μὴ ὥρισται) in the same context, "Necessity" is obviously an affirmative divine name applied to Zeus from subsequent things rather than a property that he has *per se*.

35 *Leg.* II. 6, 64. 5–11. The same argument can be found at *De differentiis* 332. 24–333. 5 (Lagarde 1973). Plethon takes up the broader question of fate in his *Letter to Bessarion* (Mohler 1923), 461–463.

36 *Leg.* II. 6, 70. 17–24.

its relation to the next term in the sequence – the body – but determined in relation to the previous term – the gods;[37] and second, on the assumption that the human soul is determined with respect to the best actualization of its possibilities, but free with respect to inferior actualizations.[38] Plethon's argument therefore makes it possible to maintain, while accepting the notion that causation is equivalent to determination, that human beings can pray to the gods not to fall short of their fate – the falling short or not falling short being within the sphere of human freedom – but cannot pray to them to surpass that fate – the fate foreseen and planned by the gods being already the best.[39]

Bibliography

Alexandre, C. (ed.) (1858) *Pléthon: Traité des Lois, Ou recueil des fragments, en partie inédits, de cet ouvrage*, trans. A. Pellissier, Paris.

Bertozzi, M. (2003) "George Gemistos Plethon and the Myth of Ancient Paganism, From the Council of Ferrara to the Tempio Malatestiano in Rimini," in L. Benakis and C. P. Baloglou (eds.), *Proceedings of the International Congress on Plethon and His Time, Mystras 26–29 June 2002* (in Greek), Athens and Mystras, 177–185.

Blum, W. (2003) "Plethon der Heide, als Theologe," in L. Benakis and C. P. Baloglou (eds.), *Proceedings of the International Congress on Plethon and His Time, Mystras 26–29 June 2002*, Athens and Mystras, 95–104.

Blum, W. and Seitter, W. (eds.) (2005) *Georgios Gemistos Plethon (1355–1452): Reformpolitiker, Philosoph, Verehrer der alten Gőtter*, Zurich and Berlin.

Carabă, V. A. (2010) *Pletho Apostata, Die Ablehnung des Christentums durch Georgios Gemistos Plethon (ca. 1355–1452) und dessen Konversion zur griechischen Religion*, Giessen.

Codoñer, J. S. (2000) *Jorge Gemisto Pletón (ca. 1355/1360–1452)*, Madrid.

Couloubaritsis, L. (1997) "La métaphysique de Pléthon: Ontologie, théologie, et pratique du mythe," in A. Neschke-Hentschke (ed.), *Images de Platon et lecture de ses oeuvres. Les interprétations de Platon à travers des siècles*, Louvain-la-Neuve, 117–152.

(2005) "Prolegomena zur Kosmologie Plethons," in Blum and Seitter (2005), 69–76.

Dannenfeldt, K. H. (1957) "The Pseudo-Zoroastrian Oracles in the Renaissance," *Studies in the Renaissance* 4: 7–31.

Demetracopoulos, Y. (2004) *Plethon and Thomas Aquinas* (in Greek), Athens.

[37] *Leg.* II. 6, 70. 24–74. 3. Cf. Tambrun-Krasker and Tardieu (1995), 2.

[38] See *Leg.* III. 34, 146. 14–20 and *Leg.* III. 34, 148. 2–6.

[39] See especially *Mag. log.* 4, 6. 8–10 (Tambrun-Krasker and Tardieu 1995) interpreting the oracle: "Do not increase your destiny" (μὴ σύ γ'αὔξανε σὴν εἱμαρμένην).

Dodds, E. R. (ed. and trans.) (1933) *Proclus: The Elements of Theology*, Oxford; 2nd edn., Oxford 1963.

Ficino, M. (1576) *Opera omnia*, 2nd edn., Basel.

Lagarde, B. (ed.) (1973) "Le *De differentiis* de Pléthon d'après l'autographe de la Marcienne," *Byzantion* 43: 312–343.

Masai, F. (1956) *Pléthon et le platonisme de Mistra*, Paris.

Mohler, L. (1923) *Kardinal Bessarion als Theologe, Humanist und Staatsmann, Funde und Forschungen*, vol. III: *Aus Bessarions Gelehrtenkreis, Abhandlungen, Reden, Briefe*, Paderborn.

Nikolaou, T. (1982) "Georgios Gemistos Plethon und Proklos, Plethons 'Neuplatonismus' am Beispiel seiner Psychologie," in *XVI. Internationaler Byzantinisten-Kongress, Wien 4–9 Okt. 1981, Akten II. 4 = Jahrbuch der Österreichischen Byzantinistik* 32: 387–399; Greek version in Nikolaou (2004), 67–81.

(2004) *Plēthōnika* (in Greek), Thessalonika.

Panaino, A. (2003) "Da Zoroastro a Pletone: la prisca sapientia, persistenza e sviluppi," in *Sul ritorno di Pletone, Un filosofo a Rimini, Atti del ciclo di conferenze, Rimini 22 novembre–20 decembre 2000*, Rimini, 105–121.

Saffrey, H.-D. and Westerink, L. G. (eds.) (1968–1997) *Proclus: Théologie platonicienne*, 6 vols., Paris.

Siniossoglou, N. (2011) *Radical Platonism in Byzantium: Illumination and Utopia in Gemistos Plethon*, Cambridge.

Tambrun, B. (2006) *Pléthon: Le retour de Platon*, Paris.

Tambrun-Krasker, B. and Tardieu, M. (ed. and trans.) (1995) *Magika Logia tōn apo Zōroastrou magōn*, Athens and Paris.

Woodhouse, C. M. (1986) *George Gemistos Plethon, The Last of the Hellenes*, Oxford (English translation of *De differentiis*, 191–214).

PART II.4 *Medieval Georgian philosophy*

CHAPTER 8

Ioane Petritsi

Lela Alexidze

Ioane Petritsi's *Commentary on Proclus' Elements of Theology*: themes and sources

In the twelfth century Proclus' *Elements of Theology* was translated into Georgian by Ioane (John) Petritsi, who wrote a commentary on each chapter along with an introduction and an epilogue. Petritsi was also known as an author and translator of other works. For instance, it is thought that he wrote a book on Georgian grammar and translated Aristotle's *Topika* and *Peri hermeneias*. Nevertheless, nowadays we possess only two translations and one original work that can reliably be attributed to him. These are: (1) a translation of Nemesius of Emesa's *Peri physeos anthropou*;[1] (2) a translation of Proclus' *Elements of Theology*;[2] (3) a commentary composed by Petritsi himself on each chapter of *Elements* together with what can be termed a *Prologue* and an *Epilogue*.[3]

From Petritsi's *Commentary* we can make an informed guess as to why he translated and interpreted Proclus. Petritsi wanted to familiarize the Georgian reader with Proclus' philosophy through an exact translation of his works and doctrines, commenting upon them and teaching them. He also wished to further elaborate Georgian philosophical terminology in order to reflect the meaning of Greek philosophical concepts more adequately than – as he thought – had previously been done by any other author.[4] Moreover, in his commentary on the *Elements*, Petritsi set out to demonstrate the metaphysical priority of the One over all other

I am very grateful to Stephen Gersh, István Perczel, and Michael Hayes † for help and very useful advice in the preparation of this chapter.

[1] Gorgadze (1914).

[2] Kauchtschischvili (1940) – henceforth referred to as "Petritsi, I" + chapter, page.

[3] Kauchtschischvili and Nutsubidze (1937) – henceforth referred to as "Petritsi, II" + chapter, page or as *Prologue* or *Epilogue* + page. See the following books about Petritsi's work published in European languages: Iremadze (2004); Gigineishvili (2007); Günther (2007); Alexidze and Bergemann (2009), all of them including bibliography on Petritsi's work.

[4] Petritsi, II, *Prologue*, p. 6; ch. 50, p. 107; ch. 140, p. 171; *Epilogue*, p. 220.

hypostases, together with the One's omnipresence and the dependence on it of everything else including matter.[5]

Proclus was as important to Petritsi as Plato was to Proclus. Petritsi certainly knew Proclus' *Platonic Theology*, his commentaries on the *Timaeus*, *Parmenides*, and probably his other works.[6] For Petritsi, there was no other philosopher more important than Proclus. He no more criticized Proclus than he criticized Plato. However, for Petritsi Proclus was probably an even greater philosopher than was Plato. Why? Because Proclus seemed to him to have revealed and exposed clearly the truth and the wisdom concerning the One that Plato had sought and hinted at only in a veiled form through his dialogues.[7]

In Petritsi's opinion Proclus and Plato belonged to the same group of "Platonic theologians," to whom he also assigned Orpheus, Aglaophamos, Pythagoras, the philosophers of Elea, Plotinus, Porphyrius, Iamblichus, and Asclepius.[8] Although Petritsi had a high regard for certain aspects of Aristotle's philosophy (especially his logic), admitted that in certain cases there were no contradictions between Platonic and Aristotelian theories, and often based his own interpretations on Aristotelian concepts such as the relationship between form and matter, δύναμις ("potency") and ἐνέργεια ("activity"), the overall status of Aristotle was lower, in his eyes, than that of Plato.

With respect to topics of the greatest importance to him such as the difference between corporeal and incorporeal substances, the independence of the incorporeal from the corporeal, the self-constitution of the soul, the importance of the creative cause, the relationship between Αἰών ("Eternity") and Χρόνος ("Time"), and the importance of not discussing theological subjects in a way appropriated for the material world, Petritsi always tried to prove that Plato and his successors spoke with more authority than did Aristotle, the Peripatetics, the Stoics, and Alexander of Aphrodisias. Moreover, Petritsi did not refer to Aristotle as a "theologian" or "divine" in the same manner as he spoke of Plato and Proclus.

A complete list of the Greek philosophers or philosophically orientated thinkers explicitly mentioned by Petritsi would comprise the following: Orpheus, Aglaophamos, Pythagoreans, Hippocrates, Parmenides, Empedocles, Socrates, Plato, Aristotle, Peripatetics, the Stoics, the Epicureans – the last group being held in disfavor because they neglected

[5] Petritsi, II, *Prologue*, p. 3; ch. 57, p. 125.

[6] On Petritsi's ancient philosophical sources see Alexidze (1997b); Alexidze (2008a) – on Proclus as source especially see pp. 134–225.

[7] Petritsi, II, *Prologue*, p. 5.

[8] Petritsi, II, ch. 41, p. 100; ch. 50, pp. 107–108.

the power of the divine providence –[9] Plotinus, Porphyry, Iamblichus, and Asclepius.

How can we assess the significance of Greek philosophy as a whole for Petritsi? Probably by saying that, in spite of all the differences and controversies between the ideas of individual philosophers, the Greek philosophical tradition as a whole can be viewed as some sort of preparation for Proclus' teaching. Indeed, the variety and complexity of the Greek philosophers' doctrines can be seen in some respect as harmonizing with Proclus' philosophy.

Neoplatonic and Christian aspects of Petritsi's *Commentary*

The philosophical themes that were of primary importance to Petritsi and therefore discussed in depth by him include the doctrines of the transcendent One together with the teaching regarding the one in us and the one in other beings on the basis of which we and the other beings relate to the supreme One, and those of Limit and Infinity, of the Henads, of True Being, of Intellect, of Soul, of the degrees of knowledge, of participation, of providence, of eternity and time, of the relationship between cause and effect, and of matter and its dependence on the supreme One.

But how precisely did Petritsi interpret these themes? Did he try to show a correspondence between Christian theology and Proclus' philosophy, for example as Berthold of Moosburg did in his Latin commentary on Proclus' *Elements*?

From the viewpoint of the difference between ancient Neoplatonism and Christian thought, it is probably true to say that the philosophical problems of the greatest importance for Petritsi – at least as far as the *Commentary* together with the *Prologue* are concerned but not taking account of the *Epilogue* – were approached primarily from the angle of ancient Neoplatonism. Some of the most important issues are the following:

(1) In Petritsi's *Commentary* the One is the most important principle. There is no other hypostasis as important for him as the transcendent One. The Holy Trinity is not discussed in the *Commentary* (as opposed to in the *Epilogue*).

(2) Petritsi's metaphysical system is strictly hierarchical in that the lower levels are subordinate to the higher ones. Theoretically there is no room left for the idea of the consubstantiality of the Trinity or for the co-equality of God the Father and the Son.

[9] Petritsi, II, *Epilogue*, p. 211.

(3) The hypostases in Petritsi's metaphysical system are self-constituted. They are not placed in God; nor are they simply manifestations of the relations (σχέσεις) which can be viewed in the created things – for example, as Nicholas of Methone believed in the case of the First Limit and First Infinity.[10] According to Petritsi's *Commentary*, the hypostases are self-constituted and complete in themselves, albeit ultimately dependent on the transcendent One.

(4) Petritsi considered Proclus to be the most important thinker, being convinced that the truth contained in Proclus' works required no proof or justification through any alternative or superior authority. Other ancient theories could illustrate his teaching, serving as models for its exposition, and Petritsi did indeed use the ideas of the Greek philosophers for this purpose. However, he quoted the Bible in the *Commentary* just a few times and did not mention the Church Fathers at all, trying to explain Proclus' philosophy according to internal rather than external criteria.

(5) The inner logic of Petritsi's *Commentary* and the way in which he interprets the strictly hierarchical relationship between body and soul and between the divine and material worlds would not lead the reader to the Christian doctrine of God's Incarnation. Indeed, as a commentator who remained close to the internal logic of the text being studied, Petritsi would have seen the necessity of discussing the two natures of Christ or the combination of his divine and human as contradictory to the overall sense of the *Commentary*.

(6) As far as we can tell from Petritsi's *Commentary*, matter is the lowest level in the hierarchy of emanation from the One. It has no form or figure, is not differentiated in itself, and therefore has no plurality. In fact, the absence of any specific form and the lack of plurality are the reasons why matter and the One have something in common. Although he sees matter as totally dependent on the One,[11] he does not say that God is its Creator. Nor does he refer – at least clearly and definitely – to the notion of creation from nothing.[12] Such an approach is quite untypical for the Georgian texts of Petritsi's epoch and also for the pro- and anti-Proclean literature of the contemporary Byzantine milieu.

(7) Petritsi avoided speaking about the will of the Creator, seemingly regarding the creation as something of an ontological necessity rather

[10] Nicholas of Methone, *Refutation of Proclus' Elements of Theology* (Angelou 1984), ch. 93, p. 92; ch. 94, p. 93 (further referred to as "Nic. Meth." + chapter, page).

[11] Petritsi, II, ch. 57, pp. 124–125.

[12] Chapter 39 is quite ambiguous. See below, p. 236.

than the result of God's free exercise of will. More precisely, the will of the Creator was understood by Petritsi as an expression of His essence and as manifested in the world as providence.[13]

(8) The world is everlasting according to Petritsi's commentary,[14] such an interpretation placing him on the side of Proclus and in opposition to John Philoponus.

(9) According to Petritsi, the soul is separable from the body, being able to return to itself while the body is unable to do this.[15] On the basis of this view alone of the relationship between the body and soul, it would be difficult to imagine Petritsi as believing in the resurrection of the body or as considering the latter as something positive. If he believed as a Christian in the resurrection of the body, he probably had to reserve a position for this belief somewhere outside the framework of his *Commentary*, a situation giving rise to the so-called problem of the "double truth." The last chapters (209–210) of the *Commentary* leave us to suppose that Petritsi even entertained the possibility of metempsychosis, although he obviously could not write about this topic. Perhaps he did not admit to himself that he could actively consider such a theory.

(10) Adam's sin was considered by Petritsi primarily as an ontological necessity, this sin resulting more from the fact that the first man's reason (intellect: νοῦς) was not independent from the body than that he was subject to temptation with respect to his free will and choice.[16]

(11) Petritsi did not avoid speaking about the demons that were frequently mentioned by Proclus, having included a chapter in which the demons are mentioned in his version of the *Elements* and written a commentary on it.[17] Moreover, he made no attempt to ascribe the features of Proclean demons to the angels in the manner of Isaac Sebastokrator,[18] or to represent the demons as those creatures who became evil because of their free will and choice in the manner of Nicholas of Methone.[19]

(12) Petritsi openly spoke about the "gods." In so doing, he also differed from Isaac Sebastokrator, who avoided speaking of them, and from

[13] Petritsi, II, ch. 31, p. 82; *Epilogue*, pp. 212ff.; Alexidze (2008a), 212–225.

[14] Petritsi, II, ch. 13, p. 45. [15] Petritsi, II, ch. 186, p. 194.

[16] Petritsi, II, chs. 209, 211, pp. 205–206.

[17] Petritsi, I, ch. 129, p. 79; Petritsi, II, ch. 129, p. 165. On the possibility of authenticity of this chapter (against Dodds' arguments) see Alexidze (1984a), 41–47; Alexidze (1984b), 47–53; and Alexidze and Bergemann (2009), 20–24.

[18] Rordorf (1983), 239–244. [19] Nic. Meth., ch. 13, p. 19; ch. 17, p. 24.

Nicholas of Methone, who made specific attacks on "polytheism";[20] Petritsi was convinced that, although there are "gods" in Proclus, the presence above them of the transcendent One acquitted Proclus of the real charge of "polytheism."[21] Moreover, Petritsi did not replace the names of the Greek gods with the names of the natural phenomena on the lines of Isaac Sebastokrator's treatment of Apollo and the sun.[22]

(13) Unlike Nicholas of Methone in his *Anaptyxis*,[23] or John of Scythopolis and Thomas Aquinas in their scholia on the *Corpus Dionysiacum*,[24] Petritsi did not identify the divine Forms or Ideas with God's wills.

It seems interesting that Petritsi said very little about the will, something quite unusual by the standard of contemporary Georgian theological texts. The question arises why this was the case, given that even Proclus wrote extensively on the topic? The answer seems to be that Petritsi feared that emphasizing this theme might render the all-important thesis of the One's omnipotence more problematic. On the one hand, a treatment of the will could lead us to doubts regarding the perfection of divine providence, this perfection deriving from that of the One according to Petritsi. On the other hand, treatment of the will could lead us to doubts regarding the identity of the divine will and the divine essence (οὐσία); Petritsi himself holding these to be the same. The activity of providence extends as far as the material world, although its power and activity are not so visible for us in the sphere of accidental events that prevent the fulfillment of the providential plan. In fact, Petritsi believes that he has had personal experience of this in the failure of both the Greeks and the Georgians to appreciate the importance of his work. According to the *Epilogue*, if both Greeks and Georgians had not impeded him in fulfilling his intellectual ambitions, his work would have been in harmony with the divine providence.[25] Despite all this, Petritsi always tries to show how powerful providence is, and how deeply it penetrates into everything, starting from the One and reaching the formless matter.

Although the relations between Neoplatonic and Christian elements in Petritsi's text are reasonably clear in the case of the aforementioned arguments, doubts remain in connection with certain other points that may be noted here:

[20] Nic. Meth., ch. 122, p. 117. [21] Petritsi, II, ch. 122, p. 155. [22] Maltese (1992), 614.
[23] Nic. Meth., ch. 77, p. 80. [24] In *De div. nom.* 5, 8 *Patrologia Graeca* 4, 329B; Pera (1950), 249.
[25] Petritsi, II, *Epilogue*, p. 222.

(1) The *Epilogue*: Petritsi's so-called *Epilogue* is a difficult text.[26] Although there are many parallels between the *Commentary* and the *Epilogue*, there is one principal difference between them. In the *Epilogue* – a text that is much more "Christian" and "biblical" in character – Petritsi moderated his Neoplatonism since he tried to demonstrate the compatibility of Proclean philosophy with the theology of the Trinity. Whereas in the *Commentary* he proved the omnipresence of the One, in the *Epilogue* he proved the same idea relating to the Trinity and illustrated it with examples from theology, geometry, arithmetic, music, and even military science.[27] Here he argued that all kinds of wisdom – of the Hebrews, the Greeks, and the Chaldaeans – should be regarded as columns in an edifice of which Christ represents the cornerstone.[28] In the *Commentary* Petritsi only hinted at the analogy between Proclus' One and God the Father, on the one hand, and between the Proclean Being (τὸ ὄν) and the Son-Logos on the other.[29] But in the later *Epilogue* he expressed this idea with greater clarity. Here he argued that the One corresponds to the Father, Being – to the Son, and Power (Potency: δύναμις) – to the Holy Spirit.[30]

(2) Chapter 29: This chapter is exceptional in being more explicitly orientated towards the Bible and Christian theology than is any other chapter of the *Commentary*. Here, Petritsi argues that the Logos (or the Son) is "the unchangeable image of the One" (or the Father) meaning, as he further suggests, his "infinite and most intensive likeness," or an image that "carries in itself the whole richness of the Father."[31] Since this implies that the Son as image of the Father is his equal, Petritsi is at this point in his discussion striving to maintain the orthodox Christian position. But in all other cases, when discussing the relations between ontological hypostases described by Proclus, Petritsi does not hint at their equality. In conclusion, we can say that Petritsi is a Neoplatonist in writing about Proclus' metaphysical hierarchy, and interpreting the One, Limit–Infinity, Being, and so forth as a subordinated order, yet he is orthodox in thinking about the relation between God the Father and the Son.[32]

26 D. Melikishvili supposes that a part of the so-called *Epilogue* was written by Petritsi as an introduction to his (lost) translation of the Psalms. See Melikishvili (1988), 169–180. For the relationship between Neoplatonic and Christian aspects in Petritsi's *Commentary* see Alexidze (2002), 429–52; Alexidze (2008b), 7.

27 Petritsi, II, *Epilogue*, pp. 209–218.

28 Petritsi, II, *Epilogue*, p. 208.

29 Petritsi, II, ch. 29, p. 78.

30 Petritsi, II, *Epilogue*, p. 210.

31 Petritsi, II, ch. 29, p. 78.

32 Alexidze (1997a), 131–132.

(3) Chapter 39: In this chapter Petritsi says that the One produces Being from Non-Being.[33] Although it is difficult to determine whether Petritsi here means absolute nothingness or the matter as a privation of being, he certainly does not speak about creation of the matter itself.[34]

(4) As a possible argument against my interpretation of the relation between Neoplatonism and Christianity in Petritsi, one should note one aspect of his theory of creation. This might be expressed in the form of a question: Did the Georgian think that life had been created only because the Creator was essentially good and perfect or also for the sake of creation, that is, the created world itself? In the same chapter 39 Petritsi explains the reasons for the creation of living beings as described in *Timaeus* in this way: "first, [the life has been created for the reason] that the fertile and productive image of the One *does not remain inactive*;[35] secondly, [it has been created] for the sake of the stable and eternal existence."[36] Maybe Petritsi's suggestion that the Creator was creating the world not only because his essence was "good" but also because he cared for the beings to be created indicates that his Neoplatonism is not quite "orthodox." But even this was not typical for this commentator. In Chapter 25 he explains the creation of the lower levels definitely through emanation and as a consequence of the fullness of the higher hypostases. Similarly, he explains the creative activity of the demiurge in the *Timaeus*, interpreting it as "fullness of his goodness [directed] towards the created beings."[37] The problem is: What was more important for Petritsi's theory of creation: the *essential* "fullness of the goodness" of the demiurge or the fact that goodness was *willingly* directed towards the beings to be created? It is probable that Petritsi did not differentiate between these two concepts.

So how can we finally define Petritsi's work from the point of view of the relationship between ancient Neoplatonic and Christian doctrines? Does it represent a kind of "double truth"? What does this precisely mean in

[33] Petritsi, II, ch. 39, p. 93.

[34] Cf. chapter 3: here Petritsi makes a reference to Aristotle and describes as production of beings from absolute non-being any kind of production of new beings that did not exist before, natural as well as artificial ones. He opposes this to the other type of production, which is not a production of some new being but a change of an existing being from one accidental condition into another, for example, from a cold into a warm one. Petritsi, II, ch. 3, pp. 25–26. But cf. also ch. 139, p. 171.

[35] Here I follow the manuscripts and correct the text as it has been published by S. Kauchtschishvili. There was no negation in his version ("remains inactive") – something that completely changed the meaning (Petritsi, II, ch. 39, p. 93).

[36] Petritsi, II, ch. 39, p. 93.

[37] Petritsi, II, ch. 25, p. 68.

Petritsi's case? Was he, on the one hand, a genuine Christian theologian when writing the *Epilogue* and, on the other, "simply" a good exegete of Proclus when writing the *Commentary*? Did these two personalities exist independently of one another in his case? It seems difficult to interpret him in this way, because Proclus' philosophy was for him not a part of the truth and wisdom, and not a preparation or introduction to it, but tantamount to truth and wisdom as such. For Petritsi, just as logic and physics were a preparation for the higher levels of philosophy, similarly philosophy (metaphysics) was not a "servant" of theology. Moreover, for Petritsi, a "correct" philosophy such as that of Proclus was at the same time the true theology and metaphysically the real truth itself. I think Petritsi wished to be a good commentator and interpreter of Proclus who could explain his ideas according to the inner criteria of his philosophy, and with minimal reference to the Bible. Two or even three reasons could have motivated the writing of the commentary in such a way: (1) Petritsi was convinced that Proclus' philosophy was the perfect one. (2) He was a good commentator who judged the text *not* by means of any external criterion or any other authority but by itself alone. (3) – a possibility that does not exclude (1) and (2) but presupposes them – There really are two kinds of truth for Petritsi: the truth of Proclus' philosophy and the truth of the Bible, and it is not always possible to reconcile them. Whatever the reason, as an intelligent exegete, Petritsi avoids comparing Proclus' ideas with biblical or patristic texts in his *Commentary*. Like Proclus, he acknowledges the existence of the hierarchical order throughout the whole Universe, from the transcendent One down to formless matter. Therefore, it would not be logical to speak in his *Commentary* about the Holy Trinity or about the consubstantiality or co-equality of God the Father and God the Son. It would be premature to conclude that Petritsi was not an orthodox Christian. He probably managed somehow to believe that both Christianity and Neoplatonism were true. However, it is difficult to say whether Petritsi wrote the *Epilogue* in order to make his Neoplatonic attitude less striking and more understandable to readers or whether he really believed in such a correspondence between Christianity and Neoplatonism. Perhaps both explanations are possible.

So, what did Petritsi really think outside the frame of his *Commentary*? Did he sincerely believe in what he wrote in his *Epilogue*? It seems likely that he did. But how did he reconcile in himself the two conflicting attitudes? Was it a kind of Heraclitean ability to detect harmony where the differences were more obvious? The answer is unclear. However, it is likely that the *Epilogue* was written in part by Petritsi as a form of self-rehabilitation and as a precautionary measure against possible or real accusations resulting from his Neoplatonic standpoint and admiration of Proclus.

But not only is Petritsi's *Commentary* an interesting text for the study of the heritage of Proclus' philosophy in the medieval world and the modes of its interpretation. In addition, his translation of the *Elements* deserves to be considered by specialists of the Greek versions of Proclus' text. Given that the oldest manuscript of the Georgian version of the *Elements* dates from the thirteenth century, this version casts light on the Greek manuscript tradition by allowing us to reconstruct the Greek text that Petritsi must have used. There are at least two important differences between the Georgian translation and the Greek original text as published by Dodds. On the one hand, the Georgian version includes a chapter 129 that does not occur in the Greek manuscripts. On the other hand, the Georgian version does not contain chapter 149 of the Greek version. Yet Petritsi was not the kind of translator and interpreter who would take it upon himself to change Proclus' text, adding and removing a chapter here and there. Since there are also other reasons to suppose that Petritsi used a Greek version of the *Elements* which corresponded to his translation, it is quite possible to conclude that the Greek version used by Petritsi was in actual fact the most authentic one.[38]

Petritsi's translation of the *Elements*

Petritsi's translation of Proclus' *Elements* is also an interesting text when considered in the broader context of Georgian–Armenian cultural relationships. In the thirteenth century this version of the *Elements* was translated into Armenian. In the seventeenth century a commentary in Armenian was written on the basis of the thirteenth-century Armenian translation of the Georgian version. Finally, in the eighteenth century the Armenian version of the *Elements* was re-translated into Georgian.[39] By that time Petritsi's philosophy had achieved a measure of popularity and esteem in Georgia. With respect to research into the continuity and transformation of Neoplatonism through the Middle Ages and up to modern times, a study of the two Georgian versions and the Armenian version of the *Elements* together with a study of their interrelationships would be extremely useful.

Let us now answer a question concerning Petritsi's *Commentary* in the context of the medieval philosophical and theological thought of both

[38] Alexidze (1984a), 41–47; Alexidze (1984b), 47–53; Alexidze and Bergemann (2009), 20–24; 291–293; Günther (1999), 46–54; Günther (2007), 18–25.

[39] Rapava (1999), 274–279.

Georgia and Byzantium: Was Petritsi's work typical for Georgia and Byzantium or not?

Petritsi's *Commentary* in the context of Byzantine philosophy

Greek philosophy was not the main subject of interest for Georgian scholars and writers. At the present time we possess only two complete old-Georgian translations of Greek (non-Christian) philosophical works. The first is the commentary of Ammonius, son of Hermeias, on Aristotle's *Categories* and on Porphyry's *Isagoge*, translated into Georgian in the twelfth century,[40] and the second is Proclus' *Elements of Theology*, translated and commented on by Petritsi. Since it is difficult to imagine that Petritsi, for all his love and knowledge of ancient Greek philosophy, was unique among his peers, it seems probable that other ancient philosophical texts had been translated into Georgian, although it is also possible that certain Georgian theologians read Greek philosophical texts in the original without translating them. It is also significant that the names of Greek philosophers were mentioned in the medieval Georgian epic poems, since this proves that professional theologians were not the only people who knew something about them. Nevertheless, patristic thought was certainly much more important to the Georgians than was pagan Greek philosophy, and what the Georgians learned about Greek philosophical and theological ideas was derived mainly through the Georgian translations of Greek patristic texts. Thus, translation of such writings as the theological works of the Cappadocian Fathers, Athanasius of Alexandria, pseudo-Dionysius, Maximus the Confessor, Nemesius of Emesa, John Damascene, and others contributed much to the elaboration of Georgian theological, philosophical, and logical terminology. But Petritsi's *Commentary* remains unique in its high estimation of non-Christian Greek philosophy.

Therefore, Petritsi's interest in Proclus' philosophy cannot be explained simply as a product of the Georgian intellectual tradition. Since we know that he studied in Constantinople, it seems reasonable to conclude that his *Commentary* reflects the knowledge of ancient philosophy available in the Byzantine capital. Moreover, Petritsi's *Commentary* would have depended on the availability of Greek philosophical manuscripts in a center such as Constantinople. The *Commentary* may also reflect indirectly the controversies surrounding Proclus' philosophy in Byzantine intellectual society.

[40] Rapava (1983).

But at this point some remarks are necessary concerning Petritsi's *Commentary* in the context of Byzantine philosophy of the eleventh to thirteenth centuries. Are there any significant differences between the Georgian commentator and the mainstream of Byzantine philosophy?

As far as we know, no Byzantine scholar of the eleventh to twelfth centuries claimed to be a follower of Plato. Even Michael Psellos, who confirmed that he read the works of Plato, denied being exclusively a follower of his teachings.[41] The situation with respect to Proclus was similar: Byzantine scholars read, studied, and made copies of his works although none of them claimed to have exclusively followed his philosophy. Moreover, no Byzantine scholar ever praised Proclus as freely and clearly as did Petritsi. The project of disseminating Proclean philosophy (and thereby also Platonism in its entirety) embraced by Ioane Petritsi seems very radical when considered in the context of Byzantine philosophy of the same epoch.[42] In the period immediately after Psellos when Petritsi was active, people read and used Proclus' works surreptitiously.[43] But, as far as we know, nobody attempted to introduce his *Elements* openly into the educational programs of philosophy. Petritsi must have done precisely this, since he wrote his *Commentary* in a form of lectures. Although it seems to have been impossible to express such public admiration for Proclus' philosophy at Byzantium during this period, the tolerant attitude towards philosophical, scientific, and religious ideas in Georgia between the eleventh and thirteenth centuries that resulted from the state politics of king David IV made it possible for Petritsi to work freely. Nevertheless, the *Epilogue* notes that the author lived among both Greeks and Georgians, neither of whom showed appreciation for his work.[44]

Evidently, it is not only Proclus' Byzantine admirers but also his Byzantine opponents who had an influence on Petritsi. In the middle of the twelfth century Nicholas, bishop of Methone, wrote his so-called *Anaptyxis* (*Refutation*) as a critical commentary on Proclus' *Elements*. Although the commentaries of Nicholas and Petritsi have a similar form and subject matter – both commenting on each chapter of Proclus' work in sequence – their purposes were quite different. The following are some of the main differences:

(1) Nicholas wished to prove that Proclus' ideas contradicted the theology of the Trinity. Petritsi in his so-called *Epilogue* tried to demonstrate their harmony with Christian dogma.

[41] Cacouros (1998), 1366. [42] Alexidze and Bergemann (2009), 13–15.
[43] Podskalsky (1976), 515–523. [44] Petritsi, II, *Epilogue*, p. 222.

(2) Nicholas very often compared Proclus' ideas unfavourably with pseudo-Dionysius' theology. Although it can be said with certainty that Petritsi was familiar with Dionysius' works, he did not mention him in this connection.

(3) Unlike Nicholas, Petritsi explained and evaluated Proclus' philosophy on the basis of that selfsame philosophy rather than according to external criteria. In his *Commentary* his intention was not to show either the harmony or difference between Proclus' teaching and Christian theology.

(4) Sometimes Nicholas obscured the subject matter of Proclus' argumentation. For example in chapter 3 of the *Elements* Proclus discussed τὸ γινόμενον ἕν ("that which becomes one"). In his refutation of this chapter, Nicholas transferred Proclus' conclusion with respect to τὸ γινόμενον ἕν to the transcendent One and the Trinity, an interpretation that gave him stronger grounds for a criticism of Proclus.[45] However, because of the confusion of the subject of the discussion, this criticism is really groundless. Unlike Nicholas, Petritsi generally did not obscure the subject matter of Proclus' arguments and did not transfer an argument specifically appropriate to one topic to something quite different.

(5) For Nicholas, many of the ontological levels distinguished by Proclus are assimilated to God, so that the self-constituted substances turn into relations of some kind.[46] Unlike Nicholas, Petritsi interpreted the hierarchical levels of Proclean ontology as self-constituted hypostases, albeit always acknowledging the One as transcendent cause of everything.

(6) Nicholas criticized Proclus in his use of the word "first" in such a manner as to imply polytheism.[47] Petritsi, however, argued that Proclus' primary cause is the transcendent One, and that his philosophy has nothing in common with polytheism. In the commentary on chapter 112 of Proclus' *Elements* he wrote: "Where are those who accuse the wise men of teaching the notion of a plurality of gods, those whose ignorance even makes them happy? Here [Proclus] proves that the transcendent One is [just] one. From [the One there proceeded] two creative sources that are above Being, the Henads [also proceeding] from the One, Gods from the transcendent God, and Saints from the transcendent Saint."[48]

[45] Nic. Meth., ch. 3, p. 7.
[46] Nic. Meth., ch. 93, p. 92.
[47] Nic. Meth., ch. 11, p. 15.
[48] Petritsi, II, ch. 112, p. 155.

(7) Discussing the transcendent One, Nicholas preferred the apophatic to the cataphatic method.[49] Petritsi did not discuss the differences between these two methods, although when characterizing the Proclean One he mainly used the apophatic method.

(8) Unlike Petritsi, Nicholas sometimes did not appreciate the difference between Proclus' categorical and hypothetical propositions and therefore criticized their content equally.[50]

(9) For Nicholas the will of God was much more important than it was for Petritsi.

(10) The interest in ancient Greek philosophy was much greater on the part of Petritsi than on that of Nicholas.

If we accept E. Chelidze's theory, according to which Petritsi wrote his *Commentary* at the end of the twelfth and at the turn of the thirteenth century and not in the late eleventh and early twelfth centuries as has traditionally been supposed,[51] we may perhaps entertain the possibility that Petritsi composed this work as a response to Nicholas of Methone's criticism of Proclus. It was therefore a kind of refutation of the *Refutation*.[52]

Petritsi's *Commentary* seems to be a unique testimony to the very high estimation of ancient Greek philosophy, and especially of Platonism, among the medieval Christian commentators on Proclus. For Petritsi, this philosophy was valuable on its own terms and required no justification through comparison with the ideas of the Church Fathers. From this point of view Petritsi has perhaps more in common with Byzantine Humanist philosophers of the fourteenth–fifteenth centuries, such as George Gemistos Plethon, than with the Byzantine philosophers of his own day,[53] although Petritsi did not share Plethon's goal of restoring paganism. Interestingly, both Petritsi and Plethon remained unique phenomena in their native cultures. In practical terms, neither left any direct or long-term heirs to his philosophy.

Bibliography

Alexidze, L. (1984a) "The Grades of Knowledge in the Works of Proclus and Ioane Petritsi," *Matsne (Journal of the Georgian Academy of Sciences, Series for Philosophy and Psychology)* 2: 41–47 (in Georgian, summary in Russian).

[49] Nic. Meth., ch. 8, p. 12.
[50] Nic. Meth., p. lix. See also ch. 116, p. 113.
[51] Chelidze (1994), 113–126; Chelidze (1995), 76–89.
[52] Alexidze (2007), 237–252; Alexidze and Bergemann (2009), 15–18.
[53] Alexidze (2009), 19–30.

(1984b) "Das Kapitel 129 der 'Elemente der Theologie' des Proklos bei Ioane Petrizi," *Georgica (Journal for Culture, Language, and History of Georgia and the Caucasus)* 17: 47–53.

(1997a) "'Bild Gottes' in den Kommentaren des Ioane Petrizi zur 'Elementatio theologica' des Proklos," *Stimme der Orthodoxie = Festschrift für Fairy von Lilienfeld* 3: 131–132.

(1997b) "Griechische Philosophie in den Kommentaren des Ioane Petrizi," *Oriens Christianus* 81: 148–168.

(2002) "Zum Verhältnis zwischen Neuplatonischem und Christlichem im Prokloskommentar des Ioane Petrizi," *Metaphysik und Religion. Zur Signatur des spätantiken Denkens* (Akten des Internationalen Kongresses vom 13.-17. März in Würzburg), Leipzig and Munich, 429–452.

(2007) "Ioane Petritsi in the Context of Eleventh–Twelfth Century Byzantine Philosophy," in N. Makharadze and T. Dolidze (eds.) *Byzantine Studies in Georgia. Dedicated to Simon Khaukhchishvili* (in Georgian, summary in English), Tbilisi, 237–252.

(2008a) *Ioane Petrizi und die antike Philosophie* (in Georgian, summary in German), Tbilisi.

(2008b) "Did Petritsi 'Baptize' Proclus?," in Forrai, R. (ed.), *Hellenism: Alien or Germane Wisdom?*, ESF Exploratory Workshop convened by the Center for Hellenic Traditions, Central European University, Budapest, Department of Medieval Studies, *Annual of Medieval Studies* at CEU, 14, Abstracts, p. 7.

(2009) "Antiquity in Fourteenth–Fifteenth Centuries' Byzantine Humanism: Some Parallels with Petritsi's Philosophy," in N. Makharadze and M. Giorgadze (eds.) *Byzantine Studies in Georgia 2. Dedicated to Academician Grigol Tsereteli*, 2 vols., Tbilisi, vol. 1, 19–30 (in Georgian, summary in English).

Alexidze, L. and Bergemann, L. (eds. and trans.) (2009) *Ioane Petrizi, Kommentar zur Elementatio theologica des Proklos*, Amsterdam and Philadelphia.

Angelou, A. D. (ed.) (1984) *Nicholas of Methone: Refutation of Proclus' Elements of Theology*, Leiden and Athens.

Cacouros, M. (1998) "De la pensée grecque à la pensée Byzantine," in A. Jacob (ed.), *Encyclopédie philosophique universelle*, vol. IV: *Le discours philosophique*, Paris, 1362–1384.

Chelidze, E. (1994) "On Petritsi's Life and Work," *Religia* 3/4/5: 113–126 (in Georgian).

(1995) "On Petritsi's Life and Work [continued]," *Religia* 1/2/3: 76–89 (in Georgian).

Gigineishvili, L. (2007) *The Platonic Theology of Ioane Petritsi*, Piscataway, NJ.

Gorgadze, S. (ed.) (1914) *Nemesius of Emesa: On the Nature of Man*, translated by Ioane Petritsi (in Georgian), Tbilisi.

Günther, H.-C. (1999) "Zu Ioane Petrizis Proklosübersetzung," *Georgica (Journal for Culture, Language, and History of Georgia and the Caucasus)* 2: 46–54.

(2007) *Die Übersetzungen der Elementatio Theologica des Proklos und ihre Bedeutung für den Proklostext*, Leiden and Boston.

Iremadze, T. (2004) *Konzeptionen des Denkens im Neuplatonismus. Zur Rezeption der Proklischen Philosophie im deutschen und georgischen Mittelalter: Dietrich von Freiberg, Berthold von Moosburg, Joane Petrizi*, Amsterdam and Philadelphia.

Kauchtschischvili, S. (ed.) (1940) *Ioannis Petritzii Opera*, vol. I: *Procli Diadochi ΣΤΟΙΧΕΙΩΣΙΣ ΘΕΟΛΟΓΙΚΗ*, versio Hiberica (in Georgian), Tbilisi.

Kauchtschischvili, S. and Nutsubidze, T. (eds.) (1937) *Ioannis Petritzii Opera*, vol. II: *Commentaria in Procli Diadochi ΣΤΟΙΧΕΙΩΣΙΝ ΘΕΟΛΟΓΙΚΗΝ*, textum Hibericum (in Georgian), Tbilisi.

Kechakhmadze, N. and Rapava, M. (eds.) (1983) *Ammonius Hermeias' Works in Georgian* (in Georgian, summary in German and Russian), Tbilisi.

Maltese, E. V. (1992) "Isaac le Sébastokrator," in Jacob, A. (ed.), *Encyclopédie philosophique universelle*, vol. V, 3: *Les oeuvres philosophiques*. Dictionnaire. Volume edited by J.-F. Mattéi, vol. I, Paris.

Melikishvili, D. (1988) "On the Structure of Ioane Petritsi's 'Epilogue' and Some New Sources," *Volume of the Chair of Old-Georgian Language* 27: 169–180 (in Georgian).

Pera, C. (ed.) (1950) *S. Thomae Aquinatis In librum Beati Dionysii De divinis nominibus expositio, curo introductione historica P. Caramello et syntheri doctrinali C. Mazzantini*, Turin and Rome.

Podskalsky, G. (1976) "Nikolaos von Methone und die *Proklosrenaissance* in Byzanz (11./12. Jh.)," *Orientalia Christiana Periodica* 42/1: 509–523.

Rapava, M. (1999) "About the Identity of Petritsi – Amelakhos," in Z. Alexidze (ed.), *Mravaltavi, Philological-Historical Researches* 18, Tbilisi, 274–279 (in Georgian, summary in Russian).

Rordorf, W. (1983) "Sind Dämonen gut oder böse? Beobachtung zur Proklos-Rezeption bei Isaak Sebastokrator," in H.-D. Blume and F. Mann (eds.) *Platonismus und Christentum. Festschrift für Heinrich Dörrie = Jahrbuch für Antike und Christentum*, Suppl. 10, Münster, 239–244.

PART II.5 *Medieval Western philosophy*

CHAPTER 9

William of Moerbeke, translator of Proclus

Carlos Steel

After centuries of indirect and diffuse influence (through the work of Dionysius the Areopagite and, from 1200 onwards, through the Latin-Arabic treatise *De causis*) Proclus entered directly into the Latin philosophical world thanks to the translations of William of Moerbeke (*c.* 1225–1286).[1] William was originally from Flanders, but his first activities are attested in the eastern Mediterranean region, as we learn from colophons of two dated translations: Nicaea, April 24, 1260 and Thebe, December 23, 1260.[2] At that time Constantinople was still capital of the Latin empire that had been established at the fourth crusade but would not be for much longer, as the city would be recaptured by the Byzantines in 1261. The presence of William in Nicaea, the capital of the Byzantine empire during the same period, may indicate that he belonged to a Latin delegation at the court. One might suppose that William, once he entered the Dominican order, was sent to the East for intensive training in Greek. The newly founded mendicant orders played an important role in the ecclesiastical organization of the Latin empire. At the end of 1267, as we know from the next dated translation, Moerbeke resided at the papal court at Viterbo, where he held the important office of apostolic penitentiary under pope Clement IV. There are good reasons to believe that Moerbeke was already at the court of Urban IV in Orvieto around 1264.[3] At that time he may have first met his confrere Thomas Aquinas, who was lecturing at the *studium generale* in that city. If the traditional claim that William made his translations "at the request of Thomas" is exaggerated, it is undeniable that there was for some time an intensive contact between the two Dominicans. Thomas seems to have been the first to profit from many of William's

[1] The *Elementatio physica* was already translated in the middle years of the twelfth century, but it found almost no readers in the Middle Ages. See Boese (1958).

[2] On the life and work of Moerbeke see the proceedings edited by Brams and Vanhamel (1989), and in particular the contribution of Paravicini Bagliani and the excellent bibliography of Vanhamel in that volume.

[3] See Cordonnier and Steel (2012), n. 29.

new translations and he played an essential role in their circulation at the university in Paris.[4] The position of apostolic penitentiary at the curia involved heavy administrative tasks, and one wonders when William could find the time for his intensive translation work. Fortunately, there was the long period of vacancy of the holy see (November 29, 1268 – September 1, 1271) which allowed him some leisure. We have more evidence regarding his activities towards the end of 1271. In 1274 William participated as an expert in Greek matters at the council of Lyon, where the union with the Byzantine Church was on the agenda. At the council he met his compatriot Henry Bate of Mechelen, with whom he remained in correspondence later on.[5] Bate is also a privileged user of Moerbeke's translations. Back in Viterbo William became acquainted with the Polish scholar Witelo, who dedicated to him his *Perspectiva*. In 1278 William was appointed bishop of Corinth, where he resided for some years. In 1283–1284 he was active again at the papal court, and it remains unclear whether he returned to Greece. He may have died in Italy in 1286.

Moerbeke is first known for his translations and revisions of Aristotle's complete work, which became for about two centuries the standard text for university teaching. He also translated some of the great commentaries on Aristotle by Alexander of Aphrodisias, Themistius, Philoponus, and Simplicius. A remarkable scientific achievement is his translation of Archimedes, Eutocius, and Ptolemy. More surprising is his interest in the Platonist Proclus. William translated the *Elements of Theology*, the three treatises on providence, free choice, and the problem of evil, and the commentaries on the *Parmenides* and the *Timaeus*. However, only his translation of the *Elements of Theology* had some impact on medieval philosophy, this being mainly due to its link with the *Liber de causis,* which was a required text in the university curriculum. Moerbeke's other translations remained largely unnoticed.[6] Though their historical influence is limited, these translations are of great value for the transmission of Proclus' work, since they are based on Greek manuscripts that are now lost.

The *Elements of Theology*

According to the subscription this translation was completed on May 12, 1268 in Viterbo.[7] The first reader of this translation was probably Thomas

[4] See Steel (1989). [5] On Bate see the introduction in this volume.

[6] On the limited importance of the discovery of Proclus in the late Middle Ages see Sturlese (1987) and Steel (1997).

[7] The translation was edited by Boese (1987), who also devoted a separate study to the complicated tradition of the text (1985).

Aquinas. When he left for his second stay in Paris after the summer of 1268 Thomas must have had a copy of this new Platonic translation in his luggage. He used it in Paris for the composition of his commentary on the *De causis* (which was composed in early 1272).[8] In fact, the new translation made it possible to detect the source of this famous treatise on the first causes, which was traditionally attributed to Aristotle and considered to be a supplement to the *Metaphysics*. As Thomas notices in his preface:

> In Greek we find handed down a book of this type by the Platonist Proclus, which contains 211 propositions and is entitled *The Elements of Theology*. In Arabic, however, we find the present book, which is called *On Causes* among Latin readers, [a work] known to have been translated from the Arabic and not to be extant at all in Greek. Thus, it seems that one of the Arab philosophers excerpted it from the aforementioned book of Proclus, especially since everything that is contained in the present book, is found much more fully and much more diffusely in that [of Proclus].[9]

Thomas would never have known that there was such a Greek text by Proclus, an author unknown among Latin scholars, if William had not brought it to his attention. In any case, Thomas himself made a comparative study of the *Elementatio* together with the *De causis*, as is evident in his commentary, where he quotes all the relevant propositions and demonstrations from Proclus that are needed in order to provide the background of the argument of the *De causis*. Thomas' comments show that he intensively studied the two texts in confrontation with one another. Thus at prop. 11 of the *De causis*, p. 73, 21–23, he observes: "the author of this book has conflated these two propositions [172 and 174 from Proclus] into one, and, while he sought brevity, he introduced obscurity." At prop. 21, p. 113, 23, he notes that "the author of this book bypasses the first part of this proposition," and at prop. 22, p. 115, 15–16, he observes that, whereas Proclus offers two arguments to demonstrate the proposition [115], "the author of this book is content with a general proof alone." Even more remarkably, Thomas also notes that the author of the *De causis* is not just a paraphraser of Proclus but modifies his argument and puts some new accents, sometimes motivated by his own views on the divine cause. As Thomas says, "the author sometimes

[8] See Saffrey (1954), xxxv–xxvi.

[9] *Et in Graeco quidem invenitur sic traditus liber Procli Platonici, continens ccxi propositiones, qui intitulatur Elementatio theologica; in arabico vero invenitur hic liber qui apud Latinos De causis dicitur, quam constat de arabico esse translatum et in graeco penitus non haberi: unde videtur ab aliquo philosophorum arabum ex praedicto libro Procli excerptus, praesertim quia omnia quae in hoc libro continentur, multo plenius et diffusius continentur in illo* (*In De causis, prooemium*, p. 3, 3–10 ed. Saffrey [1954]). Translation Guagliardo, Hess, and Taylor (1996), slightly modified.

departs from what Proclus said and rather approaches the common views of Platonists and Peripatetics" (*recedit auctor huius libri ab intentione Procli et magis accedit ad communes sententias et Platonicorum et peripateticorum*, prop. 2, p. 14, 18–20). And at prop. 3, p. 20, 22, Thomas observes that the author follows Dionysius in rejecting a multiplicity of gods. See also what is said at prop. 4, pp. 28, 24–25 and 33, 12–13: "according to the opinion of Dionysius, which the author of this book seems to follow when he does not place any distinction in the divine being." The same point is made at prop. 6, p. 44, 17: *auctor huius libri non concordat cum Platonicis* (see also prop. 12, p. 80, 7 and 21; prop. 16, p. 95, 1–6). At prop. 5, p. 41, 16–25, Thomas confronts the Platonic view (cf. Proclus, *El. theol.*, prop. 196) that there is an incorruptible body always connected with the soul with the position of the author of the *De causis*, which is "better" (*melius*); for according to this author the human body is corruptible because "the impression" it receives from the soul in this life is too "weak." Only when the soul has been perfected through its conjunction with the first divine cause after this earthly life can it provide the body with immortal life. This position of the *De causis* "corresponds to the Catholic faith on the resurrection of the body," whereas Proclus' view does not. All this gives ample evidence of Thomas' profound study of the newly translated Proclus text.[10] Proclus is also quoted in the treatise *De substantiis separatis*, which was composed in the same period as the commentary.

It is probably through Thomas' influence that the translation of the *Elementatio* started circulating at the University of Paris. It is undoubtedly the Proclus translation with the largest diffusion and most quotations. There are twenty manuscripts with the complete text (including two with the commentary of Berthold of Moosburg), and seven with an incomplete text. The success of the *Elementatio* is to be explained by its connection with the *Liber de causis*, which was required reading in the university curriculum. Even after it became known that the *De causis* was not an Aristotelian treatise but depended on Proclus' *Elementatio*, it remained a standard text in the university curriculum and was commented upon until the Renaissance, whereas the *Elementatio* would have to wait until Berthold of Moosburg to receive the commentary it deserved.[11] In the text tradition of the translation three different branches may be distinguished, which according to the editor, Helmut Boese, correspond to different versions of the translation. In fact, it seems that Moerbeke later introduced some corrections in his

[10] As Boese has shown, there are influences of Thomas' reading of Proclus in annotations in the margin of two manuscripts: Erfurt, Ampl. 2°26 and Paris, BNF lat. 16097. See Boese (1985), 55–59.

[11] On Berthold see Chapter 11 in this volume.

translation and even made use of another Greek model to correct the first version. This careful revision of the translation (comparable to what happened in many of the Aristotle translations) shows that Moerbeke considered the *Elementatio* to be an authoritative text. Besides the Paris university tradition (which seems to be related to the copy owned by Thomas Aquinas), there is an independent tradition that goes back to Moerbeke's autograph in Italy. The main representative of this tradition is the magnificent copy that Gonzalvo Pétrez (or Gudiel), archbishop of Toledo, acquired in Viterbo in 1280.[12] According to Boese it may have been the exemplar dedicated to pope Clement IV or a copy thereof. The third branch of the tradition (which corresponds to Moerbeke's final version) is represented by the copy owned by Henry Bate. Bate quotes the full text of the *Elementatio* in the twelfth part of his philosophical encyclopedia, *Speculum divinorum*, which was composed by the end of the thirteenth century.[13] Bate probably received a copy directly from Moerbeke himself, with whom he had become acquainted at the council of Lyon (1272). The manuscript owned by Berthold of Moosburg and used for his commentary became lost, but a copy of it is the Ampl. 4° 290 in Erfurt. Berthold worked with a text that basically belonged to the Parisian tradition but corrected it with a manuscript linked to the tradition of Bate's copy and did not hesitate to modify the text himself. Cusanus had a copy and annotated it: *Cus.* 195.[14] Other humanist scholars, such as Coluccio Salutati and Giovanni Marchanova, possessed copies of the text, as did Ficino, who used the Latin translation in his earlier work.[15]

Tria opuscula

Once William was settled as archbishop in Corinth, he started working on a translation of the three treatises Proclus devoted to problems of providence, fate, self-determination, and evil.[16] In their colophons the three translations are all dated in Corinth, respectively the 4th, the 14th, and the 21st of February 1280, which suggests an incredibly short time in which to accomplish the translation of such long and complicated texts (unless the dates refer only to the final version of the translation?). We are greatly indebted to William because the original Greek text of the *Opuscula* no longer exists. Despite the fact that they discuss topics of great interest for medieval thinkers (the problems of providence and fate, of freedom, and

[12] See on archbishop Gudiel, Hernández and Linehan (2004).
[13] See Boese's edition in Boese and Steel (1990). [14] See Senger (1986).
[15] See Steel (2013). [16] The translation is edited by Boese (1960); see also Strobel (2014).

of evil), the *Tria opuscula* were not commonly known in the late Middle Ages. The reason may be that they were translated at the end of Moerbeke's career and had no chance of entering into the university milieu.

The Latin translation is preserved in fourteen manuscripts. The best witness of the text is a late copy (A) made in Italy around 1500 (*Vat. Lat.* 4568), which also contains in the margin Greek annotations that may go back to Moerbeke's autograph itself (see for a similar case the *Ambrosianus* A 167 sup., which contains the translation of the Parmenides commentary). Two fourteenth-century manuscripts of Italian origin go back to a common model which is also derived from Moerbeke's autograph: (O) Oxford, *Bodleian Library, Digby* 236 (on which more below) and (S) Macerata, *Biblioteca Comunale* 361, which once belonged to Coluccio Salutati. Finally, there is a third branch in the transmission of the translation represented by the Parisian manuscript *Arsenal* 473 and its tradition. The Arsenal manuscript once belonged to the Augustinian convent in Paris. According to R. Wielockx the copy is made by a Parisian hand.[17] This does not necessarily mean that the manuscript was copied from a model in Paris, for a Parisian hand could have made a copy in Italy, at a place where Moerbeke's autograph was preserved. The presence of the manuscript in the library may explain why the Augustinian James of Viterbo quotes the *Opuscula* in his *Quodlibeta* and his *Quaestiones de praedicamentis in divinis*, which were composed during his regency in Paris, between 1293 and 1299. As the quodlibeta were held between 1293 and 1296,[18] the manuscript must have reached Paris before 1293. It is possible that James himself acquired a copy from the original in Viterbo, where he was lecturing between 1283 and 1287. James shows a great interest in Proclus, and he also often quotes from the *Elementatio*. His confrere, Giles of Rome quotes the opening text of the first *opusculum* in the preface of his *De renunciatione papae*, which can be dated in 1297. Berthold of Moosburg had a copy made of the Arsenal manuscript during his stay in Paris : it is still preserved as *Basel Univ.bib* F IV 31. He often quotes the *Opuscula* in his commentary on the *Elements of Theology*. References in the German mystical writer Tauler derive from his reading of Berthold.[19]

We find early quotations of the translation in some works of the Dominican Remigius of Florence (*c.* 1235–1319).[20] Having studied in Paris, probably with Thomas Aquinas, Remigius was mainly active in Florence but returned to Paris in 1297–1300 and then to Italy again. Around 1303–1307 he was

[17] See Wielockx (1994). [18] See the edition of Ypma (1968–1975).

[19] See Sturlese (2007), 181–8.

[20] On Remigius of Florence see Gentile (2001) and the website of father Panella.

lecturing at the papal court in Perugia. He refers to Proclus' *Opuscula* in his *De modis rerum* (composed before 1301)[21]; in the sermon *De tempore* (1314–1315), *De peccato usurae* (1305–1306), and *De via paradisi* (1301–1314). The quotations are quite literal and seem to indicate that Remigius used a manuscript that was neither A nor the model of O and S. This means that he still had access to Moerbeke's autograph.[22] This access may have been during his stay in Viterbo in the autumn of 1289 or perhaps in Perugia, where the papal curia had moved to. There are also frequent quotations in the commentaries on the psalms by Thomas Waleys (*c.* 1290–1349), who may have had access to the model of O and S when he was lector in Bologna in 1326–1327.[23]

The *Opuscula* were known to Renaissance scholars. Ficino refers to them in his letter to Martin Prenninger in which he recommends Platonic works available in Latin: *legentur etiam utcunque traducta Elementa theologiae Proculi atque ipsa eius Theologia et liber De providentia simul atque fato.*[24] Floriano Montini asks in a letter to Erasmus (1525) if he could provide him with a better copy of Proclus *De fato*: "The text which I found at Rome was full of errors."[25]

The commentary on the *Timaeus*

That Moerbeke translated Proclus' commentary on the *Timaeus* was first proposed as a hypothesis by Alexander Birkenmajer.[26] The starting-point of his argument was a passage in a letter sent by the Faculty of Arts in Paris, a few weeks after the death of Thomas Aquinas (1274), to the general chapter of the Dominicans in Lyon. Having expressed their praise for Thomas and their condolences, the masters of the faculty asked to obtain some of the works Thomas had started writing before he left Paris for Italy in 1269, and in particular some texts that he had promised to send them: *et specialiter Commentum Simplicii super librum De celo et mundo et Exposicionem Timei Platonis ac librum De aquarum conductibus et ingeniis erigendis, de quibus*

[21] On this work see Gavrič (2006).

[22] A collation of the literal quotations with the Boese edition shows that Remigius' copy had, for instance, neither the omission of A in 5,30; nor the other variant readings of A in *Dub.* 18,7; *Mal.* 30,21; nor the errors of OS in *Prov.* 51,1 and 7. Interestingly it has as V *factam] factum* in *Mal.* 36,22 (which may be the original reading).

[23] See Steel in Geoffroy and Steel (2001), 85, 87.

[24] See Klibansky (1981), 47.

[25] See Letter 1552, *Collected Works of Erasmus* 11 (Toronto 1994), 47–48.

[26] See Birkenmajer (1970a), 277–311.

nobis similiter speciali promissione fecerat mencionem.[27] The first work mentioned must be Moerbeke's translation of Simplicius' commentary, which was completed at Viterbo in 1271. Thomas undoubtedly had a copy of this translation since he used it in his own commentary on the *De caelo*, which he left unfinished at his death.[28] Birkenmajer assumed that the two other works requested in the letter are also translations of William of Moerbeke. Although no author's name is mentioned, it is reasonable to assume that the "Expositio Timaei" refers to a Latin version of Proclus' commentary on the *Timaeus*. A copy of the Greek text of this commentary was also present in the papal library in Avignon, which contained many Greek manuscripts that Moerbeke had used for his translations. In the catalogue of 1295 we find Proclus' *Timaeus* commentary under nr. 432: *item comentum Procli super Timoeum Philonis*, and in that of 1311 under nr. 598: *item comentum Procli succesoris Ethimeon Platonis*. Birkenmajer's hypothesis has been confirmed by the discovery of two manuscripts containing selections of texts from the *Timaeus* commentary in Moerbeke's translation: *Toletanus*, Bibl. Capituli 47–12, ff. 71r–74v and *Leidensis*, B.P.L. 64, ff. 137v–138v. The excerpts are introduced as *De commento Procli super Timeum Platonis sunt excerpta que sequuntur.*[29] Although the name of the translator is not given, a stylistic analysis makes evident that the translation is Moerbeke's work, as is also indirectly confirmed by the transmission of the text. The Toledo manuscript belongs to the famous collection of manuscripts that Archbishop Gonzalvo Gudiel acquired in 1280 in Viterbo.[30] Many of them are copies from autographs Moerbeke had left there after his departure for Corinth in 1278. All translated excerpts come from book II of the *Timaeus* commentary. The first long extract is the interesting digression on the utility of prayer (*In Tim.* 2, 207,21–212,28). This section is followed in the Toledo manuscript by two passages (219,2–11 and 236,20–28) wherein Proclus examines in what sense we have to understand Plato's affirmation that the world is generated (*genêtos*). Finally, four other extracts are taken from the commentary on *Tim.* 28a: 241,28–31; 242,24–243,1; 243,29–253,16; 253,26–257,9. They discuss different forms of cognition, namely sense perception, opinion, discursive reason, intellect, and the problem of the "criterion" of truth. The way in which the extracts are introduced shows that they were not taken by some copyist from an existing Latin

[27] Birkenmajer (1970a), 280.
[28] On Moerbeke's translation of Simplicius' commentary on the *De caelo* see Bossier (2004).
[29] The texts are edited by Steel (1985).
[30] See Hernández and Linehan (2004) with inventory of the manuscript collection on 487–496.

translation but had been selected by the translator himself, after browsing through the Greek text of the commentary. In fact, the excerpts are chosen not accidentally but deliberately in a functional relationship with certain subjects that the translator may have considered of philosophical interest, such as the question of prayer, the problem of the eternity of the world, the distinction between forms of cognition, and the criterion of truth. We know that Moerbeke translated other excerpts from large works because of their particular interest, perhaps the urgent request of Thomas Aquinas or some other scholar asking him if he knew of any discussion of these subjects in Greek commentaries. Thus, Moerbeke translated a large section from Simplicius' commentary on *De caelo* (495,25–504,32), which deals with the explanation given by Eudoxus, Calippus, and Aristotle of the doctrine of the concentric spheres. Later on he made a full translation of this bulky commentary. Thomas gratefully used the partial translation in the explanation of the notoriously difficult chapter *Metaph.* XII 8 on the immobile movers and later also received the complete translation for his own work on the *De caelo*.[31] Other examples of partial translations by Moerbeke are Philoponus, *On the Intellect*, and the chapters from the *Eudemian Ethics* and *Magna moralia*, later known as *De bona fortuna*.[32] We could find no trace of the partial translation of the *Timaeus* commentary in Thomas' work. Moerbeke did send, however, a copy of the digression on prayer to his compatriot Henry Bate of Mechelen.[33] In fact, Bate inserts this digression in his philosophical encyclopedia *Speculum divinorum*, in part XI, ch. 24; XXIII, ch. 10; and XXIII, ch. 25. The other extracts seem to have remained unknown to Bate. The manuscript of the university library of Leiden (*Universiteitsbibliotheek*, B.P.L. 64; dated early fourteenth century), which may have come from Bate's own collection, contains only the digression on prayer, and not the other excerpts that we find in the Toledo manuscript. A comparative analysis of the vocabulary used by the translator and the fact that he left so many open spaces in the text when he was uncertain how to translate some technical terms set the translation in the early period of Moerbeke's translation work, probably when he was staying at Viterbo, around 1264. It was at this same time that he also made the partial translation of Simplicius and the extracts of the *Eudemian Ethics*.

There are, however, strong indications that Moerbeke later also produced a complete translation of Proclus' commentary.[34] The translation of

[31] See Bossier (2004). [32] See Cordonier and Steel (2012).

[33] On Bate see the introduction to this volume.

[34] I summarize in this paragraph the main arguments I will develop in a forthcoming study together with Barbara Bartocci.

Simplicius' commentary offers again an interesting parallel. As in the latter case, Moerbeke may first have translated some excerpts of the *Timaeus* commentary that could be of immediate interest for scholars, only making a complete translation some years later.[35] The above-quoted passage in the letter of the Faculty of Arts seems to refer to a complete commentary, not to some excerpts. This remains, however, a speculative hypothesis as long as no manuscripts have been found. Birkenmajer originally believed that he had discovered a copy of Moerbeke's translation in a manuscript at the University Library of Leiden, the *Vossianus* F. 100.[36] This codex, which dates from the beginning of the sixteenth century, contains indeed a Latin translation of Proclus' commentary, albeit without indication of the translator. Having examined the translation style of the anonymous scholar, Birkenmajer came to the conclusion that this translation was a work by Moerbeke. But some years later, in 1925, he revised his views after criticism from Fr. Pelster, who had told him that the translation of Greek particles in the *Vossianus* was not characteristic of Moerbeke. The decisive argument against Moerbeke's authorship was Birkenmajer's discovery of a long section from Proclus' commentary in the encyclopedia *Speculum divinorum* of Henricus Bate.[37] If Bate quotes the authentic text of Moerbeke's translation, the Leiden translation could not, he concluded, be Moerbeke's work, since it is definitely different. In my view Birkenmajer too easily gave up his first view. He should have investigated further the possibility he raised in his first study, namely that the Leiden manuscript offers a humanistic rewriting of a medieval translation, of which there are many other examples.[38] The discovery of the supplementary fragments contained in the *Toletanus* copy makes it possible to compare many more texts of Moerbeke with the *Vossianus* than Birkenmajer was able to do. A minute comparison of the translation in the Vossianus with all excerpts of Moerbeke leaves no doubt: the Leiden translation is a humanistic revision of Moerbeke's translation. The anonymous author modified the Moerbeke version, removing Grecisms, rewriting too literal constructions, and replacing medieval terms with classic Latin vocabulary. But all these modifications cannot hide the fact that the author used Moerbeke's translation as substrate for his own version. When the *Vossianus* departs from Moerbeke in rendering the text more freely, one never has the impression that the translator consulted the Greek text. On the contrary, in his rewriting he renders the translation

[35] See Bossier (2004), xxii–l. [36] See De Meyier (1973), 219–220.

[37] See Henricus Bate, *Speculum divinorum* XI, ch. 24 (Boese and Steel [1990], 84–85); *Spec. div.* XXIII, ch. 10; ch. 25 (Steel and Guldentops [1996], 421–425, 508).

[38] Birkenmajer (1970a), 295.

less accurate and sometimes gets it completely wrong. My claim that the *Vossianus* is a remake of a (now lost) complete translation of Moerbeke is based on a comparison of the *Vossianus* text with the existing partial translation. It is, however, a plausible hypothesis that the author of the *Vossianus* did not just follow Moerbeke in the sections where there exists a partial translation – which he certainly did not know – but for the whole of the text. Therefore one has to postulate a now lost complete translation by Moerbeke. It should be noticed, however, that, whenever Moerbeke made an integral translation of a text of which he had previously made only a partial translation, he did not simply integrate the partial version in the complete version but translated it anew and improved it. This may explain why some omissions and empty spaces found in the edited extracts are not in the corresponding *Vossianus* version. We know that the manuscript of Leiden was once in the possession of Giovanni Battista Rasario (1517–1578). Rasario was professor of Greek in Venice and in Padua and himself a translator of Greek commentaries on Aristotle and of medical texts, Galen in particular. He must have had an interest in the *Timaeus*, as he himself composed a commentary on this dialogue. In the preface to his edition of pseudo-Galen's *In libros Hippocratis* (Venice, 1562) he refers to his own commentary on the *Timaeus*: *et nos disseruimus in eo commentario quem in Timaeum eddidimus* (f. 5E). I could find no trace of this commentary, unless Rasario meant by it his rewriting of Proclus' commentary.

The hypothesis that a version of Moerbeke's complete translation still circulated in Italy in the sixteenth century was recently confirmed by the research of Barbara Bartocci on the translation of Proclus' commentary made by Paolo Beni (1553–1623). Beni is known as author of the most extensive modern commentary on the *Timaeus*, but he also made, while he started working on his own commentary, a partial translation of Proclus' commentary when he was in Milan in 1593.[39] The translation is preserved in two copies in the "archivio segreto" of the Vatican.[40] When working on this translation Beni became more and more disappointed with Proclus' allegorical theological interpretations of the *prooemium* of the *Timaeus*. As he says, he had started in good faith, hoping that the study of this commentary might have helped him to better understand the dialogue and thus prepare his own commentary, hoping also that the work would be of some interest to other Platonic scholars, given that no Latin translation of this commentary so far existed (exception made of Leonico Tomeo's

[39] On Beni's commentary on the *Timaeus* see von Perger (2005) and Bartocci (2013).

[40] Beni's translation (dated August 6, 1593) is preserved in the "Archivio Segreto Vaticano," fondo Archivio Beni II, MSS. 110 and 111.

partial translation published in 1526). Unfortunately, Beni was exasperated by Proclus' "ecstatic" mode of philosophy and his use of allegories and other *chimaerae* which are of no use for a philosopher interested in explaining nature; it seemed that Proclus, instead of doing philosophy, took pleasure in theogonies and telling mythological stories (*aniles fabulas enarrare*). He stopped translating at the lemma where Proclus entered into a detailed explanation of the Atlantis story (*In Tim.* 1, 75,27f.).[41] He resumed, however, his translation with the second book which he translated entirely. Although he declares that he was the very first to translate Proclus' commentary into Latin – apart from a partial translation by Leonico – a comparative study of the sections that correspond to the Moerbeke fragmentary translation shows that Beni, independently from the *Vossianus*, used Moerbeke's translation as substrate for his own translation, though he occasionally also corrects the translation with the edition of the Greek text (Basel, 1534).

We may thus conclude that Moerbeke not only made a partial translation of the *Timaeus* commentary in his earlier career (around 1264), but also a complete translation, which unfortunately only survives in a humanistic editing. The complete translation may have been made during his stay in Corinth, possibly before the commentary on the *Parmenides*.[42]

The commentary on the *Parmenides*

This translation is not dated but may have been the last work of Moerbeke. In his *Speculum divinorum* Henry Bate informs us that Moerbeke had once mentioned to him Plato's *Parmenides*, a dialogue not yet known among the Latins, probably in a discussion on the problem of participation, and Moerbeke had promised to send him a copy of his translation, but that this was unfortunately prevented by his death.[43] Although there is no reference to Proclus here, it is most plausible to believe that Moerbeke meant the

[41] Cf. ASV, ABII, MS 110, f. 1r: *Etenim tam facile hic Author divertit ad orphicas genealogias ac nenias, quibus complet commentarium, tum prolixas Homericas fabulas cum solidis Platonis decretis coniungit, Poesimque cum Phisiologia miscet, tam intemperanter (id quod multo deterius est) somnia quaedam vel potius chimaeras in axiomatum habet loco, ex quibus nova semper praecepta, vel potius somnia sphingisque derivat et comminiscitur, ut non posset me suscepti laboris non paenitere praesertim vero quia, dum tam multa profert, ac nihil probat, mihi quidem non tam Philosophari videatur, quam aniles fabulas enarrare* (collation by B. Bartocci).

[42] Paravicini Bagliani (1989), 46–47.

[43] *Verum in Parmenide Platonis, qui liber nondum apud nos communiter habetur, plura forsan de hiis continentur, prout ab interprete illius libri seu translatore dudum intellexi, qui michi promiserat eum transmittere, sed morte preventus non transmisit* (Bate, *Speculum divinorum* XI, ch. 12, 53–57, ed. Boese).

Parmenides together with Proclus' commentary. Moerbeke's translation is based upon a Greek manuscript that was more complete and much better than the very mediocre copy on which the whole Greek tradition of the text depends. Thus, only Moerbeke has the important last section of the commentary on negative theology, which is missing from all the Greek manuscripts. For an edition of the Greek text the use of Moerbeke's translation is of crucial importance. After Moerbeke's death this Greek manuscript probably entered the papal collection, as happened with his commentary on the *Timaeus*.[44]

Moerbeke's translation of this seminal Neoplatonic work had a very limited success in the Middle Ages. Only six copies are preserved of this translation. The most reliable copy of the text is also the most recent: the *Ambrosianus A 167 sup.* (A), which was copied in 1508 in Ferrara, most probably directly from Moerbeke's autograph. Yet apart from its first owner, the Milanese humanist, Cesare Rovidio, the copy seems to have had no readers. The oldest copy is the *Oxford Bodleian Library, Digby* 236 (O), which was probably copied in Bologna around 1340. It also contains the *Tria opuscula*, and, at the end, some rare treatises of Averroes. As we have seen, for the *Opuscula* the Oxford manuscript is related to the Macerata codex (*Bibl. Com.* 361) and both derive from the same model. This model may also have contained the commentary on the *Parmenides*. The copy is the work of an English scholar with a keen interest in Platonism, as is shown by his annotations.[45] After the copy of the *Parmenides* commentary he added a list of all the Platonic dialogues to which he had found a reference in Proclus, with the names of the speakers. He also notes Proclus' views on the difference between the purpose of the *Parmenides* and the *Timaeus*.[46] It was not possible to identify this "English Platonist." He may have belonged to the group of English friars with a keen interest in ancient culture,[47] to which the Dominican Walley mentioned earlier also belonged. Interestingly, Berthold of Moosburg refers three times to the commentary on the *Parmenides* in his commentary on the *Elements of Theology*. He must have had access to a manuscript, perhaps when he was in England. Was it the copy now preserved in the *Bodleian*?

The third branch in the tradition is represented by a group of manuscripts associated with Nicholas of Cusa. The *Vaticanus latinus* 3074 (V) is a copy produced in the early fifteenth century in Northern Italy. It was

44 In the catalogue of 1295 it is mentioned under nr. 437 *expositio Procli super Parmenidem*; in the catalogue of 1311 under nr. 597: *comentum Procli Parmenidem Platonis*.

45 On this manuscript and its fascinating history, see Steel in Geoffroy and Steel (2001), 83–91.

46 See Steel (1982–1985), vol. 1, 5*–8*.

47 Smalley (1960).

for some time in the hands of Cusanus, as is shown by some annotations. He probably did not own it, for it entered the library of Pope Nicholas V before 1455. In any case, Cusanus had a copy made for himself from this *Vaticanus*, the present *Cusanus* 186 (C). The German humanist Johannes of Dalberg (1445–1503) made his own copy from this manuscript, when it was already in the library of Cues (*Leipzig, Stadtbibliothek* 27). Finally, there is an Italian manuscript from the late fifteenth century, the *Vaticanus latinus* 11600 (R), which contains a copy of the commentary made from the same model [y] that was used by the copyist of V. Of this model, R is the most reliable, V the most deficient copy. When studying Proclus' text in his own manuscript, a copy of V, Cusanus was in such despair that he asked his collaborator, John Bussi, to make a revision of the text. Bussi introduced some conjectures of his own but made most of his corrections from a collation of C with another manuscript. There are good arguments to conclude that Bussi made use of the now lost manuscript [y] to correct C. Cusanus studied the commentary intensively, as is evidenced by his numerous annotations in his own copy, now preserved at Cues.[48] In the works he composed during the last period of his life, when he was staying in Italy (from the September 30, 1458 until his death in 1464), Cusanus shows that he is deeply influenced by his reading of Proclus' commentary and of the *Parmenides* in general, of which he had also an integral translation made by George of Trebizond. This influence is most evident in the treatise *Tu quis es* (*De principio*) from 1459 and *De venatione sapientiae* from 1463.

Surprisingly even the great Renaissance Platonist Marsilio Ficino always relied on Moerbeke's translation in his study of Proclus' commentary on the *Parmenides* and never seems to have used a Greek manuscript of this text.[49] Already by the time he was working on the *Philebus* commentary (1464–1466) Ficino had intensively studied Proclus in the medieval translations available to him. For metaphysical arguments about the first principle of all things, the One or Good, he mainly relied on Proclus' *Elements of Theology*, of which he summarized the propositions 1–20. For arguments in favor of the doctrine of the ideas he used the third book of Proclus' commentary on the *Parmenides*. It is plausible that the young Ficino knew from Cusanus how important the digression in Proclus' commentary was for a correct understanding of the Platonic doctrine of the ideas; for only someone having read the whole commentary (as did Cusanus three times) could have discovered the relevant sections on the ideas. But even in his own

[48] See Bormann (1986). [49] I defend this prima facie implausible conclusion in Steel (2013).

commentary on the *Parmenides*, which closely follows Proclus' argument, Ficino seems to have relied only on Moerbeke's translation.

Finally, also Giovanni Pico della Mirandola knew Moerbeke's translation. The last of his celebrated *Conclusiones* of 1486 is a passage taken from Proclus' prologue (*In Parm.*, 3, 10–15).

Bibliography

Bartocci, B. (2013) "L'In Platonis Timaeum e le altre opere inedite di Paolo Beni da Gubbio," *Recherches de théologie et philosophie médiévales* 80 (1): 163–217.

Bataillon, L. J. (1989) "Quelques utilisateurs des textes rares de Moerbeke (*Philopon, Tria opuscula*) et particulièrement Jacques de Viterbe," in Brams and Vanhamel (1989), 107–112.

Birkenmajer, A. (1970a) "Der Brief der Pariser Artistenfakultät über den Tod des hl. Thomas von Aquin," in A. Birkenmajer, *Études d'histoire des sciences et de la philosophie du Moyen Âge* (*Studia Copernicana* 1), Wrocław, Warsaw, and Kraków, 277–311 (reprint of 1922).

(1970b) "Neues zu dem Brief der Pariser Artistenfakultät über den Tod des hl. Thomas von Aquin," in A. Birkenmajer, *Études d' histoire des sciences et de la philosophie du Moyen Age* (*Studia Copernicana* 1), Wroclaw, Warsaw, and Kraków, 513–528 (reprint of 1925).

Boese, H. (ed.) (1958) *Die mittelalterliche Übersetzung der Stoicheiōsis physikē des Proclus*, Berlin.

(ed.) (1960) *Procli Diadochi Tria opuscula (De providentia, libertate, malo) latine Guillelmo de Moerbeke vertente et graece ex Isaacii Sebastocratoris aliorumque scriptis collecta*, Berlin.

(1985) "Wilhelm von Moerbeke als Übersetzer der *Stoicheiosis theologike* des Proclus," *Abhandlungen der Heidelberger Akademie der Wissenschaften, Philos.-Hist. Klasse* 5, Heidelberg.

(ed.) (1987) *Proclus: Elementatio theologica, translata a Guillelmo de Morbecca*, Leuven.

Boese, H. and Steel, C. (eds.) (1990) Henricus Bate, *Speculum divinorum et quorundam naturalium*, Pars XI–XII *On Platonic Philosophy*, Leuven.

Bormann, K. (1986) *Cusanus-Texte III, Marginalien, 2. Proclus Latinus: Die Exzerpte und Randnoten des Nikolaus von Kues zu den lateinischen Übersetzungen der Proclus-Schriften; 2.1 Expositio in Parmenidem Platonis*, Heidelberg.

Bossier, F. (ed.) (2004) *Simplicius: Commentaire sur le traité du ciel d'Aristote, traduction de Guillaume de Moerbeke*, vol. 1, Leuven.

Brams, J. and Vanhamel, W. (eds.) (1989) *Guillaume de Moerbeke. Recueil d'études à l'occasion du 700e anniversaire de sa mort (1286)*, Leuven.

Cordonier, V. and Steel, C. (2012) "Guillaume de Moerbeke. Traducteur du *Liber de bona fortuna* et de l'*Éthique à Eudème*," in A. M. I. van Oppenraay (ed.), *The Letter before the Spirit, The Importance of Text Editions for the Study of the Reception of Aristotle*, Leiden, 401–446.

De Meyier, K. (1973) *Codices Vossiani Latini*, vol. I, Leiden.

Gabrič, A. (2006) *Une métaphysique à l'école de Thomas d'Aquin: le "de modis rerum" de Remi de Viterbe*, Fribourg.

Gentile, S. (2001) "Remigio de' Girolami," in *Dizionario biografico degli Italiani*, vol. LVI, Rome, 531–541.

Geoffroy, M. and Steel, C. (2001) *Averroès: La béatitude de l'âme*, Paris.

Guagliado, V. A., Hess, C. R., and Taylor, R. C. (eds. and trans.) (1996) *St. Thomas Aquinas: Commentary on the Book of Causes*, Washington, DC.

Hernández, F. J. and Linehan, P. (2004) *The Mozarabic Cardinal, The Life and Times of Gonzalo Pérez Gudiel*, Florence.

Klibansky, R. (1981) *The Continuity of the Platonic Tradition during the Middle Ages*, London (reprint of 1939).

Luna, C. (2009) "L'utilizzazione di una traduzione greco-latina medievale per la constituzione del testo greco: la traduzione di Guglielmo di Moerbeke del commento di Proclo *In Parmenidem*," *Documenti e studi sulla tradizione filosofica medievale* 20: 449–546.

Paravicini Bagliani, A. (1989) "Guillaume de Moerbeke et la cour pontificale," in Brams and Vanhamel (1989), 23–50.

Perger, M. von (2005) "Paolo Benis Timaios-Kommentar: eine christliche Kritik an aristotelischen und neuplatonische Interpretationen," in T. Leinkauf and C. Steel (eds.), *Plato's Timaeus and the Foundations of Cosmology in Late Antiquity, the Middle Ages and Renaissance*, Leuven, 407–451.

Saffrey, H.-D. (ed.) (1954) *Sancti Thomae de Aquino super librum de causis expositio*, Fribourg and Leuven.

Senger, H. G. (ed.) (1986) *Cusanus-Texte III, Marginalien, 2. Proclus Latinus: Die Exzerpte und Randnoten des Nikolaus von Kues zu den lateinischen Übersetzungen der Proclus-Schriften; 2.1 Theologia Platonis, Elementatio theologica*, Heidelberg.

Smalley, B. (1960) *English Friars and Antiquity in the Early Fourteenth Century*, Oxford.

Steel, C. (ed.) (1982–1985) *Proclus: Commentaire sur le Parménide de Platon, traduction de Guillaume de Moerbeke*, vol. I: *Books I to IV*; vol. II: *Books V to VII*, Leuven and Leiden.

(1985) "Proclus: Extraits du commentaire sur le Timée," in Steel (1982–1985), vol. II, 561–587.

(1989) "Moerbeke et saint Thomas," in Brams and Vanhamel (1989), 57–82.

(1997) "Das neue Interesse für den Platonismus am Ende des 13. Jahrhunderts," in Kobusch T. and Mojsisch B. (eds.), *Platon in der abendländischen Geistesgeschichte. Neue Forschungen zum Platonismus*, Darmstadt, 120–133.

(2013) "Ficino and Proclus: Arguments for the Platonic Doctrine of the Ideas," in J. Hankins and F. Meroi (eds.), *The Rebirth of Platonic Theology*, Florence, 63–118.

Steel, C. and Guldentops, G. (eds.) (1996) Henricus Bate, *Speculum divinorum et quorundam naturalium*, parts XX–XXIII: *On the Heavens, the Divine Movers, and the First Intellect*, Leuven.

Strobel, B. (2014) *Proklos, Tria opuscula, Griechische Retroversion mit Kommentar* (*Commentaria in Aristotelem Graeca et Byzantina* 6), Berlin.

Sturlese, L. (1987) "Il dibattito sul Proclo latino nel medioevo fra l'università di Parigi e lo studium di Colonia," in G. Boss and G. Seel (eds.), *Proclus et son influence, Actes du colloque de Neuchâtel, juin 1985*, Zurich, 261–285.

(2007) *Homo divinus, Philosophische Projekte in Deutschland zwischen Meister Eckhart und Heinrich Seuse*, Stuttgart.

Wielockx, R. (1994) "Une collection d'autographes de Gilles de Rome," in P. Chiesa and L. Pinelli (eds.), *Gli autografi medievali, Problemi paleografici e filologici*, Spoleto, 207–248.

Ypma, E. (ed.) (1968–1975) *Jacobi di Viterbo O.E.S.A.: Disputationes de quolibet*, Würzburg.

CHAPTER 10

The University of Paris in the thirteenth century

Proclus and the Liber de causis

Pasquale Porro

Premise

Proclus was known to the Parisian masters of the thirteenth century mainly in two different ways. He was known directly, through the translations made by William of Moerbeke between 1268 and 1280 (*Elementatio theologica, Tria opuscula*, a part of the commentary *In Parmenidem*, a fragment of the commentary *In Timaeum*), to which should be added the translation of the *Elementatio physica* already made in the twelfth century by an anonymous translator who was active in Salerno and in Sicily, he collaborated with Henricus Aristippus, and he might perhaps be identified with the translator of Ptolemy's *Almagest.*[1] Proclus was also known indirectly, through the *Liber de causis*. This last, as is well known, is the Latin translation of the *Kalām fī maḥḍ al-ḫayr* (*Discourse on Pure Goodness*), which in its turn is a short text in Arabic based on Proclus' *Elements of Theology* and composed in the ninth century in the circle of al-Kindī, or even, as has been suggested, by al-Kindī himself.[2] For the sake of completeness, to the indirect transmission of Proclean ideas might be added the wide diffusion of the *Corpus Dionysianum*,[3] insofar as the works of pseudo-Dionysius include themes derived from Proclus. The Latin Masters, however, could not really perceive this doctrinal affinity between Proclus and Dionysius, with the partial exceptions of Albert the Great and Thomas Aquinas.[4] I shall therefore leave aside this third and very indirect tradition and consider the first two, taking into account first the relatively limited impact

I wish to express my gratitude to Friederike Schmiga, Lisa Adams, and Stephen Gersh for their invaluable help in preparing the English version of this chapter.

[1] See Boese (1958). [2] D'Ancona (1995), 155–194.

[3] On the diffusion of the *Corpus Dionysianum* in Paris see Dondaine (1953), Faes de Mottoni (1977), Bojadjiev, Kapriev, and Speer (2000).

[4] See, for instance, Siedler, Kübel, and Vogels (1978), 183, 192, and 221, and Thomas Aquinas' preface to his commentary on pseudo-Dionysius' *Divine Names* (Pera 1950). On Aquinas and the "Platonists" see Henle (1956), Kremer (1966), and Hankey (2002).

of the Latin translations of Proclus' genuine texts (mainly, in Paris, the *Elementatio theologica*), and then that of the *Liber de causis*. In actual fact, the latter entered the Latin world before Moerbeke's versions of Proclean works: *De causis* had already been translated in Toledo in the twelfth century by Gerard of Cremona (1114–1187), probably between 1167 and 1187.[5] But its connection with Proclus' *Elements of Theology* remained unnoticed for many decades. Only after Moerbeke's translation of the Proclean work was Aquinas the first to recognize, in his commentary on the *Liber de causis* (1272), that the text was a compilation based on Proclus' work.[6] Furthermore, Aquinas' discovery did not receive much attention from the Parisian masters of his generation or the following one. Surprisingly enough, many of them (including Aquinas' master, Albert the Great) seem to ignore or at least not mention Proclus as the source of the propositions of *De causis*.[7]

Rather than presenting a more or less complete survey of the ways in which the Parisian masters quote or use Proclus' work on the one hand or *De causis* on the other – a task which has already been carried out in a more than satisfactory way[8] – the scope of this chapter will be to recapitulate, in the next section, some of the essential dates of the reception of the corpus of Proclus' works, as well as (on pp. 276–278) those of *De causis* in the West, in order to focus our attention only on some specific aspects. These are: (i) the use of some propositions of the *Elementatio* in the late twelfth-century debates over the problem of the self-motion of the will, paying special attention to Henry of Ghent and James of Viterbo, the Parisian master who displays more than anyone else familiarity not only with the *Elementatio*, but also with the *Tria opuscula* (see pp. 269–275); and (ii) the debate over the correct interpretation of the fourth proposition of the *Liber de causis* ("The first of created things is being, and there is nothing else created before it"), an issue which will allow us to locate a tension between the *Liber* itself and its Proclean source which is at least implicit in the Latin reception (see pp. 278–294).

[5] See D'Ancona and Taylor (2003) for all the essential bibliographical references; see also D'Ancona (2011).

[6] See Guagliardo, Hess, and Taylor (1996), 4: "Thus we find a collection of writings on first principles that are divided into different propositions, in a way similar to the procedure of those examining certain truths one at a time. And in Greek we find handed down a book of this type by the Platonist Proclus, which contains 211 propositions and is entitled The Elements of Theology. And in Arabic we find the present book which is called On Causes among Latin readers, [a work] known to have been translated from Arabic and not [known] to be extant at all in Greek. Thus, it seems that one of the Arab philosophers excerpted it from this book by Proclus, especially since everything in it is contained much more fully and more diffusely in that of Proclus."

[7] What Giles of Rome states in his *Commentary on De causis* is emblematic (Giles of Rome [1550], 7r): *Sed de expositione Procli non sit nobis ad praesens curae . . .*

[8] See below, notes 20 and 44.

The arrival of Proclus in the Latin world: Moerbeke's translations and the role of Thomas Aquinas

It has already been pointed out that, except for the *Elementatio physica*, which had practically no impact on the Parisian debates, even though it had already been translated in Sicily in the twelfth century, the direct arrival of Proclus' texts in the Latin world is due to the activities of the translator William of Moerbeke. The translation of the *Elementatio theologica* was completed by Moerbeke in Viterbo, at the papal court, in 1268, and so at a time when Moerbeke was working on the translation of Neoplatonic commentaries. The translation of the *Tria opuscula* can be dated to the year 1280, when Moerbeke had already been nominated Archbishop of Corinth (April 9, 1278). Actually, the only information about the Dominican's journey to Corinth is contained in the colophons of the translations of these *opuscula*.[9] In this way we know that the translations of the latter works were completed on February 4 (*De decem dubitationibus circa providentiam*), February 11 (*De providentia et fato et eo quod in nobis*), and February 21, 1280 (*Liber de malorum subsistentia*). As far as the *Commentary on Plato's Parmenides* is concerned, the dates are less certain: from an annotation made by Henry Bate of Mechelen (Malines) we can conclude that the translation was left incomplete because of the translator's death, or at least that Moerbeke died before he could send Bate a copy of his translation.[10] Since the hypothesis that Moerbeke had returned to the Holy See before his death is more likely than that he died in Greece, one may assume that the translation was made at the papal court.[11] Moerbeke has also been credited with the translation of a fragment of the *Commentary on Plato's Timaeus*, which is certain to have been made before 1274.[12] It has been suggested that the latter translation may actually precede that of the *Elementatio*, although this opinion is not shared by Boese, to whom we owe the critical edition of the Latin text of the *Elementatio*.[13]

It is quite likely that the translations of Proclus (together with those of Themistius and Simplicius) began circulating in Paris thanks to the intervention of Thomas Aquinas.[14] To be more precise, Aquinas was probably the first to obtain a copy of the *Elementatio*, which he seems

[9] See Brams (2003), 108. [10] See Van de Vyver (1960), XIV; Klibansky (1943), 289, n. 1.

[11] See Paravicini Bagliani (1989), 46–47 (the library of Boniface VIII possessed copies of Proclus' commentaries on *Parmenides* and *Timaeus*).

[12] In Paravicini Bagliani's opinion, this version of the *Commentary on Plato's Timaeus* was translated during Moerbeke's second stay at the papal court. See Paravicini Bagliani (1989), 46–47. See also Birkenmajer (1922); Verbeke (1953); Vanhamel (1989), 360–361.

[13] See Boese (1985), 10. [14] See Steel (1989), 71–72.

to have brought with him to Paris from Italy towards the end of the summer of 1268. Moreover, we can presume that Aquinas had intended to introduce in Paris the part of the translation of the commentary on the Timaeus which had already been completed. In the famous letter dated May 2, 1274, which the Parisian Masters of the Faculty of Arts, reunited at Lyon after the death of Aquinas, addressed to the General Chapter of the Dominicans, they requested some texts which Aquinas himself had promised to send from Italy: in addition to the commentary by Simplicius on *De caelo* and a text entitled *De aquarum conductibus et ingeniis erigendis*, which has not yet been precisely identified,[15] a *Commentary on the Timaeus* is mentioned, which may be assumed with some likeliness to be the one by Proclus partially translated by Moerbeke. Perhaps Aquinas had the intention of using this last work for his commentary on *De caelo*, although in fact there are no traces in the part completed by the Dominican master which could serve to document such a state of affairs.[16]

It should be mentioned, however, that Aquinas draws heavily on Proclus only in the *Commentary on De causis*, when he sets himself the task of locating – in general with great precision – the propositions of the *Elementatio* from which the author of *De causis* draws and constructs his own propositions. Apart from the *Commentary on De causis*, Aquinas seems to quote Proclus only twice: namely, in chapter 20 of *De substantiis separatis*, first in connection with the aerial bodies of demons (or rather, in connection with the fact that the souls of the dead possess perpetual and incorruptible bodies – this is a reference to prop. 196 of the *Elementatio*)[17] and secondly in connection with the fact that all substances of an intellectual nature are completely immune from temporality (this is a reference to prop. 169 of the *Elementatio*,[18] quoted together with prop. 2 of *De causis*).[19] Ultimately this does not amount to much, given the great importance accorded to *De causis* itself in the totality of Aquinas' work.

A systematic account of the citations of Proclus in the Parisian scholastic production of the thirteenth century has been provided by Sturlese, and

15 Birkenmajer's proposal of identifying the text with Hero of Alexandria's *Pneumatica* has been rejected by Grant: see Birkenmajer (1922), Grant (1971). The work might consist of a partial translation of Pappus' *Collectio*, or in a collection of passages from Anthemius; see Steel (1989), 72, n. 39; Vanhamel (1989), 372–376.

16 Quotations from Proclus' *Elementatio* can instead be found in Peter of Auvergne's continuation of Aquinas' commentary on *De caelo*.

17 *El. theol.* 171 (Dodds 1963): "Every participated soul makes use of a first body which is perpetual and has a constitution without temporal origin and exempt from decay."

18 *El. theol.* 147: "Every intelligence has its existence, its potency and its activity in eternity."

19 Guagliardo, Hess, and Taylor (1996), 12: "Every higher being is higher than eternity and before it or is with eternity or is after eternity and above time."

it would be superfluous to repeat his findings here in detail.[20] According to Sturlese, after an initial period in which they were received with great interest in Paris (by Aquinas and Siger of Brabant, for instance),[21] Proclus' texts were quickly "neutralized" and expelled from the contemporary philosophical debates as early as the late 1270s. This process of marginalization is thought to have been due, on the one hand, to the "editorial failure" of the commentary on the Parmenides and the *Opuscula* and, on the other, to the reduction, or "stylization," of the topics of the *Elementatio* to a few commonplaces, insofar as they are repeated in an almost formulaic way by the Parisian theologians. These commonplaces include the relation between one and many, the conversion to itself of incorporeal beings, and to a lesser degree, the topic of essential causality, the doctrine of providence, and the concepts of eternity and time. A similar situation is also registered by Sturlese (with some exceptions, starting with the above-mentioned Siger) in the Faculty of Arts, having been already discussed by Grabmann in his research.[22] However much the Proclean echoes in the production of the *artistae* may be relevant, the success of the *Elementatio* even in this milieu, according to Sturlese, never led to any real attempt at a deeper understanding of the Neoplatonic philosopher. Indeed, the fact that the arrival of Proclus' work ended with Moerbeke's death shows in itself that the mechanism through which later texts were introduced and disseminated did not always function very well. For Sturlese, the true medieval reception of Proclus must therefore be sought outside the Parisian context, in culturally peripheral areas, such as Brabant or Germany, and in relation to such figures as Henry Bate of Mechelen, Dietrich of Freiberg, Meister Eckhart, and obviously Berthold of Moosburg.[23]

There is not much to add to Sturlese's reconstruction, and little to modify in his account, which still seems more than well founded even when seen from the distance of some years, and even though the assumption that Proclus' metaphysics had been "embalmed" and put "into a corner in the museum of relics" within a few years seems a little too severe. In reality, at least two aspects of the "second reception" of Proclus in Paris (which took

[20] See Sturlese (1987). See also the two volumes Boss and Seel (1987) and Bos and Meijer (1992).

[21] According to Sturlese, Aquinas and Siger embody two different attitudes towards the arrival in Paris of the Proclean texts: while Aquinas shows a "substantially tactical and defensive attitude," insofar as he derives from the new works a confirmation of the superiority of Aristotle over the Platonists, Siger (together with Albert the Great) seems to adopt a more pacific and conciliatory approach, aimed at softening, through Proclus, the differences between Aristotle and Plato; see Sturlese (1987), 267 and 269.

[22] See, for instance, Grabmann (1936), 413–423; (1946), esp. 156ff.

[23] See Chapter 11 in this volume on Berthold of Moosburg. Concerning Eckhart, see Retucci (2008).

place after the generation of Aquinas, Albert the Great, and Siger) merit attention. The first concerns the significant use which James of Viterbo makes of Proclus, a fact which escaped the attention neither of Sturlese nor of Bataillon after him.[24] The second concerns the way in which some Proclean propositions were used within the bounds of a particularly lively debate in the last decades of the thirteenth century, a use which was neither stylized, nor banal. This was the debate over the self-motion of the will. In what follows I will confine myself to complementing Sturlese's analysis, not by adding quotations, which have become accessible in the meantime, but by discussing briefly the two aspects just mentioned. These intersect and overlap, often to the point of merging with one other.

The conversion of the incorporeal and the self-motion of the will

With respect to the context outlined by Sturlese for the second Parisian reception, James of Viterbo (active between 1293 and 1303) seems to represent a significant exception. For one thing, his use of Proclus' works does not stop with the *Elementatio* but includes the *Tria opuscula de providentia*, which enjoyed only limited success in Paris and the Latin world in general. Boese, the editor of the Latin version of the *Opuscula*, lists only a few citations: in the fourteenth century, Remigius of Florence (de' Girolami, active in Paris and Florence)[25] and later Berthold of Moosburg; in the fifteenth century, John Marcanova (Johannes de Marcanova or Marchanova, *c.* 1410–1467) and Marsilio Ficino.[26] Sturlese has subsequently demonstrated the presence of Proclean themes deriving from *De providentia*, at the beginning of the fourteenth century, in James of Thérines (from the mode of operation can be deduced the mode of existence) and William of Alnwick (the superiority of knowledge through causes). He observes, however, that in both cases what can be found are indirect citations that can be traced ultimately to James of Viterbo. Bataillon, to whom we owe the identification of another citation of the *Opuscula* in Giles of Rome (at the beginning of *De renunciatione pape*), has further confirmed this dependency by emphasizing James' particular interest in Proclus.[27] It may be appropriate here – in support of Sturlese's and Bataillon's findings – to

[24] See Bataillon (1989).

[25] The most interesting citation can be found in q. 15 of *Quodl.* II (*Utrum dampnati in inferno magis appetant non esse quam esse*), where an argument drawn from *De malorum subsistentia* (*melius non esse omnino quam semper male esse*) is remarkably closely associated with Matt. 26:24 (and with the *Glossa ordinaria* on the same verse). Remigius' *Quodlibet* II was presumably disputed in Perugia between 1304 and 1307.

[26] See Boese (1960), XI–XIII, XVI–XVII.

[27] See Bataillon (1989).

provide a short summary of the major occurrences (taking into account only those texts which are already available in a critical edition)[28] in order to sketch a meaningful picture of the Proclean themes which James considered worthy of attention.

From *De providentia*, James derives:

- the way of conceptualizing unity, not as that which excludes number, but as that which contains all numbers virtually (in other words, as anterior to multiplicity) in the same way that the circumference is present in its centre (*Quodl.* I, q. 2 and *De divinis praedicamentis*, q. 3; the reference is to *De decem dubitationibus circa providentiam* [q. 1], 5);
- the certainty that nothing can exist below the level of prime matter (*Quodl.* I, q. 2 and *De div. praed.*, q. 3; the reference is to *De decem dubitationibus circa providentiam* [q. 3], 10);
- the idea that the noblest form of knowledge is that which proceeds from the cause of a thing rather than from the thing itself (*Quodl.* I, q. 5; the reference is to *De decem dubitationibus circa providentiam* [q. 2], 8);
- the fact that the world is constituted by intelligence and necessity, taking the latter to mean fate, or the influence of the celestial bodies (*Quodl.* I, q. 7; the reference is to *De fato et providentia* 13);
- the claim that the mode of knowing a thing can be deduced from the mode of that thing's existence – an argument which is used to support the incorruptibility of the soul (*Quodl.* I, q. 11; the reference is to *De decem dubitationibus circa providentiam* [q. 2], 7).

It may be noteworthy that the references to the *Opuscula* seem to occur prevalently in James' first *Quodlibet*. From the *Elementatio*, by contrast, James takes the following doctrinal elements (not all of them being shared by him, evidently, and some of them functioning merely as arguments):

- that every incorporeal being is convertible to itself, and that conversion indicates not only the capacity of self-motion, but also the simplicity of incorporeal beings themselves (*Quodl.* I, q. 7, in reference to props. 15, 17, and 32; *Quodl.* I, q. 11, in reference only to prop. 17; *Quodl.* III, q. 14, in reference to props. 15 and 17; *Quodl.* IV, q. 4, in reference to prop. 14; *De div. praed.*, q. 14, in reference to prop. 17);
- that perfection is a part of goodness and not vice versa, and that the perfect as such imitates the good (*Quodl.* I, q. 8; the reference is to prop. 25);
- that every good brings with it the unification (*unitio*) of the participants with itself (*Quodl.* I, q. 8; the reference is to prop. 13);

[28] See in particular Ypma (1968), (1969), (1973), (1975), (1983), (1986).

- that just as time and eternity are distinct with respect to that which is measured, so they are distinct with respect to the mode of measurement (*Quodl.* I, q. 9; the reference is to prop. 54 and comm.); and that there exist several intrinsic times (*Quodl.* I, q. 9; the reference is to prop. 53 and comm.);
- that every soul is an incorporeal substance that can be separated from its body (*Quodl.* I, q. 11; the reference is to prop. 186);
- that the mere fact of producing things is not the cause of the producer's perfection, but instead is a sign, or effect, of its perfection, and that perfect goodness is followed by its communication (*Quodl.* II, q. 10; the reference is to prop. 7);
- that, because three Persons can be distinguished in God and because every multitude is posterior to unity, it seems possible that one could, in some respects, speak of anteriority and posteriority also in God (*Quodl.* III, q. 9; the reference is to prop. 5: every multitude is posterior to the one);
- that the most universal and remote cause is superior to the particular causes, insofar as the former is the cause of the latter's causality (*Quodl.* III, q. 13; the reference is to prop. 56);
- that every true agent acts without diminution or change (*Quodl.* III, q. 14; the reference is to prop. 26);
- that the one and that which is unified are distinct (*De div. praed.*, q. 3; the reference is to props. 2 and 4);
- that the one contrasts with multiplicity and is its cause; indeed, every multiplicity participates in the one (*De div. praed.*, q. 3; the reference is to prop. 21);
- that the multiplicity of created things does not imply any multiplicity in God (*De div. praed.*, q. 4; the reference is to prop. 22, together with prop. 20 of *De causis*);
- that the relation between God and creatures is not real (*De div. praed.*, q. 1; the reference is to prop. 122, comm.: "what acts in virtue of its being acts without relation");
- that without something in common, there is no necessity for a real and objective relation (*De div. praed.*, q. 15; the reference is to props. 122 and 141: there is order and hence a real relation only when there is something in common).

There is at least one case in which *De providentia* and the *Elementatio* are cited in conjunction, and this is the question of whether God should be called One (and Good) with greater legitimacy than Being: Proclus is cited in support of the first hypothesis, together with pseudo-Dionysius, in opposition to John Damascene (*De div. praed.*, q. 3; the reference is to *De decem dubitationibus circa providentiam* [q. 3], 10 and *El. theol.*, prop. 13: "Every good tends to unify what participates in it; and all unification is a good; and the Good is identical with the One").

Perhaps the most interesting of all the aspects mentioned above is the use of those propositions from the *Elementatio* which are concerned with the conversion of incorporeal beings (especially prop. 17, which is sometimes also cited in conjunction with props. 14, 15, and 32). This is certainly one of the most frequently mentioned Proclean topics in the thirteenth century; what is peculiar about it here is that it is used not only in a general sense, in reference to the movement of spiritual substances, but also in reference to the much more technical and delicate case of the self-motion of the will – the most heatedly discussed topic in the debates between "intellectualists" and "voluntarists" in the last quarter of the thirteenth century. In general, the "intellectualists" adhere faithfully to the Aristotelian principle that everything that moves is moved by something else: thus, the will also moves (i.e. decides to incline towards something) only insofar as it is moved by the intellect, or to be more precise, by the intellectual apprehension of an object as desirable. For the "voluntarists," on the other hand, if this were really the case, the will would never be truly free but would be forced simply to follow more or less faithfully the direction indicated by the intellect. In order to avoid this form of "psychological determinism," the "voluntarists" tend to concede in general that the will is capable of moving itself by itself and is not dependent upon any external movers. Proclus is cited explicitly in this matter by someone who could be considered the most convinced and tenacious upholder of the self-motion of the will, Henry of Ghent. Though he had already treated the same topic several times (in particular in q. 22 of *Quodl.* IV, and in q. 5 of *Quodl.* IX), Henry proposes – in q. 9 of *Quodl.* X (Advent 1286), which is actually dedicated to a different question[29] – a distinction between three meanings of motion: by motion one can refer, first of all, in the strict sense of the word, to a local and corporeal movement composed of successive parts, but one can also, in a broader sense of the word, refer to an instantaneous change of place, simple and deprived of parts, and finally, in the broadest sense of the word, to the spiritual operation performed by a spiritual agent on a passive term which is equally spiritual. Only in this sense can the will be said to move itself, through a sort of spiritual reversion to itself, just like the

[29] See Macken (1981), 220–255: *Utrum subiectum per se possit esse causa sufficiens sui accidentis* ("Whether a subject could by itself be a sufficient cause of its accident").

one to which Proclus refers in prop. 17 of the *Elementatio*: *Omne se ipsum movens primo ad se ipsum est conversum* ("Everything originally self-moving is capable of reversion upon itself"). Henry also uses the commentary on the lemma to emphasize the difference between the cases of the will (and of incorporeal agents) and that of heavy or light bodies. For instance, in the latter case, one part moves another, and this is why the whole cannot really be said to move itself by itself: what we have is only the appearance of self-motion and not a true instance of it. Only that which reverts as a whole to itself can be both mover and moved in a complete sense.[30] Shortly afterwards, in the same question, Henry has recourse to prop. 131: *omnis deus a se ipso propriam operationem orditur* ("Every god begins his characteristic activity with himself"): the will could not move anything other than itself, spiritually or physically, without having first moved itself spiritually, just as light does not illuminate other things without shining in itself, or just as any other spiritual agent does not act towards another thing without first having completed its own operation in itself. Indeed, in the commentary on the lemma of prop. 131, Proclus observes that "the quality which marks its presence in secondary beings is displayed first in itself, and it is indeed for this reason that it communicates itself to others, in virtue of the superabundance of its own nature."[31] The topics of the conversion of the incorporeal and that of the initial self-disposition of every "god" towards its appropriate operation thus become for Henry the conceptual tools with which to sidestep the Aristotelian interdict concerning the possibility of self-motion.

This claim of Henry's (which was shared by many Franciscan masters of the same period) was heavily attacked by the most radical intellectualist of the time, Godfrey of Fontaines (for instance, in q. 7 of *Quodl.* VI, 1289),[32] who assumed the unconditional and unassailable validity of the Aristotelian principle: if something were capable of self-motion, it would be in potency and in act at the same time, which is impossible (for Henry, as we have already seen, the limitation imposed by Aristotle applies only to corporeal entities).

James of Viterbo refers to this debate for the first time in q. 7 of *Quodl.* I (*Utrum motus voluntatis in finem sit actus voluntatis vel intellectus*), where Henry's claim, according to which the impossibility of self-motion does not apply to incorporeal beings, is recapitulated.[33] Significantly, James does not limit himself, as Henry does, to citing only prop. 17 of the

30 Macken (1981), 233, 54–69. 31 Macken (1981), 251, 85–88.
32 See De Wulf and Hoffmans (1914), 148–172. 33 Ypma (1968), 89, 325–328.

Elementatio[34] but also adduces prop. 15 ("All that is capable of reverting upon itself is incorporeal")[35] and prop. 32 ("All reversion is accomplished through a likeness of the reverting terms to the goal of reversion" – the same "likeness" which seems to occur in the case of movement).[36] Nevertheless, James observes that this kind of argumentation does not seem sufficient to some (*ista responsio non videtur sufficiens aliquibus*), because act and potency belong to every being, including the incorporeal; thus, the Proclean theme of the reversion of the incorporeal would not allow us to escape the inconvenient conclusion that everything which moves itself must be presumed to be in act and in potency at the same time. In the case in point, James opts for another solution, inspired by Anselm of Canterbury, according to whom the will moves itself through its affections.

In q. 4 of *Quodl.* III (*Utrum actioni voluntatis correspondeat aliqua passio*), James recapitulates explicitly the argument taken from prop. 17 of the *Elementatio*.[37] Here, the treatment of the problem is more sophisticated, as the objections of the "intellectualists," and of Godfrey in particular, are discussed. It is true that, just like any corporeal thing, no incorporeal thing can really "transmute" itself, that is, carry itself from potency to act. Nevertheless, on Proclus' hypothesis, according to which the incorporeal reverts to itself, this reversion, or "conversion," is not to be understood as a veritable transmutation, but in the sense that every incorporeal thing conforms to itself and is its own term. One could concede – according to James – that the will moves itself by itself insofar as it desires itself; however, this is not the sense in which Proclus' principle is used by Henry and it is confuted by the "intellectualists."[38]

[34] Ypma (1968), 89, 334–336 (prop. 17: "Everything originally self-moving is capable of reversion upon itself").

[35] Ypma (1968), 89, 329–330. [36] Ypma (1968), 89, 336–338.

[37] James mentions the argument according to which only spiritual beings are capable of reversion to themselves, and therefore of self-motion see Ypma (1973), 58, 69–74: *unde Proclus dicit quod "omne se ipsum movens primo est ad se conversum." Et ita supponit quod aliquid sit movens se ipsum primo. Et dicit quod tale est ad se conversivum et per consequens incorporeum. Unde, cum voluntas sit res incorporea, non est inconveniens dicere quod moveat se ipsam primo.*

[38] Ypma (1973), 73, 500–510: *Ad illud igitur quod obicitur contra primam responsionem sumptam ex verbis Procli, dicendum est quod sine dubio responsio illa non facit ad propositum, quia neque corporeum neque incorporeum transmutat se ipsum. Et tamen verum est quod ait Proclus, videlicet quod incorporeum movet se ipsum. Accipit enim movere se non modo transmutationis, secundum quem nihil se movet educendo se de potentia ad actum, sed illo modo quo finis dicitur movere, scilicet secundum rationem termini. Nam se ipsum movere secundum intentionem Procli est ad se ipsum converti. Hoc autem est sibi ipsi conformari et esse terminum sui ipsius. Et hoc modo cum intellectus intelligit se, vel cum voluntas vult se, dicitur movere se. Iste autem modus non est ad propositum.*

By way of analogy, in q. 4 of *Quodl.* IV (*Utrum idem subiecto posset movere se ipsum*), James stresses that nothing can wholly move itself: this being despite the assumption of prop. 17, which must be explained in a different way, even though James does not elaborate on this point here.[39]

The explanation in question is brought forward (or rather restated) shortly afterwards, in q. 15 (*Utrum aliquae relationes secundum rationem possint vere dici de Deo*): "conversion" must not be understood as veritable motion, but as the act of conforming or assimilating oneself to oneself according to one's own operations.[40] James' strategy ultimately consists in maintaining both the Aristotelian principle, according to which nothing moves itself, *together with* the validity of the Proclean notion of the conversion of the incorporeal, though separating it from the case of self-motion.

So, if Proclus, in Henry's eyes, offers an unexpected conceptual instrument for liberating the will from the necessity of having to be moved by something other than itself, James understands this same principle in a completely different way: "conversion" is not really synonymous with self-motion, but simply with dynamic self-identity – in other words, with the fact that every corporeal being tends to assimilate itself, or conform to itself, according to its proper operations. It is precisely this difference of interpretation which shows how at least one topic of the *Elementatio* (moreover, not a secondary theme, such as that of the conversion of the incorporeal) was being used in Paris in the 1280s and 1290s[41] – that is, just when Proclus' metaphysics seems to have been relegated, once and for all, to the "museum of relics" – and also that it was being used in a way which was neither stock, neutral, nor stylized. Indeed, it was one of the arguments to be addressed within the bounds of one of the most heated debates of the period, thus becoming much more than a simple "commonplace."

39 James rejects the thesis of those who deny that something could be self-moving, because in this case it would be at one and the same time in act and in potency: see Ypma (1975), 21, 207–210: *Propter hanc autem rationem nullum etiam totum potest movere se ipsum primo, id est ratione totius, quamvis Proclus, doctrinam Platonis sequens, dicat esse aliquid movens se ipsum primo. Quod quidem verum intellectum habere potest, quem ad praesens explicare non oportet.*

40 Ypma (1975), 237, 782–789: . . . *ille modus est, ut si aliquid esset se ipsum movens primo; quod Proclus videtur concedere, sed accipit motum aliter. Unde dicit propositione quod: "Omne se ipsum movens primo est ad se ipsum conversivum." Accipit enim ibi moveri pro assimilari secundum operationem, ut cum aliquid se ipsum intelligit, dicitur se movere quia sibi conformatur secundum operationem. Et tale est ad se conversivum.*

41 James' four *Quodlibeta* were disputed between 1293 and 1297 (or 1299 at the latest); the *Quaestiones de divinis praedicamentis* were composed between 1293 and 1295.

The *Liber de causis* in Paris

In the case of *De causis*, too, I will confine myself to recapitulating some of the essential dates of its Scholastic reception, before moving on to consider the specific case of the discussions concerning the interpretation of the fourth proposition.

The wide circulation of the *Liber de causis* in the Latin West is attested by the fact that there are more than 230 extant manuscripts of the Latin version.[42] The great success of the work is related to the fact that it circulated mainly under the name of Aristotle and entered the corpus of his works. As such, it was adopted in the Parisian curriculum of the Faculty of Arts after the Statutes of 1255 and was collocated after the *Metaphysics*, as a kind of "theological" complement to the entire Aristotelian doctrine (a position which the Book had already acquired in the first half of the thirteenth century, as shown by the *Guide to the Student* of the MS Ripoll 109).[43] However, in the manuscript tradition the attribution to Aristotle was not univocal: some manuscripts considered Aristotle as the author solely of the lemmata (propositions), while the commentaries were attributed to another philosopher (mainly, al-Fārābī); in other cases, al-Fārābī is indicated as the author of the whole text. Some manuscripts attribute the work to Proclus, but they are probably posterior to Thomas Aquinas' commentary. As already mentioned, Aquinas was the first to realize, after Moerbeke's translation of *Elements of Theology* (1268), that the *Liber de causis* was an Arabic compilation based on the work of Proclus. Interestingly enough, at least one manuscript gives Proclus as author of the lemmata, and al-Fārābī as author of the commentaries. Finally, isolated manuscripts attribute the *Liber de causis* to Gilbert of Poitiers, Avendauth, Auever, and David. It is also worth recalling that the *Liber* did not circulate just within the Aristotelian corpus but was also associated with the *Liber XXIV Philosophorum* and *De intelligentiis*, initially attributed to Witelo by his editor, Baeumker. In this case too the aim of this small corpus was to offer, through a peculiar combination of Hermetic and Neoplatonic texts, mediated by the Arabic tradition, a sort of "theological accomplishment" of Aristotelian philosophy.

The commentaries, however, are not the only texts which attest to the influence of the *Liber de causis* in the Parisian milieu. Citations from *De causis* can already be found in texts dated between the end of the twelfth

[42] See Taylor (1983). [43] See Grabmann (1928), esp. 32–33; Lafleur and Carrier (1997).

and beginning of the thirteenth century, especially in the *Liber de causis primis et secundis* and in the works of Alain of Lille. The *Liber* is also quoted by the most important masters of the first half of the thirteenth century: William of Auxerre, Philip the Chancellor, William of Auvergne, and the Dominican master Roland of Cremona, who was apparently the first to quote explicitly the work under the title *Liber de causis*. The first Franciscan masters also refer to some propositions in the *Liber*, as is shown both by the *Summa Halensis* (a collective work by the first Franciscan master, Alexander of Hales, together with some collaborators) and Bonaventure, who already shows a selective attitude: while some themes are accepted as such – the primacy and omnipresence of the first universal cause (props. 1 and 19[20]), the identification of being with the first created thing (prop. 4), the description of the intelligences and their way of knowing – the idea of creation through intermediate causes (prop. 3) is explicitly rejected as heretical.

A sufficiently ample and detailed recognition of the position of thirteenth-century masters towards the *Liber de causis* has already been compiled by Cristina D'Ancona and Richard Taylor,[44] and it would be beyond the scope of this chapter to repeat them here.

Likewise, an exhaustive list of Scholastic commentaries on the *Liber de causis*, up to the late sixteenth century, has been compiled by R. Taylor.[45] Since our interest here is confined to the thirteenth century, the following commentaries are relevant (bearing in mind that at least three of them, by Roger Bacon, Adam of Bocfled, and Albert the Great – have their true place outside the Parisian context):

Roger Bacon, *Quaestiones super librum de causis* (probably 1241–1245);[46]

Anonymous (pseudo-Henry of Ghent), *Quaestiones in librum de causis* (*c.* 1250);[47]

Master Adam (Adam de Bocfeld?), *Scriptum super librum de causis* (*c.* 1250; still unedited);[48]

Albert the Great, *Liber de causis et processu universitatis a prima causa* (1264/67–1268; in fact only the Second Book is a commentary or paraphrase of *De causis*);[49]

44 See D'Ancona and Taylor (2003).

45 See Taylor (1983), 81–84; D'Ancona and Taylor (2003), 620–623.

46 Steele and Delorme (1935).

47 Zwaenepoel (1974). See also Joly (2005).

48 On the commentaries by Roger Bacon, ps.-Henry of Ghent and [ps.?]-Adam of Bocfeld see D'Ancona (1995), 195–228.

49 Fauser (1993). See also Fauser (1994), de Libera (1990).

Thomas Aquinas, *Super librum de causis expositio* (1272);[50]
Siger of Brabant, *Quaestiones super librum de causis* (probably 1274–1276);[51]
Anonymous ([pseudo-]Peter of Auvergne), *Quaestiones super librum de causis* (still unedited, end of the thirteenth century);[52]
Giles of Rome, *Expositio super auctorem de causis alpharabium* (1290?);[53]

To this list may also be added, for temporal closeness,

William of Leus, *Scriptum et expositio totius libri de causis* (1305–1309; still unedited).[54]

Some of these commentaries have already been the subject of accurate and valuable research, which has highlighted their specific aspects. So here too, I will proceed by selecting just one topic, namely the interpretation of the famous lemma of the fourth proposition: "The first of created things is being, and there is nothing else created before it" – a topic which seems to force the Latin masters to choose between the original position of Proclus, on the one hand (even though the latter is not recognized as such, which is what happens in most cases), and its reworking in *De causis*, on the other.

"The first of created things is being": the debate on the fourth proposition of *De causis* (and its Proclean background)

The fourth proposition of De causis *and Proclus'* Elementatio theologica

Like many other propositions, the fourth proposition of the *Liber de causis* (*Prima rerum creatarum est esse et non est ante ipsum creatum aliud*) is the result of a combination of various propositions from Proclus' *Elementatio theologica*, two of which were already and with characteristic precision identified by Thomas Aquinas: prop. 138, which posits explicitly the primacy of being within the order of realities participating in the divine, as well as its superiority with respect to intellect and life (a theme which also occurs in props. 39, 101, and 139); and prop. 89, according to which everything which is being, in the veritable sense of the word, is derived from the finite and from the infinite (which is precisely what prop. 138 postulates). Apart

50 Saffrey (2002). See Vansteenkiste (1958), Taylor (1979), Elders (1989), D'Ancona (1992), then also in D'Ancona (1995), 229–258; Decossas (1994), Ewbank (1994), Selner-Wright (1994–1995), Taylor (1998), Schäfer (2002).

51 Marlasca (1972). See Imbach (1996), Piché (1999), Calma (2003).

52 The text is contained in MS Wien, *Österreichische Nationalbibliothek, Vindob. Lat. 2330*, ff. 107r-109v. Against the attribution to Peter see Dondaine and Bataillon (1966), esp. 213–214.

53 Giles of Rome (1550).

54 Città del Vaticano, *Biblioteca Apostolica Vaticana, Borgh. 352*. See Carron-Faivre (forthcoming).

from the propositions cited so far, we could also cite others, as Cristina D'Ancona has already shown;[55] prop. 177, for instance, in which the differentiation of intellects is determined by the degree of universality of the intelligible forms which each intellect possesses (something which is also indicated in props. 170 and 180); props. 125 and 129, which suggest that superior principles influence inferior ones (though it should be noted that, in these two instances, Proclus discusses the case of the gods); and finally props. 111 and 160, which might have suggested to the author of the *Liber* – though not without straining the original sense – the idea of identifying the first effect with an intelligence. It seems to me, however, that these propositions do not really equate being, conceived of as the first effect, with either intellect or intelligence; this is an element more likely to have been taken from prop. 161, to which I shall return shortly.

Despite all these shared elements, as D'Ancona has rightly pointed out, the fourth proposition of *De causis* differs profoundly in many respects from Proclus' framework, given that his work includes neither a discussion of creation nor the identification of the first principle and pure being. Moreover, even though the topic of differentiation between intellects or intelligences is common to both the *Elementatio* and the *Liber*, it should be noted that the diversity of intelligible forms in Proclus is placed in an upward relation, so to speak, with the divine character of the various henads, whereas in *De causis* it is placed in a downward relation with the infinite multiplicity of individuals in the lower world. But more importantly, Proclus' doctrine of the *ontōs on* or *prōtōs on*, in other words, of the primacy of being as intelligible form, superior to the intellect, is completely absent from the *Liber*. By contrast, this doctrine constitutes one of the salient features of the *Elementatio*. The explication of prop. 161 ("All the true Being which is attached to the gods is a divine Intelligible, and unparticipated") leaves no room for doubt in this respect: being is a divine Intelligible (and therefore the supreme intelligible form), because it is the first to participate in the unifying character proper to the gods and because it completes, in itself, the intellect, which is such insofar as it is saturated by being. According to Proclus, this means that "while the Intelligence is an existent because of primal Being, this primal Being is itself separate from the Intelligence, because Intelligence is posterior to Being. Again, unparticipated terms subsist prior to the participated: so that prior to the Being, which is consubstantial with the Intelligence there must be a form of Being which exists in itself and beyond participation. For true Being is intelligible

[55] D'Ancona (1986), 203–204.

not as coordinate with the Intelligence, but as perfecting it without loss of transcendence . . . " (prop. 161). The author of *De causis*, by contrast, wishing to emphasize divine mono-causality by removing separate intelligible forms, seeks to attenuate this hierarchical gap: being is an intelligence and depends directly on the First Cause, just as the commentary on the fourth proposition explains.

However, this operation is not free of ambiguity. First of all, as already pointed out, the term "being" is used in *De causis* to designate the First Cause as well as its first effect: no matter how common the initial identification (between the First Cause and pure being) was to become, both in the *falsafa* and in Latin thought, the problem of determining whether the usage of the same term to designate both cause and effect must be understood in an equivocal, univocal, or analogical way persists (at least starting from the period in which something like the doctrine of the analogy of being begins to enter the Scholastic lexicon). As late as in the works of Meister Eckhart, to name but one example, it is precisely the double usage of "being" in the fourth proposition of *De causis* that legitimizes, time and again, the identification of God with being, as well as God's claim to superiority over being.[56] Secondly, even though the author of the *Liber* allows created being to coincide with Intelligence ("All the part of it [i.e. of created being] that follows the first cause is *achili*, that is, an intelligence, complete and ultimate in power" [= *'aql*]), a residue of the original structure developed by Proclus survives and surfaces in the commentary on the fourth proposition, which begins with the admission that "being is above sense, above soul, and above intelligence" and that "after the first cause there is no effect more extensive or prior to it." These affirmations conflict to no small degree with the claims stated in the lemma of the proposition: either Being as a whole is complete Intelligence, in which case it could not precede the latter; or, if Being precedes Intelligence, it must be understood as partially distinct from Intelligence, which is precisely what prop. 161 of the *Elementatio theologica* states, in which case one could not say that Being resolves itself completely in Intelligence, but that it is a form (indeed, the most general and common form) in which Intelligence itself participates and which precedes everything else that can be found in Intelligence. Thus, even though the author of the *Liber* does not stick faithfully to Proclus' scheme of the triad being–life–intellect, he nevertheless makes use of the same hierarchical structure: being is more universal and extensive than life, life is more extensive than thought. The fourth proposition thus suggests

[56] On the presence of the *Liber de causis* in Eckhart see more in general Retucci (2008).

a profound dilemma to its interpreters: is being, as the first created thing, a universal form (being in general) or is it rather the highest being, namely the Intelligence?

The first created being in Pseudo-Henry of Ghent, Albert the Great, and Thomas Aquinas

In what is usually considered, in the chronology of the Latin world, the first commentary on *De causis* (1241–1245), namely the one written by Roger Bacon at Oxford, the problem seems to be only touched upon. Though it is true that the relevant part of Bacon's commentary is lacking a bifolium, the preserved section relative to the fourth proposition shows clearly that Bacon interprets the first created being as the being of the Intelligence, without considering the possibility of other interpretations: the fact that this being is presented in the *Liber* as the broadest and most extensive of all created things (*latius in creaturis*) is understood simply as the recognition of the greater ontological dignity of the Intelligence (*virtute et potestate et dignitate vel mensura*) with respect to all other created things. Indeed, Bacon then focuses his attention on questions concerning eternity, that is, on the level at which the *Liber* locates the being of the Intelligence, for instance, by asking whether there exist several eternities and whether there exists an intermediate measure between eternity and time.[57]

The question is raised explicitly in the *Commentary on De causis* by Pseudo-Henry of Ghent (the composition of which dates to c. 1250): is the being which is created first a universal form that is participated in by the rest or is it a determinate creature?[58] The anonymous commentator introduces the problem by raising two objections. First, it seems contradictory to maintain both that the being which is caused first is the Intelligence and that nevertheless being is above the Intelligence. Second, when saying that being is the first created thing, being has to be either taken in its universal meaning or reduced to an Intelligence (or some other existing thing). Now, it seems impossible that the author of the *Liber* is referring to a "contracted" being, namely the being of the Intelligence, because he says that nothing is more extensive (*latius*) than the being which is the first created thing, and "extensive" is evidently the opposite of "contracted." On the other hand, it seems equally impossible that he should be referring to the being which is common to all things, because this being is universal, and the universal, according to Averroes, is always "posterior": every universal is always produced in one of its particulars, and has its being only in them.

[57] See Steele and Delorme (1935), 37–39.
[58] Zwaenepoel (1974), q. 25, 61.

Pseudo-Henry's reply is based on the possibility of distinguishing between two different meanings of creation, understanding it either as an act which ends in something that exists *in itself* or as an act which ends in something that exists *in something else*. In the first sense, "created" is said only of that which has complete being through its specific form (and this is creation in the strict sense of the word); in the second sense "created" is said of all the essential properties that can be found in what is created in the first mode, these properties being therefore called "con-created" or created *in something else*. Thus, when the explication of the fourth proposition states that the first effect is an Intelligence, "creation" is used in the first sense, whereas the *theorem* itself refers to creation in the second sense: in the *lemma* of the proposition, in other words, the being which is first among created things designates the first substantial form residing in the first created thing that exists *per se*. This priority of being should obviously not be understood in a chronological sense, but instead in a causal sense, insofar as being is the first (*intrinsic*) cause of every existing thing. Pseudo-Henry understands the theorem in the following way: being is the first of all created things, because it is that which is first *in* all created things, that is, insofar as it constitutes the term of an act of creation, not in itself, but in something else. In this way the author can bring together two apparently contradictory directions which seem to coexist in the *Liber*: the Intelligence is the first created thing from the point of view of that which is caused *as subsistent in itself*, whereas being is that which is created first, according to nature, insofar as it is the first intrinsic cause of that which exists first in itself. Hence, the being designated in the fourth proposition is universal being, and not being contracted to a determinate creature; yet it is not universal in terms of predication (i.e. the universal which is gained by abstraction from the suppositions, as the second objection mentioned above clarifies), but universal in terms of causality, because being is precisely the first intrinsic cause of everything and is that which is created first in everything – whether intelligence, soul, or anything else. In the end, for pseudo-Henry, the being which is the first created thing does not coincide, in the strict sense of the word, with an Intelligence (*Simpliciter enim esse in quantum creatur primo habet rationem causae particularis, non concernendo esse intelligentiae vel animae nobilis, se per indifferentiam se habendo ad unumquodque*),[59] even though *the first created thing in itself* is in fact an Intelligence.

[59] Zwaenepoel (1974), 63, 100–102.

Within a few years, pseudo-Henry's attempt at reconciliation had split into two radically opposed interpretive hypotheses, one by Albert the Great, the other by Thomas Aquinas. When Albert confronts the fourth proposition of *De causis* in his *De causis et processu universitatis a prima causa* (1264/67–1268; II, tract. 1, chs. 17–23),[60] his choice is unequivocal: the being which constitutes the first created being and thus the being which is properly created (insofar as created is that which is produced without presupposing anything else) is the first indeterminate concept, rather than a particular created thing. As Albert observes, the first created being is that which admits of nothing prior to itself, either on the level of nature or on the level of concepts. Now, being is the last term in every process of resolution, whether this occurs according to the order of formal causes, or according to the order of anteriority and posteriority (both on the level of *nature* as well as *concept*), or else in the process of reducing a particular to a universal. And because that which is last in the process of resolution is first in the process of composition, one can say that all things in the process of composition proceed from being. Being is thus a simple and absolutely indeterminate concept of the mind (*Esse enim simplex mentis conceptus est ad nihil formatus vel determinatus*),[61] and it is precisely the concept through which one can make the claim that something exists, thereby responding to the question *an sit*. Everything that follows this concept, which is indeterminate to the highest degree, does so in virtue of being informed or determined by it, and it is in this sense that one can say that everything that follows being is not properly created but rather comes into being through information. Being is not "a" being, an existing thing (in which case it would entail a form of composition); it is the most simple term, and even though it has the same degree of simplicity as the First Cause, it cannot be resolved into something else, since it possesses a root of potentiality and a disposition towards nothingness: the being which is created does not in fact exist *per se* but depends on the First Cause, which in turn is pure being, that is, being completely deprived of potentiality. Between the being which is created and the being of the First Cause there is no community of genus and hence no univocity, but instead a community of analogy, which is here explicitly understood by Albert as an analogy *unius ad alterum* (i.e. as a relation of imitation). Likewise, the being which is created does not serve as a genus for all the beings which follow it, but as a principle, thereby establishing with them a further relation of analogy.

60 See Fauser (1993), 80–90. On the issue see Sweeney (1980), Bonin (2013), Vargas (2013).
61 Fauser (1993), 81, 19–20.

Thus, the affirmation of *De causis*, according to which being is an intelligence composed of the finite and the infinite, is understood by Albert as meaning that being is more simple than everything which follows and informs it, while it is limited to the degree to which it conserves a potentiality towards nothingness. Nevertheless, the question of why the author of *De causis* designates being as *intelligentia* has not yet been answered. Albert does not evade the question; the *Liber* here speaks of *intelligentia* in the sense of a concept (just as in the Latin version of *De anima*) and not in the sense of intellectual substance.[62]

The *Liber* adds, however, that the superior intelligences influence those below them, which seems to apply to the separate intellectual substances rather than to the sphere of concepts. This claim too is interpreted by Albert with reference to a hierarchy of concepts determined by greater or lesser extension: being is the most extensive concept, which includes in itself the other intelligible forms, for example living, feeling, thinking; in the concept of being, those forms are broader and more universal than in themselves. In the opposite sense, following the way of composition, the concept of being is determined by all the other concepts or successive forms, which contract or restrict its original "*confuse*" indetermination. "Superior intelligences" and "inferior intelligences" are thus concepts which stand to each other in an order of greater or lesser universality and of greater or lesser indeterminacy, following a purely conceptual or formal approach, which Albert reaffirms in the end, when restating his interpretation of the fourth proposition in chapter 23: *esse, quod est creatum primum, secundum totum sui est intelligentia in lumine intellectus agentis constituta.*[63]

The interpretation suggested by Aquinas in his *Commentary on De causis* differs radically from this. Indeed, Aquinas does not have any doubt that the *Liber* regards the first created thing as an intelligence, not in the sense of a concept, but in the sense of a separate intellectual substance: the fourth proposition refers unequivocally to the being which is with eternity, and the being which is with eternity is that of the intelligences. Thus, for Aquinas, the problem is diametrically opposed to what Albert thought: what has to be explained is not the fact that *esse* is called *intelligentia*, but the reason why an intelligence can be called being.

[62] See Fauser (1993), 83, 61–69: *Quando autem dicimus esse intelligentiam simplicem, non intelligimus, quod sit intelligentia, quae substantia intellectualis est in decem ordines multiplicata, sicut in anteriori libro determinatum est, sed quod est intelligentia, hoc est, forma a lumine intellectus agentis in esse producta et in simplici illo lumine per intentionem accepta, sicut dicimus esse intelligentiam primam et vivere intelligentiam secundam et sensibile intelligentiam tertiam et sic deinceps.*

[63] Fauser (1993), 88, 18–20.

The first thing Aquinas notes is that the author proceeds in this matter in a slightly different manner from his usual one, not by demonstration but by division.[64] He begins by positing something which is common, proceeds by dividing it, and ends by expounding the differences between the elements of the division itself. That which is common to all the intelligences, and which is posited first, is precisely being. As we have already seen, Aquinas not only recognizes the origin of this claim in Proclus (prop. 138: "Of all the principles which participate the divine character, and are thereby divinized the first and highest is Being") but also explains perfectly the meaning of the anteriority of being in the Neoplatonic scheme. The Platonists, as Aquinas emphasizes here too, used to judge the degree of separation of a principle with recourse to its commonness: the more common it is, the more separate it is, and therefore it should also be considered as anterior to the others which participate in it.

After Good in itself and the One in itself, which are established as the first and most common principles (because they are such that they can also be predicated of non-being, namely of matter, which Plato assimilates to non-being), they posited Being in itself. Aquinas also sees this hierarchy preserved in pseudo-Dionysius, who, while abolishing separate ideas, maintained the same order in those perfections which all things receive by participating in the First Principle. Thus, if Good occupies the first place among divine names, Being occupies the first place among those perfections in which God lets all things participate. According to Aquinas, this is the meaning of the fourth proposition of *De causis*: Being is superior to all created realities, because it is that which is the most common and also that which is most intensely "unified," namely the simplest of all. Yet this apparent convergence must not lead into deception: "Nevertheless, it seems that it is not his intention to speak about some separate being, as the Platonists did, nor about the being that all existing things participate commonly, as Dionysius did, but [rather] about being participated in the first grade of created being, which is higher being."[65]

Thus, for Aquinas, the first created being is only that being which is participated in by Intelligence – a being which is unified in the highest degree, because this kind of intelligence is the peak of creation, that which is closest to the First Cause. The final part of the fourth proposition then explains how Intelligence divides itself and thus becomes manifold; if it were absolutely simple, it could not subdivide itself, whereas the division is possible precisely because it is composed of the finite and the

[64] See Saffrey (2002), 27, 1–7. [65] See Saffrey (2002), 31–32.

infinite: an Intelligence is infinite in its potential being, whereas the being which it receives is finite. The difference between the elements of the division (i.e. between the various intelligences) is, however, twofold: on the one hand with regard to their nature, and on the other with regard to the intelligible species through which they achieve thought. In this way Aquinas can conclude that, just as the First Cause exerts its influence on the superior Intelligences, so the latter exert their influence on the inferior Intelligences.[66]

One could add that the opposition between these two interpretive strategies is slightly paradoxical, because Albert, who is not aware of the Proclean source (and, as has already been pointed out, never mentions Proclus in relation to *De causis*, even after Aquinas' discovery), interprets the being about which the *Liber* speaks in the fourth proposition in its most extensive form, almost in Proclus' terminology; Aquinas, by contrast, who is aware of the propositions taken from Proclus, adheres to the letter of the *Liber*, even though the *Liber* itself deviates in this instance from the spirit and structure of Proclus' *Elementatio*.

Being and creation in Henry of Ghent and Giles of Rome

We do not possess an authentic commentary by Henry of Ghent on *De causis*, even though many of the propositions of the *Liber* recur frequently both in the *Quodlibeta* and in the *Summa* [*Quaestiones ordinariae*]. The fourth proposition is quoted by Henry in art. I, q. 2 of the *Summa*, where it is pointed out that the first intention that the intellect can understand is the *ratio entis*, which can be understood without considering any other intention because, while it is included in all the others, it does not include any other intention in itself.[67] From the first articles of his collection of *Ordinary Questions* onwards, Henry thus suggests a noetic interpretation of the fourth proposition of *De causis*, where being is understood as the first level of intentional analysis which admits an object below itself. However, it is the dispute with Giles of Rome on the distinction between being and essence that henceforth marks the time when recourse to the above-mentioned proposition of *De causis* becomes crucial. In q. 7 of *Quodlibet* X (Christmas 1286)[68] Henry distinguishes four different "intentions" (i.e. four quidditative "elements" which can be conceptualized in distinct ways without being distinct in reality) in the structure of the created world:

[66] See Saffrey (2002), 34, 24–28.
[67] See Wilson (2005), vol. 1, 2, 37–38, 176–190.
[68] Macken (1981), 145–197 (*Utrum ponens essentiam creaturae esse idem re cum suo esse potest salvare creationem*).

- *esse essentiae* (the being that belongs to essence due to the latter's external relation to the Divine Intellect, i.e. to God as formal cause);
- the being-something by essence (the objective content of every possible essence, that which allows us to place it in a determinate genus);
- *esse existentiae* (the actual being that belongs to essence due to the latter's temporal relation to the Divine Will, i.e. to God as efficient cause);
- the being-something by existence (the objective content of every actually existing essence).

Between these intentions there exists a sort of parallelism: *esse essentiae* is in potency (or represents a species of the potential substratum) with respect to *esse existentiae*, just as the being-something by essence is in potency with respect to the being-something by existence. But because, in one and the same thing, being precedes by nature being-something and existence precedes a thing's existence as something determinate, it must be conceded that essential being, which is in potency with respect to existential being, is created before being-something by essence, which is in potency with respect to being-something by existence.

It is in this respect that Henry returns to the fourth proposition of *De causis*: being is the first created thing and there is nothing else which is created in the strict sense of the word.[69] Thus, Henry proposes a model of intentional analysis which is close enough to the argumentation developed by Albert the Great in his *De causis*: in every reality there are several distinct intentions, such as being, living, feeling, thinking; being does not presuppose any of these and it is closer, in the order both of nature and of thought, to the first pure and true being. Whenever something which is composed of several intentions is brought to resolution, the process will always end with being: in this way being is the first effect of the First Cause, and it is therefore the only true effect in the strict sense of the word. For Henry, just as for Albert, being is the first and simplest concept, deprived of all information and of all determination, and as such – precisely insofar as it is the first – it cannot inform or determine any other thing; on the contrary, it is open to being informed or determined by all other things. Thus, within Henry's conceptual horizon, the fact that living, feeling, and thinking are drawn from being corresponds to the fact that being-something is drawn from being, or to put it differently, that being is in potency with respect to being-something. In this sense, being-something is not something which is created out of nothing: only being is truly produced out of nothing; all the rest is produced from being and hence is produced through information

[69] Macken (1981), q. 7, 171, 12–16.

rather than through creation. This is what the author of the *Liber* also underlines explicitly in the exposition of the eighteenth proposition: "the first being is at rest and the cause of causes. If it gives being to all things, then it gives [it] to them by way of creation. And the first life gives life to those which are under it, not by way of creation, but by way of form. Likewise, an intelligence gives knowledge and the remaining things to those which are under it only by way of form."[70] In short, Henry derives from *De causis* the main pillar of support for his own complex metaphysical program: being is a divine participation to which the proper nature of every other thing is added as a further intention. Naturally, the being to which Henry refers here is essential being, that is, quidditative being taken in its broadest sense, which, though lacking a true and proper form characteristic of it in the Neoplatonic system, is something very similar to it – namely an intention which is a quasi-form: *esse essentiae est quaedam divina participatio secundum rationem causae formalis, quasi forma substantialis eius quod est aliquid per essentiam.*[71]

The position espoused by Henry in q. 7 of *Quodlibet* X is meticulously confuted by Giles of Rome in q. 12 and q. 13 of his *Quaestiones de esse et essentia.*[72] In q. 12 especially, Giles rejects Henry's interpretation of the fourth proposition of *De causis*; Giles' basic hypothesis is relatively simple: whoever wishes to rely on the authority of the *Liber* with respect to the distinction between being and essence should affirm

- that all created things are in reality composed of essence and being;
- that being is received by a given essence and not vice versa;
- that being informs a given essence and not vice versa.

In order to support his interpretation, Giles (like Aquinas before him) has recourse to what is said in the explication of the ninth proposition (in the Latin enumeration): *intelligentia est habens yliathim*, every intelligence possesses a material principle as well as something which serves as its form.[73] The material principle in this case is the form of the intelligence itself, which is thus in potency with respect to a further formal element, which is being. For Giles, just as for Aquinas, the author of *De causis* thereby intends to affirm that intelligence is composed of form and being, in other words, of an essence and being. Moreover, given that this composition can already be found in the intelligences, there is good reason to expect it with even greater legitimacy in all inferior beings.[74]

[70] Guagliardo, Hess, and Taylor (1996), 111. [71] Macken (1981), 171, 1–3.
[72] Giles of Rome (1503). See Paulus (1940–42), König-Pralong (2006).
[73] On the meaning of this proposition see D'Ancona (1995), 97–119.
[74] Giles of Rome (1503), 28vb–29ra.

However, the *Liber* does not only posit that there is (a form of) composition in the intelligences but also clarifies the mode of composition: being is what is received in their essence to inform them and not vice versa. In this case, too, the point of reference is first and foremost the ninth proposition: if it is really essence which is in potency with respect to being and if it is being which is to serve as act, it follows that the act informs the potency and is received in the latter, just as perfection is received in that which is being perfected. According to Giles, as far as the three points distinguished above are concerned, *De causis* teaches us the exact opposite of what Henry maintains.[75]

At this point, however, Giles has to clarify in what sense the author can legitimately maintain in the fourth proposition that being is the first of all created things. The Augustinian master makes use of two different strategies. The first consists in showing that the being treated in the fourth proposition is not being distinct from essence, but being in the most general and common sense, which includes in itself both types of being: that of existence and that of essence. For Giles, the evidence for this rests on the fact that the proposition is valid for the plurality of intelligences: every multiplicity (just as Proclus teaches) presupposes participation in a unity, and the unity in which the intelligences participate is being. In other words, in the fourth proposition the author does not refer to that being which can combine with an essence, but to being in general, in which all the intelligences converge and which is adduced in order to explain the origin of their multiplicity. From this point of view, according to Giles, Henry's argument completely misses the point. Still, if one wanted to uphold the claim that the being in question is the being which combines with an essence – and we thereby move to the second strategy – one could say that in the things which are produced through a single act, the act of producing concerns primarily the act and not the potency. Even though light and colors, for instance, are always perceived together, light may nevertheless be considered the first of all these visible and created things, because colors can never be perceived without it, whereas the opposite is not true. In analogy, one can say that even though being and essence are produced simultaneously, being can still be considered the first of created things because it represents the act of a given essence. Thus, in the second interpretation too, Henry's recourse to *De causis* can be considered counterproductive: being is the first created thing only because it has a

[75] Giles of Rome (1503), 29ra.

greater degree of actuality than essence, and that which is more "actual" is always received in that which is potential, and not the other way around.[76]

Moreover, in Giles' eyes, Henry claims that essence signifies a thing insofar as it is a reality in itself and being insofar as it is a reality in act in virtue of its relation to an agent. From this perspective, being would merely add a relation to essence. Nevertheless, if an essence were received in being and if only being were created, while all the rest were to add themselves to being through information, a relation would be posited as the foundation of all things – a hypothesis which nobody could ever possibly maintain.[77]

Ultimately, Giles' confutation unfolds on three levels:

(a) Henry misunderstands the sense of the fourth proposition of *De causis*, which does not refer to being combined with an essence, but rather to being in more general terms, comprising essence;
(b) even if Henry's interpretation were correct, it would still go against his own intentions;
(c) the combination of the hypothesis according to which being is the first created thing with the hypothesis according to which being consists of a relation leads to an absurd conclusion, namely that a relation is the foundation of every reality.

Nevertheless, Giles' strategy presupposes at least two decisions: first, that prop. 4 of *De causis* should be interpreted on the basis of prop. 9; and second, that the being in question in prop. 4 is not that being which renders all things in act (being which combines with essence – regardless of how this composition is understood), but being in a more general, universal and common sense, which precedes every other intention. For Giles this is the correct interpretation of prop. 4. In reality, paradoxical as it may appear, this is also what Henry is suggesting. Indeed, the first created being is not, for Henry, *esse existentiae*, which renders all essences in act, but *esse essentiae*, the most general, universal and *confuse* intention, which precedes every other intention.

So it does not come as a surprise that in his reply to Giles, in what constitutes (at least for us) the last act of their controversy over the distinction between being and essence (q. 3 of *Quodl.* XI), Henry decides to return precisely to this point: the first created being is not existential being, but *esse* in a broader sense.[78]

[76] Giles of Rome (1503), 29ra. [77] Giles of Rome (1503), 29rb.

[78] Henry of Ghent (1518), XI, 3, 442vE: *Sed dico ego quod ratio nostra dicta bene est ad propositum, quia bene et directe probat quod esse existentiae quod creatur in essentia ut accidens eius secundum quod illi dicunt, non principaliter creatur, sed potius aliquid aliud ut esse latissimum quod se tenet ex parte essentiae respectu esse existentiae, et sic ratio non procedit in aequivoco, licet esse quod principalius probat creari sit aequivoce dictum esse cum esse latissimo.*

Henry declares that his main intention in q. 7 of *Quodl.* X was precisely to show in what way essence can be called "created" with greater justification than can the being of existence (regardless of how the latter is understood): essence is created in the moment in which it *informs* being, here understood in the broader sense of the word, rather than in the moment in which it *is informed* by *esse existentiae*, which is accidental with respect to essence as such. Based on these reflections, Henry is in a position to reply (a) that he never sought to claim that being does not combine with essence; (b) that he never denied that being is an accident; (c) that he never claimed that being signifies, strictly speaking, the same thing as essence, as if the two terms were synonymous.[79] Everything depends on the correct order of intentions: the first created being is not actual being, or the being of existence (which is how Giles seems to interpret Henry's position), but being in the broader sense: *esse essentiae*. It is precisely the latter insofar as it is essentially informed by an essence (with which it coincides) to receive *esse existentiae*, which adds accidental information to it. In this way Henry can respond to Giles that he agrees perfectly with the fact that actual being is received in essence and informs it, but that he had claimed something completely different: namely, that essential being (being in the broadest sense) precedes essence at the level of intentions, and that only at this level does essence inform being, rather than the other way around. Thus, for Henry, *esse essentiae* is the first intention in absolute terms (the first created thing), and receives two kinds of information, one of which is essential and derived from essence itself, while the other is accidental and derived from *esse existentiae*. Thus, the act of creation, in the strict sense of the word, is the constitution of essence in its being: the coming of actual being signals only the successive addition of a new relation. In this way Henry manages to reject the accusation of having made a relation the foundation of every other reality.

Giles' attempt to interpret the fourth proposition of *De causis* with reference to the greater actuality, or perfection, of being is equally unacceptable to Henry, since what is at stake in this case is the true determination of that which is created first. In order to establish such anteriority, it is necessary to consider the *terminus a quo* and not the *terminus ad quem* of the act of creation (a distinction which seems to take us back to the one we encountered earlier in the commentary by pseudo-Henry between that which is created in itself and that which is created in something else): only *esse* is such, in the broadest sense of the word, to the extent to which it does

[79] Henry of Ghent (1518), XI, 3, 443rE.

not, in contrast with all the rest, inform any supposit. It follows that Giles is mistaken in maintaining that the reason for the process of production always derives from act rather than potency; and although this is true for all productions which presuppose a pre-existing reality, it does not hold true for the act of creation, in which nothing is presupposed. Once created, it is being in the broadest sense which constitutes the potency of all things: existential potency with respect to essence, accidental potency (as already mentioned) with respect to *esse existentiae.*[80]

Thus, Henry rejects Giles' second strategy, while he can easily appropriate the first: if the author of the *Liber de causis* really had intended, as Giles himself concedes, to speak about being in the broadest sense, and not about the being of existence, then recourse to the *Liber* is both legitimate and pertinent, and so is the recognition that the first created being is indeterminate and universal being, rather than the actual being of a particular creature, that is, of an Intelligence.

As mentioned above, q. 3 of *Quodl.* XI is the last chapter (or at least the last which can be documented) of the confrontation between Giles and Henry on the distinction between being and essence. Nevertheless, only a few years later, Giles had the opportunity to return to the specific question of how the priority of being in the order of creation should be understood, in his commentary on *De causis*, which he finished in Bayeux probably around 1291.[81] Though no longer in direct confrontation with Henry, Giles uses the occasion to emphasize the salient points of his interpretation, which he had already expounded in q. 12 of the *Quaestiones de esse et essentia*, departing from the conviction that the true topic of proposition 4 is that of distinguishing the intelligences, and that being is brought into the discussion only insofar as it is that in which all existing things converge and insofar as it may serve to explain plurality. Hence, the author does not really intend to speak about being: *non videtur esse sua intentio principalis hic determinare de esse, sed ex esse quod in se est quid unum vult descendere ad declarandum quomodo plurificatum est in intelligentiis, et facta est diversitas intelligentiarum.*[82] Secondly, Giles affirms once again that the *ratio* of every process of production derives from act rather than from

80 Henry of Ghent (1518), XI, 3, 443rF.

81 Giles' *Super De causis* is certainly posterior to his *De mensura angelorum*, whereas it precedes dist. 1 of his commentary on the second book of the *Sentences*. According to the Venetian edition, dating from 1550, it was finished on January 31, 1291, but the indication is not confirmed by other references. It is more likely that it was completed before September 22, 1291, in line with the dedication to Benedetto Caetani, then Cardinal of San Nicola in Carcere (from that date onward, Caetani was nominated Cardinal of S. Martino ai Monti).

82 Giles of Rome (1550), 13vA.

potency, given that a thing may be called caused or produced only insofar as it receives its being. Finally, Giles clarifies that the word *esse* can be understood to refer either to *ens* – in which case it is clear that being is the first created thing, because a thing is produced, first of all, insofar as it is a being, and only after insofar as it is one, and so forth (in other words, before all the other determinations which add themselves to an existing thing); or it can be understood to refer to being itself, which is participated in by all existing things – in which case being would be the first of all created things because the first major *ratio creationis* is derived from it: the reason for calling something created is precisely that it receives its being from the First Cause. At this point, the example of light and colors already encountered in the *Quaestiones de esse et essentia* returns: *Hoc ergo modo prima rerum creatarum est esse, sicut prima rerum visarum est lux, quia lux est prima et principalis ratio quare aliquid videatur.*[83]

The difference between Henry's and Giles' interpretation of the fourth proposition of *De causis* depends clearly on their respective choices concerning the ways in which being and essence combine, although it enters into a debate which was already thriving in the preceding decades. From this point of view Henry is closer to the interpretation of Albert the Great: the being in question in the fourth proposition is being in the most general, *confuse*, and indeterminate sense, the true product of an act of creation, to which all the rest adds itself through various acts of information. Henry not only uses a terminology which is very similar to that used by Albert but also explicitly justifies the primacy of being on the basis of the fact that being itself is the last term of any process of resolution and thus the first term of any process of composition, just as Albert had done. Not surprisingly, alongside all these parallels, there is also an element which cannot be found Albert, namely the notion of *esse essentiae* as a technical term (the being which constitutes the essences of all created things insofar as God considers his own essence as potentially imitable). By contrast, Giles seems to adopt an approach which is much more similar to the one drawn by Aquinas: prop. 4 is interpreted essentially in the light of prop. 9, with the result that one of the larger themes of the *Liber* is located in the project of positing a clear distinction between essence (in the specific case under discussion, the essence of separate substances, their form, understood as material principle – *yliathim* – with respect to being) and being itself. Nevertheless, in his attempt to confute Henry, Giles concedes that the intention of the

[83] Giles of Rome (1550), 13vc. On the entire debate between Henry and Giles concerning the interpretation of prop. 4 of *De causis* let me refer to Porro (forthcoming).

author of the *Liber* in prop. 4 seems to be to refer not to the being which combines with an essence, but to being in the broadest and most common sense of the word, which comprises in itself the essence as well as the being of existence – which is precisely what Henry seeks to maintain. In this way Giles ends up, against his will and contrary to what he declares explicitly in q. 12, in the later commentary on *De causis*, with the recognition that his adversary's interpretation may well be the most plausible, and ultimately with Albert's choice over that of Aquinas.

However, this is not the only paradoxical aspect of the debate: in a certain way, through this debate, Proclus could take a partial and indirect revenge on his unknown Arabic epigone, who tried to remove or neutralize one of his most characteristic doctrines: that of the *ontōs on* or *prōtōs on*. Thus, the interpretive differences with respect to the fourth proposition of *De causis* ultimately show how the Parisian masters (and with them Albert) discerned a certain tension between the *Liber* and its Proclean source, even in those cases in which they did not explicitly recognize this source, and how they took this tension to such a point as to restore some hypotheses of the *Elementatio* (even though with some modifications) which had been concealed or altered in the Arabic tradition.

Bibliography

Bataillon, L.-J. (1989) "Quelques utilisateurs des textes rares de Moerbeke (*Philopon, Tria opuscula*) et particulièrement Jacques de Viterbe," in J. Brams and W. Vanhamel (eds.), *Guillaume de Moerbeke. Recueil d'études à l'occasion du 700e anniversaire de sa mort (1286)*, Leuven, 107–112.

Birkenmajer, A. (1922) "Der Brief der Pariser Artistenfakultät über den Tod des hl. Thomas von Aquino," in A. Birkenmajer, *Vermischte Untersuchungen zur Geschichte der mittelalterlichen Philosophie*, Münster, 1–32. Reprinted in A. Birkenmajer, *Études d'histoire des sciences et de la philosophie du Moyen Âge* (*Studia Copernicana 1*), Wrocław, Warsaw, and Kraków (1970), 277–311.

Boese, H. (ed.)(1958) *Die mittelalterliche Übersetzung der Stoicheiōsis phusikē des Proclus: Procli Diadochi Lycii Elementatio physica*, Berlin.

(ed.) (1960) *Procli Diadochi Tria opuscula (De providentia, libertate, malo), latine, Guillelmo de Moerbeka vertente, et graece, ex Isaacii Sebastocratoris aliorumque scriptis collecta*, Berlin.

(ed.) (1987) *Proclus: Elementatio theologica, translata a Guillelmo de Morbecca*, Leuven.

Boiadjiev, T., Kapriev, G., and Speer, A. (eds.) (2000) *Die Dionysius-Rezeption im Mittelalter. Internationales Kolloquium, Sofia, 8–11 April 1999*, Turnhout.

Bonin, T. (2013) "Albert's *De causis* and the Creation of Being," in I. M. Resnick (ed.), *A Companion to Albert the Great. Theology, Philosophy, and the Sciences*, Leiden and Boston, 688–694.

Bos, E. P. and Meijer, P. A. (eds.) (1992) *On Proclus and His Influence in Medieval Philosophy*, Leiden, New York, and Cologne.

Boss, G. and Seel, G. (eds.) (1987) *Proclus et son influence. Actes du colloque de Neuchâtel, juin 1985*; with an introduction by F. Brunner, Zurich.

Brams, J. (2003) *La riscoperta di Aristotele in Occidente*, Milan.

Calma, D. (2003) "Siger de Brabant et Thomas d'Aquin: note sur l'histoire d'un plagiat," *Freiburger Zeitschrift für Philosophie und Theologie* 50: 118–134.

Carron-Faivre, D. (forthcoming) "Guillaume de Leus, commentateur du *Liber de causis*," *Bulletin de philosophie médiévale* 54.

D'Ancona, C. (ed.) (1986) *Tommaso d'Aquino: Commento al Libro delle cause*, Milan.

(1992) "Saint Thomas lecteur du *Liber de causis*. Bilan des recherches contemporaines concernant le *De causis* et analyse de l'interprétation thomiste," *Revue Thomiste* 92: 611–649. Reprinted in D'Ancona (1995), 229–258.

(1995) *Recherches sur le Liber de causis*, Paris.

(2011) "Nota sulla traduzione latina del *Libro di Aristotele sull'esposizione del bene puro* e sul titolo *Liber de causis*," in S. Perfetti (ed.), *Scientia, Fides, Theologia. Studi di filosofia medievale in onore di Gianfranco Fioravanti*, Pisa, 89–101.

D'Ancona, C. and Taylor, R. C. (2003) "Le *Liber de causis*," in R. Goulet (ed.), *Dictionnaire des philosophes antiques*. Supplement to vol. 1, Paris, 599–647.

De Wulf, M. and Hoffmans, J. (eds.) (1914) *Les Quodlibet Cinq, Six et Sept de Godefroid de Fontaines*, Leuven.

Decossas, B. (1994) "Les exigences de la causalité créatrice selon l'*Expositio in Librum de causis* de Thomas d'Aquin," *Revue Thomiste* 94: 241–272.

Dodds, E. R. (ed. and trans.) (1963) *Proclus: The Elements of Theology*, 2nd edn., Oxford.

Dondaine, H. (1953) *Le corpus dionysien de l'Université de Paris au XIIIe siècle*, Rome.

Dondaine, H. and Bataillon, L.-J. (1966) "Le manuscrit *Vindob. Lat.* 2330 et Siger de Brabant," *Archivum Fratrum Praedicatorum* 36: 153–261.

Elders, L. (1989) "Saint Thomas d'Aquin et la métaphysique du *Liber de causis*," *Revue Thomiste* 89: 427–442.

Ewbank, M. B. (1994) "Doctrinal Precisions in Aquinas's *Super librum De causis*," *Archives d'histoire doctrinale et littéraire du Moyen Âge* 61: 7–29.

Faes de Mottoni, B. (1977) *Il Corpus Dionysianum nel Medioevo. Rassegna di studi 1900–1972*, Bologna.

Fauser, W. (ed.) (1993) Albertus Magnus, *De causis et processu universitatis a causa prima. Alberti Magni Opera Omnia 17/2*, Münster.

(1994) "Albert the Great's Commentary on the *Liber de causis*," *Bulletin de philosophie médiévale* 36: 38–44.

Giles of Rome (Aegidius Romanus) (1503) *De esse et essentia, De mensura angelorum, De cognitione angelorum*, Venice. Reprinted Frankfurt am Main 1968.

(1550) *Super librum De causis*, Venice. Reprinted Frankfurt am Main 1968.
Grabmann, M. (1928) "Mittelalterliche lateinische Aristotelesübersetzungen und Aristoteleskommentare in Handschriften spanischer Bibliotheken," *Sitzungsberichte der Bayerischen Akademie der Wissenschaften, philos.-philol. und hist. Klasse* 5, Munich. Reprinted in M. Grabmann, *Gesammelte Akademieabhandlungen*, Paderborn, Munich, and Vienna (1979), vol. 1, 391–402, 427–428.
(1936) "Die Proklosübersetzungen des Wilhelm von Moerbeke und ihre Verwertung in der lateinischen Literatur des Mittelalters," in M. Grabmann, *Mittelalterliches Geistesleben. Abhandlungen zur Geschichte der Scholastik und Mystik*, Munich, 413–423.
(1946) *Guglielmo di Moerbeke O.P. il traduttore delle opere di Aristotele*, Rome.
Grant, E. (1971) "Henricus Aristippus, William of Moerbeke and Two Alleged Mediaeval Translations of Hero's *Pneumatica*," *Speculum* 46: 656–669.
Guagliardo, V. A., Hess, C. R., and Taylor, R. C. (eds. and trans.) (1996) *St. Thomas Aquinas: Commentary on the Book of Causes*, Washington, DC.
Hankey, W. J. (2002) "Aquinas and the Platonists," in S. Gersh and M. J. F. M. Hoenen (eds.), *The Platonic Tradition in the Middle Ages. A Doxographic Approach*, Berlin and New York, 279–324.
Henle, R. J. (1956) *Saint Thomas and Platonism. A Study of the "Plato" and "Platonici" Texts in the Writings of Saint Thomas*, Den Haag.
Henry of Ghent (Henricus de Gandavo) (1518) *Quodlibeta*, 2 vols., Paris. Reprinted Leuven 1961.
Imbach, R. (1996) "Notule sur le commentaire du *Liber de causis* de Siger de Brabant et ses rapports avec Thomas d'Aquin," *Freiburger Zeitschrift für Philosophie und Theologie* 43: 304–323.
Joly, É. (2005) "L'âme noble et l'âme humaine dans le commentaire du pseudo-Henri de Gand sur le *Livre des causes*," *Recherches de théologie et philosophie médiévales* 72: 29–53.
Klibansky, R. (1943) "Plato's *Parmenides* in the Middle Ages and the Renaissance," *Mediaeval and Renaissance Studies* 1: 281–332. Reprinted New York 1982.
König-Pralong, C. (ed.) (2006) *Henri de Gand, Gilles de Rome, Godefroid de Fontaines. Être, essence et contingence*, Paris.
Kremer, K. (1966) *Die neuplatonische Seinsphilosophie und ihre Wirkung auf Thomas von Aquin*, Leiden.
Lafleur, C. (ed., avec la collaboration de J. Carrier) (1997) *L'enseignement de la philosophie au XIIIe siècle. Autour du "Guide de l'étudiant" du ms. Ripoll 109*, Turnhout.
Libera, A. de (1990) "Albert le Grand et Thomas d'Aquin interprètes du *Liber de causis*," *Revue des sciences philosophiques et théologiques* 3: 347–378.
Macken, R. (ed.) (1981) Henricus de Gandavo, *Quodlibet X, Henrici de Gandavo Opera omnia 14*, Leuven and Leiden.
Marlasca, A. (1972) *Les Quaestiones super Librum de causis de Siger de Brabant. Édition critique*, Leuven and Paris.

Paravicini Bagliani, A. (1989) "Guillaume de Moerbeke et la cour pontificale," in J. Brams and W. Vanhamel (eds.), *Guillaume de Moerbeke. Recueil d'études à l'occasion du 700e anniversaire de sa mort (1286)*, Leuven, 23–52.

Paulus, J. (1940–42) "Les disputes d'Henri de Gand et de Gilles de Rome sur la distinction de l'essence et de l'existence," *Archives d'histoire doctrinale et littéraire du moyen âge* 13: 323–358.

Pera, C. (ed.) (1950) Thomas de Aquino, *In librum Beati Dionysii De divinis nominibus expositio, cum introductione historica P. Caramello et synthesi doctrinali C. Mazzantini*, Turin and Rome.

Piché, D. (1999) "*Causa prima* et *esse* dans le *Liber de causis* selon Thomas d'Aquin et Siger de Brabant," *Dialogue* 38: 75–97.

Porro, P. (forthcoming) "*Prima rerum creatarum est esse.* Henri de Gand, Gilles de Roma et la quatrième proposition du *De causis*," in V. Cordonier and T. Suarez-Nani (eds.), *Henri de Gand et Gilles de Rome: aspects de leur débat*, Fribourg.

Retucci, F. (2008) "Her ûf sprichet ein heidenischer meister in dem buoche, daz dâ heizet daz lieht der liehte: Eckhart, il *Liber de causis* e Proclo," in L. Sturlese (ed.), *Studi sulle fonti di Meister Eckhart*, vol. 1, Fribourg, 135–166.

Saffrey, H.-D. (ed.) (2002) Thomas d'Aquin, *Super librum de causis expositio*, 2nd edn., Paris.

Schäfer, C. (2002) "Die ontologische Realdistinktion im *Liber de causis.* Zum philosophiegeschichtlichen Ursprung eines metaphysischen Hauptgedankens bei Thomas von Aquin und den Thomisten," *Theologie und Philosophie* 77: 518–531.

Selner-Wright, S. C. (1994–1995) "Thomas Aquinas and the metaphysical inconsistency of the *Liber de causis*," *The Modern Schoolman* 72: 323–336.

Siedler, D., with Kübel, W., and Vogels, H. G. (eds.) (1978) *Summa theologiae sive De mirabili scientia Dei*, vol. 1, part 1: *Quaestiones 1–50A, Alberti Magni Opera Omnia 34/1*, Münster.

Steel, C. (1989) "Guillaume de Moerbeke et saint Thomas," in J. Brams and W. Vanhamel (eds.), *Guillaume de Moerbeke. Recueil d'études à l'occasion du 700e anniversaire de sa mort (1286)*, Leuven, 57–82.

Steele, R. (ed.) with Delorme, F. M. (1935) Roger Bacon, *Quaestiones supra librum de causis*, Oxford.

Sturlese, L. (1987) "Il dibattito sul Proclo latino nel Medioevo fra l'Università di Parigi e lo Studium di Colonia," in Boss and Seel (1987), 261–285.

Sweeney, L. (1980) "*Esse primum creatum* in Albert the Great's *Liber de causis et processu universitatis*," *The Thomist* 44: 599–646.

Taylor, R. C. (1979) "St. Thomas and the *Liber de causis* on the Hylomorphic Composition of Separate Substances," *Mediaeval Studies* 41: 506–513.

(1983) "The *Liber de causis*: A Preliminary List of Extant mss," *Bulletin de philosophie médiévale* 25: 63–84.

(1988) "Aquinas, the *Plotiniana Arabica*, and the Metaphysics of Being and Actuality," *Journal of History of Ideas* 59: 217–239.

Van de Vyver, E. (ed.) (1960) Henricus Bate, *Speculum divinorum et quorundam naturalium*, Leuven and Paris.

Vanhamel, W. (1989) "Biobibliographie de Guillaume de Moerbeke," in J. Brams and W. Vanhamel (eds.), *Guillaume de Moerbeke. Recueil d'études à l'occasion du 700e anniversaire de sa mort (1286)*, Leuven, 301–383.

Vansteenkiste, C. (1958) "Il *Liber de causis* negli scritti di S. Tommaso," *Angelicum* 35: 325–374.

Vargas, R. E. (2013) "Albert on Being and Beings: The Doctrine of *Esse*," in I. M. Resnick (ed.), *A Companion to Albert the Great. Theology, Philosophy, and the Sciences*, Leiden and Boston, 627–648.

Verbeke, G. (1953) "Guillaume de Moerbeke traducteur de Proclus," *Revue philosophique de Louvain* 51 (1953), 349–373.

Wilson, G. A. (ed.) (2005) Henricus de Gandavo, *Summa [1] (Quaestiones ordinariae), art. 1–5. Henrici de Gandavo Opera omnia 21*, Leuven.

Ypma, E. (ed.) (1968) Jacobus de Viterbio O.E.S.A., *Disputatio prima de quolibet*, Rome.

(ed.) (1969) Jacobus de Viterbio O.E.S.A., *Disputatio secunda de quolibet*, Rome.

(ed.) (1973) Jacobus de Viterbio O.E.S.A., *Disputatio tertia de quolibet*, Rome.

(ed.) (1975) Jacobus de Viterbio O.E.S.A., *Disputatio quarta de quolibet*, Rome.

(ed.) (1983) Jacobus de Viterbio O.E.S.A., *Quaestiones de divinis praedicamentis. I–X*, Rome.

(ed.) (1986) Jacobus de Viterbio O.E.S.A., *Quaestiones de divinis praedicamentis. XI–XVII*, Rome.

Zwaenepoel, J. F. (1974) *Les Quaestiones in Librum de causis attribuées à Henri de Gand. Édition critique*, Leuven and Paris.

Manuscripts

Città del Vaticano, *Biblioteca Apostolica Vaticana, Borgh. 352*.

Wien, *Österreichische Nationalbibliothek, Vindob. Lat. 2330*.

CHAPTER 11

Dietrich of Freiberg and Berthold of Moosburg

Markus Führer and Stephen Gersh[1]

Dietrich of Freiberg

Dietrich of Freiberg was born sometime between the years 1240 and 1250 in Freiberg in Saxony. Not much is known about his youth except that he joined the Dominican order at an early age. He was educated at the Dominican convent in Freiberg and then taught in the convent school around the year 1271. Dietrich journeyed to Paris, where he studied theology from 1272 until 1274. He returned to Germany and was recorded as being a lector at Trier from 1280 until 1281, when he returned to Paris and began lecturing on Peter Lombard's *Sentences*. Dietrich remained in Paris, most probably teaching, until around the year 1293. He was then made Provincial Superior for Germany in 1293. He held this post until 1296, when he was made a master of theology in Paris sometime between 1296 and 1297. Dietrich remained in Paris and taught until 1300. He was made Vicar Provincial of Germany in 1310. All records of him end in the same year. The date of his death is not known.

General influence of Proclus on Dietrich

Dietrich's access to the writings of Proclus was confined to the *Elements of Theology*, which had been rendered into Latin by William of Moerbeke as *Elementatio theologica* and dated May 18, 1268.[2]

The most notable influence of Proclus on the philosophical thought of Dietrich of Freiberg is found in his identification of God with the One in Proclus' doctrine. For Dietrich, God is a reality than which nothing is superior. Understood in this way God holds an absolutely unique place in the hierarchy of being. This idea of the ineffability of divinity as absolute

[1] In this collaborative essay the section on Dietrich of Freiberg was written by Markus Führer and that on Berthold of Moosburg by Stephen Gersh.

[2] See Boese (1987).

unity is understood not only as the principle of the hierarchy of being but of created being itself. Here Dietrich seems to be following a Proclean idea that he most likely found in the *Liber de causis*.

In differentiating the various kinds of beings that constitute the hierarchical universe, Dietrich also follows Proclus. God, understood as the ineffable One, is followed by the intelligences, then by souls, and finally by material bodies. Relying heavily on Proclus, Dietrich explains that these four types of being form an order of procession as follows. The first intelligence proceeds from the divine unity. Here the first stage in the procession has been reached and a kind of rank is established which corresponds to the traditional *nous* of Proclus' metaphysics. From this first intelligence the second intelligence flows forth along with the soul of the first celestial sphere and the first celestial sphere itself. This is the second stage. Then the process is repeated with the emanation of the third intelligence, the soul of the second heaven, the second heaven itself, on down through all the celestial worlds until the intelligence and soul of the lowest heaven and the lowest heaven itself is reached. This intelligence, Dietrich explains, causes the substance of the sublunary beings that suffer generation and corruption – namely material bodies.[3] The entire universe of beings is therefore in a state of active procession from the divine unity. The influence of Proclus' general metaphysics is seen in all of this.

Concerning the return of all creatures to the divine unity Dietrich makes a modified use of Proclus. He explains that the second hypostasis, namely the first emanated intelligence, is identified with desire and is the cause of the return of all things to the divine unity. Citing Proclus directly he notes that intellect is what is desirable to all things and that all things proceed from intellect, as well as return through it.

Dietrich thus develops a particular version of the hierarchy of being based on Proclus' idea of the One and its particular relation with the hierarchy of being. By identifying the One of Proclus' *Elements of Theology* with the creative God of Christian theology, Dietrich introduces a dynamic element into the hierarchy of being, in which God brings beings into existence out of nothing and marks them with a resemblance or similitude to himself. The universe is thus like God and each productive being in its hierarchically ordered series of causes is also like God. Dietrich specifically cites props. 146 and 147 of Proclus, as well as the comment on prop. 147, all of which emphasize the role of similitude in this hierarchy:[4]

[3] See Mojsisch *et al.* (1977–1985), vol. 1, 144.

[4] See Dietrich of Freiberg, *De visione beatifica*, ed. B. Mojsisch (Mojsisch *et al.* 1977–1985), vol. 1, 13.

Prop. 146: In the procession of all divine things the ends are assimilated to their beginnings, sustaining a circle without beginning and without end by turning to the beginnings.[5]

Prop. 147: The highest of all the divine orders are assimilated to the last of those positioned above them.[6]

Comment on prop. 147: For if there must be continuity of the divine procession and each order must be connected by the proper middle terms, it is necessary that the highest terms of the secondary ranks be joined to the last terms of the first ranks. Conjunction, however, occurs through likeness. Thus likeness occurs between the first of the lower order and the last of the higher one.[7]

Proposition 146 makes it clear that at each stage of the hierarchy of being the effect is like the cause just as each creature is like God. Furthermore, just as there is a built-in bias, as it were, of an effect in relation to its cause in terms of a "turning" to its principle, so all creatures have a bias to return to the source or principle of their being.

Proposition 147, together with its comment, allows Dietrich a hierarchy that is continuous in such a way that this continuity is due solely to the likenesses that exist between the ranks of being.

Besides adopting the Proclean doctrine of similitude for the sake of maintaining the continuity of being, Dietrich introduces his own principle of linkage in the *De intellectu*. There he identifies the operation of each creature with its end. This operation, he explains, is the end of the thing, for the sake of which the thing exists. Then he goes on to reveal how he conceives this operation to link one being with another: by means of this operation a thing tends beyond itself. It is because of this operation that there is found in each thing not only being and truth, but also goodness. Thus each thing is interchangeably being, true, and good. Consequently, it is a being with respect to itself, true as ordered to the intellect, and good insofar as it actively overflows into something beyond itself. This is a remarkable view of operation and end, but it is Proclean in spirit. The operation of a creature always lies in moving beyond itself and this is its end or purpose. Just as in Proclus, nothing is static in Dietrich's universe; everything is moving, attempting to return to its initial principle.

[5] See Boese (1987), *El. theol.* 72: *Omnium divinorum processuum fines ad sua principia assimilantur, circulum sine principio et sine fine salvantes per conversionem ad principia.*

[6] See *El. theol.* 73: *Omnium divinorum ornatuum summa ultimis assimilantur superpositorum.*

[7] See *El. theol.* 73: *Si enim oportet continuitatem esse divini processus et propriis medietatibus unumquemque ordinem colligari, necesse summitates secundorum copulari finibus primorum; copulatio autem per similitudinem. Similitudo ergo erit principiorum submissi ordinis ad ultima superlocati.*

Creatures do not have their end in themselves; everything is for the sake of something else and that something else is ultimately the divine unity. Insofar as a creature follows its proper operation it will be led out of itself and back to this unity.

It is interesting that the voluminous direct citations by Dietrich of Proclus' *Elements*, along with almost equally prolific indirect references to the same work, are found in his writings dealing with intellectual or spiritual substances. For example, he cites the *Elements* directly twelve times in his *De visione beatifica*, fifteen times in his *De intellectu et intelligibili*, eighteen times in his *De cognitione entium separatorum*, five times in the *De substantiis spiritualibus*, and seven times in the *De animatione caeli*. In his works dealing with subjects other than the intellect the references are not so prolific. While he does use Proclus throughout his writings, the concentration of emphasis on the intellectual suggests that Dietrich read Proclus with a particular concern. This seems to be confirmed by Dietrich's numerous citations of the *Liber de causis* in the same works just cited. But Dietrich knew that Proclus' *Elements* was the source for the *Liber de causis*, so any analysis of the influence of Proclus on Dietrich must take account of this identity.[8]

The special influence: Dietrich's theory of the intellect

Dietrich made particular use of Proclus in his treatise on the intellect. He locates his analysis of intellect by introducing a distinction between what he calls *ens reale* and *ens conceptionale*. He claims in his *De visione beatifica* that this is the first division of being.[9] *Ens conceptionale* includes the objects of the intellectual act as well as the intellectual act itself. It is a semi-creative power that is coextensive with the universe of beings insofar as it exemplifies all the modes of natural being. Furthermore, it forms a conceptional hierarchy of its own, which finds the external senses at the bottom of the hierarchy, followed by the interior senses, the discursive power, the possible intellect, and finally the agent intellect at the top of the schema. Kurt Flasch notes in his introduction to the first volume of the *Opera omnia* of Dietrich that the distinction between *ens reale* and *ens conceptionale* replaces the old scholastic distinction between *ens naturae*

[8] See Dietrich of Freiberg, *De cognitione entium separatorum et maxime animarum separatarum*, 8, ed. H. Steffan (Mojsisch *et al.* 1977–1985), vol. II, 174, 33–35: *Et hoc habemus manifeste ex* Libro de causis *et ex libro Procli, unde videtur sumptus* Liber de causis.

[9] See *De vis. beat.* 96.

and *ens rationis*.[10] According to this old distinction, being as found in the mind is dependent upon an extra-mental reality. But Dietrich's distinction denies this and establishes that the mental or conceptional includes the real or extra-mental. This may be one of the primary influences of Proclus' metaphysics upon Dietrich's analysis of intellect.

The semi-creative power of intellect also has Proclean overtones. Intellect, according to Dietrich, is an emanative activity, which he calls *emanatio simplex*. It is similar to, and yet distinct from, divine creation, upon which it is dependent.[11] Intellect is capable of an emanation that is as vast as that of the creative emanation of the divine unity in the order of real beings. It might be better to say that it re-creates, or mirrors, a conceptional world rather than creates a world of real beings, as does the divine unity. This emanative activity results in what Dietrich will come to call the *universitas entium*.[12]

Following Proclus, Dietrich claims that intellects fall immediately beneath the divine unity in the hierarchy of being. It is this proximity to the creative unity of God as the One that accounts for the particular essence of intellect. Dietrich uses Proclus' doctrine that essence is convertible with being in act, to draw the conclusion that the operation of intellect will have something deiform or "god-like" about it.[13] He makes it clear, however, that this god-like operation is just that. It is not creative in the sense of bringing something into being from nothing. Appealing to Proclus' prop. 56, he insists it is dependent upon secondary agents.[14] Yet it is causal in its own way.[15] He develops this idea of the unique nature of intellectual causation in the *De intellectu*, where he relies directly on Proclus:

> Above at the beginning of Proposition 171 Proclus clarifies the issue of the intellect's being the cause of something. For as he says, "Every intellect in understanding establishes the things that come after it and its producing is to understand, and its understanding is to produce." And he proves this in the same place in the commentary as follows: "For intellect and being

[10] See K. Flasch "Einleitung" to Mojsisch *et al.* (1977–1985), vol. I, xii, xvii, and xxi.

[11] See Dietrich of Freiberg, *De animatione caeli*, 7, ed. L. Sturlese (Mojsisch *et al.* 1977–1985), vol. III, 18–19.

[12] See *De intellectu et intelligibili*, ed. B. Mojsisch (Mojsisch *et al.* 1977–1985), vol. I, 174–175.

[13] See *De intell. et intellig.* 146, where Dietrich cites prop. 140 of Proclus' *Elements* in order to arrive at the conclusion that lower things, in this case intellects, are identified by participation with what comes before them in the hierarchical order, in this case the divine unity. He also argues that intellects are a likeness of the whole of being.

[14] *De intell. et intellig.* 144.

[15] See Dietrich of Freiberg, *De vis. beat.* 13.

> are identical. Consequently, if it produces through its being and its being is understanding, then it produces through understanding."[16]

Using Proclus in this way, Dietrich establishes that there are two orders of non-creative causation, one governing intellectual causation and the other all the other forms of natural interaction. But perhaps more important is his identification of intellect and being. As noted above, this identification allows him to develop a metaphysics that is quite different from any metaphysics based solely on the concept of being. This new metaphysics can be found also in his younger contemporary, Meister Eckhart and later in Nicholas of Cusa. It would have a profound influence upon the development of European philosophy in the late medieval period.

According to Dietrich's account, intellects not only cause other non-intellectual beings, but they have a causal relationship to each other. Again he relies directly on Proclus' *Elements* to develop his analysis. Laying particular stress upon prop. 31 of that work, which states that "Everything that proceeds from another according to its essence, returns to that from which it proceeds," he establishes the relationship of effect to cause as a kind of conscious-appetitive relationship within the order of intellects.[17] He relies on Proclus' commentary on prop. 31 in order to do this. This commentary argues that individuals desire their own cause. Now, it is not clear that Proclus intends this desire to be intellectual or even conscious. But Dietrich draws exactly such a conclusion. He cites the commentary and then argues:

> From this remark one can argue for the present matter as follows: Every intellect that proceeds from another returns to it as to its cause. But such a return occurs only through desire. And every desire of an intellect is only intellectual, because it does not occur except in the manner in which it knows. Therefore, such a return of the intellect to its cause is intellectual.[18]

Intellectual procession as well as intellectual reversion involves conscious desire. These operations do not occur automatically as a kind of *élan vital*

[16] *De intell. et intellig.* 195: *Quantum ad intellectum, qui est alicuius causa, patet ex Proclo, sicut . . . principium inductum est ex propositione 171. Sic dicit*: Omnis intellectus in intelligendo instituit, quae sunt post ipsum, et factio intelligere et intelligentia facere. *Et probatur istud* ibid*em in commento sic*: Etenim intellectus et ens, quod in ipso idem. Si igitur facit per esse, esse autem intelligere est, facit per intelligere. Note: the correct reference is to prop. 174 and its commentary.

[17] *Cf. De intell. et intellig.* 195–196.

[18] *De intell. et intellig.* 196: *Ex hoc arguitur ad propositum sic:* Omnis intellectus procedens ab alio convertitur in ipsum tamquam in causam suam. Talis autem conversio non est nisi per appetitum. Omnis autem appetitus intellectus non est nisi intellectualis, quia non est nisi secundum modum, quo cognoscit. Ergo talis conversio intellectus in causam suam est intellectualis.

that could operate independently of conscious choosing and desiring. It seems to be Dietrich's intention here to use Proclus to establish what might be called a "personalized" concept of the order of intellects. Intellects are not just blind forces in the hierarchy of the universe. They are beginning to take on the aspect of what must be called "persons."

Intellects can of course be divided into those that operate as efficient causes in relation to material bodies and those that do not. The later class of intellects Dietrich identifies as separate substances. These are simple substances, which he defines as intellects that are always in act through their essence. They overflow into the beings below themselves in the order of formal causation. He uses the term *ebullitio* (boiling over), for which he cites the authority of Proclus, to describe this operation of emanation.[19] They also revert upon themselves through their very act of understanding.[20] Such intellects, he claims, Proclus identifies as intellectual hypostases (*intellectuales hypostases*).[21]

When Dietrich comes to the question of the relationship of consciousness to the human agent intellect he wonders what kind of causal affinity there might be between the agent intellect and the soul, which is its immediate object of causation. He uses Proclus' explanation of the principles of generation within the hierarchy of being in order to explain this affinity. The agent intellect, according to Proclus, is the intrinsic efficient cause of the soul.[22] The human soul, of course, governs a material body. And here the order of cosmic procession ends and the return of all things through the hierarchy of intellects begins.

Berthold of Moosburg

Berthold of Moosburg was for a long time a shadowy figure in the history of medieval philosophy, although his work at least has become available in a printed edition during the last thirty-five years. We know that he was a member of the Dominican province in Germany who was sent by his order to discharge various functions in both Cologne and in Oxford and died in 1361. His main claim for recognition is based on the fact that he wrote a philosophically acute and immensely learned commentary on

[19] *De intell. et intellig.* 142.

[20] *De intell. et intellig.* 142. He cites the authority of the *Liber de causis*, prop. 15 to support this claim. He also claims the authority of prop. 34 of the *Elements.*

[21] *De intell. et intellig.* 142. The reference here is to the term νοεραὶ ὑποστάσεις, which is found in props. 20, 191 comm., and 201 comm. of Proclus' *Elements.*

[22] See Mojsisch *et al.* (1977–1985), vol. 1, 51–53.

Proclus' *Elements of Theology* as translated by Moerbeke, which survives in two manuscripts: *Vat. Lat. 2192* and *Oxford, Balliol 224B.*[23] A further manuscript now in Basel[24] containing among other works Proclus' *Tria opuscula* and Macrobius' *Commentarius in Somnium Scipionis* – two texts that are also extensively utilized in the commentary on the *Elementatio theologica* – can be traced back to Berthold's library.[25] The fact that there are only two extant manuscripts of his commentary and that confusion even arose regarding his name suggests that his work, despite its undeniable erudition, found few readers inside or outside the later medieval schools. Since Nicholas of Cusa in his *Apologia doctae ignorantiae* includes Berthold's name in a list of authors that he considers to be philosophically valuable but dangerous for unwary readers, he presumably knew his work.[26] Apart from that, Berthold has been forced to wait for modern scholarship and its thesis regarding the unique philosophical tradition of the German Dominican School of the late Middle Ages in order to obtain the recognition that he properly deserves.[27]

The introductory material of Berthold's Expositio in Elementationem theologicam Procli

The intellectual direction of Berthold's *Expositio in Elementationem theologicam Procli* can be gauged by a careful examination of the introductory materials to the commentary.[28] These materials, which are sufficiently extensive to amount to a treatise in their own right, comprise a *prologus*, an *expositio tituli*, and a *praeambulum.* The most significant feature of the "prologue" to Berthold's *Expositio* is his attempt to justify the doctrine of Proclus' text by inserting it into a panoramic discussion of what might be termed the "Latin Platonic tradition" to date. In line with a tradition established by the so-called "School of Chartres" in the early twelfth century but

[23] The critical edition has been done in stages, over a lengthy period, and by many hands under the guidance of L. Sturlese. See Sturlese (1974), M-R. Pagnoni-Sturlese and Sturlese (1984), Sturlese, Pagnon-Sturlese, and Mojsisch (1986), Sannino (2001), Zavattero (2003), Jeck and Tautz (2003), Retucci (2007), Retucci (2011).

[24] *Basel F IV 31.* [25] See Sturlese (1974), xxiv–xlii.

[26] Nicholas of Cusa, *Apologia doctae ignorantiae* (h II) 44, 29. 14–30. 3 (for the style of references to Nicholas' works see n. 3 of Chapter 12). Nicholas actually gives the author's name here as *Iohannes de Mossbach.* This does not prove that he knew of Berthold only by hearsay, as some have argued. The confusion of the name had already arisen in the manuscripts, one of which Nicholas had presumably used.

[27] On Berthold's position as the definitive figure of the German Dominican school see especially de Libera (1984), 325 and Sturlese (2007), 175.

[28] For a more detailed analysis of these materials see Gersh (2001).

including much updating as a result of the wider range of texts available in his own day, Berthold here attempts to show that the teachings of the *Elementatio theologica* can be incorporated seamlessly into a kind of universal body of doctrine shared by the great thinkers of the past. These thinkers consist of some whom modern historians would call "Platonists" and others whose thought can easily be assimilated to "Platonism." Given that he subscribes to the traditional Augustinian view that the *Platonici* were the ancient thinkers most in agreement with Christian doctrine, Berthold can synthesize his universal doctrine on the one hand from Christian Platonic writings such as Augustine's *Confessions*, philosophical dialogues, and scriptural commentaries, Calcidius' *Commentarius in Timaeum*, or Boethius' theological tractates and *De consolatione philosophiae*; and on the other hand from non-Christian Platonic texts such as Apuleius' *De deo Socratis*, the *Asclepius* attributed to "Hermes Trismegistus," and Macrobius' *Commentarius in Somnium Scipionis.* Berthold goes beyond the Chartrian Platonists of the twelfth century and approaches the Platonism of Nicholas of Cusa a hundred years after his own day in employing a complex of doctrines drawn indirectly from the Carolingian thinker Iohannes Scottus Eriugena as a kind of catalyst for further textual harmonization. This complex includes: the *Clavis physicae* attributed to "Theodorus" but actually a work by Honorius Augustodunensis summarizing Eriugena's *Periphyseon*, the *De causa causarum* attributed to al-Fārābī but really a work by an Anonymous of the early thirteenth century influenced by Eriugena,[29] the *Homilia in prologum Iohannis* attributed to Origen but actually by Eriugena, and various glosses on Dionysius the Areopagite that also derive from Eriugena's *Periphyseon.* The second introductory section: the "Exposition of the Title" moves along a different trajectory. Here, Berthold's main task is to explain that the name *Proclus* can be interpreted to mean "having widespread fame" (via *procul* + *cluens*), the name *Diadochus* to mean "noble glory" (via *dia* + *doxa*), and the name *Lycius* to mean "associated with Apollo";[30] and also to explain that the title *Elementa* can be understood as signifying either the propositions' role as foundation of argument (via *ylementa*) or their ability to elevate the mind (via *elevamenta*).[31] In this section Berthold also assesses Proclus' contribution to the history of Platonism. Building on some historiographical information derived from Augustine's *Contra academicos*, he argues that whereas Plotinus had succeeded in removing the

[29] Most often known to modern scholars as the *Liber de causis primis et secundis*.

[30] *Expos. in El. theol.*, exp. tit., A (37, 10–13), E (41, 156–160), F (42, 198–43. 201) (Pagnoni-Sturlese and Sturlese 1984).

[31] *Expos. in El. theol.*, exp. tit., I (45, 285–291) and K (47, 343–348).

"coverings" (*integumenta*) placed on the true doctrines by the members of the New Academy, the greater achievement of Proclus was to organize the truths that had previously been covered up into propositions and axioms.[32] The most important aspect of the "preamble" to Berthold's *Expositio* is his attempt to justify the method of Proclus' text by situating it within a fictive debate between Aristotelians and Platonists about first principles. For the Aristotelians, the study which is called "Metaphysics" (*metaphysica*) deals with being *qua* being and employs a combination of "intellect" (*intellectus*) and "knowledge" (*scientia*), whereas for the Platonists the comparable study which is called "Divine Super-Wisdom" (*divinalis supersapientia*) deals with the One or Good and employs "simple intuition" (*simplex inspectio*).[33] Given that Proclus must be understood to adhere to the more Platonic rather than the more Aristotelian of the two positions described, the entire argument of his *Elementatio theologica* can now be traced back to two principles that are assumed rather than stated formally within the body of the text: namely, that multiplicity exists, and that productivity exists.[34] According to Berthold, the argument unfolds in accordance with the first assumption by showing that the One must exist in props. 1–6 and then in accordance with the second assumption by showing that the Good must exist in prop. 7, this order of discussion being necessary because the One is a principle which is superior to a cause whereas the Good is merely a cause.[35] Finally, Berthold clarifies the entire position by characterizing the two assumptions underlying the text as general principles, as opposed to a most general principle like the law of contradiction,[36] and also by comparing the two assumptions on the one hand to principles derived from sensation and on the other to articles of faith.[37]

In the three introductory sections of his commentary Berthold states the basic premises underlying his approach to the *Elementatio theologica.* However, certain fundamental ideas that appear in the introductory sections but only take on real significance as the commentary itself progresses are equally important. Among these the first idea of importance is a distinction between "natural providence" (*providentia naturalis*) and "voluntary providence" (*providentia voluntaria*) derived originally from Augustine's *De genesi ad litteram,* book VIII. At least according to Berthold's reading, the distinction between natural providence and voluntary providence can be

[32] *Expos. in El. theol.*, exp. tit., A (37. 14–29).

[33] *Expos. in El. theol.*, prae. B (56. 111–119), C (65. 422–429), C (65. 430–432), C (65. 452–66. 458), C (66. 462–471), C (67. 504–68. 528), C (68. 539–540).

[34] *Expos. in El. theol.*, prae. A (53. 13–20).

[35] *Expos. in El. theol.*, prae. A (53. 6–12).

[36] *Expos. in El. theol.*, prae. C (61. 305–62. 326).

[37] *Expos. in El. theol.*, prae. A (53. 15–20).

exemplified – in a manner building on Augustine's own distinction between God's operation through seminal reasons and through angelic and human mediation[38] – in the distinction between primordial causes together with their participants and angelic interpreters of the divine mind together with human souls.[39] In the course of this discussion he introduces a passage of Proclus' *De malorum subsistentia* to illustrate not the natural providence – as one might expect – but the voluntary providence. Given that this interpretation of the distinction cuts across one current in the earlier German Dominican school whereby natural and voluntary providence represent the spheres studied by natural and dogmatic theology respectively,[40] it is not surprising to find that Berthold can understand Proclus' *Elementatio theologica* as making a contribution to *both* philosophy and theology understood in the later medieval sense and not simply to the former. A second topic of importance introduced but not developed in the introductory part of the commentary is the role of the pseudo-Dionysius in the philosophical-theological synthesis of the *Expositio* as a whole. Remarks in the *expositio tituli* have shown that Berthold knew that Proclus lived after Plotinus and developed his thought.[41] Given that Berthold also knows through Augustine that Plotinus was active subsequent to the rise of Christianity, and also subscribes to the universally held medieval opinion that "Dionysius the Areopagite" was a writer of the apostolic age, he must have believed that the obvious similarities of doctrine between Dionysius and Proclus resulted from the influence of the former on the latter. As we read on in the commentary, we accordingly discover that Berthold is justifying the study of Proclus' doctrine on the grounds of its similarity to that of Dionysius and that the relation between the pagan and the Christian Platonist further exemplifies the relation between natural and voluntary providence.[42] Now, conferral of a primal theological authority on Dionysius had been especially characteristic of writers following in the tradition of Albert the Great, and Berthold's legitimization of Proclus as *the* commentator on Dionysius can therefore be seen as a natural development of this viewpoint. In fact, by presenting what amounts to the first ever "axiomatization" of Dionysian thought, Proclus emerges as a Dionysian commentator uniquely adapted to the scholastic mentality. A third idea of importance is the role played

38 Augustine, *De genesi ad litteram* VIII. 9, 243. 25–244. 20 (Zycha 1894).

39 Berthold, *Expos. in El. theol.*, prol. 5 (13. 252) – 6 (14. 285). Cf. *Expos. in El. theol.*, prop. 161C (12. 41–13. 62).

40 For example, see Dietrich of Freiberg, *De subiecto theologiae* 281–282, ed. L. Sturlese (Mojsisch *et al.* 1977–1985, vol. III). On the interpretation of this text see de Libera (1989), 56–62.

41 See pp. 307–308 above.

42 Although these two relations will not be exactly parallel.

by authorities nearer to Berthold's own time and within his own religious order in influencing his thought. Here, the lists of *doctores ecclesiae* and *philosophi famosi* respectively that are placed at the end of the *Expositio* in the two manuscripts but have been more conveniently placed at the beginning by the modern editors turn out to be important indicators.[43] Although names such as *Dominus Albertus Teutonicus, Frater Ulricus de Argentina,* and *Magister Thomas Anglicus minor* appear in the list of church teachers, Berthold does not by explicit citation indicate the passages where in reality he can be found paraphrasing or excerpting from Albert the Great's *Summa theologiae*, Ulrich of Strasbourg's *De summo bono*, and Thomas of York's *Sapientale.* However, Berthold's dependence for lengthy passages of his commentary on previous doctrinal *summae* is an important fact to be borne in mind when evaluating the combinations of more ancient authorities that are used to bolster particular arguments. For example, the conviction running through Thomas of York's *Sapientale* that the writings attributed to "Hermes Trismegistus" contained a quasi-Christian insight into the highest truths[44] also lies behind Berthold's specific strategies in employing clusters of Hermetic citations in order to reinforce the argument of Proclus' text.[45]

General tendencies in Berthold's interpretation of Proclus

Given the grand scale of Berthold's *Expositio* and the limited scope of the present discussion, it will only be possible to outline a few of the most interesting features of the reading of Proclus' philosophy in the main body of the commentary. In the remainder of this chapter, we will consider just one example each of three kinds of interpretation occurring there. These might be characterized very approximately as (a) expansion, (b) restriction, and (c) alteration of Proclus' doctrine, these modifications being important indices of the commentator's understanding of Platonism and of its relation to Aristotelianism.

(a) *Expansion of Proclus' doctrine.* Prop. 174 of the *Elements of Theology* reads: "Every intellect produces the intellects subsequent to it by intellection. Its making is vested in its intellection, and its intellection

[43] Berthold, *Expos. in El. theol.* (3. 1–4. 48).
[44] Thomas of York, *Sapientale* I. 6 (MS *Firenze, Conv. soppr.* A VI 437, 6rb–6vb) and I. 14 (ibid. 14ra–14va).
[45] For example, see *Expos. in El. theol.*, prop. 131 (190. 1–191. 44 and 192. 76–194. 103) (Retucci 2011). Cf. *Expos. in El. theol.*, prol. 8 (14. 296) ff. (Pagnoni-Sturlese and Sturlese 1984).

is vested in its making."[46] The proof is based on the prior assumptions first, that the intelligible object and the intellect are the same as one another;[47] second, that each intellect's being is identical with its intellection;[48] third, that each intellect's making is vested in its being; and fourth, that each intellect causes in virtue of being what it is.[49] In *supp. 1* of his commentary on this proposition[50] Berthold makes a survey of the different definitions of *intellectus* leading to that of what is termed the "universal agent intellect" (*intellectus universaliter agens*).[51] *Supp. 2* contrasts the cognitive activity of this intellect with that of other intellects. Berthold argues that in the case of other intellects the intellectual objects are not identical with the intellectual subject itself, these objects being *a.* constituted by accidental – i.e. external – relations and *b.* embodying intentional or conceptual rather than real or existent relations. These intellects have the character of non-essential causes. In the case of the agent intellect the intellectual objects are identical with the intellectual subject, these objects being *a.* constituted by essential – i.e. internal – relations and *b.* embodying intentional or conceptual as well as real or existent relations. The agent intellect has the character of an "essential cause." In order to unfold the implications of the proposition in this manner, Berthold introduces a number of citations from Dietrich of Freiberg's *De intellectu et intelligibili* that are themselves based on the creative use of a number of ideas taken from Proclus. These Proclean ideas include the notion that a cause is identifiable with its effect in the sense of pre-containing the latter in a higher mode,[52] that it has a cognitive character through its process of reverting to itself,[53] that it proceeds from itself through an overflow resulting from perfection,[54] and that

[46] Proclus, *El. theol.* 174, 152. 8–9 πᾶς νοῦς τῷ νοεῖν ὑφίστησι τὰ μετ᾽αὐτόν, καὶ ἡ ποίησις ἐν τῷ νοεῖν, καὶ ἡ νόησις ἐν τῷ ποιεῖν = *Omnis intellectus in intelligendo instituit quae post ipsum, et factio in intelligere et intelligentia in facere* (Moerbeke) (Boese 1987).

[47] Prop. 167. [48] From prop. 169 pr. [49] From prop. 26 pr.

[50] The commentary on most of the propositions in the *Elementatio* is divided into two parts sometimes but not always labeled the *suppositum* and the *propositio*, each of which is itself most often divided into three parts (the overall division being therefore notated as *supp.* 1, 2, 3, and *prop.* 1, 2, 3, etc.). The *supposita* sections of the commentary tend to contain the most wide-ranging (and intertextual) discussions of each Proclean proposition.

[51] Berthold, *Expos. in El. theol.* 174A (136. 10–137. 53). The sense of "universal" is ambiguous here for reasons to be examined in our next paragraph.

[52] See Dietrich of Freiberg, *De cogn. ent. separ.* 237 For a useful tabulation of the passages in Dietrich citing Proclus and the passages in Proclus cited see Calma (2010), 277–342. The passages of Dietrich can be found in English translation in Führer (1992).

[53] See above p. 305. [54] See above p. 305.

it produces its effect through an activity identical with rather than distinct from its substance.[55] Dietrich had been able to develop his more radically idealistic reading of Proclus by bringing into greater relief the notions that the relation between cause and effect can be identified with that between intellective subject and object, and that the emanative process is one in which essence and existence cannot be completely distinguished from one another.[56] In *supp.* 3 of the commentary on the present proposition, Berthold notes that the above criteria do not apply to a substance that is intellectual only "through participation" (*per participationem*).[57] *Prop.* 1/1 argues that, because of the inseparability of its substance and its activity, the agent intellect understands eternally and immutably.[58] In *prop.* 1/2 Berthold concludes that, since the activity of this intellect is directed both to the interior and to the exterior, and this activity is the final cause of the intellect, then intellect's causality with respect to its effect is inherently purposive. For this reason it is similar to the primal Good. This argument shows Berthold as continuing to follow Dietrich of Freiberg in inverting Proclus' normal viewpoint by treating finality as something that the cause finds in the effect rather than the effect in the cause.[59] *Prop.* 1/3 argues that every intellect causes things subsequent to it by intellection that is strictly active and emanating to the exterior, this intellection being "in the order of essential causality" (*in ordine essentiali causali*).[60] In *prop.* 2/1 Berthold emphasizes that the causal activity of the agent intellect is to be distinguished from normal efficient causality because no motion is implied in its activity.[61] *Prop.* 2/2 proposes a qualified application of the simile of an artificer to the activity of this intellect.[62] In *prop.* 2/3 Berthold concludes that the causal activity of this intellect can be considered either as intellection or as making with emphasis on the internality or the externality of the process respectively.[63]

(b) *Restriction of Proclus' doctrine.* According to prop. 20 of the *Elements of Theology*, "beyond all bodies is the substance of Soul, beyond all

[55] See above pp. 303–304.
[56] Berthold, *Expos. in El. theol.* 174B (137. 54–140. 120) (Jeck and Tautz 2003).
[57] Berthold, *Expos. in El. theol.* 174C (140. 121–129).
[58] Berthold, *Expos. in El. theol.* 174D (140. 135–150).
[59] Berthold, *Expos. in El. theol.* 174E (140. 151–141. 183).
[60] Berthold, *Expos. in El. theol.* 174F (141. 184–142. 192).
[61] Berthold, *Expos. in El. theol.* 174G (142. 197–143. 230).
[62] Berthold, *Expos. in El. theol.* 174H (143. 231–262).
[63] Berthold, *Expos. in El. theol.* 174I (144. 263–284).

souls the nature of Intellect, and beyond all intellectual hypostases the One."[64] The proof moves through the following stages: first, Soul is shown to be superior to bodies because the former is self-moved;[65] second, Intellect is shown to be superior to souls on the one hand because the Intellect is unmoved[66] and on the other because souls have intellection only by participation;[67] and third, the One is shown to be superior to intellects because participation in unity is more universal than participation in intellect.[68] In commenting on this proposition, Berthold again introduces ideas derived from Dietrich of Freiberg.[69] As the latter had argued in *De visione beatifica*, the most fundamental division of being is into "real" and "conceptional" being.[70] Given that conceptional beings include not only the objects but the subjects and activities of intellection,[71] that there is an analogous relation between the causal process by which God's intellect produces the hierarchies of both real beings and conceptional beings and that by which created intellects produce the hierarchy of conceptional beings,[72] and that the distinction between the real and conceptional increases progressively as the hierarchy descends,[73] then conceptional beings are clearly more than the traditional *entia rationis.* At any rate, Berthold uses the distinction between real and conceptional being in order to restrict the realist interpretation of the relations within and between the hypostases of intellect and soul typical of Proclus' own work. With respect to the "horizontal" relations within Proclean hypostases, Berthold argues that all intellects (for him the second level of being) and all souls (for him the third level of being) can be considered as "one" intellect and "one" soul as a *maneries* (i.e. as a conceptional being) but not as an *ens reale.*[74] With respect to the "vertical" relations, he argues that angelic and human souls can be considered as participated intellects, being, according to the *esse naturae*, intellects that must be considered to subsist inseparably and

[64] Proclus, *El. theol.* 20, 22. 1–3: πάντων σωμάτων ἐπέκεινά ἐστιν ἡ ψυχῆς οὐσία, καὶ πασῶν ψυχῶν ἐπέκεινα ἡ νοερὰ φύσις, καὶ πασῶν τῶν νοερῶν ὑποστάσεων ἐπέκεινα τὸ ἕν = *Omnibus corporibus superior est animae substantia, et omnibus animabus superior intellectualis natura, et omnibus intellectualibus ypostasibus superius ipsum unum* (Moerbeke).
[65] From prop. 17 and pr. [66] From prop. 14, corr.
[67] From prop. 19 pr. [68] From prop. 1 and pr.
[69] Berthold, *Expos. in El. theol.* 20 (65. 1ff.) (Sturlese, Pagnoni-Sturlese and Mojsisch 1986).
[70] See above pp. 302–303. [71] See above pp. 302–303. [72] See above p. 303.
[73] Dietrich of Freiberg, *De vis. beat.* 28–29, ed. Mojsisch (Mojsisch *et al.* 1977–1985, vol. 1).
[74] Berthold, *Expos. in El. theol.* 20B (68. 129–139), 20E (70. 192–196) (Sturlese, Pagnoni-Sturlese and Mojsisch 1986).

in alio but, according to the *esse conceptionale*, intellects that subsist *per se* and separately.[75]

(c) *Alteration of Proclus' doctrine.* Prop. 43 of the *Elements of Theology* reads: "Everything that is capable of reversion to itself is self-constituted."[76] The proof is based on the prior assumption that everything that reverts according to its nature performs its reversion towards that from which the procession of its own substance was derived.[77] In *supp.* 1 of his commentary on this proposition, Berthold identifies the self-reverting with the intellectual nature and then notes that there are three levels of things that revert to themselves: the "intellectual hypostases" (*intellectuales hypostases*) which have no relation to body, the agent and possible intellect which have no relation to body yet a relation to something else in the order of reality, and the "total souls" (*animae totales*) which have a relation to body. In the course of explaining these levels, Berthold notes that things reverting to themselves – and especially the agent and possible intellects – are conceptional beings in the sense of cognitive subjects that establish cognitive objects.[78] *Supp.* 2 compares the self-reversion of the agent and possible intellects, noting that the former reverts to itself "essentially" (*essentialiter*) – involving no externality of the form or object of its cognition – whereas the latter reverts to itself "intentionally" (*intentionaliter*) – implying some externality of its cognitive form or object. This argument would imply that there is less of a distinction between the real and the conceptional in the case of the agent intellect and more of that distinction in the case of the possible intellect.[79] In *supp.* 3 of his commentary Berthold returns to the question of the levels of things that revert to themselves specifically in order to clarify the status of the total souls as self-reverting things. Here, he compares the total souls, on the one hand, with the primal Good or One and the unities which revert "as wholes wholly" (*toti totaliter*) – the former reverting "in a simple manner" (*simpliciter*), the latter "in a contracted manner" (*contracte*); and, on the other hand, with the intellectual hypostases – as opposed to the agent intellect – which revert "as wholes not wholly" (*toti non totaliter*). The intellectual hypostases have a self-reversion which includes reversion in an infinite,

[75] Berthold, *Expos. in El. theol.* 20G (71. 213–229).

[76] Proclus, *El. theol.* 43, 44. 25: πᾶν τὸ πρὸς ἑαυτὸ ἐπιστρεπτικὸν αὐθυπόστατόν ἐστιν = *Omne quod ad se ipsum conversivum est authypostatum est* (Moerbeke).

[77] Prop. 34. [78] Berthold, *Expos. in El. theol.* 43A (66. 1–67. 54) (Sannino 2001).

[79] Berthold, *Expos. in El. theol.* 43B (67. 55–69. 134).

substantial, vital, and intellectual manner, the total souls themselves having a threefold manner of self-reversion: the psychic, the intellectual, and the divine.[80] *Prop.* 1 explains how a self-constituted principle could be its own "cause of being" (*causa essendi*) in the sense of being both a form and an agent. If self-constitution means having no higher cause at all, then only the Good or One would really be self-constitutive; but if self-constitution means having no higher cause of its form, then all incorporeal things are self-constitutive.[81] In *prop.* 2 of his commentary Berthold emphasizes the connection between self-reversion and separation and then distinguishes self-reversion "in a single intention" (*in una intentione*) – which applies in a simple manner to the Good or One and in a contracted manner to the goodnesses – from self-reversion "in a multiplicity of intentions" (*in pluribus intentionibus*). The latter can be associated in one way with the intellectual hypostases that are completely separate from body, and in another with the agent intellect that is separate from body and therefore self-reverting when considered in itself but not separate from body and therefore not self-reverting when considered as part of the partial soul.[82] *Prop.* 3 distinguishes three types of self-reversion: self-reversion "through essential cognition" (*per essentialem cognitionem*) or "absolutely" (*absolute*), self-reversion "through an intention" (*per intentionem*) or "according to conceptional being" (*secundum esse conceptionale*), and self-reversion "through self-motion" (*per sui ipsius motionem*) or "by reason of separation" (*ratione separationis*). The first type of self-reversion applies to the intellectual hypostases – and is consistent with their reversion in an infinite, existential, vital, and intellectual manner, the second applies to the possible intellect, and the third to the total souls.[83] It is obvious that throughout this commentary on Proclus' prop. 43, Berthold is extracting numerous ideas from Proclus' already far-ranging discussion of self-reversion and recombining them in order to produce a doctrine more compatible with late medieval views about cognition. Moreover, he maintains his dependence on Dietrich of Freiberg not only in applying the distinction between conceptional and real being to the notion of self-reversion but also in introducing Aristotle's *De anima* and

[80] Berthold, *Expos. in El. theol.* 43C (69. 135–70. 154).
[81] Berthold, *Expos. in El. theol.* 43D (70. 158–71. 176).
[82] Berthold, *Expos. in El. theol.* 43E (71. 177–191).
[83] Berthold, *Expos. in El. theol.* 43F (71. 192–72. 223).

Augustine's *De Trinitate* as supplementary authorities for the definition of the cognitive subject.

Bibliography

Biard, J., Calma, D., and Imbach, R. (eds.) (2009) *Recherches sur Dietrich de Freiberg (Studia Artistarum 19)*, Turnhout.

Boese, H. (ed.) (1987) *Proclus: Elementatio theologica translata a Guillelmo de Morbecca*, Leuven.

Calma, D. (2010) *Le poids de la citation, Étude sur les sources arabes et grecques dans l'oeuvre de Dietrich de Freiberg*, Fribourg.

Flasch, K. (ed.) (1984) *Von Meister Dietrich zu Meister Eckhart*, Hamburg.

(2007) *Dietrich von Freiberg: Philosophie, Theologie, Naturforschung um 1300*, Frankfurt a. M.

Führer, M. L. (trans.) (1992) *Dietrich of Freiberg: Treatise on the Intellect and the Intelligible (Tractatus de intellectu et intelligibili)*, translated from the Latin with introduction and notes, Milwaukee.

Gersh, S. (2001) "Berthold of Moosburg on the Content and Method of Platonic Philosophy," in J. A. Aertsen, Emery, K., and Speer, A. (eds.), *Nach der Verurteilung von 1277, Philosophie und Theologie an der Universität von Paris im letzten Viertel des 13. Jahrhunderts = Miscellanea Mediaevalia* 28, Berlin and New York, 493–503. Reprinted in Gersh (2005).

(2005) *Reading Plato, Tracing Plato: From Ancient Commentary to Medieval Reception*, Aldershot.

Iremadze, T. (2004) *Konzeptionen des Denkens im Neuplatonismus, Zur Rezeption der Proklischen Philosophie im deutschen und georgischen Mittelalter: Dietrich von Freiberg, Berthold von Moosburg, Joane Petrizi*, Amsterdam and Philadelphia.

Jeck, U. R. and Tautz, I. J. (eds.) (2003) Berthold von Moosburg, *Expositio super Elementationem theologicam Procli, props. 160–183*, Hamburg.

Kandler, K.-H., Mojsisch, B., and Stammkötter, F.-B. (eds.) (1999) *Dietrich von Freiberg, Neue Perspektiven seiner Philosophie, Theologie und Naturwissenschaft*, Amsterdam and Philadelphia.

Libera, A. de (1984) *Introduction à la mystique rhénane, D'Albert le Grand à Maître Eckhart*, Paris.

(1989) "Philosophie et théologie chez Albert le Grand et dans l'école dominicaine allemande," in A. Zimmermann (ed.), *Die Kölner Universität im Mittelalter, Geistige Wurzeln und soziale Wirklichkeit = Miscellanea Mediaevalia* 20, Berlin and New York, 49–67.

Mojsisch, B. (1977) *Die Theorie des Intellekts bei Dietrich von Freiberg*, Hamburg.

Mojsisch *et al.* (eds.) (1977–1985) Dietrich von Freiberg, *Opera omnia*, vols. I–IV, in *Corpus Philosophorum Teutonicorum Medii Aevi*, Hamburg.

Pagnoni-Sturlese, M.-R. and Sturlese, L. (eds.) (1984) Berthold von Moosburg, *Expositio super Elementationem theologicam Procli, prol., props. 1–13*, with Introduction by K. Flasch, Hamburg.

Retucci, F. (ed.) (2007) Berthold von Moosburg, *Expositio super Elementationem theologicam Procli, props. 136–159*, Hamburg.
(ed.) (2011) Berthold von Moosburg, *Expositio super Elementationem theologicam Procli, props. 108–135*, Hamburg.
Sannino, A. (ed.) (2001) Berthold von Moosburg, *Expositio super Elementationem theologicam Procli, props. 35–65*, Hamburg.
Sturlese, L. (ed.) (1974) Bertoldo di Moosburg, *Expositio super Elementationem theologicam Procli, 184–211, De animabus*, Rome.
(1986) "Der Prokloskommentar Bertholds von Moosburg und die philosophische Probleme der Nacheckhartschen Zeit," in K. Ruh (ed.), *Abendländische Mystik im Mittelalter, Symposium Kloster Engelberg 1984, Stuttgart 1986*, 145–161. Reprinted in Sturlese (2007), 137–154.
(1987) "Tauler im Kontext, Die philosophische Voraussetzungen des 'Seelengrundes' in der Lehre des deutschen Neuplatonikers Berthold von Moosburg," *Beiträge zur Geschichte der deutschen Sprache und Literatur* 109: 390–426. Reprinted in Sturlese (2007), 169–197.
(2007) *Homo divinus, Philosophische Projekte in Deutschland zwischen Meister Eckhart und Heinrich Seuse*, Stuttgart.
Sturlese, L., Pagnoni-Sturlese, M.-R., and Mojsisch, B. (eds.) (1986) Berthold von Moosburg, *Expositio super Elementationem theologicam Procli, props. 14–34*, Hamburg.
Thomas of York (Thomas Eboracensis), *Sapientale*, in MS *Firenze, Biblioteca Nazionale Centrale, conv. soppr.* A. VI. 437.
Zavattero, J. (ed.) (2003) Berthold von Moosburg, *Expositio super Elementationem theologicam Procli, props. 66–107*, Hamburg.
Zycha, J. (ed.) (1894) Augustine, *De Genesi ad Litteram libri duodecim, eiusdem libri capitula* (*Corpus Scriptorum Ecclesiasticorum Latinorum* 28/1), Vienna.

CHAPTER 12

Nicholas of Cusa

Stephen Gersh

In considering the relation between Nicholas of Cusa and Proclus, one should emphasize from the outset that the fifteenth-century writer has a core of early philosophical doctrine that was not altered substantially during his later career, and that this teaching is stated most fully in the treatise *De docta ignorantia* (1440) and the writings immediately following it. Given that Nicholas was a profoundly creative thinker who read widely and transformed everything that he read, one has to be cautious in any attempt to trace his most essential thought back to earlier writers. Nevertheless, the earlier philosophical doctrine of Nicholas of Cusa does depend heavily on a blend of twelfth-century Latin Platonism[1] and the theology of pseudo-Dionysius the Areopagite,[2] and includes the first tentative steps in an interpretation of Proclus that emerges more clearly in writings of the period after 1450.

First encounters with Proclus

According to its author's explicit summary, the system underlying *De docta ignorantia* is based on a relation between three terms: the "absolute maximum," the "contracted maximum," and the "absolute and contracted maximum." These three terms are studied in the three successive books of *De docta ignorantia* and, to the extent that they correspond very loosely to God, the universe, and Christ, they represent ultimate realities, although to the extent that they correspond more precisely to God seen through the universe, the universe seen through God, and the combination of

[1] See Beierwaltes (1985), 368–384. Useful but more restricted in scope is McTighe (1980).
[2] Fundamental for this subject is Baur (1940–1941). For philosophical analysis see Beierwaltes (1998), 130–171; for historical context Monfasani (1987) and Senger (2002), 228–252.

these viewpoints, they represent ultimate concepts.[3] *De docta ignorantia I* exploits the doctrine of pseudo-Dionysius – a writer whom Nicholas reports himself to have studied eagerly at a crucial point in his life.[4] Here, it is argued that God can be understood and described by using either negative terms such as "not-Being" or affirmative terms such as "Being," and further argued that negative terms are applied more truly and affirmative terms less truly to God.[5] Nicholas follows Dionysius in identifying the negation "not-*x*" with the superlative "more than *x*," yet he innovates in treating the negation as an indication of the infinity of God.[6] *De docta ignorantia II* follows the teaching of Thierry of Chartres – a writer whom Nicholas describes as the most brilliant of all those he has studied.[7] Here it is argued that the totality can be considered from four viewpoints: as the "absolute necessity" of God, as the "necessity of complication" of the Forms, as the "determinate possibility" of particulars, and as the "indeterminate possibility" of matter.[8] Nicholas follows Thierry in maintaining that the four viewpoints are moments of both the divine and the human mind's contemplation, but he innovates in identifying both absolute necessity and indeterminate possibility with God.[9] In addition to these central ideas derived from pseudo-Dionysius and Thierry of Chartres, the enigmatic descriptions of God in the Hermetic *Liber XXIV Philosophorum* are the source of important developments. For Nicholas, God is the infinite sphere whose center is everywhere and whose circumference is nowhere,[10] the opposition to Nothing through the mediation of Being,[11] and so forth.

[3] *De docta ignorantia* I. 2 (h I, 7. 1–8. 17 [= Hoffmann and Klibansky 1932]). All citations of Nicholas' works will be from the Heidelberg Academy edition: *Nicolai de Cusa Opera omnia iussu et auctoritate Academiae Litterarum Heidelbergensis*, Hamburg: F. Meiner 1932–2005. Individual works are cited by the traditional book and chapter numbers, with volume, section (or page), and line numbers of the Heidelberg edition (= h) given in parentheses.

[4] *Apologia doctae ignorantiae* 17 (h II, 12. 19–24 [= Klibansky 1932]). Nicholas here states that the crucial notion of learned ignorance came to him by a direct intuition (see n. 20) and before engaging in an intensive study of Dionysius. However, the working-out of this idea at length in *De docta ignorantia*, at least, gives clear indications of Dionysian influence.

[5] *De doct. ign.* I. 24–26 (h I, 48. 1–56. 20).

[6] *De doct. ign.* I. 3 (h I, 8. 18–9. 28); I. 12ff. (h I, 24. 10ff.); I. 26 (h I, 54. 19–55. 12); II. 1 (h I, 61. 1–65. 10); II. 5 (h I, 77. 7–23).

[7] *Apol. doct. ign.* 35 (h II, 24, 6–9).

[8] *De doct. ign.* II. 7–10 (h I, 81. 16–99. 12). Cf. *De doct. ign.* I. 17 (h I, 33. 18–20) and I. 23 (h I, 46. 22–47. 5.

[9] *De doct. ign.* II. 8 (h I, 87. 21–88. 8).

[10] *De doct. ign.* I. 23 (h I, 46. 1–47, 28).

[11] *De doct. ign.* II. 2 (h I, 66. 7–23).

The ideas that we have distinguished as foundational in *De docta ignorantia* and in the writings immediately following it are drawn from a variety of sources within the broad tradition of medieval Platonic thought. They do not reveal any specific indebtedness to Proclus' doctrines. The same can probably be said regarding two other ideas formulated during the 1440s that are not only foundational with respect to Nicholas' thought as a whole but constitute some of his most audacious philosophical innovations: namely, the notion of "conjecture" (*coniectura*) and the principle of "coincidence of opposites" (*coincidentia oppositorum*).

Nicholas outlines his understanding of the notion of conjecture in the prologue, first chapter, and several later passages of *De coniecturis* (1442–1443).[12] Here he contrasts the maximal and infinite Truth with our finite apprehension of truth and argues that, since there is no proportion between the latter and the former, human beings are forced to conjecture. He quickly reduces this statement to the more concise form of a contrast between the unity of Truth and the otherness of conjecture: a move which will permit him later to define conjecture as "an affirmative statement that, together with otherness, participates in Truth as it is."[13] Employing this reduction, he goes on to qualify the disproportional relation between the unity and the otherness, and to establish a structural parallelism between divine creativity and human conjecturing. With respect to the qualification of the disproportionate relation, he notes that at present the unity of Truth is known by the otherness of conjecture whereas in the future the otherness of conjecture will be seen through the unity of Truth, adding that a disproportional relation holds not only between the unity of Truth and the otherness of conjecture but between the individual conjectures embodying that otherness. With respect to the establishment of structural parallelism, he notes that just as the activity of the divine mind produces the real world so does that of the human mind produce the conjectural world, adding that the more closely our mind approaches God's the more closely will its conjectures of otherness approach the Truth of unity. The remainder of *De coniecturis* consists of a series of individual conjectures in the form of demonstrations and diagrams. Nicholas argues that, since number derives from the unity, equality, and connection of the divine nature and also forms the basis not only of reason's making but of reason

[12] Koch (1956) and Sfez (2102) provide detailed commentaries on this work. For brief orientation see Haubst (1970) and De Gandillac (1972).

[13] *De coniecturis* I (h III, 57. 10–11) (= Koch, Bormann, and Senger 1972) *positiva assertio in alteritate veritatem, uti est, participans.*

itself, conjectural thinking is best executed through the manipulation of symbolic numbers.[14]

Although the notion of conjecture has no obvious parallel in Proclus, it is worth noting that some of the earliest unambiguous evidence regarding Nicholas' study of late ancient Platonism emerges around the time when the notion of conjecture itself was being elaborated. One of the most important arguments in *De coniecturis* states that the doctrine of a dynamic proceeding and reverting relation between the hypostases of One, Intellect, Soul, and Body can be reinterpreted as a kind of "conjectural" covering of the inner truth represented by his own Christian conception of the simultaneously transcendent and immanent relation of the creator God to created things.[15] The important figure "P" of *De coniecturis*, in its depiction of the metaphysical relation between unity and otherness in terms of a spatial relation between light and darkness where a pyramid with its apex at the bottom (representing diminishing unity/light) is superimposed on a pyramid with its apex at the top (representing increasing otherness/darkness), is employed by Nicholas as a powerful graphic illustration of this conjecture.[16] Now, it is a curious fact that the four levels of Being that are here interpreted as a conjectural covering are stated most compactly in prop. 20 of Proclus' *Elementatio theologica*, a passage that can also be shown to have been of particular interest to Nicholas on the basis of certain of his *marginalia*.[17]

The notion of a *coincidentia oppositorum*[18] which had been frequently employed albeit rarely defended in late ancient Platonism assumes the role

[14] Less arcane examples of conjecturing can be found in Nicholas' *Idiota de mente*. Here, conjectures typically vary in their scale between single statements and elaborate theories. For the former see *Id. de mente* 7 (h V, 102. 11–20) (= Steiger 1983) (that forms are obscured by the variability of matter), and for the latter see *Id. de mente* 2 (h V, 65. 5–68. 16) (that there are transcendent as well as abstracted forms). They can also vary in their area of application: for example, to the physical or logical domain (see *Id. de mente* 7 [h V, 102. 11–13]). Conjectures can deal with abstract metaphysical issues – for example, concerning mind (see *Id. de mente* 1 [h V, 56. 8–13]) and number (see *Id. de mente* 6 [h V, 94. 1–16]) – and with historical interpretive questions – for example, the relation between Plato's and Aristotle's thought (see *Id. de mente* 2 [h V, 66. 1–20]).

[15] The program is worked out at considerable length in *De coni.* I. 4–I. 8 (h III, 12. 1–36. 12) and elaborated from a more subjectivist viewpoint in *De coni.* II. 14 (h III, 140. 1–145. 21).

[16] See *De coni.* I. 9 (h III, 41. 8ff.) for the figure, *De coni.* I. 9 (h III, 37. 1–40. 16) for the relation between unity and otherness, and *De coni.* I. 9 (h III, 43. 1–53. 12) for the *explicatio* of the figure. Nicholas also suggests at *De coni.* I 5 (h III, 20. 1–16) that the base of the pyramid of light specifically represents an object to which at the same time two contradictory terms can be applied.

[17] Sfez (2012), 116–127 sees the influence of Proclus as crucial to Nicholas' philosophical approach in *De coniecturis*. However, the influence is perhaps in the sphere of the conjectured doctrines rather than the method of conjecture as such (which is influenced more by Llull and Nominalism).

[18] The phrases coincidence of "opposites" (*opposita*) and coincidence of "contradictories" (*contradictoria*) seem to be used interchangeably. For example, see *De visione Dei* 9 (h VI, 36. 1–37. 13) (= Riemann 2000).

of an explicit fundamental principle for the first time in the history of philosophy with Nicholas of Cusa.[19] For this reason, the latter was perhaps justified in describing it in one passage as a kind of personal revelation.[20] The concept of such a coincidence seems to occur with two distinguishable but not disconnected emphases, depending upon whether it is seen more metaphysically as the simultaneous transcendence and immanence of God or more methodologically as a symbolic pointer towards this incomprehensible Deity.[21] Examples of opposites treated as a coinciding relation in the earlier writings include maximum and minimum and infinite and finite.[22] The metaphysical aspect of their coincidence is emphasized in *Apologia doctae ignorantiae* (1449) when God is said to be everywhere in such a manner that he is nowhere,[23] and where these opposite predications are said to circumvent the law of contradiction.[24] Nicholas is able to argue in the language of the early *De coniecturis* that the coincidence of opposites applies *a.* to the One and *b.* to Intellect,[25] as he does in the language of the later *De visione Dei* (1453) that God is *a.* equivalent to and *b.* superior to the coincidence,[26] the fact that any point in the dynamic process of emanation that coincidence attempts to represent can be denoted equally

[19] Among the many discussions of this topic see especially Wilpert (1953), Beierwaltes (1964), Flasch (1972), Beierwaltes (1977), Beierwaltes (1988), Haubst (1989), Stallmach (1989), Beierwaltes (1997), Flasch (1998), 430–443.

[20] See *De doct. ign.* III (h I, 163. 6–13) "Letter to Cardinal Julian" and *Apol. doct. ign.* 16 (h II, 12. 14–18). The coincidence of opposites discussed here is specifically the so-called "learned ignorance."

[21] For the combination of metaphysical and methodological approaches see n. 31 below.

[22] For the former see *De doct. ign.* I. 2 (h I, 7. 1–25); I. 4 (h I, 10. 25–11. 22); I. 16 (h I, 30. 5–32. 27); I. 18 (h I, 36. 27–37. 7); *Apol. doct. ign.* 12–13 (h II, 9. 24–10. 20). For the latter see *Apol. doct. ign.* 12–13 (h II, 10. 1–3). Similar pairs are: universal and singular (*Apol. doct. ign.* 12–13 [h II, 9. 18–10. 3]), actual and possible (*Apol. doct. ign.* 46 [h II, 31. 16–27]), distinct and indistinct (*Apol. doct. ign.* 25 [h II, 24. 1–27]).

[23] *Apol. doct. ign.* 18 (h II, 13. 20–26) and 25 (h II, 17. 20–18. 3). The statements that God enfolds all things or somehow *is* all things at *Apol. doct. ign.* 12 (h II, 9. 15) and 39–40 (h II, 26. 25–27. 14) are elliptical references to the same principle. Nicholas finds authority for the principle in both Augustine (*Apol. doct. ign.* 18 (h II, 13. 11–19) and 22 (h II, 15. 19–22) and Dionysius (*Apol. doct. ign.* 24–25 (h II, 17. 3–18. 3) and 29 (h II, 19. 25–20. 15). He also notes that the same principle when enunciated by Meister Eckhart did not imply a pantheistic identification of God and creature (*Apol. doct. ign.* 36–37 (h II, 25. 1–26. 25)).

[24] *Apol. doct. ign.* 20–22 (h II, 14. 20–15. 22) and 42 (h II, 28. 11–17).

[25] At *De coni.* I. 6 (h III, 24. 1–26) this is equated with speaking of God as an "intellectual unity" and as an "absolute unity" respectively. Nicholas adds that the former expression was typical of *De docta ignorantia* whereas the latter is utilized in *De coniecturis.* For coincidence of opposites in God see also *Apol. doct.ign.* 29 (h II, 20. 2–15) – together with the passages cited in nn. 23–24. For coincidence of opposites in intellect see also *De coni.* I. 6 (h III, 22. 1–24. 26) and I. 10 (h III, 52. 1–13).

[26] At *De vis. Dei* 17 (h VI, 74. 1–75. 14) (= Riemann 2000) God is said to have a distinctness that is beyond the coincidence of distinctness and indistinctness. This idea is more succinctly expressed at *Apol. doct. ign.* 21 (h II, 15. 15–16) and *De vis. Dei* 13 (h VI, 54. 9–10), where God is said to be "the opposition of opposites" (*oppositorum oppositio*).

as a logical structure of *both . . . and* or of *neither . . . nor* seeming to permit the simultaneous maintenance of positions *a* and *b*.[27] The methodological aspect of the coincidence of opposites is emphasized in the same *De visione Dei*, where the coincidence is compared to a wall separating us from the God,[28] and where a supra-intellective vision is necessary to carry us through the barrier of opposites.[29] Examples of opposites treated as a coinciding relation in the earlier writings include comprehensible and incomprehensible and revealed and hidden.[30] Of course, the "learned ignorance" that provided the title of Nicholas' most celebrated work also falls within this category.[31]

Those interested in the sources of Nicholas of Cusa's notions of conjecture and coincidence of opposites should turn to Raimund Llull[32] and Dionysius the Areopagite[33] respectively although, given Nicholas' general tendency to transform everything that he reads in personal ways, any influence upon him of these two thinkers will be found in this case also to be as oblique as it is profound. In fact, his exploitation of Llull is largely with respect to methodology rather than metaphysics, that is, in pursuing the organization of discourse through the manipulation of graphic figures. Likewise, his reading of Dionysius is mainly in the Eriugenian manner, emphasizing a dialectical rather than an affective type of

27 In fact, the coincidence of opposites tends to unfold into a fourfold schema whose logical structure is *A*, both *A* and *B*, *B*, neither *A* nor *B*. For good illustrations see *De doct. ign.* I. 6 (h I, 14. 1–6) (where it is applied to the existence of the maximum), *De coni.* I. 11 (h III, 58. 1–60. 6) (where it is applied to participation in unity), and *De vis. Dei* 11 (h VI, 45. 1–46. 11) (where it is applied to the mind's contemplation of God).

28 At *De vis. Dei* 9 (h VI, 37. 1–13) this wall is identified as the "wall of paradise" (*murus paradisi*). At *De vis. Dei* 10 (h VI, 42. 7–9) the wall's opposites are beginning and end, at 11 (h VI, 45. 5–11) enfolding and unfolding, at 12 (h VI, 49. 1–16) creating and created, and at 17 (h VI, 74. 1–5) distinctness and indistinctness. At *De vis. Dei* 10 (h VI, 40. 1–42. 19) the circularity of the wall is stressed. See also *De vis. Dei* 23 (h VI, 101. 1–6).

29 At *De vis. Dei* 9 (h VI, 37. 9–10) the "spirit of reason" (*spiritus rationis*) presiding over the barrier must be vanquished, and at *De vis. Dei* 17 (h VI, 75. 9–10) the wall of coincidence is "the limit of all intellectual power" (*claudere . . . potentiam omnis intellectus*). Cf. also *De vis. Dei* 12 (h VI, 48. 4–5). According to *De vis. Dei* 12 (h VI, 47. 1–48. 19), etc., what lies beyond the wall can only be "seen" (*videri*). Cf. also *Apol. doct. ign.* 20–21 (h II, 14. 11–15. 16).

30 For the former see *De vis. Dei* 16 (h VI, 68. 1–70. 14). For the latter see *De vis. Dei* 17 (h VI, 79. 1–15). Similar pairs are: visible and invisible (*De vis. Dei* 12 [h VI, 43. 1–13]), intelligible and unintelligible (*Apol. doct. ign.* 16 [h II, 12. 9–11]), and light and darkness (*De vis Dei* 9 [h VI 38. 1–14] and 13 [h VI, 53. 10–12], *Apol. doct. ign.* 29–30 [h II, 19. 25–21. 4]), etc. The last item is a metaphorical expression of all the previous.

31 What we have been calling the metaphysical and methodological approaches to the coincidence of opposites are sometimes explicitly combined by Nicholas. See the extended discussion of the *interrelation* (metaphysical) between divine and human *seeing* (methodological) that begins *De visione Dei* at *De vis. Dei* pr.-2 (h VI, 1. 2–8. 18) and 5–6 (h II, 13. 1–21. 23).

32 See Koch (1956), 14; Sfez (2012), 44, etc.

33 See Baur (1940–1941), 51.

non-discursivity.[34] However, even if Proclus is found to have initially stimulated neither the doctrines of conjecture and of coincidence of opposites nor the other ideas that were fundamental to *De docta ignorantia* and immediately subsequent writings, it is an indisputable fact that Proclus' characteristic doctrines would eventually be absorbed into the Cusan synthesis to such an extent and in such a manner that that synthetic doctrine would acquire a new kind of historical legitimacy as the definitive statement of Platonic Christianity. We must now turn to consider the primary evidence for that absorption.

The extracts from Proclus in MS *Strasbourg, cod. lat. 84*

Four translated extracts from Proclus' writings copied by Nicholas' own hand into a small codex preserved in the *Bibliothèque municipale* of Strasbourg were first noted by E. Vansteenberghe[35] and then discussed in detail by R. Haubst.[36] On the basis of certain doctrinal similarities between the extracts and *De coniecturis*, it is generally assumed that these extracts were made during Nicholas' earlier career in or before 1442–1443.[37]

One passage is taken from William of Moerbeke's translation of Proclus' *Commentarius in Parmenidem*, which it abbreviates in places.[38] Nicholas' extract begins at the point where the commentator is asking how the One can be described as "unlimited" (*infinitum*) and excluding the sense in which other things might be characterized in this manner. Here, the statement that the One is unlimited is justified by considering the nature of opposites. It is argued that the One must be either elevated above both opposites or assigned the name of the better of the two opposites, since the One is the best of all things. Thus, the One must be either elevated above cause and caused or named as "cause" (which is better than caused).[39] Now, negations applied to the highest – among which the *un*limited is included – imply not deficiency but superiority. Therefore, the One must be either elevated above the unlimited and limit or named as "unlimited" (which is better than limit). The question of a possible conflict with a passage of

34 On the Eriugenian tendency in Nicholas' reading of Dionysius see Gersh (2012).

35 Vansteenberghe (1928). 36 Haubst (1961).

37 For a summary of the historical discussion and for illuminating philosophical commentary see Beierwaltes (2000).

38 Proclus, *In Parm.* VI. 1123–1124 (Steel 2007–2009). The extract in the Strasbourg MS and the corresponding passage in Moerbeke's translation are reproduced in Steel (1982–1985), vol. 1, 19*–20*.

39 Alternatively: elevated above unity and multiplicity or named as "unity" (which is above multiplicity).

Plato's *Laws* stating that the One is the "measure" (*mensura*) of all things is considered. However, the notion of measure there implies that the One is limit with respect to other things, in the sense of being their final cause, but unlimited with respect to itself, in the sense of having no prior cause.

Three further passages are taken from a translation, which is assumed to be by Ambrogio Traversari, of Proclus' *Theologia Platonica*.[40] The first translated extract from the *Theologia Platonica* is a heavily abbreviated paraphrase of the original Greek text at a point where, in order to characterize the subject matter of theology, an account of reality inviting comparison with that in *De Coniecturis* is presented.[41] Having briefly stated an argument to the effect that principles must be incorporeal and indivisible, this text establishes partly through a consideration of motion and time an ascending hierarchy of four terms each of which is causally dependent on the higher. These terms are: "body" (*corpus*) which is moved by another in time, "soul" (*anima*) which is moved by itself in time, "intellect" (*intellectus*) which has eternal motion, and "unity" (*unio*).[42] This fourfold hierarchy is immediately re-stated in terms of "participation" (*participari*) since everything is said to participate in unity, but not everything in intellect, and not everything in soul.[43] In a descending sequence[44] the passage now refers to the three "unities" (*unitates*)[45] above body and the three specific series of "numbers" (*numeri*)[46] – the unitary, the intellectual, and the psychic – to which these unities give rise. In an ascending sequence[47] the passage next speaks of the joining of body to soul, of soul to intellect, and of intellect to unity.[48] Some new terminology is introduced when the first principle is characterized as the "indivisible/unparticipated unity" (*impartibilis unitas*).[49] Various intermediate levels are also introduced when soul is said to be joined to "intellectual forms" (*intellectuales species*), and through

[40] This identification first proposed by Haubst (1961), 40–42 has generally been accepted.

[41] Proclus, *Theol. Plat.* I. 3, 13. 6–15. 16 (Saffrey and Westerink 1968–1997).

[42] The last term is said to have been introduced by Plato.

[43] Proclus' original discussion, which maps the different ranges of participation in more detail, is heavily abbreviated by Nicholas or the translator.

[44] The motion of procession is indicated by the Latin verb "leading down" (*deducere*).

[45] The translator merges the *henades* and the *monades* of the original – which are technically distinct – into the single Latin term *unitates*.

[46] The numbers are "appropriate" (*proprii*) or "congruent" (*congrui*) with the unities.

[47] The motion of reversion is indicated by the Latin verb "convert" (*convertere*) – in addition to "join" (*copulare*) and "conjoin" (*coniungere*).

[48] In this part of the translation, two separate descriptions of the four levels (*Theol. Plat.* I. 3, 14. 13–16 and *Theol. Plat.* I. 3, 14. 21–15. 6) have been combined. However, the general sense of the argument is not seriously compromised.

[49] The Greek reads: "unparticipated henad." With the Latin *impartibilis*, the translator is combining two ideas – division and participation – that are distinct in the original passage.

the latter to "the unities of beings" (*unitates entium*), while "the summit of intellect, its flower, and its subsistence" (*summitas intellectus, flos et subsistentia eius*)[50] is said to be joined to the unities of beings and through the latter to the "hidden union of the divine unities" (*divinarum unitatum abscondita unio*). Finally, it is noted that the nature of the gods[51] can be grasped by neither "sense" (*sensus*) nor "imagination" (*imaginatio*)[52] nor "rational intellect" (*rationalis intellectus*),[53] given that this nature is borne above the beings attainable by the faculties mentioned and stands isolated in its "union of wholes" (*universorum unio*).[54]

The second translated extract from the *Theologia Platonica* follows the original much more closely. Starting from the traditional epistemological notion that like is known by like – a principle said to be applicable at all levels between sensation and opinion and union and ineffability – this text quotes Socrates' statement in the *Alcibiades* that the soul "contracted to itself" (*in sese contracta*)[55] sees all things including God. Looking within at its "unity and the center of its entire life" (*unio, centrum totius vitae*), and shaking off the "multiplicity and variety of its powers" (*multitudo et varietas virtutum*), the soul ascends to the highest vantage point of beings. Following a comparison with two stages of the mysteries, where the initiates first encounter the multiple and variegated forms of the gods and then participate in the divine radiance itself,[56] the contrast between the soul's movements to the exterior and to the interior is elaborated further. In the former case, the soul is said to perceive the "shadows and images" (*umbrae atque simulacra*) of beings. In the latter case, it is said to "bring together its own essence and its reasons" (*essentiam propriam atque rationes sui colligere*) in such a manner that, first, it contemplates "itself alone" (*se ipsam tantum*) and – with expansion of its cognition – "its intellect and the

[50] In both the original and the translation, this indicates a highest phase of intellection distinguished within intellect itself.

[51] In the original, these gods are equivalent to the "unities of beings" and the "divine unities" mentioned earlier.

[52] The original's intermediate cognitive levels of δόξα and διάνοια are omitted by the translator.

[53] This translates νόησις μετὰ λόγου ("intellection together with reason") in the original.

[54] The phrase ἕνωσις τῶν ὅλων in the original refers to the henads' function of providing unification to the lower terms – beings, intellects, souls – that participate in them. It is doubtful that such a meaning would emerge from the Latin translation taken in isolation.

[55] The term *contracta* (which seems to translate the συννεύουσα in the next line of the Greek rather than the εἰσίουσα of the present passage) is a technical term in Nicholas' thought. It is perhaps one of his most notable borrowings from the *Expositio in Elementationem theologicam* of Berthold of Moosburg in which a parallel usage is fairly common.

[56] The translation and the original text seem to envisage the two stages differently. For the former these are the approaches to the many gods and to the one God respectively, and for the latter the approaches to the demons and the gods respectively.

orders of beings" (*intellectus et entium ordines*); and, second, it explores and contemplates "the divine order and the unities of beings" (*genus deorum atque entium unitates*). After stating as a kind of general principle that all things are in us in the manner of soul, the passage continues by stating that the purpose of humanity is to know all things by arousing our powers and the images of all things, and that it is lawful for us to ascend to the point where we may be conjoined with "the ineffable and most excellent Good . . . the supreme principle of things" (*ineffabile . . . excellentissimum bonum . . . supremum rerum principium*).[57] Having reached this point, we may descend again through the "realm of beings" (*entium dimensio*) by collecting the multiplicity of Forms. Moreover, by examining the "unities and numbers" (*unitates et numeri*) of the Forms, and understanding intellectually how each thing depends on its own specific unity and how the "gods' causality" (*deorum origines*) relates to beings and the "beings' distinctions" (*entium discretiones*) to the gods,[58] we will achieve the most perfect knowledge of the divine.

The four translated extracts[59] from Proclus in the Strasbourg manuscript, which are obviously of great importance for understanding Nicholas' relation to Proclus, raise as many problems as they solve. Although it is beyond doubt that certain notions appearing in the extracts correspond with ideas developed in Nicholas' own writings, it remains to be established whether the passages had originally been excerpted and then inspired these ideas, or whether the ideas were developed independently and then stimulated the excerpting of these passages as corroboration. Obviously, this question is closely implicated in the further question regarding the dating which has, in fact, attracted most of the scholarly interest in the past.

The *marginalia* to Proclus' *Commentarius in Parmenidem* and *Elementatio theologica*

If the extracts in the Strasbourg manuscript represent a modest documentation of one early stage in Nicholas' encounter with Proclus, the

57 This phrase alters the πάντων ἐπέκεινα τῶν ὄντων of the original (a) by substituting "the Good" for "the Beyond of beings," (b) by introducing the notion of the maximum. However, with the second alteration – introducing a favorite notion of Nicholas' – the translator may be attempting to render ἐπέκεινα.

58 The translator here obscures the technical sense of πρόοδοι (= "processions") by translating the latter term as *origines*.

59 We have not felt it necessary to discuss the third extract from the *Theologia Platonis* which is extremely brief (*Theol. Plat.* I. 11, 47. 10–12). This merely re-describes the fourfold hierarchy of the first extract in new terminology. Here, the first principle is "one" (*unum*), intellect "one [as] many" (*unum multa*), soul "one and many" (*unum et multa*), and body "many and one" (*multa et unum*).

marginalia to Proclus provide evidence of a more extensive and continuous engagement with the Greek philosopher. These *marginalia* comprise annotations in Nicholas' own handwriting that have been identified in various manuscripts of Proclus' translated works formerly owned by him and now housed either in the library of the St. Nicholas Hospital at Bernkastel-Kues, which he himself founded, or elsewhere.[60] Now, the annotations on Pietro Balbi's translation of Proclus' *Theologia Platonica* and on William of Moerbeke's translation of Proclus' *Commentarius in Parmenidem* in the MSS *Cusanus Hospitalis S. Nicolai 185* and *186* are among the most extensive *marginalia* in any of Nicholas' manuscripts. However, there are problems in using these marginal glosses to supplement the fifteenth-century thinker's original writings. First, there are questions surrounding the dating of the *marginalia*. Although the annotations on the *Theologia Platonica* can be given a single collective *terminus post quem*, those on the *Commentarius in Parmenidem* seem to have arisen on three different occasions.[61] Secondly – and with potentially greater interpretive ramifications – it is difficult to establish whether individual *marginalia* are preparation for or a consequence of the elaboration of similar ideas in Nicholas' original writings. Thirdly, there are questions raised by the scale of the *marginalia*. Here, the very extensive annotations on the *Commentarius in Parmenidem* may be contrasted with the brief and incomplete ones on the *Elementatio theologica*. As a means of postponing certain questions that can be resolved and of evading certain others that cannot, we will treat the Proclus-*marginalia* as a largely independent body of evidence.

The copy of William of Moerbeke's translation of Proclus' *Commentarius in Parmenidem*[62] in the MS *Cusanus Hospitalis S. Nicolai 186* contains 620 *marginalia* in Nicholas' handwriting according to their modern editor's count. Among the numerous philosophical issues treated in these annotations, there are at least four that are particularly noteworthy in the light of parallel developments in the original treatises of Nicholas of Cusa: (1) the distinction between discursive and non-discursive thinking; (2) the application of negative language to God; (3) the status of opposition; and (4) the disproportion between God and created things.[63]

60 For the texts of these glosses and introductory notes see Senger (1986) and Bormann (1986). Among earlier philosophical discussions of these *marginalia*, see especially Beierwaltes (1987), 290–291 and Beierwaltes (1998), 630–631.

61 The three chronological stages of the latter glosses are suggested by differences of handwriting style and color of ink. See Klibansky (1928–1929), 27–28.

62 For a description of this manuscript see Marx (1905).

63 On Nicholas and the Moerbeke translation of the Parmenides see Steel (1977); Steel (1982–1985), vol. I, 12*–22*, 36*–37*; Steel (1982–1985), vol. II, 529–555. Nicholas later commissioned a translation

A distinction between the non-discursive thinking characteristic of "intellect" (*intellectus*) and the discursive thinking characteristic of "reason" (*ratio*) is emphasized in a number of Nicholas' marginal notes on the fifth book *in Parmenidem*. At one point, he distinguishes the two faculties in terms of a descending relation where intellect is connected to reason through the "utterance" (*locutio*) or "revelation" (*revelatio*) of the former that underlies definition.[64] In a later comment he distinguishes the same two faculties in terms of an ascending relation by observing that what we call logical theory is "an exercise with a view to intellectual cognition" (*exercitatio ad intellectualem cognitionem*).[65] The discursive aspect of reason is suggested by the reference to definition in the first comment and the reference to logic in the second. The non-discursive character of intellect is shown when Nicholas observes pointedly that "the most primal Forms are not defined. They are only intellectual and contemplated by simple intuition. Definition and division are concerned with their images."[66] In his notes on the fifth book Nicholas makes some further observations about the distinction between intellect and reason. In particular, he draws attention to passages where Proclus brings intellect and reason closer together by distinguishing various modes of "dialectic" (*dialectica*) – the method peculiar to reason – that are less discursive or more discursive in nature.[67]

The ideas about the distinction between non-discursive and discursive thinking elaborated in these *marginalia* are paralleled in the original writings of Nicholas of Cusa from a relatively early date.[68] A definitive

of the entire dialogue *Parmenides* by George of Trebizond. On the two translations of the *Parmenides* used by Nicholas see Klibansky (1943) and Ruocco (2003). Ruocco argues that the later translation had an impact on Nicholas' work, although the evidence for this is rather uncertain.

64 *Marginalia in Parmenidem*. # 351 (on Proclus: *In Parm.* [Moerbeke] 296. 25ff. / Proclus: *In Parm.* 986). Moerbeke's translation (= M) is cited in the edition and pagination of Steel (1982–1985), Proclus' original in the edition of Steel (2007–2009) but using the pagination of Cousin (1864) reproduced by Steel.

65 *Marg. in Parm.* # 358 (on Proclus: *In Parm.* [M] 302. 22ff. / Proclus: *In Parm.* 993–994).

66 *Marg. in Parm.* # 353 (on Proclus: *In Parm.* [M] 296. 36ff. / Proclus: *In Parm.* 986) *Primissimae species non definiuntur. Sunt enim solum intelligentiales et simplici intuitione speculantur. Definiens autem et dividens ad imagines ipsarum respicit.* Cf. *Marg. in Parm.* # 349 (on Proclus: *In Parm.* [M] 295. 3ff. / Proclus: *In Parm.* 985) for a briefer statement of the same point. See *Marg. in Parm.* # 352 (on Proclus: *In Parm.* [M] 295. 3ff. / Proclus: *In Parm.* 985) for an explanation why the intellectual Forms cannot be defined.

67 See *Marg. in Parm.* # 356 (on Proclus: *In Parm.* [M] 298. 5ff. / Proclus: *In Parm.* 989) "the works of dialectic" (*opera dialecticae*). Cf. *Marg. in Parm.* # 368 (on Proclus: *In Parm.*[M] 313. 74ff. / Proclus: *In Parm.* 1007) contrasting the higher dialectic of Plato's *Parmenides* and the lower dialectic of the Peripatetics, and *Marg. in Parm.* ## 378 and 380 (on Proclus: *In Parm.* [M] 330. 8ff. and 330. 80ff. / Proclus: *In Parm.* 1027–1028), where the contrasting methods of Parmenides, Zeno, and Socrates are noted.

68 For example, see *De doct. ign.* I. 24, where intellect grasps the unity of the various divine names but reason handles them as distinct.

example can be found in *Apologia doctae ignorantiae*,[69] where the writer compares intellect to sight and reason to hearing and emphasizes the distinction between the two faculties by arguing that the latter maintains the opposition between unity and multiplicity, point and line, center and circumference – having a "discursiveness bounded between an initial and a final point"[70] – whereas the former allows these extremities to coincide, reason being characterized as the unfolding of intellect.[71] There are also parallels in Nicholas' earlier writings to ideas concerning the application of negative language to God[72] that occur in a further set of *marginalia*.

Nicholas' marginal notes on the sixth book *in Parmenidem* show his interest in the kinds of human language that must be employed in order to speak properly about the transcendent One. In two consecutive comments he explains that when affirmative language is applied to the first principle by Plato, this affirmation is understood as indicating the principle's causality with respect to subsequent things to it, and that when Plato applies negative language to the first principle, this negation is understood to indicate the principle's superiority with respect to subsequent things.[73] The latter approach is dominant in the *Parmenides*[74] since "negations are prior to affirmations in the divine sphere."[75] Nicholas therefore draws attention to Proclus' arguments[76] (1) that there are three kinds of non-being: *a.* that which is superior to being, *b.* that which is coordinate with being, and *c.* that which is inferior to being, and three corresponding kinds of negation; and (2) that the non-being of type *a.* can be subdivided into the non-being *i.* that is not considered in relation to any being and the non-being *ii.* that is considered in such a relation to being:

[69] *Apol. doct. ign.* 20–21 (h II, 14. 10–15. 16).

[70] *Apol. doct. ign.* 21 (h II, 15. 5–6) *discursus . . . terminatus inter terminos a quo et ad quem.*

[71] Nicholas also refers here to his own earlier discussion in *De coniecturis*. This more extended treatment compares the unity of intellect with the unity of reason, emphasizes the connection between the two faculties by arguing that the former is the "presupposition" (*praesupponere*) and the "precision" (*praecisio*) of the latter, and characterizes reason as the unfolding of intellect. See *De coni.* I. 6 (h III, 23. 1–25. 25); I. 10 (h III, 50. 1–52. 13); I. 11 (h III, 57. 1–17).

[72] For examples of such parallels see the passages cited on pp. 318–319.

[73] *Marg. in Parm.* ## 497–498 (on Proclus: *In Parm.* [M] 392. 46ff. / Proclus: *In Parm.* 1109–1110).

[74] *Marg. in Parm.* # 518 (on Proclus: *In Parm.* [M] 407. 20 / Proclus: *In Parm.* 1128).

[75] *Marg. in Parm.* # 434 (on Proclus: *In Parm.* [M] 365. 12ff. / Proclus: *In Parm.* 1074) *Negationes in divinis praeferuntur affirmationibus.* Cf. *Marg. in Parm.* # 430 (on Proclus: *In Parm.* [M] 364. 74ff. / Proclus: *In Parm.* 1072). Cf. *Marg. in Parm.* # 437 (on Proclus: *In Parm.* [M] 366. 43ff. / Proclus: *In Parm.* 1075–1077), where affirmations are said to be prior to negations in the sensible sphere. For further notes on the different usages of negative and affirmative predications with respect to the intelligible and sensible spheres see *Marg. in Parm.* ## 614–615 (on Proclus: *In Parm.* [M] 517. 49ff. / Proclus: *In Parm.* 68. 16ff. [Klibansky-Labowsky 1953]).

[76] Of course, he does not repeat the entire argument in his marginal note.

> Note that "non-being" and "negation" are both said in three ways. For just as non being is said in the sense of "above being," so negation is said in the sense of "above affirmation". . . . Non-being – in the sense of elevated above being – is twofold: namely, as participated and as considered together with no being.[77]

In two further consecutive comments, Nicholas notes that the linguistic forms in which affirmative and negative language are applied to the first principle by Plato correlate with cognitive states in which intellect knows itself and surpasses itself respectively.[78] In fact, we may even accept the formulation that "understanding of God, since he 'is not,' is negation."[79]

Nicholas' marginal notes on the sixth book *in Parmenidem* also return frequently to the questions regarding the status of opposition. The application of affirmative and negative language to God that has been discussed in connection with the previous set of notes obviously introduces this topic, and in further comments we find Nicholas developing this theme particularly with respect to the opposites of limit and infinity. Since Proclus had been compelled to maintain on the basis of Plato's *Philebus* that the One was superior to limit and infinity while conceding that this principle was also itself limit according to the *Laws* and infinity according to the *Parmenides*, Nicholas seizes the opportunity of simultaneously introducing the fully developed theory of "coincidence of opposites" and recasting Proclus' polytheistic hierarchy of principles as the Christian monotheistic order of divine names.[80] For the fifteenth-century writer, the fact that God can be understood not only as equivalent to the opposites of finite and infinite[81] but also as superior to that opposition[82] results from the facts that negation is a *polysemous* term.[83] As the "in-" of infinity, this negation can signify *a.* both one of two and both of two opposites treated as coordinate, and

77 *Marg. in Parm.* ## 432–433 (on Proclus: *In Parm.* [M] 365. 86ff. / Proclus: *In Parm.* 1073) *nota: tripliciter dici non ens et ita negationem. Nam sicut non ens dicitur quia supra ens, ita et negatio supra affirmationem . . . duplex non ens supra ens exaltatum, scilicet participatum et nulli entium connumeratum.*

78 *Marg. in Parm.* ## 443–444 (on Proclus: *In Parm.* [M] 370. 43ff. / Proclus: *In Parm.* 1080).

79 *Intelligentia dei, quia non est, negatio est.*

80 See the series of comments from *Marg, in Parm.* # 510 (Proclus: *In Parm.* [M] 403. 15ff. / Proclus: *In Parm.* 1123–1124). These deal with the section of Proclus' text from which Nicholas had also made an extract in the MS *Strasbourg 84*. See above.

81 *Marg. in Parm.* # 514 (on Proclus: *In Parm.* [M] 403. 15 ff. / 1123–1124). In this passage God is also said to be – introducing another typical opposition – both maximum and minimum.

82 *Marg. in Parm.* # 509 (on Proclus: *In Parm.* [M] 402. 65ff. / Proclus: *In Parm.* 1121). Cf. *Marg. in Parm.* # 517 (on Proclus: *In Parm.* [M] 406. 10ff. / Proclus: *In Parm.* 1127).

83 For the identification of negation and infinity see *Marg. in Parm.* # 435 (on Proclus: *In Parm.* [M] 366. 19ff. / Proclus: *In Parm.* 1074). See above.

b. the superior of two opposites treated as superior and inferior respectively.[84] This dialectic underlies the following note:

> If you also consider how one and the same thing can simultaneously mean "not *x*" and "very *x*," then you will be able to penetrate the meaning of this statement: namely, that negation is superior to affirmation. Thus, God is said to be "infinite," in the sense of *not* finite and *very* finite. Note that "in-" represents the coupling or uniting of affirmation and negation. Just as "in-" unites the initial letters *i* of the word *ita* ["yes"] and *n* of the word *non* ["no"], so it signifies both affirmation and negation.[85]

The ideas regarding the status of opposition elaborated in these *marginalia* are paralleled in the original writings of Nicholas of Cusa from a relatively early date.[86] There are also parallels in Nicholas' earlier writings to ideas concerning the disproportion between God and created things that occur in a further set of *marginalia*. For example, the teaching of *De docta ignorantia I* that a *quasi*-geometrical symbolism may be applied to God,[87] being based on the notions that "all inquiry proceeds by means of a comparative proportion"[88] between what is known and what is unknown, that the infinite *qua* infinite is unknown because it escapes proportionality, and that a cognitive approach to the infinite God must therefore be achieved by a " transumptive proportion"[89] not proportional in the conventional mathematical sense,[90] has numerous parallels in the *marginalia.*

Similarly, a note on the seventh book *in Parmenidem*, by extracting the statement that the One is "incomparable with all things" (*incomparabile omnibus*) and "not coordinate with multiplicity" (*neque coordinabile*

84 Many of Nicholas' *marginalia* deal with the polysemy of infinity. See *Marg. in Parm.* ## 504–505 (on Proclus: *In Parm.* [M] 398. 42ff. / Proclus: *In Parm.* 1117–1118) and # 516 (on Proclus: *In Parm.* [M] 403. 15ff. / Proclus: *In Parm.* 1123–1124).

85 *Marg. in Parm.* # 439 (on Proclus: *In Parm.* [M] 366. 43ff. / Proclus: *In Parm.* 1075–1077) *Si simul consideras ut unum et idem sit non et valde, tunc subintrare poteris intellectum huius, scilicet quomodo negatio est plus quam affirmatio, ut cum deus dicitur infinitus id est non et valde finitus. Nota "in" est copulatio sive unio affirmationis et negationis, sicut enim prima elementa de "ita" et "non," scilicet "i" et "n" in se unit, ita et utriusque significatum.* The marginal note continues with some remarks about the use of figures – of which the verbal prefix "in-" in the present note is an instance – to express something transcending figure.

86 For examples of such parallels see the passage cited on pp. 322–323.

87 *De doct. ign.* I. 1 (h I, 5. 1–6. 24) and *De doct. ign.* I. 10–23 (h I, 19. 15–47. 28).

88 *De doct. ign.* I. 1 (h I, 5. 23–6. 1) *omnis . . . inquisitio in comparativa proportione . . . existit.*

89 *De doct. ign.* I. 11 (h I, 22. 18) *transumptiva proportio.*

90 Nicholas illustrates the application of these principles at even greater length in *De coniecturis* where he argues that the disproportion between man and Truth is the origin of the *quasi*-arithmetical method of conjecture. See *De coni.* I, prol. (h III, 2. 1–6. 19). For the distinction between mathematical and disproportional proportion see *De coni.* I. 9 (h III, 39. 1–40. 16) and *De coni.* I. 10 (h III, 52. 1–13). See also *De coni.* I. 6 (h III, 24. 1–26).

multiplicatis),[91] points to the topic of proportional knowledge in the *marginalia*. In the course of his annotations Nicholas argues that there is a disproportion between God and created things that can be expressed by saying in a more logical manner that the One is neither the same nor other with respect to other things or even itself,[92] or in a more mathematical manner that the One is neither greater than, nor lesser than, nor equal to other things.[93] That the One cannot be the same in any of these ways is justified on the grounds that this relation depends upon the presence of a "formal identity" (*specifica identitas*) which is incompatible with the One's status,[94] and that the One cannot be greater or lesser on the grounds that these relations depend upon the presence of sameness "according to tension or relaxation" (*secundum intensionem et remissionem*), which is likewise incompatible.[95] Nicholas obviously conceives of the lack of proportion between God and created things explicitly in terms of geometrical figures, since he draws attention to Proclus' comment that equality among geometers means that two things are measured by the same measures.[96]

The copy of William of Moerbeke's translation of Proclus' *Elementatio theologica* in the MS *Cusanus Hospitalis S. Nicolai 195*[97] contains seventy-three *marginalia* in Nicholas' handwriting according to the modern editor's count. These notes differ from the set considered previously in several ways. They are more abbreviated, often consisting of very few words, or of a graphic symbol calling attention to certain words in the text, or of the single word *nota*. They are also distributed more sparsely. Moreover, they indicate a reading of only the first two-thirds of Proclus' translated text, ending with the comment on prop. 139. There are perhaps two philosophical issues treated in these annotations that can be considered significant on the basis of parallel developments in Nicholas' original treatises: (1) the hierarchy of four levels of reality, and (2) the relation of participation.

91 *Marg. in Parm.* ## 583–584 (on Proclus: *In Parm.* [M] 467. 73ff. / *In Parm.* 1207–1208).
92 *Marg. in Parm.* # 573 (on Proclus: *In Parm.* [M] 453. 55ff. / Proclus: *In Parm.* 1187) and # 576 (on Proclus: *In Parm.* [M] 454. 86ff. / Proclus: *In Parm.* 1188).
93 *Marg. in Parm.* # 588 (on Proclus: *In Parm.* 472. 76ff. / *In Parm.* 1211).
94 *Marg. in Parm.* # # 571–572 (on Proclus: *In Parm.* [M] 452. 10ff. / *In Parm.* 1185–1186) – at *Marg. in Parm.* # 581–582 (on Proclus: *In Parm.* [M] 469. 58ff. / Proclus: *In Parm.* 1207) the various senses of sameness are listed. It should be noted that Nicholas does not here – at least as evidenced by any *marginalia* – take up the parallel question with respect to otherness. However, cf. his comments on the One's "transcendence" (*supereminentia*) in *Marg. in Parm.* ## 566–568 (on Proclus: *In Parm.* [M] 450. 60ff. / Proclus: *In Parm.* 1183–1185).
95 *Marg. in Parm.* # 588 (on Proclus: *In Parm.* [M] 472. 76ff. / Proclus: *In Parm.* 1211).
96 *Marg. in Parm.* # 580 (on Proclus: *In Parm.* [M] 468. 27ff. / Proclus: *In Parm.* 1206).
97 For a description of this manuscript see Marx (1905).

That the hierarchy of four levels of reality presented in prop. 20 of the *Elementatio theologica* has caught Nicholas' attention is indicated by a sequence of short verbal notes and graphic symbols. He begins by noting Proclus' statement that the substance of "soul" (*anima*) is superior to all bodies, the nature of "intellect" (*intellectus*) superior to all souls, and "the One itself" (*ipsum unum*) superior to all intellectual hypostases.[98] His next comments draw attention to the fact that the two primary criteria used by the Greek writer to distinguish each higher level from the level below it are motion and participation. From the viewpoint of motion, body is moved by another, soul is self-moved, and intellect is unmoved; and from the viewpoint of participation, body is self-moved "by participation" (*secundum participationem*) and soul is self-moved "in essence" (*secundum essentiam*).[99] Nicholas continues by noting the original source's references to intellect as the "unmoved mover" (*movens immobilis*)[100] and as the cause of all knowing,[101] in the former case possibly shifting the original's meaning somewhat towards his own notion of a coincidence of opposites.[102]

The ideas concerning the hierarchy of four levels of reality developed in these *marginalia* are paralleled in the original writings of Nicholas of Cusa from a relatively early date.[103] There are also parallels in Nicholas' earlier writings to ideas concerning the relation of participation that occur in a further set of *marginalia*. For example, the teaching of *De docta ignorantia I*[104] that participation must be approached in terms of learned ignorance[105] has certain parallels in the *marginalia*. According to this teaching, the multiple and mediated relation of "participation" (*participatio*) between

98 *Marg. in El. theol.* # 8 (on Proclus: *El. theol.*, prop. 20 = *El. theol.* [M] 20. 1–3 / *El. theol.* 22. 1–3) (Dodds 1933). Moerbeke's translation (= M) will be cited in the edition and pagination of Boese (1987), Proclus' original in the edition of Dodds (1933).

99 *Marg. in El. theol.* ## 9–10 (on Proclus: *El. theol.*, prop. 20 = *El. theol.* [M] 20. 4–18 / *El. theol.* 22. 4–18). Nicholas makes a relatively insignificant substitution of *substantia* for *essentia*.

100 *Marg. in El. theol.* # 11 (on Proclus: *El. theol.*, prop. 20 = *El. theol.* [M] 20. 17–18 / *El. theol.* 22. 18).

101 *Marg. in El. theol.* # 12 (on Proclus: *El. theol.*, prop. 20 = *El. theol.* [M] 20. 27–29 / *El. theol.* 22. 26–28).

102 It is worth noting that Nicholas also comments on the hierarchy of four levels of reality as presented in the *Parmenides* commentary. At *Marg. in Parm.* # 167 (on Proclus: *In Parm.* [M] 151. 90ff. / Proclus: *In Parm.* 808) it is given an epistemological emphasis and combined with the doctrine of Plato's *Epistula II*. At *Marg. in Parm.* ## 69–71 (on Proclus: *In Parm.* [M] 98. 42ff. / Proclus: *In Parm.* 739–740) and ## 81–82 (on Proclus: *In Parm.* [M] 107. 16ff. / Proclus: *In Parm.* 749–753) the four levels are associated with types of opposition. At *Marg. in Parm.* # 144 (on Proclus: *In Parm.* [M] 142. 93ff. / Proclus: *In Parm.* 795–796) the four levels are intellect, soul, nature, and body.

103 For an example in an original work see p. 321, and for an example in an extract see p. 325.

104 *De doct. ign.* I. 17–18 (h I, 33. 1–37. 10) and *De doct. ign.* II. 4–5 (h I, 72. 23–78. 29). A much more elaborate discussion of participation along the same lines can be found at *De coni.* I. 11–13 (h III, 54. 1–69. 11).

105 *De doct. ign.* I. 17 (h I, 35. 1–12).

an unparticipated term and its participant(s) is transformed into a simple and immediate relation of "contraction" (*contractio*) between the absolute and contracted maximum,[106] thereby giving the traditional doctrine that everything is in everything else a novel sense.[107]

In fact, Nicholas' marginal notes on the *Elementatio theologicam* perhaps return to the question of participation more frequently than to any other topic. By drawing attention to the statements that "an effect participates in its cause" (*causatum participat causam*)[108] and is perfected by participation,[109] these *marginalia* identify participation with the basic form of causation that obtains within a hierarchical order of metaphysical principles. Nicholas also notes that participation can be conceived of as a threefold structure of unparticipated, participated, and participating terms or as a twofold structure of unparticipated and participated (or participating) terms, the "unparticipated" (*ametecton*) term being one not derived from any earlier term within its own series,[110] and the single unparticipated term and the multiplicity of participated terms together constituting that "series" (*seira*).[111] The annotator's attention is further drawn to Proclus' notion that the various structures of participation can be applied to different levels of reality. Thus, unity can be treated as the unparticipated unity, the participated unities, and the beings participating the unities,[112] while being, life, and intellect can be treated either as an unparticipated being, life, or intellect or as existent, living, and intellectual things.[113] Finally, Proclus' idea that the threefold structure of participation can be identified with other triads attracts the annotator's attention. For example, causation can be understood as a sequence comprising a whole before the parts, a

106 *De doct. ign.* II. 4 (h I, 72. 23–75. 18). The notion of an emanative hierarchy which is corrected by that of a process of contraction is here associated with Avicenna. The transformation of the one system into the other is mediated through the interpretation of the transcendent Forms as modalities of a single Form that is associated with Thierry of Chartres (see *De doct. ign.* I. 17 [h I, 33. 15–20]). This is shown by the introduction at this point, precisely along the lines of Thierry's Boethian commentaries, of a quotation of Plato's *Phaedo* via Calcidius.

107 *De doct. ign.* II. 5 (h I, 76. 1–78. 29).

108 *Marg. in El. theol.* # 27 (on Proclus: *El. theol.*, prop. 28 = *El. theol.* [M] 28. 9–10 / *El. theol.* 32. 20–21).

109 *Marg. in El. theol.* # 20 (on Proclus: *El. theol.* 25 = *El. theol.* [M] 25. 6–7 / *El. theol.* 28. 27–28).

110 *Marg. in El. theol.* # 59 (on Proclus: *El. theol.*, prop. 99 = *El. theol.* [M] 99. 5–6 / *El. theol.* 88. 24–25).

111 *Marg. in El. theol.* ## 60–61 (on Proclus: *El. theol.*, prop. 100 = *El. theol.* [M] 100. 1–7 / *El. theol.* 90. 1–6).

112 *Marg. in El. theol.* # 71 (on Proclus: *El. theol.*, prop. 137 = *El. theol.* [M] 137. 2–3 / *El. theol.* 120. 32–34). Cf. *Marg. in El. theol.* # 18 (on Proclus: *El. theol.* [M] 24. 11–13 / *El. theol.* 28. 18–20).

113 *Marg. in El. theol.* # 62 (on Proclus: *El. theol.*, prop. 101 = *El. theol.* [M] 101. 5–7 / *El. theol.* 90. 20–22).

whole of parts, and a whole in the part,[114] or as one comprising a term according to cause, a term according to substance, and a term according to participation.[115]

It is worth asking why Nicholas' *marginalia* on the *Elementatio theologica* are more abbreviated and sparse than those on the *Commentarius in Parmenidem*. It seems implausible to suggest that the philosophical ideas in the former work were simply of less interest to Nicholas than those in the latter. It is perhaps more reasonable to think that the axiomatic methodology of Proclus' treatise seemed inappropriate for articulating a paradoxical "Dionysian" theology. However, the real reasons for Nicholas' forbearance as a commentator with respect to the *Elementatio* may have been of a purely practical nature. After all, Proclus' treatise had clearly been studied extensively in the oral lectures of Heimeric de Campo, with whom Nicholas had studied in Cologne,[116] and had also been the subject of a massive written *expositio* by Berthold of Moosburg with which he had some acquaintance,[117] as well as having been a classic text among the German Albertists for over a century.[118] The *Commentarius in Parmenidem* was, by contrast, a document not yet absorbed into the mainstream.

The citations of Proclus in Nicholas of Cusa's own writings

The earliest of Nicholas of Cusa's original works to contain an explicit citation[119] of Proclus is *De beryllo* (1459).[120] The context is provided by Nicholas' characterization of the beryl that gives the work its title – a kind of optical instrument serving as a visual analogy for the coincidence

114 *Marg. in El. theol.* # 44 (on Proclus: *El. theol.*, prop. 69 = *El. theol.* [M] 69. 6–8 / *El. theol.* 64. 30–32).

115 *Marg. in El. theol.* # 66 (on Proclus: *El. theol.*, prop. 103 = *El. theol.* [M] 103. 5–6 / *El. theol.* 92. 17–18).

116 See Colomer (1961), 11–17 for Heimeric's use of Proclus' *Elementatio theologica* in works such as the *Compendium divinorum* and *Theoremata totius universi*. As Colomer shows ([1961], 1–46), Heimeric's work in general mirrors that of Nicholas in combining Proclean doctrines with Lullian methodology, although it is not easy to determine who influenced whom. See also Colomer (1964).

117 For a comparison of Berthold's and Nicholas' respective ways of reading Proclus see Riccati (1993).

118 On Nicholas and the Albertist tradition see Haubst (1952).

119 In this section we will concentrate upon *explicit citations* of Proclus. From 1459 onwards we also encounter frequent allusions (or possible allusions) to Proclus' works, the sermon-treatise *De aequalitate* being a particularly interesting case. See *De aequ.* 2 (h X 1, 5. 13–14 [= Senger 2001]) on the identification of intellect and the intelligible (cf. Proclus, *El. theol.* 167, 144. 22–23); *De aequ.* 4 (h X 1, 8. 9–11) on the transcendence by the *ens seu unum absolutum* of all quantity and quality (cf. Proclus, *In Parm.* 1047); and *De aequ.* 14 (h X 1, 19. 103) on the One as cause of itself and all things (cf. Proclus, *In Parm.* 1143. 37–39).

120 For brief listing and discussion of the texts in which Nicholas cites Proclus see Santinello (1966), 15–50; Santinello (1993); Cranz (1996); Beierwaltes (1998), 633–634; D'Amico (2007).

of opposites – as one of those mystical matters of which Plato forbids disclosure to the ignorant.[121] Nicholas then inserts a paraphrase of two passages in Plato's *Epistula II*.[122] In the first passage he notes the Greek philosopher's argument that all good things exist together with the King of all who represents their cause but that, when the human mind desires to understand what sort of things these are, it observes things related to them that are not self-sufficient and therefore different from the things in the King himself.[123] In the second passage he interprets the hierarchy of three principles mentioned by Plato as consisting of (1) the Father, God, or cause of all things which is a threefold efficient, formal, and final cause; (2) the beginning of all things, begotten as Son by the Father, the creative intellect which is the first creature, is the mediator between the primal cause and sensible caused things, and executes the will of the Father; and (3) the Spirit or motion connecting all things.[124] The evidence for Nicholas' familiarity with Leonardo Bruni's translation of Plato's *Epistulae* is strong.[125] However, the addition of the words "as Proclus adds" (*ut addit Proclus*) to the first citation suggests that one of the later Greek philosopher's own references to Plato in his *Commentarius in Parmenidem* is the indirect source for both passages.[126] Moreover, a later citation of the same *Epistula* within a more extensive treatment of Proclus reinforces this hypothesis.[127]

The sermon-treatise *Tu quis es?* (*De principio*), dating from the same year as the treatise mentioned above, documents a close reading of Proclus' *Commentarius in Parmenidem*.[128] In considering the important question whether the term "principle" (*principium*) can be applied to the One,[129] Proclus' discussion of the relations between the "self-constituted" (*authypostaton – per se subsistens*), the absolute One, and the transcendent Forms catches the cardinal's attention. The relation between the self-constituted and the absolute One is explained by saying, on the one hand, that the notion of self-constitution does not really befit the absolute One because

121 *De beryllo* 1 (h XI/1, 4. 1–4 [= Senger and Bormann 1988]).

122 Plato: *Epist. II*, 312e–313a (Burnet 1900–1907).

123 *De ber.* 15 (h XI/1, 14. 17–21).

124 *De ber.* 23 (h XI/1, 27. 19–28. 7). Both (1) and (2) are described as creative intellect in the present passage, (1) being creative in a non-mediating and (2) in a mediating sense. Of course, these ambiguities result from Nicholas' attempt to read Plato's triad as the Christian Trinity.

125 Nicholas' own copy of Bruni's translations of Plato's *Apologia Socratis*, *Crito*, and *Phaedo* is extant in the library of the St. Nicholas Hospital at Bernkastel.

126 At *De ber.* 11 (h XI/1, 12. 10–11) Nicholas explicitly cites "Proclus in his commentary on the *Parmenides*" (*Proculus . . . in commentariis Parmenidis*).

127 See *De non aliud* 20 (h XIII, 48. 17–20 [= Baur and Wilpert 1944]), where Nicholas refers to "Plato in the *Letters* which Proclus also summarizes in his commentary on the *Parmenides*" (*Plato in epistolis . . . quae Proculus quoque in Parmenides commentariis resumit*).

128 For discussion of this text see Cranz (1996) and Bormann (2001).

129 *De principio* (h X 2b, 19. 1–16 [= Bormann and Riemann 1994]).

self-constitution implies duality and division whereas the absolute One is prior to all "otherness" (*alteritas*).[130] On the other hand, the concept of self-constitution befits the absolute One more truly than it does anything else, given that in comparison with that cause none of the other things caused either exists or is determinate "in itself" (*per se*).[131] The relation between the self-constituted and the transcendent Forms is explained by noting that the term "self-constituted" befits the First only to the extent that it is the cause of things that are self-constituted.[132] These self-constituted things are primarily the "Forms" (*species*) – for example, that of man – that are enfolded in the First as in their cause or fount but unfolded eternally or intellectually in Eternity and temporally or sensibly in the eternal world.[133] Nicholas' interpretation of the relation between the self-constituted and the absolute One is broadly in line with the views of the ancient Platonist. However, the cardinal's interpretation of the relation between the self-constituted and the transcendent Forms, apparently based on the use of the prefix "in itself" in both cases,[134] represents a significant departure from Proclus' own teaching.

The argument about the nature of self-constitution leads into a more extensive discussion of the question – also raised by the *Commentarius in Parmenidem* – whether there is a multiplicity of self-subsistent principles co-eternal with the absolute One.[135] Nicholas' general strategy here is to turn Zeno's and Parmenides' refutation of plurality against Proclus himself, although some of the ancient Platonist's more specific arguments are seen in a positive light. In one passage the cardinal argues in opposition to Proclus that there cannot be a multiplicity of things co-eternal with the One – except in the case of "its own three hypostases" (*tres suae hypostases*)[136] – because the eternal is equivalent to Eternity, which itself cannot be multiplied.[137] Elsewhere, Nicholas adopts Proclus' usual metaphysical distinction between the "unparticipated" (*imparticipabile*) One and the "participated" (*participabile*) One[138] but transforms it subtly by associating the former with "existence itself" (*ipsum esse*) and the latter

[130] *De princ.* (h X 2b, 20. 1–3). Cf. Proclus, *In Parm.* (M) 424. 19ff. (Steel 1982–1985) (*In Parm.* 1150, 1183–1184 [Steel 2007–2009]).

[131] *De princ.* (h X 2b, 20. 3–9).

[132] *De princ.* (h X 2b, 24. 1–3).

[133] *De princ.* (h X 2b, 24. 3–7) and *De princ.* (h X 2b, 21). Cf. Proclus, *In Parm.* (M) 145. 2ff.; 147. 37ff.; 392. 46ff.

[134] In the case of the self-constituted, the phrase "in itself" normally has an existential sense, whereas in that of the transcendent Forms it is used in a predicative manner. Proclus treats these two usages of the prefix *auto-* as quite distinct.

[135] *De princ.* (h X 2b, 25. 1–30. 22).

[136] I.e. the three persons of the Trinity.

[137] *De princ.* (h X 2b, 25. 1–3).

[138] *De princ.* (h X 2b, 28. 1–13). Cf. Proclus, *In Parm.* (M) 71. 11–72. 31 and 75, 24ff.

with "any existent thing" (*quodlibet entium*),[139] and also by suggesting that the former has multiplicity "enfolded" (*complicari*) within it.[140] In another passage the cardinal argues in agreement with Proclus that no determination can be assigned to God – who is above both affirmation and negation – although we may apply the name of "one" to him not through intellectual thinking but "somehow divining his subsistence" (*divinando aliqualiter hypostasim eius*) through our endless desire for unity.[141]

The dialogue *Directio speculantis sive De non aliud* (1461) provides even more striking evidence of Proclus' importance in Nicolas' mind. This evidence is composed in the first instance by the work's dramatic setting, for it is reported near the beginning of the text that the four interlocutors – whose number makes the work, technically speaking, into a "tetralogue" (*tetralogus*) – have all been occupied with profound studies. The interlocutors and their studies are identified as "the Abbot" – John Andrea Vigevius, abbot of Sezadium, who has been occupied with Plato's *Parmenides* and Proclus' *Commentarius in Parmenidem*; "Peter" – Pietro Balbi of Pisa, later bishop of Tropaea – who has been devoting himself to Proclus' *Theologia Platonis* which he is translating into Latin; "Ferdinand" – Ferdinand Matim of Portugal, the cardinal's personal physician – who has been busy with Aristotle; and "Nicholas" – Nicholas of Cusa himself – who has been continuing his studies of Dionysius the Areopagite.[142] Each of the interlocutors comes to prominence somewhere in the text, and the intervention of "Peter" is especially significant. At this point the Pisan scholar explains that he has been translating "Proclus the Platonist" (*Proculus ille Platonicus*) into Latin and that, since he has found many similarities of doctrine and expression with the Dionysian material summarized earlier by Nicholas, he would like to have some more information about Proclus' *Theologia Platonica.* Nicholas replies by saying that it is certain that Proclus lived at a later date than did Dionysius, although it is uncertain whether the Platonist had actually read any of the writings by St. Paul's famous convert.[143]

The actual discussion of Proclus' doctrine begins in chapter 20 of the dialogue and forms part of an argument to prove that the *quasi*-concept[144]

139 *De princ.* (h X 2b, 29. 1–4). 140 *De princ.* (h X 2b, 30. 1–5).

141 *De princ.* (h X 2b, 26. 1–27. 11). For the One as unnameable see Proclus, *In Parm.* (M) 456. 49ff.; 514. 44ff., and 518. 72ff.; for the One as above negation and affirmation see *In Parm.* (M) 403. 16ff. and 519. 2ff.; for the inapplicability of the name "one" to the First see *In Parm.* (M) 511. 60ff., and for the applicability of the name "one" because of the First's desirability see *In Parm.* (M) 511. 60ff.

142 *De non aliud* 1–2 (h XIII, 3. 1–6. 27) (Baur and Wilpert 1944).

143 *De non aliud* 20 (h XIII, 47. 16–26).

144 See p. 341 and n. 157. Nicholas himself describes the non-other most frequently as an "enigma" (*aenigma*) at *De non aliud* 5 (h XIII, 12. 2), 8 (h XIII, 18. 22), and 11 (h XIII, 23. 24).

of "non-other" (*non aliud*), although suggested by one of Aristotle's texts,[145] only comes into play in an adequate form in the writings of Plato, Dionysius, and Proclus.[146] As developed in this dialogue, the *non aliud*[147] is a later variant on the theme of coincidence of opposites that had always been so important for Nicholas.[148] Like the coincidence of opposites, the *non aliud* occurs with two distinguishable but interconnected emphases, depending on whether it is seen more metaphysically as the simultaneous transcendence and immanence of God or the simultaneous inherence of his attributes, or else more methodologically as a symbolic pointer towards this incomprehensible Deity.[149] In the present dialogue[150] the first metaphysical sense of *non aliud* is associated with Proclus when the One is said to be "not other than" (*non aliud quam*) the One-Being, the Being not other than beings, and the Cause not other than the caused,[151] and the second metaphysical sense of *non aliud* with Proclus when attribute x is said to be "not other than" (*non aliud quam*) attribute y in the first principle but other than the attribute y in the second principle.[152] The relation to the ancient Platonist is made less explicit in the methodological than in the metaphysical sense of the non-other. This methodological sense of *non aliud* emerges when Nicholas argues that the non-other is not yet another name of the

145 See Aristotle: *Metaph.* B. 1, 996a5–9 and Z. 1, 1028b 2–4 (Ross 1924) quoted at *De non aliud* 18 (h XIII, 44. 1–18).

146 For reasons of space, we can only take up the question of the relation to Proclus here. At *De non aliud* 20 (h XIII, 48. 1–4) Nicholas notes as a general characteristic of Proclus' mode of thinking the constant search for prior terms: for example, Intellect prior to Soul, and the One prior to Intellect.

147 On the interpretation of this difficult notion in Nicholas' work see especially Wyller (1970); Beierwaltes (1970); Beierwaltes (1977), 14–28; Beierwaltes (1987), 291, n. 7; Beierwaltes (1998), 645ff. Wyller's essay argues well for the close relation between the non-other and infinity, but less convincingly for the derivation of the idea from George of Trebizond's complete translation of the *Parmenides.* Beierwaltes' contribution suggestively explores the status of the non-other as an "absolute concept." Unfortunately, even Beierwaltes' more sensitive reading tends to miss or evade the really important point: that the non-other (as a later variant of the coincidence of opposites) stands on the borderline between metaphysical concept and methodological tool and ushers in a hermeneutic of an almost "proto-Heideggerian" character. See, however, Beierwaltes (1977), 38–39.

148 It also has affinities with the enigma of "identity" (*idem*) discussed in Nicholas' of Cusa's *De genesi.* See the comments at *De non aliud* 5 (h XIII, 13. 13–14) to the effect that "this" (*hoc*), "that" (*id*), and "the same" (*idem*) imitate the non-other.

149 The non-other also shares with the coincidence of opposites the possibility of being compared with an optical device. See *De non aliud* 8 (h XIII, 18. 24–28) and 11 (h XIII, 23. 27–25. 17).

150 Nicholas assumes a general connection with Proclus at this point without citing specific texts. See *De non aliud* 20 (h XIII, 48. 17–20) and *De non aliud* 22 (h XIII, 52. 14–24). However, the notion that the One is *not* other in the sense of being above "otherness" (*heterotēs*) is common in the *Commentary on the Parmenides.* See Proclus, *In Parm.* (M) 442. 71ff.

151 *De non aliud* 20 (h XIII, 48. 20–49. 14). Cf. *De non aliud* 6 (h XIII, 13. 22–15. 7).

152 *De non aliud* 10 (h XIII, 21. 13–23. 9); 15 (h XIII, 38. 10–40. 11); 16 (h XIII, 41. 22–29). Nicholas also applies the non-other to the relation between the persons of the Trinity at *De non aliud* 5 (h XIII, 12. 15–27).

First but that "through" (*per*) which he discloses the name(s),[153] and he shows that the non-other is not itself a concept[154] but stands between a concept fusing opposite notions[155] and an expression combining different words.[156] In fact, the non-other performs in a more obvious manner the role of a "symbol" (*symbolon/sunthēma*) pointing to the First that the Greek Platonist had attributed to the name of unity.[157]

The treatise *De venatione sapientiae* (1462) is the first of the cardinal's works to reveal a close reading of Proclus' *Theologia Platonica*.[158] Here, the connection between the human soul and the Deity through the mediation of the "intelligible Idea" (*intelligibilis idea*) is noted,[159] as also the notion that the intellective soul sees God and all things within itself, the latter point being referred back to Plato's *Alcibiades*.[160] Attention is paid to the details of Proclus' theology where being, life, and intellect are treated as "creating gods" (*conditores dei*),[161] where the second god is called the "cause of beings" (*causa entium*)[162] or the "creative intellect" (*conditor intellectus*)[163] and is identified with Jupiter,[164] and where numerous "celestial, cosmic, and other eternal gods" (*caelestes et mundani et alii . . . aeterni dei*) are established.[165]

153 *De non aliud* 22 (h XIII, 52. 9–13) – note especially the remark: "But regarding the First itself, I reveal to you the name of my concept through the 'non other' itself" (*sed de ipso primo conceptus mei nomen per ipsum "non aliud" tibi patefacio*) at *De non aliud* 22 (h XIII, 52. 11–12). Cf. *De non aliud* 24 (h XIII, 58. 4–5), where the non-other reveals the "way" (*via*) to the First.

154 At *De non aliud* 20 (h XIII, 49. 16–27) it is argued that the non-other cannot be conceived, is above concept, and is an absolute concept.

155 See *De non aliud* 5 (h XIII, 11. 6–28), 7 (h XIII, 15. 14–30), and 22 (h XIII, 52. 14–53. 4) for sameness and difference and *De non aliud* 7 (h XIII, 16. 15–22) for conjunction and disjunction.

156 Unlike the conventional divine names, *non* + *aliud* is an inherent duality.

157 See pp. 339–340 and n. 144. Cf. also the references to *hen* and *Ad Ad* as symbols in this manner at Proclus, *In Parm.* 50 and 60 (Klibansky and Labowsky 1953).

158 The work is cited by name at *De venatione sapientiae* 8 (h XII, 21. 9 [Klibansky and Senger 1982]) and 22 (h XII, 62. 8–9). At *De ven. sap.* 22 (h XII, 62. 16–17) Nicholas notes that Proclus "came after Dionysius" (*post Dionysium venit*), the evidence for this being that he cites Origen (i.e. in *Theologia Platonica* II. 4).

159 *De ven. sap.* 1 (h XII, 3. 11–16). See Proclus, *Theol. Plat.* II. 7, 47. 11–27. It is not always possible to determine the exact passages in Proclus' work that are being cited. However, Nicholas' *marginalia* to the *Theologia Platonica* – to be discussed below – often provide a clue. Some of these will be cited in the notes to follow.

160 *De ven. sap.* 17 (h XII, 49. 3–7). See Proclus, *Theol. Plat.* I. 3, 15–16. Cf. *Marg. in Theol. Plat.* ## 10–12. For Nicholas' earlier use of this passage see above.

161 *De ven. sap.* 8 (h XII, 21. 1). See Proclus, *Theol. Plat.* III. 6, 24, and 29 and IV. 3, 15. Cf. Nicholas of Cusa, *Marg. in Theol. Plat.* ## 198–199 and 261.

162 *De ven. sap.* 8 (h XII, 21. 4). See Proclus, *Theol. Plat.* III. 10, 9–10. Cf. Nicholas of Cusa, *Marg. in Theol. Plat.* # 219.

163 *De ven. sap.* 8 (h XII, 21. 6). See Proclus, *Theol. Plat.* V. 3, 15–17 and V. 16, 57–59. Cf. Nicholas of Cusa, *Marg. in Theol. Plat.* ## 322 and 347.

164 *De ven. sap.* 8 (h XII, 21. 6–7). See Proclus, *Theol. Plat.* IV. 5, 21 and V. 3, 15–17. Cf. Nicholas of Cusa, *Marg. in Theol. Plat.* ## 263 and 322.

165 *De ven. sap.* 8 (h XII, 21. 7–8). See Proclus, *Theol. Plat.* I. 10, 43. Cf. Nicholas of Cusa, *Marg. in Theol. Plat.* # 26.

Nicholas explicitly cites the *Theologia Platonica* for these doctrines,[166] and also for the notions that the creative intellect is called "word" (*logos*),[167] that the "one-many" (*unum plura*) is one in essence but many in power,[168] and that "limit" (*finitum*) and "infinity" (*infinitum*) immediately follow the One.[169] As a general characterization of this theology, he notes that those terms which Christians attribute to the one God differing "only according to reason and by no means in reality" (*non nisi ratione et nequaquam re differentia*) are declared by Proclus to be "different gods according to the differential relation among attributes" (*deos asserere diversos propter diversam attributorum rationem*).[170] Finally, the denial of unity and goodness to the First because of the latter's complete ineffability is noted,[171] as also the notion that the absolute One is in a certain sense "intelligible in itself" (*per se intelligibile*), Proclus being said to follow Dionysius on the former point.[172]

The *marginalia* to Proclus' *Theologia Platonica*

The primarily doxographical character of these references to Proclus' *Theologia Platonica* is reflected in the *marginalia* written by Nicholas in his copy of Pietro Balbi's translation.[173] Among his *marginalia* to book I, Nicholas draws attention to Proclus' historical account of ancient Greek theology as a continuous tradition transmitted from Orpheus through

[166] *De ven. sap.* 8 (h XII, 21. 9) "in his six-book *'On Plato's Theology'*" (*in sex libris de Theologia Platonis*).

[167] *De ven. sap.* 9 (h XII, 24. 1–3). See Proclus, *Theol. Plat.* II. 9, 59. Cf. Nicholas of Cusa, *Marg. in Theol. Plat.* # 182.

[168] *De ven. sap.* 12 (h XII, 31. 16–17). See Proclus, *Theol. Plat.* III. 9, 39 and IV. 35–36, 104–106. Cf. Nicholas of Cusa, *Marg. in Theol. Plat.* ## 222 and 302.

[169] *De ven. sap.* 29 (h XII. 88. 14–17). See Proclus, *Theol. Plat.* III. 8, 31–32 and 34. Cf. Nicholas of Cusa, *Marg. in Theol. Plat.* ## 201–207.

[170] *De ven. sap.* 8 (h XII, 21. 10–17). In an important gloss Nicholas goes on to contrast the Peripatetic and Platonic approaches on this question.

[171] *De ven. sap.* 22 (h XII, 64. 8–12). Nicholas here notes that Proclus summarizes Plato's doctrine in the *Parmenides* (i.e. in Proclus' *Platonic Theology* II) regarding the primacy of the negative method. See Proclus, *Theol. Plat.* II. 9. 60. Cf. Nicholas of Cusa, *Marg. in Theol. Plat.* # 184.

[172] *De ven. sap* 36 (h XII, 107. 11–14). See Proclus, *Theol. Plat.* II. 4, 33. Cf. Nicholas of Cusa, *Marg. in Theol. Plat.* ## 157–158.

[173] MS *Cusanus Hospitalis S. Nicolai 185.* This contains, according to the editor's count, 390 *marginalia*. According to an MS note, the first version of this translation was completed on March 22, 1462. Further copies of the translation are in MSS London, British Library, *Harleiensis 3262* and Bergamo, Biblioteca civica, *Gamma IV.* For details of these see Saffrey (1955); Saffrey (1979); Saffrey and Westerink (1968–1997), vol. 1, viii ff.

Aglaophamos and Pythagoras to Plato,[174] and to his explanation that the "name of 'god'" (*denominatio deorum*) was applied by Plato not only to super-substantial but also to intellectual and to psychic things,[175] two comments that suggest the possibility of treating pagan religion as an external symbolization of the inner truth of Christianity. One of Nicholas' glosses on *Theologia Platonica* II marks Proclus' statement that the One surpasses both sameness and difference with the comment: "in place of the 'non-other'" (*pro non aliud*),[176] the abbreviated nature of this remark suggesting that Nicholas is relating his own doctrine subsequently to Proclus' text rather than deriving it from that source in the first place.[177] Most of the *marginalia* on book III deal with questions that were also the subject of the cardinal's annotations on the *Commentarius in Parmenidem*, although one is struck by the extent to which Nicholas draws attention to the triadic structures in Proclus' account of the intelligible world.[178] One of Nicholas' glosses on *Theologia Platonica* IV notes "the coincidence of contraries in the one" (*coincidentia oppositorum in uno*) implied by Proclus' description of the second triad of the intelligible-and-intellectual sphere,[179] there being no doubt that Nicholas is here relating his own long-established doctrine subsequently to Proclus' text rather than deriving it from that source in the first place. Among his *marginalia* to book V, Nicholas draws attention to Proclus' observation that Socrates was being humorous in describing the relations between the gods Saturn and Jupiter in the *Cratylus*,[180] and to his advocacy of the hermeneutic principle that myths are "demonstrative of mystical

[174] Nicholas of Cusa, *Marg. in Theol. Plat* # 21 (Proclus, *Theol. Plat.* I. 5, 25). Balbi's translation will be cited in the edition (extracts) of Senger (1986). Proclus' original is in the edition of Saffrey and Westerink (1968–1997).

[175] *Marg. in Theol. Plat.* ## 123–124 (Proclus, *Theol. Plat.* I. 26, 114–116). Possibly connected with this note is Nicholas' reference at *De non aliud* 20 (h XIII, 48. 1–3) to Proclus' teaching that Plato was a humanized god.

[176] *Marg. in Theol. Plat.* # 190 (Proclus, *Theol. Plat.* II. 12, 70).

[177] It is because the notion expressed by Proclus in his text actually corresponds to only one aspect of Nicholas' "not-other" that this passage alone could not have been the source of the latter's extremely complex *quasi*-concept. At *Marg. in Theol. Plat.* ## 143 and 174–175 (Proclus, *Theol. Plat.* II. 3, 26 and II. 7, 48, and 50), Nicholas seems to draw attention deliberately to a similar phrase "nothing other" (*nihil aliud*) in Balbi's translation expressing the self-identity of the One. A similar passage speaking of the self-identity of the "mixed" occurs in *Marg. in Theol. Plat.* # 208 on book III (Proclus, *Theol. Plat.* III. 9, 35).

[178] See *Marg. in Theol. Plat.* ## 231, 237–240, 245, 249–250, 253–254, 257 (Proclus, *Theol. Plat.* III. 11, 44; III. 13, 47; III. 18, 61; III. 22, 79; III. 24, 84–85; III. 27, 94), etc. As in the case of Plato's *Epistula II*, Platonic triads are presumed to be intimations of the Christian Trinity.

[179] *Marg. in Theol. Plat.* # 302 (Proclus, *Theol. Plat.* IV. 35–36, 105).

[180] *Marg. in Theol. Plat.* # 320 (Proclus, *Theol. Plat.* V. 3, 15–17).

doctrines" (*mysticarum sententiarum demonstrativa*),[181] two comments that explain his own preoccupation with the pagan theology expounded in this book.

The majority of the extensive *marginalia* on book V – totaling seventy-six in the modern editor's enumeration – call attention to the general doctrine of divine intellection. Here, Nicholas' comments on the ancient Platonist's account of the so-called intellectual gods may be assigned to two broad categories relating to the hierarchical status of intellect and to the nature of intellect's activity respectively, the former category especially representing an avenue of thinking that the cardinal had not pursued in his earlier sets of annotations.[182] The hierarchical status of intellect is particularly at issue in *marginalia* dealing with the relations between Saturn, Rhea, and Jupiter corresponding to those between the three terms of the first triad of the intellectual gods,[183] with the relation between the "creator god" (*conditor deus*) and the "paradigm" (*exemplar*) corresponding to that between the third term of the first triad of the intellectual gods and the third triad of the intelligible gods,[184] and with the relations between Jupiter = the creator god and Soul, the cosmic gods, and the visible world corresponding to those between the third term of the first triad of the intellectual gods and the various super-mundane and mundane principles.[185] Nicholas is clearly attempting to read the complex divine hierarchy described by Proclus – which comprises at least twenty-five terms ($2 \times 9 + 7$) when the intelligible-and-intellectual gods are included – as equivalent to the second of the three principles mentioned in Plato's *Epistula II*.[186] Moreover, it is

181 *Marg. in Theol. Plat.* # 328 (Proclus, *Theol. Plat.* V. 3, 17–19).

182 Because the latter category represents less of an innovation we will not discuss it here. However, the reader may like to examine *Marg. in Theol. Plat.* ## 321 and 336 (Proclus, *Theol. Plat.* V. 3, 15–17; V. 5, 22–23) (relation between intellection and desire), ## 334–337 (Proclus, *Theol. Plat.* V. 5, 20–23) (self-intellection = intellection of the prior), ## 340 and 361 (Proclus, *Theol. Plat.* V. 5, 23–24 and V. 17, 62–63) (simultaneity of intellection), # 351 (Proclus, *Theol. Plat.* V. 16, 57–59) (intellection as limit, infinity, and mixed), ## 359 and 362 (Proclus, *Theol. Plat.* V. 17, 60–62 and V. 17, 62–64) (contrast between intellection and ratiocination).

183 See *Marg. in Theol. Plat.* ## 315–318, 321–325, 333, 339–341 (Proclus, *Theol. Plat.* V. 3, 14–17; V. 5, 20–24).

184 See *Marg. in Theol. Plat.* ## 345, 350, 354–355, 360, 365, 372 (Proclus, *Theol. Plat.* V. 16, 54–55; V. 17, 62–64; V. 19–20, 71–76). Strictly speaking, the third member of the intellectual triad is not itself divided into a further triad, the result being a hebdomatic rather than enneadic structure for the intellectual triad as a whole.

185 See *Marg. in Theol. Plat.* ## 322, 349–350, 352, 365, 369, 372, 374 (Proclus, *Theol. Plat.* V. 3, 15–17; V. 16, 52–60; V. 19–20, 71–76).

186 See *Marg. in Theol. Plat.* # 338 (Proclus, *Theol. Plat.* V. 5, 22–23) where the interpretation of Plato's letter by "noble Amelius" (*nobilis Amelius*) occasions the note.

undoubtedly because of the intertextual relation established between the texts of Proclus and Plato that the cardinal is willing to find Trinitarian allusions in Proclus' frequent references to the paternal function[187] and occasional references to the connective function of the different intellects.[188] With this extensive discussion of the intellectual hierarchy in mind, it is interesting to speculate on the direction that Nicholas' thought might have taken under the influence of the *Theologia Platonica* if his literary career had not come to an end only two years after receiving his copy of its Latin translation.

Bibliography

Baur, L. (ed.) (1940–1941) *Cusanus-Texte III, Marginalien, 1. Nicolaus Cusanus und Ps.-Dionysius im Lichte der Zutate und Randbemerkungen des Cusanus = Sitzungsberichte der Heidelberger Akademie der Wissenschaften, phil.-hist. Klasse* 4, Heidelberg.

Baur, L. and Wilpert, P. (eds.) (1944) Nicholas of Cusa, *Directio speculantis seu De non aliud (Opera omnia XIII)*, Leipzig.

Beierwaltes, W. (1964) "Deus oppositio oppositorum (Nicolaus Cusanus, *De visione Dei xiii*)," *Salzburger Jahrbuch für Philosophie* 8: 175–185.

(1970) "Cusanus und Proklos. Zum neuplatonischen Ursprung des non-aliud," in *Nicolò Cusano agli inizi del mondo moderno, Atti del Congresso internazionale in occasione del V centenario della morte di Nicolò Cusano, Bressanone 6–10 settembre 1964*, Florence, 137–140.

(1977) *Identität und Differenz, Zum Prinzip cusanischen Denkens (Rheinisch-Westfälische Akademie der Wissenschaften*, G 220), Opladen.

(1985) *Denken des Einen, Studien zur neuplatonischen Philosophie und ihrer Wirkungsgeschichte*, Frankurt a. M.

(1987) "Das seiende Eine, Zur neuplatonischen Interpretation der zweiten Hypothesis des platonischen Parmenides: das Beispiel Cusanus," in G. Boss and G. Seel (eds.), *Proclus et son influence, Actes du colloque de Neuchâtel, juin 1985*, Zurich, 287–297.

(1988) *Visio facialis, Sehen ins Angesicht: Zur Coincidenz des endlichen und unendlichen Blicks bei Cusanus*, Munich.

(1997) *Der verborgene Gott: Cusanus und Dionysius*, Trier.

(1998) *Platonismus im Christentum*, Frankfurt a. M.

[187] See *Marg. in Theol. Plat.* ## 318, 343, 349 (Proclus, *Theol. Plat.* V. 3, 14–15; V. 16, 54–55; V. 16, 57–59).

[188] See *Marg. in Theol. Plat.* ## 366–367 (Proclus, *Theol. Plat.* V. 19–20, 73–74). Cf. also *Marg. in Theol. Plat.* # 365 (Proclus, *Theol. Plat.* V. 19–20, 71–73) noting Proclus' reference to the visible cosmos as "only-begotten" (*unigenitum*).

(2000) "Centrum Tocius Vite: zur Bedeutung von Proklos' *Theologia Platonis* im Denken des Cusanus," in A.-Ph. Segonds and C. Steel (eds.), *Proclus et la Théologie platonicienne, Actes du colloque international de Louvain (13–16 mai 1998) en l'honneur de H.-D. Saffrey and L. G. Westerink*, Leuven and Paris, 629–651.

Boese, H. (ed.) (1987) Proclus, *Elementatio theologica translata a Guillelmo de Morbecca*, Leuven.

Bormann, K. (ed.) (1986) *Cusanus-Texte III, Marginalien, 2. Proclus Latinus: Die Exzerpte und Randnoten des Nikolaus von Kues zu den lateinischen Übersetzungen der Proclus-Schriften, 2.2 Expositio in Parmenidem Platonis*, Heidelberg.

(2001) "Affirmation und Negation: Der *Parmenides*-Kommentar des Proklos in Nikolaus von Kues' Schrift *Tu quis es*," *600 Jahre Nikolaus von Kues (1401–2001), Tradition und Aktualität Negativer Theologie = Theologische Quartalschrift* 181: 84–96.

Bormann, K. and Riemann, A. D. (eds.) (1994) Nicholas of Cusa, *Opuscula II. 2, De Deo unitrino principio, De Theologicis Complementis (Opera omnia X/2a)*, Hamburg.

Burnet, J. (ed.) (1900–1907) *Platonis Opera*, 5 vols., Oxford.

Colomer, E. (1961) *Nikolaus von Kues und Raimund Llull, Aus Handschriften der Kueser Bibliothek*, Berlin.

(1964) "Nikolaus von Kues und Heimeric van den Velde," *Das Cusanus-Jubiläum in Bernkastel-Kues vom 8. bis 12. August 1964 =Mitteilungen und Forschungsbeiträge der Cusanus-Gesellschaft* 4: 198–213.

Cousin, V. (ed.) (1864) *Procli philosophi Platonici opera inedita*, 2nd edn., Paris.

Cranz, F. E. (1996) "The *De aequalitate* and *De principio* of Nicholas of Cusa," in G. Christianson and T. M. Izbicki (eds.), *Nicholas of Cusa on Christ and the Church, Essays in Memory of Chandler McCuskey Brooks for the American Cusanus Society*, Leiden, 271–280.

D'Amico, C. (2007) "Nikolaus von Kues als Leser von Proklos," in K. Reinhardt and H. Schwaetzer (eds.), *Nikolaus von Kues in der Geschichte des Platonismus*, Regensburg, 33–64.

De Gandillac, M. (1972) "Les conjectures de Nicolas de Cues," *Revue de métaphysique et de morale* 77: 356–364.

Dodds, E. R. (ed.) (1933) *Proclus: The Elements of Theology*, Oxford; 2nd edn. 1963.

Flasch, K. (1972) "Nikolaus von Kues, Die Idee der Koinzidenz," in J. Speck (ed.), *Grundprobleme der grossen Phiosophen, Philosophie des Altertums und des Mittelalters*, Göttingen, 221–261.

(1998) *Nikolaus von Kues, Geschichte einer Entwicklung*, Frankfurt a. M.

Gersh, S. (2012) "Rewriting the *Proslogion*. Nicholas of Cusa's Transformation of Anselm of Canterbury's Proof of the Existence of God," *Epekeina: International Journal of Ontology, History and Critics* 1: 1–40.

Haubst, R. (1952) "Zum Fortleben Alberts des Grossen bei Heymerich von Kamp und Nikolaus von Kues," in H. Ostlender (ed.), *Studia Albertina, Festschrift für Bernard Geyer zum 70. Geburtstage = Beiträge zur Geschichte der Philosophie und Theologie des Mittelalters, Suppl.-Bd.* 4, Münster, 420–447.

(1961) "Die Thomas- und Proklos-Exzerpte des 'Nicolaus Treverensis' in codicillus Strassburg 84," *Mitteilungen und Forschungsbeiträge der Cusanus-Gesellschaft* 1: 17–51.

(1970) "Zur Interpretation von *De coniecturis*. Zusammenfassende theologische Erwägungen," *Mitteilungen und Forschungsbeiträge der Cusanus-Gesellschaft* 8: 192–198.

(1989) "Die erkenntnistheoretische und mystische Bedeutung der 'Mauer der Koinzidenz'," *Mitteilungen und Forschungsbeiträge der Cusanus-Gesellschaft* 18: 167–195.

Hoffmann, E. and Klibansky, R. (eds.) (1932) Nicholas of Cusa, *De docta ignorantia (Opera omnia I)*, Leipzig.

Klibansky, R. (1928–1929) "Ein Proklos-Fund und seine Bedeutung," *Sitzungsberichte der Heidelberger Akademie der Wissenschaften, philos.-hist. Klasse* 5, Heidelberg.

(ed.) (1932) Nicholas of Cusa, *Apologia doctae ignorantiae (Opera omnia II)*, Leipzig; 2nd edn., Hamburg 2007.

(1943) "Plato's *Parmenides* in the Middle Ages and the Renaissance, A Chapter in the History of Platonic Studies," *Mediaeval and Renaissance Studies* 1.2: 281–335.

Klibansky, R. and Labowsky, C. (eds.) (1953) *Parmenides usque ad finem primae hypothesis nec non Procli Commentarium in Parmenidem, pars ultima adhuc inedita interprete Guillelmo de Moerbeke*, London.

Klibansky, R. and Senger, H.-G. (eds.) (1982) Nicholas of Cusa, *De venatione sapientiae, De apice theoriae (Opera omnia XII)*, Hamburg.

Koch, J. (1956) *Die Ars coniecturalis des Nikolaus von Kues*, Cologne.

Koch, J., Bormann, K., and Senger, H.-G. (eds.) (1972) Nicholas of Cusa, *De coniecturis (Opera omnia III)*, Hamburg.

McTighe, T. P. (1980) "Thierry of Chartres and Nicholas of Cusa's Epistemology," *Proceedings of the PMR Conference (Villanova University)*, 5: 169–176.

Marx, J. (1905) *Verzeichnis der Handschriften-Sammlung des Hospitals zu Cues bei Bernkastel a. Mosel.* Trier. Reprinted Frankfurt a. Main 1966.

Monfasani, J. (1987) "Pseudo-Dionysius the Areopagite in Mid-Quattrocento Rome," in J. Hankins, J. Monfasani, and F. Purnell (eds.), *Supplementum Festivum, Studies in Honor of Paul Oskar Kristeller*, Binghamton, NY, 189–219.

Nicholas of Cusa (1932–2005) Nicolai de Cusa, *Opera omnia iussu et auctoritate academiae litterarum Heidelbergensis*, Leipzig and Hamburg.

Riccati, C. (1993) "La presenza di Proclo tra neoplatonismo arabizzante e tradizione dionisiana (Bertholdo di Moosburg e Niccolò Cusano," in G. Piaia (ed.), *Concordia Discors, Studi su Niccolò Cusano e l'umanesimo Europeo offerti a G. Santinello*, Padua, 23–38.

Riemann, A. D. (ed.) (2000) Nicholas of Cusa, *De visione Dei (Opera omnia VI)*, Hamburg.

Ross, W. D. (ed.) (1924) *Aristotle's Metaphysics*, 2 vols., Oxford.
Ruocco, I. (2003) *Il Platone latino: Il Parmenide, Giorgio di Trebisonda e il cardinale Cusano*, Florence.
Saffrey, H.-D. (1955) "Sur la tradition manuscrite de la *Théologie platonicienne* de Proclus," *Autour d'Aristote, Recueil d'études de philosophie ancienne et médiévale offert à Monseigneur A. Mansion*, Leuven, 387–430.
(1979) "Pietro Balbi et la première traduction latine de la *Théologie platonicienne* de Proclus," in P. Cockshaw, M.-C. Garand, and P. Jodogne (eds.), *Miscellanea Codicologica F. Masai dicata MCMLXXIX*, vol. 1, Ghent, 425–437. Reprinted in Saffrey (1987), 189–201.
(1987) *Recherches sur la tradition platonicienne au Moyen Âge et à la Renaissance*, Paris.
Saffrey, H.-D. and Westerink, L. G. (eds.) (1968–1997) *Proclus: Théologie platonicienne*, 6 vols., Paris.
Santinello, G. (1966) *Saggi sull "umanesimo" di Proclo*, Bologna.
(1993) 'Il neoplatonismo di Niccolò Cusano', in P. Prini (ed.), *Il Neoplatonismo nel Rinascimento*, Rome, 103–115.
Senger, H.-G. (ed.) (1986) *Cusanus-Texte III, Marginalien, 2. Proclus Latinus, Die Exzerpte und Randnoten des Nikolaus von Kues zu den lateinischen Übersetzungen der Proclus-Schriften, 2.1 Theologia Platonis, Elementatio theologica*, Heidelberg.
(ed.) (2001) Nicholas of Cusa, *De aequalitate (Opera omnia X/1)*, Hamburg.
(2002) *Ludus sapientiae. Studien zum Werk und zur Wirkungsgeschichte des Nikolaus von Kues*, Leiden, Boston, and Cologne.
Senger, H.-G. and Bormann, K. (eds.) (1988) Nicholas of Cusa, *De beryllo (Opera omnia XI/1)*, Hamburg.
Sfez, J. (2012) *L'art des conjectures de Nicolas de Cues*, Paris.
Stallmach, J. (1989) *Ineinsfall der Gegensätze und Weisheit des Nichtwissens*, Münster.
Steel, C. (1977) " La place du *Vat. lat. 11600* dans la tradition latine du commentaire *In Parmenidem* de Proclus," *Scriptorium* 31: 262–266.
(ed.) (1982–1985) *Proclus: Commentaire sur le Parménide de Proclus, Traduction de Guillaume de Moerbeke*, 2 vols., Leuven and Leiden.
(ed.) (2007–2009) *Procli In Platonis Parmenidem commentaria*, 3 vols., Oxford.
Steiger, R. (ed.) (1983) Nicholas of Cusa, *Idiota de sapientia, Idiota de mente (Opera omnia V)*, Hamburg.
Vansteenberghe, E. (1928) "Quelques lectures de jeunesse de Nicolas de Cues," *Archives d'histoire doctrinale et littéraire du moyen âge* 3: 275–284.
Wilpert, P. (1953) "Das Problem der coincidentia oppositorum in der Philosophie des Nikolaus von Cues," in J. Koch (ed.), *Humanismus, Mystik und Kunst in der Welt des Mittelalters*, Leiden and Cologne, 39–55.
Wyller, E. (1970) "Zum Begriff des 'non aliud' bei Cusanus," in *Nicolò Cusano agli inizi del mondo moderno, Atti del Congresso internazionale in occasione*

del V centenario della morte di Nicolò Cusano, Bressanone 6–10 settembre 1964, Florence, 419–441.

(1974) "Nicolaus Cusanus' 'De non aliud' und Platons Dialog 'Parmenides.' Ein Beitrag zur Beleuchtung des Renaissance-Platonismus," in K. Döring and W. Kullmann (eds.), *Studia Platonica, Festschrift für Hermann Gundert zu seinem 65. Geburtstag*, Amsterdam, 239–251.

PART II.6 *The Renaissance*

CHAPTER 13

Marsilio Ficino

Michael J. B. Allen

Ficino, Dionysius the Areopagite, and Proclus

Marsilio Ficino expressed an unqualified admiration of Plotinus, who had no anti-Christian record, and who could even be co-opted as a crypto-Christian on the evidence that he and Origen, the great Greek Church Father, had both been disciples of Ammonius Saccas.[1] Plotinus' one error was his toying, however figuratively, with the notion of the transmigration of rational souls. By contrast Ficino responded to Proclus in two much more guarded ways. First, he saw him as a non-Christian Platonist, however productive and subtle as a commentator; and he continuously under-referenced him even when he was continuously indebted to him. Second, he assumed that the Platonism of Proclus was profoundly derivative, not in the sense that many modern historians of Greek philosophy have viewed Proclus as essentially a systematizer and scholastic elaborator of Plotinus, but in the more radical sense that he was reproducing or imitating, so Ficino believed, the philosophical principles, the "Platonic theology" of Dionysius the Areopagite, "the greatest of all the Platonists" and one of the greatest of the Christian saints.[2] This Dionysius was known to the Middle Ages and the Renaissance as the Areopagite, because he was identified with the convert of St. Paul in Acts 17:34 who had heard the apostle preach on the hill of Ares beside the Acropolis.[3] Later he was said to be present in Jerusalem at the death and Assumption of the Virgin; and he became,

[1] There is the possibility that Ammonius himself was a Christian. I wish to take this opportunity to thank John Monfasani for his eagle-eye and several important references to Scutellius, Harmonios, and others.

[2] See Cristiani (1993), 185–203, Vasoli (2001), and Podolak (2009) with further references. Since Ficino thought of Dionysius as the Areopagite, I shall not refer to him as the pseudo-Areopagite (or as the pseudo-Dionysius).

[3] For Dionysius in the Middle Ages and Renaissance, see, for example, Gersh (1978), the important article by Monfasani (1994b[1987]), and Makris (2000), 3–39.

reputedly, the first bishop of Athens.[4] Most significantly, he was held to be the first-century AD author of four profoundly Platonic treatises and of ten letters, the tenth being to John the Apostle in exile on Patmos, though in reality they were all composed in the late fifth or early sixth century AD by a monophysite follower of Proclus (412–485).[5]

Predated and misattributed in this way, the treatises had a profound impact on Ficino, since they were the best evidence for the flowering of an integral Christian Platonism immediately after Christ's death, one that Plotinus was to inherit in the third century and Proclus in the fifth. Proof of this Platonism could also be found in St. Paul's epistles, and even more convincingly in St. John's gospel and epistles. Their appeal to Ficino, and to the medieval and Renaissance worlds in general, was decisive, and it took many decades, beginning in the later sixteenth century, to uproot the whole notion of Dionysius' apostolic Platonism with its array of Proclean features. As Kristeller duly observed a quarter of a century ago, "wherever we find traces of Neoplatonic influence on medieval and early modern thought, down to Cusanus, Ficino and Lefèvre, the first source to be considered is always the Areopagite."[6] The obvious consequence for Ficino and his contemporaries was that Proclus was deprived of much of his stature as the last great ancient Neoplatonist. Or rather, he was eclipsed by the Areopagite, even though his work, particularly his long commentaries on the *Timaeus*, *Parmenides*, and *Republic*, had deployed, in a systematic and definitive way, the panoply of Neoplatonic arguments. It was an ironic case of the master being supplanted by the disciple.

Even so, we must take note of the important role Proclus played for Ficino as a doxographer. He was a rich and often unique source for what the ancients had debated, providing as he did a vivid sense of the range and the differences of opinion in the ancient schools, Platonic and non-Platonic, and an account too of their succession. He also cast light on the Neoplatonists' hierarchizing of the dialogues and its reflection in their teaching cycle(s), one that had conferred a special role on the *Timaeus* and above all on the *Parmenides*, as well as giving subordinate but still prominent roles to the *Philebus*, the *Sophist*, and even the *Alcibiades*. In sum,

4 Entangling matters further, this hybridized Dionysius was then confounded with St. Denis, patron saint of France and a cephalophore.

5 The bibliography on this Dionysius is immense. For some recent studies and collections in English, see Rorem (1993), Schäfer (2006), Klitenic Wear and Dillon (2007), Perl (2007), and Coakley and Stang (2009).

6 Kristeller (1987), 196. To this masterly article, with its host of detailed references, I am much indebted in the sections on pp. 355–361 below. It is reprinted in Kristeller (1996), 115–137. I shall refer to the pagination of the original article.

Proclus helped to establish in Ficino's mind the Neoplatonic perspective on the entire Plato canon, dominated as it was by the later dialogues and by the notion of their essential unity, complementarity, and shared wisdom.

The legacy of William of Moerbeke

To understand the depth of Ficino's encounter with Proclus, we must begin with the Proclean works that had captured the attention of the Aristotelian Scholastics in the thirteenth and fourteenth centuries, and that continued to engage Ficino and other Quatrocento thinkers. The most important late medieval translations of Proclus were those by the Flemish Dominican, William of Moerbeke. In May 1268 Moerbeke finished rendering Proclus' *Elements of Theology*, which now survives in at least twenty-seven manuscripts and was the most widely diffused of his translations. Salutati and Cusanus, for instance, both owned copies, and manuscripts of the original Greek commentary were owned by Bessarion, Pico, and Patrizi.[7] The translation was cited by Thomas Aquinas, Henry of Ghent, and others, and it was made the object of several commentaries, the most extensive being that by Berthold of Moosburg. Ficino too cited the translation in one of his earliest writings and made excerpts from the Greek text as well as a new Latin translation of the work which is now lost.[8] Pico used the *Elements* in his *Conclusiones* and Francesco Patrizi (1529–1597) published a new translation of the work, as later did Aemelius Portus, the first editor of the Greek text.[9] In the twelfth century Nicolaus of Methone had written a *Refutatio* attacking it which also circulated widely in the Renaissance. In a manuscript of this *Refutatio* which Ficino himself owned (*Paris: Greek MS 1256*), we even have his notes, scanty though they are, on Proclus' first six propositions.[10] A Latin translation of this refutation, or rather a free paraphrase, survives by Bonaventura Vulcanius.[11]

Moerbeke also translated the three influential short treatises on providence, fate, and the existence of evil, completing the task in Corinth in February 1280.[12] These survive in at least thirteen manuscripts; and the Greek original, long considered lost, has been partially excavated from an attack on Proclus compiled by Isaac Sebastokrator.[13] Ficino made explicit references to the treatises in his commentary on the Areopagite's great

[7] Kristeller (1987), 197–198. [8] Kristeller (1987), 197–198 [9] Kristeller (1987), 197–198.
[10] Sicherl (1986), 226–227. See also Förstel (2006), 82–83. [11] Kristeller (1987), 198–199.
[12] Boese (1960). [13] Kristeller (1987), 199.

work *On the Divine Names*, which we now realize was indebted to the treatises.

Moerbeke's Latin rendering of Proclus' *In Timaeum* is fragmentary and exists in only two manuscripts, though three excerpts occur in Henricus Bate's *Speculum divinorum*. Whether Moerbeke translated more than the surviving excerpts is unknown. Kristeller suggests that the work remained eclipsed by the continuing impact of Calcidius' Middle Platonic *In Timaeum*, widely consulted and repeatedly copied in the Middle Ages and printed several times in the sixteenth century.[14] Still, the Greek text of Proclus' *In Timaeum* also circulated in the Renaissance, and we have copies owned by Bessarion and Ficino and excerpts by Patrizi. Ficino had access in fact to two manuscript copies: the one he owned is partial in that it is missing the second half of the third book, the other, recently identified, is complete.[15] Gentile's recent edition of the second book of Ficino's letters has a number of references to Proclus' *In Timaeum*[16] and this suggests an indebtedness that needs further exploration in other Ficino texts, including of course Ficino's own *In Timaeum*. Interestingly, Pico quotes extensively from Proclus' *In Timaeum* in the *Conclusiones* he attributed to Porphyry and Iamblichus – that is, he is clearly using it as a doxographical resource. In the sixteenth century in northern Italy it was translated into Latin anonymously.[17]

The last of Moerbeke's Proclus translations was that of the massive *In Parmenidem*, which comments on everything in the dialogue up to the end of the first hypothesis at 142a8.[18] Of particular note is the fact that Moerbeke includes translated lemmata from the *Parmenides* and thus provides us with an important addition to the small list of Platonic dialogues that were accessible in Latin, in whole or in part, to the medieval West. Second, his rendering preserves the last portion of Proclus' commentary – that on 141e7–142a8 – which has been lost in the original Greek.[19] The work survives in six manuscripts, one of them owned by Cusanus, who annotated it[20] and who later ordered the Greek émigré George of Trebizond (1394–1472/3)

14 Kristeller (1987), 199.

15 MSS *Riccardiana 24* and *Chigiana R VIII 58* respectively. See Megna (2003), Megna (2004). See also Gentile, Niccoli, and Viti (1984) 25–26.

16 Gentile (2010), 171–172.

17 Kristeller (1987), 199–200.

18 See Steel (1977), 262–266; and Steel (1982–1985); also Klibansky and Labowsky (1953). For the diffusion of Moerbeke's translation, see Sturlese (1987).

19 This final part has been edited (with a modern retroversion into Greek) in Steel (2007–2009), vol. III, 279–355. See also Luna and Segonds (2007–2011) for a competing edition of Proclus' *In Parmenidem*. Scholarship hitherto has been indebted to Cousin's 1864 edition.

20 The annotations are now in Steel (2007–2009), vol. II, 529–557.

to do a translation of the dialogue itself, which was completed in 1459.[21] A decade later, the Greek Bessarion (*c.* 1403–1472) used the Neoplatonic interpretation of the *Parmenides* to convince his Italian audience that Plato was superior to Aristotle and closer to Christianity.[22] Ficino used Proclus' *In Parmenidem* in composing his own long commentary,[23] and he did so using Moerbeke's rendering in whole or in part: indeed, Carlos Steel, the authority on Moerbeke, has recently argued for his extensive use of it.[24] We shall address the issue of Ficino's quasi-Proclean interpretation of the dialogue below.

To Moerbeke's Latin corpus of Proclus' writings, the fifteenth century added the huge *Platonic Theology*, arguably his *magnum opus*. The translation was begun by Ambrogio Traversari at the behest of Cusanus, and the specimen translation of two chapters of book I made just before Traversari died in 1439 survives in a copy penned by Cusanus himself.[25] A complete translation, again at the behest of Cusanus, was undertaken by a longtime member of Bessarion's household, Petrus Balbus Pisanus, from 1463 the bishop of Tropea in southern Italy.[26] Balbi completed this on March 26, 1462 before Cusanus' death in 1464 and dedicated it to King Ferrante of Naples. Of the three extant manuscripts, two belonged to the Cardinal and the third went to Ferrante with a preface declaring that Balbi had translated the work at Cusanus' request.[27] Ficino apparently knew of Balbi's translation.[28] He and Bessarion, Pico, Giles of Viterbo, Patrizi, and Holstenius all had access to Greek manuscripts of the original;[29] indeed, we have Ficino's own *marginalia* on the Riccardiana's 70.[30] Though Proclus'

21 See Monfasani (1984), 167–170; Monfasani (2004b[2002]) – p. 221 deals with Bessarion's notes on George's translation of the *Parmenides*. These are in a unique codex which also contains the notes of George's son Andreas Trapezuntius and those of Cusanus.

22 For the *Parmenides* and Nicholas of Cusa, George of Trebizond, and Bessarion, see Klibansky (1943), 306–312; Monfasani (1984); Monfasani (2004b[2002]); and Ruocco (2003).

23 Two editions of this Ficinian commentary have just appeared: Lazzarin (2012) and Vanhaelen (2012). See their introductions and also the comments in Lazzarin (2003).

24 Contrast Steel's cautious remarks in his Moerbeke edition (1982–1985), vol. 1, 38*–42* with the new evidence he presents in his 2013 article. Vanhaelen (2012), p. li, assumes that Ficino mainly worked from the Greek text except for the missing end portion. In 1521 Proclus' *In Parmenidem* was again translated by Scutellius (1490–1542).

25 Kristeller (1987), 201; Monfasani (2004b[2002]), 218.

26 See Pratesi (1963), 378–379; Saffrey (1979–1980); and Monfasani (2008), 252 and n. 21.

27 Kristeller (1987), 201.

28 See Ficino's 1489 letter to Martin Prenninger (*Opera* [1576], 899), where he lists the works of Proclus available in Latin: *Leguntur etiam utcumque traducta Elementa theologiae Proculi atque ipsius Theologia et liber de providentia simul atque fato.*

29 Kristeller (1987), 201.

30 This contains Proclus' *Platonic Theology*, the *Elements of Theology* and the *Elements of Physics*, along with Ocellus Lucanus' *De natura universi*. See Saffrey (1959) with an edition of Ficino's annotations

masterpiece provided the Florentine with the title for his own *magnum opus* – the subtitle "On the immortality of souls" came from Plotinus and Augustine – the two *Platonic Theologies* are nevertheless quite different and I have not found that Ficino is much indebted to his predecessor's work, though Proclus' deployment of material from Plato's *Phaedrus* deserves perhaps a second look.[31] This is striking given that Proclus was – after Plato, the Areopagite, and Plotinus – the Platonic authority to whom Ficino was most indebted, even though he often concealed the debt or adduced it only by way of disagreement.

The vast majority of the fifty-five *Conclusiones* that Pico attributed to Proclus himself – some of them consisting of specific phrases or sentences, others synopsizing whole sections in a deliberately elusive manner – are culled from books three to six of Proclus' *Platonic Theology*. Indeed, this seems to have been the Proclus text that most obsessed Pico when compiling his *conclusiones secundum Proclum*, and his knowledge of it, and especially of the later books, was arguably unique – one wonders whether Bessarion or Ficino had read them as carefully. Patrizi later made extracts from the work and "the great fragment" (i.e. 1.11 to 2.4)[32] was re-translated by Scutellius in 1520. The Greek text was quoted extensively by Augustinus Steuchus in his *De perenni philosophia*; and it was finally published in 1618, with a new Latin translation, by Aemelius Portus, though the edition was criticized by Holstenius in his manuscript notes.[33]

Ficino's translations of Proclus

Ficino himself contributed four extant additions to the Latin corpus of Proclus' works besides coming up with his own translations of Proclus' *Hymns*, of the *Elements of Theology*, and of the *Elements of Physics* (*De motu*), none of which has survived.[34]

In 1488–1489 he translated a short text he entitled *De sacrificio et magia* (*Opera*, 1928–1929), and he made some substantial selections from Proclus'

on pp. 168–179. Saffrey argues that Ficino would not have known this manuscript until 1492, while Gentile's entry 26 in Gentile, Niccoli, and Viti (1984) argues that Ficino had read and annotated it before 1463.

31 See Allen (1984), 249–254.

32 Ed. and trans. Saffrey and Westerink (1968–1997), I.11, 54.26–II.[2]31.4.

33 Kristeller (1987), 201–202.

34 See Kristeller (1937), vol. 1, cxlv; Kristeller (1987), 197–198. There are several anonymous translations of Proclus' *Hymns*, however, from the fifteenth and sixteenth centuries, including one now attributed to Janus Lascaris. This is found in MS *Laur. 36.35*, ff. 23v–25v, alongside translations of the Orphic *Hymns* and the *Chaldaean Oracles* that are also attributed to Lascaris. See Gentile's entry no. 20 in Gentile, Niccoli, and Viti (1984).

commentary on Plato's *First Alcibiades* (*Opera*, 1908–1928).[35] Both of these translations were widely diffused, accompanied as they were by Ficino's translation of Iamblichus' *De mysteriis* and of other Neoplatonic works in a volume published by Aldus Manutius in 1497 and often reprinted. A translation of the commentary on the *First Alcibiades* up to 1.58.8 (ed. Segonds) was made by Scutellius (though misattributed in the past to Gogava, the translator of Aristoxenus and Ptolemy).[36] The *De sacrificio* was long deemed to be a rendering of a lost Greek original (and Kroll even reconstructed the Greek from the Latin); but the Greek text has been rediscovered in two manuscripts used and owned by Ficino. Kristeller supposed it was probably an excerpt made not by Proclus but by Psellus from a longer work now lost.[37] The *De sacrificio* seems to have influenced Ficino's *De vita* book III and thereby played a seminal role in Renaissance theories of natural and demonic magic.[38]

In mid 1492 Ficino came upon the first half of a codex containing Proclus' huge *In Rempublicam*. The codex was originally four hundred leaves or more and dated from the ninth or tenth century. But it was later divided and owned by Armonios or Harmonios of Athens, the nephew of Theodore Gaza.[39] The first half – now the first volume in the standard two-volume edition by Wilhelm Kroll – contained dissertations I–XII on the first seven books of the *Republic*; and it was in excellent condition when it was bought by Janus Lascaris in 1492 for the Medici library in Florence. It is now the Laurenziana's MS *80.9*.[40] Ficino must have borrowed the new acquisition almost immediately, for we have a note of July 7 to that effect.[41] In less than a month he had translated some extracts, "plucking flowers from its delightful meadows," which he then sent in a letter to Martinus Uranius (Prenninger) dated August 3, 1492. This letter he incorporated into the eleventh book of his *Letters* (published in 1495 and thereafter repeatedly reprinted). The first half of the *In Rempublicam* – dissertations I–XII – was translated again by Scutellius; and Conrad Gesner translated another section defending Homer against Plato's strictures.[42]

35 Kristeller (1937), vol. 1, cxxxiv–cxxxv. Megna (2004) has identified Ficino's exemplar as the Vatican's *Palatinus gr. 63*.

36 Kristeller (1987), 203. The standard edition is by Segonds (1985–1986).

37 Kristeller (1987), 203 citing "Proclus sur l'art hiératique" in Bidez (1928).

38 See Copenhaver (1988a), 279; and, for a fuller analysis, Copenhaver (1988b).

39 See Papanicolaou (1998).

40 See Gentile's entry no. 117 in Gentile, Niccoli, and Viti (1984).

41 See Viti's entry no. 160 in Gentile, Niccoli, and Viti (1984).

42 It survives in a rare printed edition apparently known to Thomas Taylor; see Kristeller (1987), 203–204.

The second half of the codex, the half containing dissertations XIII–XVII, has a different story. This did not come to the West until many years later, certainly long after Ficino's death in 1499. It was first owned by the Salviati, whom Holstenius blamed in 1640 for its bad condition, before passing into the hands of the Colonna family and thence in 1821 to the Vatican where it is now MS *Vat. Gr. 2197*.[43] We should note that, although Ficino wrote a long and intricate treatise on the fatal number enigmatically referred to by Plato in the *Republic* VIII at 546a1–d1, he knew nothing of Proclus' recondite analysis of that number's enigmas in the so-called *Melissa*, the thirteenth treatise of the *In Rempublicam*. He relied instead on other sources, including parts of Proclus' *In Timaeum* and their detailed analysis of mathematical passages in the *Timaeus*. Proclus' *In Rempublicam* had no role to play either (predictably so, given Ficino's late encounter with it in the summer of 1492) in the orchestration of his *argumenta* for the ten books of the *Republic* in his 1484 Plato volume.

Finally, Ficino contributed a Latin version of an intriguing and substantive scholion for the *Sophist* which he attributed to Proclus. It is probably by Olympiodorus, whose commentary on the *Sophist* was still available to the Arabic translators.[44] We will take a detailed look at this scholion below.

As a footnote, we might note that Proclus' *In Cratylum* was owned and excerpted by Patrizi but never translated in the Renaissance, and whether Ficino engaged it or Proclus' *In Euclidem* awaits exploration.

Kristeller properly remarks that, in surveying the *fortuna* of Proclus in the fifteenth, sixteenth, and seventeenth centuries we continually run up against the same scholars, those interested, predictably, in Neoplatonism: Cusanus, Ficino, Pico, Scutellius, Patrizi, Aemilius Portus, and Holstenius, the translator of Porphyry.[45] Even so, the search for citations of Proclus by Renaissance thinkers has barely begun, and even establishing the range of Pico's Proclean *Conclusiones* is still in the pioneering stage.

Kristeller proceeds to draw our attention to some features of the impact of Proclus (and of the Areopagite) on medieval philosophical terminology. *Existentia* does not occur in Aquinas, for example, but becomes common in the fourteenth century in the modern sense as opposed to essence. It

[43] It remained in the Vatican, to all intents and purposes hidden from the scholarly world, until a defective version of it appeared in 1886 edited by Richard Schoell. It was then authoritatively edited by Kroll in 1901 – in the second volume of his edition – though the text is full of lacunae and conjectural reconstructions, necessarily so given the damage to the manuscript's upper borders.

[44] See Westerink (1976–1977), vol. 1, 22 – Olympiodorus' commentary on the *Phaedo*. I am indebted to L. G. Westerink for this reference.

[45] Kristeller (1987), 204. Holstenius published nothing on Proclus, but he eagerly collected and annotated many Proclus manuscripts.

was used by Moerbeke to render *hyparxis*, a term coined by the Stoics but unknown to Plato or Aristotle. *Processus* and *conversio* also came to be used in the metaphysical Proclean sense. Kristeller observes that the theory of the soul's ascent through several degrees of contemplation to union with the One was first formulated by Plotinus, while it was "hidden away" in Proclus (not even being mentioned in the *Elements*). The ascent's prevalence in medieval thought was due then not to Proclus but to the influence of the Areopagite.[46]

Ficino also followed Porphyry, Iamblichus, and above all Proclus in assuming that the writings attributed to the Chaldaeans, Orphics, and Pythagoreans – writings we now consider apocryphal – were authentic witnesses to the ancient theology that culminated in Plato and then, for Ficino, in Christ. This view had deeply affected Psellus and Pletho and it shaped Ficino's radical recasting of the history of theology and philosophy alike. Thereafter it had an impact on Pico, Steuchus, and others. Although Proclus was not the only source for this view – which, incidentally, did not include a recognition of the claim of Hermes Trismegistus or the Egyptian tradition to a prominent place in the transmission of the *prisca theologia*[47] – the Proclean perspective may nonetheless account for Ficino's decision midway through his career to promote Zoroaster, the putative inspirer if not the author of the *Chaldaean Oracles*, as the first of the ancient theologians, and thus as the *fons et origo* of the ancient Platonic wisdom.[48] Elsewhere I have emphasized the importance of Zoroaster to Ficino, given his triumphant assumption that the Three Magi in the Epiphany story were Zoroastrians who had come to Bethlehem to worship the Christ child as the new Zoroaster, as the perfection of the ancient wisdom, as the King-Magus-Priest who would initiate a new covenant and reign over the coming age of grace.[49]

Proclus' In Parmenidem

Ficino's most important encounter with Proclus involved the *In Parmenidem*.[50] Let us turn to the introduction (*argumentum*) he wrote

46 Kristeller (1987), 205–206. 47 Kristeller (1987), 205.

48 His authority here was Pletho's commentary on the Chaldaean Oracles; see Tambrun (1999), 9–48.

49 Allen (1998), 26–41. See now Hanegraaff (2012), chapter 1.

50 Ficino's personal copy of Proclus' *Parmenides* commentary has not yet been identified. Vanhaelen (2012), xv–xvi, notes that at least two copies of the Greek text circulated in Florence: the Laurenziana's *Conv. Soppr. 103* (a Byzantine manuscript which was purchased by the Florentine Antonio Corbinelli and bequeathed to the Badia after 1425); and the Laurenziana's *Pluteus 85. 8* (copied by John Rhosos

for the *Parmenides* in the early 1460s,[51] the *Parmenides* being the climactic dialogue in the first batch of ten dialogues that Ficino hurried to translate for the ailing Cosimo in 1464, and the one which he apparently read to his patron, along with the *Philebus*, on his deathbed! This consolatory "reading" amounted to little more, surely, than Ficino's being asked to provide Neoplatonic muzak, given Cosimo's freshman Latin, his declining condition, and the convolutions of the arguments! Even so, as part of Cosimo's own *ars moriendi*, it makes for a dramatic story.

Ficino later reused the *argumentum* as the introduction for his *Parmenides* translation as it appeared in the *Platonis Opera omnia* of 1484, and then again as the preface for his own long *In Parmenidem* published with other Plato commentaries in 1496.[52] As early as the 1460s, however, the *argumentum* was already testifying to the awe investing the *Parmenides* for Ficino, given its primacy among the dialogues, and its role as Plato's compendium of universal theology. More pertinently, it demonstrates that Ficino was already familiar with the Proclean account of the dialogue's structure and its account of the second part's elaboration of the nine interconnected hypotheses predicated on the presence of the One or on the consequencies of postulating its absence.

The *argumentum* begins: "though Plato scattered the seeds of all his wisdom through all his dialogues," he assembled the principles of moral philosophy in the *Republic* and all the knowledge of the natural world in the *Timaeus*. But "in the *Parmenides* he included the universal theology. This (as Proclus says) might seem unbelievable to other people but is most certain for those in the [Platonic] family (*familiaribus*)." Even so, Ficino did not accord the dialogue quite the same status as Proclus had conferred upon it. For Proclus had argued that the *Parmenides* was the consummation and perfection of all the other dialogues, and that, once mastered, it made reading the others unnecessary or at least supererogatory. Ficino was too much in love with the Platonic mysteries buried in the other dialogues, not only in the *Republic* and *Timaeus* as suggested above, but pre-eminently in the *Symposium*, *Phaedrus*, *Phaedo*, *Statesman*, and *Letters*, to commit himself exclusively to this view of the *Parmenides*. Nonetheless,

in 1489 at the request of Lorenzo de' Medici). Ficino also had access to William of Moerbeke's translation as we have seen.

[51] *Opera*, 1136–1137. I have explored the following *Parmenides* material in Allen (1983) and (1986), both of which have been reprinted in Allen (1995a). But see now Etienne (1997); Beierwaltes (2002); 389–410; Lazzarin (2003) and (2004) (with a critical edition and Italian translation of Ficino's *argumentum in Parmenidem*). For the contretemps with Pico, see Raphael Ebgi's comments in Baccelli and Ebgi (2010), 124–137; also Vanhaelen (2009).

[52] See Vanhaelen's note on the text of the *argumentum* in her edition pp. 237–239.

he recognized it as the sovereign embodiment of Plato's ontology and thus of his metaphysical theology.[53]

In the other dialogues Plato puts a wide gap between himself and the other philosophers, Ficino argues, but in the *Parmenides* he "finally seems to excel even himself... for he appears to have been divinely inspired to produce this heavenly work from the sanctuaries of the divine mind and from philosophy's innermost shrine." This suggests that, while composing in this hierophantic frame, he was in a higher state of consciousness, and functioning as a seer rather than a philosopher. And the *argumentum* goes on to observe correspondingly that "Whoever embarks on the sacred reading of this text should prepare himself with soberness of soul and liberty of understanding (*sobrietate animi mentisque libertate*) before daring to take up the mysteries of this heavenly work." That is, the soul must be tempered and the mind liberated from bodily involvement before a disciple can even embark on a "sacred reading" (*sacra lectio*) of such a celestial work. In effect, the text is being accorded the status of scripture, and any person embarking on reading it must prepare himself inwardly, as a priest prepares to officiate at Mass. Ficino accords no other dialogue quite this privileged status, though we must bear in mind that the Platonic tradition inherited from Pythagoreanism a commitment to inward preparation and discipleship: to the notion of a disciplined and guided initiation into correct interpretation. Indeed, we should recall that Ficino was constantly aware of the Pythagorean strains in Platonism, from Pythagoras himself to the Eleatics, particularly Parmenides and Melissus, and on to Plato and the succession of later Platonic exegetes, to end in Proclus himself. From this perspective, the later interpretation of the *Parmenides* was one of the triumphs of Pythagoreanism, and Proclus emerged as a lineal descendant of the Pythagoreans.

The challenge, says Ficino, is that the divine Plato has confronted us with a "most subtle series" of arguments concerning the One as the one principle of all and the source of all; for Plato examines how the One is outside all and within all, and how all exist from it, through it and for it."[54] This obviously refers to the challenges of the dialogue's second part beginning at 137c4 with the young Aristotle (not the Stagirite) as the respondent and not to the theory of Ideas explored in the first part with the young Socrates. It underscores the fact that Ficino was apprized of the Neoplatonic reading from early on, that is, from the early 1460s when he completed his rendering

[53] Were their *Parmenides* commentaries the last Plato commentaries respectively of Proclus and Ficino?

[54] Ed. Vanhaelen (2012), 2–9 (= *Opera*, 1136–1137). See Allen (1995b[1983]), 24.

of the dialogue for Cosimo and prepared the *argumentum* to accompany it. In other words, the *skopos* of the dialogue is not *De ideis*, as was mooted on occasions in antiquity, and as we might anticipate from reading only the first part of the dialogue; but rather *De uno*, the One being the subject of the second part by way of both affirmation and negation, and the source of the Ideas. Plato leads us from Zeno's concern with the principle of unity in sensibles, to Socrates' corresponding concern with the same principles in intelligibles, and thus to a consideration of the Ideas "in which the unities of things consist." Finally, Parmenides, the eldest of the speakers, turns to the reason or rational principle underlying the Ideas (or, more literally, to "the entire reason" of the Ideas), not in order to refute Zeno or Socrates, but to bring their unfinished contemplation to completion. That is, we are taken to successively higher levels of viewing unity; and the triple inquiry climaxes with Parmenides himself advancing the primary questions about the existence and nature of the Ideas.

The second part is concerned with the transcendent One, the One beyond the unity immanent in the Ideas. From a Neoplatonic point of view, the history of the correct interpretation of the dialogue is the result of a series of interpretive breakthroughs, culminating with that of Plutarch of Athens (*c.* 350–430) and Syrianus (d. 437), the teacher of Proclus; and it has been well analyzed by Saffrey, Westerink, and others. That Ficino was familiar with this account is clear not only from the *argumentum* but from chapters 37, 52, and 56 of his own *In Parmenidem*. But here he distances himself from Proclus in that the latter had followed Syrianus "in supposing that individual mysteries were hidden in individual words and that the number of individual conclusions usually corresponded to the number of individual divinities (37.2)," an interpretation which is keyed to the conclusions attendant on the second hypothesis (52.3, 56.3), and which Ficino rejects (80.3).[55]

Finally, the *argumentum* exhorts us to follow Pythagorean precedent and to recognize that Plato uses the terms "one" and "other" in the dialogue in various oppositional ways: "one," for instance, can refer not only to the transcendent One but to the two grand hypostases free of matter, namely Mind and Soul and all they embrace. "Other" may refer to matter or to material forms. We have to bear this always in mind lest we mistake the dialogue's content and structure, which are so matched that we cannot

[55] Cf. 80.3: "we do not intend to introduce as many divinities as there are conclusions" lest we end up siding with Proclus in postulating eight gods from the tenses of "to be" and "to become."

understand them apart: hence the requirement that we acquire an inward sobriety and liberty.[56]

Decades later, after November 7, 1492, Ficino began to compile his own full-scale *Parmenides* commentary, which he completed before August 1494 and published in 1496. The *proemium*, which immediately follows his *argumentum*, raises the contentious question as to why a work that was "for the most part theological" is cast in a dialectical form (giving rise of course to the ancient notion that the work was merely a dialectical or logical exercise). Ficino retorts that "it was the custom of Pythagoras, of Socrates, and of Plato to conceal divine mysteries everywhere in figures and veils." The result was "jesting in seriousness" and "playing in earnest" – a philosophical wittiness that evoked Lucian and Apuleius as well as Plato and Plotinus, and that reminds us of the reference in the *Laws* 803c to the "playful gods" who use men as their puppets. Correspondingly, we have to cultivate an inner *laetitia* or playfulness if we are to interpret correctly. Even so, it comes as a surprise to see Ficino referring to the wit of the *Parmenides* as if it were the supreme example of Plato at play or of the ultimate Platonic game designed to "exercise the wit" and incite it to "the contemplation of divine dogmas." Ficino clearly thinks that Plato had remained faithful to Pythagorean example in mixing themes and motifs in imitation of nature's variety. In particular the *Parmenides* melds matters divine with demonstration, the highest dialectical strategy that "is based on universal not particular principles." In other words, Parmenides himself is a dialectician instructing us in the most advanced procedure of inquiry even as he is initiating us into the proper subject of that skill, the highest matters of theology. Ficino notes by way of further confirmation that the *Republic* too mixes theology and dialectic together. The proem is a justification, in short, of the dialogue's logical format in terms of the arresting notion of Platonic play, a notion that Ficino also saw at the heart of Proclus' brimming analyses – not surprisingly given the cognate notion that playing in seriousness was the very hallmark of what Ficino thinks of as the Platonic family.[57]

Again, it was Proclus who gave Ficino the notion of a succession of Platonists who had established the theological status of the whole dialogue, and especially of its second part, and who had detected a sublime order in what Raymond Klibansky, an expert in the history of the *Parmenides*, was

[56] Allen (1995c[1986]), 432–437.

[57] For Platonic play, cf. *Opera*, 1129 (the dedicatory proem to Lorenzo for the 1484 Plato edition which later also served as the proem for Ficino's Plato commentaries).

still calling in 1943 "the bewildering array of [its] conflicting hypotheses."[58] On the basis of Proclus' account in the *Platonic Theology* I.1, Ficino tells us at the close of ch. 38 that Plato's successors, his *familiares*, elevated the One and the Good over Being and Intellect; and that they included "each and every upright Platonist": Plutarch [of Chaeronea], Ammonius, Plotinus, Amelius, Porphyry, Iamblichus, Theodorus of Asine, and their followers."[59] Ficino also toys with the idea of what he calls an "old school," which must have included the figures listed above, and a "new school," which stemmed from Syrianus and Proclus, "eminent men indeed who were in agreement," and which later also included Hermias, Damascius,[60] and Olympiodorus. The old school is not the Old Academy or a later Academy, but the "school" of eminent philosophers stemming from Plutarch of Chaeronea who maintained correctly that Plato had elevated the One above Being and Intellect. Though they had not yet arrived at the full-fledged Syrianian account of the *Parmenides* with its nine hypotheses, still they had interpreted it metaphysically and thus in large part correctly.

In ch. 51, which is entitled *Dispositio propositionum Parmenidis apud Plutarchum*,[61] Ficino turns to the other, the later Plutarch, the Plutarch of Athens from Proclus' account; and proceeds to treat in detail the first five hypotheses in the second part of the *Parmenides* 137c4–160d2. He begins with the notion that the first three treat the three substances separated from matter – the One, Intellect, and Soul – as "one," while the next two treat corporeal form and matter, fulfilling as they do their work from within matter, as "other." The first three serve as prime causes, the last two as accompanying causes. The last four of the nine hypotheses by contrast, 160d3–166c5, demonstrate that, if the One did not exist, then various absurdities would ensue: hypotheses 2 to 5 and 6 to 9 correspond, while the first hypothesis is unique. Ficino is in fact lucidly paraphrasing a passage in book VI of Proclus' *In Parmenidem*.[62]

The end of ch. 52 introduces a further refinement that in a way recaptures the first hypothesis. The first and fifth hypotheses, Ficino writes, proceed by way of negations: the first denies all things of the One, using negation to signify the sublime power of the cause and its incomparable excellence. The fifth denies all things of the last [i.e. of matter] and uses negation

58 Klibansky (1943), 307.

59 Ed. Saffrey and Westerink (1968–1997), I.1, 6,16–24. Ficino adds Plutarch [of Chaeronea] and Ammonius to Proclus' list.

60 No evidence suggests that Ficino knew of Damascius' *Parmenides* commentary, the other important late Neoplatonic interpretation, especially of the second hypothesis; see Saffrey and Westerink (1968–1997), vol. III, lxxviii–xciv; vol. IV, xlvi–lxiii; vol. V, xxxviii–lvi; and vol. VI, xci–xcvii.

61 *Opera*, 1165 (where the chapter is misnumbered 55).

62 Cousin (1864), 1058–1060.

to signify privation, inadequacy, and defect. The second and fourth use only affirmations: the second as exemplars, the fourth as images. The third hypothesis as the mean accords with Soul as the mean, and because of this is composed of affirmations and negations together.[63] This passage depends in part on Proclus' *Platonic Theology* 1.12[64] and supplies us with decisive evidence that Ficino knew both the *In Parmenidem* and the *Platonic Theology* and could work back and forth between them.

In sum, Proclus provided Ficino with the substance and history of the Neoplatonic search for the ultimate reading of the *Parmenides*; and Ficino in turn became the Renaissance scholar who best understood Proclus – more profoundly so than even Cusanus and Bessarion, let alone the haughty young Pico, who had rushed, according to the older Ficino, into a rash and ill-informed interpretation of Plato's greatest dialogue based on a logical and not a truly metaphysical reading. If it was the "inmost sanctuary" of Plato's thought for Ficino, for Pico it was apparently "nothing but a dialectical exercise" (*nihil aliud est quam dialectica quaedam exercitatio*),[65] and one that was especially vulnerable to the violence of "arbitrary and precipitate commentaries" (*arbitrariae et violentae enarrationes*). In espousing this latter view, Pico was of course reviving an ancient perspective on the dialogue, one adopted, for example, by Alcinous (Albinus), who had interpreted it as essentially eristical or obstetrical and not, or not primarily, as dogmatic or doctrinal.

However indebted to Proclus' complex interpretation of the dialogue, Ficino nonetheless takes interesting issue with Proclus and the *Syrianici* in general and is at pains to distinguish his views from theirs. In ch. 37 he declares that he cannot accept the *Syrianici*'s view that every word in the dialogue is theologically significant.[66] For Plato had mingled logical and theological difficulties and had selected Socrates not as a mature initiate, but as a youth still awaiting instruction: Plato, that is, had mingled various elements together that had to be interpreted in various ways. The commitment to maintaining that "individual mysteries lie hidden away in every single word and that the number of propositions equals the number of divinities" was the error, "however understandable," of Syrianus and his most prolific disciple, Proclus.[67] Ficino is referring, one assumes, to

[63] 52.4 (ed. Vanhaelen) = *Opera*, 1167.1.

[64] Ed. Saffrey and Westerink (1968–1997), I.12, 57.22–58.3.

[65] Garin (1942), 390.

[66] Vanhaelen (2009) has advanced a problematic thesis that chapter 37 is the first of thirteen intruded chapters specifically aimed at refuting Pico's arguments.

[67] Cf. Ficino's *In Parmenidem* 90.2, 94.2–4: "one should not derive individual gods from each little clause" (ed. Vanhaelen).

Proclus' assumptions: (a) that everything denied of the One in the first hypothesis is secretly being predicated of the second hypostasis Mind; (b) that all negation in the dialogue is inverted affirmation; and (c) that every abstraction or attribution signifies a divinity in a particular category of gods, hypercosmic or encosmic. But Proclus had been wrong to regard every word as a theological cipher and had in consequence interpreted the text too rigidly, because too literally.

Ficino contests this literalist view just as he had contested the ancient Albinian and the modern Piconian error at the other extreme. In taking pains to separate himself from the *Syrianici*, he is going to tread, he says, "the middle path" on the assumption that there is "only as much underlying theology as the artifice, or what is commonly called the dialectic, allows." For Ficino, judgments about divine matters are not "wholly or continuously or ubiquitously present" but rather are divulged on occasions (37.2). Thus, although the *Syrianici* can serve as guides, Ficino says at the end of the discussion of the first hypothesis, to interpret the remaining hypotheses any interpreter must rely on himself and on God. Here we should bear in mind that the *terminus ad quem* for Proclus' commentary is the *Parmenides* 142a8. In other words, Ficino adheres yet again to the notion of a playful Plato who only intermittently reveals dogmas in "a serious and businesslike game" (*ludum serium negociosumque*) that weaves together theological with logical concerns and requires a flexible, intuitive response that can only come from sobriety of soul and liberty of understanding (37.2).[68] In a way we must toy with the *Parmenides* and its mysteries as the gods delight to toy with men.

In the opening of ch. 103, in taking up the sixth hypothesis, Ficino sees this challenge in terms of poetry, not surprisingly given that Parmenides himself was a poet. His fragmentary *Poema* tells of a chariot ride up through the gates of Night and Day to encounter an anonymous goddess, who then instructs him in the ultimate mysteries. It is against the backdrop of the *Poema* and other poetic fragments attributed to Parmenides that Ficino therefore interprets what he thinks of as the poetry of the dialogue: "Parmenides was not only a philosopher but also a divine poet . . . and in this dialogue he also played the poet." As evidence, Ficino boldly links the choice of nine hypotheses with the number of the Muses, and he plays with the Pythagorean-Neoplatonic interpretation of Apollo, the Muses' leader, as "the not of many." Other poetic features include the varying of terms and their meanings – of "one" and "other" as we have already mentioned – but

[68] Cf. *argumentum* 2.

above all the feigning of "what does not exist and could never exist" – the traditional failing of poets, though some would declare it their traditional calling. Additionally, Parmenides frequently resorts to poetic "paradoxes" and to the "hiding of one thing under the name of another" and by "name" here Ficino takes him to mean terms such as the Good and the One (as ch. 40 makes clear). Parmenides "delighted in metaphors," says Ficino, and "used them to attribute untypical or unexpected (*aliena*) meanings to things. The result of the deployment of all these poetic techniques is that "almost every aspect of the words requires allegory." For "under the dialectical form, he often adds mystical dogmas, not in every sentence but in different passages . . . everywhere however he feigns difficulties and sets out paradoxes."[69] Again, while this certainly points to the complexity and variety of the verbal surface of the dialogue, it is not aligning itself with Proclus' literal response to words that require non-literal allegorization and figurative exegesis. Ficino adduces the *Theaetetus* 166c–168c, where, he says, we should strive not to be deceived by the art Plato has deployed, and not to "take both the words and what they signify in a sense at variance from what Plato himself intends." Plato in short, like Parmenides before him, was a poet and hence we must interpret him as a poetic philosopher. And this Proclus had failed to do.

Before turning to a detailed exposition of the last four of the nine hypotheses, Ficino asks provocatively in ch. 103: "What do a dialectician and a poet have in common?" And he answers, "almost everything" (*certe quam plurimum*); for both the dialectician and the poet "busy themselves with their own conceits and their own devices; and both are deemed divine and possess something of madness." Hence in the *Parmenides* we find something of madness too; for it depicts the old man as a poet and it is itself the masterpiece of a Plato who had begun his career as a poet. Witness the abundance of poetry in the *Phaedrus*, which was purportedly for Ficino Plato's first dialogue; and witness too the youthful poetic tragedies that Plato is said to have burned. Again, the failure of the *Syrianici* and of Proclus was the failure both to recognize the essential poetry of this great dialogue, and to respond to it in a sufficiently flexible way – and this despite their profound insight into the relationship of the hypotheses to the hypostases and their determination of the correct number of the hypotheses.

This attack on Proclus is all the more striking given the praise accorded Dionysius in the *In Parmenidem* 37.3 as the authoritative reader of the dialogue, praise for an achievement that, Ficino supposed, had long predated

[69] *In Parmenidem* 90.2–4, 103.1–2 (ed. Vanhaelen).

Proclus' attempt. This is of course ironic, given what we now know of the true dating. Since Dionysius was the object of veneration as the greatest of all the Platonists and the teacher of a Christian Platonism already perfected in the first century AD, Proclus and the *Syrianici* must have learned about the structure of the *Parmenides* from reading Dionysius, who, Ficino affirmed, had completely understood Plato's supreme work and drawn upon its arguments. Indeed, Dionysius' negative theologizing was the triumphant outcome of his understanding of Plato's deployment of negations. He had even transcended the poetic reading Ficino had been advocating earlier in the first embedded proem; for he had come to understand the power of the apophatic, of the radical nay-saying that amounts to a kind of poetry by way of denial and concealment. Whereas Proclus by contrast had been led to an excessively particular interpretation, Dionysius long before him had understood that the dialogue undermines all such predication: that everywhere it deploys the poetry of no-thing-ness, of non-being, of "absence, darkness, death, Things which are not" – to co-opt Donne's haunting phrases. This is at the opposite end of the spectrum from the merely "dialectical exercise" that Pico had brushed aside as effectively subordinate to the greater works of Aristotle. For its apophaticism is the divine night of a poetry beyond being, the deep but dazzling darkness of a Sinai where for forty days and nights Moses had been an ecstatic poet, prophet, and dialectician.

All this points yet again to Kristeller's observation that for Ficino and for the Renaissance at large the "source" of what seems to be a Proclean idea should always be first referred to the Areopagite,[70] the Christian Proclus who had preceded the pagan Proclus by five centuries.

Ficino and Proclus' metaphysical system

We should not leave the *Parmenides*, however, without briefly taking up several of Kristeller's arguments – advanced on several occasions and reiterated in his "Proclus as Reader" article – that directly bear upon Ficino's interpretation of the dialogue's metaphysics. Most notable is his marginalization of the role of Proclus in shaping Ficino's theory of the fivefold hierarchy of being, and his suggestion that Proclus did not consistently hold to the fivefold model himself or did so only in the *In Parmenidem*. This is a major issue given the importance of the hierarchy to Ficino and given the centrality of Soul in his thought. Kristeller is correct, I have argued,

[70] Kristeller (1987), 196.

in emphasizing the importance of the fivefold structure, but incorrect in supposing it to be something that Ficino engineered independently.[71]

Firstly, he assumes that Ficino read Proclus only after composing his own *Platonic Theology* and therefore that he had already formulated his fivefold metaphysical scheme. But the evidence suggests to the contrary that Ficino encountered the scheme early on in Proclus' *Elements of Theology* and more pertinently, in his *In Parmenidem*. We should recall that Ficino had translated the *Parmenides* before Cosimo died in 1464 and written the accompanying *argumentum*, which clearly testifies to his having already understood and embraced a number of Proclus' arguments with regard to the dialogue. We should note that he had similarly engaged the Platonism of Plotinus long before he actually sat down to translate the *Enneads* and to compile his commentary on them.

In his *Platonic Theology* 3.1.1–11 and 4.1.25 Ficino deploys a metaphysical pentad, albeit in a Christian version: namely God, Angel, Soul, Quality, and Body. But he does so on the basis of a Pythagorean-Proclean definition of this pentad in terms of one, one-many, one-and-many, many-and-one, and many. In arguing that this pentad is Ficino's not Proclus', Kristeller turns to seven propositions in Proclus' *Elements of Theology*, where, he maintains, we are presented only with a tetrad: the One, Nous, Soul, and corporeal Nature.[72] But the seven propositions are in actuality concerned with various aspects of the relationships between and among the subordinate hypostases and their relationship with the One.[73] Most importantly, Matter in all of the propositions, though necessarily outside such relationships since it is prior to and inferior to being, is nonetheless understood as the last of five and not of four hypostases. The Ficinian scheme is problematic only in that it assigns the Pythagorean category many-and-one to Quality, many alone to Body, and nothing to Matter, whereas Proclus ignores Quality and assigns many-and-one to Body and many alone to Matter. Ficino's

[71] Allen (1995b[1983]), 19–22, 41–44. [72] Allen (1995b[1983]), 19–22, 41–44. and n. 101.

[73] Prop. 20 does present us with a tetrad, but a tetrad focused on motion: being moved (Body), self-motion (Soul), unmoved moving (Mind), and being unmoved (the One). Prop. 21 treats the monad as "an originative principle" in Nature, Soul, intellective Essence, and the One. Prop. 62 addresses the fact "that a manifold nearer to the One has fewer members than manifolds more remote." Prop 109 is concerned only with the participation of the particular in the universal. Prop. 111 deals with the distinction between the more and the less perfect members of any level of being; it does not mention the One at all. Prop. 129 treats the henads and "divine bodies." And prop. 139 treats deity as "it exists on the corporeal, the psychical, and the intellective levels." The corollary of prop. 72 introduces Matter as "the basis of all things proceeding from the cause of all things" and presents us with a tetrad: the One, Soul, Body, and Matter. But it omits Mind altogether, even though Mind is integral to any Platonic metaphysical scheme. In sum, none of the propositions serves the argument.

independence from Proclus consists not in his medial positioning of Soul, which he saw, I believe, as a Platonic and not just a Proclean commonplace, but rather in his insertion of Quality as the fourth hypostasis.[74]

Kristeller also argues: (a) that Proclus reports earlier views without subscribing himself to the notion that the hypotheses of the second part of the *Parmenides* signify "various entities" or "levels of being," that is, are concerned with the five hypostases; and (b) that, when Proclus does in fact speak "in his own name," he adduces only the tetrad of One, Nous, Soul, and Body."[75] And here Kristeller cites two references. The first is to a passage in the *In Parmenidem*[76] where Proclus presents us in fact with a pentad not a tetrad of hypostases, and he presents it, moreover, as the scheme he himself subscribes to! And he does so by again invoking the aforementioned Pythagorean sequencing that descends from one (the One) to one-many (Intellect), to one-and-many (Soul), to many-and-one (Bodies collectively as Body), and to many alone (Matter). In other words, Proclus deploys the same sequencing of the "Pythagorean" categories that Ficino uses in his *Platonic Theology* 3.1.1 in order to differentiate his Christian pentad (though with the complication introduced by the insertion of Quality).

For his second reference to the notion that Proclus only speaks "in his own name" when postulating a tetrad of hypostases, Kristeller turns to Proclus' *Platonic Theology* I.11.[77] But here Proclus is not speaking *in propria persona*, but rather outlining Syrianus' interpretation of the *Parmenides'* second hypothesis, even as he is redeploying the Pythagorean one-many sequencing. Moreover, though he does not mention Matter in this particular passage, Matter is nonetheless implied in the notion of the Many at the furthest extreme from the One. For Proclus certainly believed, *pace* Kristeller,[78] that the lowest hypostasis was Matter not Bodies or Body (Matter in extension); and more particularly so, since pure or chaotic matter was the subject of the fifth hypothesis at 159b5–160d2, the fifth being the last of the positive hypotheses in what was for Proclus the definitive analysis of the dialogue by Plutarch of Athens and Syrianus.[79] Proclus' *In Parmenidem* is committed to this account of Matter as Ficino's own *In Parmenidem* testifies, e.g. 51.2 and 52.4.

74 For the role of Quality, see Kristeller's exploratory analysis in Kristeller (1964), 106–108, 233, 400–401.

75 Kristeller (1987), 206 and n. 100.

76 Cousin (1864), 1089.32–1090.3.

77 Ed. Saffrey and Westerink (1968–1997), I.11, 47.10–12.

78 Kristeller (1987), 207.

79 Similarly, in Amelius' breadown of the *Parmenides*'s second part into eight hypotheses, and again in Porphyry's and Iamblichus' separate breakdowns of it into nine hypotheses, it was assigned the seventh hypothesis.

In sum, Kristeller is mistaken in seeing Ficino's pentadic metaphysical scheme as original, for the reverse is true. Ficino was deeply indebted to Proclus: (a) for his articulation of the fivefold scheme; (b) for arguing that it was Plato's own; and (c) most notably for anchoring it in the *Parmenides*, the dialogue which thus served as the unassailable bulwark for the Platonic argument that Soul is the universal mean, the third of five universal hypostases.[80] Furthermore, Ficino's *Parmenides argumentum* provides us with irrefutable evidence of his having engaged Proclus' complex analysis at an early stage in his career as a commentator.

The *Sophist* scholion

Finally, there is the issue of the *Sophist* scholion which invokes "the great Iamblichus" and which, significantly, Ficino attributed to Proclus. Having translated it into Latin, he used it, we might note, as a *praefatio* to his own introduction for the *Sophist*; and as such it appears in his Plato editions of 1484 and 1491 and then in the editions of his own *Opera omnia*.[81] For a study of Ficino and the scholion, may I alert colleagues to the third chapter of my *Icastes*.[82] Suffice it to say that the scholion served as the point of entry for any Renaissance reader embarking on a reading of the *Sophist*, the dialogue that Ficino came to regard as the companion piece of the *Parmenides*, and whose speaker, the Eleatic Stranger, he identified (on the basis of the allusion at *Theaetetus* 180e) with Melissus, one of Parmenides' most accomplished disciples. Far from being a curious oddity, the scholion was thus the golden key to an understanding of a central Platonic mystery concerning the very nature of imitations, dreams, and images, and the veracity, or at least validity, of illusions and of illusion itself. In this regard it was a radical corrective to the *Republic*'s overly simple contrast between the flickering shadows of the cave and the blinding sunlight – in other words, between men as prisoners fettered to illusions and men as liberated philosophers gazing upwards at the dazzling brightness of the Good. For Proclus' scholion problematizes this straightforward polarity by transforming the basic notion of a sophist: Love, Nature, Pluto, even Jupiter are all in a way sophists. Hence the *Sophist* is concerned, Proclus argues, with "a nobler subject than it might first appear." Iamblichus, for instance, had opined that its real concern was with the sophist as demiurge;

80 Kristeller (1987), 207.
81 It is oddly missing, however, from the *Sophist* material in the 1496 *Commentaria in Platonem*.
82 Allen (1989), 83–116 (plus epilogue at 205–210).

"for the sophist is a fashioner of idols, a purifier of souls, a shape-exchanger, forever separating souls from contrary arguments or reasons."[83]

Along with these mingled and ambivalent, even negative aspects, the scholion also asserts that, while the sophist "loves what is truly false, namely matter, he regards at the same time what truly and really exists"; for he is described as many-headed, and as such he lays claim to many essences and many lives. In other words, he cannot be easily dismissed or even categorized; for he "is a magus in generation, enchanting and enticing souls," and as such he is like Love – or, to put it the other way round, Love is a sophist just as Nature is a sophist. Plato's intent, the Proclean scholion is affirming, is "to proclaim the sophist in every way." Even "the philosopher too is a sophist in that he imitates both the celestial craftsman and the craftsman of generation"; and if this is so, then the essential nature of man himself is that of a sophist or rather a philosopher-sophist.[84]

The scholion concludes by noting that the Eleatic Stranger in the dialogue represents the supercelestial, absolute father of these two lower craftsmen, the celestial and the subcelestial. Hence the two people in the dialogue listening to the Stranger represent the twin understandings of that sublime craftsman – the first listener represents the jovian understanding, the second listener, "being an interpreter and a geometer," the saturnian understanding of "the angelic nature." And since craftsmanship (demiurgy) "commences with the imperfect but ends with the perfect," so the Stranger "turns to converse first with Theodorus and then with Socrates."[85]

Thus we have the twin themes of the sophist as magus and as demiurge. Later in his *Sophist* commentary, Ficino will take up the notion of the sublunar demiurge as the creator-craftsman of the whole world of shadows and images and of the pregnant notion that God Himself is in a way the *phantastes*, the master of illusion. Indeed, one of the persuasive arguments that Proclus was the author of the scholion is a statement that Ficino encountered in Proclus' *Platonic Theology* 1.5 to the effect that the *Sophist* tells us about the sublunar world of change and the proper condition of the gods who have received it as their domain.[86] All this would seem to link the *Sophist* more with the *Timaeus* than with the *Parmenides*; but the scholion effectively serves to position the *Sophist* as a bridge between the cosmological concerns of the one and the engagement with non-being of

83 Allen (1989), 90–91, 217.
84 Allen (1989), 90–91, 217.
85 Allen (1989), 90–91, 217.
86 Saffrey and Westerink (1968–1997), vol. 1, 25.

the other in that the *Sophist*'s demiurges are demiurges of creation's "non-being," that is, of the whole realm of fleeting images and imitations, and of sublunar change and motion.

Who is the mysterious sublunar demiurge referred to in the Proclean scholion? For Ficino he has to be identified with the reference to Hades/Pluto in the scholion's first line. To interpret this, Ficino must have turned to Proclus' *In Timaeum* 1.74.15, 1.95.13ff., 1,124,20ff., and 2.56.21ff., and perhaps to the *In Cratylum*, where Proclus takes up the references in the *Timaeus* to the "father" (e.g. at 41a) by identifying a Father demiurge, that is, Mind or Cronus (the Father of the "old demiurgy") and a triad of filial demiurges in the "new demiurgy": Zeus, Poseidon, and Hades.[87] Here Poseidon, appropriately as the god of the seas and earthquakes, is the god of the realm of sublunar flux, while his brother Hades is the lord of the subterranean realm of shadows and illusions. Elsewhere I have suggested that Ficino probably identified these two fraternal deities Poseidon and Hades as a single sublunar demiurge or at least as a hybrid Poseidon-Hades, more particularly since Plutarch of Chaeronea had referred to the entire realm below the Moon as the realm of Hades.[88]

That there is a link between the *ars praeclarissima* of sophistry – whether the sophist is love, or nature, or magic, or Poseidon, or Hades, or Zeus himself – and the art of Platonic dialectic, the capstone of the sciences, would seem at first glance to be deeply problematic. We must recall, however, first that the *Sophist* is the dialogue that Plato paired with the *Parmenides* as the culminating achievement of Platonic dialectic; and second that Parmenides and Melissus are the twin masters of the Eleatic school of what Ficino saw, following Proclus, as Pythagorean-Platonists. That is, the two dialogues are not just complementary but profoundly interconnected. This suggests that the way of the philosopher is ultimately the way of the sophist also; and that the *Sophist* itself, in Ficino's view, was exploring the negative theology that Plato would also explore in the second part of the *Parmenides*. In other words, the *Sophist* as interpreted by Proclus would have been for Ficino the *Sophist* that had already engaged Dionysius the Areopagite in that its profound me-ontological mysteries were the very mysteries that the Areopagite had also taken up in his *De divinis nominibus*. This (mis)interpretation is perhaps inevitable given the (mis)dating of the *Dionysiaca*.

[87] The *Timaeus* itself merely refers at 42de to the new and younger gods who are the Demiurge's children.

[88] *De facie in orbe lunae* 942C–F and *De genio Socratis* 519A-C; cf. *De E apud Delphos* 393A ff.

Conclusion

Our chapter on the Ficinian Proclus must end therefore where it began – with Proclus' most illustrious pupil, or rather (for Ficino) with Proclus' most accomplished teacher, Dionysius. That the Florentine deliberately understated his debts to Proclus must be set over and against the fact that he took the very notion of a Platonic theology from Proclus in entitling his own masterwork, and that he did indeed make careful use of a great deal of Proclus' wide-ranging analyses. Nonetheless, Ficino never wavered in the conviction that his most profound debts were not to Proclus but to Plato, the Areopagite, and Plotinus. However, when he died in 1499 nothing resembled the Diadochus' work, ironically, so much as his own *Opera omnia* in the folio splendor eventually of the Basel edition with its all but 2,000 pages – and this is leaving aside the massive Plato and Plotinus translations. The eminent Florentine scholar-philosopher-magus had indeed become, in many arresting and fundamental respects, the Proclus of the European Renaissance.

Bibliography

Allen, M. J. B. (1984) *The Platonism of Marsilio Ficino*, Berkeley and Los Angeles.

(1989) *Icastes: Marsilio Ficino's Interpretation of Plato's Sophist*, Berkeley and Los Angeles.

(1995a) *Plato's Third Eye: Studies in Marsilio Ficino's Metaphysics and Its Sources,* Aldershot.

(1995b[1983]) "Ficino's Theory of the Five Substances and the Neoplatonists' *Parmenides*," reprinted in Allen (1995a), item XVIII.

(1995c[1986]) "The Second Ficino–Pico Controversy: Parmenidean Poetry, Eristic and the One," reprinted in Allen (1995a), item X.

(1998) *Synoptic Art: Marsilio Ficino on the History of Platonic Interpretation*, Florence.

Allen, M. J. B. and Hankins, J. (eds.) (2001–2006) *Marsilio Ficino: Platonic Theology*, I Tatti Renaissance Library, 6 vols., Cambridge, MA.

Baccelli, F. and Ebgi, R. (eds.) (2010) *Pico della Mirandola: Dell'Ente e dell'Uno*, Milan.

Beierwaltes, W. (2002) "L'interpretazione ficiniana del Parmenide platonico," in M. Barbanti and F. Romano (eds.), *Il Parmenide di Platone e la sua tradizione. Atti del III colloquio internazionale del Centro di Ricerca sul Neoplatonismo (Università degli Studi di Catania, 31 maggio-2 giugno 2001)*, Catania, 389–410.

Bidez, J. (ed.) (1928) "Proclus, *De arte sacrificiali*," in *Catalogue des manuscrits alchimiques grecs*, vol. VI, Brussels.

Boese, H. (ed.) (1960) *Procli Diadochi Tria opuscula (De providentia, libertate, malo) latine Guillelmo de Moerbeka vertente et graece ex Isaacii Sebastocratoris aliorumque scriptis collecta*, Berlin.

Coakley, S. and Stang, C. (eds.) (2009) *Re-thinking Dionysius the Areopagite*, Chichester.

Copenhaver, B. (1988a) "Astrology and Magic," in C. B. Schmitt, Q. Skinner, E. Kessler, and J. Kraye (eds.), *The Cambridge History of Renaissance Philosophy*, Cambridge, 264–300.

(1988b) "Hermes Trismegistus, Proclus, and the Question of a Theory of Magic in the Renaissance," in I. Merkel and A. G. Debus (eds.), *Hermeticism and the Renaissance: Intellectual History and the Occult in Early Modern Europe*, London and Washington, DC, 79–110.

Cousin, V. (ed.) (1864) *Procli philosophi Platonici opera inedita*, 2nd edn., Paris.

Cristiani, M. (1993) "Dionigi dionisiaco: Marsilio Ficino e il *Corpus Dionysianum*," in P. Pini (ed.), *Il Neoplatonismo nel Rinascimento*, Rome, 185–203.

Etienne, A. (1997) "Marsile Ficin, lecteur et interprète du Parménide à la Renaissance," in A. B. Neschke-Hentschke (ed.), *Images de Platon et lectures de ses oeuvres: les interprétations de Plato à travers les siècles*, Paris and Leuven, 153–185.

Ficino, M. (1576) *Ficini Opera omnia*, 2nd edn., Basel.

Förstel, C. (2006) "Marsilio Ficino e il Parigino greco 1816 di Plotino," in S. Gentile and S. Toussaint (eds.), *Marsilio Ficino: Fonti, Testi, Fortuna*, Rome, 65–88.

Garin, E. (ed.) (1942) *Giovanni Pico della Mirandola: De hominis dignitate, Heptaplus, De ente et uno, e scritti vari*, Florence.

Gentile, S., Niccoli, S., and Viti, P. (eds.) (1984) *Marsilio Ficino e il ritorno di Platone: Mostra di manoscritti, stampe e documenti 17 maggio – 16 giugno 1984*, Florence.

(ed.) (2010) *Marsilio Ficino: Lettere II*, Florence.

Gersh, S. (1978) *From Iamblichus to Eriugena: An Investigation of the Prehistory and Evolution of the Pseudo-Dionysian Tradition*, Leiden.

Hanegraaff, W. F. (2012) *Esotericism and the Academy: Rejected Knowledge in Western Culture*, Cambridge.

Hankins, J. (1990) *Plato in the Italian Renaissance*, 2 vols., Leiden.

Klibansky, R. (1943) "Plato's *Parmenides* in the Middle Ages and the Renaissance," in *Mediaeval and Renaissance Studies* 1.2: 281–335.

Klibansky, R. and Labowsky, C. (eds.) (1953) *Parmenides usque ad finem primae hypothesis . . . interprete Guillelmo de Moerbeka*, London.

Klitenic Wear, S. and Dillon, J. (eds.) (2007) *Dionysius the Areopagite and the Neoplatonist Tradition: Despoiling the Hellenes*, Aldershot.

Kristeller, P. O. (1937) *Supplementum Ficinianum*, 2 vols., Florence.

(1964) *The Philosophy of Marsilio Ficino*, Gloucester, MA.

(1987) "Proclus as a Reader of Plato and Plotinus, and His Influence in the Middle Ages and in the Renaissance," in J. Pépin and H.-D. Saffrey (eds.),

Proclus: lecteur et interprète des anciens, Actes du colloque international du CNRS, Paris, 2–4 Octobre 1985, Paris, 191–211.
(1996) *Studies in Renaissance Thought and Letters*, vol. IV, Rome.
Lazzarin, F. (2003) "Note sull'interpretazione ficiniana del *Parmenide* di Platone," *Accademia* 5: 17–37, with errata in *Accademia* 6 (2004), 34.
(2004) "L'*Argumentum in Parmenidem* di Marsilio Ficino," *Accademia* 6: 7–33.
(ed. and trans.) (2012) *Marsilio Ficino, Commento al "Parmenide" di Platone*, Immagini della Ragione 15, Florence.
Luna, C. and Segonds, A.-Ph. (2007–2011) *Proclus: Commentaire sur le Parménide de Platon*, 3 vols., Paris.
Makris, G. (2000) "Zwischen Hypatios von Ephesos und Lorenzo Valla. Die areopagitische Echtheitsfrage im Mittelalter," in T. Boiadjiev, G. Kapriev, and A. Speer (eds.), *Die Dionysius-Rezeption im Mittelalter: Internationales Kolloquium in Sofia vom 8. bis 11 April 1999 unter der Schirmherrschaft der Société Internationale pour l'Étude de la Philosophie Médiévale*, Turnhout, 3–39.
Megna, P. (2003) "Marsilio Ficino e il Commento di Proclo al *Timaeo*," *Studi medioevali e umanistici* 1: 93–135.
(2004) "Per Ficino e Proclo," in F. Bausi and V. Fera (eds.), *Laurentia laurus: per Mario Martelli*, Messina, 313–362.
Monfasani, J. (1984) *Collectanea Trapezuntiana: Texts, Documents and Bibliographies of George of Trebizond*, Binghamton, NY.
(1994a) *Language and Learning in Renaissance Italy*, Aldershot.
(1994b[1987]) "Pseudo-Dionysius the Areopagite in Mid-Quattrocento Rome," reprinted in Monfasani (1994a), item IX.
(2004a) *Greeks and Latins in Renaissance Italy*, Aldershot.
(2004b[2002]) "Nicholas of Cusa, the Byzantines, and the Greek Language," reprinted in Monfasani (2004a), item VIII.
(2008) "Some Quattrocento Translators of St. Basil the Great: Gaspare Zacchi, Episcopus Anonymus, Pietro Balbi, Athanasius Chalkeopoulos, and Cardinal Bessarion," in *Filanagnostes: Studi in onore di Marino Zorsi*, in C. Maltezou, P. Schreiner, and M. Losacco (eds.), Venice, 249–264.
Papanicolaou, M. (1998) "Harmonios ho Athenaios: Bibliofilo e copista, maestro di greco e diplomatico," in *Studi in onore di Mgr. Paul Canart per il LXX compleanno, 2, Bollettino della Badia Greca di Grottaferrata*, N.S. 52: 283–301.
Perl, E. D. (2007) *Theophany: The Neoplatonic Philosophy of Dionysius the Areopagite*, Albany, NY.
Podolak, P. (2009) "*Unitas apex animae*: il commento ficiniano allo ps. Dionigi Areopagita: fra Aristotelismo, Platonismo e Mistica Medioevale," *Accademia* 11: 27–60.
Pratesi, A. (1963) entry in *Dizionario biografico degli Italiani*, vol. v, Rome.
Rorem, P. (1993) *Pseudo-Dionysius: A Commentary on the Texts and an Introduction to Their Influence*, New York.
Ruocco, I. (2003) *Il Platone Latino. Il Parmenide: Giorgio di Trebisonda e il cardinale Cusano*, Florence.

Saffrey, H.-D. (1959) "Notes platoniciennes de Marsile Ficin dans un manuscript de Proclus," *Bibliothèque d'humanisme et de Renaissance* 21: 161–184.

(1979–1980) "Pietro Balbi et la première traduction latine de la *Théologie platonicienne* de Proclus," in P. Cockshaw, M.-C. Garand, and P. Jodogne (eds.), *Miscellanea codicologica F. Masai dicata*, 2 vols., Ghent, 425–437.

Saffrey, H.-D. and Westerink, L. G. (eds.) (1968–1997) *Proclus: Théologie platonicienne*, 6 vols., Paris.

Schäfer, C. (2006) *The Philosophy of Dionysius the Areopagite: An Introduction to the Structure and the Content of the Treatise On the Divine Names*, Leiden and Boston.

Segonds, A.-Ph. (ed.) (1985–1986) *Proclus: Sur le Premier Alcibiade de Platon*, 2 vols., Paris.

Sicherl, M. (1986) "Zwei Autographen Marsilio Ficinos: Borg. Gr. 22 und Par. Gr. 1256," in G. Garfagnini (ed.), *Marsilio Ficino e il ritorno di Platone: Studi e documenti*, 2 vols., Florence, vol. 1, 221–228.

Steel, C. (1977) "La place du Vat. Lat. 11600 dans la tradition de la traduction latine du commentaire *In Parmenidem* de Proclus," *Scriptorium* 31: 262–266.

(ed.) (1982–1985) *Proclus: Commentaire sur le Parménide de Platon, traduction de Guillaume de Moerbeke*, 2 vols., Leuven and Leiden.

(ed.) (2007–2009) *Procli In Platonis Parmenidem commentaria*, 3 vols., Oxford.

(2013) "Ficino and Proclus: Arguments for the Platonic Doctrine of the Ideas," in J. Hankins and F. Meroi (eds.), *The Rebirth of Platonic Theology*, Florence, 63–118.

Sturlese, L. (1987) "Il dibatitto sul Proclo latino nel Medioevo fra l'Università di Parigi e lo Studium di Colonia", in G. Boss and G. Seel (eds.), *Proclus et son influence: Actes du colloque de Neuchâtel, juin 1985*, Zurich, 261–285.

Tambrun, B. (1999) "Marsile Ficin et le *Commentaire* de Pléthon sur les *Oracles chaldaïques*," *Accademia* 1: 9–48.

Vanhaelen, M. (2009) "The Pico–Ficino Controversy: New Evidence in Ficino's Commentary on Plato's *Parmenides*," *Rinascimento*, 2nd ser. 49: 301–339.

(ed. and trans.) (2012) *Marsilio Ficino: Commentaries on Plato*, vol. II: *Parmenides*, I Tatti Renaissance Library, 2 vols., Cambridge, MA.

Vasoli, C. (2001) "L'Un-Bien dans le commentaire de Ficin à la *Mystica theologia* du Pseudo-Denys," in P. Magnard (ed.), *Marsile Ficin: les Platonismes à la Renaissance*, Paris, 181–193.

Westerink, L. G. (ed. and trans.) (1976–1977) *The Greek Commentaries on Plato's Phaedo*, 2 vols., Amsterdam and New York.

CHAPTER 14

Francesco Patrizi

Thomas Leinkauf[1]

I

Francesco Patrizi da Cherso (1529–1597) is undoubtedly one of the most knowledgeable scholars of ancient philosophy in the second half of the sixteenth century.[2] Even in an age characterized by an awareness of language, philological Eros, and a longing for autonomy, his extensive and very thorough analysis of the Aristotelian philosophy in the *Discussiones peripateticae* (1581) represents an extraordinary accomplishment. Patrizi not only creates a critical *Vita Aristotelis* but also and most importantly presents an entirely distinct and new arrangement of the entire *Corpus aristotelicum*, which resulted from internal textual comparisons and confrontations with the tradition of critical ancient commentary. What should be pointed out in particular are his distinct arrangement and organization of the *Metaphysics* books, which bring about similar results long before Werner Jaeger's pioneering suggestions.[3] His actual reference point in ancient thought,

[1] Translation by Thomas Stefaniuk, revised and corrected by Stephen Gersh.

[2] According to Schmitt (1976), 100. The texts of Patrizi will be cited as follows: *NUP* = *Nova de universis philosophia in qua Aristotelica methodo non per motum, sed per lucem & lumina, ad primam causam ascenditur. Deinde propria Patricii methodus tota in contemplationem venit Divinitas, postremo methodo Platonica rerum universitas a conditore Deo deducitur*, Ferrara (Benedictus Mammarellus) 1591 (= Patrizi 1591), within which *PAU* = *Panaugia*, *PAR* = *Panarchia*, *PP* = *Pampsychia*, *PC* = *Pancosmia*, respectively with folio page (recto/verso) and with column (a/b), e.g. *PAR* XI, 13ra. There is an appendix: *Ingens divinae sapientiae thesaurus* with the following texts in each case having its own paging: *Z* = *Zoroastris oracula CCCXX ex Platonicis collecta* (7r–11v); *H* = *Hermetis Trismegisti libelli et fragmenta* (4r–51v); *A* = *Asclepius Hermetis Trismegisti dialogus ab Apuleio Madaurensi platonico in latinum conversus* (1r–6v); *As* = *Asclepius discipuli tres libelli* (2r–5v); *M* = *Mystica Aegyptiorum, a Platone voce tradita, ab Aristotele excerpta et perscripta philosophia* (4r–40v); *Ordo* = *Platonicorum dialogorum novus penitus a Francisco Patricio inventus ordo scientificus* (44v–48v). *DP* = *Discussionum peripateticarum tomi IV, quibus Aristotelica philosophiae universa historia atque dogmata cum veterum placitis collatam eleganter & erudité declarantur*, Basileae (Perna) 1581 (= Patrizi 1581). *ET* = *Procli Lycii Diadochi Platonici Philosophie Eminentissimi Elementa theologica et physica*, Ferrara (Mammarellus) 1583 (see below n. 14).

[3] See for the division of the *Corpus aristotelicum* in the *DP* Pandzic (1999), xxiv–xxx, especially p. xxvii. On Aristotle criticism, its strategy, and its main ideas see Leinkauf (1990), 15–22, 72–86.

however, is Platonic philosophy and especially Neoplatonic thought. Even more specifically, and equally in the singular knowledge of the texts as well as in the hermeneutical depth of penetration, this reference point is the complicated theoretical configuration of the late Neoplatonists: Syrianus, Proclus, and Damascius. In comparison, Marsilio Ficino, in the case of Plotinus, performed similarly thorough preparatory work through translation, commentary, and transposition into his own thought. There was possibly nobody with a better knowledge of these authors of late Neoplatonism and their theoretical configuration before the time of the great philologists in the early nineteenth century, that is, before Friedrich Creutzer (1777–1858) and Victor Cousin (1792–1867).[4] Patrizi certainly ranks with Ficino, Holstenius, Portus, Cudworth, More, and the aforementioned Creutzer and Cousin. His knowledge and consideration of Damascius, to whom no reception history in the philosophy of the Middle Ages and the early modern period is generally attributed, is moreover unique.[5]

II

If one wants to highlight the presence of Proclean thought in Patrizi's main work, the *Nova de universis philosophia* (1591),[6] a considerable difficulty arises: Patrizi brings Syrianus, and especially Proclus and his successor Damascius, into a close synthesis, even treating them perhaps as a unified theoretical configuration. This emerges in connection with the concepts derived from Plato's *Parmenides* regarding the "One-Being" and its systematic transformation into the *unum enti coordinatum.* Such a synthesis therefore often results in global references, in which Patrizi groups together the later Platonists Plotinus, Amelius, Theodore of Asine, Porphyry, Iamblichus, Proclus, and Damascius albeit in variegated constellations (for example, see *PAR* IX, 19va: XVI, 33va, etc.). On the whole,

[4] See Creutzer (1820–1822); Cousin (1820–1827). [5] On this cf. Leinkauf (2011).

[6] In the following, only the *NUP* and especially the *PAR* with the doctrine of principles are at the center of my analyses. This can be justified by the fact that Patrizi especially draws upon theorems and systematic conceptions of the late Neoplatonists in his doctrine of principles, indeed drawing almost exclusively upon Proclus and Damascius. Proclus is explicitly named in the *PAR* many times – ff. 16r, 19r, 19v, 25v, 33v, 34v, 45r, 50v, 59r – but his presence extends into the core domain of argumentation as well as the terminology of the entire discussion of principles. This presence as well as that of the other Neoplatonists has always been apparent, and most recently Anna L. Puliafito has repeatedly made connections, cf. Puliafito (1988), although this discussion remains fundamentally in the domain of philological references, questions concerning the systematic function of Neoplatonic theorems being left unexplored. The works of Puliafito came out at the same time as my first explorations of Patrizi, and therefore we were unfortunately unable to have any exchange with each other. Cf. Leinkauf (1990).

the humanistic reintroduction of the later Neoplatonists should be seen as a replacement of the conventional discourse of medieval thought, contrived for the most part indirectly and surreptitiously beneath Christian pretensions, by a *direct* philological-critical discussion that achieves its completeness on a newly unveiled textual basis – here, the texts of Dionysius the Areopagite should be mentioned first, especially *De divinis nominibus*, but also the *Liber de causis* and the partial translation of Proclus' *Commentary on Plato's Parmenides* by William Moerbeke.[7] This is true with respect to interest in the texts themselves and also with respect to the impulse and motivation for new translations that we find in Nicholas of Cusa,[8] and it especially distinguishes the translation project of Marsilio Ficino that stands out as exemplary until this very day. Now, Ficino's focus was primarily on the work of Plotinus. This was partially a result of the task assigned to him, with regard to Neoplatonism, by the Medici, and we are grateful to him not only for this milestone in the art of translation but also for a vigorous commentary and adaptation of Plotinus' thought into his own "system." However, Ficino also possessed a few texts of the late Neoplatonists, of Syrianus as well as of Proclus himself, such as the latter's *Elementatio theologica*, *Timaeus* and *Parmenides* commentaries, and *Theologia Platonica*[9] and translated a selection from them which then partially went into the various editions of the *Opera omnia*.[10] One cannot claim, however, that Syrianus, Proclus, or even Damascius stood at the center of his theoretical

[7] The (i) *Corpus Dionysiacum*, which contains many fundamental ideas of Proclean Neoplatonism, was often turned into Latin and also commentated upon in the Middle Ages. As a result it was mediated to the Humanism and the Renaissance of the fifteenth and sixteenth centuries through a certain trajectory of Christianism, cf. the translations of Johannes Scotus Eriugena, Johannes Saracenus, Robert Grosseteste, then, already in the fifteenth century, those of Ambrogio Traversari and Marsilio Ficino. As Kristeller rightly and succinctly pinpointed: "Wherever we find traces of Neoplatonic influence in medieval and early modern thought, the first source to be considered is always the Areopagite" (Kristeller [1987], 196). On (ii) the *Liber de causis* (originally also called *De bono*), which represents a compilation of Proclus that stems from the Arabic tradition and greatly influenced Alkindi, Alfarabi, and Avicenna see Bardenhewer (1882); then the edition of Pattin (1966), 90–203 and especially Thomas Aquinas, *Expositio super librum de causis* (Saffrey 1954). On the translations (iii) of William Moerbeke see Klibansky and Labowsky (1953). Moerbeke translated parts of the *Parmenides* and *Timaeus* commentaries, the three treatises on destiny and evil as well as the *Elementatio theologica*. For the structure and tradition of the Parmenides translation see the "Introduction," in Steel (1982–1985), vol. 1, 1*–62*. See also the portrayal by Grabmann (1936), 413–423; more generally on the presence of Proclus see Gersh (1986).

[8] Cusanus invited Ambrogio Traversari to translate the *Theologia Platonica*, which at first remained incomplete. Then Petrus Balbus Pisanus, also at the behest of the cardinal, produced a full translation. Two of the three available manuscripts were also found in the possession of the Cusan.

[9] See Boese (1985), 112–114, who also substantiates the possession of this work by Salutati and Cusanus.

[10] Ficino (1576), ff. 1873–1939, 1968–1978 (Iamblichus, Proclus, Porphyry, Synesius).

development.[11] The purpose they served for him was primarily as means of transmission for the texts of the *Oracula chaldaica* and the Orphic hymns that interested him more. In this regard, Ficino could find himself factually in agreement with a basic concern of Proclus, who, following Porphyry and Iamblichus, considered the texts of the Chaldeans, Orphics, and Pythagoreans as evidence of an antique theology, a "prisca theologia," or of a primeval doctrine of wisdom (*prisca sapientia*), Proclus being of interest here not as a systematic writer but primarily as an authority with respect to their common purpose. However, in those areas where Proclus became systematically important for Ficino – in the doctrine of principles and the theory of the One – parallels to Patrizi's approach can definitely be found.[12] After Ficino, a strand of philosophical engagement with Plotinus and also Proclus continues all the way down to Patrizi, who was of course very familiar with it. However, it does not amount to a synthesis of edition, translation, and especially integration into the speculative doctrine of principles comparable to that which we find in the humanist from Ragusa. Instead we find – to the extent that an overview can be obtained – editions and translations, such as those of Simon Grynaeus (1493–1541) or of Francesco Barocci (*c.* 1538–*c.* 1587).[13] Patrizi possessed a very extensive library of antique, late antique, and medieval manuscripts, in which the presence of many of Proclus' works can be verified, including those that otherwise had less distribution or were never translated, such as the *Cratylus* commentary. In addition to this commentary, these works include the *Elementatio theologica*, the *Elementatio physica* – Patrizi translated both of these[14] – the *Timaeus commentary* (excerpts in Vat. Barb. gr. 179), the *Theologica Platonica* (excerpts in Vat. Barb. gr. 179), the *Commentaria in Alcibiadem*, and the *Commentaria in Parmenidem.*[15]

11 Ficino translated: excerpts from the *Alcibiades I* (1488/89), a few excerpts from Proclus' *Republic* commentary (1492) and a short text *De sacrificio et magia* (actually an excerpt of Michael Psellos from an unknown text), both of these in the edition of translations of Neoplatonic authors handled by Aldo (Plotinus, Porphyry, Synesius, Proclus), Venice 1497 and often reprinted; see Kristeller (1987), 201ff.

12 On the significance of Proclus for Ficino see Beierwaltes (1985), 217–222.

13 Here we are dealing especially with the editions that Simon Grynaeus, partly together with Johannes Oporinus (1507–1568), organized: *Opera omnia Platonis* together with the commentaries of Proclus on the *Timaeus* and on the *Republic* (Grynaeus and Oporinus 1534), *Euclidis Opera* together with Proclus' Euclid commentary (Grynaeus 1533). Cf. Barocius (1560). See also the introduction in Saffrey and Westerink (1968–1997), vol. 1, 91–94; Muccillo (1986) and especially 653ff.

14 Cf. Patrizi (1583).

15 Cf. the evidence from Patrizi's own library, which he had to sell to the Spanish Crown because of financial hardship (MS Escurial) in Jacobs (1908) at nos. 12–14; Barbagli (1975), appendice: lista di libri manoscritti del Signor Francesco Patritio, 554–555.

III

For a mode of thought such as that of Francesco Patrizi, but of course also for that of Nicolaus Cusanus and Marsilio Ficino, the significance of the Neoplatonic school's approach to thinking cannot be overestimated. It is this school of thinkers that thought through the idea of metaphysical unity to its furthest point in terms of its systematic ramifications. It is this school of thinkers that also, particularly in its later forms but also beginning already with Porphyry, reflected thoroughly on the systematic possibilities of differentiation that can demonstrate an ontology based on the theory of Spirit as opposed to a pure doctrine of being, the complete and mutual interpenetrations of central core-functions such as Being–Life–Intellect (οὐσία–ζωή–νοῦς) being thought of according to the model of Aristotle's noology and at the same time synthesized with the unity-based theoretical implications of Pythagorical-Platonic thought. The result of this is a complex system of variegated ternary relationships, whose moments are of equal value in themselves (horizontal equivalence) given that each of them contains or implies the other, but which when considered as total relations are arranged hierarchically, because in any one of the factical unfoldings two members are always placed under the index of the first and are dominated by it (vertical gradation, see subsection 4 below, pp. 395–398). Accordingly, Patrizi introduces two categories based on this differentiation: the *ordo coordinationis aequalium* and the *ordo subordinationis inaequalium* (*PAR* III, 5vb).[16] The difference-quotient of this gradation and differentiation is founded on the ontological and spirit-theoretical basic ideas of the completed unfolding (totality), where "Being" is thought of as agency, and whose absolute implication is "Life" and – building on this in the same pattern of devolution – "Thought." If everything is put under the index of Being, then "Life" and "Thought" are to be understood in terms of Being; if everything is put under the index of Life, then "Being" and "Thought" are to be seen as living self-realization; and if everything is put under the index of Thought, then "Being" and "Life" are to be thought of as *modi cogitandi*, as reflection, and as the sublimation of presuppositions into suppositions. Although the ternary or tripartite basic form of this complex structure was first configured and reflected in Plotinus (as the

[16] How close Patrizi comes in this, as in many of his other hermeneutical activities, to the results of later research, can be shown by a glance at the book on Proclus by Werner Beierwaltes. Here, with regard to the fundamental ontological structural aspect (*Strukturmoment*) of the triad/triads and their "dynamic ontological identity," recourse to the phrase "subordinate arrangement" can also be found, see Beierwaltes (1965), 34ff.

synthesis of Aristotle's idea of the thought of thought and the link between being and life in Plato),[17] it was systematically developed by Porphyry,[18] Iamblichus, and then especially by Proclus.[19] It is no wonder then that we find again and again this Neoplatonic ternarity – handed down primarily by Augustine and then Dionysius Areopagita – in Cusanus, Ficino, and Patrizi.[20] In addition to this systematic and functional significance of the tripartite form of mediation, which is typical for Neoplatonism and which, for theological-dogmatic reasons (doctrine of the Trinity), came to have immediate significance for all Christian authors, we find in Patrizi's thought a clear, unmistakable positioning towards a metaphysic of unity. The obvious ties to the late Neoplatonic model of thought were of course noticed by the Readers of the Holy Office, who subsequently forced Patrizi to retract and emend.[21] One of these retractions is the removal of the emphatic passage in the dedication to Pope Gregory XIV in the first edition Ferrara 1591, where Patrizi gives special attention to Plotinus, Proclus, and Damascius and praises each one of them in particular for his unique approach to thought – Plotinus for his astuteness, Proclus for his *Elementatio theologica* and its mathematical-deductive method, and Damascius for his doctrine of principles and his divine orders. Patrizi explicitly portrays all of these Platonists, however, as theologians with a close affinity to Christianity.[22] In his doctrine of principles, contained in the twenty-two books of the *Panarchia*, he especially develops a metaphysic of unity that is

17 Cf. Hadot (1960).

18 Smith (1993), fr. 366; Halfwassen (2004), 142–152. We find here the basic approach of a matrix structure, which, in connection with the thought of predominance, will play a central role in the philosophy of the Middle Ages (especially in the work of Raimundus Lullus) and in that of the early modern period:

Index	Being Permanence	Life	Thought
Being	Being-Being	Life-Being	Thought-Being
Life	Being-Life	Life-Life	Thought-Life
Thought	Being-Thought	Life-Thought	Thought-Thought

19 See Beierwaltes (1965), 48–164 on the triads in general, and on the ternarity mentioned pp. 93–118.

20 I have cited and discussed a few of these passages in Leinkauf (2009).

21 On this, see Firpo (1950), 150–173, 390–401; Gregory (1953); Gregory (1955), 402–414 on the *Apologia* and 417–424 on the *Declarationes*; Rotondò (1982); Puliafito (1993).

22 Patrizi *NUP*, *Praefatio*, fol. a 3r: *Plotini libri omnes, sacram quandam continent verius Theologiam, quam philosophiam. Neque argumentationum viribus philosopho ulli cedit, alios omnes acutie superat. Theologica Procli elementa, quae nos ante paucos annos Latina fecimus, ad instar mathematicarum demonstrationum sunt contexta. Et cum iis ipsis de certitudine certant. Deus Bone, quam sacrosancta, quam admiranda est apud Damascium Opere De principiis, de Deo, de Trinitate, de divinis ordinibus Theologia*; see on the emendation, the version dating between 1593 and 1596, revised and made accessible by Puliafito, where in reference to this passage it states *epistolam totam . . . detraxi*, Puliafito (1993), xliii.

very closely aligned with Proclus and Damascius and which he at the same time modifies in view of central Christian theological doctrines (Trinity, creation). In the following discussion, only hints of the presence of the Proclean theorems, or theorems advocated by Proclus in conjunction with the tradition originating with Plotinus, can be provided.[23] What must be highlighted above all else is the clear fact that Patrizi directly adopts the *systematic form* of post-Porphyrian Neoplatonism. This separates him from Ficino, who mostly sought to preserve the order of Being that had fundamentally originated with Plotinus. In the *Nova de universis philosophia* we find a hypostatically conceived basic order of existence that is oriented towards Proclus and especially towards Damascius. We can schematically represent this as follows:[24]

Panarchia	*unum tantum*
	unitas primaria
	unum essentiale
	———
	essentia (primaria)
	vita (primaria)
	mens (primaria) / intellectus primus
Pampsychia	*anima/animus*
	here, Patrizi differentiates according to classical theories of the soul: *anima rationalis, phantasia, imaginatio, sensatio*, etc.
Pancosmia	*natura*
	qualitas
	forma
	corpus
	———
	[*materia*]

In the repeated presentation of an *ordo entium* tiered in such a manner, Patrizi aligns himself directly with similar statements by Marsilio Ficino,[25] a fact that was alluded to by Paul Oskar Kristeller.[26] On the other hand, the other elements in the makeup of the Patrizian "system" point to a direct recourse to texts of Damascius, who formally intensifies still further the accomplishment of differentiation that we find in Proclean thought. Patrizi is familiar with the analogous systematizations of Plotinus (*Enneads*

[23] I have already discussed a large part of the relevant passages here from the *oeuvre* of Patrizi in Leinkauf (1990), 23–71. I have further elaborated on the theses and considerations stated there in the following works: Leinkauf (1999), 173–187; Leinkauf (2008a); Leinkauf (2010). On Patrizi see Kristeller (1965); Vasoli (1989) (collection of his essays/presentations on Patrizi).

[24] Cf. for Patrizi, *PAR* I, 2r–v; XI, 23v; XII, 27v; *PP* I, 49v; for Proclus, *Theol. Plat.* I 12; III 6; for the passages in Damascius see Leinkauf (1990), 25ff.

[25] Ficino, *De amore* I, 3 (Ficino [1978], 139) and II, 3 (Ficino [1978], 147); *Theologia Platonica* XIII, ch. 2 (Ficino [1964–1970], vol. II, 207) and XV, ch. 2 (Ficino [1964–1970], vol. III, 21).

[26] Kristeller (1965), 121.

V 1, 1; V 2, 1) as well as Proclus' approaches (*Theologia Platonica* I 12, 56–57; I 21, 100; III 6, 20) (Saffrey and Westerink [1968–1997]), but he aligns himself, as I was able to demonstrate years ago, with Damascius' treatment in *De rerum principiis*, a text that he at times follows step by step.[27] We thus find in the doctrine of principles, but also in the theory of the soul and cosmology, a complex synthesis of Proclus' reflections and systematizations: these are broadly aligned with Plotinus and concern the tripartite structure of being, with the basic ternarity of *esse–vivere–intelligere* and the ternarity derived from it of *essentia–virtus–operatio*, which for the philosophy of the early modern period is even more important.[28] We also find here the formally didactical and at the same time highly speculative texts of Damascius which, going to extremes, are aligned with Proclus. In the systematic outline, a main field of reflection creates the internal differentiation of the One, which Patrizi continuously confronts (and had to confront – for this see subsection 2 below, pp. 389–392) with the basic approach of Trinitarian theology. The argumentation of the *Nova de universis philosophia*, however, is completely permeated and saturated, and this fact should (1) be briefly illuminated in terms of the principles (*propositiones, axiomata*) of Neoplatonic philosophy, especially in the form that Proclus gave them in the *Elementatio theologica.* Following this will be (2) Patrizi's discussion of the notions of unity and principle, (3) the problematics of the relations of this One and principle to the multiplicity that results from it (the world as *mundus intelligibilis* and *sensibilis*), and (4) Patrizi's fundamental theses on the structure and composition of this world: its distinction into *authypostata* and *eterostata*, the basic ternarities *esse–vivere–intelligere* and *essentia–virtus–operatio.*

1. *Fundamental theorems of ontology and noology*

The main Latin texts of Patrizi, especially his doctrine of principles, point to a continual presence of typically Neoplatonic fundamental theorems,

[27] Leinkauf (1990), 25–27; Leinkauf (2011), *passim.*

[28] Patrizi, *PAR* II, 3v; XI, 23rv; XIX, 40va–b; *PP* I, 49v; *PC* XIV, 95r, especially; the universal, especially also the nature-theoretical validity of this ternarity is evident in passages such as *PAU* I, 1rv: *Inter sensus, et naturae nobilitate, et virium praestantia, et actionum dignitate, visus est primarius.* Here seeing, like all other sense activities, is thought of as a complex ternary form of explication and expression of the spiritual: *naturae (= essentiae) nobilitas, virium (= virtutum) praestantia, actionum (= operationum) dignitas.* On this point, see Leinkauf (1990), 39–44, here with reference to Patrizi; Leinkauf (2009), here with a special consideration of Cusanus, Ficino, and Bruno. For Ficino see *Commentaria in Ionem Platonis, Opera* 1282 (Ficino 1576): *Ut enim ab ipso uno quod omnium principium est unitatem quandam sortita est, quae omnem essentiam eius, vires, actionesque unit, a qua et ad quam, ita caetera quae in anima sunt, se habent, sicut a centro et ad centrum circuli lineae.*

whose specific explanation, structure, and evaluation of reality is thus tightly interwoven with Patrizi's own theses. These Neoplatonic fundamental theorems are found in his work alongside the perhaps even more extensive presence of dicta and quotations from the wisdom teachings of the *Oracula chaldaica*, the writings of Hermes Trismegistus, the Orphics, and Zoroaster – one example for many is *PAR* IX, 18r–20r, where the Christian idea of the Trinity is traced back to the "holy" sayings of this tradition. If these λόγια, however, are categorically assigned to an author, for example Hermes, Zoroaster, or Orpheus (who, especially through his great antiquity and the primordiality of his teachings, serves as an authority), then the Neoplatonic theorems that are essentially more important in their systematic significance appear mostly *without* explicit reference to their provenance. This form of adaptation of a form of thought experienced normatively, which is not identified by quotations or reference to names, is also typical of the work of Marsilio Ficino and other authors of this time. Since Patrizi dealt with Ficino very early on, and especially with his *Theologia Platonica* (whose title reminds us of Proclus), this form of largely affirmative reception may have perhaps been so formative for Patrizi because of the Florentine's style of argumentation.[29] Most of these theorems are identical with basic propositions in Proclus' *Elementatio theologica*, a few are taken from the *Liber de causis*, and others from the material of the commentaries. These theorems (in the form of propositions), usually presented in a sentence structure easy to memorize, generally highlight or indicate basic ontological facts such as the *inferiority of all things secondary with respect to the primary*, of the copy with respect to that which it copies, of that which has come to be with respect to that which has not come to be or that from which it came to be, the similar with respect to the identical or the same, the multiple with respect to Unity or that which displays more unity than does itself, and so forth.[30] These basic facts directly result from a systematic approach to thinking based on a theory of unity but nevertheless refer to the multiplicity that results from the One in that multiplicity's variegated structure and nature. They can be described as

[29] On Patrizi–Ficino see Muccillo (1986); I have given references to this issue in Leinkauf (1990), *passim*.

[30] Cf. e.g. Patrizi, *PAU* III, 5va: *Omne enim producens, praestantius est producto. Productum tamen semper similis est producenti*; *PAR* XVI, 36rb: *omne enim producens excellentius superiusque sit suo producto* with Proclus, *El. theol.*, prop. VII (and Patrizi's translation, *ET* 2r: *omne productivum excellentius superiusque sit suo producto*), cf. also prop. XI, XXXVI; *PAR* XVIII, 40va: *omnis productio, non ad supera, sed ad infera . . . progreditur; PAR* IX, 20r: *multitudo autem omnis ab unitate nascitur* with Proclus, *El. theol.*, prop. V*; PAR* III, 6vb–7ra: *oportet autem ubique id quod participat, inferius esse participato, & id quod ordinat, antiquius eo, quod ordinatur* and with Proclus, *El. theol.*, prop. XXIV. See also the next comment.

fundamental assumptions (*axiomata*), since they are formally either strict *universal propositions* (*y* is true for all *x*: *omne producens... est excellentius... suo producto*) or *necessary assertions* (it is necessary that *y* is true for all *x*: *oportet autem, quod...*). And since they categorically determine *universal* relations of being: the active is of a greater importance than the non-active or than that which is activated through the active; the origin or the beginning is of more importance (dignity) than that which originates from it; and the principle generally ranks higher in being than all things that have principle – nothing is higher or before the One, all coming forth and bringing forth occurs in a Being that is ontologically more profound, and so on.[31] Alongside the principles there are also of course purely direct terminological extractions from Proclus and Damascius: for example, the notion of "*infinitipotens*" or "*potentia infinita*"[32] from ἀπειροδύναμις; the use of the term "*hyparxis*"[33] as a direct adoption of ὕπαρξις; the common use of "*uniter*"[34] as the translation of ἑνιαίως; or the introduction of the pair of terms αὐθυπόστατον–ἑτερόστατον, which is discussed below (subsection 4 on pp. 395–398). These things unfortunately still await a more intensive scholarly analysis.

2. *The One and the "internal structure" of the domain of unity*

In Patrizi's reflections on the First Principle (*primum principium*), especially in the fundamental deliberations of *PAR* I–VIII, we find a complex internal differentiation of the domain of unity, which extends between (i) absolute, pure One, the *unum tantum* and (ii) the essential *unum essentiale* which

[31] Patrizi, *PAR* II, 3ra: *omne enim quod est, vires habet aliquas* – this is a direct conversion of the Plotinian-Proclean basic thought of the dynamic fundamental constitution of being; II, 3ra: *nihil est superius, aut prius uno*; III, 8ra: *virtus unita, fortior est divisa*; *PAU* IX, 20rb: *multitudo omnis, ab unitate nascitur*; IV 9vb: *prima enim in uno quoque entium genera, sunt etiam summa* (this accords with Ficino's basic principle of *Primum in aliquo genere*, which the latter had derived from Plotinus, Thomas Aquinas, and the *Liber de causis*). *Et quod primo propinquius est, & principialius est, & potentius; ibid: sed est aliquid in se prius, postea praesens fit alicui*; *PAU* IV, 10va und V, 13rb: *omne enim productum, producenti partim est simile, partim dissimile.* Proclus himself, for example, uses such tenets, which he had systematically arranged in the *Elementatio theologica*, in his Plato commentaries, especially in the *Timaeus* and *Parmenides* commentaries. On this point see Martijn (2008), 63–153.

[32] Patrizi, *PAR* VII, 14ra: *infinitipotens*, cf. Proclus, *In Parm.* 1118,19; 1119,25; 1120,8; 1124,17–22 (Cousin 1820–1827). In what follows I will give in parentheses the references to the edition of Steel, Mace, and d'Hoine (2007–2009); here, see this edition, vol. III, 102, 104, 110.

[33] Patrizi, *PAR* V, 9ra; VII, 12vb–13ra; VIII, 16ra; X, 20vb, 21rb; XI, 23ra: *prior hyparxis quam passio*, 23va; XIII, 29ra, among others.

[34] Patrizi, *PAR*, VII, 13ra; X, 21ra: translated into Christian terms: *in Patre uno, uniter sunt omnia, & una indistincte.* We find it in connection with *uniter* but also *indistincte*, which may correspond to the Proclean ἀδιακρίτως, cf. Proclus, *In Parm.* 757,8; 760,4–5 (Cousin 1820–1827).

directly gives the individual entity its substantial unity. The pure or "only" One is *nihil aliud quam ipsum*, it is without any deficiency (*omni caret indigentia*), and is "principle to itself and to everything else" (*principium sibi, & aliis, PAR* V, 9rv).[35] After this pure One that exists exclusively as one, *quod ab omnibus est separatum, & omnia supereminet*, Patrizi introduces (ii) a "second One" (*secundum unum*), which is now also expressed terminologically as *unitas primaria* (*PAR* V, 9v); this emanates from the First (*a primo*) into essence (*essentia*).[36] After this he establishes (iii) an entire series of unities (*unitates*), which can indeed be linked to Proclus' henads (*PAR* XIII, 29r). They are *unitates . . . inter unum, & ens positae*, whose function it is, to unite that which has being with the One (*entia cum uno uniunt*): that is, to "turn them back" to the One (*ad ipsum ea convertunt, PAR* XIII, 29r).[37] The (i) pure One is "mythologically" assigned to the Father, the domain from the second One down to the many unities (ii–iii) is assigned to the Son and designated as *multitudo unialis* or *multitudo uniformis* (*PAR* XIII 29r). Furthermore, this domain of unities *in* the One is more often seen together with the *paternum profundum* (πατρικὸς βύθος) of the *Oracula chaldaica* and of Proclus (the Bythos being for Proclus the domain of the intelligible and noetic).[38] It is undoubtedly a direct recourse to the Neoplatonic interpretation of the first two hypotheses of the Platonic *Parmenides* that we find here in Patrizi's texts, this being substantially more pronounced and assertive in his own thought than we observe to be the case in that of Ficino (who implements this teaching more in his commentaries, and not so much in the *Theologia Platonica* or *De triplici vita*). The second One is the "One-Being", which "is in beings" (*unum, quod est in entibus*), and which is to be thought of as *iunctum essentiae* and as *unum essentiale* (*PAR* I, 2r–v; V, 9v).[39] If everything is one in the pure One,

[35] Cf. Plotinus: *Enneads* III 8, 10, 22; V 3, 13, 34f.: τὸ ἁπλῶς ἕν; τὸ ἁπλούστατον ἁπάντων (Henry and Schwyzer 1951–1973); Proclus, *Theol. Plat.* II, 1; II 2, 20 (Saffrey and Westerink 1968–1997); *In Parm.* 1179–1180 (Cousin 1820–1827), especially 1180,6–10 (vol. III, 188 [Steel, Mace and d'Hoine 2007–2009]) on the self-sustained, self-standing, absolute being of the πρώτως ἕν. On this point, see Beierwaltes (1965), 68ff.; Beierwaltes (1985), 38–72.

[36] Cf. Proclus, *Theol. Plat.* I 10, 42–43 (Saffrey and Westerink 1968–1997).

[37] On this point see Proclus, *El. theol.*, props. 114–115 (Dodds 1933). Cf. also Patrizi, *PAR* XI, 23v; XV, 31r the differentiation of the unities of being according to *proprietates* – one may surmise that the ontological-categorical basic structures of all existence should be formulated here – in this case ideal differences of type and manner. I will also use the indexing (i), (ii), (iii), etc. in the following for the identification of the basic structure.

[38] See Leinkauf (1990), 36–38 on the *paternum profundum* and on the exegesis of *Oracula chaldaica* fr. 7 des Places. Proclus, *In Parm.* 962,61ff.; 965,14 (Cousin 1820–1827); *In Tim.* II, 92 Diehl (1903–1906): ὁ ἐκεῖ νοῦς . . . ἔμεινεν ἐν τῷ πατρικῷ βυθῷ.

[39] On the "existing one" in Proclus' *Theol. Plat.* I 4; II 10; III 24–26 (Saffrey and Westerink 1968–1997). Cf. Beierwaltes (1985), 193–225, on Proclus 201–211.

and indeed in an absolutely *undivided* manner, everything in the second One-Being is one in a *differentiated* manner.[40] The (i) One only is absolute unity, a unity transcending every propositionality as the absolute enveloping of everything. Therefore the concept *unitas*, which Patrizi applies to unfolded or developed forms of the One, cannot be assigned to it, since unities are always ideal multiplicities. In the (ii) second One, the Son (*Logos, Verbum*) of the Christian Trinity, the non-unfolded and undivided togetherness of everything in the pure One is brought, according to Patrizi, into an ideal and intelligible determinateness and differentiation, through the addition of otherness, difference, and relationality. Through this, he integrates the Plotinian idea of intellect as a hypostatic κόσμος νοητός, and especially the speculative and differentiated reflection on the relation of unseparateness–separateness in ideal entities which was carried out by Proclus, into the Christian Trinity.[41] The first two hypostases of the Plotinian approach – the doctrine is essentially the same in the later systems – must be "synthesized," against the backdrop of the Christian idea of God, into a basic Trinitarian form, in which the strict unity of the One, the ternary differentiation of the *Nous* (in thinker, thought, and execution of thought), as well as the gradation of intellect in terms of the three fundamental agencies: Father, *dynamis*, intellect/Demiurge that is already developed in Middle Platonism (particularly by Numenius) is maintained.[42] If for Plotinus the One is not strictly speaking Intellect but is rather the basis or principle of Intellect that is positioned *before* Intellect, it is also not as such – ἰδίως, *sensu proprio* – that which essentially constitutes this Intellect: namely, thinking, loving, willing, acting. The One can only "be" these genuinely intellectual actualizations in an inauthentic, hyperbolic sense, just as in the same sense Intellect is not and cannot be a one, in the way that the One itself is. Concerning God's thought or comprehension, Patrizi says (*PAR* XVI, 36va): *nullo ergo modo Deus pater intelligit, nec cognoscit, quia nec se ipsum . . . nec alia cognoscit aut intelligit.* However, just as Plotinus in *Enneads* VI 8 attributes thinking, willing, and so on, to the One, as far as this is possible without the abandonment of his basic approach, Patrizi adds in direct connection with the above: *Non se, non ignorat alia, etiam si,*

[40] On the pure One: Patrizi, *PAR* V, 10r; VII, 13r: *omnia uni insunt, & uniter, & une, & indistincte; indivisa* with Proclus, *El. theol.*, prop. 25; 118 (Dodds 1933); *Theol. Plat.* V 8 (Saffrey and Westerink 1968–1997): πλῆθος ἑνιαῖον; on the second one *PAR* XV, 31r: *omnia iam inter se distincta, & unita*; as ideal multiplicity, see XIII, 29r.

[41] Plotinus, *Enneads* V 3, 14, 19 (Henry and Schwyzer 1951–1973) τὸ ἓν πάντα; V 4, 2, 13–20 on the differentiation of aspects in the Nous through the act of thought; Proclus, *In Parm.* 756–757 (Cousin 1820–1827), see Leinkauf (1990), 35ff.

[42] See Halfwassen (1994).

nec se intelligat, nec alia, nec sensu, nec ratiocinio comprehendat... Se ipsum se ipso novit. Seipso itidem novit omnia, supereminentissimo, & sibi proprio modo (*PAR* XVI, 36vb).[43] Patrizi transfers the distinction between pure, absolute One and first, absolute Multiplicity, which itself is a unity, into the Trinity: the One is the Father, the first, absolute Multiplicity as unity is the Son or the Word. For the Father the rule applies, that no "actual" intellection or structure of intellect as reflection can occur. Of the *Verbum Dei*, however, it can be said: *in Verbo vero, & Spiritu, ubi distincta iam erant omnia, cadere intellectio potuit, & utrumque intellectum facere* (*PAR* XIX, 41v). Thinking is differentiated – just as it is with Proclus – into an "absolute thinking," which, in the sense of the thought of ὑπερνόησις, is to be positioned above thinking, and which actually is a non-thinking,[44] and a "highest thinking": a thinking that is completely mediated in and of itself (which is thinking in the proper sense), and in which a first Multiplicity, whose difference and otherness is, however, eternally overcome or sublimated, appears as a sort of first theophany.[45] The Spirit or Intellect, to the extent that it is in the latter sense real thinking, as the reflecting-recognizing mediation of different moments into a One, is thus also to be seen as the "seat of ideas" (Plotinus, *Enneads* I 6, 9, 34ff.) or "fullness of ideas" (Proclus, *Commentarius in Parmenidem* 800,14 (Steel, Mace, and d'Hoine [2007–2009], vol. 1, 210): ποῦ πρῶτον ὑπέστη τὸ πλήρωμα τῶν ἰδεῶν). Only the (absolute) Spirit/Intellect "is" also that which it thinks, namely the ideas as intelligible being.[46]

3. *The Relation of the Absolute Principle to That which is derived from the Principle to be thought in a dialectical-speculative manner*

The relationship of One and Many, considered in a dialectic-speculative way (as one-many, one and many, many-one) transcends the unilinear

[43] See Leinkauf (1990), 56ff., together with the reference noted there to Marsilio Ficino, *Theol. Plat.* II, ch. 9 (Ficino [1964–1970], vol. 1, 99).

[44] Cf. Proclus, *In Parm.* 72,9 (Klibansky and Labowsky 1953); *In Parm.* 1079,35–1080,10 (Cousin 1820–1827) (Steel, Mace, and d'Hoine [2007–2009], vol. III, 51–52); on the dual manner of knowing (διττὰς γὰρ ἔχει τὰς γνώσεις) in the Nous, it "recognizes" or "thinks" the One ἀποφατικῶς ... ὡς μὴ νοῦς; *Theol. Plat.* II, 12, 114, 37 (Saffrey and Westerink 1968–1997). Consequently, it is therefore stated in the Ἐκλογαί concerning the Chaldaean Oracles (des Places [1971] 209, 29): "It [*sc.* the One] should be thought of as non-thinking" – τὸ νοεῖν ἐκεῖνο μὴ νοεῖν ἐστιν.

[45] Leinkauf (1990), 57. The guideline concerning this in the thought of Plotinus, the differentiation of a non-thinking, pure One, to which perhaps a ὑπερνόησις corresponds, and an actual thinking of Nous, was made very clear by Beierwaltes (1985), 43–47.

[46] Patrizi, *PAR,* XV 32rb: *omnia ergo intelligibilia, ei sunt intrinseca. Et extra ipsum nihil est eorum, quae sui natura intelliguntur, cum ipse ea sit, & omnia*; on this point cf. also Plotinus: *Enneads* V 9, 5, 7–13 (Henry and Schwyzer 1951–1973).

causality that is asserted in the basic propositions or theorems. Every principle in this regard was placed in order *before* that which was derived from it and is therefore also ontologically distinct from it: in the cosmos there must be an order like the causal sequence.[47] For order, structure, and form of process to exist, there must be differences, othernesses, and negations, even if, as in Platonic-Aristotelian thought, the differences are *mediated* through the thought of participation (μέθεξις, participatio), the archetype-image-structure (εἰκών, *imago*) or similarity (ὁμοιότης, *similitudo*), the (seminal) implication (σπέρμα, προέχειν, *semen*, *praehabere*), or the return (ἐπιστροφή, *conversio/reditus*).[48] In Patrizi's view, however, this cannot be claimed for the Absolute Principle of everything, for the One itself. In this case, it should much rather be said and with complete awareness of the paradoxicality: "the principle is in that which was derived from it and is *simultaneously* not in it," that is to say, it is "outside (*ultra*) that which is derived from the Principle as well as with (*cum*) it," or "going through everything, it is simultaneously separated from everything."[49] The theoretical model that serves as the basis for such phrases was essentially evolved by Plotinus, in his reflection towards a strict, but not absolutely uncoordinated unity of the One and to a relation of the One to everything non-one, other, and multiple. The basic idea is that the One is present to everything in various ways that correspond to each respective existence but is also nevertheless not present in everything as it itself is.[50] This was then taken over by the Neoplatonic School and especially by Proclus

[47] Patrizi, *PAR* VI, 10va: *Ergo res mundanae omnes ordine constant aliquo, & sunt suis numeris, formis, molibus, qualitatibus, & ornatae, & ordinatae. At ubi ordo, ibi primum, & secundum, & tertium est, & reliqua deinceps.*

[48] Systematically speaking, reversion and the foregoing self-differentiation therefore belong together, cf. Proclus, *El. theol.*, prop. 35, pr., 38. 22: Πῶς τὸ μὴ διακριθὲν ἐπιστρέφειν δυνατόν (Dodds 1933). For Patrizi, these structures of order, which in substance are identical with the theorems from subsection 1 (see pp. 387–389), are manifoldly verified, as in the case of the theorem concerning the meaning of the seed, cf. *PAR* IV, 7vb: *in semine prius sunt omnia occulta, quae postea in natis manifest sunt*; 8ra: *in eo (semine) insunt ita unita, ut extra prodeunt distincta.* The criteria are laid out in their classic form in Proclus: uniform–different, concealed–evident, internal–external.

[49] Patrizi, *PAR* V, 10rb: *ipsum autem principium, & ultra principiata est, & cum principiatis, & haec in ipso sunt, & cum ipso, & ab ipso*; *PAR* XIX, 42va: *est enim (sc. bonum ipsum) ab omnibus entibus separatum: sed omnibus etiam est praesens . . . sua tamen supereminentia, ab omnibus se impermistum, in sua unitate permanens, conservat. Dum vero se ipsum ita conservat, servat etiam alia, in se omnia statuens, illaque complectens*; XX, 43rb: *Si Deus est in omnibus, Deus est ubique. Si in ipso sunt omnia, Deus est nullibi*; 44vab: *Igitur Deus modis hisce (sc. ipso sui esse, ipsa sui potentia, ipsa sui operatione) est ubique, non autem, ut Aristoteles voluit, tantum alicubi, supra coeli culmen, & extra coelum. Est etiam nullibi, quia nullibi est affixus, nullibi locatus. Sed per omnia means, ab omnibus est segregatus, & ab omnibus seiunctus, in suae dignitatis, & supereminentiae abysso, se se a nostris sensibus, a nostris etiam cogitationibus, in altum rapuit.*

[50] Cf. Plotinus, *Enneads* III 9, 4: πανταχοῦ καὶ οὐδαμοῦ; V 2, 1; VI 8, 18, 17f.; VI 4, 11, 20: ἔστι γὰρ παρεῖναι χωρὶς ὄν (Henry and Schwyzer 1951–1973).

in the *Elementatio theologica* (props. 140–143) in particular, which Patrizi himself translated (cf. Patrizi, *ET* 38r–v).[51] Proclus, however – and this is typical for the differentiations that the later Neoplatonism directly after Plotinus, namely in Porphyry, added to Plotinus – distinguishes between the transcendent, absolute unity of the One (for Patrizi's handling of this, see pp. 389–392 above) and the relative, correlative, unity of the "One-Being" – which is coordinated (σύντακτον, coordinatum) with Being or beings – or alternatively that of the divine sphere or the sphere of the gods.[52] The latter is dialectically mediated with respect to Being and thereby with respect to Multiplicity and again to the Totality of beings. It is the origin, from which everything emerges by simultaneously remaining in it, and it has proceeded as founding principle, without being processive. Everything is in it, as it, this One, itself is. It is in everything as that which turns all existing things into this one Being, however, without their being this Being itself. Patrizi clearly shows – even if he has problems maintaining with his Christian approach a pure, uncoordinated transcendence of the One – a very good knowledge of Proclus' and Damascius' texts pertinent with respect to this problem. He calls this towards the beginning of his doctrine of principles, the problem "of finding the way (*modus*) in which the principle itself is One as well as All."[53] It is clear that he takes this *modus essendi* for itself from the guidelines of Proclus and Damascius. This is especially true for a partial aspect of the dialectical relation: that of the *pre-existence* or *pre-being* (*praeesse*, προυπάρχειν, προεῖναι) of that which is derived *from* a principle *in* its principle – this in regard to everything that exists, as far as it, as being, containing a principle of its being: *Hoc demonstratum antea, in principio entia omnia praefuisse, antequam de principio profluerent aut prodirent* (*PAR* VI, 12rb).[54] Patrizi pictures the structure of this relation of One-Many according to the (Platonic-Neoplatonic) model of enfolding

[51] But also cf. Proclus, *Theol. Plat.* II 8, 56, 16–19 (Saffrey and Westerink 1968–1997), VI 14, 6, 68–72, especially 69ff. (Saffrey and Westerink 1968–1997); *In Tim.* I, 209,13–28 (Diehl 1903–1906); Damascius, *De rerum principiis (Dubitationes et solutiones)* I. 80,13ff. (Westerink and Combès 1986); Marsilio Ficino, *Theol. Plat.* II, ch. 11 (Ficino [1964–1970], vol. 1, 108–109; IV, ch. 1 (Ficino [1964–1970], vol. 1, 157) *aeque omnibus communis et ab omnibus soluta (sc. prima causa).*

[52] Proclus, *In Tim.* I, 209, 13–29 (Diehl 1903–1906): everything is produced by the gods (πάντα τὰ ὄντα θεῶν ἐστιν ἔκγονα), this, i.e. the divine, (τὸ θεῖον) is absolutely present (παρόν, πανταχοῦ) and at the same time everything existing is "rooted" in the divine, because although it emerges, it does so without separating itself absolutely: προέλθοντα δὲ πάντα ἐκ θεῶν οὐκ ἐξελήλυθεν ἀπ' αὐτῶν, ἀλλ' ἐνερρίζονται ἐν αὐτοῖς. It is, according to Proclus, in a "wonderful" or "wondrous" way "how everything emerges and does not emerge" (καὶ προῆλθε πάντα καὶ οὐ προῆλθεν).

[53] Patrizi, *PAR* V, 10rb: *Et modus est inveniendus quo ipsum principium, & unum sit, & omnia.*

[54] Cf. also *PAR* VII, 13r: *unum uniter est omnia, et unum . . . est UNOMNIA*; VIII, 15v: *prius in uno*; X, 20v: *omnia in se praehabuit;* Proclus, *El. theol.*, prop. 118: *Omne quodcumque fuerit in Diis secundum eorum proprietatem praeexistit in ipsis, & est proprietas ipsorum uniformis & superessentialis* (31v Patrizi); *In Tim.* I, 8,17–27; 209,24–25 (Diehl 1903–1906). Cf. Leinkauf (1990), 46–49.

and unfolding. In the (i) One (only as One) everything multiple is undistinguished (*indistincte, indiscrete*), uniform (*uniter*) and enfolded (*complicite*). On the other hand in the (ii) One-Being, in the (iii) units coordinated with it, and in the (iv) Many that is itself unified (always composed of units), this multiplicity is gradual, that is, variously graded in intensity (*distincte, discrete*), manifold (*multiformis*) and unfolded (*explicate*). Here we find Neoplatonic terms unambiguously attested in Proclus and Damascius, such as *uniformis*, which directly takes up the Greek ἑνιαίως, but also *occulte*, which captures in Latin the frequently used term κρυφίως.[55] The greater proximity to Proclus also shows itself in the fact that Patrizi discusses the One-Being in its relationship to the Being of the Many without bringing into his argument the "systematic position" adopted by Plotinus – the second hypostasis or Intellect – into the discussion. He thereby exposes the difference between himself and his predecessor. This difference lies in the fact that the One, thought of strictly transcendentally and as an only-One, cannot turn into a relation to the non-One that is to be thought of *as* a relation (i.e. implying a duality of aspects or *relata*). For Plotinus, Intellect as absolute unity of unity and multiplicity must always timelessly fulfill this relation – thought of as fundamental identity of Thinking and Being (Parmenides fr. 3) and as the absolutely complex intertwining and interpenetration of all its aspects.[56] A further Neoplatonic idea that Patrizi takes over from Ficino and Proclus is the thought, originally credited to the genius of Plotinus, that the One is at the same time "everywhere and nowhere" (πανταχοῦ καὶ οὐδαμοῦ),[57] a thought conceived in regard to the totality of Being, because there is a real being everywhere where there is a unity: *Si Deus est in omnibus, est ubique. Si in ipso sunt omnia, est nullibi... Igitur Deus... est ubique. Est etiam nullibi, quia nullibi affixus, nullibi locatus. Sed per omnia means, ab omnibus est segregatus, & ab omnibus seiunctus* (*PAR* XX, 43rb–44va).

4. *The structure of multiplicity and the world*

Provided that Intellect is Thinking and applies to Thinking: *intellectus vero intelligendo in se veluti circulo convertitur, & agnoscit se cognoscere, & intelligit*

[55] Proclus, *In Tim.* I, 8, 209, 234: ἑνιαίως καὶ κρυφίως (Diehl 1903–1906); *Theol. Plat.* V 18, 5, 65 (Saffrey and Westerink 1968–1997): ἑνιαῖον πλῆθος; *El. theol.*, prop. 65 (Dodds 1933) (ET 18v), 118 (ET 31v), 138.

[56] Plotinus, *Enneads* V 1, 8; V 3, 5 and 13; V 8, 4; V 9, 5, 29ff.; VI 2, 3 (Henry and Schwyzer 1951–1973). On this issue cf. Beierwaltes (1967); Beierwaltes (1991); Halfwassen (2004), 59–97.

[57] Plotinus, *Enneads* III 9, 4; V 2, 1; VI 4, 11 (Henry and Schwyzer 1951–1973) among others; Proclus, *Theol. Plat.* II 8, 56 (Saffrey and Westerink 1968–1997); *In Tim.* I, 209,13–29 (Diehl 1903–1906); *El. theol.*, props. 140–143 (Dodds 1933) (38r–v Patrizi).

se intelligere (*Panarchia* XVI, 36r), then intellect, whether as transcendent, hypostatic Spirit (*Nus*, *Verbum/Logos*), or as psychic, incorporated intellect (*mens humana*, *intellectus humana*), is fundamentally determined by reflexivity. It is, to the extent that it is itself the highest object of thought, activity turned *into itself*, self-relation as and through real relation, and in so far as it thinks its own Being and is this Being itself.[58] Patrizi construes this circular reflexivity as *a fundamental structure of reality overall*: it is to be thought of as absolute reflexivity in the Divine Intellect, as temporal-discursive process in the *mens humana*, and as temporal-bodily process in Nature.[59] The continuous unfolding of ontologically "higher" unities into "lower" ones according to the consistency of the structure – in this case, of the unity of unity and multiplicity and of reflexivity as the form of action – allows all authors who argue in the mode of thinking originated by Plotinus to construe human intellect as an agency that is structurally analogous to an absolute or divine intellect, image-like, and intelligible.[60] It also, however, allows the actuality or reality of this Being to be construed as a reflexivity that is mediated in itself, dynamic, and

[58] Cf. also Patrizi, *PAR* XV, 31rb: *haec enim est propria intellectus operatio, in se, & in suam causam conversio* [crossed out in the emendated version, cf. p. XLIV!]; this *conversio* however, directly brings an absolute pattern to expression that precedes every spiritual return and reflection. This consists of the primordial "return" of the "word" that emerges from the father/One. According to Patrizi, this emergence is only not imperfect when it includes or perceives itself: *sentire, persentire*, 31rb. What essence and life cannot do: to perceive and include itself in emergence, that is the original achievement of the spirit or intellect! 31rb: *Ea persentiscentia (ut ita vocem) in se vertitur, & in patrem, armore ardentissimo, convertitur*; 31va: *cognitio . . . non aliud quid esse, quam conversio, & intensio cognoscentis in cognoscibile*. On parallels with Proclus and Damascius cf. Leinkauf (1990), 58–62.

[59] Patrizi, *PC* XVII, 104vb: *mentis motus intrinsecus . . . est circularis, animus mentis motum imitatur, idem & natura facit . . . in gyrum ergo natura, naturaliter movet sua corpora.*

[60] Thus, the human intellect is for Nicholas of Cusa an "imago" of the divine intellect, *Idiota de mente* 4, 74 (= h V, 113–114), *De venatione sapientiae* 27, 82 (= h XII, 79); for Ficino, the *mens humana* is thus a *scintilla mentis superioris, Theol. Plat.* XI, ch. 2 (Ficino [1964–1970], vol. II, 95); for Cornelius Gemma the intellect is the basic form of existence, in which the universal structure of the intelligible becomes primarily or primordially manifest for all existing things of a paradigmatic circular form, *De arte cyclognomica, Prooem.* 5–6, *pars* I, 4, 27; ch. 5, 47; ch. 8, 116 (Gemma 1569). See (among others) regarding this: Leinkauf (2008b); for Patrizi, the rational soul (the ontological "place" of human intellect) is a *progenies mentis, PC* XVII, 104vb. Patrizi distinguishes (cf. *PAR* XVII, 37ra) between the – potentially endless multiplicity of – "created" intellects (*creatis mentibus*), which are "intellects in their essential form (or nature)" (*sua essentia sunt mentes*), and the likewise "created" intellects, which only on the basis of "participation" (*participatio*) are intellects (*de participatis mentibus*). The first of these are discussed in the Panarchia and therefore still belong to the principial-logical domain – it deals with the hierarchy of angelic essence (basic reference here is Dionysius Areopagita); the latter, on the other hand, have their place in the Pampsychia and are an integral part of the created essence-totality of the "human." It can also be surmised that the "actual place" (*suus locus*), of which Patrizi speaks in the beginning of *Panarchia* XVII is to be sought in the no longer extant treatise *De humana philosophia*. On the concept of intellect in general in Patrizi see Puliafito (1988), on human spirit/intellect, especially 198ff.

of the nature of process. This state of being mediated was also thought of by Proclus, in line with Plotinus and Porphyry, as a threefold, ternary (triadic), and continuous[61] mediation. In unfolding this threefold basic structure of Being, it is striking that Patrizi, like Cusanus, Ficino, Pico, Reuchlin, and others before him, does not employ to any great extent the ternarity *esse–vivere–intelligere* (*essentia–vita–intellectus*, οὐσία–ζωή–νοῦς), but instead that of *essentia–potentia/virtus–operatio/actio*[62] favored by Proclus. Only an actual Being that is in and of itself a one (and derivative from the One) can be the means or kernel for the dynamic unfolding of such a ternary complex. For it is true that a being or substance anticipatively enfolds into itself, as a unity, the aspects of potentiality and operationality, and that such a being must therefore be independent or an αὐθυπόστατον (see below) – these are all thoughts that in the early modern debate point directly towards Leibniz's notion of the "unum per se," and building on that, to that of the monad. The ternarity exhibits the characteristics: (1) the irreversibility of the explicative consequences of the individual aspects; (2) the penetration of identity and difference as categorical determinations in every component of the ternarity – the power (*virtus*) is nothing other than the essential form that emanates from itself (explicative identity) but at the same time is not identical with that which it founds ontically (explicative difference); (3) the dynamic basic form that conceives of actuality (*actualitas*) as action (*actio* – also in the sense of the Aristotelean ἐνεργεῖν) but considers this as the definite expressive and unfolding horizon of a presupposed substantial essence. Thus, the being of actuality can be construed as a shining through of the essential in a peripheral and contingent appearance, Nature therefore being the expression of *natura naturans*.

A further fundamental differentiation that concerns the entire pluralistic, ternary actuality is that of *per se stantia* (*authypostata*) and *non per se stantia* (*heterostata*). Patrizi uses this typical Proclean differentiation numerous times. In its original intention for Proclus it served the distinction of those forms of being that are in the position to have their being as result, product, and instantiation of its *self-relation*. An αὐθυπόστατον is an existence that possesses a self-reflexive basic structure and therefore possesses its being through itself without this having to be caused or brought about "from outside" or "from others." It is thus of a higher dignity than that which is established through another (ἑτερόστατον). Because it is, in terms of its essence, *out of and through itself*, it is a more intense picture of the One itself,

[61] This was paradigmatically highlighted by Beierwaltes (1965), 24–164.

[62] Patrizi, *PAR* II, 3v; XIX, 40v; *PP* I, 49v; *PC* XIV, 95r among others see Leinkauf (1990), 39–44, also 25–27; Leinkauf (2013), *passim*.

even though it is radically dependent on the One or the First Principle in an absolute sense.[63] Patrizi uses this conceptual distinction in exactly this form and, like Proclus and Damacius after him, also attaches great importance to the fact that it is Intellect that, in an intelligible-intellectual and thus pre-eminent way, possesses such an existence:[64] *Quae* (*sc.* αὐθυπόστατα) *propria sua hyparxi, & essentia, propriisque viribus innixa, nullo egent alterius ullus adminiculo, ut sint, quam Deo productore, & creatore . . . Haec autem sunt omnia incorporea, quae in mundo sunt Archetypo, Ideae, & unitates, essentiae, vitae, & intellectus, & etiam animae.*[65] In Patrizi's approach to thinking we therefore have, as the central constitutive structural aspects of the actuality that originates from the One, the mutally and objectively conditioning structures of (a) henological self-reliance (opposition of *authypostata–heterostata*), (b) the dynamic triadicity (*essentia–virtus–operatio*), and the (c) noetic reflexivity (*circularitas*). All of these structural aspects are the direct expression of the unfolding of the One itself, actuality being nothing other than action and agency of the One.

IV

On the whole it can be said that Patrizi's theory of principles and theory of the soul represent a congenial adaptation of Neoplatonic thought into a philosophical system, which, as "new philosophy," claims to adequately capture the actuality of the early modern world. What makes the thought of Francesco Patrizi so important is the opposition to a purely naturalistic interpretation of the world, whether it sees itself as Neo-Atomism in connection with the increasingly heated dispute concerning Lucretius (whose culmination will be seen in the works of Pierre Gassendi and Thomas Hobbes), or whether it articulates itself as a Neo-Stoicism that is part of the naturalizing tendencies in ethics and the understanding of nature (whose influence is much more comprehensive). Patrizi's thought is also the firm renunciation of the Aristotle of scholastic philosophy and of a theory of nature tied to locomotion, substantial forms, and a hierarchical gradation of elements that occurs around the same time. This opposition seemed to Patrizi only to be possible by recourse to the highly complex,

[63] Proclus, *El. theol.*, props. 40–51, 42. 8–50. 6 (Dodds 1933), especially prop. 43, 44, 25 Dodds: πᾶν τὸ πρὸς ἑαυτὸ ἐπιστρεπτικὸν αὐθυπόστατόν ἐστιν; see on this point Beierwaltes (1965), 119ff. On the connection Proclus–Patrizi see Leinkauf (1990), on the concept of "intellect," 171ff.

[64] For Proclus cf. *El. theol.*, props. 43–44 (Dodds 1933); *In Tim.* II, 243,9ff. (Diehl 1903–1906) on the self-reference and self-sufficiency of the intellect.

[65] Patrizi, *PAR* XVIII, 39ra, cf. also XII, 25vb in the context of explicit Proclus exegesis.

unity-metaphysical, and especially *dynamic* ontology of Neoplatonism, in which the theoretical approaches of Aristotle that are allied to Plato are themselves retained – an achievement especially of the Neoplatonic commentators of Aristotle, it should not be forgotten. He was thus able to align himself directly with Ficino and his school, though he distinguishes himself from Ficino and the *Platonici* of the sixteenth century through his independent re-evaluation and productive adoption of the works of Proclus as well as Damascius. The reception history of Patrizi in the seventeenth century has until now hardly been researched, but it extends from Francis Bacon, Robert Fludd, Thomas Hobbes, Herbert of Cherbury,[66] Athanasius Kircher,[67] and Amos Comenius up to the Cambridge Platonists. It remains to be investigated to what extent Neoplatonic, Proclean thought permeated the discussions of the seventeenth century, especially the newer theories on nature and the dynamization of theories of Being, through the reading of Patrizi's texts.

Bibliography

Barbagli, D. A. (ed.) (1975) *Francesco Patrizi da Cherso, Lettere ed opuscoli inediti*, Florence.

Bardenhewer, O. (ed.) (1882) *Die ps.-aristotelische Schrift Über das Gute, bekannt unter dem Namen Liber de causis*, Freiburg.

Barocius, F. (1560) *Procli in primum Euclidis elementorum librum commentariorum libri III*, Patavii.

Beierwaltes, W. (1965) *Proklos, Grundzüge seiner Metaphysik*, 2nd edn., Frankfurt/M.

(1967) "Einleitung," in W. Beierwaltes (ed.), *Plotin: Über Ewigkeit und Zeit (III 7)*, Frankfurt/M.

(1985) *Denken des Einen, Studien zur neuplatonischen Philosophie und ihrer Wirkungsgeschichte*, Frankfurt/M.

(1991) *Selbsterkenntnis und Erfahrung der Einheit, Plotins Enneade V 3*, Frankfurt/M.

Boese, H. (ed.) (1985) *Wilhelm von Moerbeke als Übersetzer der Stoicheiosis theologike des Proclus*, Heidelberg.

Cousin, V. (ed.) (1820–1827) *Procli philosophi Platonici opera*, vol. I: *Opuscula tria*, Paris 1820; vols. II–III: *In primum Alcibiadem*, Paris 1820–21; vols. IV–VI: *Commentarius in Parmenidem Platonis; Supplementum Damascii*, Paris 1821–1827.

Creutzer, F. (ed.) (1820–1822) *Initia philosophiae et theologiae ex Platonicis fontibus ducta, Pars prima: In Alcibiadem priorem commentaria*, Frankfurt 1820: *Pars secunda: Institutio theologica*, Frankfurt 1822.

[66] Dilthey (1957), 251–263. [67] Leinkauf (1993).

Cusanus (Nicholas of Cusa) (1932–2005) *Opera omnia, iussu et auctoritate academiae litterarum Heidelbergensis*, Leipzig and Hamburg (cited as h, with volume and pages).

Des Places, É. (ed.) (1971) *Oracles chaldaiques avec un choix de commentaires anciens*, Paris.

Diehl, E. (ed.) (1903–1906) Proclus, *In Platonis Timaeum commentaria*, 3 vols., Leipzig.

Dilthey, W. (1957) *Die Autonomie des Denkens im 17. Jahrhundert*, in W. Dilthey, *Gesammelte Schriften*, vol. II, Göttingen.

Dodds, E. R. (ed. and trans.) (1933) *Proclus: The Elements of Theology*, Oxford; 2nd edn., Oxford 1963.

Ficino, M. (1576) *Opera omnia*, Basel. Reprint: Société Marsile Ficin, Paris 2000.

(1964–1970) *Théologie platonicienne de l'immortalité des âmes*, trans. Raymond Marcel, 3 vols., Paris.

(1978) *De amore, Commentaire sur le banquet de Platon*, trans. Raymond Marcel, Paris.

Firpo, L. (1950) "Filosofia italiana e controriforma," *Rivista di Filosofia* 41: 150–173; "II. La condanna di Francesco Patrizi," 159–173.

Gemma, C. (1569) *De arte cyclognomica*, Antwerp.

Gersh, S. (1986) *Middle Platonism and Neoplatonism, the Latin Tradition*, 2 vols., Notre Dame, IN.

Grabmann, M. (1936) *Die Proklos-Übersetzungen des Wilhelm von Moerbeke und ihre Verwertung in der lateinischen Literatur des Mittelalters, in Mittelalterliches Geistesleben*, vol. II, Munich, 413–423.

Gregory, T. (1953) "L' 'Apologia ad Censuram' di Francesco Patrizi," *Rinascimento* 4: 89–104.

(1955) "L' 'Apologia ad Censuram' e le 'Declarationes' di Francesco Patrizi," in *Medioevo e Rinascimento, Studi in onore di Bruno Nardi*, vol. I, Florence, 402–424.

Grynaeus, S. (ed.) (1533) *Euclidii Opera*, Basel.

Grynaeus, S. and Oporinus, J. (eds.) (1534) *Opera omnia Platonis*, Basel.

Hadot, P. (1960) "Être, vie et pensée chez Plotin et avant Plotin," in *Les Sources de Plotin, Entretiens sur l'Antiquité Classique, Fondation Hardt* 5, Vandoeuvres and Geneva, 105–157.

Halfwassen, J. (1994) *Geist und Selbstbewußtsein, Studien zu Plotin und Numenios*, Mainz and Stuttgart.

(2004) *Plotin*, Munich.

Henry, P. and Schwyzer, H.-R. (eds.) (1951–1973) *Plotini Opera*, 3 vols., Leiden.

Jacobs, E. (1908) "Francisco Patricio und seine Sammlung griechischer Handschriften in der Bibliothek des Escorial," *Zentralblatt für Bibliothekswesen* 25: 19–47.

Klibansky, R. and Labowsky, C. (eds.) (1953) *Parmenides usque ad finem primae hypothesis nec non Procli Commentarium in Parmenidem, pars ultima adhuc inedita interprete Guillelmo de Moerbeke*, London.

Kristeller, P. O. (1965) "Patrizi," in P. O. Kristeller, *Eight Philosophers of the Italian Renaissance*, London, 110–123.

(1987) "Proclus as a reader of Plato and Plotinus, and His Influence in the Middle Ages and in the Renaissance," in J. Pépin and H.-D. Saffrey (eds.), *Proclus: lecteur et interprète des anciens*, Paris, 191–211.

Leinkauf, T. (1990) *Il neoplatonismo di Francesco Patrizi come presupposto della sua critica ad Aristoteles*, Florence (originally presented 1987).

(1993) *Mundus combinatus. Untersuchungen zur Struktur der barocken Universalwissenschaft am Beispiel Athanasius Kirchers SJ*, Berlin; 2nd edn. 2009.

(1999) "Francesco Patrizi (1529–1597), Neue Philosophien der Geschichte, der Dichtung und der Welt," in P. R. Blum (ed.), *Philosophen der Renaissance*, Darmstadt, 173–187.

(2008a) "Zum Begriff des 'Geistes' in der Frühen Neuzeit. Überlegungen am Beispiel Francesco Patrizi da Chersos," in J. Dillon and M.-L. Zovko (eds.), *Platonism and Forms of Intelligence*, Berlin, 159–178.

(2008b) "Cornelius Gemma: Philosophie und Methode, Eine Analyse des ersten Buches der Ars cyclognomica," in H. Hirai (ed.), *Cornelius Gemma, Cosmology, Medicine, and Natural Philosophy in the Renaissance*, Leuven, Pisa, and Rome, 127–147.

(2009) "Der Ternar 'essentia-virtus-operatio' und die Essentialisierungen der Akzidentien," in G. Radke-Uhlmann and A. Schmitt (eds.), *Philosophie im Umbruch, Der Bruch mit dem Aristotelismus im Hellenismus und im späten Mittelalter*, Stuttgart, 131–153.

(2010) "Platon in der Renaissance: Marsilio Ficino und Francesco Patrizi," in A. Neschke-Hentschke (ed.), *Argumenta in dialogos Platonis*, vol. 1: *Platoninterpretation und ihre Hermeneutik von der Antike bis zum Beginn des 19. Jahrhunderts*, Basel, 285–300.

(2011) "Die Rezeption des Damaskios im Denken des Francesco Patrizi," *Accademia* 13: 47–65.

Martijn, M. (2008) *Proclus on Nature, Philosophy of Nature and Its Methods in Proclus' Commentary on Plato's Timaeus*, Leiden.

Muccillo, M. (1986) "Marsilio Ficino e Francesco Patrizi da Cherso," in S. Gentile, S. Niccoli, and P. Viti (eds.), *Marsilio Ficino e il ritorno di Platone, Studi e documenti*, Florence, vol. 1, 615–674.

Pandzic, Z. (1999) "Introduction," in *Franciscus Patricius, Discussiones peripateticae* (reprint of Basel 1581 edn.), Cologne and Vienna.

Patrizi, F. (1581) *Discussionum peripateticarum tomi IV, quibus Aristotelica philosophiae universa historia atque dogmata cum veterum placitis collatam eleganter & erudité declarantur*, Basel.

(1583) *Procli Lycii Diadochi Platonici philosophie eminentissimi Elementa theologica et physica. Opus omni admiratione prosequendum quae Franciscus Patricius de Graecis fecit latina*, Ferrara.

(1591) *Nova de universis philosophia in qua Aristotelica methodo non per motum, sed per lucem & lumina, ad primam causam ascenditur. Deinde propria Patricii methodus tota in contemplationem venit Divinitas, postremo methodo Platonica rerum universitas a conditore Deo deducitur*, Ferrara.

Pattin, A. (ed.) (1966) "*Le Liber de causis*," *Tijdschrift voor Filosophie* 28: 90–203.

Puliafito, A. L. (1988) "'Principio primo' e 'principi principiati' nella Nova de universis philosophia di Francesco Patrizi," *Giornale critico della filosofia italiana* 67: 154–201.

(1993) *Francesco Patrizi da Cherso, Nova de universis philosophia. Materiali per un'edizione emendata*, Florence.

Rotondò, A. (1982) "Cultura umanistica e difficoltà di censori. Censura ecclesiastica e discussioni cinquecentesche sul platonismo," in *Le pouvoir et la plume, Incitation, contrôle et répression dans l'Italie du XVIe siècle*, Paris, 15–50.

Saffrey, H.-D. (ed.) (1954) Thomas von Aquin, *Expositio super librum de causis*, Fribourg.

Saffrey, H.-D. and Westerink, L. G. (eds.) (1968–1997) *Proclus: Theologie platonicienne*, Paris.

Schmitt, C. B. (1976) "L'introduction de la philosophie platonicienne dans l'enseignement des universités à la Renaissance," in *Platon et Aristote à la Renaissance (XVIe Colloque international de Tours)*, Paris, 93–104.

Smith, A. (ed.) (1993) *Porphyrios, Fragmenta*, Stuttgart and Leipzig.

Steel, C. (ed.) (1982–1985) *Proclus: Commentaire sur le Parménide de Platon, traduction de Guillaume de Moerbeke*, 2 vols., Leuven and Leiden.

Steel, C., Mace, C., and d'Hoine, P. (eds.) (2007–2009) *Procli in Platonis Parmenidem commentaria*, 3 vols., Oxford.

Vasoli, C. (1989) *Francesco Patrizi da Cherso*, Rome.

Westerink, L. G. and Combès, J. (eds. and trans.) (1986) Damascius, *De rerum principiis (Dubitationes et solutiones)*, vol. 1, Paris.

Index of names

Index of subjects

Printed in Great Britain
by Amazon

19944456R00241